Personal Finance

The Prentice Hall Series in Finance

Adelman/Marks
Entrepreneurial Finance

Andersen
Global Derivatives: A Strategic Risk Management Perspective

Bekaert/Hodrick
International Financial Management

Berk/DeMarzo
*Corporate Finance**

Berk/DeMarzo
*Corporate Finance: The Core**

Berk/DeMarzo/Harford
*Fundamentals of Corporate Finance**

Boakes
Reading and Understanding the Financial Times

Brooks
*Financial Management: Core Concepts**

Copeland/Weston/Shastri
Financial Theory and Corporate Policy

Dorfman/Cather
Introduction to Risk Management and Insurance

Eiteman/Stonehill/Moffett
Multinational Business Finance

Fabozzi
Bond Markets: Analysis and Strategies

Fabozzi/Modigliani
Capital Markets: Institutions and Instruments

Fabozzi/Modigliani/Jones/Ferri
Foundations of Financial Markets and Institutions

Finkler
Financial Management for Public, Health, and Not-for-Profit Organizations

Frasca
Personal Finance

Gitman/Joehnk/Smart
*Fundamentals of Investing**

Gitman/Zutter
*Principles of Managerial Finance**

Gitman/Zutter
*Principles of Managerial Finance—Brief Edition**

Goldsmith
Consumer Economics: Issues and Behaviors

Haugen
The Inefficient Stock Market: What Pays Off and Why

Haugen
The New Finance: Overreaction, Complexity, and Uniqueness

Holden
Excel Modeling in Corporate Finance

Holden
Excel Modeling in Investments

Hughes/MacDonald
International Banking: Text and Cases

Hull
Fundamentals of Futures and Options Markets

Hull
Options, Futures, and Other Derivatives

Hull
Risk Management and Financial Institutions

Keown
*Personal Finance: Turning Money into Wealth**

Keown/Martin/Petty
*Foundations of Finance: The Logic and Practice of Financial Management**

Kim/Nofsinger
Corporate Governance

Madura
*Personal Finance**

Marthinsen
Risk Takers: Uses and Abuses of Financial Derivatives

McDonald
Derivatives Markets

McDonald
Fundamentals of Derivatives Markets

Mishkin/Eakins
Financial Markets and Institutions

Moffett/Stonehill/Eiteman
Fundamentals of Multinational Finance

Nofsinger
Psychology of Investing

Ormiston/Fraser
Understanding Financial Statements

Pennacchi
Theory of Asset Pricing

Rejda
Principles of Risk Management and Insurance

Seiler
Performing Financial Studies: A Methodological Cookbook

Shapiro
Capital Budgeting and Investment Analysis

Sharpe/Alexander/Bailey
Investments

Solnik/McLeavey
Global Investments

Stretcher/Michael
Cases in Financial Management

Titman/Keown/Martin
*Financial Management: Principles and Applications**

Titman/Martin
Valuation: The Art and Science of Corporate Investment Decisions

Van Horne
Financial Management and Policy

Van Horne/Wachowicz
Fundamentals of Financial Management

Weston/Mitchel/Mulherin
Takeovers, Restructuring, and Corporate Governance

*denotes MyFinanceLab titles   Log onto www.myfinancelab.com to learn more

Personal Finance

Turning Money into Wealth

Sixth Edition

Arthur J. Keown

Virginia Polytechnic Institute and State University
R.B. Pamplin Professor of Finance

PEARSON

Boston Columbus Indianapolis New York
San Francisco Upper Saddle River Amsterdam Cape Town
Dubai London Madrid Milan Munich Paris Montréal
Toronto Delhi Mexico City São Paulo Sydney
Hong Kong Seoul Singapore Taipei Tokyo

Editorial Director: Sally Yagan
Editor-in-Chief: Donna Battista
Acquisitions Editor: Tessa O'Brien
Editorial Project Managers: Jill Kolongowski and Amy Foley
Editorial Assistant: Elissa Senra-Sargent
Director of Marketing: Maggie Moylan
Marketing Assistant: Ian Gold
Senior Managing Editor: Nancy H. Fenton
Senior Production Project Manager: Meredith Gertz
Permissions Project Supervisor: Estelle Simpson
Permissions Editor: Joanna Green
Art Director: Jonathan Boylan

Cover Designer: Gretchen Irmiger
Cover Images: ©Shutterstock/Brandon Alms and ©Shutterstock/Fotofermer
Image Manager/Image Asset Services: Rachel Youdelman
Photo Research: PreMedia Global
Senior Manufacturing Buyer: Carol Melville
Director of Media: Susan Schoenberg
Content Lead, MyFinanceLab: Miguel Leonarte
Senior Media Producer: Melissa Honig
Production Coordination, Composition, and Art Creation: Cenveo Publisher Services/Nesbitt Graphics, Inc.

Credits and acknowledgments borrowed from other sources and reproduced, with permission, in this textbook appear on appropriate page within the text.

Photo credits: Page 3, Ron Jaffe/CBS/Everett Collection; page 33, AF Archive/Alamy; page 63, AF Archive/Alamy; page 95, Jamste/PR NewsFoto/AP Images; page 137, Mark Ralston/AFP/Getty Images/Newscom; page 167, KRT/Newscom; page 201, STR/AP Images; page 233, AF Archive/Alamy; page 291, 20th Century Fox/Everett Collection; page 337, Heidi Huber/East Valley Tribune/AP Images; page 369, Doug Pensinger/Getty Images; page 401, Creatas/Comstock; page 429, AP Images; page 457, AF Archive/Alamy; page 489, Ben Margot/AP Images; page 525, Frank Augstein/AP Images; page 563, Peter Muhly/Reuters/Corbis, page w-2 (Web chapter), New Line/Everett Collection.

Many of the designations by manufacturers and sellers to distinguish their products are claimed as trademarks. Where those designations appear in this book, and the publisher was aware of a trademark claim, the designations have been printed in initial caps or all caps.

Library of Congress Cataloging-in-Publication Data

Keown, Arthur J.
 Personal finance : turning money into wealth / Arthur J. Keown. -- 6th ed.
   p. cm. -- (The Prentice Hall series in finance)
 Includes index.
 ISBN 978-0-13-271916-2 (alk. paper)
 1. Finance, Personal. 2. Investments. I. Title.
 HG179.K47 2013
 332.024--dc23

                                   2011042276

10 9 8 7 6 5 4 3

www.pearsonhighered.com

ISBN-10: 0-13-271916-9
ISBN-13: 978-0-13-271916-2

*To Barb, my partner and my love—
for showing me happiness that money can't buy*

About the Author

Arthur J. Keown is the R. B. Pamplin Professor of Finance and Finance Department Head at Virginia Polytechnic Institute and State University. He received his bachelor's degree from Ohio Wesleyan University, his MBA from the University of Michigan, and his doctorate from Indiana University. An award-winning teacher, he is a member of the Academy of Teaching Excellence at Virginia Tech, he has received five Certificates of Teaching Excellence, the W. E. Wine Award for Teaching Excellence, and the Alumni Teaching Excellence Award, and in 1999 he received the Outstanding Faculty Award from the State of Virginia. Professor Keown is widely published in academic journals. His work has appeared in *Journal of Finance, Journal of Financial Economics, Journal of Financial and Quantitative Analysis, Journal of Financial Research, Journal of Banking and Finance, Financial Management, Journal of Portfolio Management,* and many others. Two of his books are widely used in college finance classes all over the country—*Financial Management* and *Foundations of Finance: The Logic and Practice of Financial Management.* Professor Keown is a Fellow of Decision Sciences Institute and head of the Finance Department. In addition, he has served as the co-editor of both *Journal of Financial Research,* and the Financial Management Association's *Survey and Synthesis Series.* He was recently inducted into Ohio Wesleyan's Athletic Hall of Fame for wrestling. His daughter and son are both married and live in Madison, Wisconsin, and Dubai, while he and his wife live in Blacksburg, Virginia, where he collects original art from *Mad* magazine.

Brief Contents

Contents

Preface

For many students, the Personal Finance course is their initial and only exposure to personal finance, so it is important that the material is presented in a way that leaves a lasting impression. Tools, techniques, and equations are easily forgotten, but the logic and fundamental principles that drive their use, once understood, will remain and will become part of a student's "financial personality." *Personal Finance: Turning Money into Wealth*, Sixth Edition empowers students, through the presentation of the ten fundamental principles of personal finance, to successfully make and carry out a plan for their financial future. Throughout the rest of their lives, students will have the ability to draw upon these principles that will help them effectively deal with an ever-changing financial environment.

Hallmarks of *Personal Finance: Turning Money into Wealth*

- ◆ **The Ten Principles of Personal Finance**—Each chapter of the text touches back on the ten principles introduced in Chapter 1 and shows how to apply those principles to particular situations.
- ◆ **The Personal Finance Workbook**—A companion workbook is also available for this text. This workbook contains tear-out worksheets to provide a step-by-step analysis of many of the personal finance decisions examined in the book. Instructors can use them for homework assignments or to guide students through actual decisions. Icons in the text indicate content areas as well as cases and problems that utilize the worksheets. Every worksheet is also available electronically on the Instructor's Resource Center at **http://www.pearsonhighered.com/irc**. The workbook also includes **Your Financial Plan**, which guides the student through a series of exercises that utilize the worksheets (available in the workbook and on the Instructor's Resource Center) and will generate a very basic financial plan to explore where students are today, where they will want to be in the future, and what they need to do to get there. Finally, the workbook includes a section on how to use a financial calculator.
- ◆ **Easy-to-Follow Advice**—The proactive checklists, which appear throughout the text, serve as a useful learning tool for students. These boxes identify areas of concern and questions to ask when buying a car, getting insurance, investing in mutual funds, and performing other personal finance tasks.
- ◆ **MyFinanceLab**—MyFinanceLab, a fully integrated online homework and tutorial system, enables students to complete problems and receive immediate feedback and help. See the inside front cover for details.

Other Points of Distinction

Learning Objectives   Each chapter opens with a set of action-oriented learning objectives. As these objectives are covered in the text, an identifying icon appears in the margin.

Stop and Think   These short boxes provide the student with insights as to what the material actually means—its implications and the big picture.

Money Matters Boxes placed within each chapter are written by Marcy Furney, CFP, and provide checklists of things to do—in effect, free advice from a certified financial planner.

Be a Financial Planner—Discussion Cases Each chapter closes with a set of two mini-cases that provide students with real-life problems which tie together the chapter topics and require a practical financial decision.

Be a Financial Planner—Continuing Case: Cory and Tisha Dumont The book is divided into five parts, and at the end of each part a Continuing Case provides an opportunity to synthesize and integrate the many different financial concepts presented in the book. It gives the student a chance to construct financial statements, analyze a changing financial situation, calculate taxes, measure risk exposure, and develop a financial plan.

Ten Financial Life Events The concepts and tools in this book are all tied together in Web Chapter 18 through the ten "Financial Life Events." Here the student gains a broad perspective and overview on how personal finance affects almost all parts of his or her life. The student will clearly see that in the course of a lifetime he or she will experience many events that will change goals, affect financial resources, and create new financial obligations or opportunities. While there are a great number of life-changing events, we focus on ten of the most common, such as getting married, having a child, and retiring, and with each one we present a comprehensive step-by-step discussion of how to respond to them—pulling material from throughout the book and thereby tying it all together into an action plan.

New to the Sixth Edition

Since the last edition of *Personal Finance: Turning Money into Wealth*, a lot has changed in the world of personal finance and much of this was driven by the crash of the financial markets and the worst downturn in the economy since the Great Depression. Unemployment soared, housing prices dropped, consumer debt (including mortgage debt) reached $12.5 trillion, more than doubling in just 10 years. Foreclosures became commonplace, and of those homeowners who took out second mortgages almost 40 percent are under water on their loans—owing more on their homes than they are worth. In response to this crisis the government passed a number of new laws aimed at protecting consumers and bringing about stability in the financial markets. This new legislation includes tax laws that impact not only what your annual income taxes are but also what happens to your estate when you die. If that weren't enough in the way of changes, in 2010 Congress passed and President Obama signed into law the Affordable Care Act. In light of all these changes, the new edition of this text includes the following revisions:

◆ **Coverage of lessons from the recent economic downturn.** The opening chapter includes a new section on the lessons learned from the recent economic downturn, which brought about a swift rise in unemployment, a dramatic loss of wealth both in the stock and real estate markets, and a disruption in our financial markets that made borrowing extremely difficult. Not only is this covered in the first chapter, but also in Chapters 5, 7, 8, 11, 13, and Web Chapter 18.

◆ **Expanded coverage of the use of financial calculators to calculate the rate of return and number of periods.** In addition, Chapter 3 introduces and Chapters 7 and 8 expand on nonannual compounding, which allows for the calculation of the number and size of payments and the interest rate—for example, calculation of the number of months to pay off a loan, the size of a monthly mortgage payment, and the annual interest rate on a monthly loan. Further, the size of the problem set in Chapter 3 was doubled to provide students with a better learning experience.

◆ **Coverage of the Credit Card Accountability, Responsibility, and Disclosure (CARD) Act of 2009.** Signed into law by President Obama on May 22, 2009, this act attempts, among other things, to protect consumers against arbitrary interest rate hikes, to prevent the use of misleading terms, to eliminate excessive fees, and to outlaw the use of gifts and promotional items (such as coupons for free pizza) to entice college students to take on debt by applying for their credit cards. Much of the coverage of this new law can be found in Chapter 6.

◆ **Coverage of the creation of the Consumer Financial Protection Bureau (CFPB).** As part of the Dodd-Frank Wall Street Reform and Consumer Protection Act, the CFPB was signed into law in July 2010 and serves to regulate consumer financial products and services. Coverage of the CFPB is offered primarily in Chapter 6.

◆ **A reexamination of debt.** Chapter 8 includes a new section on debt that ties together the discussion of credit card debt, consumer loans, home mortgages, home equity loans, auto loans, and student loans and examines why the problem has become more acute. It also presents six rules for successful debt management.

◆ **Examination of the implications of the 2010 Affordable Care Act.** Presented in Chapter 9, the goals of the Affordable Care Act are to provide new consumer protections, improve quality and lower costs, increase access to affordable care, and hold insurance companies accountable. This is an extensive piece of legislation that goes into effect gradually through 2018 and, among other provisions, includes guaranteed coverage to those with preexisting health conditions, the creation of insurance exchanges to increase the number of people with access to insurance, tax credits to small businesses and the poor and middle class for insurance purchases, and requirements for employers with more than 50 workers to offer insurance.

◆ **Chapters on investing completely revised.** The chapters on investing, Chapters 11 through 15, were thoroughly updated to reflect the drama in the investments markets since the previous edition of the book, with the DJIA hitting a low of 6,547 in March 2009 then almost doubling by May 2011. While the stock market gyrated, interest rates dove and the rate of inflation was actually negative for the year 2009.

◆ **Changes in estate tax laws.** A major revision of Chapter 17 reflects legislation changes including estate taxes disappearing in 2010, only to reappear at levels below the pre-2010 level in 2011 and 2012, and a feature that allows for portability of the estate tax exemption. Then in 2013 estate tax laws are scheduled to jump dramatically.

◆ **Web Chapter 18 dramatically streamlined and completely rewritten.** Chapter 18 now solely focuses on ten financial life events and how to deal with them, pulling together all the different topics in the book. This is followed by a discussion of 12 key decisions to financial success.

Major Content Update

Chapter 1 A new section, "Lessons from the Recent Economic Downturn," in Chapter 1 details how a dramatic and swift rise in unemployment and a disruption of our financial markets resulted in loss of wealth and a level of difficulty in borrowing that has not been experienced since the Great Depression. This section then looks at the lessons learned from this crisis—the importance of emergency funds and of controlling debt and the concerns revolving around retirement and health care. In addition, Principle 9 was rewritten and is now "Mind Games, Your Financial Personality, and Your Money" with new focus added to the importance of your financial personality in determining how much you save, how much you spend, and how you view money. Finally, a new section, "Women and Personal Finance," looks at the unique financial challenges faced by women including the fact that they generally earn less money, are less likely to have pensions, qualify for less income from Social Security, and live longer than men.

Chapter 2   This chapter begins with a new introduction that focuses on the dramatic difference in spending habits between Sarah Jessica Parker and the character she plays in the *Sex and the City* movies and HBO series. In addition to updating the statistics in the chapter, emphasis was switched from using a spreadsheet for budgeting and managing your money to doing it through free Web-based personal financial planning tools that allow for the consolidation of all your financial information. The site that is presented and suggested is Mint.com, which can be used to create a budget, track expenditures, plan for goals, and track all your investments.

Chapter 3   A new section in Chapter 3 deals with solving for I/Y and N using a financial calculator, thus allowing the student to solve for the rate of return and the number of payments. Another new section discusses the calculation of monthly and other nonannual payments on amortized loans, teaching students how to determine the monthly payments on a home mortgage using a financial calculator. In addition, the number of problems included in the "Develop Your Skills— Problems and Activities" section was doubled.

Chapter 4   The tax chapter has been simplified through the elimination of unnecessary detail and updated to reflect all changes in the tax laws since the previous edition. The section on education credits has also been updated and expanded to include a direct comparison of the American Opportunity Credit and the Lifetime Learning Credit.

Chapter 5   This chapter begins with a new introduction that focuses on the value of an emergency fund, taken from the ABC special "Unbroke," featuring Antonio Banderas and Marisa Tomei. It also discusses how the lack of an emergency fund exacerbated the financial problems faced by many during the recent economic downturn. A new section on overdraft protection outlines the new rules for debt and ATM card overdrafts that came out of the recent financial crisis and includes a table that presents these changes in a straightforward manner.

Chapter 6   With a new introduction on the use of credit cards, Chapter 6 deals extensively with the impact of the CARD Act of 2009 and exactly what the new credit card rules mean. The chapter also examines the Consumer Financial Protection Bureau (CFPB), which was established under the Dodd-Frank Act. In addition, another new section looks at both the FICO and VantageScore credit scoring methods.

Chapter 7   The student loans section is entirely new and now covers Stafford loans for students and Direct PLUS for parents. Included is a comparison of the different federal student loan programs focusing on both the program details and the annual award limits. In addition, the section dealing with payday loans was revised to reflect recent efforts by payday lenders to circumvent the laws. The calculation of monthly payments on installment loans using a financial calculator is now demonstrated in Chapter 7.

Chapter 8   Coverage of the use of financial calculators to determine monthly payments—in this case focusing on installment and auto loans—continues in this chapter. The discussion on housing now also examines subprime loans and real estate short sales. Finally, a new, comprehensive section ties together the discussion on debt presented earlier in the book. This section looks at the debt trap—how debt was both a cause and consequence of the recent economic downturn and also exacerbated the pain that individuals felt during the downturn. In addition, this section examines the consequences of too much debt and includes the six keys to successful debt management.

Chapter 9 After extensive revisions, the coverage in Chapter 9 now reflects the provisions of the 2010 Affordable Care Act, much of which goes into effect in 2014, and when fully implemented, will provide health coverage to over 32 million Americans who are currently without health insurance. Table 9.5 outlines the major benefits provided by the Affordable Care Act along with the dates these measures become law: new consumer protections, improved quality and lower costs, increased access to affordable care, and accountability for insurance companies. Chapter 9 also includes a new section on appealing health insurance claim decisions.

Chapter 10 Updated and revised, Chapter 10 now reflects changes in property and liability insurance. The discussion of insurance credit scores now includes additional visual presentation to reflect the impact of your insurance credit score in the determination of what you pay in the way of insurance.

Chapter 11 The ever-changing world of investments is reflected in the updating of this chapter. Since the last edition the financial markets crashed and the economy suffered the worst downturn since the Great Depression. The revised chapter reflects the current state of the financial markets and also clarifies the discussion of investing versus speculating.

Chapter 12 This chapter has been updated to reflect the changing nature of the securities market. The revisions include updates to the discussion of how individuals use the Web as a source of investment information, focusing on Yahoo! Finance, CNNMoney, the Motley Fool, and EDGAR.

Chapter 13 In this chapter we examine the crash and rebound in the stock market along with the dramatic increase in volatility since the previous edition of the book. During this period the value of a typical stock dropped by 50 percent with the DJIA hitting a low of 6,547 in March 2009 and then almost doubling by May 2011. The historical focus of the chapter was moved forward, looking at a more representative period, the period since 1950.

Chapter 14 This chapter examines the volatility in the bond market as witnessed by the dramatic rise in the price of bonds in 2008, with long-term Treasury bonds climbing by about 26 percent, followed in 2009 by a drop in their price by about 15 percent. In addition, the use of online listings as a source for bond prices is presented along with an annotated table showing the types of bond pricing information that is available online.

Chapter 15 This chapter has been updated to reflect movements in the markets and in the mutual fund industry. In addition, it offers new coverage of hedge funds, reflecting their increased popularity among some investors. A deeper explanation of ETFs is also provided along with a new table that compares ETFs and mutual funds. The discussion dealing with the selection of mutual funds has been rewritten with emphasis, along with two new tables, placed on mutual fund information on the Web and Web sources for screening mutual funds.

Chapter 16 This chapter now includes the latest information on retirement planning and corporate pension funds and the increased difficulties that most Americans—women in particular—face in meeting their retirement goals as a result of the recent economic downturn. In addition, more emphasis is provided on the role of online retirement planning.

Chapter 17 Chapter 17 begins with a new introduction, looking at George Steinbrenner and the fact that he died during the year when there wasn't a federal estate tax. The chapter then looks at the current and upcoming changes in federal estate tax laws, the new portable estate tax exemption, and the implication of those changes for estate planning and the use of trusts.

Web Chapter 18   Chapter 18 has been updated to reflect the changing financial markets and tax laws. In addition, it has been dramatically shortened to allow it to focus on the ten financial life events, using those life events to provide a capstone for the book. The chapter then presents a dozen keys to financial success, including the use of Mint.com or some other online budgeting tool to make financial control a reality.

For Instructors

The following supplements are available to adopting instructors.

Instructor's Resource Center   Register. Redeem. Log in. **www.pearsonhighered.com/ irc** is the Web site where instructors can download, in a digital format, a variety of print, media, and presentation resources that are available with this text. For most texts, resources such as Blackboard, WebCT, and Course Compass are also available for course management platforms.

It Gets Better.   Once you register, you will not have additional forms to fill out or multiple usernames and passwords to remember in order to access new titles and/ or editions. As a registered faculty member, you can log in directly to download resource files and receive immediate access and instructions for installing course management content to your campus server.

Need Help?   Our dedicated technical support team is ready to assist instructors with questions about the media supplements that accompany this text. Visit: **http://247pearsoned.custhelp.com/** for answers to frequently asked questions and toll-free user support phone numbers. The following supplements are available to adopting instructors. Detailed descriptions of these supplements are provided on the Instructor's Resource Center:

◆ Instructor's Manual—Prepared by John Grable and Sonya Britt of Kansas State University. The Instructor's Manual contains many features to aid with the navigation of this rich text. Among the features included for each chapter are a brief overview of the chapter's content (Chapter Summary), insight into how the chapter integrates with the other chapters in that part and the entire text (Chapter Context), a teaching outline of the concepts and terms to assist with chapter reviews (Chapter Outline), an explanation of the principles in the order they appear in the chapter (Applicable Principles) and sample solutions for all end-of-chapter questions, problems, and cases, along with suggested solutions for the Continuing Cases. There are also suggested in-class activities as well as hands-on individual and group projects to be completed outside of class (Classroom Applications).

◆ Test Item File—Prepared by Diann Moorman, an award-winning professor and Lilly Teaching Fellow in the Housing and Consumer Economics Department at the University of Georgia and checked for accuracy by Laurel Tech and Kathleen Reiter at Southwest Community College. The Test Bank for each chapter contains approximately 50–75 questions consisting of short-answer vocabulary, true/ false, multiple choice, and scenario-based questions.

◆ TestGen—The computerized TestGen package allows instructors to customize, save, and generate classroom tests. The TestGen program permits instructors to edit, add, or delete questions from the test bank, analyze test results, and organize a database of test and student results. This software allows for extensive flexibility and ease of use. It provides many options for organizing and displaying tests along with search and sort features. Instructors can download the software and the test banks from the Instructor's Resource Center (**www .pearsonhighered.com/irc**).

◆ Instructor PowerPoint slides—Prepared by John Grable and Sonya Britt of Kansas State University. The PowerPoint slides provide the instructor with individual lecture outlines to accompany the text. The slides include many of the figures and tables from the text. Instructors can use these lecture notes as is or can easily modify the notes to reflect specific presentation needs.

For Students

Personal Finance Workbook   The first section of this workbook is made up of a set of worksheets that provide you with the opportunity to answer problems from the book and develop and implement your own financial plan. Reference to the worksheets can be found throughout the text. The second section of this workbook contains Your Financial Plan, which guides you through a series of exercises that utilize the worksheets (also available online) and electronic calculators (found on **www.myfinancelab.com**). The third section contains step-by-step calculator keystrokes to help you calculate important personal finance formulas.

MyFinanceLab   *Personal Finance,* Sixth Edition, is also available with MyFinanceLab. MyFinanceLab, a fully integrated homework and tutorial system, solves one of the biggest teaching problems in finance courses: students learn better when they practice by doing homework problems, but grading complex multipart problems is time-consuming. MyFinanceLab offers:

- ◆ Textbook problems online
- ◆ Algorithmically generated values for more practice
- ◆ Partial credit
- ◆ Personalized study plans
- ◆ Extra help for students
- ◆ Online gradebook
- ◆ Chapter 18 is now in MyFinanceLab

Selected end-of-chapter problems, including Develop Your Skills—Problems and Activities, and the Discussion Cases, as well as additional bonus problems that provide assessment and practice opportunities are available in MyFinanceLab.

Acknowledgments

I gratefully acknowledge the assistance, support, and encouragement of those individuals who have contributed to *Personal Finance: Turning Money into Wealth.* Specifically, I wish to recognize the very helpful insights provided by many of my colleagues. For their careful comments and helpful reviews of the text, I am indebted to:

Allen Arnold, University of Central Oklahoma

Mike Barry, Boston College

Karin Bonding, University of Virginia

Craig Bythewood, Florida Southern College

Ronald J. Cereola, James Madison University

Stephen Chambers, Johnson County Community College

Lynda S. Clark, Maple Woods Community College

Michael Collins, University of Wisconsin–Madison

Bobbie D. Corbett, Northern Virginia Community College

Charles P. Corcoran, University of Wisconsin–River Falls

Julie Cumbie, University of Central Oklahoma

Kathy J. Daruty, Los Angeles Pierce College

Richard A. Deus, Sacramento City College

Yuhong Fan, Weber State University

Beverly Fuller, Portland State University

Caroline S. Fulmer, University of Alabama

Michael Gordinier, Washington University in St. Louis

Clayton R. Griffin, Metro State College of Denver

Ramon Griffin, Metropolitan State College of Denver

Jack Griggs, Abilene Christian University

Carolyn M. Hair, Wake Tech. Community College

Neil D. Holden, Ohio University

Marilynn E. Hood, Texas A&M University

Joe Howell, Salt Lake Community College

Randal Ice, University of Central Oklahoma

Robert Jensen, Metropolitan Community Colleges

Ernest W. King, University of Southern Mississippi

Katherine Kocher, University of Central Oklahoma

Sophie Kong, Western Washington University

Karen Korins, University of Northern Colorado

Edward Krohn, Miami-Dade Community College

Karen Lahey, University of Akron

Frances Lawrence, Louisiana State University

K.T. Magnusson, Salt Lake Community College

James E. Mallett, Stetson University

Abbas Mamoozadeh, Slippery Rock University of Pennsylvania

Robert McCalla, University of Wisconsin–Madison

James A. Milanese, University of North Carolina, Greensboro

Mitch Mokhtari, The University of Maryland

Diann Moorman, University of Georgia

Dianne R. Morrison, University of Wisconsin–LaCrosse

James Muckell, Nyack College

Frederick H. Mull, Fort Lewis College

David W. Murphy, Madisonville Community College

David Overbye, Keller School of Management

Eve Pentecost, University of Alabama

Ted Pilger, Southern Illinois University

Jack Popovich, Columbus State Community College

Robert Rencher, Liberty University

Irving E. Richards, Cuyahoga Community College

Greg Richey, California State University, San Bernardino

Clarance Rose, Radford University

Pat Rudolph, American University

Nick Sarantakes, Austin Community College

Daniel L. Schneid, Central Michigan University

Thomas M. Springer, Florida Atlantic University

James C. Thomas, Indiana University Northwest

Shafi Ullah, Broward Community College

Same Veit, University of Wisconsin–Madison

Dick Verrone, University of North Carolina Wilmington

Sally Wells, Columbia College

Alex White, Virginia Tech

Martha A. Zenns, Jamestown Community College

I would like to thank a wonderful group of people at Prentice Hall. I must thank my editor-in-chief, Donna Battista, who has provided leadership from the top and has kept all the parts moving. Donna has transformed the finance list at Prentice Hall, making it the best in the industry, and in doing so has helped make this book live up to its potential. I would also like to thank Tessa O'Brien, my editor, who has been great to work with. Under Tessa's guidance, I believe we have produced the finest possible textbook and supplements package. Tessa is truly creative, insightful, and demanding—never settling for anything but the best. As if that was not enough, I must also thank Tessa for her role as marketing manager—Tessa never ceases to amaze me. As marketing manager, she has shown an impressive understanding of the market, coupled with an intuitive understanding of what the market is looking for. I also thank Amy Foley who served as the project manager on this revision. Amy has been great to work with. She continuously offered insights and direction, often serving as a sounding board for revisions and new ideas. Even more, she is a great person and was fun to work with, always keeping me on task. It seemed that a day did not go by when I didn't call Amy to ask her advice or help on something, and she was always able and willing to help out. To Meredith Gertz, the production editor, I express a very special thank you for seeing the book through a complex production process and keeping it all on schedule while maintaining extremely high quality. In addition, I owe a debt of gratitude to Nancy Fenton, the managing editor, who made this a much better book. Miguel Leonarte and Nicole Sackin, who worked on MyFinanceLab, also deserve a word of thanks for making MyFinanceLab flow so seamlessly with the book. They have continued to refine and improve MyFinanceLab, and as a result of their efforts, it has become a learning tool without equal.

I should also thank Paul Donnelly and David Cohen. Paul is a past editor and good friend, without whom this project would never have been started. Dave served as the developmental editor and helped mold this book into a text that is fun to read. My thanks also go to Mary Sanger of Nesbitt Graphics who served as copy editor for this edition. Mary did an outstanding job of providing a consistency in presentation that has helped the book greatly. Simply put, she is one of the best.

My appreciation to the people at Prentice Hall would be incomplete without mention of the highly professional Prentice Hall field sales staff and their managers. In my opinion, they are the best in the business, and I am honored to work with them. In particular, I must single out Bill Beville, retired national editorial advisor. He is one of the most dogged and delightful people I have ever met. Bill pursued me relentlessly until I agreed to do this book. I will always owe Bill a debt of gratitude. Bill, I'm glad you're on my side.

I also owe a great debt to John Grable, the Vera Mowery McAninch Professor of Human Development and Family Studies at Kansas State University where he serves as the director of the Institute of Personal Financial Planning at Kansas State, and Sonya Britt, an assistant professor of family studies and human services at Kansas State University and president of the newly established Financial Therapy Association. In addition to preparing the PowerPoint slides and revising the Instructor's Manual, John and Sonya oversaw the revision of the end-of-chapter material. In doing so, they went well beyond the call of duty by refining, revising, and simplifying the end-of-chapter material and thereby greatly improving it. Their efforts made a meaningful impact on the book—strengthening it and making it more user friendly—and, as a result, they have improved the student experience. In addition, they were always there to provide advice and opinions, which greatly improved this edition of the book. Moreover, they are two of the nicest and hardest working individuals I have ever worked with. I am hoping this is a relationship that will carry on long into the future.

I must also thank Diann Moorman at the University of Georgia. She not only prepared the Test Item File, but she also provided excellent insights into the behavioral aspects of personal finance that were incorporated into the book.

Finally, I must extend my thanks to my friend and colleague Ruth Lytton. While her role on this edition was limited, her efforts in the past helped produce the outstanding cases and end-of-chapter material currently in the book. Because she is a perfectionist and an award-winning teacher, her efforts result in a pedagogy that works. When working with Ruth, I am constantly in awe of her effortless grasp of the many aspects of personal finance and of her ability to make complex concepts accessible to any student. She is truly one of the "gifted ones." Her suggestions and insights made a profound impact on the book, from start to finish, and greatly added to its value.

In past editions Derek Klock joined Ruth in working on the case and end-of-chapter material. Derek is exceptional! If you can think of a trait you would like a coworker to have, Derek has it. On top of all that he is one of the nicest people I have ever had the opportunity to work with.

A salute goes also to Marcy Furney for her exceptional work on the "Money Matters" boxes. She also read and reviewed the manuscript and provided insights and comments that materially improved the book.

As a final word, I express my sincere thanks to those using *Personal Finance: Turning Money into Wealth* in the classroom. I thank you for making me a part of your team.

Arthur J. Keown

Personal Finance

PART 1
Financial Planning

It's easy to avoid thinking about financial planning—after all, sometimes just financial existence seems like a victory. The problem is that by avoiding financial planning, you are actually creating more financial problems for your future. It's just too easy to spend money without thinking—it's saving money and planning that take some thought and effort. The problem is that most of us have no background in financial planning.

Part 1: Financial Planning will begin your introduction to personal finance. We will present some of the personal finance problems you will face in the future, along with a five-step process for budgeting and planning. You will also be introduced to ten fundamental principles of personal finance in Chapter 1 that reappear throughout the book. While the tools and techniques of personal finance may change or be forgotten over time, the logic that underlies these ten principles, once understood, will become part of your "financial personality," and you will be able to draw upon these principles for the rest of your life.

In Part 1, we will focus on the first four principles:

Principle 1: The Best Protection Is Knowledge—After all financial advice is everywhere; the hard part is differentiating between the good and bad advice, and without that ability, you're ripe for a financial disaster.

Principle 2: Nothing Happens Without a Plan—Financial planning doesn't happen without a plan, so you're going to want to begin by measuring your financial health by finding out where you stand financially, setting your goals, putting together a plan of action, and then putting that plan into play with a budget. Because without a plan, nothing will happen.

Principle 3: The Time Value of Money—In order to understand why it is so important to begin saving early you need to understand how powerful the time value of money is. Once you understand this concept, saving becomes much more fun.

Principle 4: Taxes Affect Personal Finance Decisions—Like it or not, taxes are part of life, and as a result, your financial plan must take taxes into account.

The Financial Planning Process

Learning Objectives

 1 **Explain** why personal financial planning is so important.

 2 **Describe** the five basic steps of personal financial planning.

 3 **Set** your financial goals.

 4 **Explain** how career management and education can determine your income level.

 5 **Explain** the personal finance lessons learned in the recent economic downturn.

 6 **List** ten principles of personal finance.

7 **Understand** that achieving financial security is more difficult for women.

O n the TV show *How I Met Your Mother*, Marshall and Lily play the part of loving, but somewhat goofy, newlyweds. Marshall is a young lawyer and Lily is a kindergarten teacher, who, along with their friends, Robin, Ted, and Barney, get into some improbable predicaments, but the financial problems they face are, unfortunately, all too realistic.

Marshall has his law degree, is loaded with student loan debt, and has to make a decision whether to take his low-paying dream job with the non-profit NRDC, or a high-paying job with an evil law firm. It's a choice of money versus his dream, and he ends up taking the money. Meanwhile, Lily is back at their apartment with girlfriend Robin, looking over some of her new purchases. Robin asks, "How can you afford such expensive clothes?" The answer is as you might expect, on credit, and apparently Lily has a lot of debt. As Robin says, "Lily, you have debt the size of Mount Waddington!" "Waddington?" Lily responds. "It's the tallest mountain in Canada. It's like 4,000 meters high," Robin explains. "Meters?" Lily responds—apparently Lily knows about as much about meters as she does about personal finance.

Clever and improbable plot line? Not really. Unfortunately, personal financial problems and their avoidance are all too common. It's much easier to postpone dealing with money problems than to confront them. In fact, Lily said she was intending to take care of her credit card debt just as soon as she finished furnishing their apartment. As Robin responded, "You should be on a reality show."

How much do you know about personal finance? Hopefully more than Lily, but probably not enough. That's pretty much how it is for everyone until they've made a real effort to learn about personal finance.

Being financially secure involves more than just making money—life will be easier when you learn to balance what you make with what you spend. Unfortunately, financial planning is not something that comes naturally to most people. This text will provide you with the know-how to avoid financial pitfalls and to achieve your financial goals, whether they include a new car, a vacation home, or early retirement. In addition to providing the necessary tools and techniques for managing your personal finances, you will also learn the logic behind them, allowing you to understand why they work. To make life a little easier, you will be introduced to ten basic principles, which reinforce this underlying logic. If you understand these principles, you are well on your way to successful financial planning. It's just too bad Lily didn't take this class.

Facing Financial Challenges

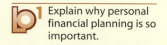
Explain why personal financial planning is so important.

How big are the financial challenges you face? You may be gaining an appreciation for the cost of college. College tuition and fees at a private school average around

3

$27,300 per year; at a public school, the average is $7,605 per year. Add to this the cost of housing and food, textbooks and computer equipment, and the "essentials"—a minirefrigerator, a parking permit, lots of change for the laundry, a bit more cash to cover library fines, and late-night pizza money. How do most students finance the cost of college? The answer is, by borrowing.

Today, the typical grad with loans—and that's about half of all college students—will leave college with both a diploma and about $24,000 in debts, and many students are far more in debt than that. Take, for example, Sheri Springs-Phillips, who was written about in the *Wall Street Journal.* She's a neurology resident at Loyola University Medical Center. On her 11-year journey from the South Side of Chicago to becoming a doctor, she piled up $102,000 in debt. Although her friends think she's got it made, she worries about the $2,500 monthly loan payments that begin when she finishes her residency. Fortunately, Sheri is an exception, but just the average level of debt can be daunting. However, with a solid financial plan, even this level of debt is manageable.

Financial planning may not help you earn more, but it can help you use the money you do earn to achieve your financial goals. Say you really hope to buy a Jeep when you graduate—one with a stereo loud enough to wake the neighbors (and the dead). That's a financial goal, and a good financial plan will help you achieve it. A solid financial plan could also help you save enough to spend the summer in Europe, or help you balance your budget so maybe someday you won't have a roommate. It may even help you pay off those student loans! Whatever your financial goals, the reality is this: Either you control your finances, or they control you—it's your choice.

Managing your finances isn't a skill you are born with. And, unfortunately, personal finance courses aren't the norm in high school, and in many families money is not something to talk about—only to disagree on. In fact, financial problems can be a major cause of marital problems. Disagreements about money can instill a fear of finance at an early age, and a lack of financial education just makes matters worse. As a result, most people grow up feeling very uncomfortable about money. But there is nothing to be afraid of; personal financial management is a skill well worth learning.

When we first attempt to understand the subject of personal finance, we are often intimidated by the seemingly unending number of investment, insurance, and estate planning options, as well as by the fact that the subject has a language of its own. How can you make choices when you don't speak the language? Well, you can't. That's why you're reading this text and taking this course—to allow you to navigate the world of money. Specifically, this text and this course will allow you to accomplish the following:

> ### STOP & THINK
>
> Why do people *need* to make a financial plan? Because it's always easier to spend than to save. According to a survey by Thrivent Financial, more than half of non-retired adult Americans have less than $10,000 saved for retirement. On top of that, 54 percent said they've never tried to determine how much money they will need to save for retirement. How do you see yourself in retirement? Now, do you think you need a plan?

◆ **Manage the unplanned:** It may seem odd to plan to deal with the unexpected or unplanned. Hey, stuff happens. Unfortunately, no matter how well you plan, much of what life throws at you is unexpected. A sound financial plan will allow you to bounce back from a hard knock instead of going down for the count.

◆ **Accumulate wealth for special expenses:** Travel, a big wedding, college for your children, or buying a summer home are all examples of events that carry expenses for which you'll have to plan ahead financially. Financial planning will help you map out a strategy to pay for a house by the beach or a trip around the world.

- **Save for retirement:** You may not think much about it now, but you don't want to be penniless when you're 65. A strong financial plan will help you look at the costs of retirement and develop a plan that allows you to live a life of retirement ease.

- **"Cover your assets":** A financial plan is no good if it doesn't protect what you've got. A complete financial plan will include adequate insurance at as low a cost as possible.

- **Invest intelligently:** When it comes to investing savings, arm yourself with an understanding of the basic principles of investment. And beware: There are some shady investments and investment advisors out there!

- **Minimize your payments to Uncle Sam:** Why earn money for the government? Part of financial planning is to help you legally reduce the amount of tax you have to pay on your earnings.

The Personal Financial Planning Process

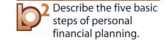 Describe the five basic steps of personal financial planning.

Financial planning is an ongoing process—it changes as your financial situation and position in life change. However, there are five basic steps to personal financial planning we should examine before we continue.

Step 1: Evaluate Your Financial Health

A financial plan begins with an examination of your current financial situation. How much money do you make? How much are you spending, and what are you spending it on? To survive financially, you have to see your whole financial picture, which requires careful record keeping, especially when it comes to spending.

Keeping track of what you spend may simply be a matter of taking a few minutes each evening to enter all of the day's expenses into a book or a computer program. Is this record keeping tedious? Sure, but it will also be revealing, and it's a first step toward taking control of your financial well-being. In Chapter 2 we take a closer look at the record-keeping process.

Step 2: Define Your Financial Goals

You can't get what you want if you don't *know* what you want. The second step of the financial planning process is defining your goals, which entails writing down or formalizing your financial goals, attaching costs to them, and determining when the money to accomplish those goals will be needed. Unfortunately, establishing personal financial goals is something most people never actually do, perhaps because the subject is intimidating, or because they have absolutely no idea how to achieve these goals. Although it is not a difficult task, it's an easy one to put off. However, only when you set goals—and analyze them and decide if you're willing to make the financial commitment necessary to achieve them—can you reach them.

> **STOP & THINK**
>
> According to a recent Retirement Confidence Survey, retirement was the number one savings goal for Americans. It was listed 3½ times more often by those surveyed than the number two savings goal, which was a child's or grandchild's education. But while Americans feel retirement savings are important, they don't seem to be making much progress saving. That same survey showed that 54 percent of all workers had saved less than $25,000 (not including the value of their primary residence), and 63 percent of Americans aged 55 and older have less than $100,000 in savings. Only 30 percent of this same group have an annual income of more than $25,000; 45 percent have an annual income of less than $15,000! And these figures include Social Security benefits! Retirement is only one of many reasons financial planning is so important. As Carl Sandburg once wrote, "Nothing happens unless first a dream." Why do you think goals are so important?

Step 3: Develop a Plan of Action

The third step of the process is developing an action plan to achieve your goals. A solid personal financial plan includes an informed and controlled budget, determines your investment strategy, and reflects your unique personal goals. Although everyone's plan is a bit different, some common factors guide all sound financial plans: flexibility, liquidity, protection, and minimization of taxes.

Flexibility   Remember when we mentioned planning for the unplanned? That's what flexibility is all about. Your financial plan must be flexible enough to respond to changes in your life and unexpected events, such as losing your job or rear-ending the Honda in front of you. An investment plan that doesn't allow you to access your money until you retire doesn't do you much good when you suddenly get fired for using your office computer to play Portal 2 or Shogun 2: Total War.

Liquidity

The relative ease and speed with which you can convert noncash assets into cash. In effect, it involves having access to your money when you need it.

Liquidity   Dealing with unplanned events requires more than just flexibility. Sometimes it requires immediate access to cold, hard cash. **Liquidity** means the ability to get to your money when you need it. No one likes to think about things such as illness, losing a job, or even wrecking your car. But as we said earlier, stuff happens, so when it does, you need to make sure you have access to enough money to make it through.

Protection   What if the unexpected turns out to be catastrophic? Liquidity will pay the repair bill for a fender bender, but what if you are involved in a serious accident and you wind up badly injured? What if the cost of an unexpected event is a lot more than you've got? Liquidity allows you to carry on during an unexpected event, but insurance shields you from events that threaten your financial security. Insurance offers protection against the costliest unforeseen events, such as flood, fire, major illness, and death. However, insurance isn't free. A good financial plan includes enough insurance to prevent financial ruin at reasonable rates.

> ### STOP & THINK
>
> It's much easier to be satisfied if you think of working toward goals rather than working toward becoming "rich." That goes back to Ecclesiastes 5:10, "He that loveth silver shall not be satisfied with silver." What do you think this means?

Minimization of Taxes   Finally, your financial plan must take taxes into account. Keep in mind that a chunk of your earnings goes to the government, so if you need to earn $1,000 from an investment, make sure it yields $1,000 *after taxes*. While you want to pay as little in tax as possible, your goal in effect is not to minimize taxes but to maximize the cash that is available to you after taxes have been paid.

Step 4: Implement Your Plan

Although it's important to carefully and thoughtfully develop a financial plan, it is equally important to actually stick to that plan. While you don't want to become a slave to your financial plan, you will need to track income and spending, as well as keep an eye on your long-term goals.

Keep in mind that your financial plan is not the goal; it is the tool you use to achieve your goals. In effect, think of your financial plan not as punishment but as a road map. Your destination may change, and you may get lost or even go down a few dead ends, but if your map is good enough, you'll always find your way again. Remember to add new roads to your map as they are built, and be prepared to pave a few yourself to get to where you want to go. Always keep your goals in mind and keep driving toward them.

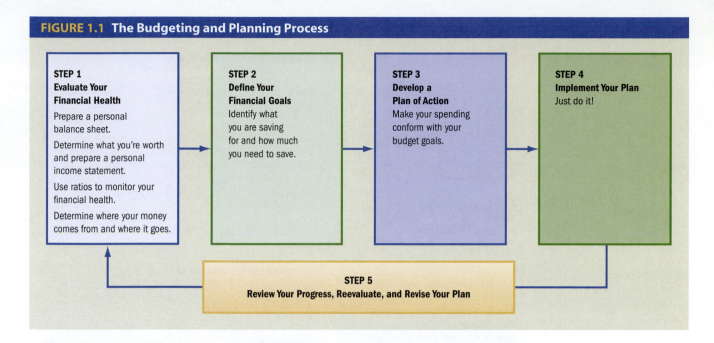

FIGURE 1.1　The Budgeting and Planning Process

STEP 1
Evaluate Your Financial Health
Prepare a personal balance sheet.
Determine what you're worth and prepare a personal income statement.
Use ratios to monitor your financial health.
Determine where your money comes from and where it goes.

STEP 2
Define Your Financial Goals
Identify what you are saving for and how much you need to save.

STEP 3
Develop a Plan of Action
Make your spending conform with your budget goals.

STEP 4
Implement Your Plan
Just do it!

STEP 5
Review Your Progress, Reevaluate, and Revise Your Plan

Step 5: Review Your Progress, Reevaluate, and Revise Your Plan

Let's say that on your next vacation you'd like to explore Alaska, but the only road map you have of that state is decades old. Well, to stay on course you'd better get a new map! The same is true for your financial strategy. As time passes and things change—maybe you get married or have children—you must review your progress and reexamine your plan. If necessary, you must be prepared to get a new map—to begin again and formulate a new plan. Remember, your financial plan is not the goal; it is the tool you use to achieve your goals. It's a road map to your dreams. Your destination may change, and you may get lost or even go down a few dead ends, but if your map is clear, you'll always be able to get back on course.

Figure 1.1 summarizes these five basic steps to financial planning.

Establishing Your Financial Goals

Financial goals cover three time horizons: (1) short term, (2) intermediate term, and (3) long term. Short-term goals, such as buying a television or taking a vacation, can be accomplished within a 1-year period. An intermediate-term goal may take from 1 year to 10 years to accomplish. Examples include putting aside college tuition money for your 12-year-old or accumulating enough money for a down payment on a new house. A long-term goal is one for which it takes more than 10 years to accumulate the money. Retirement is a common example of a long-term financial goal.

Figure 1.2 is a worksheet that lists examples of short-, intermediate-, and long-term goals. You can use it to determine your own objectives. In setting your goals, be as specific as possible. Rather than aim to "save money," state the purpose of your saving efforts, such as buying a car, and determine exactly how much you want saved by what time. Also, be realistic. Your goals should reflect your financial and life situations. It's a bit unrealistic to plan for a $100,000 Porsche on an income of $15,000 a year.

Once you've set up a list of goals, you need to rank them. Prioritizing goals may make you realize that some of your goals are simply unrealistic, and you may need to reevaluate them. However, once you have your final goals in place, they become the cornerstone of your personal financial plan, serving as a guide to action and a benchmark for assessing the effectiveness of the plan.

FIGURE 1.2 Personal Financial Goals Worksheet

Short-Term Goals (less than 1 year)

Goal	Priority Level	Desired Achievement Date	Anticipated Cost
Accumulate Emergency Funds Equal to 3 Months' Living Expenses	_____	_____	_____
Pay Off Outstanding Bills	_____	_____	_____
Pay Off Outstanding Credit Cards	_____	_____	_____
Purchase Adequate Property, Health, Disability, and Liability Insurance	_____	_____	_____
Purchase a Major Item	_____	_____	_____
Finance a Vacation or Some Other Entertainment Item	_____	_____	_____
Other Short-Term Goals (Specify)	_____	_____	_____

Intermediate-Term Goals (1 to 10 years)

Goal	Priority Level	Desired Achievement Date	Anticipated Cost
Save Funds for College for an Older Child	_____	_____	_____
Save for a Major Home Improvement	_____	_____	_____
Save for a Down Payment on a House	_____	_____	_____
Pay Off Outstanding Major Debt	_____	_____	_____
Finance Very Large Items (Weddings)	_____	_____	_____
Purchase a Vacation Home or Time-Share Unit	_____	_____	_____
Finance a Major Vacation (Overseas)	_____	_____	_____
Other Intermediate-Term Goals (Specify)	_____	_____	_____

Long-Term Goals (greater than 10 years)

Goal	Priority Level	Desired Achievement Date	Anticipated Cost
Save Funds for College for a Young Child	_____	_____	_____
Purchase a Second Home for Retirement	_____	_____	_____
Create a Retirement Fund Large Enough to Supplement Your Pension So That You Can Live at Your Current Standard	_____	_____	_____
Take Care of Your Parents After They Retire	_____	_____	_____
Start Your Own Business	_____	_____	_____
Other Long-Term Goals (Specify)	_____	_____	_____

The Life Cycle of Financial Planning

As we said earlier, people's goals change throughout their lives. Although many of these changes are due to unexpected events, the majority are based on a financial life cycle pattern. Figure 1.3 illustrates an example of a financial life cycle. Looking at this figure and thinking about what your own financial life cycle may look like allows you to foresee financial needs and plan ahead. Consider retirement. If you're a college student, retirement may be the furthest thing from your mind. However, if you think about your financial life cycle, you'll realize that you need to make retirement funding one of your first goals after graduation.

The first 17 or 18 years of our lives tend to involve negative income (and you thought it was only you). You can think of this as the "prenatal" stage of your financial life cycle. During this period most people are in school and still depend on their parents to pay the bills. After high school, you may get a job, or attend college, or do both. Regardless, once your education is completed, your financial life cycle may begin in earnest. This first stage can be decades long, and centers on the accumulation of wealth. For most people this period continues through their mid-50s. During this time, goal setting, insurance, home buying, and family formation get the spotlight in terms of planning.

FIGURE 1.3 A Typical Individual's Financial Life Cycle

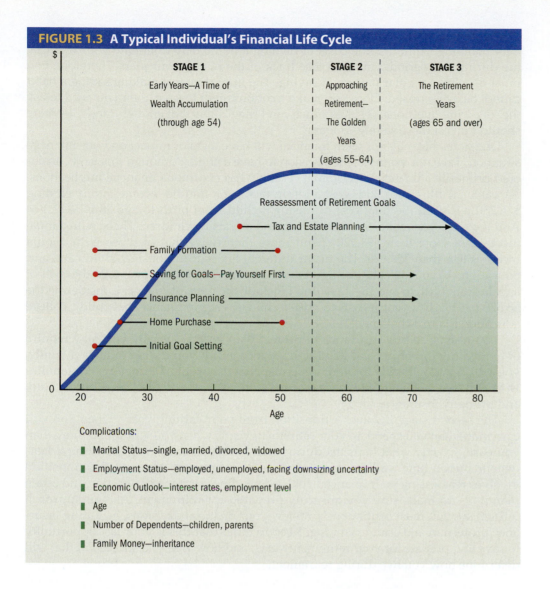

Complications:

- Marital Status—single, married, divorced, widowed
- Employment Status—employed, unemployed, facing downsizing uncertainty
- Economic Outlook—interest rates, employment level
- Age
- Number of Dependents—children, parents
- Family Money—inheritance

The second and third stages are shorter. During the second stage, which for some people may begin in their early 50s, financial goals shift to the preservation and continued growth of the wealth you have already accumulated. You may begin to think about **estate planning**, that is, planning for the passage of your wealth to your heirs. The third and final stage, retirement, often begins in the mid- to late-60s. During retirement you are no longer saving; you are spending. However, you must still allow for some growth in your savings simply to keep **inflation** from eating it away.

Think of the financial life cycle in terms of a family life cycle. Consider a couple that marries in their 20s or 30s, has kids shortly thereafter, spends the next 18 or 20 years raising the kids and putting them through college, and then settles down as a couple again when the kids move out to form their own families. Obviously, a typical individual's experiences don't fit everyone perfectly. Today, with more single-parent families and more young people postponing marriage, it simply isn't reasonable to refer to any family experience as typical. However, regardless of how unusual your life is, you'll be surprised at how much it has in common with a typical financial life cycle.

The early years are different for everyone. For many people, however, the biggest investment of a lifetime, purchasing a home, occurs during these early years.

Estate Planning
Planning for your eventual death and the passage of your wealth to your heirs.

Inflation
An economic condition in which rising prices reduce the purchasing power of money.

With a house comes a long-term borrowing commitment and your introduction to debt planning. Although the costs of owning a home may dominate your financial life during this period, you can't lose track of the rest of your plan. Therefore, you must develop a regular pattern of saving. The importance of making saving a habit cannot be overstressed. Once you make a commitment to save, then you need to ask the following questions: (1) How much can I save? (2) Is that enough? and (3) Where should I invest those savings dollars?

Decisions that may not seem financial will have a major impact on your financial situation. Take, for example, the decision to have a child. Although this isn't considered primarily a financial decision, it certainly has enormous financial implications. As Table 1.1 illustrates, kids cost a lot. In fact, for a middle-income family earning $76,250 per year, the total cost of raising a child from birth to age 18 is $222,360. And the more you make, the more you spend on raising children. Those with annual incomes of more than $98,120 spend more than twice that of those with annual incomes less than $56,670. The major differences occur in housing, child care, and education. As you look at these figures, keep in mind that they cover only the costs of a child from birth to age 18—they don't include the costs of college. Considering the $8,570 to $19,410 a year it costs to raise a child, saving to finance that child's college education is a real challenge!

You must also buy insurance to protect your assets. Initially you may require only medical, disability, and liability insurance, but if you decide to have a family, you will need to provide for your dependents in the event of a tragedy. For families with children, adequate life insurance is essential. You will also need home, auto, and property insurance.

The second stage involves a transition from your earning years, when you will earn more than you spend, to your retirement years, when you will spend more than you earn. Exactly what happens during this transition stage and how long it lasts depends upon how well you are prepared for retirement. Much of this transition involves reassessing your financial goals—including insurance protection and estate planning—to make sure you are truly prepared for retirement. As you approach retirement, you must continuously review your financial decisions, including insurance protection and estate planning. Keep in mind that this is your last opportunity to save and prepare for your retirement years, and how well you succeed at that will determine how you live during retirement.

TABLE 1.1 The Cost of Raising a Child

These calculations are for the second child in a two-child family. For families with only one child, the costs of raising that child are more and can be determined by multiplying the totals by 1.24. For families with two or more children, the costs of an additional child can be determined by multiplying the totals by 0.77.

Annual Income	Annual Expenses First 3 Years	Total Expenses First 18 Years	Total Spent Over 18 Years For						
			Housing	Food	Transportation	Clothing	Health Care	Child Care and Education	Other[a]
Less than $56,670	$ 8,570	$160,410	$53,280	$29,760	$20,790	$10,980	$13,230	$21,720	$10,650
$56,670–$98,120	11,700	222,360	70,020	35,970	28,590	13,260	17,760	37,740	19,020
More than $98,120	19,410	369,360	126,540	45,570	41,790	18,750	20,460	81,210	35,040

[a]Other expenses include personal-care items, entertainment, and reading material.

Source: Expenditure on Children by Families, 2009 Annual Report, U.S. Department of Agriculture, Agricultural Research Service, www.cnpp.usda.gov/Publications/CRC/crc2009.pdf.

In the last stage, during your retirement years, you'll be living off your savings. Certainly, the decision about when to retire will reflect how well you have saved. Once you retire, your financial focus is on ensuring your continued wealth, despite not having income. As always, you'll spend much of your time overseeing the management of savings and assets, but now your concern will be making sure you don't run out of money. You'll be dealing with the question of how much of your savings can you tap into each year without ever running out of money, and your investment strategy will probably become less risky as you now need to preserve rather than create wealth. In addition, your insurance concerns may now include protection against the costs of an extended nursing home stay.

Finally, estate planning decisions become paramount. Things like wills, living wills, health proxies, power of attorney, and record keeping should all be in place to help protect you along with your assets for your heirs. These estate planning tools will help ensure that your wishes are kept as you reach the end of your life. They'll also allow you to pass on your estate to whomever you want while keeping your estate taxes at a minimum.

FACTS OF LIFE

Forty-five percent of those in the United States aged 65 and older are financially dependent on relatives and another 30 percent live on charity. If you're like most young people, fresh out of college, you probably will have an urge to spend all that cash that you may be making for the first time in your life. Feel free to spend, as long as you manage to save for your goals, and *make sure you begin planning for your financial future now*. The key is to start the personal financial planning process early in life and make saving a habit.

MONEY MATTERS

Tips from Marcy Furney, ChFC, Certified Financial Planner™

THE ABC'S OF FINDING AN ADVISOR

Analyze your needs. Are you a "do-it-yourselfer" who needs just a basic plan to follow, or do you need assistance in implementing any recommendations? Are you just starting out, or do you have a family and estate planning needs? Perhaps you have both personal and business concerns, such as a professional practice or your own firm.

Decide what type of advisor you want. Are you set on a "fee only" planner? Do you like the idea of a general practitioner, or does your situation dictate the need for a highly specialized individual, such as an estate attorney? Once you've figured out what type of advisor you want, attend seminars, or better yet, ask for referrals from friends and family.

Visit with one or more advisors before you make a decision. Most offer a complementary initial consultation. Caution: Don't feel you have to keep shopping if you're fortunate to find the right person on the first try.

Investigate your candidates. Ask for an explanation of services or a sample plan. Check for complaints and resolutions through the Better Business Bureau or regulatory bodies such as the CFP Board of Standards. Find out how long the firm has been in business. (Will they be there when you need them?) How is the advisor compensated?

Set a deadline for selecting your advisor and stick to it. I have met people who admit to spending 5 or more years searching for the "perfect planner."

Open your mind! Gray hair and wrinkles don't always mean wisdom, and peach fuzz is not synonymous with fresh ideas. If the candidates are relatively new in practice, make sure they have, or are pursuing, a professional designation and that they have associates who can take over for them if they don't continue in the practice.

Rely on your knowledge and instincts. If you're not comfortable enough with the person to reveal all your financial details, run, don't walk, away. Annoying "faults" and suspicions become major roadblocks with time. Select someone you like, trust, and respect—someone you think could be your lifetime financial advisor. As Mom always said, "Don't date 'em if you wouldn't marry 'em."

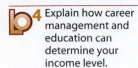

4 Explain how career management and education can determine your income level.

Thinking About Your Career

Career planning is the process of identifying a job that you feel is important and that will lead to the lifestyle you want. When considering which career is right for you, think about the kind of work you find enjoyable and satisfying. It is also important to choose work that provides the standard of living you hope to achieve. In general, your first job isn't the one you'll spend the rest of your life doing. Most careers involve a series of positions that give you the opportunity to display your skills, that lead to a job that you find satisfying, and that allow you to balance work and your personal life. Figure 1.4 is a Job Search Worksheet that will help you manage your career.

Choosing a Major and a Career

The first steps in career planning are self-assessment and developing an understanding of what you want. First, consider your interests, skills, values, personal traits, and desired lifestyle. What activities do you enjoy? How do you like to spend your time? What other skills do you have that might be of value in a career? Look, too, at your educational record. Which courses did you like most and which did you like least? Which courses did you do the best in? From there, take a look at your work experience. Make a list of all the jobs you've had and all the volunteer activities you've taken part in. Think about each of these and determine what about them you found satisfying and not so satisfying. Why did you leave any of these situations?

Conducting an effective self-assessment means looking at many aspects of your life honestly. Once you are through, you will have a good idea of your skills and interests. Now you can research career alternatives and identify those in which your abilities are valued. Once you've narrowed down a list of options, look at both the positive and negative aspects of these professions. Do they offer the status and earning potential you are looking for? Are they part of a stable industry? Might they require travel or frequent relocation? Talk to people in the occupations you've targeted to learn more about what they do as well as what they like and dislike about their jobs.

Once you've made a self-assessment, looked at career options, and talked to people in the workplace, you may be ready to decide on a career field that fits your interests and that is realistically achievable. If you are a college student who has not yet chosen a major, you will want to consider which major puts you in line for the kind of job you'd like when you graduate. You may want to talk to the people at your school's career center to find out more about how specific college majors relate to different occupations. While you want to make sure you choose a career that fits your interests, it is also good to have an idea of what that job pays when you're making this decision. Let's take a look at the average annual earnings of full-time employed college graduates with only a bachelor's degree based upon their college major. As you can see from Table 1.2, the major you choose can affect how much you eventually earn. While looking at these numbers, keep in mind that these are averages—you might earn more or less than the figure given. And picking one of the "low earners" in terms of majors doesn't mean you won't be successful and earn a good wage—just look at Carly Fiorina who served as the CEO of Hewlett-Packard from 2000 through 2005 and is now a business commentator on Fox Business Network. She was a medieval history and philosophy major! Also keep in mind that while money isn't everything, it shouldn't be ignored.

If you're still lost, you might want to try the Internet, which offers a wealth of career advice. *The Career Guide to Industries*, published by the

FIGURE 1.4 Job Search Worksheet

Notes

The Search (Complete items 1–3 on this checklist before starting
your job search.)

1. Identify Occupations
- List your work and life experience.
- Review information on jobs—find out what types of jobs are hiring.
- Identify jobs that use your talents.   _____

2. Identify Employers
- Tell relatives and friends that you are job hunting—you never
  know who may have a lead!
- Go to your state employment service office for assistance.
- Use the Internet or contact employers to get company and
  job information.   _____

3. Prepare Materials
- Write your résumé. Tailor it, if necessary, using job announcements
  to "fit" your skills with job requirements.
- Write cover letters or letters of application.   _____

The Daily Effort

4. Contact Employers
- Call employers directly (even if they're not advertising openings).
  Ask to speak to the person who would supervise you if you
  were hired. Make note of names.
- Go to companies to fill out applications.

The Interview (Complete items 5–8 when you have interviews.)

5. Prepare for Interviews
- Check out the Internet and learn about the company you're
  interviewing with.
- Review job announcements to determine how your skills will
  help you do the job.
- Assemble résumés, application forms, etc. (make sure everything
  is neat).   _____

6. Go to Interviews
- Dress right for the interview—that, of course, will depend on the
  job you're applying for.
- Go alone.
- Be positive.
- Thank the interviewer.   _____

7. Evaluate Interviews
- Send a thank-you note to the interviewer within 24 hours of
  the interview.
- Think about how you could improve the interview—remember,
  this may not be your last interview.   _____

8. If You Have to Take Tests for the Job—Be Ready
- Find out about the test(s) you're taking.
- Prepare for the test and brush up on job skills.
- Relax and be confident.   _____

9. Accept the Job!
- Be flexible when discussing salary (but don't sell yourself short).
  If you're expecting more than they offer, ask for it. The worst that
  can happen is that they will say no.
- *Congratulations!*   _____

TABLE 1.2 What Different College Majors Earn

Choice of Major	Mean Annual Earnings (for all workers—regardless of experience)[a]
Chemical Engineering	$87,903
Physics/Astronomy	$80,963
Accounting	$73,847
Financial Management	$72,900
Marketing	$66,611
Political Science	$66,261
History	$59,878
Nursing	$59,292
Psychology	$58,111
English	$56,861
Secondary School Teacher	$52,120
Parks, Recreation, Leisure, and Fitness Studies	$49,352
Dramatic Arts	$48,360
Social Work	$44,006

[a]2011 dollars.

Source: National Science Foundation, 2003 National Survey of College Graduates, updated by Neeta Fogg, Paul Harrington, and Thomas Harrington, *College Majors Handbook*, 2nd ed. (St. Paul, MN: JIST Works, 2004) and Bureau of Labor Statistics, National Compensation Survey—2010, www.bls.gov/ncs/ncswage2010.htm.

U.S. Department of Labor, is a good source for career advice. This guide is located at **www.bls.gov/oco/cg** and provides information on available careers by industry, including the nature of the industry, working conditions, employment, occupations in the industry, training and advancement, earnings and benefits, and employment outlook along with lists of organizations that can provide additional information. It's comprehensive, too; in fact, it discusses over 42 industries, accounting for over 7 out of every 10 wage and salary jobs.

Getting a Job

Getting your first real job is a job in itself. One of the most important things to remember is to *start early*. Remember what Woody Allen once said, "Eighty-five percent of success is simply showing up." That means that if you're graduating in May, you have to put your résumé together the summer before your senior year.

Why start that early? There are three reasons. First, the beginning of fall semester is generally hectic, so if you wait until then to create your résumé, you may get delayed by a month or two. Beginning in the summer guarantees you'll be prepared to start your job search in the fall. Second, when you begin submitting your résumé before other seniors, you send a message to potential employers that you are both serious and organized—two traits employers love. Third, for many companies, the fall is the beginning of their recruiting cycle.

When you are selected for an interview, the key is to be prepared. While you can't be ready for every question, there are some relatively standard questions that you should be equipped to answer. Recently, resumedoctor.com surveyed over 2,000 recruiters and hiring managers to find out what questions they ask during job interviews. Table 1.3 lists the top 15 interview questions.

TABLE 1.3 Most Common Interview Questions

1. Describe your ideal job and/or boss.
2. Why are you looking for a job? Why are you leaving your current position?
3. What unique experience or qualifications separate you from other candidates?
4. Tell me about yourself.
5. What are your strengths and weaknesses?
6. Describe some of your most important career accomplishments.
7. What are your short-term/long-term goals?
8. Describe a time when you were faced with a challenging situation and how you handled it.
9. What are your salary requirements?
10. Why are you interested in this position? Our company?
11. What would your former boss/colleagues say about you?
12. What are the best and worst aspects of your previous job?
13. What do you know about our company?
14. What motivates you? How do you motivate others?
15. Are you willing to relocate?

Source: Resumedoctor.com accessed June 22, 2011, www.resumedoctor.com/ResourceCenter.htm#interviewsurvey.

If possible, practice interviewing. Many college career development offices provide courses or help in developing the interpersonal skills that are necessary for a good interview. Next, use the library or the Internet to find as much information as possible about the company you're interviewing with. Understand how the company makes its money, know its history and its financial status, and read up on any new developments. And be sure to make a good first impression. Dress appropriately and get a good night's rest before your interview. Plan to arrive about 30 minutes early to guard against any unexpected delays. Display strong body language: A firm handshake, good eye contact, and straight but relaxed posture are all part of a confident image. When the interview is ended, make sure you thank the interviewer for his or her time and for giving you the opportunity to meet. Finally, when you get home, send a follow-up letter, thanking the interviewer again, and reiterating your interest in the position.

FACTS OF LIFE

According to a recent recruiting survey, the most common mistake job interviewees make is: talking too much.

Being Successful in Your Career

If you are just starting out, it is likely that you'll work for at least three or four different companies and have more than ten different jobs over the course of your working life. You may switch jobs or even careers for many reasons: You may be offered great opportunities, your personal interests may shift, or the job market in your industry may change. In this era of regular corporate restructuring, job security is not what it used to be. To protect yourself, be sure to keep your skills marketable through education and by keeping up with changing technology. To increase your value as an employee:

◆ Do your best work.
◆ Project the right image—an image aligned with the organization's values and wants.
◆ Gain an understanding of the power structure so that you can work within it.
◆ Gain visibility. Make those with power aware of your contributions.
◆ Take new assignments. Gain experience and an understanding of the various operations of the organization.

◆ Be loyal to and supportive of your boss. Remember, your boss controls your immediate future.

◆ Continually acquire new skills, in particular, skills that are not easy to duplicate.

◆ Develop a strong network of contacts in case you ever need to look for a new job.

◆ Pay attention to ethics because the most damaging event you, as an employee, can experience is a loss of confidence in your ethical standards. Ethical violations end careers.

The bottom line is that managing your career is an ongoing process that will end only when you finally retire.

What Determines Your Income?

What you earn does not determine how happy you are, but it does determine the standard of living you can afford. However, there is great variation in what different people earn at the same job with different companies. But, one thing is clear, the more specialized skills and training a job requires, the higher it tends to pay.

Without question, the key differentiating factor in determining your eventual salary is how well educated you are as Figure 1.5 shows. Right now, you may be making the best single investment you will ever make—your education. Interestingly, being married is also a trait of the wealthy. Whereas a married couple heads 70 percent of the middle class households, that number climbs to 85 percent for wealthy households. Your financial plan must be realistic and it must be based on your income. Let's look at some basic principles of a solid financial strategy.

STOP & THINK

A recent survey conducted by *Family Circle* magazine found that 84 percent of those surveyed felt that doing work they love was more important than making money, and 88 percent said they valued health and a happy home life above wealth. There's no reason you shouldn't have both, provided you take what you learn in this book and this course, and put together and implement a financial plan. Are you ready to try it?

Keeping a Perspective—Money Isn't Everything

Your personal financial plan allows you to extend your financial strategy beyond the present—to allow you to achieve goals that are well off in the future. In effect,

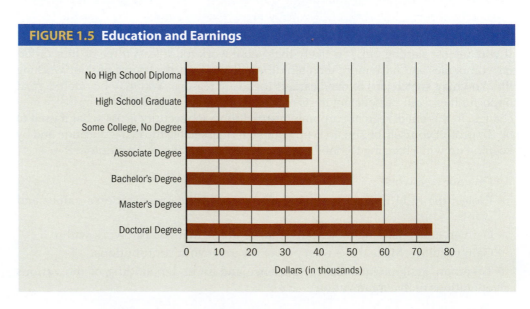

FIGURE 1.5 Education and Earnings

Dollars (in thousands)

- No High School Diploma
- High School Graduate
- Some College, No Degree
- Associate Degree
- Bachelor's Degree
- Master's Degree
- Doctoral Degree

personal financial planning allows you to be realistic about your finances—to act your wage. Unfortunately, for some people financial goals become all consuming. They see nothing but dollar signs and lose a healthy perspective on what is actually important in life. In the first version of the movie *Arthur* there is an exchange between Dudley Moore and Liza Minnelli in which Moore, who plays Arthur Bach, says "money has screwed me up my whole life. I've always been rich, and I've never been happy." To this Minnelli, who plays Linda Marolla (Arthur's girlfriend), replies, "Well, I've always been poor, and I've usually been happy." Arthur's mother then steps in and responds, "I've always been rich, and I've always been happy!" It's true: Money does not equal happiness. In fact, the *Wall Street Journal* reported the results of an international happiness survey and found respondents from Forbes's annual list of the 400 richest Americans score 5.8 on the happiness scale. That's the same score reported by the Inuit of northern Greenland and the hut-dwelling Masai of Kenya. But keep in mind, while money doesn't necessarily bring happiness, facing college expenses or retirement without the necessary funding certainly brings anxiety.

> **STOP & THINK**
>
> Wealth is "like seawater: the more you drink, the thirstier you become."—Arthur Schopenhauer, philosopher in *The Wisdom of Life*. What do you think Schopenhauer meant by this?

Lessons from the Recent Economic Downturn

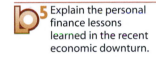

5 Explain the personal finance lessons learned in the recent economic downturn.

The economic downturn that started in 2008 has had a painful impact on all Americans in one way or another. This pain has two root causes: first, a dramatic and swift rise in unemployment and, second, a disruption of our financial markets. Together, these two events have resulted in loss of wealth and a level of difficulty in borrowing that has not been experienced since the great depression. At one point, stocks had dropped in value by over 50 percent and banks were not lending money—in short, it has been a financial disaster of historic proportion. Unfortunately, no one can change the past, but the question remains: Can the lessons learned be used to change your financial future? If not, you will be destined to relive the past over and over again.

In December 2010, a Rockefeller Foundation report[1] detailed how Americans were impacted by the recession that began in 2008. The report focuses not only on financial hardship, but also on citizens' worries, stress, and concerns for the future. Why is it so important that we take a close look at the impact of the recent downturn on Americans? First, it paints a frightening picture of how vulnerable Americans are. Second, it gives you an idea of the deep concerns Americans have about their retirement. For students, retirement is generally the farthest thing from your mind—after all, you don't even have a job yet, retirement is years and years away, and you know things will work out because they always seem to. But by looking at the financial fears of those a generation ahead of you, you can get a clearer picture of what you might face in the future if you don't take action now. Finally, when it comes to pain, we all have short memories. As we move out of the recession and the memory of the financial pain fades, we are destined to repeat the past if we don't learn from it, falling into the old habits that brought on all the financial pain—overspending, not saving, and acquiring too much debt.

---

[1]Jacob S. Hacker, Philipp Rehm, and Mark Schlesinger, *Standing on Shaky Ground, Americans' Experiences with Economic Insecurity* (New York: Rockefeller Foundation, 2010). **www.rockefellerfoundation.org/uploads/files/dea8c178-62d9-4b30-8c58-76b5e9033e04.pdf**.

Let's take a look at some of the findings. First, let's look at how Americans felt about their financial situation:

◆ From March 2008 to September 2009, 93 percent of households experienced a financial shock either in the form of a substantial decline in their wealth or earnings, or a huge increase in spending, most often from medical expenses or from monetarily assisting family members.

◆ Twenty-three percent of households reported a drop of at least one-quarter of their annual household income.

◆ Not just the poor were affected; the middle class was also impacted: More than half of families with incomes of $60,000 to $100,000 who experienced medical expenses or a job loss said they were unable to meet at least one basic economic need such as food, shelter, or medical care.

Clearly, all Americans were affected by this recession.

Now let's look at Figure 1.6, which examines how long a household can go without income before hardship sets in. From that figure you can see:

◆ Just over 29 percent of Americans reported that their household could be maintained 6 months or longer without experiencing hardship if their earnings were to stop tomorrow.

◆ Nearly half of households could not be maintained longer than 2 months without hardship setting in.

◆ About 1 in 5 households could only go 2 weeks without experiencing hardships.

What lesson can we learn from all this? First, in looking back at the recent economic downturn it becomes evident that too many of us have insufficient emergency funds—one of your first financial goals should be to put together an emergency fund that is sufficient to carry you through a financial emergency. We will talk about that in the next chapter, and it will form the foundation for one of our Ten Principles of Personal Finance, which will be introduced in the next section.

What financial issues do Americans worry about the most? According to the Rockefeller Foundation report, without question, the answer is retirement. Over 50 percent of Americans worry about their ability to pay for retirement, with about 60 percent of those who were worried saying they were "very worried." Retirement concerns rise above employment, housing value, debt, medical costs,

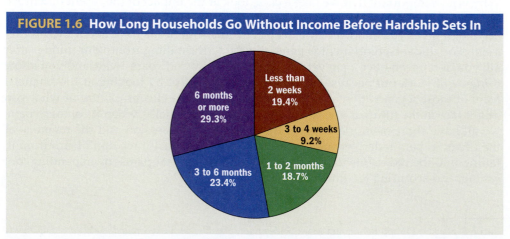

FIGURE 1.6 How Long Households Go Without Income Before Hardship Sets In

Source: Jacob S. Hacker, Philipp Rehm, and Mark Schlesinger, *Standing on Shaky Ground, Americans' Experiences with Economic Insecurity* (New York: Rockefeller Foundation, 2010) www.rockefellerfoundation.org/uploads/filesdea8c178-62d9-4b30-8c58-76b5e9033e04.pdf.

and health care in terms of areas of concern. For that reason we will provide you with a strong foundation in personal finance directly related to retirement planning. While retirement may be many years away, a comfortable and secure retirement won't come without a plan coupled with an early start.

Too much debt and health care were also identified as major concerns for Americans, with approximately 40 percent of Americans indicating that they are worried about their ability to make their debt payments. In addition, both the ability to secure adequate health insurance and to pay medical bills also showed up as a worry for about 40 percent of Americans.

Without a doubt, the economic recession of the late 2000s not only exacerbated the financial problems of most Americans, but it also gave us a look into the future by shedding light on the problems that will again haunt us if we do not prepare for them. Fortunately, with some financial planning, things like having sufficient emergency funds available when you need them; being able to afford a comfortable retirement and being able to retire when you want to; avoiding too much debt; and having adequate health insurance—all currently major concerns for many Americans—won't be worries for you.

Ten Principles of Personal Finance

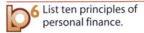

6 List ten principles of personal finance.

To the first-time student of personal finance, this text may seem like a collection of tools and techniques held together solely by the binding on the book. Not so! In fact, the techniques and tools we use to teach personal financial management are all based on very straightforward logic. We can sum up this logic in ten simple principles. *Although it's not necessary to understand personal finance in order to understand these principles, it's necessary to understand these principles in order to understand personal finance.*

These principles are used throughout the text to unify and relate the topics being presented, which will help you better understand the logic behind why the tools work. Let's face it, your situation and the personal finance challenges you'll face won't fit into a simple formula. You have to understand the logic behind the material in the book in order to apply it to your life.

Let's identify the ten principles that form the foundations of personal finance. Some are as much statements of common sense as they are theoretical statements. If all you remember from this course are these principles, you'll still have an excellent grasp of personal finance and, thus, a better chance of attaining wealth and achieving your financial goals.

Principle 1: The Best Protection Is Knowledge

Finding advice on personal finance isn't hard—the hard part is differentiating between the good and bad advice. The Internet, radio, television, newspapers, magazines, and even old-fashioned books are teaming up with financial gurus and guru wannabees, showering you with the latest advice on what to do with your money. While much of that advice will make someone rich, it may not be you; it may be the advice giver instead—and even worse, that someone may be getting rich at your expense. You can turn to a professional financial planner to help you establish a lifetime financial plan, but it will be up to you to manage it. The bottom line is that you need to understand the basics of personal financial management if you are going to achieve your financial goals—it's also the only way you can protect yourself. A solid understanding of personal finance will:

- ◆ Enable you to protect yourself from the danger of an incompetent investment advisor.
- ◆ Provide you with an understanding of the importance of planning for your future.

♦ Give you the ability to make intelligent investments and take advantage of changes in the economy and interest rates.

♦ Allow you to extract the principles you learn here and elsewhere and apply them to your own situation.

Because financial problems in real life seldom perfectly reflect textbook problems and solutions, you must be able to abstract what you learn in order to apply it. The only way you can effectively abstract something is to understand it. As with most else in life, it's much easier to do it right if you understand what you're doing and why you're doing it.

And when you know what you're doing you don't have to rely on insurance salespeople, personal financial advisors, and stockbrokers—after all, they may actually be acting in *their own* interests rather than in *your* best interest. For example, an insurance salesperson, motivated by a potential commission, may try to sell you insurance you don't need. A personal financial advisor may try to sell you financial products, such as mutual funds, that are more expensive than similar products because he or she receives a hefty commission on them.

That doesn't mean you should avoid insurance salespeople or financial planners but you should choose them carefully. Pick a financial planner just as you pick a competent and trustworthy doctor—look for one that fits your needs and has a proven record of ethical and effective assistance to clients. If you trust your doctor—or financial planner—you have to believe he or she has your best interests at heart. Just keep your eyes open, and of course, be aware of ulterior motives when making financial decisions.

Principle 2: Nothing Happens Without a Plan

Most people spend more time planning their summer vacation than they do planning their financial future. It's easy to avoid thinking about retirement, to avoid thinking about how you're going to pay for your children's education, and to avoid thinking about tightening your financial belt and saving money. We began this book with the statement that it is easier to spend than to save. We can go beyond even that and say it is easier to think about how you're going to spend your money than it is to think about how you're going to save your money.

If you're like most people, you can probably spend money without thinking about it, but you can't save money without thinking about it. That's the problem. Saving isn't a natural event: It must be planned. Unfortunately, planning isn't natural either. Begin with a modest, uncomplicated financial plan. Once the discipline of saving becomes second nature, or at least accepted behavior, modify and expand your plan. The longer you put off devising a financial plan, the more difficult accomplishing goals becomes. When goals appear insurmountable, you may not even attempt to reach them.

Principle 3: The Time Value of Money

Perhaps the most important concept in personal finance is that money has a time value associated with it. Simply stated, because you can earn interest on any money you receive, money received today is worth more than money received in, say, a year. For example, if you earn $1,000 today, and invest that money at 5 percent, 1 year from today that $1,000 will be worth $1,050. If, however, 1 year from today you earn another $1,000, that will be worth just that $1,000—$50 less than the $1,000 you earned today. Although this idea is not a major surprise to most people, they simply don't grasp its importance. The importance of the time value of money is twofold. First, it allows us to understand how investments grow over time. Second, it allows us to compare dollar amounts in different time periods. If you can't do that, you'll be lost in personal finance.

TABLE 1.4 Importance of Starting Early—Just Do It!—to Accumulate $1 Million by Age 67 Investing Your Money at 12%

Making Your Last Payment on Your 67th Birthday and Your First When You Turn	Your Monthly Payment Would Have to Be
20	$ 33
21	37
22	42
23	47
24	53
25	60
26	67
27	76
28	85
29	96
30	109
31	123
32	138
33	156
34	176
35	199
40	366
50	1,319
60	6,253

In this text, we focus on ways to create and preserve wealth. To create wealth, we invest savings and allow it to grow over time. This growth is an illustration of the time value of money. In fact, much of personal finance involves efforts to move money through time. Early in your financial life cycle you may borrow money to buy a house. In taking out that home mortgage, you are really spending money today and paying later. In saving for retirement, you are saving money today with the intention of spending it later. In each case money is moved through time. You either spend in today's dollars and pay back in tomorrow's dollars, or save in today's dollars and later spend in tomorrow's dollars. Without recognizing the existence of the time value of money, it is impossible to understand **compound interest**, which allows investments to grow over time.

You'll also find that time is your ally. If you are 20 right now, plan on retiring at 67, and you are earning 12 percent on your investments, you'll end up with $1 million if you begin today and save $33 a month, begin at age 40 and save $366 a month, or begin at age 50 and save $1,319 a month, as shown in Table 1.4. As you can see, it's a lot easier if you start early. This is all because of the time value of money.

Compound Interest
Interest paid on interest. This occurs when interest paid on an investment is reinvested and added to the principal, thus allowing you to earn interest on the interest, as well as on the principal.

Principle 4: Taxes Affect Personal Finance Decisions

Because taxes help determine the realized return of an investment, they play an important role in personal finance. No investment decision should be made without first knowing the effect of taxes on the return of that investment. Thus, you must look at all your alternatives on an after-tax basis. Taxes aren't the same on all investments, so you will find that effective personal financial planning requires you to have an understanding of the tax laws and how they affect investment decisions.

Principle 5: Stuff Happens, or the Importance of Liquidity

Although much of the focus of personal financial planning is on long-term investing for lifetime goals, you must also plan for the unexpected. This means that some of your money must be available to you at any time, or *liquid*. If liquid funds are not available, an unexpected need, such as job loss or injury, may push you to have to cash in a longer-term investment. You may need to act immediately, which might entail, for example, having to sell a rental property when real estate prices are low. And what if you don't have something to sell? In that case you'll have to borrow money fast. That kind of borrowing may carry a high interest rate. It will also mean making unexpected loan repayments, which you may not be financially prepared to make. Generally, unplanned borrowing is tough to pay off; it is just one reason to have adequate liquid funds available and that generally means having enough liquid funds to cover 3 to 6 months of living expenses; exactly how much is needed will be discussed in the next chapter.

Principle 6: Waste Not, Want Not—Smart Spending Matters

Personal finance and managing your money involves more than just saving and investing—it also involves spending, specifically smart spending. If you're going to work hard for your money, you don't want to waste it. Unfortunately, smart spending isn't always practiced. In fact, studies estimate that over 1 in 20 of us—that's over 17 million Americans—are shopaholics; that is, they can't control their urge to shop.

When we talk about smart shopping we will not only be talking about the four-dollar lattes, the two-pack-a-day cigarette habit, the magazines, and the 450 extra satellite channels; we'll also talk about buying a car and a house, and getting the most out of every dollar you spend.

The first step in smart buying is to differentiate want from need and understand how each purchase fits into your life. The second step involves doing your homework to make sure what you get has the quality that you expect. The third step involves making a purchase and getting the best price, and finally, the last step involves maintaining your purchase.

Principle 7: Protect Yourself Against Major Catastrophes

The worst time to find out that you don't have the right amount or right kind of insurance is just after a tragedy occurs. Just look at the flood victims in New Orleans, after Hurricane Katrina, who didn't have flood insurance. As you'll see, insurance is an unusual item to purchase. In fact, most people don't "buy" insurance, they're "sold" insurance. It's generally the insurance salesperson who initiates the sale and leads the client through the process of determining what to purchase.

What makes this process a problem is that it is extremely difficult to compare policies because of the many subtle differences they contain. Moreover, most individuals have insurance but have never read their policies. To avoid the consequences of a major tragedy, you need to buy the kind of insurance that's right for you and to know what your insurance policy really says.

The focus of insurance should be on major catastrophes—those events that, although remote, can be financially devastating. Hurricanes, floods, earthquakes, and fires are examples. These are the events you can't afford, and these are the events insurance should protect you against.

Principle 8: Risk and Return Go Hand in Hand

Why do people save money? The answer is simple: People generally save money and invest it in order to earn interest and grow their money so they will have even more money in the future. What determines how much return or interest you get on your money? Well, investors demand a *minimum return* greater than the anticipated level of inflation. Why? If inflation is expected to be 6 percent and the expected returns on the investment are only 2 percent, then the return isn't enough to cover the loss of purchasing power due to inflation. That means the investor has, in effect, lost money, and there's no sense in making an investment that loses money.

Now that you know what the minimum return is, how do you decide among investment alternatives? While all investments are risky to some degree, some are safer than others. Why would investors put their money in a risky investment when there are safer alternatives? The answer is they won't unless they are compensated for taking that additional risk. In other words, investors demand additional expected return for taking on added risk. Notice that we refer to "expected" return rather than "actual" return. You may have expectations and even assurances of what the returns from investing will be, but because risk exists, you can never be sure what those returns are actually going to be.

Let's face it, when it comes to investing, nothing is guaranteed in the future, and some investments have more uncertainty or risk—that is, there's a greater chance that the fat return you're expecting may not turn out. Just look at investing in government bonds versus bonds issued by General Motors. In each case you're lending money—that's what you're doing when you buy a bond because a bond is just like a loan. The person that issues the bond is borrowing the money and the person that buys the bond is lending the money. Because there is more risk with GM bonds—that is, there's a greater chance GM might not be able to pay you back—GM bonds pay a higher rate of interest than government bonds do; otherwise, no one would buy GM bonds. After all, you know the government will be around to pay off its loans, but GM may not be. It's that added incentive of additional interest that convinces some investors to take on the added risk of a GM bond rather than a government bond. The more risk an investment has, the higher its expected return should be. This relationship between risk and expected return is shown graphically in Figure 1.7.

Fortunately, **diversification** lets you reduce, or "diversify away," some of your risk without affecting your expected return. The concept of diversification is illustrated by the old saying, "Don't put all your eggs in one basket." When you diversify, you are spreading your money in several investments instead of putting all your money in one. Then, if one of those investments goes bust, another—you hope—goes boom to make up for the loss. In effect, diversification allows you to weather the ups

Diversification
Acquisition of a variety of different investments instead of just one to reduce risk.

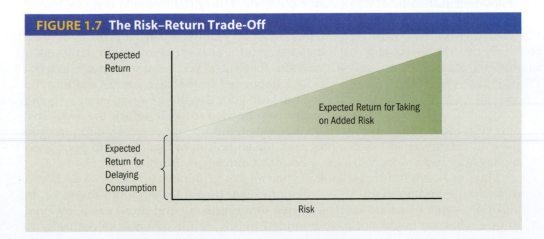

FIGURE 1.7 The Risk–Return Trade-Off

and downs of investing. You don't experience the great returns, but you don't experience the great losses either—instead, you receive the average return.

How much risk can you afford to take? In general, the longer you intend to hold an investment for, the more risk you can afford to take on. Take stocks, for example. Over the past 82 years, large-company stock prices have risen an average of 10.4 percent per year. However, it has not been a smooth ride. The problem with stocks is that "an average" may not be what you actually get. You may, for whatever reason, put your money in the stock market during the wrong period. If you need your money for your child's college education, which begins next year, the stock market is not the right place to invest it. You do not want to stake your child's college education on the hope that this will be a good year—or, more important, that this will not be a bad year.

However, if you are in your 20s and saving for your retirement, investing in the stock market makes sense. Although the market will surely vary over time, in the long run, your money is likely to grow more in the stock market than it would if you invested it in safer investments such as money markets or bonds.

Principle 9: Mind Games, Your Financial Personality, and Your Money

Sure you want to avoid financial mistakes—the problem is a lot of those mistakes are built right into your brain. In recent years a lot has been discovered about how our behavioral biases can lead to big financial mistakes. In effect, your mind can get in the way of good financial decision making. Take for instance what's called "mental accounting." Mental accounting refers to the tendency for people to separate money into different mental accounts, or buckets, each with a different purpose. How does this impact your personal finance decisions? It shows itself when you keep money in a savings account that pays 3 percent interest, while not paying off your credit card that charges you 14 percent interest. It also shows up when you get your tax return and you view it as "mad money" and promptly go out and spend it, while at the same time you are pinching pennies to save for your child's education.

This idea of "mental accounts" is just one of several behavioral biases and mental shortcuts that lead us unknowingly down the path to major financial mistakes. Let's look at another one of these behavioral biases, the "sunk cost effect"—once we put money into something, we become attached to it and are more likely to spend good money after bad money. For example, you just bought a very used car for $1,000, and almost immediately after buying it the transmission goes out. A new transmission is going to cost $1,500. This bias leads you to want to make the repair, even though the repair will cost more than the car is worth. That's because if you don't repair your car, that $1,000 you spent for it is wasted. But what's happened in the past doesn't matter; you want to base your decisions on what they're going to produce in the future. In effect, the sunk cost effect can cause you to make decisions based on the amount of money and time you have already invested in something, and the end result of that can be to pour good money after bad money into a car, a house, or almost anything.

Making all this harder is that everyone relates to money and financial decisions differently—and for many, it is difficult to separate out the emotions involved. In addition, some of us are more sensitive to advertising and more easily swayed to buy what we might not have intended to buy, while others take naturally to

STOP & THINK

Envy and "the comparison complex" are two behavioral traits we all have that make us focus on what others have rather than on what is important in life. Studies have shown that watching TV makes people more likely to feel that happiness is based upon wealth and what you can buy, and as a result, they become less content with their lives. Have you ever felt that way? Think of an example.

financial discipline. Unfortunately, your financial personality is tough to change. At an early age, many people seem to become "financially wired" in ways that make it hard to save while others find it hard to spend. Our views on spending and saving and whether we have a fear of money-related issues resulting in the tendency to "just not think about it" will go a long way toward determining our financial success. In fact, there are also people who view money as an evil and feel uncomfortable with wealth. Recognizing your financial personality will allow you to gain control over your financial life and help you to make decisions based on choice rather than emotion and habit. Moreover, when you recognize what your financial personality is and how it impacts your decisions, you won't have to repeat the same financial mistakes for the rest of your life. Just look at Lily in the introduction to this chapter—she simply couldn't stop spending, in spite of the fact that she didn't have any money.

Throughout the book we will try to alert you to some of the things that might be going on in your brain that you don't know about—at least those things that impact your financial decisions. If you understand these biases, you can control them, and if you recognize what your financial personality is, you can take it out of the process and avoid some of the pitfalls you'd otherwise be subject to. In fact, the last principle that we will look at is based upon one of these behavioral biases, and it's made tougher for some because of their financial personality.

Principle 10: Just Do It!

Making the commitment to actually get started may be the most difficult step in the entire personal financial planning process. In fact, people are programmed against taking on unpleasant tasks—it's one of the behavioral biases that we all have—because of a natural desire to procrastinate. If you don't believe that, just think of the last term paper you had to write—more likely than not, much of it was written the night before it was due, even though you knew that it would be due weeks before. However, the positive reinforcement associated with making progress toward your goals and taking control of your financial affairs generally means that, once you take the first step, the following steps become much easier.

It's much easier to save than to spend, right? No, just checking—you know the opposite is true. For most people, savings are a residual. That means that you spend what you like and save what is left, and the amount you save is simply what you earn minus what you spend. When you pay yourself first, what you spend becomes the residual. That is, you first set aside your savings, and what is left becomes the amount you can spend—that's the first step in putting your financial plan into play.

> **FACTS OF LIFE**
>
> Saving early can make a big difference. Save $50 a month at 10 percent.
>
> Start at 25, by 65 you'll have: Start at 45, by 65 you'll have:
> **$316,204**   **$37,968**

Women and Personal Finance

The basic principles of personal finance are the same for men and women, as is the desire for financial security. However, the effort needed to achieve your financial goals does differ: It's much tougher to achieve financial security if you're a woman. Some of the reasons for this are that women generally earn less money, are less likely to have pensions, qualify for less income from Social Security because they generally earn less over their lifetime, and live longer than men. As a result, planning for their financial independence, in particular during their retirement years, is more difficult for women than it is for men.

 Understand that achieving financial security is more difficult for women.

Consider these facts:[2]

- Over 90 percent of all women will take sole responsibility for their financial decisions at some point in their lives.
- Women live, on average, 7 years longer than men.
- Almost 45 percent of all nonmarried (divorced, widowed, or never married) women 65 and older get 90 percent of their income from Social Security compared to 35 percent of comparable men.
- Twenty percent of all women never marry.
- Forty-seven percent of first marriages and 49 percent of second marriages end in divorce.
- Seventy-five percent of women do not know how much they need to save for retirement.
- Only 28 percent of women 65 and older receive pension benefits, versus 45 percent of men, and the median amount of men's pension income is twice that of women.
- Women tend to be more conservative with their investments, which means their investments tend to earn less.
- At age 65, women outnumber men by 3 to 2, and at 85 they outnumber them 5 to 2.
- Seventy-five percent of married women eventually end up widowed, and the average age of widowhood is 56.
- Although only about 12 percent of all elderly people live in poverty, about three-fourths of them are women.
- Eighty percent of all widows who are now living in poverty were not living in poverty when their husbands died.
- In 2009, the median personal income for women 65 and older was $15,209. For men in the same age group, it was $25,409.
- For every dollar of wealth owned by single men, single women own 36 cents.
- More single young women ages 21–34 (53 percent) said they were living from paycheck to paycheck than did single young men (42 percent).

What does all this mean? It means it's not a fair world out there and women have to take charge of their money and their financial future. Unfortunately, it will take more than the Lilly Ledbetter Fair Pay Act,[3] signed into law in 2009, to fix the fact that women on average earn 78 cents for every dollar men earn. So, where does a woman start?

The first step is to acquire knowledge; remember **Principle 1: The Best Protection Is Knowledge**—that's what this book is all about. You'll notice that this book is filled with action ideas—put them to use—you'll learn how to track your spending, make financial decisions, and take the mystery out of investing. You might also want to join an investment club, which is a great way to learn more about investments and

---

[2]**www.wiserwomen.org**, **www.heinzfamily.org/programs/wiser.html**, **www.ncrw.org**, **www.msmoney.com/home.htm**, **www.wife.org**, **www.pay-equity.org**, **www.census.gov/prod/2008pubs/acs-09.pdf**.

[3]The Lilly Ledbetter Fair Pay Act of 2009 was named for a supervisor in a tire factory in Alabama who after 20 years of employment, received an anonymous note containing the salaries of three male supervisors. Lilly was the sole female supervisor and in spite of the fact that she had more seniority than some of the other 15 male supervisors, she earned $3,727 per month while her male counterparts earned between $4,286 and $5,236 per month. On January 29, 2009, President Obama signed this act into law stating, "Lilly knows this story isn't just about her. It's the story of women across this country still earning just 78 cents for every dollar men earn—women of color earn even less—which means that today, in the year 2009, countless women are still losing thousands of dollars in salary, income, and retirement savings over the course of a lifetime."

get some hands-on experience. If you do decide to join a club, look for one whose members are all women. Remember, over 90 percent of all women take sole responsibility for their financial decisions at some point in their lives. When that time comes for you, you'll want to know what you're doing.

The next step is to make things happen. That means you need a plan. As we know from **Principle 2: Nothing Happens Without a Plan.** The principles in this text apply to both men and women. Although the principles are gender neutral, there are some essential actions you should consider if you're a woman. You want to make sure your plan recognizes that women live longer than men and that half of all marriages end in divorce. If you are married, make sure you're involved in your husband's pension decisions, and make sure you fund any employer-sponsored retirement plans and spousal IRAs to the fullest. Finally, if you aren't convinced about the soundness of your financial situation, see a financial planner about your specific concerns. An advisor will be able to build your confidence and give you direction. Just as important, a financial advisor can serve as a great motivator.

Summary

Explain why personal financial planning is so important.
Personal financial planning will allow you to (1) manage the unplanned, (2) accumulate wealth for special expenses, (3) realistically save for retirement, (4) "cover your assets," (5) invest intelligently, and (6) minimize your payments to Uncle Sam.

Describe the five basic steps of personal financial planning.
There are five basic steps to personal financial planning:

1. Evaluate your financial health.
2. Define your financial goals.
3. Develop a plan of action.
4. Implement your plan.
5. Review your progress, reevaluate, and revise your plan.

In fact, the last step in financial planning is often the first, because no plan is fixed for life.

Set your financial goals.
To reach your financial goals you must first set them. This process involves writing down your financial goals and attaching costs to them, along with identifying when the money to accomplish those goals will be needed. Once you have set your goals, they will become the cornerstone of your personal financial plan, a guide to action, and a benchmark for evaluating the effectiveness of the plan.

Over your lifetime your goals will change and you will see that a general financial life cycle pattern applies to most people, even you. There are three stages in the financial life cycle: (1) the early years—a time of wealth accumulation, (2) approaching retirement—the golden years, and (3) the retirement years.

Explain how career management and education can determine your income level.
In general, the more educated you are, the more you will earn. This is because the more specialized skills and training needed for a job, the higher it tends to pay.

5 Explain the personal finance lessons learned in the recent economic downturn.

The recent economic downturn demonstrated that too many of us have insufficient emergency funds. In addition, it showed that the financial issue that most Americans worry about is retirement. Other major problems that surfaced involved having too much debt and inadequate health insurance. A lack of financial planning left many Americans ill-prepared for the economic downturn.

 6 List ten principles of personal finance.

There are ten principles on which personal financial planning is built and that motivate the techniques and tools introduced in this text.

 7 Understand that achieving financial security is more difficult for women.

Without question, it's much tougher to achieve financial security if you're a woman. That's because women generally earn less, are less likely to have pensions, qualify for less income from Social Security because they generally earn less, and live longer than men. As a result, it is of the *utmost importance* that women take responsibility for their financial future.

Review Questions

1. Why is financial planning, or just plain money management, a challenge for most people?

2. Review the six financial accomplishments that may result from studying personal finance. In your opinion, which three are most important? Why?

3. Summarize the five steps that make up the financial planning process.

4. What three steps are required to define financial goals? Once identified, why is it important to rank goals?

5. List and explain the four common concerns that should guide all financial plans.

6. How does Step 5 of the financial planning process contribute to the idea that "financial planning is an ongoing process"?

7. Explain the time horizon for short-term, intermediate-term, and long-term goals. Give an example of each.

8. Why are financial goals the cornerstone of a financial plan?

9. List and characterize the stages of the financial life cycle. What three financial concerns are addressed across all three stages?

10. Define career planning. How is it related to financial planning?

11. Explain why planning for financial independence is more difficult for women than men.

12. Summarize two strategies that women should implement to compensate for the unique financial challenges they face.

13. List three reasons why college seniors returning to campus for the fall semester should have a résumé already prepared.

14. Describe a good, or effective, job interview.

15. What do you think will be the five most important strategies for success in your career field?

16. List and describe two important factors that help determine your current and future income.

17. Why is financial knowledge the best protection when faced with daily financial decisions?

18. Explain why it is important to review past economic downturns when studying personal finance.

19. What are the two reasons investors demand compensation when saving money or making an investment? Explain how Principles 3 and 8 impact the choice to delay consumption. Why might investors who ignore these principles lose money?

20. Define the terms "diversification" and "liquidity." Give an example to illustrate each concept.

21. Describe the "sunk cost effect" and why this is considered a financial bias.

Develop Your Skills—Problems and Activities

These problems are available in MyFinanceLab.

1. What financial strategies should you develop as a result of studying personal financial planning? What financial problems might you avoid?

2. List the five steps in the financial planning process. For each, list an activity, or financial task, that you should accomplish in each stage of the financial life cycle.

3. Financial goals should be specific, realistic, prioritized, and anchored in time. Using these characteristics, identify five financial goals for yourself.

4. As the cornerstone of your financial plan, goals should reflect your lifestyle, serve as a guide to action, and act as a benchmark for evaluating the effectiveness of your plan. For one of the goals identified in Problem 3, explain this statement.

5. The goal of financing the cost of education is obviously important in your present stage of the financial life cycle. Explain how this goal might continue to be important in future stages.

6. For three of the questions in Table 1.3, write a concise and descriptive response. Practice your answers and then present them to someone willing to give you suggestions for improving your responses or your delivery.

7. Explain how **Principle 5: Stuff Happens, or the Importance of Liquidity** and **Principle 7: Protect Yourself Against Major Catastrophes** may be related. What are you currently doing to protect yourself, and your financial future, from "stuff and other major catastrophes"?

Learn by Doing—Suggested Projects

1. Interview three heads of household, each from a household representing a different stage of the life cycle or socioeconomic status. Inquire about their financial planning process and their strategies to identify and save for short-term, intermediate-term, and long-term goals. Report your findings.

2. You can think of a financial plan as a "financial road map to guide you through life." Develop a visual display that illustrates this concept and the five steps of the financial planning process. Try to incorporate examples that illustrate how the "new roads" on the map may change over the life cycle.

3. Visit your campus career counseling office to learn about the services available to assist you with your career search and your job search. What career management services, if any, are available after you graduate?

4. Jason Zweig, author of *Your Money and Your Brain* (2007), poses the question, which animal is responsible for the greatest number of deaths in the United States annually? The options given are alligator, bear, deer, shark, or snake. But how is the question related to money? Just as inflation should be the larger worry for anyone investing for retirement or other long-term future goals, investors tend to focus on the "attack" of a significant stock market drop as the more dangerous of the two. Similarly, most people are influenced by the biases of recent or vivid events when responding to Zweig's question. Most don't recognize that the deer, typically not associated with fear or fierce attacks, is responsible for 130 times more deaths than the other four animals combined. To learn more about behavioral finance and neuroeconomics, conduct an Internet search or visit your local library.

5. As a foundation for your financial planning, visit the U.S. Department of Labor Career Guide to Industries at **www.bls.gov/oco/cg** to determine the earnings, benefits, and employment outlook for a position in your career field. What educational requirements are necessary for entry and advancement in the field? Don't have a chosen field? Then check out the resources on the Internet or your campus career services office to start your career self-assessment. You can't plan your finances without an income (to learn more, visit **www.payscale.com** or other Internet sites with salary data)—and remember, it's hard to plan for career success in a job you hate!

6. As a group project, have each member of the group visit a financial professional (e.g., benefits officer, stockbroker, insurance company representative, loan officer, banker, financial planner, etc.). Present the list of ten principles that form the foundations of personal finance. Ask the professional to pick the three to five principles that he or she considers to be most important to personal financial success. Share the results in your group and prepare an essay or oral report of your findings. Which principles appear to be most important?

Be a Financial Planner—Discussion Case 1

This case is available in MyFinanceLab.

Jimmy, an accountant, and Bethany just returned from their honeymoon in the Bahamas. They celebrated their marriage and the completion of Bethany's M.B.A. program. They have been encouraged by their parents to establish some personal and financial goals for their future. However, they do not know how to set or achieve these goals. They know that they would like to own their own home and have children, but those are the only goals they have considered. Jimmy knows of a financial advisor who might be able to help with their predicament, but they don't think they can afford professional help.

Questions

1. If you were serving as the couple's financial advisor, how would you explain the five steps in the financial planning process and their importance to future financial success?

2. What financial goals (short term, intermediate, and long term) would you determine to be the most important or least important to Jimmy and Bethany considering their current life cycle stage? Support your answer. (*Hint:* See Worksheet 1 or Worksheet 2.)

3. What four common concerns should guide the development of their financial plan? How do these relate to Principles 4, 5, and 7?

4. List five tips for Bethany to keep in mind when preparing for interviews. *(Hint:* Review Worksheet 3.)

5. Identify three important strategies for young professionals such as Jimmy and Bethany to remember to ensure success in their chosen careers. Why do "ethical violations end careers"?

6. Why is Principle 10 the most important principle? Why is it equally relevant to financial and career planning?

Be a Financial Planner—Discussion Case 2

This case is available in MyFinanceLab.

Nicholas and Marita Delgado, from Rochester, Minnesota, are the proud new parents of twin daughters. This was quite a shock to them and 2-year-old Jarred. They were not prepared for twins and this has muddled their financial plans as well as most everything else! They had planned to pay for education costs, but now they are unsure of how to prepare for having three children in college at the same time. They love their family, and truly believe that money isn't everything, but their dream to retire early and travel seems to be fading with every new expense. They need help with Step 5: Review Your Progress, Reevaluate, and Revise Your Plan. Marita has told Nicholas that she wants to attend a personal finance class at the community center, but Nicholas thinks they should seek assistance from a financial planner. As Nicholas points out, although expenses are rising, they both have good jobs with the potential for rapid advancement and salary increases.

Questions

1. Explain to Nicholas and Marita why personal financial planning is crucial to their future. Why are Principles 1 and 2 important if they choose to seek professional advice? How might the behavioral finance biases of mental accounting and sunk costs influence their response to the professional's advice?

2. Using the information in Table 1.1, estimate the cost of raising Jarred and the twins from birth to age 18 if the Delgados' current annual income is approximately $95,000 and both parents plan to continue working full-time.

3. Explain how understanding and applying Principles 3 and 8 will be critical to funding the children's education.

4. Setting financial goals involves specifically defining the goal, its future cost, and the future time when the money will be needed. Write a specific and realistic goal for funding the children's education.

5. In addition to funding the children's education, name two other short-, intermediate-, and long-term goals the Delgados should consider as they revise their financial plan.

6. With three children to consider, how might Principles 5, 6, and 7 pertain to the Delgados' situation?

Measuring Your Financial Health and Making a Plan

Learning Objectives

1 **Calculate** your level of net worth or wealth using a balance sheet.

2 **Analyze** where your money comes from and where it goes using an income statement.

3 **Use** ratios to identify your financial strengths and weaknesses.

4 **Set** up a record-keeping system to track your income and expenditures.

5 **Implement** a financial plan or budget that will provide for the level of savings needed to achieve your goals.

6 **Decide** if a professional financial planner will play a role in your financial affairs.

I f you've ever seen one of the *Sex and the City* movies, or one of the TV episodes, you know it revolves around Carrie Bradshaw and her friends living, working, and shopping in New York. One scene finds Carrie Bradshaw taking a break from the pressures of trying to come up with a down payment to buy her apartment by doing what she does best, shoe shopping with her friend Miranda.

"Where did all my money go? I know I made some."

Holding up a pair of Manolo Blahnik shoes, Miranda replies, "At four hundred bucks a pop how many of these do you have? Fifty? One hundred?"

"Would that be wrong?"

"One hundred times four hundred, that's your down payment," Miranda replies.

"Well, that's only . . . four thousand."

"No, that's forty thousand," corrects Miranda.

"I spent forty thousand dollars on shoes and have no place to live!"

How many of us have thought at one time or another, "Where does all my money go?"

It doesn't matter how much or how little you make, the key to financial success is control. Today, Sarah Jessica Parker, who played Carrie Bradshaw, leads a relatively frugal life and has financial security well in hand. Perhaps that's because Ms. Parker wasn't always wealthy and appreciates her current status, and also because she and her TV counterpart have dramatically different financial personalities, with Carrie being a spender and Ms. Parker being a saver. Ms. Parker has said, "I remember being poor. There was no great way to hide it. We didn't have electricity sometimes. We didn't have Christmases sometimes, or we didn't have birthdays sometimes, or the bill collectors came, or the phone company would call and say, 'We're shutting your phones off.'"

While Sarah Jessica Parker is doing well, there are plenty of other celebrities who have proven that making money doesn't guarantee financial success. For example, rapper M. C. Hammer, who earned $33 million in 1990, declared bankruptcy in 1996 with $13.7 million in debts. In that same decade bankruptcy also bit film stars Kim Basinger and Burt Reynolds, as well as Shannen Doherty of *Beverly Hills, 90210* fame. Then, in 2003, former heavyweight champ Mike Tyson filed for bankruptcy. And in 2010, *The Real Housewives of New Jersey* diva Teresa Giudice and her husband Joe filed for bankruptcy. While the Giudices made about $79,000 a year (plus $120,000 in "assistance" from family members), they owed over $10.8 million. Their credit card debt totaled over $100,000 including $20,000 to Bloomingdale's, Neiman Marcus, and Nordstrom. How does this all relate to you? Well, you don't have to be rich to lose control of your money. As we've said, it's easy to avoid thinking about our financial future—dealing with the present is difficult enough. However, don't forget **Principle 2: Nothing Happens Without a**

Plan. If you're like most people, you can probably spend money without thinking about it, but you can't save money without thinking about it. For Carrie Bradshaw, that certainly was the case. Saving isn't a natural event. It must be planned.

Planning and budgeting require control—they don't come naturally. Without the ability to measure our financial health and develop a plan and budget, we will not achieve our financial goals. Showing financial restraint isn't as much fun as spending with reckless abandon, but it's a lot more fun than winding up broke and homeless. Making and sticking with a plan isn't necessarily easy, and it often involves what some people would consider sacrifices, such as getting a job over spring break instead of going down to Panama City to be on MTV's *Spring Break*, or just skipping that daily designer coffee. The fact is, though, that the rewards of taking financial control are worth any small sacrifices and more. After all, you don't want to share Carrie's fate, who at the end of the *Sex and the City* scene lamented, "I will literally be the old woman who lived in her shoes."

In this chapter we begin the budgeting and planning process that was first outlined in Figure 1.1, specifically, working on Steps 1 and 3 as shown in Figure 2.1. We begin by measuring our wealth using a personal balance sheet and then a personal income statement to help figure out where our money came from and where it went. With this information in hand, we will use ratios to check into the status of our financial health and look at ways to keep track of all this. Finally, we will set up and implement a cash budget.

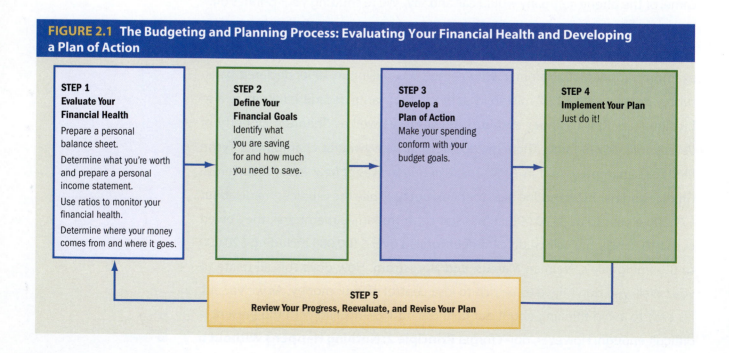

FIGURE 2.1   The Budgeting and Planning Process: Evaluating Your Financial Health and Developing a Plan of Action

STEP 1
Evaluate Your Financial Health
Prepare a personal balance sheet.
Determine what you're worth and prepare a personal income statement.
Use ratios to monitor your financial health.
Determine where your money comes from and where it goes.

STEP 2
Define Your Financial Goals
Identify what you are saving for and how much you need to save.

STEP 3
Develop a Plan of Action
Make your spending conform with your budget goals.

STEP 4
Implement Your Plan
Just do it!

STEP 5
Review Your Progress, Reevaluate, and Revise Your Plan

Using a Balance Sheet to Measure Your Wealth

1 Calculate your level of net worth or wealth using a balance sheet.

Before you can decide how much you need to save to reach your goals, you have to measure your financial condition—what you own and what you owe. Corporations use a balance sheet for this purpose, and so can you. A **personal balance sheet** is a statement of your financial position on a given date—a snapshot of your financial status at a particular point in time. It lists the **assets** you own, the debt or **liabilities** you've incurred, and your general level of wealth, which is your **net worth or equity**. Assets represent what you own. Liabilities represent your debt or what you owe. To determine your level of wealth or net worth, you subtract your level of debt or borrowing from your assets. Figure 2.2 is a sample balance sheet worksheet. We will now look at each section.

Assets: What You Own

The first section of the balance sheet represents your assets. All your possessions are considered assets whether or not you still owe money on them. When you estimate the value of all your assets, list them using their **fair market value**, not what they cost or what they will be worth a year from now. The fair market value can be more or less than the price you paid for a given asset, depending on what others are willing to pay for that asset now. Remember, a balance sheet is a snapshot in time, so all values must be current.

Monetary Assets   There are a number of different types of assets. The first type of asset listed on the balance sheet is a monetary asset. A monetary asset is basically a liquid asset—one that is either cash or can easily be turned into cash with little or no loss in value. Monetary assets include the cash you hold, your checking and savings account balances, and your money market funds. These are the cash and cash

Personal Balance Sheet
A statement of your financial position on a given date. It includes the assets you own, the debt or liabilities you have incurred, and your level of wealth, which is referred to as net worth.

Assets
What you own.

Liabilities
Something that is owed or the borrowing of money.

Net Worth or Equity
A measure of the level of your wealth. It is determined by subtracting the level of your debt or borrowing from the value of your assets.

Fair Market Value
What an asset could be sold for rather than what it cost or what it will be worth sometime in the future.

FIGURE 2.2 Personal Balance Sheet

Assets (What You Own)

A.	Monetary Assets (bank account, etc.) (Chapter 5)	_____
B.	Investments (Chapters 11–15)	+ _____
C.	Retirement Plans (Chapter 16)	+ _____
D.	Housing (market value) (Chapter 8)	+ _____
E.	Automobiles (Chapter 8)	+ _____
F.	Personal Property	+ _____
G.	Other Assets	+ _____
H.	Your Total Assets (add lines A–G)	= _____

Liabilities or Debt (What You Owe)

Current Debt

I.	Current Bills	_____
J.	Credit Card Debt (Chapter 6)	+ _____

Long-Term Debt

K.	Housing (Chapter 8)	_____
L.	Automobile Loans (Chapter 8)	+ _____
M.	Other Debt (Chapter 7)	+ _____
N.	Your Total Debt (add lines I–M)	= _____

Your Net Worth

H.	Total Assets	_____
N.	Less: Total Debt	− _____
O.	Equals: Your Net Worth	= _____

equivalents you use for everyday life. They also provide the necessary liquidity in case of an emergency.

Investment   The second major category of assets, investments, refers to such financial assets as common stocks, mutual funds, or bonds. In general, the purpose of these assets is to accumulate wealth to satisfy a goal such as buying a house or having sufficient savings for a child's college tuition or your retirement. You can usually determine the value of your investments by checking their current price on Internet sites such as **finance.yahoo.com** or in financial newspapers such as the *Wall Street Journal*. Your insurance policy may also be an investment asset if it has a cash surrender value. This type of insurance policy can be terminated before the insured's death, at which time the policyholder will receive the cash value of the policy. If you have this type of insurance policy, then its cash surrender value should be included as part of your investment assets. Finally, any real estate purchased for investment purposes should also appear as an asset. The common thread among all these assets is that they are not meant for use, as you would use a car or a house. Instead, they have been purchased for the purpose of generating wealth.

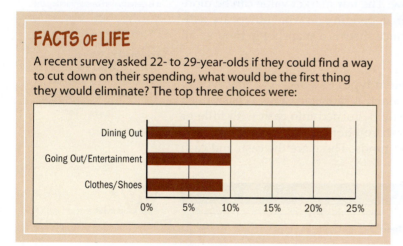

FACTS OF LIFE

A recent survey asked 22- to 29-year-olds if they could find a way to cut down on their spending, what would be the first thing they would eliminate? The top three choices were:

Retirement Plans   These include investments made by you or your employer aimed directly at achieving your goal of saving for retirement. Retirement plans are usually in the form of IRAs, 401(k) or 403(b) plans, Keogh plans, SEP-IRA plans, and company pension plans, which we will discuss in detail in Chapter 16. Typically, retirement plans issue quarterly statements, which list their current value.

The current value of your stake in your company's pension plan should also be included as a retirement plan asset. If you work for a company that offers a pension plan, the easiest way to value your stake in the plan is to call up your benefits office and ask them how much it's worth.

Housing   Your house, if you own it, comprises another asset category. Although a house is an asset that you use—a **tangible asset**—it usually holds the majority of your savings. The value of your house recorded on the balance sheet should be its fair market value, even though at that price it may take several months for it to sell. You might consult with a real estate agent or look on **www.zillow.com** for help in valuing your home. Keep in mind that even if you owe money on your home, it's still yours.

Tangible Asset
A physical asset, such as a house or a car, as opposed to an investment.

Automobiles   Your car, truck, motorcycle, or other vehicle also gets its own asset category. Similar to your home, your vehicle is a tangible asset—one you probably use daily. However, unlike your home, your vehicle is likely to be worth less than you paid for it. The fair market value for vehicles almost always goes down, often starting right after you take it home from the showroom. You can find the fair market value for most vehicles in an automotive **blue book** or try **www.edmunds.com**. Do not include any cars you lease as assets. If the car is leased, you don't hold title to it and thus don't actually own it. Likewise, a company car that you get to use but don't own wouldn't count as an asset.

Blue Book
A listing of used-car prices, giving the average price a particular year and model sells for and what you might expect to receive for it as a trade-in.

Personal Property   This category consists of tangible assets. Basically, personal property is all your possessions—furniture, appliances, jewelry, TVs, and so forth. In general, although you may have spent a good deal of money on these items, their fair market value will be only a fraction of the purchase amount.

Other Assets   The "other" category includes anything that has not yet been accounted for. As an example, you might own part of a business or you have a massive collection of semivaluable (or so you think) Pez dispensers, or you might be owed money by a deadbeat friend. All of these count as assets and must appear at their fair market value on your balance sheet. Of course, if your friend is really a deadbeat, the amount owed shouldn't appear as an asset—since you'll never see it!

Summed up, these asset categories represent the total value of everything you own.

Liabilities: What You Owe

A liability is debt that you have taken on and that you must repay in the future. Most financial planners classify liabilities as current or long-term. Current liabilities are those that must be paid off within the next year, and long-term liabilities come due beyond a year's time. In listing your liabilities, be sure to include only the *unpaid* balances on those liabilities. Remember, you owe only the unpaid portion of any loan.

Current Debt   In general, the current debt category is comprised of the total of your unpaid bills including utility bills, past-due rent, cable TV bills, and insurance premiums that you owe. The unpaid balance on your credit cards represents a current liability because it's a debt that you should pay off within a year. Even if you have not yet received a bill for a purchase you made on credit, the amount you owe on this purchase should be included as a liability.

Long-Term Debt   This category tends to consist of debt on larger assets, such as your home or car or student loan. Because of the nature of the assets it finances, long-term debt almost always involves larger amounts than does current debt. If you think about it, the very reason long-term debt covers the long term is that it involves sums too large for the average individual to be able to pay off within 1 year. The largest debt you ever take on, and thus the longest-term debt you ever take on, will probably be the mortgage on your home. Car loans are another major category of long-term debt. Just as a leased car is not considered an asset, the remaining lease obligation should not be considered a liability, or something that you owe. In effect, you are "renting" your car when you lease it. However, it's a very fine line between a debt obligation and a lease contract—if the lease simply can't be broken, no matter what, it may be considered debt. Keep in mind that future lease payments, future insurance payments, and future rent payments are something you may owe in the future, but they are not something you owe right now.

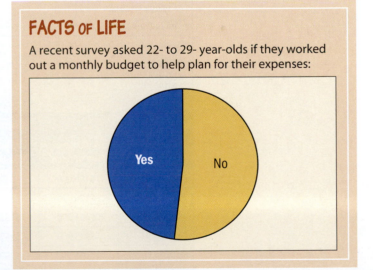

FACTS OF LIFE

A recent survey asked 22- to 29- year-olds if they worked out a monthly budget to help plan for their expenses:

Finally, any other loans that you have outstanding should be included. For example, student loans, loans on your life insurance policy, bank loans, and installment loans are liabilities. Together, long-term debt and current liabilities represent what you owe.

Net Worth: A Measure of Your Wealth

Insolvent
The condition in which you owe more money than your assets are worth.

To calculate your net worth, subtract your total debt from your total assets. This represents the level of wealth you have accumulated. If your liabilities are greater than the value of your assets, then your net worth has a negative value, and you're considered **insolvent**. Insolvency results from consuming more than you take in financially, and in some instances it can lead to bankruptcy.

What is a "good" level of net worth? That depends upon your goals and your place in the financial life cycle. You would expect a 25-year-old to have a considerably lower net worth than a 45-year-old. Likewise, a 45-year-old who has saved for college for three children may have a higher net worth than a 45-year-old with no children. Which one is in better financial shape? The answer doesn't necessarily rest on who has the larger net worth, but on who has done a better job of achieving financial goals. Just to give you an idea of where most people stand, Table 2.1 presents the average annual salary and net worth for individuals along with some other financial data.

Your goal in financial planning is to manage your net worth or wealth in such a way that your goals are met in a timely fashion. The balance sheet enables you to measure your progress toward these goals, and to monitor your financial well-being. It also allows you to detect changes in your financial well-being that might otherwise go unnoticed and correct them early on.

TABLE 2.1 How Do You Compare?

Average annual salary:	
High school graduate or GED	$33,801
College graduate	$55,656
All households (total for all household members)	$62,857

If your family income is at least …	then you're in the top …
$180,000	5%
$100,240	20%
$62,725	40%

Family Net Worth and Income					
Age	Average Net Worth	Median Net Worth	Head of Household Education Status	Average Net Worth	Median Net Worth
Less than 35	$106,000	$11,800	No high school diploma	$142,900	$33,200
35 to 44	$325,600	$86,600	High school diploma	$251,600	$80,300
45 to 54	$661,200	$182,500	Some college	$365,900	$84,700
55 to 64	$935,800	$253,700	College degree	$1,097,800	$280,800
65 to 74	$1,015,200	$239,400			
75 or more	$638,200	$213,500			
All families		$120,300			

Average annual amount spent by full-time college students on beer and pizza …	$1,900
Average annual cost of college—tuition, room, and board at an in-state university …	$19,388
Projected cost in 18 years …	$54,779

Source: CollegeBoard.com; Federal Reserve Board, 2011; Survey of Consumer Finances, 2007; EBRI 2010 Retirement Confidence Survey; U.S. Census Bureau, *Percent Distribution by Households, by Selected Characteristics within Income Quartiles,* 2009; and Department of Education, National Center for Educational Statistics, *The Condition of Education 2010* (NCES 2010-028).

Sample Balance Sheet for Larry and Louise Tate

To illustrate the construction and use of a balance sheet, we have a sample from Larry and Louise Tate shown in Figure 2.3. Remember, a balance sheet provides a snapshot of an individual's or a family's financial worth at a given point in time. As investment values fluctuate daily with the movements in the stock market, so does net worth. The balance sheet in Figure 2.3 was constructed on December 31, 2011, and reflects the value of the Tates' assets, liabilities, and net worth on that specific date.

Worksheet

Using an Income Statement to Trace Your Money

Analyze where your money comes from and where it goes using an income statement.

Income Statement
A statement that tells you where your money has come from and where it has gone over some period of time.

The second step in creating a personal financial plan is to trace your money. A balance sheet is like a financial snapshot: It tells you how much wealth you have accumulated as of a *certain date*. An **income statement** is more like a financial motion picture: It tells you where your money has come from and where it has gone over some *period of time*. Actually, although it's generally called an income statement, it's really an income and expenditure, or net income, statement because it looks at both what you take in and subtracts from that, or "nets out," what you spend, with what is left over being the amount available for savings or investment.

An income statement can help you stay solvent by telling you whether or not you're earning more than you spend. If you're spending too much, your income statement shows exactly where your money is going so that you can spot problem areas quickly. Of course, if you don't have a spending problem, your income statement tells you how much of your income is available for savings and for meeting financial goals. With a good income statement, you'll never end another month wondering where all of your money went.

Personal income statements are prepared on a cash basis, meaning they're based entirely on actual cash flows. You record income only when you actually receive money, and you record expenditures only when you actually pay money out. Giving someone an IOU wouldn't appear on an income statement, but receiving a paycheck would. Buying a stereo on credit wouldn't appear on your income statement, but making a payment to the credit card company would. As a result, a personal income statement truly reflects the pattern of cash flows that the individual or family experiences.

To construct an income statement, you need to record your income only for the given time period and subtract from it the expenses you incurred during that period. The result tells you the amount you have available for savings. Figure 2.4 shows a general outline for an income statement.

Worksheet

Income: Where Your Money Comes From

For your income statement, income, or cash inflows, will include such items as wages, salary, bonuses, tips, royalties, and commissions, in addition to any other sources of income you may have. Additional sources of income might include family income, payments from the government (e.g., veterans' benefits or welfare income), retirement income, investment income, and those yearly checks you get for winning the Publishers' Clearinghouse Sweepstakes.

Some of your income may not ever reach your pocketbook. Instead, it may be automatically invested in a voluntary retirement plan, used to pay for insurance you buy through work, or be sent to the government to cover taxes. For example, if your total earnings are $50,000 and you automatically have $4,000 deducted for insurance

FIGURE 2.3   A Balance Sheet for Louise and Larry Tate, December 31, 2011

Assets (What They Own)

MONETARY ASSETS

A. Total Monetary Assets	A.	=	3,590

INVESTMENTS

Mutual Funds			5,600
Individual Stocks and Bonds		+	9,500
Investment Real Estate (REITs, partnerships)		+	0
Other (life insurance—cash value, REITs, other)		+	0
B. Total Investments	B.	=	15,100

RETIREMENT PLANS

401(k) and 403(b), Keough Plan			2,500
Company Pension		+	8,000
IRA		+	8,000
C. Total Retirement Plans	C.	=	18,500

HOUSING

Primary Residence			170,000
Time-Shares/Condominiums, and Second Home		+	70,000
D. Total Housing (market value)	D.	=	240,000

AUTOMOBILES

E. Total Automobiles	E.	=	12,000

PERSONAL PROPERTY

F. Total Personal Property	F.	=	11,000

OTHER ASSETS

G. Total Other Assets	G.	=	0

TOTAL ASSETS

H. Total Assets (add lines A–G)	H.	=	300,190

Liabilities or Debt (What You Owe)

CURRENT BILLS

I. Current Bills (unpaid balance)	I.	=	350

CREDIT CARD DEBT

J. Total Credit Card Debt	J.	=	1,150

HOUSING LOANS

First Mortgage			105,000
Second-Home Mortgage		+	52,000
Home Equity Loan		+	9,000
K. Total Housing Loans	K.	=	166,000

AUTOMOBILE LOANS

L. Total Automobile Loans	L.	=	3,000

OTHER DEBT

College Loans			4,000
Other Loans (installment, bank, other)		+	1,000
M. Total Other Debt	M.	=	5,000

TOTAL DEBT

N. Total Debt (add lines I–M)	N.	=	$175,500

Your Net Worth

TOTAL ASSETS

H. Total Assets	H.	+	$300,190

LESS: TOTAL DEBT

N. Less: Total Debt	N.	−	$175,500

EQUALS: NET WORTH

O. Equals: Net Worth	O.	=	$124,690

Assets: This includes everything they own.

The Tates' primary investments are their home and their vacation condominium in Vail, which have market values of $170,000 and $70,000, respectively.

Adding all the assets together shows that the Tates own or have total assets of $300,190.

Liabilities: This includes everything they owe.

Just as the Tates' homes make up their primary assets, their mortgages on these homes make up their primary liabilities. Their mortgage loans total $166,000.

The Tates' total liabilities, or what they owe, equals $175,500.

We use net worth to gauge financial progress. If in future balance sheets the Tates' net worth is higher, the Tates are accumulating more wealth.

Net Worth: This is the difference between assets and liabilities and is a measure of your wealth.

If the Tates sold off all their assets and paid off all their debts, they would have $124,690 in cash—that is their net worth.

FIGURE 2.4 A Simplified Income Statement

Your Take-Home Pay

A.	Total Income		A. _____
B.	Total Income Taxes	−	B. _____
C.	After-Tax Income Available for Living Expenditures or Take-Home Pay (line A minus line B)	=	C. _____

Your Living Expenses

D.	Total Housing Expenditures		D. _____
E.	Total Food Expenditures	+	E. _____
F.	Total Clothing and Personal Care Expenditures	+	F. _____
G.	Total Transportation Expenditures	+	G. _____
H.	Total Recreation Expenditures	+	H. _____
I.	Total Medical Expenditures	+	I. _____
J.	Total Insurance Expenditures	+	J. _____
K.	Total Other Expenditures	+	K. _____
L.	Total Living Expenditures (add lines D–K)	=	L. _____

Total Available for Savings and Investments

C.	After-Tax Income Available for Living Expenditures or Take-Home Pay		C. _____
L.	Total Living Expenditures (add lines D–K)	−	L. _____
M.	Income Available for Savings and Investment (line C minus line L)	=	M. _____

and a retirement fund, and $8,000 deducted in taxes, then your income would be $50,000 even though your take-home pay is only $38,000. You must make sure to record the full amount of what you earned—your full earnings and taxes paid, not just the dollar value of your paycheck. Any money you receive, even if you automatically spend it (even for taxes), is considered income at the point in time when it is received.

Next, include the total amount of money you pay in federal, state, and Social Security income taxes. Then, subtract your taxes from your earnings. This is your take-home pay, or the money you have available for expenditures.

Expenditures: Where Your Money Goes

Although income is usually very easy to calculate, expenditures usually are not. Why? Because many expenditures are cash transactions and do not leave a paper trail. It's hard to keep track of all the little things you spend your money on. But to create a valuable personal financial plan, you must understand where your money goes. Look at the categories of expenditures in Figure 2.4 to get an idea of the ways living expenses can be categorized and tracked.

Some financial planners also classify living expenses as **variable** or **fixed expenditures**, depending on whether you have control over the expenditure. These classifications are appealing, but not all expenses fit neatly into them. For example, it's difficult to categorize car or home repairs as being either variable (you have a choice in spending this money) or fixed (you have no choice in spending this money). They may be postponable but probably not for too long.

Where does all our money go? Turns out that what the average American household spends its money on depends on how much it earns. The more we earn, the more we spend on such things as education and entertainment. Figure 2.5 provides a breakdown of spending for the average U.S. household or, as the government calls it, consumer unit. It shows that housing is the major expenditure, accounting for 34.4 percent of all expenditures. Under the heading of housing, shelter is the main item, with utilities, fuels, and public services following next in importance. The category that comes

Variable Expenditure
An expenditure over which you have control. That is, you are not obligated to make that expenditure, and it may vary from month to month.

Fixed Expenditure
An expenditure over which you have no control. You are obligated to make this expenditure, and it is generally at a constant level each month.

FIGURE 2.5 How Americans Spent Their Money in 2010

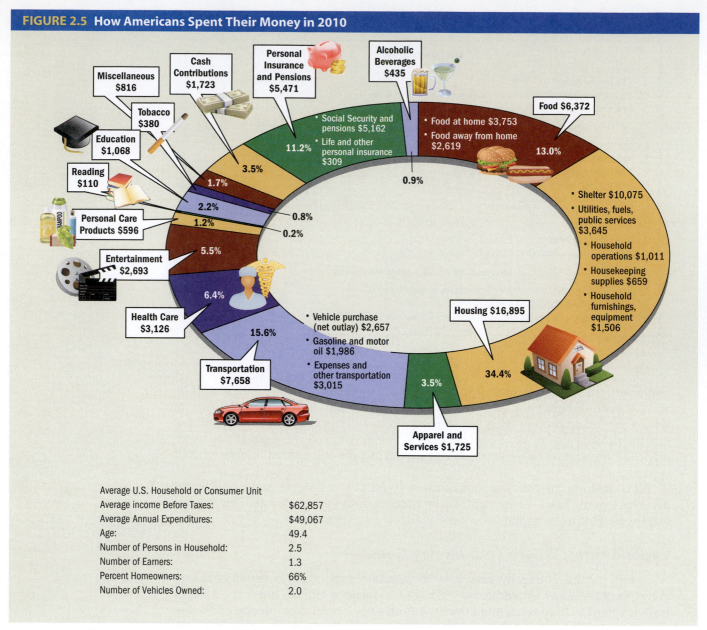

Average U.S. Household or Consumer Unit	
Average income Before Taxes:	$62,857
Average Annual Expenditures:	$49,067
Age:	49.4
Number of Persons in Household:	2.5
Number of Earners:	1.3
Percent Homeowners:	66%
Number of Vehicles Owned:	2.0

Source: Consumer Expenditure (U.S. Department of Labor, U.S. Bureau of Labor Statistics, 2010).

in second in terms of money spent is transportation, which accounts for 15.6 percent of all expenditures, followed by food, which accounts for 13 percent of all expenditures. Interestingly, but probably not a surprise, 41.1 percent of food expenditures, or an average of $2,619 per year, is spent away from home at restaurants.

Why the difference between income before taxes and average annual expenditures shown in Figure 2.5? One big reason is that neither taxes nor savings are included. How much are taxes on average? Federal, state, and local income taxes consumed 9.2 percent of all personal income in 2009. On top of that, it's also possible to spend even more by borrowing money—just by putting it on your credit card. One thing to keep in mind with these figures is that they represent the averages, not median or middle income. Why is that important? If you calculate the average income for 100 people, you add up the income for all 100, then divide that by 100. However, if there are some people like Warren Buffett who make a ton of money in that population of 100, they would raise the average income of the entire population above what the 50th ranked person earned. What that 50th ranked person earned is the median of the population. You can think of that as what the "Average Joe" earns. For the United States, the median household income is less than the $62,857 shown in Figure 2.5; it's actually only about $49,777. If you look at what is considered "family households," it is pretty close to $61,265, and for "non-family households" (someone living alone or unrelated people living together), it is only $30,444. Still, this figure gives you a good idea of what some of the typical expenditures are for a typical household unit.

Also, keep in mind that the amounts in Figure 2.5 are spending averages, and that they vary across the country. For example, people living in San Francisco spend quite a bit more on food because they tend to eat out more often than those who live else-where (better restaurants, I guess). In addition, remember that when you buy some-thing, it actually costs more than you may think—at least in terms of how much money you must earn to buy it. For example, if you pay 28 percent of your income in taxes, and you want to buy a new stereo for $720, you have to earn $1,000 to pay for it. The first $280 of your $1,000 earnings went to Uncle Sam, leaving you $720 for your stereo.

Preparing an Income Statement: Louise and Larry Tate

To get a better understanding of the preparation of an income statement, take a look at the one for Louise and Larry Tate in Figure 2.6. The income statement and balance sheet can and should be used together. The balance sheet lets you judge your finan-cial standing by showing your net worth, and the income statement tells you exactly how your spending and saving habits affect that net worth. If your balance sheet shows you that you're not building your net worth as much or as quickly as you'd like, or if you're overspending and actually decreasing your net worth, your income statement can help by showing you where your money is going.

By reviewing all your expenses and spending patterns, you can decide on specific ways to cut back on purchases and increase savings. This process of setting spending goals is referred to as setting a **budget**. As you will see later in this chapter, a smart budget includes estimates of all future expenses and helps you manage your money to meet specific financial goals.

But before you can design and implement a budget plan, you first need to ana-lyze your balance sheet and income statement using ratios to better understand any financial shortcomings or deficiencies you discover.

Budget
A plan for controlling cash inflows and cash outflows. Based on your goals and financial obligations, a budget limits spending in different categories.

Using Ratios: Financial Thermometers

 3 Use ratios to identify your financial strengths and weaknesses.

The next step in creating your personal financial plan is to take the temperature of your finances. By themselves the numbers in your balance sheet and income state-ment are helpful and informative, but they don't tell you everything you need to know about your financial well-being. You need a tool to help you glean all the meaning you can from these numbers. That tool is ratios.

Financial ratios allow you to analyze the raw data in your balance sheet and income statement and to compare them with a preset target or your own previous performance. In general, you use ratios to better understand how you're managing your financial resources. Specifically, you want answers to these questions:

1. Do I have enough liquidity to meet emergencies?
2. Can I meet my debt obligations?
3. Am I saving as much as I think I am?

FIGURE 2.6 Louise and Larry Tate's Personal Income Statement

Your Take-Home Pay		
Income		
Wages and Salaries		
Wage Earner 1	$57,500	
Wage Earner 2	12,000	
= Total Wages and Salaries		69,500
+ Interest, Dividends, Royalties, Other		720
= **A. Total Income**		**$70,220**
Taxes		
Federal Income and Social Security		11,830
+ State Income		1,880
= **B. Total Income Taxes**		**$13,710**
C. After-Tax Income Available for Living Expenditures or Take-Home Pay (line A minus line B)		**$56,510**
Your Living Expenses		
Housing		
Rent		0
+ Mortgage Payments		19,656
+ Utilities, Maintenance, Taxes, Furniture, Other		10,820
= **D. Total Housing Expenditures**		**$30,476**
Food		
Food and Supplies		5,800
+ Restaurant Expenses		1,400
= **E. Total Food Expenditures**		**$ 7,200**
Clothing and Personal Care		
= **F. Total Clothing and Personal Care Expenditures**		**$ 2,590**
Transportation		
Automobile Loan Payments		2,588
+ Gas, Tolls, Parking, Repairs, Other		1,550
= **G. Total Transportation Expenditures**		**$ 4,138**
Recreation		
Vacation		2,000
Other Recreation		1,700
= **H. Total Recreation Expenditures**		**$ 3,700**
Medical Expenditures		
= **I. Total Medical Expenditures**		**$ 410**
Insurance Expenditures		
Health and Life		420
+ Automobile		1,260
+ Disability, Liability, Other		260
= **J. Total Insurance Expenditures**		**$ 1,940**
Other Expenditures		
Educational Expenditures (college loan payments)		1,600
+ Child Care, Other		180
= **K. Total Other Expenditures**		**$ 1,780**
L. Total Living Expenditures (add lines D–K)		**$52,234**
Total Available for Savings and Investment		
= **M. Income Available for Savings and Investment (line C minus line L)**		**$ 4,276**

> Your take-home pay is your after-tax income—it is what you have available to spend or save.

> Your income statement only makes sense if you know where your money goes. To determine your living expenses, keep a small notebook or some notepaper in your purse or wallet, and write down all your cash expenditures—do this for a month. You'll probably be surprised to see where your money went. In addition, make use of your credit card bills and cancelled checks to help keep track.

> If your take-home pay is greater than your living expenses, you can save and invest—but if your take-home pay is less than your living expenses, you've got some changes to make.

Question 1: Do I Have Enough Liquidity to Meet Emergencies?

If your TV died in the middle of the playoffs or that miniseries you've been watching, would you have enough cash on hand to buy another one immediately? To judge your liquidity, you need to compare the amount of your cash and other liquid assets with the amount of debt you have currently coming due. In other words, you need to look at your balance sheet and divide your monetary assets by your current liabilities. The resultant measure of your liquidity is called the **current ratio**:

$$\text{current ratio} = \frac{\text{monetary assets}}{\text{current liabilities}}$$

Current Ratio
A ratio aimed at determining if you have adequate liquidity to meet emergencies, defined as monetary assets divided by current liabilities.

We can see from Larry and Louise Tates' balance sheet that their monetary assets total $3,590 and their current liabilities (current bills and credit card debt) total $1,500. Thus, the Tates' current ratio is:

$$\text{current ratio} = \frac{\$3,590}{\$1,500} = 2.39$$

Although there's no set rule for how large the current ratio should be, it certainly should be greater than 1.0. Most financial advisors look for a current ratio above 2.0. More important than the level of the current ratio is its trend—is it going up, or of more concern, is it going down? If it is going down, you have to try to find the cause. To do this you have to see what changes have caused the ratio to decrease.

One problem with the current ratio is that people generally have a number of monthly expenses that are not considered current liabilities. For example, long-term debt payments such as mortgage payments, auto loan payments, and so forth may not be considered current liabilities but still must be paid on a monthly basis. Therefore, it's also helpful to calculate the ratio of monetary assets to monthly living expenses, called the **month's living expenses covered ratio**.

FACTS OF LIFE

A Gallup poll of U.S. adults between the ages of 22 and 29 asked: How much do you spend on entertainment (eating out, going to movies, buying music) a month?

$$\text{month's living expenses covered ratio} = \frac{\text{monetary assets}}{\text{annual living expenditures}/12}$$

Month's Living Expenses Covered Ratio
A ratio aimed at determining if you have adequate liquidity to meet emergencies, defined as monetary assets divided by annual living expenditures divided by 12.

As the name suggests, this ratio tells you how many months of living expenditures you can cover with your present level of monetary assets. Again, the numerator is the level of monetary assets, and the denominator is the annual living expenditures (as on line L of the income statement in Fig. 2.6) divided by 12. For the Tates, this ratio would be:

$$\frac{\$3,590}{\$52,234/12} = \frac{\$3,590}{\$4,353} = 0.825 \text{ months}$$

This means the Tates currently have enough cash and liquid assets on hand to cover 0.825 months of expenditures.

The traditional rule of thumb in personal finance is that an individual or family should have enough liquid assets to cover 3 to 6 months of expenditures in order to cover the untimely death of a television, a major car repair, or some other unexpected event. The Tates fall well short of this amount. However, this rule was set up long before credit cards and home equity lines of credit were as common as they are today. You set up emergency funds so that you don't need to tap into money for long-term goals. However, sufficient credit from your credit cards or a home equity line of credit to cover emergency expenses will serve the same purpose. Of course, you may have to pay high interest on any credit you use, but the return you get from having to keep less in emergency funds may be enough to compensate. Most emergency funds earn very little return, because as you gain liquidity you give up expected return. Liquid investments are low risk and low return because the money is always safe and readily available—that's the risk–return relationship we looked at in **Principle 8: Risk and Return Go Hand in Hand**.

The bottom line is that the Tates, and most people, may be better off investing most of their emergency funds in higher yielding, less liquid investments. For example, if the Tates invest their emergency funds in a money market fund paying 3 percent, those funds will grow 34 percent over the next 10 years. If they invested them in a stock fund that grew at an annual rate of 9 percent, their investment would have grown 137 percent over that same period. Thus, if you have enough credit and insurance protection to provide income in the face of an emergency, you can safely reduce the number of months of living expenses you keep in your emergency fund to three or below.

Regardless of what you do with your emergency funds, the month's living expenses covered ratio still provides a sound, easy-to-understand indication of the relative level of cash on hand. It's a better personal liquidity measure than the current ratio. You should track this ratio over time to make sure that it does not drop unexpectedly.

FACTS OF LIFE

A survey asked 22- to 29-year-olds who had finished their schooling or graduated from college the following question:
    When you first began living on your own after school, how would you rate your expenses?

Question 2: Can I Meet My Debt Obligations?

A second question ratios can answer is, "Do you have the ability to meet your debt obligations?" In other words, you saw it, you borrowed money and bought it, now can you pay for it? To answer this question you need to look at the debt ratio and the debt coverage ratio. The **debt ratio** answer tells you what percentage of your assets has been financed by borrowing. This ratio can be expressed as follows:

Debt Ratio
A ratio aimed at determining if you have the ability to meet your debt obligations, defined as total debt or liabilities divided by total assets.

$$\text{debt ratio} = \frac{\text{total debt or liabilities}}{\text{total assets}}$$

Looking at the Tates' balance sheet, we see that the level of their total debt or liabilities is $175,500, (line N of Figure 2.3), while their total assets or what they own is $300,190 (line H of Figure 2.3). Thus, their debt ratio becomes $175,500/$300,190 = 0.5846. This figure means that just over half of their assets are financed with borrowing. If you are managing your finances well, this ratio should go down as you get older.

The **long-term debt coverage ratio** relates the amount of funds available for debt repayment to the size of the debt payments. In effect, this ratio is the number of

Long-Term Debt Coverage Ratio
A ratio aimed at determining if you have the ability to meet your debt obligations, defined as total income available for living expenses divided by total long-term debt payments.

times you could make your debt payments with your current income. It focuses on long-term obligations such as home mortgage payments, auto loan payments, and any other long-term credit obligations. If credit card debt has gotten large enough, it, too, represents a long-term obligation. The denominator of this ratio represents your total outstanding long-term debt payments (excluding short-term borrowing such as credit cards and bills coming due). The numerator represents the funds available to make these payments.

$$\text{long-term debt coverage ratio} = \frac{\text{total income available for living expenses}}{\text{total long-term debt payments}}$$

For the Tates, total income available for living expenses is found on line C of their income statement and is $56,510. The only long-term debt obligations they have are their mortgage payments of $19,656 (under Housing in Figure 2.6, the income statement), their automobile loan payments of $2,588 (under Transportation in Figure 2.6, the income statement), and college loan payments of $1,600 (under Other Expenditures in Figure 2.6, the income statement). Thus, their debt coverage ratio is [$56,510/($19,656 + $2,588 + $1,600)] = 2.37 times. In general, a debt coverage ratio of less than approximately 2.5 should raise a caution flag.

You should also keep track of your long-term debt coverage ratio to make sure it does not creep downward. The Tates are at their limit in terms of the level of debt that they can manage comfortably. Such a low debt coverage ratio, though, is not surprising, because most of their assets are tied up in housing.

Another way of looking at the debt coverage ratio is to take its inverse; that is, divide the total debt payments by the total income available for living expenses. In this case, the inverse of the Tates' debt coverage ratio is 0.43, or 43 percent, indicating that 43 percent of the Tates' total income available for living expenses goes to cover debt payments.

Question 3: Am I Saving as Much as I Think I Am?

The final question you can answer using ratios is, "How much of your income are you really saving?" The answer to this question lies in the **savings ratio**, which is simply the ratio of income available for savings and investment (line M of Figure 2.6) to income available for living expenditures (line C of Figure 2.6). This ratio tells you the proportion of your after-tax income that you are saving.

Savings Ratio
A ratio aimed at determining how much you are saving, defined as income available for saving and investments divided by income available for living expenditures.

$$\text{savings ratio} = \frac{\text{income available for savings and investment}}{\text{income available for living expenditures}}$$

For the Tates, this ratio is ($4,276/$56,510) = 0.076 or 7.6 percent. This figure is in the range of what is typical in this country. Actually, for families saving for their first house it tends to be higher, and for families that have just purchased their first house and now are experiencing large mortgage payments, it tends to be lower. Again, as with the other ratios, this ratio should be compared with past savings ratios and target savings ratios to determine whether or not the Tates' savings efforts are enough.

If you're not presently saving, then you're living above your means. The only effective way to make saving work is to pay yourself first. That is, you first set aside your savings, and what is left becomes the amount you can spend.

Record Keeping

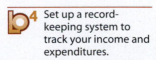
Set up a record-keeping system to track your income and expenditures.

The fourth step in creating a personal financial plan is to keep and maintain records, for three reasons. First, without adequate records it's extremely difficult

CHECKLIST 2.1
Storing Financial Files

Home File

→ **Tax Records (may be discarded after 6 years) (Chapter 4)**
- Tax returns
- Paychecks
- W-2 forms
- 1099 forms
- Charitable contributions
- Alimony payments
- Medical bills
- Property taxes
- Any other documentation

→ **Investment Records (Chapters 11–15)**
- Bank records and non-tax-related checks less than a year old
- Safety deposit box information
- Stock, bond, and mutual fund transactions
- Brokerage statements
- Dividend records
- Any additional investment documentation

→ **Retirement and Estate Planning (Chapters 16–17)**
- Copy of will
- Pension plan documentation
- IRA documentation
- Keogh plan transactions
- Social Security information
- Any additional retirement documentation

→ **Personal Planning (Chapters 2, 8–10, 17)**
- Personal balance sheet
- Personal income statement
- Personal budget
- Insurance policies and documentation
- Warranties
- Receipts for major purchases
- Home improvement receipts
- Credit card information (account numbers and telephone numbers)
- Birth certificates
- Rental agreement if renting a dwelling
- Automobile registration
- Powers of attorney
- Any additional personal planning documentation

Safety Deposit Box Storage

→ **Investment Records (Chapters 5, 13, 14)**
- Certificates of deposit
- Listing of bank accounts
- Stock and bond certificates
- Collectibles

→ **Retirement and Estate Planning (Chapters 16, 17)**
- Copy of will
- Nondeductible IRA records

→ **Personal Planning (Chapters 6–10, 17)**
- Copy of will
- Deed for home
- Mortgage
- Title insurance policy
- Personal papers (birth and death certificates, alimony, adoption/custody, divorce, military, immigration, etc.)
- Documentation of valuables (videotape or photos)
- Home repair/improvement receipts
- Auto title and new car sticker
- Listing of insurance policies
- Credit card information (account numbers and telephone numbers)

Throw Out
- Non-tax-related checks over a year old
- Records from cars and boats you no longer own
- Expired insurance polices on which there will be no future claims
- Expired warranties
- Non-tax-related credit card slips over a year old

to prepare taxes. Second, a strong record-keeping system allows you to track expenses and know exactly how much you're spending and where you're spending it. In short, if you don't know where and how much you're spending, you don't have control of your finances. Third, organized record keeping makes it easier for someone else to step in during an emergency and understand your financial situation.

Record keeping really involves two steps: tracking your personal financial dealings, and filing and storing your financial records in such a way that they are readily accessible. Very simply, if you don't know where financial records are, you won't be in control of your affairs.

In determining how best to track your personal financial dealings, you must keep in mind that the best system is one that you will use. This may sound silly, but because of the tedious nature of record keeping, anything too complex just won't be used. Do yourself a favor and keep your system simple.

In general, credit card and check expenditures are easy to track because they leave an obvious paper trail. It's the cash expenditures that cause the most concern. Cash expenditures must be tracked as they occur; if not, they will be lost and forgotten. The simplest way to keep track of all cash expenditures is by recording them in a notebook or your checkbook register as they are made, and then using these records, in addition to check and credit card transactions, to generate a monthly income statement. You then compare this monthly income statement with your annual and target income statements to determine whether or not you have any problems. Sure, the process may be tedious, but it's necessary. Remember, your budget is your best friend, because the key to controlling expenditures is to keep track of them.

Once you've tracked your expenditures, you need to record them in an organized way. How should you do this? A relatively easy way is to set up a budget book similar to the income statement shown in Figure 2.4 and manually enter your expenditures. Alternatively, a number of personal finance computer programs can track your monthly and yearly expenses and your financial position once you've entered your daily expenditures. This approach is ideal. The two most popular personal financial management programs for the personal computer (PC) are Intuit's Quicken and Microsoft's Money. However, for those without a PC, the money for such a software program, or the time to set up such a system, the manual approach works just as well.

When recording your transactions, you should have a section in your **ledger** for each month broken down by the major types of expenditures. In addition, each month should be broken down by day. The more detailed your records are, the easier it is to track your money. For example, when you spend $200 on new clothes, you should enter the expense in the new clothes subsection of the clothes and personal care section of the proper month on the day on which the expenditure occurred (it sounds more complicated than it is). At the end of the month you should add up your expenditures and compile your monthly income statement.

After you've been keeping records for a while, you'll notice that they really start to pile up. How long do you have to hang on to these records? This, of course, depends upon the item. In general, items dealing with taxes must be kept for at least 6 years after the transaction takes place; some items should be kept for life. Checklist 2.1 provides a summary of where and for how long financial records should be kept.

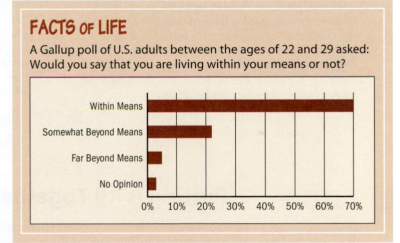

FACTS OF LIFE

A Gallup poll of U.S. adults between the ages of 22 and 29 asked: Would you say that you are living within your means or not?

Ledger
A book or notebook set aside to record expenditures.

MONEY MATTERS

Tips from Marcy Furney, ChFC, Certified Financial Planner™

FOR THE RECORD

Starting a budget and don't know what the utilities cost last summer? Having a battle with Visa regarding a credit that hasn't shown up on the bill? Even if you already use bookkeeping software, a good system for maintaining paper records could be your salvation.

Set up a place in your home for record storage. Keep everything in one location—a desk, a file cabinet, or even an extra kitchen drawer.

Create file folders for each type of monthly bill. Also make one for major purchase receipts and warranties, pay stubs, benefit and insurance documents, investment reports, bank statements, car and/or home records, and IRS-related items.

Mark on each bill the date you paid it and the number of the check used to pay it. Then file each in the appropriate folder.

Put your credit card receipts in the designated credit card folder and then use them to reconcile your monthly statement. When you pay the bill, staple the receipts to your section of the statement, and file it. Keep any credit slips to make sure the charge is reversed. Make notations on your statement regarding problems, phone calls to the credit card company, or deductibility of any charges for your next tax return.

When you call the company regarding a bill, note the date, time, with whom you spoke, and the resolution on your copy of the bill.

Don't throw away bills or receipts until you purge your files. When you file your tax return for the year, put supporting documents with your return and keep it in a separate envelope. There are many opinions regarding how long to keep tax returns; 5 to 7 years seems sufficient for most. However, those that report the purchase or sale of a home, deductions that can carry forward, or other unusual tax situations are best kept for much longer periods.

When you purge folders, remove the material that wasn't used as tax support from the spending and pay stub files. Bundle it up and store it for 1 more year. After that you should be able to throw away most of it. Use your judgment if you think something needs to be kept longer. Keep receipts for major purchases, warranties, titles, deeds, and year-end investment statements until you no longer own the item.

 5 Implement a financial plan or budget that will provide for the level of savings needed to achieve your goals.

Putting It All Together: Budgeting

Now we are ready to put our financial plan together. Chapter 1 introduced the planning cycle as a five-step process. Now that you have a better understanding of the tools involved in that process, how about a little review? Let's see how the balance sheet and income statement fit into the planning process.

The planning process begins by evaluating your financial health, which is exactly what the balance sheet and income statement are all about. Your balance sheet sums up everything you own or owe and lets you know your net worth, the basic element of financial health. Your income statement furthers your understanding by showing you where your money comes from, where it goes, and what your spending patterns are. Once you understand how much money you have coming in and how you tend to spend it, you can figure out how much you can realistically afford to save. If you don't know how much you can actually save, you can't come up with realistic financial goals, the second step of the planning process.

By providing you with information on how far you need to go to achieve a certain level of wealth and how you might realistically balance spending and saving to get there, your balance sheet and income statement not only help you set goals, but they also help you achieve them. Developing a plan of action to achieve your goals is the third step in the planning process, and for this your income statement is the key.

Your income statement helps you set up a cash budget (which we examine in more detail in the next section) that allows you to manage your saving while considering flexibility, liquidity, protection, and minimization of taxes. Once your plan is in place, you'll need to monitor your progress. Because this last step is really the same as the first, you're right back to using your balance sheet and income statement again. As you can see, without these documents, the planning process isn't nearly as effective.

STOP & THINK

What do you do if it appears that you won't reach your financial goals? You need to change either your goals or your saving pattern. Fortunately, a small change in your financial lifestyle can produce large benefits down the road. For example, if you are 22 now and you save $10 per month—that works out to about 33¢ per day—at 12 percent, by age 67 when you retire, it will have grown to over $240,000. Are there any small changes that you might make to save money?

Developing a Cash Budget

A budget is really nothing more than a plan for controlling cash inflows and outflows. The purpose of the cash budget is to keep income in line with expenditures plus savings. Your cash budget should allocate certain dollar amounts for different spending categories, based on your goals and financial obligations.

To prepare a cash budget, you begin with your most recent annual personal income statement. First, examine last year's total income, making any adjustments to it you expect for the coming year. Perhaps you expect to receive a raise, plan to take a second job, or anticipate an increase in royalty payments. Based on your income level, estimate what your taxes will be. This figure provides you with an estimate of your anticipated after-tax income available for living expenditures, which is commonly called take-home pay.

Just as your estimate of anticipated take-home pay flows from your most recent annual personal income statement, so does your estimate of living expenses. Using last year's personal income statement, identify expenditures over which you have no control—fixed expenditures. Then determine your variable expenses. These are the expenses over which you have complete control, and you can increase or decrease them as you see fit.

This is the category in which you have to start looking for ways to reduce your spending and increase your saving. For example, you can generate savings just by reducing the amount you spend on food—substitute bean dip for those exotic fresh fruits as your evening snack (of course, any savings there will probably be offset in an increase in exercise equipment this year). You must also keep in mind that when you buy on credit, you obligate yourself to future expenditures to pay off your debt. When you borrow you are spending your future income, which limits your ability to save.

Finally, subtract your anticipated living expenditures from your anticipated take-home pay to determine income available for savings and investment. Then compare your anticipated monthly savings with your target savings level, which is, as we mentioned earlier, based on a quantification of your goals. If it doesn't look as if you'll be able to fund all your goals, then you must earn more, spend less, or downsize your goals. The choice is, of course, personal; however, keep in mind that regardless of your level of income, many people live on less than what you're earning.

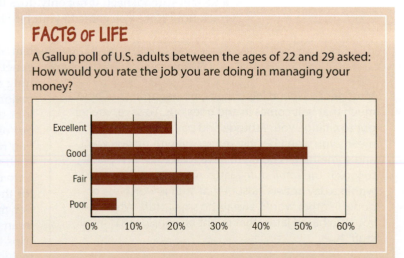

FACTS OF LIFE

A Gallup poll of U.S. adults between the ages of 22 and 29 asked: How would you rate the job you are doing in managing your money?

How do Louise and Larry Tate develop a cash budget? First, assume that the only change in income they expect for the coming year is a $5,000 increase in wages and salaries from $69,500 to $74,500. Last year, the Tates paid approximately 20 percent in federal and state income taxes. If they pay the same percentage this year, their $5,000 raise will result in an increase in take-home pay of $4,000, with 20 percent of the raise, or $1,000, going to pay increased taxes.

The Tates' personal income statement is shown in Figure 2.6. If there are any anticipated changes in different expenditure categories, they must adjust their personal income statement—and the changes can involve increases in planned spending. A cash budget, then, does not necessarily curb spending in all areas. Instead, it allows you to decide ahead of time how much to spend where.

Assume that the Tates' target level of savings for the entire year is $6,400. If the Tates stick to this cash budget, they will exceed their target. Were this not the case, they would have been forced to adjust their budget so that it covered their target savings. To make your annual cash budget easier to control, you should break it down into monthly budgets by simply dividing by 12.

A key point to remember when budgeting is that no budget is set in stone. As **Principle 5** says, **Stuff Happens**. A TV, a car, a washer—unexpected expenditures are just that—unexpected. Conversely, you may be pleasantly surprised that you wound up spending *less* than you planned. Then again, you may change your goals—you don't want that new house, your apartment's fine for the moment, but you do want to buy a llama farm in Peru. Basically, the budgeting process is a dynamic one: You must continuously monitor the financial impact of change on your spending and saving habits.

Implementing the Cash Budget

Now that you've put together a cash budget and have your plan, how do you make it work? Essentially, you just put it in place and try to make a go of it for a month. At the end of the month, compare your actual expenditures in each category with your budgeted amounts. If you spent more than you budgeted, you may want to pay closer attention to expenditures in that category or you may want to change the budgeted amount. If you do need to increase one budgeted amount, you might try to reduce spending in another area. Keep in mind that responsibility for sticking to the budget remains with you, but by examining deviations from desired spending patterns on a monthly basis, you can focus on where you need to exert additional self-control. If you need help, see Worksheet 7, which is downloadable from the MyFinanceLab Web site (**www.myfinancelab.com**). Figure 2.7 shows a budget tracker in the form of an Excel spreadsheet. It not only does the calculations for you, but also allows you to track how close you came to your budgeted amount in each category.

If sticking to a desired budget remains a problem, one possible control method is using what's generally called the envelope system. At the beginning of each month the dollar amount of each major expenditure category is put into an envelope. To spend money in that area, simply take it out of the envelope. When the envelope is empty, you're done spending in that area.

If you are having trouble controlling spending only in certain areas, envelopes could be used just for those areas. For example, if you budgeted $120 per month for restaurant expenditures, put $120 in an envelope each month. When it is exhausted, trips to the restaurant are over for the month. This includes pizza home delivery, so no cheating!

STOP THINK

Most people spend what they earn, regardless of how much that is. It comes in and goes out. To save, you've got to change your attitude and pay yourself first. That means you won't be able to buy everything you want, and something is going to have to go. The first place to look is the *small stuff*—latte, magazines, CDs, pop—within a day or two most of that stuff is worthless or gone. In other words, sweat the small stuff. What have you purchased lately that might be considered "small stuff"?

FIGURE 2.7 Budget Tracker

The Budget Tracker is downloadable from MyFinanceLab (**www.myfinancelab.com**).

Budget Tracker: Personal Income Statement Worksheet			
Directions: *Fill in the gold cells with your data. Be careful not to modify the red cells.*			
Income	**Month Budget Income**	**Actual Income**	**Difference**
Wages and salaries			
Wage Earner 1			0
Wage Earner 2			0
=Total Wages and salaries	0	0	0
+ Interest and Dividends			0
+ Royalties, Commissions and Rents			0
+Other Income			0
=A. Total Income	0	0	0
Taxes			
Federal Income and Social Security			0
+State Income			0
=B. Total Income Taxes	0	0	0
C. After-Tax Income Available for Living Expenditures or Take-Home Pay (line A minus line B)	0	0	0
Living Expenses	**Budget Amount**	**Actual Spending**	**Difference**
Housing			0
Rent			0
+Mortgage Payments			0
+Utilities			0
+Maintainance			0
+Reas Eastate and Property Taxes			0
+Fixed Assets-furniture, appliances, televisions, etc.			0
+Other Living Expenses			0
=D. Total Housing Expenditures	0	0	0
Food			

If spreadsheets make you cringe and you like working online, take a look at **Mint .com**, which is a free Web-based personal financial planning Web site that allows you keep an eye on your financial moves and track all bank accounts, credit cards, investments, and loans together. In addition to aggregating all your financial information it creates a simple budget for you and then gently lets you know when you're stepping out of line— keeping you from spending too much on entertainment or meals out—and it does this in real time, right when you're spending your money. You'll even get a weekly summary e-mail that looks like a bank statement for all of your accounts. What happens if your checking account balance is getting low of if there is unusual spending taking place on one of your accounts? You'll receive an alert message, and you have control of how, for what, and when you receive alerts. Not only that, but it also provides a list of possible goals—retirement, travel, a wedding, education, and so forth—then lets you work toward the goals you select by entering them directly into your budget. There's even an app for smartphones and other electronic devices so you don't have to leave your financial plan at home. And what's the price of this app? Just like **Mint .com**, the app is free. Figure 2.8 provides a short description of **Mint.com** along with its features, and it also gives you an idea of what **Mint.com** looks like, with a screen shot of your income and expenses over several months.

Hiring a Professional

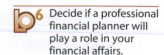

6 Decide if a professional financial planner will play a role in your financial affairs.

The goal of this course and text is to give you the understanding, tools, and motivation to manage your own financial affairs. Sometimes, though, smart management means knowing when to ask for help. When it comes to personal financial management, there's good help to be found. You have three options available regarding working with professionals: (1) Go it alone, make your own plan, and have it checked

FIGURE 2.8 Web-Based Financial Planning with Mint.com

Web site: Mint — "the best free way to manage your money"
Address: http://www.mint.com/
Features:

- ◆ Free.
- ◆ Recommended by the *Wall Street Journal* and *Businessweek*.
- ◆ Award-winning, top-rated online finance service by PC World.
- ◆ Extremely easy to use.
- ◆ Connects securely with more than 16,000 U.S. financial institutions and automatically updates all transactions.
- ◆ Spending is automatically categorized to make it easy to see how much you're spending on food, gas, groceries, entertainment, and more.
- ◆ Has a free app available for smartphones and other electronic devices.

What can you do with Mint.com?

- ◆ See all your accounts together at the same time — from checking and savings to credit cards, retirement, and more.
- ◆ Mint automatically pulls in and categorizes your transactions daily. You only need to enter your cash transactions. All other transactions are automatically entered.
- ◆ Mint can create a budget based on your actual spending, or you can create your own. Your budget works in real time allowing you to know how much you can spend while you're out.
- ◆ Avoid late fees and monitor cash flow. Mint allows you to stay up-to-date with e-mail or text alerts (your choice) for budgets, fees, due dates, low balances, unusual activity, and more.
- ◆ Mint allows you to track all your expenses at a particular merchant — for example, Starbucks — to see if you are spending more or less than usual there.
- ◆ Mint tracks all of your investments, including your brokerage and bank accounts, 401(k)s, and IRAs, keeping you up-to-date on the performance of your investments.
- ◆ Mint helps you plan for your goals — like buying a car, retirement, and buying a house — and works those goals into your budget.

by a professional; (2) work with a professional to come up with a plan; or (3) leave it all in the hands of a pro (though preferably not one with a bad toupee, leisure suit, and beat-up Ford Pinto). Although this decision need not be made until you have finished this course and have a better grasp of the process, let's take a moment to look further at the options.

What Planners Do

For relatively simple personal financial matters, computerized financial planning programs provide basic budgeting tools and advice. However, as with most standardized advice, they simply may not fit your particular situation. The more unique your situation, the greater the need for professional help.

Even if you turn over the development of your plan to a professional, however, you must understand the basics of personal financial planning in order to judge the merits of the plan and to monitor your game plan. Remember, even if you use a financial planner

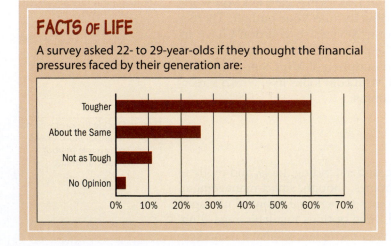

FACTS of LIFE

A survey asked 22- to 29-year-olds if they thought the financial pressures faced by their generation are:

(Bar chart)
- Tougher: ~60%
- About the Same: ~26%
- Not as Tough: ~11%
- No Opinion: ~3%

(x-axis: 0% 10% 20% 30% 40% 50% 60% 70%)

FIGURE 2.8 *(continued)*

to put together the entire plan, you are merely receiving advice. You still bear the ultimate responsibility. This brings us back to **Principle 1: The Best Protection Is Knowledge**.

It is extremely important that you find a financial planner who is competent and trustworthy. Although the overwhelming majority of financial planners are dedicated, responsible, and competent, and despite the fact that there are regulations in place meant to protect consumers, these regulations don't mean that all planners are equally qualified. Remember, financial planners may receive commissions on certain products, and they may talk up those more than others in order to receive this commission. Also be wary of those who promise you quick riches, and walk away from anyone using high-pressure tactics. Building wealth takes time and consistent attention.

Choosing a Professional Planner

Many financial planners are excellent at what they do. Some, however, are not so excellent. How do you choose a financial planner? The title "financial planner" is not legally defined—it just means that the individual offers comprehensive financial planning services and says nothing about competence. It is wise to limit your search to those who have received accreditation from a professional organization:

- *A personal financial specialist* (PFS) is a certified public accountant who has passed certification tests in personal financial planning administered by the American

Institute of Certified Public Accountants, and has 3 years of personal financial planning experience.

◆ *A certified financial planner* (CFP) has satisfactorily completed a 10-hour, 2-day exam and a minimum of 3 years of experience in the field.

◆ *A chartered financial consultant*, or ChFC, has completed coursework and ten exams administered by the American College.

After you've ascertained a planner's credentials, consider how much experience they have had. Experience can teach a planner a lot about what's best for you. Also be aware of whether the planner will give you advice tailored to your specific circumstances. And don't forget about referrals. Can the planner provide the names of people they've worked for? Do you have friends or relatives who have had good experiences with this financial planner in the past?

How Are Financial Planners Paid?   Actually, there are four common ways that planners are paid:

1. *Fee-only* planners earn income only through the fees they charge, generally running from $75 to $200 per hour. They tend to work with bigger, more involved, and specialized situations. You will personally have total control of the products purchased to complete your plan, and therefore you control commission costs. However, you have to sort through a sometimes overwhelming array of options and deal with several different vendors.

2. *Fee-and-commission* planners charge fees and also collect commissions on products they recommend. Fees may be less if you do choose to use some of their commissioned products, but if you're dealing with a less-than-ethical person, you could be directed toward higher-commission products. Be aware of what you're paying for.

3. *Fee offset* planners charge a fee, but then reduce this fee by any commissions they earn.

4. *Commission-based* planners work on a commission basis. They can provide an analysis of your personal financial situation, offer solutions to problems, and assist you in implementing the plan. You want to make sure your planner has a wide range of financial products to choose from.

If you have trouble getting recommendations, try calling the Financial Planning Association (**www.fpanet.org**) at 800-322-4237 or the CFP Board of Standards (**www.cfp.net/search**) at 800-487-1497 or 888-237-6275 for help. Remember, you bear all the consequences of bad decisions, so you must take responsibility for doing it right.

CHECKLIST 2.2

What to Ask a Financial Planner

◆ How long have you been a financial planner?
◆ What are your credentials and professional designations?
◆ How do you keep up with the latest financial changes?
◆ Can you provide references?
◆ Will you show me a copy of a financial plan you made for someone with a somewhat similar financial situation? (With names removed to preserve confidentiality, of course.)

◆ Who will I work with on a regular basis? You, or another member of your staff?
◆ Who will actually create my plan? You, a junior staffer, or a software program?
◆ How many financial companies do you represent?
◆ How are you paid—by fee or commission? How will that fee be calculated?
◆ Can you provide a written estimate of the services I can expect and the cost of those services?

Summary

 Calculate your level of net worth or wealth using a balance sheet.

A personal balance sheet is a statement of your financial position on a given date. It includes the assets you own; the debt, or liabilities, you have incurred; and your level of wealth. The difference between the value of your assets (what you own) and your liabilities (what you owe) is your net worth, the level of wealth that you or your family has accumulated.

 Analyze where your money comes from and where it goes using an income statement.

Whereas a balance sheet tells you how much wealth you have accumulated as of a *certain date*, an income statement tells you where your money has come from and where it has gone over some *period of time*. Actually, an income statement is really an income and expenditure, or net income, statement, because it looks at both cash inflows and outflows. Once you understand where your money comes from and where it goes, you'll be able to determine whether you're saving enough to meet your goals and how you might change your expenditure patterns to meet those goals. Then you'll be able to construct a budget.

 Use ratios to identify your financial strengths and weaknesses.

Financial ratios help you to identify your financial standing. These ratios are analyzed over time to determine trends and are also compared with standards or target ratios. The purpose of using ratios is to gain a better understanding of how you are managing your financial resources.

 Set up a record-keeping system to track your income and expenditures.

To keep track of your income and expenditures and to calculate your net worth, you need a sound system of record keeping. Such a system not only helps with tax preparation, but also allows you to identify how much you are spending and where you are spending it.

 Implement a financial plan or budget that will provide for the level of savings needed to achieve your goals.

Developing a plan of action involves setting up a cash budget. The starting point for the cash budget, which is the center point of the plan of action, flows directly from the personal income statement. By comparing the income available for savings and investments with the level of savings needed to achieve your goals, you can determine whether you need to alter your current spending patterns and by how much. Once you have established a plan, it's your responsibility to stick to your budget.

 Decide if a professional financial planner will play a role in your financial affairs.

If you need help in financial planning, there are professional planners out there who can provide such help. You can use professional planners simply to validate the plan you have developed, or you can hire them to put the entire plan together, from start to finish.

Review Questions

1. What are the steps of the budgeting and planning process? Describe what happens in each step.

2. Why is net worth a measure of financial health? What is the purpose of a personal balance sheet?

3. What information must you gather to develop an accurate balance sheet? What can you learn by annually updating the balance sheet?

4. Define and give examples of the seven categories of assets. How do you determine the current value of your assets?

5. What is a financial liability? How do you determine the amount owed on current and long-term liabilities? Give examples of each.

6. Why is net worth a relative and not an absolute measure? For example, why might insolvency be of less concern for a college student than for the student's parents?

7. Why might an income statement more accurately be called an income and expenditure statement or a "net" income statement? What is the purpose of an income statement?

8. What information do you need to calculate an accurate income statement? What are likely to be the four largest expenses?

9. Explain the practical difference between a fixed and a variable expense. Over which type of expense does a household have greater control?

10. Why are financial ratios important diagnostic tools? What three potential problem areas do they highlight?

11. If Larry and Louise Tate were trying to determine how long they would be able to continue paying their bills if they both lost their jobs, which financial ratio would be most useful?

12. Why are both the current measures and the trends of the ratios over time important measures of financial well-being?

13. Explain the debt coverage ratio and the inverse of the ratio. Why is the inverse ratio intuitively more informative?

14. List the three most important reasons for keeping accurate financial records.

15. Where should you keep the following records: non-tax-related checks or credit card slips, a listing of all bank accounts, your investment earnings statements, and copies of your will?

16. Summarize the steps to establish a cash budget.

17. If there is no legal requirement to be a financial planner, how might **Principle 1: The Best Protection Is Knowledge** affect your decision to seek professional assistance? What accreditations might you look for when shopping for a planner?

Develop Your Skills—Problems and Activities

These problems are available in MyFinanceLab.

1. Mike and Mary Jane Lee have a yearly income of $65,000 and own a house worth $90,000, two cars worth a total of $20,000, and furniture worth $10,000. The house has a mortgage of $50,000 and the cars have outstanding loans of $2,000 each. Utility bills, totaling $150 for this month, have not been paid. Calculate or use Worksheet 4 to determine their net worth and explain what it means. How would the Lees' age affect your assessment of their net worth?

2. Using the preceding information, calculate the debt ratio for the Lee household.

3. Ed and Marta are paid $3,250 after taxes every month. Monthly expenses include $1,200 on housing and utilities, $550 for auto loans, $300 on food, and an average of $1,000 on clothing and other variable expenses. Calculate and interpret their savings ratio. *Hint:* Prepare an income statement or use Worksheet 5 and then compute the ratio.

4. A rumor of "right sizing" at Ojai's engineering firm has him and his wife Kaya concerned about their preparation for meeting financial emergencies. Help them calculate their net worth or complete Worksheet 4 and calculate and interpret the current ratio given the following assets and liabilities:

Checking account	$2,000	Utility bills	$500
Savings account	$4,000	Credit card bills	$1,000
Stocks	$8,000	Auto loan	$2,600

5. Faith Brooks, a 28-year-old college graduate, never took a personal finance class. She pays her bills on time, has managed to save a little in a mutual fund, and with the help of an inheritance managed a down payment on a condominium. But Faith worries about her financial situation. Given the following information, prepare Worksheet 4 and Worksheet 5. Using information from these statements, calculate the current ratio, savings ratio, monthly living expenses covered ratio, debt ratio, and long-term debt coverage ratio. Interpret these financial statements and ratios for Faith. Based on your assessment, what advice would you give Faith? In addition to the following list, Faith offers these explanations:

- ◆ All short-term and long-term liabilities are unpaid.
- ◆ "Other expenses, monthly" represents cash spent without a record.
- ◆ She charges all incidentals on her credit cards and pays the balances off monthly. The balances shown below represent her average monthly balances.

Visa bill	$355	Checking account	$825
Stocks	$5,500	Quarterly auto insurance (not due)	$450
MasterCard bill	$245	Inherited coin collection	$3,250
Monthly paycheck, net	$2,400	Condominium	$65,000
Annual medical expenses	$264	Food, monthly	$225
Mortgage payment, monthly	$530	Auto	$9,000
Temple Mutual Fund	$2,100	Furnishings	$5,500
401(k) retirement account	$4,500	Mortgage outstanding	$50,000
Car payment, monthly	$265	Auto loan outstanding	$4,225
Total monthly utilities	$275	Other personal property	$8,000
Savings account	$2,300	Other expenses, monthly	$150
Clothing expense, monthly	$45		

6. Your friend Dario heard about your personal finance class and asked for your help. Explain to Dario why he should establish a budget and what information he needs.

7. If the Potinsky household spends $39,000 annually on all living expenses and long-term debt, calculate the amount recommended for an emergency fund. How might household circumstances (e.g., wage earners in the household, available credit, type and stability of employment) affect this decision?

8. Based on your projected salary, estimate and subtract 20 percent for taxes and benefits and another 10 percent for retirement. From the remainder, estimate and subtract the amount you plan to save annually for short-, intermediate-, and long-term goals. What you have left represents your income available for meeting all expenses. Now, estimate your needed emergency fund of 3 to 6 months of expenses. Realistically, how long will it take you to save the needed amount?

Learn by Doing—Suggested Projects

1. Using Worksheet 6 as a guide, talk to your parents about their record-keeping system. Offer to assist with organizing the household financial records. Do they have a balance sheet, income statement, or budget to track financial well-being? If not, offer the worksheets from the text as a starting point. Do they handle all financial matters alone or with the help of professionals? What assistance have they received and from whom?

2. Use Worksheet 7 to track your actual income and expenses for 1 month and then to develop a budget or spending plan for future months. Analyze your income and expenses to determine your spending patterns and any needed changes. (If you don't actually earn an income, consider your monthly college allowance or periodic withdrawals from summer savings.) See how long you can follow the budget. Should you consider an envelope system for some expenses? (Also, consider using the worksheet to project your finances when moving off campus, accepting a job after graduation, or changing jobs.)

3. According to this chapter, "planning and budgeting require control." Talk to several friends, family, or acquaintances about the strategies they routinely or occasionally use to control spending and saving. What's the best advice they could give to a novice financial manager? Have they automated spending or saving decisions? Share your findings as an oral or written report.

4. Locate at least three different Web sites with net worth calculators. Compare and contrast the listings of assets and liabilities. Do any of the calculators offer guidelines for interpreting results? Comment on the ease of use. Share your findings in an oral or written report.

5. The acronym GIGO—"garbage in, garbage out"—is commonly associated with computer-automated analysis. How does GIGO apply to the calculation of a balance sheet, income statement, or the ratios that are derived from both documents? Explain how an individual preparing these documents guards against GIGO.

6. To learn more about financial planners, profile a typical client, summarize the services offered by the planner, and explain the method(s) of payment for the services. Planners often include this information on their Web page, or you could call and explain that you are a student doing research for a class. How do you find a planner? Are there planners in your college community or hometown? Ask friends and family or use the "find a planner" link on the Web sites of professional groups such as the Financial Planning Association (**www.fpanet.org**), National Association of Personal Financial Advisors (NAPFA) (**www.napfa.org**), or the International Association of Registered Financial Consultants (IARFC) (**www.iarfc.org**). What does it mean to be a fee-only planner? Report your findings to the class.

7. Watch a short video on the Mint.com Web site on how to set up a Mint account. Explore the Web site to determine who funds the program. Read one or more of the personal finance blogs and write a one-page essay on what your learned from the Web site and blog(s).

8. Write a one-page essay that explains at least four reasons why you believe that people do not budget or develop even a simple plan for balancing income and expenses, including saving for goals. Review Worksheet 1 or Worksheet 2 for examples of financial objectives and goals for which households are *most* or *least* prepared.

Be a Financial Planner—Discussion Case 1

This case is available in MyFinanceLab

Sami, 34, and Ronald, 31, want to buy their first home. Their current combined net income is $65,000 and they have two auto loans totaling $32,000. They have saved approximately $12,000 for the purchase of their home and have total assets worth $55,000, which are mostly savings for retirement. Ronald has always been cautious about spending large amounts of money, but Sami really likes the idea of owning their own home. They do not have a budget but they do keep track of their expenses, which amounted to $55,000 last year including taxes. They pay off all credit card bills on a monthly basis and do not have any other debt or loans outstanding. Other than that, they do not spend a great deal of time tracking their finances.

Questions

1. What financial statements should Sami and Ronald prepare to begin realizing their home purchase goal? What records should they use to compile these statements?
2. Use the worksheets or simply calculate their net worth and income surplus. How does their net worth compare to other "thirty-somethings"?
3. Calculate and interpret their month's living expenses covered ratio and their debt ratio.
4. What other information would be necessary or helpful to develop more complete statements? Give as much detail as possible.
5. What six- to eight-step process should Sami and Ronald undertake to develop a budget?
6. Why might adopting **Principle 6: Waste Not, Want Not—Smart Spending Matters** be important to Sami and Ronald, given their goal of home ownership?

Be a Financial Planner—Discussion Case 2

This case is available in MyFinanceLab

Tim and Jill Taylor are retiring this year! Tim has worked for a utility company since his co-op job in college and has participated in all of the company's retirement savings plans. Jill has worked since the kids were in high school. Although they never consulted a financial planner, they have been careful to keep their insurance policies updated, to keep debt to a minimum, and to save regularly. As a result, the Taylors have a very large retirement portfolio—and now, without the restrictions of their companies' plans, lots of other investment options. Jill would like to live "the good life" for a while, but also is concerned about "outliving" their money. Tim says, "I earned it, I'll spend it." Now Tim and Jill think that consulting a professional might be a good idea to keep them on track through retirement. They haven't made too many plans, but know they want to help pay for college costs for their grandchildren.

Questions

1. What assessments of their financial situation should Tim and Jill expect when working with a financial planner? Given their past efforts to plan their finances and control spending, will these assessments be necessary?
2. The Taylors just received statements from their companies outlining the total value of their retirement savings. How can they use this information?
3. How might a budget ensure that they will have the necessary amount to help their grandchildren?
4. Since both their income and expenses will change, how would you suggest that they not "go overboard in living the good life," yet at the same time know that they can afford some retirement luxuries?
5. Should they manage the investment portfolio themselves or should they find a planner to manage their retirement assets and help them develop a plan for what could be 30 years in retirement? What kind of relationship with the planner and method of payment might work best for them?
6. Do the Taylors need to track their expenses more or less closely once they retire? Are their big expenses likely to remain the five reported by the average household?

Understanding and Appreciating the Time Value of Money

Learning Objectives

 Explain the mechanics of compounding.

 Understand the power of time and the importance of the interest rate in compounding.

 Calculate the present value of money to be received in the future.

 Define an annuity and calculate its compound or future value.

"Let's just do what we always do—hijack some nuclear weapons and hold the world ransom." These are the words of Dr. Evil, played by Mike Myers in the movie *Austin Powers, International Man of Mystery*. Frozen, along with his cat, Mr. Bigglesworth, in 1967 after escaping from the Electric Psychedelic Pussycat Swinger's Club in London, Dr. Evil is thawed out in 1997 and immediately resumes his evil ways.

Dr. Evil continues with his plan: "Gentlemen, it has come to my attention that a breakaway Russian republic, Ripblackastan is about to transfer a nuclear warhead to the United Nations in a few days. Here's the plan. We get the warhead, and we hold the world ransom for . . . one million dollars!"

Silence, followed by, "Umm, umm, umm" from Dr. Evil's Number 2 man, played by Robert Wagner: "Don't you think we should ask for more than a million dollars? A million dollars is not exactly a lot of money these days."

"OK, then we hold the world ransom for $100 billion."

A million dollars in 1967 certainly bought more than a million dollars in 1997 did. But consider this, if Dr. Evil had taken a million dollars in 1967 and put it in the stock market, it would have accumulated to over $30.7 million when he was thawed out in 1997. However, that $30+ million wouldn't have the same purchasing power it did 30 years earlier. In fact, given the rate of inflation over that period, it would only purchase about one-fifth of what it would have in 1967.

Three decades is a long time. The year Dr. Evil was frozen, one of the top-rated TV shows was *Bewitched*, and *The Monkees* took top honors at that year's Emmy Awards for best comedy show. The Green Bay Packers won Super Bowl I. Thirty years later Dr. Evil woke up to those same sitcoms airing on *Nick at Night* and the Green Bay Packers winning Super Bowl XXXI. But times had changed—now the world was full of personal computers, compact disks, MP3s, and cable TV.

Now look to the future: For most of you, it will be well over 30 years before you retire. If you want to work out how much you will need for your golden years, how the heck do you look at today's dollars and come up with a dollar figure? As we saw in **Principle 3: The Time Value of Money**, a dollar received today is worth more than a dollar received in the future. For one thing, a dollar received and invested today starts earning interest sooner than a dollar received and invested some time in the future. Remember, the **time value of money** means that we can't compare amounts of money from two different periods without adjusting for this difference in value. Clearly, if you want a firm grasp on personal finance, it's important to understand the time value of money.

Just how powerful is the time value of money? Think about this: If you were to invest $1,000 at 8 percent interest for 400 years, you would end up with $23 quadrillion—approximately $5 million per person on Earth. Of course, your

Time Value of Money
The concept that a dollar received today is worth more than a dollar received in the future and, therefore, comparisons between amounts in different time periods cannot be made without adjustments to their values.

investments won't span 400 years—it's doubtful that you'll be cryogenically frozen like Dr. Evil and Austin Powers—but your investments will rely on the time value of money. If you manage properly, time can be the ace up your sleeve—the one that lets you pocket more than you would have imagined possible.

In personal finance, the time value of money is just as widespread as it is powerful. We're always comparing money from different periods—for example, buying a bond today and receiving interest payments in the future, borrowing money to buy a house today and paying it back over the next 30 years, or determining exactly how much to save annually to achieve a certain goal. In fact, there's very little in personal finance that doesn't have some thread of the time value of money woven through it.

 1 Explain the mechanics of compounding.

Compound Interest and Future Values

Compound Interest
The effect of earning interest on interest, resulting from the reinvestment of interest paid on an investment's principal.

How does the time value of money turn small sums of money into extremely large sums of money? Through compound interest. **Compound interest** is basically interest paid on interest. If you take the interest you earn on an investment and reinvest it, you then start earning interest on the **principal** and the reinvested interest. In this way, the amount of interest you earn grows, or compounds.

Principal
The face value of the deposit or debt instrument.

How Compound Interest Works

Present Value (PV)
The current value, that is, the value in today's dollars of a future sum of money.

Annual Interest Rate (i)
The rate charged or paid for the use of money on an annual basis.

Future Value (FV)
The value of an investment at some future point in time.

Anyone who has ever had a savings account has received compound interest. For example, suppose you place $100, which is your **present value (PV)**, in a savings account that pays 6 percent interest annually, which is the **annual interest rate (i)**. How will your savings grow? At the end of the first year you'll have earned 6 percent or $6 on your initial deposit of $100, giving you a total of $106 in your savings account. That $106 is the **future value (FV)** of your investment, that is, the value of your investment at some future point in time. The mathematical formula illustrating the payment of interest is:

Future Value or FV_1	=	Present Value or PV	×	Amount it has increased by **in 1 year** or $(1 + i)$

$$FV_1 = PV(1 + i) \qquad (3.1)$$

In our example, you began with a present value of $100, then it grew by 6 percent, giving you $6 of interest, and when you add the interest you earned ($6) to what you began with ($100), you end up with $106. Assuming you leave the $6 interest payment in your savings account, known as **reinvesting**, what will your savings look like at the end of the second year? You begin the second year with $106, and you add the interest you earned in the second year (6 percent on $106 for a total of $6.36 in interest), and you end up with $112.36.

Reinvesting
Taking money that you have earned on an investment and plowing it back into that investment.

What will your savings look like at the end of three years? Five years? Ten years? Figure 3.1 illustrates how an investment of $100 would continue to grow for the first

FIGURE 3.1 Compound Interest at 6 Percent Over Time

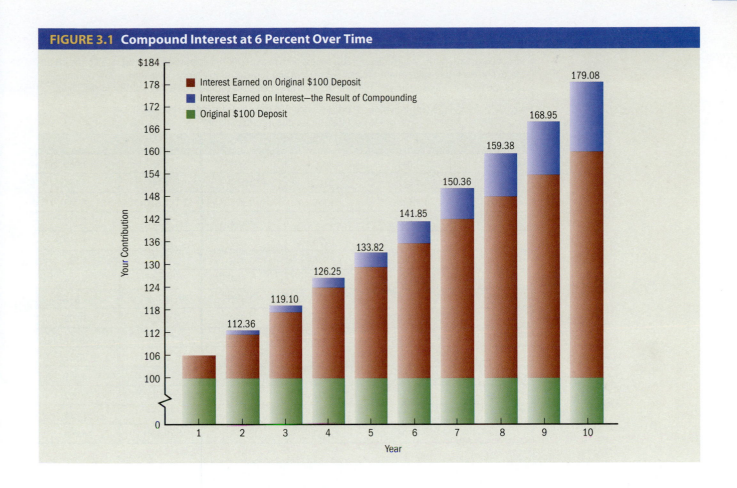

10 years at a compound interest rate of 6 percent. Notice how the amount of interest earned annually increases each year because of compounding.

Why do you earn more interest during the second year than you did during the first? Simply because you now earn interest on the sum of the original principal, or present value, *and* the interest you earned in the first year. In effect, you are now earning interest on interest, which is the concept of compound interest.

How did we determine all the future values of your investment in Figure 3.1? We took the amount we began each year with, and let it grow by 6 percent—in effect, we just multiplied the amount we began each year with by $(1 + i)$. We can generalize the future-value equation to:

Future Value or FV_n	=	Present Value or PV	×	Amount PV has increased by **in n years** or $(1 + i)^n$

$$FV_n = PV(1 + i)^n \qquad (3.2)$$

where n is equal to the number of years during which compounding occurs.

Equation (3.2) *is* the time value of money formula, and it will work for any investment that pays a fixed amount of interest, i, for the life of the investment. As we work through this chapter, sometimes we will solve for i and other times we will solve for PV or n. Regardless, equation (3.2) is the basis for almost all of our time value calculations.

TABLE 3.1 Future Value of $1 (single amount), Future-Value Interest Factor

Instructions: Each future-value interest factor corresponds to a specific time period and interest rate. For example, to find the future-value interest factor for 5 percent and 10 years, simply move down the $i = 5\%$ column until you reach its intersection with the $n = 10$ years row: 1.629. The future value is then calculated as follows:

$$\text{future value} = \text{present value} \times \text{future-value interest factor}$$
$$\text{or } FV_n = PV \text{ (future-value interest factor)}$$

n	4%	5%	6%	7%	8%
1	1.040	1.050	1.060	1.070	1.080
2	1.082	1.102	1.124	1.145	1.166
3	1.125	1.158	1.191	1.225	1.260
4	1.170	1.216	1.262	1.311	1.360
5	1.217	1.276	1.338	1.403	1.469
6	1.265	1.340	1.419	1.501	1.587
7	1.316	1.407	1.504	1.606	1.714
8	1.369	1.477	1.594	1.718	1.851
9	1.423	1.551	1.689	1.838	1.999
10	1.480	1.629	1.791	1.967	2.159
11	1.539	1.710	1.898	2.105	2.332
20	2.191	2.653	3.207	3.870	4.661
30	3.243	4.322	5.743	7.612	10.062
40	4.801	7.040	10.285	14.974	21.724
50	7.106	11.467	18.419	29.456	46.900

The Future-Value Interest Factor

Future-Value Interest Factor
The value of $(1 + i)^n$ used as a multiplier to calculate an amount's future value.

Calculating future values by hand can be a serious chore. Luckily, you can use a calculator. Also, there are tables for the $(1 + i)^n$ part of the equation, which will now be called the **future-value interest factor** for i and n. These tables simplify your calculations by giving you the various values for combinations of i and n.

Table 3.1 is one such table (a more comprehensive version appears in Appendix A at the back of this book). Note that the amounts given in this table represent the value of $1 compounded at rate i at the end of the nth year. Thus, to calculate the future value of an initial investment, you need only determine the future-value interest factor using a calculator or a table and multiply this amount by the initial investment. In effect, you can rewrite equation (3.2) as follows:

$$\boxed{\begin{array}{c}\text{Future Value} \\ \text{or} \\ FV_n\end{array}} = \boxed{\begin{array}{c}\text{Present Value} \\ \text{or} \\ PV\end{array}} \times \boxed{\text{Future-Value Interest Factor}} \quad (3.2a)$$

Let's look at an example.

Compounded Annually
With annual compounding, the interest is received at the end of each year and then added to the original investment. Then, at the end of the second year, interest is earned on this new sum.

EXAMPLE

You receive a $1,000 academic award this year for being the best student in your personal finance course, and you place it in a savings account paying 5 percent annual interest **compounded annually**. How much will your account be worth in 10 years?

We can solve this mathematically using equation (3.2) or using the future-value interest factors in Table 3.1.

Solving Mathematically Substituting $PV = \$1,000$, $i = 5$ percent, and $n = 10$ years into equation (3.2), you get:

$$
\begin{aligned}
FV_n &= PV(1 + i)^n \\
&= \$1,000(1 + 0.05)^{10} \\
&= \$1,000(1.62889) \\
&= \$1,628.89
\end{aligned}
$$

Thus, at the end of 10 years you will have $1,628.89 in your savings account. Unless, of course, you decide to add in or take out money along the way.

Solving Using the Future-Value Interest Factors In Table 3.1, at the intersection of the $n = 10$ row and the 5% column, we find a value for the future-value interest factor of 1.629. Thus:

$$
\begin{aligned}
\text{future value} &= \text{present value} \times \text{future-value interest factor} \\
FV_{10} &= \$1,000(1.629) = \$1,629
\end{aligned}
$$

You obtain the same answer using either approach.

The Rule of 72

Now you know how to determine the future value of any investment. What if all you want to know is how long it will take to double your money in that investment? One simple way to approximate how long it will take for a given sum to double in value is called the **Rule of 72**. This "rule" states that you can determine how many years it will take for a given sum to double by dividing the investment's annual growth or interest rate into 72. For example, if an investment grows at an annual rate of 9 percent per year, according to the Rule of 72 it should take $72/9 = 8$ years for that sum to double.

Keep in mind that this is not a hard and fast rule, just an approximation, but it's a pretty good approximation at that. For example, the future-value interest factor from Table 3.1 for 9 years at 8 percent is 1.999, which is pretty close to the Rule of 72's approximation of 2.0.

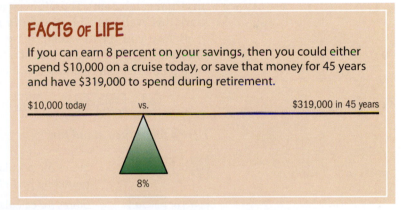

FACTS OF LIFE

If you can earn 8 percent on your savings, then you could either spend $10,000 on a cruise today, or save that money for 45 years and have $319,000 to spend during retirement.

$10,000 today   vs. $319,000 in 45 years

8%

Rule of 72

A helpful investment rule that states you can determine how many years it will take for a sum to double by dividing the annual growth rate into 72.

EXAMPLE

Using the "Rule of 72," how long will it take to double your money if you invest it at 12 percent compounded annually?

$$
\begin{aligned}
\text{numbers of years to double} &= \frac{72}{\text{annual compound growth rate}} \\
&= \frac{72}{12} \\
&= 6 \text{ years}
\end{aligned}
$$

Compound Interest with Nonannual Periods

Until now we've assumed that the compounding period is always annual. Sometimes, though, financial institutions compound interest on a quarterly, daily,

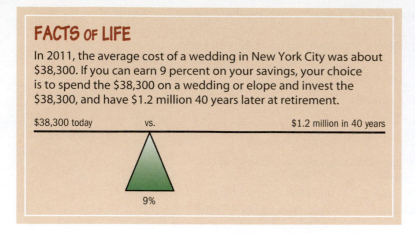

or even continuous basis. What happens to your investment when your compounding period is nonannual? You earn more money faster. The sooner your interest is paid, the sooner you start earning interest on it, and the sooner you experience the benefits of compound interest.

The bottom line is that your money grows faster as the compounding period becomes shorter—for example, from annual compounding to monthly compounding. That's because interest is earned on interest more frequently as the length of the compounding period declines.

Using an Online or Handheld Financial Calculator

Time value of money calculations can be made simple with the aid of a financial calculator. If you don't own a financial calculator, you can easily find one on the Web—there's an excellent one on the Web site that accompanies this book (**www.myfinancelab.com**). There's even a little tutorial there, and you might want to bookmark this Web site. This calculator is illustrated in Figure 3.2 below.

Before you try to whoop it up solving time value of money problems on your financial calculator, take note of a few keys that will prove necessary. There are five keys on a financial calculator that come into play:

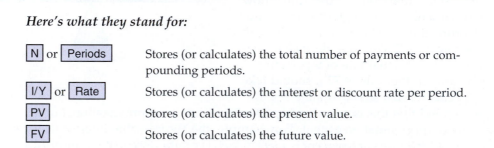

N or Periods   I/Y or Rate   PV   PMT   FV

Here's what they stand for:

N or Periods	Stores (or calculates) the total number of payments or compounding periods.
I/Y or Rate	Stores (or calculates) the interest or discount rate per period.
PV	Stores (or calculates) the present value.
FV	Stores (or calculates) the future value.

FIGURE 3.2 Time Value of Money Calculator on MyFinanceLab

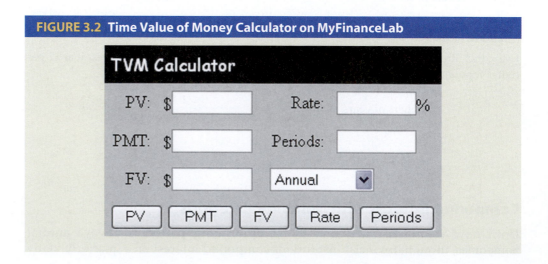

PMT

Stores (or calculates) the dollar amount of each annuity payment. (We talk about these later in the chapter, but an annuity is a series of equal dollar payments for a specified number of time periods.)

And if you're using a Texas Instruments BA II Plus calculator, here's another one you'll want to know about:

 CPT

This is the compute key on the Texas Instruments BA II Plus calculator, the calculator we use in examples in this text. If you want to compute the present value, you enter the known variables and press CPT PV.

Every calculator operates a bit differently with respect to entering variables. It is a good idea to become familiar with exactly how your calculator functions.

To solve a time value of money problem using a financial calculator, all you need to do is enter the appropriate numbers for three of the four variables and then press the key of the final variable to calculate its value.

Now let's solve an example using a financial calculator. Suppose you would like to know the rate at which $11,167 must be compounded annually for it to grow to $20,000 in 10 years. All you have to do is input the known variables, then calculate the value of the one you're looking for.

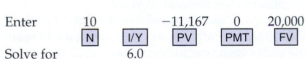

Enter	10		−11,167	0	20,000
	N	I/Y	PV	PMT	FV
Solve for		6.0			

FACTS OF LIFE

According to a recent study by Thrivent Financial for Lutherans, 59 percent of those surveyed have not calculated how much they need for retirement—the time value of money tools will help you do this.

Why the negative sign before the $11,167? When using a financial calculator each problem will have at least one positive number and one negative number. In effect, a financial calculator sees money as "leaving your hands" and taking on a *negative sign*, or "returning to your hands" and taking on a *positive sign*. You'll also notice that the answer appears as 6.0 rather than 0.06—when entering interest rates, enter them as percentages rather than decimals, that is, 10 percent would be entered as 10, not .10.

Calculator Clues

Calculators are pretty easy to use. When people have problems with calculators, it is usually the result of a few common mistakes. Before you take a crack at solving a problem using a financial calculator keep the following tips in mind:

1. Set your calculator to one payment per year. Some financial calculators use monthly payments as the default, so you will need to change it to annual payments.

2. Set your calculator to display at least four decimal places. Most calculators are preset to display only two decimal places. Because interest rates are so small, change your decimal setting to at least four.

3. Set your calculator to the "end" mode. Your calculator will assume cash flows occur at the end of each time period.

When you're ready to work a problem, remember:

1. Every problem will have at least one positive and one negative number.

2. You must enter a zero for any variable that isn't used in a problem, or you have to clear the calculator before beginning a new problem. If you don't enter a value for one of the variables, your calculator won't assume that the variable is zero. Instead, your calculator will assume it carries the same number as it did during the previous problem.

3. Enter the interest rate as a percent, not a decimal. That means 10 percent must be entered as 10 rather than .10.

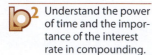

Understand the power of time and the importance of the interest rate in compounding.

Compounding and the Power of Time

Manhattan Island was purchased by Peter Minuit from Native Americans in 1626 for $24 in knickknacks and jewelry. If at the end of 1626 the Native Americans had invested their $24 at 8 percent compounded annually, it would be worth over $191.3 trillion today (by the end of 2012, 386 years later). That's certainly enough to buy back all of Manhattan. In fact, with $191.3 trillion in the bank, the $90 billion to $100 billion you'd have to pay to buy back all of Manhattan would seem like pocket change. The story illustrates the incredible power of time in compounding. Let's take a closer look.

The Power of Time

Why should you care about compounding? Well, the sooner you start saving for retirement and other long-term goals, the less painful the process of saving will be. Consider the tale of twin sisters who work at the Springfield DMV. Selma and Patty Bouvier decide to save for retirement, which is 35 years away. They'll both receive an 8 percent annual return on their investment over the next 35 years.

Selma invests $2,000 per year at the end of each year *only* for the first 10 years of the 35-year period—for a total of $20,000 saved. Patty doesn't start saving for 10 years and then saves $2,000 per year at the end of each year for the remaining 25 years—for a total of $50,000 saved. When they retire, Selma will have accumulated just under $200,000, while Patty will have accumulated just under $150,000, despite the fact that Selma saved for only 10 years while Patty saved for 25 years. Figure 3.3 presents their results and illustrates the power of time in compounding.

Let's look at another example to see what this really means to you. The compound growth rate in the stock market over the period 1951–2010 (the past 60 years) was approximately 10.8 percent. Although the rate of return on stocks has been far from constant over this period, assume for the moment that you could earn a constant annual return of 10.8 percent compounded annually on an investment in stocks. If you invested $2,500 in stocks at the beginning of 1951 and earned 10.8 percent compounded annually, your investment would have grown to $1,175,779 by the beginning of 2011 (60 years). That would make you one wealthy senior citizen.

Let's look at one example that illustrates the danger in just looking at the bottom-line numbers without considering the time value of money. One of today's "hot" collectibles is the Schwinn Deluxe Tornado boy's bicycle, which sold for $49.95 in 1962. In 2012, 50 years later, a Schwinn Tornado in mint condition is selling on eBay for $920.00, which is 18.59 times its original cost. At first glance you might view this as a 1,859 percent return—but you'd be ignoring the time value of money. At what

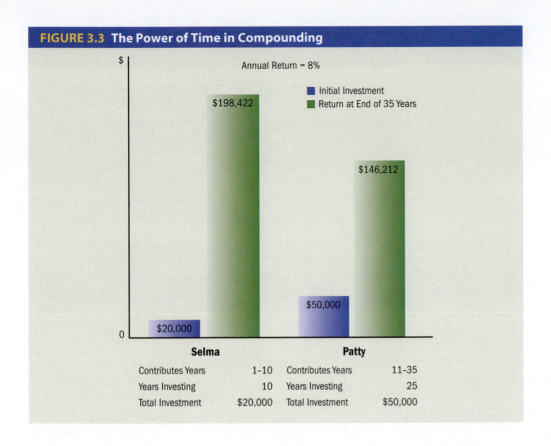

FIGURE 3.3 The Power of Time in Compounding

Annual Return = 8%

■ Initial Investment
■ Return at End of 35 Years

$198,422

$146,212

$50,000

$20,000

	Selma		**Patty**	
Contributes Years	1–10	Contributes Years	11–35
Years Investing	10	Years Investing	25
Total Investment	$20,000	Total Investment	$50,000

rate did this investment really compound? The answer is 6 percent per year, which ignores any storage costs that might have been incurred. The Schwinn may provide a great ride, but given what you just saw common stocks doing over the same period, it doesn't provide a very good return.

The Importance of the Interest Rate

It's not just time that makes money grow in value, it's also the interest rate. Most people understand that a higher interest rate earns you more money—that's why some people are willing to buy a risky bond issued by Vertis, the direct marketing firm that has experienced financial problems, that pays 11 percent rather than a very safe bond issued by the government that pays only 4 percent—but most people don't understand just how dramatic a difference the interest rate can make. This brings us back to **Principle 1: The Best Protection Is Knowledge**.

Without an understanding of investment concepts such as the time value of money, you're a prime target for bad advice. You're also at a real disadvantage because you might not be able to take advantage of good deals and even understand basic financial principles, such as those that apply to interest rates. The bottom line is it's much easier to do things correctly if you understand what you're doing. Let's take a closer look at interest rates.

Obviously, the choice of interest rate plays a critical role in how much an investment grows. But do small changes in the interest rate have much of an impact on future values? To answer this question, let's look back to Peter Minuit's purchase of Manhattan. If the Native Americans had invested their $24 at 10 percent rather than 8 percent compounded annually at the end of 1626, they would have about $228 quadrillion by the end of 2012. That's 228 moved over 15 decimal places, or

TABLE 3.2 The Daily Double

Day	"Daily Double": 1¢ at 100% Compounded Daily Would Become
1	$0.01
2	0.02
3	0.04
4	0.08
5	0.16
6	0.32
7	0.64
8	1.28
15	163.84
20	5,242.88
25	167,772.16
30	5,368,709.12
31	10,737,418.24

STOP & THINK

If you receive an inheritance of $25,000 and invest it at 6 percent (ignoring taxes) for 40 years, it will accumulate to $257,125. If you invest it at 12 percent (again ignoring taxes) over this same period, it would accumulate to $2,326,225! Almost ten times more! If the interest rate doubled, why did your investment grow almost tenfold?

$228,000,000,000,000,000. Actually, that's enough to buy back not only Manhattan Island, but the entire world and still have plenty left over!

Now let's assume a lower interest rate, say 6 percent. In that case the $24 would have grown to a mere $140.7 billion—less then one thousandth of what it grew to at 8 percent, and only one millionth of what it would have grown to at 10 percent. With today's real estate prices, you might be able to buy Manhattan, but you probably couldn't pay your taxes!

To illustrate the power of a high interest rate in compounding, let's look at a "daily double." A "daily double" simply means that your money doubles each day. In effect, it assumes an interest rate of 100 percent compounded on a daily basis. Let's see what can happen to a penny over a month's worth of daily doubles, assuming that the month has 31 days in it. The first day begins with 1¢, the second day it compounds to 2¢, the third day it becomes 4¢, the fourth day 8¢, the fifth day 16¢, and so forth. As shown in Table 3.2, by day 20 it would have grown to $5,242.88, and by day 31 it would have grown to over $10 million. This explains why Albert Einstein once marveled that "Compound interest is the eighth wonder of the world."

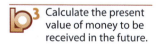 **3** Calculate the present value of money to be received in the future.

Present Value—What's It Worth in Today's Dollars?

Up until this point we've been moving money forward in time; that is, we know how much we have to begin with and we are trying to determine how much that sum will grow in a certain number of years when compounded at a specific rate. We're now going to look at the reverse question: What's the value in today's dollars of a sum of money to be received in the future? That is, what's the present value?

Why is present value important to us? It lets us strip away the effects of inflation and see what future cash flows are worth in today's dollars. It also lets us compare dollar values from different periods. In later chapters we'll use the present value to determine how much to pay for stocks and bonds.

In finding the present value of a future sum, we're moving future money back to the present. What we're doing is, in fact, nothing other than inverse compounding. In compounding we talked about the compound interest rate and the initial investment; in determining the present value we will talk about the **discount rate** and present value.

When we use the term "discount rate," we mean the interest rate used to bring future money back to the present, that is, the interest rate used to "discount" that future money back to the present. For example, if we expected to receive a sum of money in 10 years and wanted to know what it would buy in today's dollars, we would discount that future sum of money back to the present at the anticipated inflation rate. Other than that, the technique and the terminology remain the same, and the mathematics are simply reversed.

Let's return to equation (3.2), the time value of money equation. We now want to solve for present value instead of future value. To do this we can simply rearrange the terms in equation (3.2) and we get:

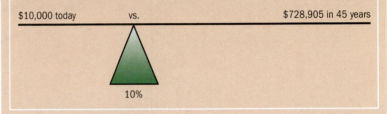

FACTS OF LIFE

In 2011, the cost of a new Honda Accord EX was about $24,000, while a used 2007 Honda Accord EX was about $14,000. If you can earn 10 percent on your savings, your choice is to spend the $24,000 on a new Honda, or save $10,000 and buy the used Honda. You could then invest the $10,000 at 10 percent and have $728,905 forty-five years later at retirement.

$10,000 today   vs. $728,905 in 45 years

10%

Discount Rate
The interest rate used to bring future dollars back to the present.

Present Value or PV	$=$	Future Value at the end of n years or FV_n	$\times$	The inverse of the Future-Value Interest Factor or $\dfrac{1}{(1+i)^n}$

$$PV = FV_n \frac{1}{(1+i)^n} \qquad (3.3)$$

Because the mathematical procedure for determining the present value is exactly the inverse of determining the future value, the relationships among n, i, and PV are just the opposite of those we observed in future value. The present value of a future sum of money is inversely related to both the number of years until the payment will be received and the discount rate. Figure 3.4 shows this relationship graphically.

To help us compute present values, we once again have some handy tables. This time, they calculate the $[1/(1+i)^n]$ part of the equation, which we call the **present-value interest factor** for i and n. These tables simplify the math by giving us the present-value interest factor for combinations of i and n. Appendix B at the back of this book presents fairly complete versions of these tables, and an abbreviated version appears in Table 3.3.

A close examination of Table 3.3 shows that the values in these tables are the inverse of the tables found in Appendix A and Table 3.1. Of course, this inversion makes sense because the values in Appendix A are $(1+i)^n$ and those in Appendix B are $[1/(1+i)^n]$. To determine the present value of a sum of money to be received at some future date, you need only determine the value of the appropriate present-value interest factor, by using a calculator or consulting the tables, and multiply it by

Present-Value Interest Factor
The value $[1/(1+i)^n]$ used as a multiplier to calculate an amount's present value.

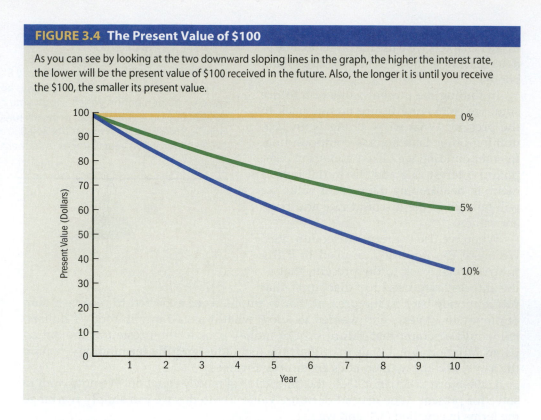

FIGURE 3.4 The Present Value of $100

As you can see by looking at the two downward sloping lines in the graph, the higher the interest rate, the lower will be the present value of $100 received in the future. Also, the longer it is until you receive the $100, the smaller its present value.

the future value. In effect, you can use the new notation and rewrite equation (3.3) as follows:

$$\begin{array}{|c|}\hline \text{Present Value} \\ \text{or} \\ PV \\\hline\end{array} = \begin{array}{|c|}\hline \text{Future Value} \\ \text{or} \\ FV \\\hline\end{array} \times \begin{array}{|c|}\hline \text{Present-Value Interest Factor} \\\hline\end{array} \quad (3.3a)$$

TABLE 3.3 Present Value of $1 (single amount)

Instructions: Each present-value interest factor corresponds to a specific time period and interest rate. To find the present-value interest factor for 6 percent and 10 years, simply move down the $i = 6\%$ column until you reach its intersection with the $n = 10$ years row: 0.558. The present value is then calculated as follows:

present value = future value × present-value interest factor

n	4%	5%	6%	7%	8%
1	0.962	0.952	0.943	0.935	0.926
2	0.925	0.907	0.890	0.873	0.857
3	0.889	0.864	0.840	0.816	0.794
4	0.855	0.823	0.792	0.763	0.735
5	0.822	0.784	0.747	0.713	0.681
6	0.790	0.746	0.705	0.666	0.630
7	0.760	0.711	0.655	0.623	0.583
8	0.731	0.677	0.627	0.582	0.540
9	0.703	0.645	0.592	0.544	0.500
10	0.676	0.614	0.558	0.508	0.463
11	0.650	0.585	0.527	0.475	0.429

MONEY MATTERS

Tips from Marcy Furney, ChFC, Certified Financial Planner™

A MILLION DOLLARS IS A MILLION DOLLARS

In my previous life, I helped enroll executives in special deferred compensation plans. They had to agree not to take a part of their pay each year in exchange for a large lump payment at retirement. One day, a 30-year-old man sat across from me to review the plan agreement. After a few minutes together he told me, "I don't need to try to support my family on any less income. My retirement plan will be worth a million dollars at 65." When I asked if he thought that would be enough, he replied, "A million dollars is a million dollars!" I was too tired from a long flight to argue. He was determined not to participate, so away he went. Later I calculated that his million dollars at 4 percent inflation would be worth only about $250,000 in current buying power. I wonder if he'll realize in a few years that sometimes a million dollars isn't a million dollars.

The moral of the story may be:

When accumulating money for a long-range goal such as retirement or a child's education, you must always include the impact of inflation. Establish your goal in today's dollars, then calculate the future amount needed using a reasonable inflation rate assumption.

Now that you've learned the magic of compounding, start saving. Even a small monthly investment at an early age will grow into a respectable sum at retirement. Just as compounding grows your money, inflation erodes it.

As soon as the opportunity presents itself, get into an employer-sponsored savings plan such as a 401(k) or SIMPLE. If your company makes a matching contribution of 50 cents for each dollar you put in, it's similar to a 50 percent rate of return in the first year. Where else can you make that kind of investment?

Save your raises. When you get a raise at work, increase your savings to include that amount. You're already used to living on your current take-home pay.

Calculate the real cost of that new iPod if paid out over a year or two on a credit card. You may find it's worth waiting until you've saved the funds.

When purchasing a big-ticket item like a car, take the initiative to do your own time value of money calculations to make sure the interest rate, number of payments, or total price is not being "adjusted" to produce an attractive payment.

If a financial calculator isn't one of your wardrobe accessories, always remember the Rule of 72. You'll be surprised by the way it comes in handy when making investment, savings, or borrowing decisions.

EXAMPLE

You're on vacation in Florida and you see an advertisement stating that you'll receive $100 simply for taking a tour of a model condominium. However, when you investigate, you discover that the $100 is in the form of a savings bond that will not pay you the $100 for 10 years. What is the present value of $100 to be received 10 years from today if your discount rate is 6 percent? By looking at the $n = 10$ row and $i = 6\%$ column of Table 3.3, you find the present-value interest factor is 0.558. Substituting $FV_{10} = \$100$ and present-value interest factor $= 0.558$ into equation (3.3a), you find:

$$PV = \$100 \times \text{present-value interest factor}$$
$$= \$100(0.558)$$
$$= \$55.80$$

Thus, the value in today's dollars of that $100 savings bond is only $55.80. Not a bad take for touring a condo, but it's not a hundred bucks.

Calculator Clues

Calculating a Present Value

Note for all calculations in this chapter: If you don't have a financial calculator handy, you can use the one that is located on the Web site that accompanies this book: **www.myfinancelab.com.**

In the example above, we're calculating the present value of $100 to be received in 10 years given a 6 percent interest or discount rate. For any value that does not appear in the calculations we'll enter a value of 0.

Enter   10   6   0   100
              [N]   [I/Y]   [PV]   [PMT]   [FV]
Solve for   −55.84

You'll notice that this calculator solution is slightly different from the answer we just got using the tables; that's just a matter of rounding error. You'll also notice we get a negative value for the answer. Remember, that's because financial calculators view money just as a bank does. You deposit money in the bank (the sign is negative because the money "leaves your hands"), and later you take money out of the bank (the sign is positive because the money "returns to your hands"). Every problem with two cash flows will have one with a positive sign and one with a negative sign.

EXAMPLE

Let's consider the impatient son of wealthy parents who wants his inheritance NOW! He's been promised $500,000 in 40 years. Assuming the appropriate discount rate (i.e., the interest rate used to bring future money back to the present) is 6 percent, what is the present value of the $500,000? To find the present value of the estate, we need only multiply the future value, which is $500,000, times the present-value interest factor for 6 percent and 40 years. To find the present-value interest factor for 6 percent and 40 years, go to the present-value interest factor table (see Appendix B) and simply move down the $i = 6\%$ column until you reach its intersection with the $n = 40$ years row: 0.097. Thus, the present value of the estate is:

$$\text{present value} = \text{future value} \times \text{present-value interest factor}$$
$$= \$500,000(0.097)$$
$$= \$48,500$$

That $500,000 the son is to receive in 40 years is worth only $48,500 in today's dollars. Another way of looking at this problem is that if you deposit $48,500 in the bank today earning 6 percent annually, in 40 years you'd have $500,000.

Calculator Clues

Calculating a Present Value

In this example, you're solving for the present value of $500,000 to be received in 40 years given a 6 percent interest or discount rate.

Enter   40   6   0   500,000
              [N]   [I/Y]   [PV]   [PMT]   [FV]
Solve for   −48,611.09

As expected, you get a negative sign on the *PV*. Try entering a higher value for *I/Y* and see what happens to the *PV*. Again, you'll notice a slight difference in the calculator solution due to rounding error and the negative sign that the solution takes on.

Keep in mind that there is really only one time value of money equation. That is, equations (3.2) and (3.3) are actually identical—they simply solve for different variables. One solves for future value, the other for present value. The logic behind both equations is the same: To adjust for the time value of money, we must compare dollar values, present and future, in the same time period. Because all present values are comparable (they are all measured in dollars of the same time period), you can add and subtract the present value of inflows and outflows to determine the present value of an investment.

Solving for *I/Y* and *N* Using a Financial Calculator

As you might expect, you can solve for *I/Y* and *N* using either the tables or a financial calculator. While solving for them using a financial calculator is relatively easy, solving for them using the tables is a bit more difficult, and, as such, an appendix to this chapter has been provided that explains this process.

> ### STOP & THINK
>
> Why should you be interested in stripping away the effects of inflation from money you receive in the future? Because the dollar value of future money is not as important as that money's purchasing power. For example, you might be excited if you were told you would receive $1 million in 20 years. However, if you then found out that in 20 years a new car will cost $800,000, your average monthly food bill will be $15,000, and a typical month's rent on your apartment will be $30,000, you would have a different view of the $1 million. Using the time value of money to strip away the effects of inflation allows you to calculate the value of a future amount in terms of the purchasing power of today's dollars. What do you think a car will cost in 20 years?

Let's assume that BMW, the owner of MINI Cooper, has guaranteed that the price of a new MINI Cooper will always be $20,000. You'd like to buy one, but currently you have only $7,752. How many years will it take for your initial investment of $7,752 to grow to $20,000 if it is invested at 9 percent compounded annually?

In this case we are solving for *N*, the number of years your money needs to grow. Just as when solving for *PV*, *PMT*, or *FV*, all you have to do is enter the variables you know into your financial calculator, and in this case solve for *N*. Remember, you must keep in mind that every problem will have at least one negative and one positive number, and in this problem you'll notice that *PV* is input with a negative sign. In effect, the $7,752 is a cash outflow (the money leaving your hands), whereas the $20,000 is money that you will receive. If you don't give one of these values a negative sign, you can't solve the problem, and if you have a TI BA II Plus calculator, you'll receive an "Error 5" message.

Calculator Clues

Solving for *N*—the Number of Payments

Solving for the number of payments using a financial calculator is simple. To solve for *N*, enter the known variables and solve. In this example, how many years will it take for $7,752 to grow to $20,000 at 9 percent?

Enter		9	−7,752	0	20,000
	N	I/Y	PV	PMT	FV
Solve for	10.998				

The answer is 10.998 or about 11 years. You'll notice we gave the present value, $7,752, a negative sign and the future value, $20,000, a positive sign. Why? Because a calculator looks at cash flows like it's a bank. You deposit your money in the bank (and the sign is negative because the money "leaves your hands"), and later you take your money out of the bank (the sign is positive because the money "returns to your hands"). As a result, every problem will have a positive and negative sign on the cash flows.

Now let's solve for the compound annual growth rate. In 10 years you'd really like to have $20,000 to buy a new MINI Cooper convertible, but you have only

$11,167. At what rate must your $11,167 be compounded annually for it to grow to $20,000 in 10 years?

Once again you have to remember that at least one of the dollar value variables, *PV*, *PMT*, or *FV*, must take on a negative value. In this case, we will enter $11,167 as a negative value since that money will "leave your hands" and later you will receive $20,000.

Calculator Clues

Solving for *I/Y*—the Rate of Return

Finding a rate of return using a financial calculator is simple. To solve for *I/Y*, enter the known variables and solve. For example, what is the growth rate of an initial investment of $11,167 that grew to $20,000 in 10 years?

Enter	10		−11,167	0	20,000
	N	I/Y	PV	PMT	FV
Solve for		6.0009			

The answer is 6.0009—about 6 percent. Just as when you solved for *N*, you gave the present value, $11,167, which was your initial investment, a negative sign and the future value, $20,000, a positive sign.

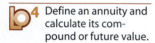
4 Define an annuity and calculate its compound or future value.

Annuity
A series of equal dollar payments coming at the end of each time period for a specified number of time periods.

Compound Annuity
An investment that involves depositing an equal sum of money at the end of each year for a certain number of years and allowing it to grow.

Future-Value Interest Factor of an Annuity
A multiplier used to determine the future value of an annuity. The future-value interest factors for an annuity are found in Appendix C.

Annuities

To this point, we've been examining single deposits—moving them back and forth in time. Now we're going to examine annuities. Most people deal with a great number of annuities. Mortgage payments, pension funds, insurance obligations, and interest received from bonds all involve annuities. An **annuity** is a series of equal dollar payments coming at the end of each time period for a specified number of time periods (years, months, etc.). Because annuities occur frequently in finance—for example, as bond interest payments and mortgage payments—they are treated specially. Although compounding and determining the present value of an annuity can be done using equations (3.2) and (3.3), these calculations can be time-consuming, especially for larger annuities. Thus, we have modified the formulas to deal directly with annuities.

Compound Annuities

A **compound annuity** involves depositing or investing an equal sum of money at the end of each year (or time period) for a certain number of years (or time periods, e.g., months) and allowing it to grow. Perhaps you are saving money for education, a new car, or a vacation home. In each case you'll want to know how much your savings will have grown by some point in the future.

Actually, you can find the answer by using equation (3.2) and compounding each of the individual deposits to its future value. For example, if to provide for a college education you are going to deposit $500 at the end of each year for the next five years in a bank where it will earn 6 percent interest, how much will you have at the end of 5 years? Compounding each of these values using equation (3.2), you find that you will have $2,818.50 at the end of 5 years.

As Table 3.4 shows, all we're really doing in the preceding calculation is summing up a number of future values. To simplify this process once again, there are tables providing the **future-value interest factor of an annuity** for *i* and *n*. Appendix C provides

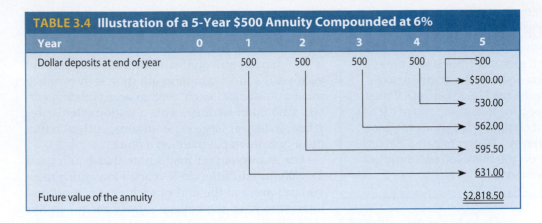

TABLE 3.4 Illustration of a 5-Year $500 Annuity Compounded at 6%

Year	0	1	2	3	4	5
Dollar deposits at end of year		500	500	500	500	500
						$500.00
						530.00
						562.00
						595.50
						631.00
Future value of the annuity						$2,818.50

a fairly complete version of these tables, and Table 3.5 presents an abbreviated version. Using this new factor, we can calculate the future value of an annuity as follows:

$$\text{Future Value of an Annuity or } FV_n = \text{Annual Payment or } PMT \times \text{Future-Value Interest Factor of an Annuity} \quad (3.4)$$

Using the future-value interest factor for an annuity to solve our previous example involving 5 years of deposits of $500, invested at 6 percent interest, we would look in the $i = 6\%$ column and $n = 5$ row and find the value of the future-value interest factor of an annuity to be 5.637. Substituting this value into equation (3.4), we get

$$\text{future value} = \$500(5.637)$$
$$= \$2,818.50$$

TABLE 3.5 Future Value of a Series of Equal Annual Deposits (annuity), Future-Value Interest Factor of an Annuity

Instructions: Each future-value interest factor of an annuity corresponds to a specific time period (number of years) and interest rate. For example, to find the future-value interest factor of an annuity for 6 percent and 5 years, simply move down the $i = 6\%$ column until you reach its intersection with the $n = 5$ years row: 5.637. The future value is calculated as follows:

future value = annual payment × future-value interest factor for an annuity

or $FV_n = PMT(FVIFA_{i\%, n\,years})$

n	4%	5%	6%	7%	8%
1	1.000	1.000	1.000	1.000	1.000
2	2.040	2.050	2.060	2.070	2.080
3	3.122	3.152	3.184	3.215	3.246
4	4.246	4.310	4.375	4.440	4.506
5	5.416	5.526	5.637	5.751	5.867
6	6.633	6.802	6.975	7.153	7.336
7	7.898	8.142	8.394	8.654	8.923
8	9.214	9.549	9.897	10.260	10.637
9	10.583	11.027	11.491	11.978	12.488
10	12.006	12.578	13.181	13.816	14.487
11	13.486	14.207	14.972	15.784	16.645

This is the same answer we obtained earlier. (If it weren't, I'd need to get a new job!)

Rather than ask how much you'll accumulate if you deposit an equal sum in a savings account each year, a more common question is, how much must you deposit each year to accumulate a certain amount of savings? This question often arises when saving for large expenditures, such as retirement or a down payment on a home.

For example, you may know that you'll need $10,000 for education in 8 years. How much must you put away at the end of each year at 6 percent interest to have the college money ready? In this case, you know the values of n, i, and FV_n in equation (3.4), but you don't know the value of PMT. Substituting these example values in equation (3.4), you find

$$\text{future value} = \text{annual payment} \times \text{future-value interest factor of an annuity}$$
$$\$10,000 = PMT(9.897)$$
$$\$10,000/9.897 = PMT$$
$$PMT = \$1,010.41$$

Thus, you must invest $1,010.41 at the end of each year at 6 percent interest to accumulate $10,000 at the end of 8 years.

For a moment, let's use the future value of an annuity and think back to the discussion of the power of time. There's no question of the power of time. One way to illustrate this power is to look at how much you'd have to save each month to reach some far-off goal. For example, you'd like to save up $50,000 by the time you turn 60 to use to go see a Rolling Stones concert. (There's a good chance they'll still be on tour and that concert tickets will cost that much.)

If you can invest your money at 12 percent and start saving when you turn 21, making your last payment on your 60th birthday, you'll need to put aside only $4.25 per month. If you started at age 31, that figure would be $14.31 per month. However, if

you waited until age 51, it would rise to $217.35 per month. When it comes to compounding, time is on your side.

Calculator Clues

Future Value of an Annuity

At the end of each year for 50 years you deposit $365 in an account that earns 12 percent.

Enter	50	12	0	365
	N	I/Y	PV	PMT	FV
Solve for					−876,006.66

As expected, you get a negative sign on the *FV*. What happens if you waited until you were 33 instead of 18 to begin? Then you'd only be investing for 35 years, so you change *N* to 35 and solve it again:

Enter	35	12	0	365	
	N	I/Y	PV	PMT	FV
Solve for					−157,557.18

Present Value of an Annuity

In planning your finances, you need to examine the relative value of all your annuities. To compare them, you need to know the present value of each. Although you can find the present value of an annuity by using the present-value table in Appendix B, this process can be tedious, particularly when the annuity lasts for several years. If you wish to know what $500 received at the end of the next 5 years is worth to you given the appropriate discount rate of 6 percent, you can separately bring each of the $500 flows back to the present at 6 percent using equation (3.3) and then add them together. Thus, the present value of this annuity is $2,106.00. As Table 3.6 shows, all we're really doing in this calculation is adding up present values. Because annuities occur so frequently in personal finance, the process of determining the present value of an annuity has been simplified by defining the **present-value interest factor of an annuity** for i and n. The present-value interest factor of an annuity is simply the sum of the present-value interest factor for years 1 to n. Tables for values of the present-value interest of an annuity have once again been compiled for various combinations of i and n. Appendix D provides a fairly complete version of these tables, and Table 3.7 provides an abbreviated version.

Using this new factor, we can determine the present value of an annuity as follows:

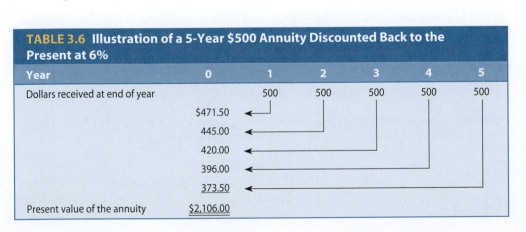

> **FACTS OF LIFE**
>
> Spending money involves a tradeoff—spending it today, or saving it and spending the amount it grows to later. For example, when you graduate, one of your first purchases might be a car. In 2011, two of your choices would be an Audi TT for about $46,000 or a 2-year-old used Toyota Camry in great shape for about $16,000. If you saved the difference at 9 percent until you retired in 40 years, you'd have about $942,000 waiting for you!
>
> $30,000 today   vs. $942,000 in 40 years
>
> 9%

Present-Value Interest Factor of an Annuity ($PVIFA_{i, n}$)
A multiplier used to determine the present value of an annuity. The present-value interest factors are found in Appendix D.

$$\boxed{\begin{matrix}\text{Present Value}\\\text{of an Annuity}\\\text{or}\\PV\end{matrix}} = \boxed{\begin{matrix}\text{Annual}\\\text{Payment}\\\text{or}\\PMT\end{matrix}} \times \boxed{\begin{matrix}\text{Present-Value Interest Factor}\\\text{of an Annuity}\end{matrix}} \qquad (3.5)$$

Using the present-value interest factor of an annuity to solve our previous example involving $500 received annually and discounted back to the present at 6 percent,

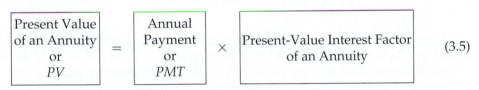

TABLE 3.6 Illustration of a 5-Year $500 Annuity Discounted Back to the Present at 6%						
Year	**0**	**1**	**2**	**3**	**4**	**5**
Dollars received at end of year		500	500	500	500	500
	$471.50					
	445.00					
	420.00					
	396.00					
	373.50					
Present value of the annuity	$2,106.00					

TABLE 3.7 Present Value of a Series of Annual Deposits (annuity), Present-Value Interest Factor of an Annuity

Instructions: Each present-value interest factor for an annuity corresponds to a specific time period (number of years) and interest rate. For example, to find the present-value interest factor of an annuity for 6 percent and 5 years, simply move down the $i = 6\%$ column until you reach its intersection with the $n = 5$ years row: 4.212. The future value is then calculated as follows:

present value = annual payment × present-value interest factor for an annuity

n	4%	5%	6%	7%	8%
1	0.962	0.952	0.943	0.935	0.926
2	1.886	1.859	1.833	1.808	1.783
3	2.775	2.723	2.673	2.624	2.577
4	3.630	3.546	3.465	3.387	3.312
5	4.452	4.329	4.212	4.100	3.993
6	5.242	5.076	4.917	4.767	4.623
7	6.002	5.786	5.582	5.389	5.206
8	6.733	6.463	6.210	5.971	5.747
9	7.435	7.108	6.802	6.515	6.247
10	8.111	7.722	7.360	7.024	6.710
11	8.760	8.306	7.887	7.499	7.139

we would look in the $i = 6\%$ column and the $n = 5$ row and find the present-value interest factor of an annuity to be 4.212. Substituting the appropriate values into equation (3.5), we find

present value = annual payment × present-value interest factor of an annuity
= $500(4.212)
= $2,106

Again, we get the same answer we previously did. (We're on a roll now!) We didn't get the same answer just because we're smart. Actually, we got the same answer both times because the present-value interest factor of an annuity tables are calculated by adding up the values in the present-value interest factor table.

EXAMPLE

As part of a class action lawsuit settlement against Lee's "Press On Abs" (they caused a nasty rash), you are slated to receive $1,000 at the end of each year for the next 10 years. What is the present value of this 10-year, $1,000 annuity discounted back to the present at 5 percent? Substituting $n = 10$ years, $i = 5$ percent, and $PMT = \$1,000$ into equation (3.5), you find

$$PV = \$1,000 \text{ (present-value interest factor of an annuity)}$$

Determining the value for the present-value interest factor of an annuity from Table 3.7, row $n = 10$, column $i = 5\%$, and substituting it into our equation, we get:

$$PV = \$1,000(7.722)$$
$$PV = \$7,722$$

Thus, the present value of this annuity is $7,722.

Calculator Clues

Present Value of an Annuity

In this example, you're solving for the present value of a 10-year, $1,000 annuity discounted back to the present at 5 percent.

Enter   10   5   1,000   0
                 N   I/Y   PV   PMT   FV
Solve for   − 7,721.73

As expected, you get a negative sign on the PV. What happens if you enter a higher value for I/Y?

As with the other problems involving compounding and present-value tables, given any three of the four unknowns in equation (3.5), we can solve for the fourth. In the case of the present-value interest factor of an annuity table, we may be interested in solving for PMT, if we know $i, n,$ and PV. The financial interpretation of this action would be: How much can be withdrawn, perhaps as a pension or to make loan payments, from an account that earns i percent compounded annually for each of the next n years if you wish to have nothing left at the end of n years?

> ### STOP & THINK
>
> One of the reasons people don't save for retirement gets back to **Principle 9: Mind Games, Your Financial Personality, and Your Money**. People tend not to save enough for retirement because retirement seems a long time away and they think they can catch up later—it's our tendency to postpone and procrastinate that is hurting us. With an understanding of the time value of money you can gain an understanding of why starting to save early is so important. Name two or three instances where you have procrastinated in the past.

Amortized Loans

You're not always on the receiving end of an annuity. More often, your annuity will involve paying off a loan in equal installments over time. Loans that are paid off this way, in equal periodic payments, are called **amortized loans**. Examples of amortized loans include car loans and mortgages.

Amortized Loan
A loan paid off in equal installments.

Suppose you borrowed $16,000 at 8 percent interest to buy a car and wish to repay it in four equal payments at the end of each of the next 4 years. We can use equation (3.5) to determine what the annual payments will be and solve for the value of PMT, the annual annuity. Again, you know three of the four values in that equation, PV, i, and n. PV, the present value of the future annuity, is $16,000; i, the annual interest rate, is 8 percent; and n, the number of years for which the annuity will last, is 4 years. Thus, looking in the $n = 4$ row and 8% column of Table 3.7 you know the present-value interest factor of an annuity is 3.312. PMT, the annuity payment received (by the lender and paid by you) at the end of each year, is unknown. Substituting these values into equation (3.5) you find:

present value = annual payment × present-value interest factor of an annuity

$$\$16,000 = PMT(3.312)$$
$$\frac{\$16,000}{3.312} = \frac{PMT(3.312)}{3.312}$$
$$\$4,831 = PMT$$

To repay the principal and interest on the outstanding loan in 4 years, the annual payments would be $4,831. The breakdown of interest and principal payments is given in the loan amortization schedule in Figure 3.5. As you can see, the interest payment declines each year as the outstanding loan declines.

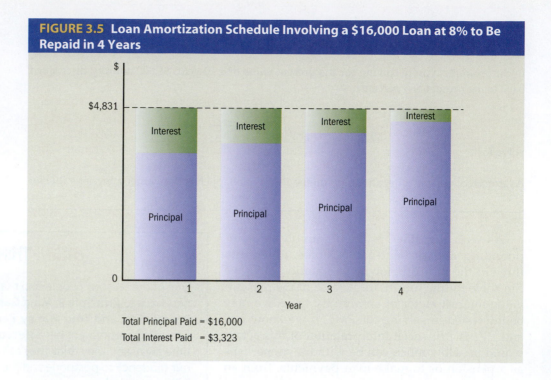

FIGURE 3.5 Loan Amortization Schedule Involving a $16,000 Loan at 8% to Be Repaid in 4 Years

Total Principal Paid = $16,000
Total Interest Paid = $3,323

Calculator Clues

Calculating a Loan Payment

Calculating loan payments is easy with a financial calculator. In the example above you want to determine the loan payments on a $16,000 loan at 8 percent that you want to pay off with four equal payments at the end of each of the next 4 years. All you need to do is plug your numbers into the calculator and solve for *PMT*. *PV* is $16,000, because that's how much you've borrowed today, and *FV* is 0 because you will have the loan paid off after 4 years.

Enter	4	8	16,000		0
	N	I/Y	PV	PMT	FV
Solve for				−4,831	

As expected, *PMT* takes on a negative sign.

Amortized Loans with Monthly Payments Using a Financial Calculator

In our examples so far, we have assumed that only one payment is made per year and that interest is compounded annually. However, many loans—for example, auto and home loans—require monthly payments. Fortunately, dealing with monthly, as opposed to yearly, payments is easy. We simply have to make sure that our measurement of periods and interest rate is consistent—that is, if we are talking about monthly payments, then the interest rate should be expressed as the interest rate per month.

To make this adjustment we can define a new variable, *m*, which is the number of times compounding occurs per year. For example, if we are taking about semi-annual compounding, *m* would be equal to 2, and if we are talking about monthly compounding, *m* would be equal to 12. Then, all we do is multiply the number of years outstanding on the loan or annuity by m, which gives us the number of times compounding occurs over the life of the loan or annuity, and this goes in your financial calculator as n, the number of periods. Then, we divide the annual interest rate by m to find the interest rate per period, and this goes in your financial calculator as i.

In effect, n is the number of periods for which the annuity will last. If the annuity payments are received annually, n will be the number of years, if the payments are received monthly, it will be the number of months. If n is expressed in terms of months, then i should also be expressed in terms of the interest rate per month. Thus, if annuity payments are received annually, i would be expressed as an annual rate; if the payments are received monthly, it would be the monthly rate.

Unfortunately, it's generally impossible to solve problems with nonannual compounding periods using the time value of money tables. That's because when we convert an annual interest rate into a monthly or daily interest rate, the monthly or daily interest rate tends to be smaller than the interest rates in the time value of money tables. For example, if we are looking at a 15-year mortgage with monthly payments at an annual interest rate of 7 percent, we are really talking about a mortgage with 180 periods (months) at a rate of 7 percent/12 = 0.5833 percent per month. Unfortunately, there aren't tables with fractional interest rates and 180 periods. As a result, when we are dealing with monthly and other nonannual payments we are forced to use a financial calculator.

Calculator Clues

Calculating a Monthly Mortgage Payment

You've just found the perfect home. However, in order to buy it, you'll need to take out a $150,000, 30-year mortgage at an annual rate of 6 percent. What will your monthly mortgage payments be?

Because there are 360 monthly periods in 30 years, 360 is entered for N, and I/Y becomes 0.5 (annual interest rate of 6 percent divided by m, which is 12).

Enter	360	0.5	150,000		0
	N	I/Y	PV	PMT	FV
Solve for				−899.33	

Calculator Clues

Calculating the Present Value When Payments Are Monthly

One of the first things you'll need to decide when shopping for a house is "how much can I really afford to spend?" This will determine which houses you look at. You figure you can afford monthly mortgage payments of $1,250, and you can get a 30-year loan at 7.2 percent. So, how big of a mortgage can you afford?

We are using 360 as the number of periods or n because there are 30 years' worth of monthly mortgage payments, and there are 360 months in 30 years. But why are we using 0.72%/12 as the value for the i? Because if the interest rate is 7.2 percent per year, it would be one-twelfth of that every month, or 7.2%/12 or 0.6 percent; remember, if n is expressed in months, then i must also be expressed as a monthly interest rate.

The easiest way to enter the interest rate here is to simply divide annual interest rate by m and then enter this number into I/Y. That way you don't have to worry about rounding error.

Enter	360	7.2 ÷ 12		1,250	0
	N	I/Y	PV	PMT	FV
Solve for			−184,152		

Perpetuities

Perpetuity
An annuity that continues forever.

A **perpetuity** is an annuity that continues forever. That is, every year from its establishment, this investment pays the same dollar amount and never stops paying. Determining the present value of a perpetuity is delightfully simple: You divide the payment amount by the discount rate. For example, the present value of a perpetuity that pays a constant dividend of $10 per share forever if the appropriate discount rate is 5 percent is $10/0.05 = $200. Thus, the equation representing the present value of a perpetuity is

$$PV = PP/i \tag{3.6}$$

where:

$$PV = \text{the present value of the perpetuity}$$
$$PP = \text{the annual dollar amount provided by the perpetuity}$$
$$i = \text{the annual interest (or discount) rate}$$

Summary

 Explain the mechanics of compounding.
Almost every decision in personal finance involves the techniques of compounding and time value of money—putting aside money now to achieve some future goal. The cornerstone of the time value of money is the concept of compound interest, which is interest paid on interest.

With the time value of money, you can determine how much an investment will grow over time using the following formula:

$$FV_n = PV(1 + i)^n \tag{3.2}$$

To simplify these calculations, there are tables for the $(1 + i)^n$ part of the equation referred to as the future-value interest factor for i and n. In effect, you can rewrite equation (3.2) as follows:

$$\text{future value} = \text{present value} \times \text{future-value interest factor} \tag{3.2a}$$

 Understand the power of time and the importance of the interest rate in compounding.
It is also important to understand the role of the interest rate in determining how large an investment grows. Together, time and the interest rate determine how much you will need to save in order to achieve your goals. You can increase your future value by increasing either the interest rate or the number of years for which your money is compounded. You can also use the Rule of 72 to determine how long it will take to double your invested money. This "rule" is only an approximation:

$$\text{number of years to double} = 72/\text{annual compound growth rate}$$

3 **Calculate the present value of money to be received in the future.**

Many times we also want to solve for present value instead of future value. We use the following formula to do this:

$$\boxed{\begin{array}{c}\text{Present Value}\\\text{or}\\PV\end{array}} = \boxed{\begin{array}{c}\text{Future Value}\\\text{or}\\FV_n\end{array}} \times \boxed{\text{Present-Value Interest Factor}} \qquad (3.3a)$$

4 **Define an annuity and calculate its compound or future value.**

An annuity is a series of equal annual dollar payments coming at the end of each year for a specified number of years. Because annuities occur frequently in finance—for example, as bond interest payments and mortgage payments—they receive special treatment. A compound annuity involves depositing or investing an equal sum of money at the end of each year for a certain number of years and allowing it to grow.

$$\boxed{\begin{array}{c}\text{Future Value}\\\text{of an Annuity}\\\text{or}\\FV_n\end{array}} = \boxed{\begin{array}{c}\text{Annual}\\\text{Payment}\\\text{or}\\PMT\end{array}} \times \boxed{\begin{array}{c}\text{Future-Value Interest Factor}\\\text{of an Annuity}\end{array}} \qquad (3.4)$$

To find the present value of an annuity, we use the following formula:

$$\boxed{\begin{array}{c}\text{Present Value}\\\text{of an Annuity}\\\text{or}\\PV\end{array}} = \boxed{\begin{array}{c}\text{Annual}\\\text{Payment}\\\text{or}\\PMT\end{array}} \times \boxed{\begin{array}{c}\text{Present-Value Interest Factor}\\\text{of an Annuity}\end{array}} \qquad (3.5)$$

Many times annuities involve paying off a loan in equal installments over time. Loans that are paid off this way, in equal periodic payments, are called amortized loans. Examples of amortized loans include car loans and mortgages.

Review Questions

1. What is compound interest? How is compound interest related to the time value of money?
2. What is "future value" and why is it important to calculate?
3. Describe how you can use the Rule of 72 to make financial planning decisions.
4. What variables are used in solving a time value of money problem with no periodic payments? Which of these variables equals zero when solving a simple present- or future-value problem with no periodic payments? Why?
5. Explain the concept of the time value of money. Explain two ways this concept is relevant in financial planning.
6. What two factors most affect how much people need to save to achieve their financial goals?
7. Why do you think that Albert Einstein once called compound interest the "eighth wonder of the world"?

8. Why might an investor require a greater expected return for an investment of longer maturity? Do you feel you can forecast inflation 2 years from now with greater accuracy than inflation in 20 years?

9. Why might you use the anticipated rate of inflation as the discount rate when calculating present value?

10. Why is the interest rate in a time value of money calculation sometimes referred to as the discount rate? Why is it also called "inverse compounding"?

11. Explain in terms of the future-value interest factor why, given a certain goal, that as the period of time to invest increases, the required periodic investment decreases.

12. What is the primary difference between an annuity and a compound annuity?

13. What is the relationship between present-value and future-value interest factors and present and future interest factors for annuities?

14. Define an amortized loan and give two common examples.

15. Why is it necessary to use a negative present value when solving for *N* (the number of payments) or *I/Y* (the rate of return)? Similarly, why does the answer have a negative sign if positive payments were used when solving for a future value on a calculator?

16. What is a perpetuity? Name an example of a perpetuity (payments or receipt of income) in personal finance.

Develop Your Skills—Problems and Activities

These problems are available in MyFinanceLab.

1. Your mother just won $250,000 for splitting a Nobel Prize with three coworkers. If she invests her prize money in a diversified equity portfolio returning 8 percent per year, approximately how long will it take her to become a millionaire, before accounting for taxes?

2. Linda Baer has saved $5,000 for a previously owned vehicle. Ignoring taxes and assuming her money is invested in a flexible withdrawal CD earning 5 percent compounded annually, how long will it take to buy a car that costs $7,755? (*Hint:* The answer is between 6 and 10 years.)

3. Paul Ramos just graduated from college and landed his first "real" job, which pays $23,000 a year. In 10 years, what will he need to earn to maintain the same purchasing power if inflation averages 3 percent?

4. Anthony and Michelle Constantino just got married and received $30,000 in cash gifts for their wedding. Use your financial calculator, or the Money in Motion calculator which is available in MyFinanceLab, to determine how much they will have on their 25th anniversary if they place half of this money in a fixed-rate investment earning 7 percent compounded annually. Would the future value be larger or smaller if the compounding period was 6 months? How much more or less would they have earned with this shorter compounding period?

5. Calculate the future value of $5,000 earning 10 percent after 1 year assuming annual compounding. Now, calculate the future value of $5,000 earning 10 percent after 20 years.

6. Ahmed Mustafa just turned 22 and wants to have $10,283 saved in 8 years by his 30th birthday. Assuming no additional deposits, if he currently has $6,000 in an intermediate-term bond fund earning a 5 percent yield, will he reach his goal? If not, what rate of return is required to meet his goal?

7. If another *Austin Powers* movie had been released in 2007, and Dr. Evil, now armed with a financial calculator, wants to hold the Earth ransom for $7,039,988.71,

what inflation rate would Dr. Evil use to make his ransom equivalent to $1 million in 1967? (*Hint:* Inflation is compounded on an annual basis.)

8. When Derek was a small child, his grandfather established a trust fund for him to receive $20,000 on his 35th birthday. Derek just turned 23. Use your financial calculator or the Money in Motion calculator, which is available in MyFinanceLab, to calculate the value of his trust today if the trust fund earns 7 percent interest. What is the present value of the $20,000 to be received in 17 years if he had to wait until age 40 to receive the money?

9. You and 11 coworkers just won $12 million ($1 million each) from the state lottery. Assuming you each receive your share over 20 years and that the state lottery earns a 6 percent return on its funds, what is the present value of your prize before taxes if you request the "up-front cash" option?

10. Richard Gorman is 65 years old and about to retire. He has $500,000 saved to supplement his pension and Social Security, and would like to withdraw it in equal annual dollar amounts so that nothing is left after 15 years. How much does he have to withdraw each year if he earns 7 percent on his money?

11. Assume you are 25 and earn $35,000 per year, never expect to receive a raise, and plan to retire at age 55. If you invest 5 percent of your salary in a 401(k) plan returning 10 percent annually, and the company provides a $0.50 per $1.00 match on your contributions up to 3 percent of your salary, what is your estimated future value? Once you retire, how much can you withdraw monthly if you want to deplete your account over 30 years?

12. Shaylea, age 22, just started working full-time and plans to deposit $5,000 annually into an IRA earning 8 percent interest compounded annually. How much would she have in 20 years, 30 years, and 40 years? If she changed her investment period and instead invested $417 monthly and the investment also changed to monthly compounding, how much would she have after the same three time periods? Comment on the differences over time.

13. Your grandmother just gave you $6,000. You'd like to see what it might grow to if you invest it.

   a. Calculate the future value of $6,000, given that it will be invested for 5 years at an annual interest rate of 6 percent.

   b. Recalculate part (a) using a compounding period that is semiannual (every 6 months).

   c. Now let's look at what might happen if you can invest the money at a 12 percent rate rather than 6 percent rate; recalculate parts (a) and (b) for a 12 percent annual interest rate.

   d. Now let's see what might happen if you invest the money for 12 years rather than 5 years; recalculate part (a) using a time horizon of 12 years (annual interest rate is still 6 percent).

14. If you deposit $3,500 today into an account earning an 11 percent annual rate of return, what would your account be worth in 35 years (assuming no further deposits)? In 40 years?

15. Sarah Wiggum would like to make a single investment and have $2 million at the time of her retirement in 35 years. She has found a mutual fund that will earn 4 percent annually. How much will Sarah have to invest today? If Sarah invests that amount and could earn a 14 percent annual return, how soon could she retire assuming she is still going to retire when she has $2 million?

16. Kirk Van Houten, who has been married for 23 years, would like to buy his wife an expensive diamond ring with a platinum setting on their 30-year wedding anniversary. Assume that the cost of the ring will be $12,000 in 7 years. Kirk

currently has $4,510 to invest. What annual rate of return must Kirk earn on his investment to accumulate enough money to pay for the ring?

17. Seven years ago, Lance Murdock purchased a wooden statue of a Conquistador for $7,600 to put in his home office. Lance has recently married, and his home office is being converted into a sewing room. His new wife, who has far better taste than Lance, thinks the Conquistador is hideous and must go immediately. Lance decides to sell it on eBay and only receives $5,200 for it, and so he takes a loss on the investment. What is his rate of return, that is, the value of *i*?

18. You are offered $100,000 today or $300,000 in 13 years. Assuming that you can earn 11 percent on your money, which should you choose?

19. In March 1963, Ironman was first introduced in issue number 39 of *Tales of Suspense*. The original price for that issue was 12 cents. By March 2012, 49 years later, the value of this comic book had risen to $9,000. What annual rate of interest would you have earned if you had bought the comic in 1963 and sold it in 2012 (49 years later)?

20. You are graduating from college at the end of this semester and have decided to invest $5,000 at the end of each year into a Roth IRA, which is a retirement investment account that grows tax free and is not taxed when it is liquidated, for the next 45 years. If you earn 8 percent compounded annually on your investment of $5,000 at the end of each year, how much will you have when you retire in 45 years? How much will you have if you wait 10 years before beginning to save and only make 35 payments into your retirement account?

21. To pay for your education, you've taken out $25,000 in student loans. If you make monthly payments over 15 years at 7 percent compounded monthly, how much are your monthly student loan payments?

22. How long will it take to pay off a loan of $50,000 at an annual rate of 10 percent compounded monthly if you make monthly payments of $600 (round up)?

23. You've just bought a new flat screen TV for $3,000 and the store you bought it from offers to let you finance the entire purchase at an annual rate of 14 percent compounded monthly. If you take the financing and make monthly payments of $100, how long will it take to pay the loan off? How much did you pay in interest over the life of the loan (that would be the difference between the total of all your payments and the amount of your payments that went toward your principle of $3,000)?

24. Chris Griffin has a $5,000 debt balance on his Visa card that charges 18.9 percent compounded monthly, and his minimum monthly payment is 3 percent of his debt balance, which is $150. How many months (round up) will it take Chris to pay off his credit card if he pays the current minimum payment of $150 at the end of each month? If Chris made monthly payments of $200 at the end of each month, how long would it take to pay off his credit card (round up)?

Learn by Doing—Suggested Projects

1. Ask older friends or relatives about the cost of specific items (e.g., a gallon of gas, a cup of coffee, etc.) during their youth. Also inquire about their average wages in the past. Compare the amounts given to current expenses and income levels. Explain your findings using the time value of money concepts.

2. Develop and solve a future-value, a present-value, a future value of an annuity, and a present value of an annuity problem. Establish the three known variables in each problem and solve for the fourth. Do not always solve for the same variable. Explain the results.

3. Using a financial calculator, determine the future value of $5,000 invested at 12 percent for 40 years with annual compounding. What rate of interest would result in the same future value if the compounding period were changed to monthly? (*Hint:* Change the compounding period and solve the equation in reverse for the interest rate.)

4. Research the cost of five products or services that were advertised in newspapers or magazines published more than 20 years ago. Then find the current cost of these items. Calculate the rate of inflation for each item between the two points in time.

5. Visit a local financial institution and record the interest rates and minimum balance requirements for the various financial products it offers. Using the information gathered, determine how much interest you would earn if you deposited $2,500 in each type of account. For each, calculate your total return subtracting any applicable service charges.

6. Assume you can save $4,000 a year (about $80 per week) after graduation. Set a financial goal for yourself and specify the time frame and cost. Calculate the interest rate required to achieve the goal. Is it possible to achieve your goal, with moderate risk, in today's financial market? If not, describe the changes that could be made to bring the goal closer to reality.

7. Investigate a specific financial planning issue or decision that involves the use of the time value of money concepts. Describe why it is necessary to make a time value of money calculation.

   Examples: Determining how much retirement income to withdraw per year over your life expectancy, calculating loan payments, calculating present pension plan contributions needed to fund future benefits, calculating future value of an IRA or 401(k), calculating present value (purchasing power) of money to be received in the future.

Be a Financial Planner—Discussion Case 1

This case is available in MyFinanceLab.

Jinhee Ju, 27, just received a promotion at work that increased her annual salary to $37,000. She is eligible to participate in her employer's 401(k) plan to which the employer matches dollar-for-dollar workers' contributions up to 5 percent of salary. However, Jinhee wants to buy a new $25,000 car in 3 years and she wants to save enough money to make a $7,000 down payment on the car and finance the balance.

Also in her plans is a wedding. Jinhee and her boyfriend, Paul, have set a wedding date 2 years in the future, after he finishes medical school. Paul will have $100,000 of student loans to repay after graduation. But both Jinhee and Paul want to buy a home of their own as soon as possible. This might be possible because at age 30, Jinhee will be eligible to access a $50,000 trust fund left to her as an inheritance by her late grandfather. Her trust fund is invested in 7 percent government bonds.

Questions

1. Justify Jinhee's participation in her employer's 401(k) plan using the time value of money concepts.

2. Calculate the amount that Jinhee needs to save each year for the down payment on a new car, assuming she can earn 6 percent on her savings. Calculate how much she will need to save on a monthly basis assuming monthly compounding. For each scenario, how much of her down payment will come from interest earned?

3. What will be the value of Jinhee's trust fund at age 60, assuming she takes possession of half of the money at age 30 for a house down payment, and leaves the other half of the money untouched where it is currently invested?

4. What is Paul's annual payment if he wants to repay his student loans completely within 10 years and he pays a 5 percent interest rate? How much more or less would Paul pay if the loans compounded interest on a monthly basis and Paul also paid the loans on a monthly basis?

5. List at least three actions that Jinhee and Paul could take to make the time value of money work in their favor.

Be a Financial Planner—Discussion Case 2

This case is available in MyFinanceLab.

Doug Klock, 56, just retired after 31 years of teaching. He is a husband and father of three children, two of whom are still dependent. He received a $150,000 lump-sum retirement bonus and will receive $2,800 per month from his retirement annuity. He has saved $150,000 in a 403(b) retirement plan and another $100,000 in other accounts. His 403(b) plan is invested in mutual funds, but most of his other investments are in bank accounts earning 2 or 3 percent annually. Doug has asked your advice in deciding where to invest his lump-sum bonus and other accounts now that he has retired. He also wants to know how much he can withdraw per month considering he has two children in college and a nonworking spouse. Because Rachel and Ronda are still in college, his current monthly expenses total $5,800. He does not intend to begin receiving Social Security until age 67 and his monthly benefit will amount to $1,550. He has grown accustomed to some risk but wants most of his money in FDIC-insured accounts.

Questions

1. Assuming Doug has another account set aside for emergencies, how much can he withdraw on a monthly basis to supplement his retirement annuity if his investments return 5 percent annually and he expects to live 30 more years?

2. Ignoring his Social Security benefit, is the amount determined in question 1 sufficient to meet his current monthly expenses? If not, how long will his retirement last if his current expenses remain at $5,800 per month? If his expenses are reduced to $4,500 per month? (*Hint:* Use the information in the appendix to this chapter to solve this problem.)

3. If he withdraws $3,000 per month, how much will he have in 11 years when he turns 67? If he begins to receive Social Security payments of $1,550 at 67, how many years can he continue to withdraw $1,450 per month from his investments?

4. If the inflation rate averages 3 percent during Doug's retirement, how old will he be when prices have doubled from current levels? How much will a soda cost when Doug dies, if he lives the full 30 years and the soda costs $1 today?

Appendix

Crunchin' the Numbers— Advanced Topics in Time Value of Money Using the Tables

Solving for I/Y and N Using the Tables

As you might expect, you can solve for I/Y and N using the tables or calculator, which was illustrated earlier in this chapter. With the tables, you first find what table value you're looking for, then you see what column (if you're solving for I/Y) or row (if you're solving for N) it is in. Take a look at the examples below.

Let's assume that the DaimlerChrysler Corporation has guaranteed that the price of a new Jeep will always be $20,000. You'd like to buy one, but currently you have only $10,805. How many years will it take for your initial investment of $10,805 to grow to $20,000 if it is invested at 8 percent compounded annually? We can use equation (3.2a) to solve for this problem as well. Substituting the known values in equation (3.2a), you find

$$\text{future value} = \text{present value} \times \text{future-value interest factor}$$
$$\$20,000 = \$10,805 \times \text{future-value interest factor}$$
$$\frac{\$20,000}{\$10,805} = \frac{\$10,805 \times \text{future-value interest factor}}{\$10,805}$$
$$1.851 = \text{future-value interest factor}$$

Thus, you're looking for a value of 1.851 in the future-value interest factor tables, and you know it must be in the 8% column. To finish solving the problem, look down the 8% column for the value closest to 1.851. You'll find that it occurs in the $n = 8$ row. Thus, it will take 8 years for an initial investment of $10,805 to grow to $20,000 if it is invested at 8 percent compounded annually.

Now let's solve for the compound annual growth rate. In 10 years you'd really like to have $20,000 to buy a new Jeep, but you have only $11,167. At what rate must your $11,167 be compounded annually for it to grow to $20,000 in 10 years? Substituting the known variables into equation (3.4a), you get

$$\text{future value} = \text{present value} \times \text{future-value interest factor}$$
$$\$20,000 = \$11,167 \times \text{future-value interest factor}$$
$$\frac{\$20,000}{\$11,167} = \frac{\$11,167 \times \text{future-value interest factor}}{\$11,167}$$
$$1.791 = \text{future-value interest factor}$$

You know to look in the $n = 10$ row of the future-value interest factor tables for a value of 1.791, and you find this in the $i = 6\%$ column. Thus, if you want your initial investment of $11,167 to grow to $20,000 in 10 years, you must invest it at 6 percent.

4 Tax Planning and Strategies

Learning Objectives

 1 **Identify** and understand the major federal income tax features that affect all taxpayers.

 2 **Describe** other taxes that you must pay.

 3 **Understand** what is taxable income and how taxes are determined.

 4 **Choose** the tax form that's right for you, file, and survive an audit if necessary.

 5 **Calculate** your income taxes.

 6 **Minimize** your taxes.

"The Trouble with Trillions" episode of the *Simpsons* begins with the family watching the 11 o'clock news.

"This is Kent Brockman at the Springfield Post Office on Tax Day. It's literally the 11th hour, 10 P.M., and tardy taxpayers are scrambling to mail their returns by midnight."

"Will you look at those morons? I paid my taxes over a year ago," Homer chimes in.

"Dad! That was last year's taxes. You have to pay again this year," Lisa replies.

"No, because you see I went ahead and . . . year-wise, I was counting forward from the last previous . . . d-oh!" Frantically putting together his tax return Homer shouts out "Marge, how many kids do we have, no time to count, I'll just estimate 9. If anyone asks you need 24-hour nursing care, Lisa is a clergyman, Maggie is 7 people, and Bart was wounded in Vietnam."

"Cool!" replies Bart.

It isn't only cartoon characters that have trouble with the IRS—just look at Willie Nelson. He has made millions of dollars and spent millions of dollars, and for quite some time he ignored his taxes entirely. That lack of attention finally caught up with him in 1990, when the IRS sent him a bill for $32 million. Yikes! But as Willie said, "Thirty-two million ain't much if you say it fast." How did Willie manage to run up such a tax bill? On bad advice, he got involved in a number of tax shelters (investments aimed at lowering your taxes) that were disallowed by the IRS because they were such blatant tax-avoidance schemes. Eventually, Willie and the IRS settled on a $9 million payment, and Willie sued the accounting firm of Price Waterhouse, claiming it had mismanaged his finances. By 1995, Willie had paid back the government, but to do it he had to auction off nearly all of his possessions—leaving him with his long hair and beard, headband, worn blue jeans, guitar, and little else.

Mention the IRS and most people cringe. Few of us relish the thought of tax planning because taxes are unavoidable, too high, and determined by a tax code that is close to incomprehensible. However, like it or not, taxes are a fact of life, and they have a dramatic impact on many aspects of your finances, in particular your investment choices.

Most of the financial decisions that you make are affected in one way or another by taxes—that's **Principle 4: Taxes Affect Personal Finance Decisions**. Given that the average American pays over $10,000 annually in taxes, limiting Uncle Sam's cut of your income is important. Remember, what you pay in April each year is based on income, expenses, and tax-planning decisions from the previous year. If you don't understand the tax system, you're probably paying more than you have to. The primary purpose of this chapter is not to teach you all the ins and outs of filing your own return but rather to help you understand how taxes are imposed, what strategies can be used to reduce them, and the role of tax planning in personal financial planning. With proper tax planning you will be able to achieve your financial goals, and avoid wasting money in tax payments as well looking at your tax bill and saying "D-oh!"

The Federal Income Tax Structure

The starting point for tax planning is looking at the overall structure of the income tax. Our present tax structure is a **progressive** or **graduated tax**, meaning that increased income is taxed at increasing rates. This system is based on the idea that those who earn more can afford to pay a higher percentage of their income taken in taxes. This is why people who earn different incomes fall into different **tax brackets**.

However, not all income is taxed. Some income is tax free because of **personal exemptions**, and other income is shielded by **itemized** or **standard deductions**. Your **taxable income** is a function of three numbers—**adjusted gross income** or **AGI**, deductions, and exemptions. From there, the tax rates determine how much of the difference between income and deductions will be taken away in taxes. Table 4.1 provides the 2011 federal income tax rates for two of several different classifications of taxpayers.

To better understand what the rates in Table 4.1 actually mean, let's see what you might have paid in taxes in 2011 if you were married with three children, had a combined income of $70,000, and were filing a joint return. First, we'll determine your adjusted gross income, which from now on we'll call your AGI. The $70,000 would be your gross income, and from that you subtract certain adjustments allowed by law to arrive at your AGI. For example, let's say you made a $2,000 deductible IRA contribution and paid $900 interest on a student loan. You subtract these figures from $70,000 to find your adjusted gross income, or AGI, of $67,100. Remember, however, that your

 1 Identify and understand the major federal income tax features that affect all taxpayers.

Progressive or Graduated Tax
A tax system in which tax rates increase for higher incomes.

Tax Brackets
Income ranges in which the same marginal tax rates apply. For example, an individual might fall into the 15 percent or 28 percent marginal tax bracket.

Personal Exemptions
An IRS-allowed reduction in your income before you compute your taxes. You are given one exemption for yourself, one for your spouse, and one for each dependent.

Deductions
Expenses that reduce taxable income.

Itemized Deductions
Deductions calculated using Schedule A. The allowable deductions are added up and then subtracted from AGI.

Standard Deductions
A set deduction allowed by the IRS regardless of what taxpayers' expenses actually were.

Taxable Income
Income subject to taxes.

Adjusted Gross Income or AGI
Your taxable income from all sources minus specific adjustments (for example, IRA deduction, student loan interest payments, and alimony paid by you), but before deducting your standard or itemized deductions.

TABLE 4.1 Tax Rates and Brackets

Single Filers		
Tax Bracket	**If Taxable Income Is:**	**The Tax Is:**
10%	Not over $8,500	10% of taxable income
15%	$8,500–$34,500	$850 plus 15% of excess over $8,500
25%	$34,500–$83,600	$4,750 plus 25% of excess over $34,500
28%	$83,600–$174,400	$17,025 plus 28% of excess over $83,600
33%	$174,400–$379,150	$42,449 plus 33% of excess over $174,400
35%	Over $379,150	$110,016.50 plus 35% of excess over $379,150

Married Filing Joint Returns and Surviving Spouses		
Tax Bracket	**If Taxable Income Is:**	**The Tax Is:**
10%	Not over $17,000	10% of taxable income
15%	$17,000–$69,000	$1,700 plus 15% of excess over $17,000
25%	$69,000–$139,350	$9,500 plus 25% of excess over $69,000
28%	$139,350–$212,300	$27,087.50 plus 28% of excess over $139,350
33%	$212,300–$379,150	$47,513.50 plus 33% of excess over $212,300
35%	Over $379,150	$102,574 plus 35% of excess over $379,150

total income of $70,000 isn't taxed nor is your AGI of $67,100; *only the difference between your AGI and your exemptions and deductions is taxed.*

Next, you subtract personal exemptions and deductions. To begin with, you receive one exemption for each family member you claim on your tax return—one for you, your spouse, and each of your three children. Each exemption allows you to subtract $3,700 from your income, resulting in a total reduction of $18,500. Next, you need to subtract your deduction, either standard or itemized, both of which we'll talk about in detail later in this chapter. Let's assume you use the standard deduction because it's higher than your itemized deduction would be. For the 2011 tax year, that would give you a deduction of $11,600. The minimum level of deductions that you have is $18,500 + $11,600 = $30,100. Subtracting these from your AGI of $67,100 leaves taxable income of $37,000.

Your deductions have brought you to the 15 percent tax bracket. Does that mean you have to pay 15 percent of your taxable income of $37,000 in taxes? No. Remember, tax rates are graduated, which means that income is taxed at increasing rates. It means that the last dollars you earned are taxed at 15 percent. As Table 4.1 shows, the first $17,000 of taxable income is taxed at 10 percent, and the next $20,000 (income from $17,000 to $37,000) is taxed at 15 percent, resulting in a total tax bill before tax credits of $4,700.00.[1]

Taxable Income: 37,000	×	Tax Rate	=	Taxes Paid
$0 to $17,000 ($17,000)	×	10%	=	$1,700
$17,000 to $37,000 ($20,000)	×	15%	=	$3,000
		Total taxes before credits	=	$4,700

Marginal Versus Average Rates

Let's take another look at the tax rates you paid in the previous example. There are two ways we measure your tax rate—we measure the average tax rate that relates taxes to taxable or overall income, and we measure your marginal tax rate that looks at the percent of the next dollar you earn that will go toward taxes. You paid taxes of $4,700 on taxable income of $37,000, so your average tax rate on *taxable income* was about 12.7 percent. Your average tax rate on your *overall* income of $70,000 was $4,700/$70,000, or about 6.7 percent. The term *average tax rate* refers to this latter figure—the average amount of your total income taken away in taxes.

While it's good to know what percent of your taxable income and what percent of your overall income goes toward taxes, it's even more important to know what percent of the next dollar you earn will go toward paying taxes. Why? Because it is the tax

STOP & THINK

It was the Massachusetts Bay Colony that first imposed income taxes in the New World in 1643. Even though taxes have been around for hundreds of years, it doesn't mean you pay more than your fair share. Do you think you have a patriotic duty to pay extra taxes? Answer: No, as Judge Learned Hand of the U.S. Court of Appeals said, "Anyone may so arrange his affairs that his taxes shall be as low as possible; he is not bound to choose that pattern which will best pay the treasury; there is not even a patriotic duty to increase one's taxes. What "tax breaks" have you taken or expect to take in the future?

---

[1]As we will see shortly, this amount drops even more because of the child tax credit, which in 2011 and 2012 provides qualifying families with a tax credit of $1,000 for each child under age 17 as of the close of each year. This tax credit offsets taxes owed on a dollar-for-dollar basis. That is, if you owe $5,000 in taxes and have a $1,000 tax credit, you only need to write the IRS a check for $4,000. You'll also notice if you use the tax tables you get a slightly different number. That's because the tax tables calculate an "average" rate over each $50 range.

rate that you pay on the next dollar of earning that is important in making financial decisions. For example, if you were looking at an additional part-time job that would produce $5,000 per year in income, you would be concerned with how much in taxes you'd pay on that $5,000. The tax rate that is important in making this decision is your **marginal tax rate** or **marginal tax bracket**, which is the percentage of the last dollar you made that goes to taxes or the tax bracket that your taxable income falls into. If your taxable income is $37,000, and $37,000 falls in the 15 percent tax bracket, then 15 percent is your marginal tax rate. If you earn $5,000 on that part-time job, it is your marginal tax rate that determines how much of that raise you have left to spend.

Marginal Tax Rate or Marginal Tax Bracket
The percentage of the last dollar you earn that goes toward taxes.

In addition, if you are in the 15 percent marginal tax bracket and have a choice of investing in tax-free bonds that earn 7 percent or taxable bonds that earn 8 percent, your marginal tax rate can help you determine which is the better investment. Even though your average tax rate may be only 6.7 percent, this additional income is taxed at your marginal tax rate, which, in this example, is 15 percent. To make a fair comparison, you must look at your after-tax returns. The tax-free bond would still return 7 percent after taxes, but the 8 percent bond would have 15 percent of its returns confiscated for taxes, resulting in a return of $8\% \times (1 - 0.15) = 6.85\%$.

STOP & THINK

Unfortunately, the Social Security system is feeling financial strains because there are more people receiving benefits than ever before, and that number is only going to grow. Forty years ago 16 workers contributed for every Social Security recipient. Today, the ratio is down to three workers for every recipient, and in another 40 years it will be down to two workers for every recipient. What types of changes in the Social Security system do you expect by the time you are ready to receive benefits?

Your marginal tax rate also becomes important when you're considering investing in a **tax-deferred** retirement plan. The government allows tax deductions for the funds you contribute to this kind of retirement plan. So, if you are in the 15-percent marginal tax bracket and you contribute $1,000 to a tax-deferred retirement plan, you would lower your taxes by $150 ($0.150 \times \$1,000$). This reduction allows you to invest the entire $1,000 rather than only $850; that is, $1,000 less $150 in taxes.

Tax-Deferred
Income on which the payment of taxes is postponed until some future date.

As you can see from Table 4.1, once you earn enough to pay taxes—have income beyond the personal exemption and standard deduction levels—there are six different

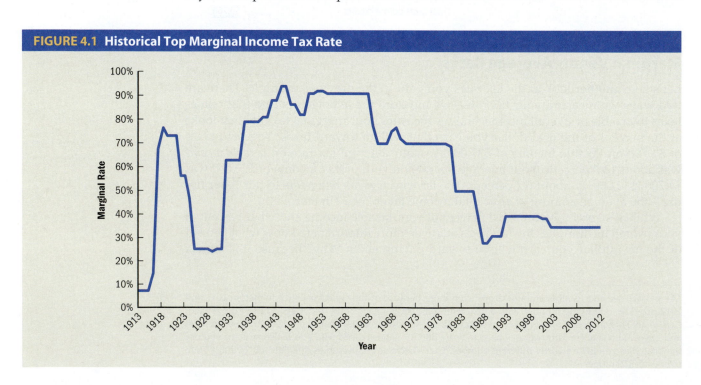

FIGURE 4.1 Historical Top Marginal Income Tax Rate

marginal tax rates ranging from 10 percent to 35 percent. However, these tax rates have only been extended through 2012, and at that point Congress will need to take action. In fact, whenever Congress wishes, it can change the tax rates and the tax code. As you can see in Figure 4.1, back in 1964 the top marginal rate was 91 percent, and in 1981 it was still at 70 percent. Needless to say, changes in the marginal tax rates have a major impact on investment strategies, so you need to keep a close eye on tax law changes.

Effective Marginal Tax Rate

Federal income taxes are not the only income-based taxes you pay. Many states impose state income taxes, some cities impose a city or a local tax, and there are also Social Security taxes. Each of these taxes is imposed at different rates. As a result of these taxes, your effective marginal tax rate—the tax rate you pay when all income tax rates are combined—is greater than the marginal tax rate on your federal income taxes.

To determine your effective marginal tax rate, you need to add up the rates of the different taxes you pay on income. Let's assume you have a marginal federal tax rate of 25 percent, a state income tax rate of 4.75 percent, and a city income tax rate of 2 percent. The tax for Social Security and Medicare is typically 7.65 percent, so your total effective marginal tax rate would be 39.4 percent (25% + 4.75% + 2% + 7.65%).[2] That means if you were to receive one more dollar of income, 39.4 cents of that dollar would go toward taxes. Alternatively, if you can shield one dollar from taxes, you'll save 39.4 cents in taxes.

> ### STOP & THINK
>
> You really should know what your marginal tax rate is. It not only tells you how much more you'll have to pay in taxes on any additional income (the bad news) but also tells you how any additional deductions will reduce your taxes (the good news). What is you marginal tax rate?

Capital Gains and Dividend Income

The income you make on your investments is taxed somewhat differently from other income. Almost any asset you own, except for certain business assets, is called a **capital asset**. A **capital gain** is what you make if you sell a capital asset for a profit. For example, if you purchase 100 shares of GM stock for $50 per share and sell them 2 years later for $70 per share, your capital gain would be $100 \times (\$70 - \$50) = \$2,000$. A **capital loss** is what you lose when you sell a capital asset for a loss. For example, if you purchase 100 shares of GM stock for $50 per share and sell them 2 years later for $30 per share, the capital loss would be $100 \times (\$50 - \$30) = \$2,000$. The tax you pay on your capital gains is called, appropriately, the **capital gains tax**. Capital losses can be used to offset capital gains. If the losses exceed the gains and you are married filing a joint return, you may deduct the excess from up to $3,000 of other income. If you hold the asset for 12 months or more it qualifies as a long-term capital gain and qualifies for a lower tax rate, otherwise the capital gain is treated as ordinary income.

The tax laws provide a lower tax rate on both the long-term capital gains and on dividends received by individuals from most domestic corporations and many foreign companies.[3] Although the long-term capital gains tax applies to profits from the sale of stocks, bonds, and most other investments, it doesn't apply to gains from the sale of collectibles. In addition, real estate investments don't necessarily receive the full benefit of the cut.

Capital Asset
An asset you own, except for certain business assets, including stocks, bonds, real estate, or collectibles.

Capital Gain/Capital Loss
The amount by which the selling price of a capital asset differs from its purchase price. If the selling price is higher than the purchase price, a capital gain results; if the selling price is lower than the purchase price, a capital loss results.

Capital Gains Tax
The tax you pay on your realized capital gains.

---

[2]The 2010 Tax Relief Act reduces the employee contribution to Social Security by 2 percent from 6.2 percent to 4.2 percent, while leaving the employee contribution to Medicare at 1.45 percent for the tax year 2011. As a result, the combined employee contribution to Social Security and Medicare dropped to 5.65 percent for 2011. Without further changes in the law, employee contributions to Social Security and Medicare will return to 7.65% beginning in 2012.

[3]For dividend income to qualify for the reduced rate, the stock issuing the dividend must be held for more than 61 days during the 120-day period beginning 60 days before the ex-dividend date (that is, when the stock sells without the dividend).

How much do capital gains or dividend income save you? That depends on your tax bracket. If you're in the 35 percent tax bracket and have long-term capital gains or dividend income of $50,000, you would pay only $7,500 in taxes. If this $50,000 of income had been from wages, you would have paid $17,500, or more than twice what you paid on long-term capital gains or dividend income.

Just as valuable as the tax break on capital gains income is the fact that you do not have to claim it—and, therefore, pay taxes on it—until you sell the asset. That is, you can decide when you want to claim your capital gains. For exam-

ple, at the end of 1994 you may have invested $17,000 in Berkshire Hathaway stock, only to see it grow in value, reaching $127,000 by early 2011. Although you've "made" $110,000 on your investment, you don't have to pay any taxes on this gain. You pay taxes only when you sell the stock and realize the gain. In effect, you can postpone your capital gains taxes. As long as you can earn interest on money you don't pay out in taxes, it's better to postpone paying taxes for as long as possible—that's what we learned in **Principle 3: The Time Value of Money**. Because the maximum tax rate on long-term capital gains is lower than the ordinary tax rate and you have the ability to postpone its tax liability, capital gains income is preferable to ordinary income.

Long-Term Capital Gains on Homes   For most homeowners, there are no capital gains taxes on the sale of their homes. There is an exemption from taxation for gains of up to $500,000 for couples filing jointly or $250,000 for those filing single on the sale of a principal residence. To be eligible for the complete exemption, the home must be your principal residence and you must have occupied it for at least 2 years during the 5 years before the sale. You are eligible for this exemption once every 2 years.

Filing Status

While Table 4.1, 2011 Tax Rates and Brackets, shows only two of the four different filing statuses, you can see that filing status plays a major role in determining what you pay in the way of taxes. But you may not have much of a choice in deciding your filing status. Filing status is somewhat akin to marital status. But, as is always the case with taxes, it's not that simple. Let's look at the different classifications.

Single   You are single at the end of the year and do not have any dependent children.

Married Filing Jointly and Surviving Spouses   You file a joint return with your spouse, combining incomes and deductions into a single return. If your spouse dies, you can still qualify for this status for up to 2 years after the year in which your spouse died if you have a dependent child living with you, you pay more than half the cost of keeping up your home, and you are not remarried. Of course, if you remarry, you can file a joint return with your new spouse.

Married Filing Separately   Married couples also have the choice of filing separately. As *Consumer Reports* noted in 2010, if you are married, it is hard to say ahead of time whether you will do better filing jointly or separately—the best ideas is to figure your taxes both ways and, of course, go with the low number. This status is often used when a couple is separated or in the process of getting a divorce.

Head of Household   Head of household status applies to someone who is unmarried and has at least one child or relative living with him or her. The advantage of this status is that your tax rate will be lower and your standard deduction higher than if you had filed with single status. To qualify for head of household status, you must be unmarried on the last day of the tax year, have paid more than half the cost of keeping up your home, and had a child or dependent live with you for at least half of the year.

Cost of Living Increases in Tax Brackets, Exemptions, and Deductions

Since 1985, tax brackets have changed annually to reflect increases in the cost of living (inflation). In addition, the standard deductions and personal exemptions are also increased to reflect the increased cost of living.

The purpose of these adjustments is to make sure your tax payments don't go up just because you've received a cost of living increase in your wages. In the past, taxpayers' incomes rose during periods of high inflation, but their purchasing power didn't. As a result, rising incomes that only kept pace with inflation nudged taxpayers into higher tax brackets. In effect, taxpayers paid more taxes while the real value of their wages remained constant.

> ### FACTS OF LIFE
>
> According to the Tax Policy Center, for the 2009 tax year approximately 47 percent of American households did not pay any federal income taxes. That was higher than in most years because of the poor economy.

The tax increase caused by inflation is referred to as **bracket creep**. For those whose earnings remain the same each year, the inflation adjustment of tax brackets actually results in lower taxes. Of course, if your earnings don't increase to keep pace with inflation, you're worse off with each passing year and probably deserve a reduced tax bill!

Bracket Creep
The movement into higher tax brackets as a result of inflation increasing wages.

Paying Your Income Taxes

Taxes are collected on a pay-as-you-go basis. Most taxes—about 70 percent of individual income taxes—are collected through withholding from wages. The idea behind withholding is to collect taxes gradually so that when your taxes are due in the spring, you won't feel the pain of paying in one lump sum. Also, without withholding, too many people would spend the money they should be saving for taxes. These withholdings also cover Social Security and state and local taxes. Other ways in which taxes are collected include quarterly estimated taxes sent to the IRS, payments with the tax return, and withholding from stock dividends, retirement funds, and prizes or gambling winnings.

You do have some control over how much is deducted for taxes from your wages. Your withholdings are determined by your income level and by the information you provide on your W-4 form. The W-4 form shows marital status, the number of exemptions you wish to claim—remember, you get one for yourself, one for your spouse, and one for each dependent—and any additional withholding you would like. Most people fill out their W-4 when they begin employment and never make changes to it. However, if you find you're paying too much in taxes at tax time, or your refund is too large, revising your W-4 to make appropriate adjustments might not be a bad idea.

> ### STOP & THINK
>
> "Isn't this exciting! I earned this. I wiped tables for it, I steamed milk for it, and it's—[opening her paycheck]—not worth it! Who's FICA? Why is he getting my money?" This is the response of Rachel Green on the TV show *Friends* upon seeing her first Central Perk paycheck on the episode "The One with George Stephanopoulos." Your first paycheck can be a real shock. Federal, state, and local taxes, in addition to FICA, a contribution to your firm's hospitalization plan, and retirement savings take a real bite out of your paycheck. Financial planning is all the more important if you're to make the best use of what's left. Are you surprised by how large FICA taxes are?

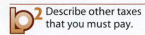

2 Describe other taxes that you must pay.

Social Security
A federal program that provides disability and retirement benefits based on years worked, amount paid into the plan, and retirement age.

Medicare
The federal government's insurance program to provide medical benefits to those over 65.

Other Taxes

Other Income-Based Taxes

Social Security or FICA   **Social Security** is really a mandatory insurance program administered by the government, which provides for you and your family in the event of death, disability, health problems, or retirement. To pay for these benefits, both you and your employer pay into the system. Each typically pays 7.65 percent of your gross salary. This deduction appears on your pay slip as "FICA," which stands for the Federal Insurance Contributions Act.[4] These funds actually go to both Social Security and **Medicare**, which is a government health care insurance program.

The FICA tax is typically deducted from your salary at 7.65 percent (6.20 percent for Social Security and 1.45 percent for Medicare) until your salary reaches a point ($106,800 in 2011)[5] where it is no longer taxed the 6.20 percent for Social Security. Medicare, however, keeps on taxing after the Social Security cap has been reached, taking an additional 1.45 percent of your total salary from both you and your employer. If you are self-employed, you have to pay both the employer and employee portion of FICA for a total rate of 15.3 percent. However, if you're self-employed, half of your contribution is tax deductible.

State and Local Income Taxes   As we said earlier, most individuals also face state and, in some cases, local income taxes. Most states impose some type of income tax, though the level varies greatly from state to state. Local income taxes are relatively uncommon and are generally confined to large cities. New York City, for example, imposes an income tax.

Non-Income-Based Taxes

In addition to paying federal income taxes, Social Security taxes, and state and local taxes, you also face excise taxes, sales taxes, property taxes, and gift and estate taxes.

Excise taxes are taxes imposed on specific purchases, such as alcoholic beverages, cigarettes, gasoline, telephone service, jewelry, and air travel. Often such taxes are aimed at reducing consumption of the items being taxed. For example, liquor and tobacco taxes are referred to as "sin taxes."

Most local taxes take the form of property taxes on real estate and personal property, such as automobiles and boats. The level of property taxes is based on the assessed value of real estate or other property.

Some states and localities also impose sales taxes on certain purchases. These taxes can range up to 8.875 percent (in New York) and in general cover most sales, with the exception of food and drugs. Because these tax rates are fixed—everyone in New York pays 8.875 percent sales tax—lower income individuals

FACTS OF LIFE

The Tax Foundation calculates what it calls Tax Freedom Day, the day by which the average American has earned enough to pay his or her total federal, state, and local taxes for the year. In 2010 Tax Freedom Day arrived on April 9th. After April 9th, the typical American has earned enough to pay off his or her taxes and can now earn money to spend on housing, food, clothing, and so forth.

Year	Tax Freedom Day	All Taxes as a Percentage of Income
1900	January 22	5.9%
1920	February 13	12.0%
1940	March 7	17.9%
1950	March 31	24.6%
1970	April 19	29.6%
1990	April 21	30.4%
2000	May 1	33.0%
2007	April 24	31.1%
2008	April 16	29.0%
2009	April 8	26.6%
2010	April 9	26.9%
2011	April 12	27.7%

Source: Tax Foundation calculations based on data from the Bureau of Economic Analysis and Congressional Budget Office.

---

[4]For 2011, the employee portion of Social Security was reduced to 4.2 percent. This only lasts for 1 year unless extended by Congress.

[5]For 2011 only, the employee portion of Social Security was 4.2 percent, and the employee portion of the FICA tax was 5.65 percent.

pay a higher *percentage* of their income in sales taxes than higher income people do. Unfortunately, these taxes are quite difficult to avoid.

Gift and estate taxes are imposed when you transfer wealth to another person, either when you die, in the case of estate taxes, or while you're alive, in the case of gift taxes. For 2011 and 2012, the tax code allows for an estate valued at up to $5 million to be transferred tax free to any heir. If the estate is valued at more than $5 million, the amount over $5 million will be taxed at 35 percent. The U.S. tax code also allows for an unlimited marital deduction for gift and estate tax purposes. This means that when a husband or wife dies, the estate, regardless of size, can be transferred to the survivor totally tax free.

Calculating Your Taxes

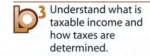 **3** Understand what is taxable income and how taxes are determined.

Must everyone file a tax return? According to IRS regulations, if your total income is more than $20,900, you need to file a return. If it's less than this amount, you may not need to file, depending on your filing status, gross income, age, and whether you can be claimed as a **dependent** on someone else's tax return. If you think you don't need to file, calculate your taxes anyway, because you may be owed a refund, which you won't receive unless you file a tax return.

Dependent
Person you support financially.

The only exception to these rules deals with dependents. The income threshold for filing a tax return is generally lower for anyone who may be claimed as a dependent. Dependents with income include children who have a job or earn investment income or elderly parents who have some investment income. If you are considered a dependent on someone else's tax return, you'll want to check carefully to make sure that you don't have to file a return.

Step 1: Determining Gross or Total Income

When you file a tax return, the first step in calculating your taxes is determining your total income. **Total** or **gross income** is the sum of all taxable income from all sources. Actually, the IRS defines three different types of income—**active income** (from wages, salaries, and tips or from a business), **portfolio** or **investment income** (from securities including dividends and interest), and **passive income** (from activities in which the taxpayer does not actively participate such as rental income and royalties). Generally, your wages are reported to you on a W-2 form, while interest and dividends are reported on a Form 1099. Total income also includes alimony, business income, capital gains, taxable IRA distributions, pensions and annuities, rental income, royalties, farm income, unemployment compensation, taxable Social Security benefits, and any other income. In short, whatever you receive in taxable income is summed to make up your total or gross income:

Total or Gross Income
The sum of all your taxable income from all sources.

Active Income
Income that comes from wages or a business.

Portfolio or Investment Income
Income that comes from securities.

Passive Income
Income that comes from activities in which the taxpayer does not actively participate.

> Gross Income = Sum of Taxable Income from All Sources

Although this calculation is relatively straightforward, it's harder than it looks because of the IRS and its lovely little rules.

Remember that not all income is taxable, and so not all income is included in total income. The main source of tax-exempt income is interest on state and local debt. Other sources include gifts, inheritances, earnings on your IRA, federal income tax refunds, child support payments, welfare benefits, and foreign income incurred by U.S. citizens living and working abroad.

FACTS of LIFE

Where's the highest tax rate you face? It's probably in your state lottery. It's not really a tax in the normal sense, but if you look at the state's "cut" as a percentage of the value of the lottery tickets (prize money plus administrative cost), it runs, on average across America, at 41.8 percent, varying from state to state. For example, Delaware's rate is about 52 percent. And that doesn't include the state and federal taxes on any winnings!

Step 2: Calculating Adjusted Gross Income (AGI)

Adjusted Gross Income or AGI
Your taxable income from all sources minus specific deductions (for example, IRA contributions, student loan interest deduction, and alimony paid by you), but before deducting your standard or itemized deductions.

Adjusted gross income (AGI) is gross income less allowable adjustments. Adjustments to gross income include payments set aside for retirement, some moving expenses, and alimony payments. In effect, the IRS allows you to reduce your taxable income when you incur specific expenses or when you contribute to certain retirement plans. The advantage of these deductions is that they lower your taxes, allowing you to invest or spend (hopefully, invest) money that you would otherwise send to Uncle Sam.

A list of the adjustments is found on Form 1040, page 1. Some of the adjustments that the IRS allows include:

IRA
An individual retirement arrangement which is a tax-deferred retirement savings account allowed by the government.

- Contributions to qualified retirement accounts, for example, **IRA**, 401(k), or **Keogh plans**.
- Interest paid on student loans.
- Moving expenses.
- Half of the Social Security and Medicare taxes for self-employed filers.

Keogh Plan
A tax-deferred retirement plan for the self-employed.

- Alimony payments.
- Health savings accounts.
- Unreimbursed expenses for educator expenses for kindergarten through grade 12 teachers.

Because adjustments to income reduce your taxes, it's important to understand these adjustments and take advantage of them. After adding up all your adjustments to income, you subtract this amount from total income to arrive at your AGI:

Gross Income = Sum of Taxable Income from All Sources

Less

Adjustments to Gross Income: Tax-Deductible Expenses and Retirement Contributions (traditional IRA, Keogh contributions, moving expenses, and so on)

Equals

Adjusted Gross Income (AGI)

Step 3: Subtracting Deductions

Once you know your AGI, the next step is to subtract your deductions. You have your choice of the standard deduction or itemizing, whichever benefits you the most. Obviously, taking the largest possible deduction is important. For example, if you're in the 33 percent marginal tax bracket and you're able to take an additional $5,000 in deductions, you've actually reduced your tax bill by $5,000 × 0.33 = $1,650. That's $1,650 that you can spend on Domino's pizza or invest for retirement—whichever seems more important.

FACTS OF LIFE

In an earlier Facts of Life box we noted that on average the "tax" on state lottery sales is over 42 percent, so given that huge tax rate, do people spend much on the lottery? The answer is yes. Nationwide the average state lottery sales per capita for 2008 were $199, and in Delaware, where the "tax" rate on the lottery is over 50 percent, the average lottery sales per capita was $846.

What's the difference between standardized and itemized deductions? On the simplest level, one is calculated for you and the other you have to calculate yourself. Of course, the answer's really more complicated than that. Let's start by taking a look at the deduction you have to calculate yourself—the itemized deduction.

Itemizing Deductions   The IRS has decided that you shouldn't be taxed on income that's used to pay for certain expenses. These are considered deductible expenses. Itemizing is simply listing all the deductions you're allowed to take. Of course, it's your responsibility to determine and document these deductible expenses.[6]

For most of us, which expenses count as deductible? Let's look at the most common ones.

- ◆ **Medical and Dental Expenses** Medical and dental expenses are deductible only to the extent that they exceed 7.5 percent of your AGI. For an individual with an AGI of $60,000, only those medical and dental expenses in excess of $4,500 (which is 7.5 percent of $60,000) would be deductible. The definition of what's considered a medical or dental expense is quite broad and includes medical treatment, hospital care, prescription drugs, and health insurance.

- ◆ **Tax Expenses** Some, but not all, tax expenses are deductible. Although the biggest chunk of taxes you pay—federal and Social Security—are not tax deductible, state and local income *or* sales taxes, along with real estate taxes, are deductible. You have the option of claiming an itemized deduction for either state and local *sales* taxes *or* state and local *income* taxes—but not both. In addition, any county or city income taxes are tax deductible. Some states impose a personal property tax—generally a tax on automobiles—which is also tax deductible.

- ◆ **Home Mortgage and Investment Interest Payments** Several types of interest are tax deductible. Interest that you pay on your home mortgage is deductible. Interest on **home equity loans** is also deductible on home equity debt up to $100,000.

Home Equity Loan
A loan that uses your home as collateral, that is, a loan that is secured by your home. If you default, the lender can take possession of your home to recapture money lost on the loan.

The last type of tax-deductible interest is investment interest, or interest on money borrowed to invest. The maximum deduction on investment interest is limited to the amount of investment income that you earn. Why does the IRS let you deduct these interest payments? Because the government wants to make it easier for you to buy a house and make investments to help the overall economy. By making home interest payments tax deductible, the government is in effect subsidizing your purchase of a home.

FACTS OF LIFE

What's the relationship between buying a home and charitable deductions? Once you buy a home, you're generally better off itemizing deductions because the home mortgage interest payments usually push you over the threshold, giving you enough deductible expenses to make itemizing worthwhile. As a result, expenses that have no value when you take the standard deduction, such as personal property taxes, charitable contributions, and the cost of a safety-deposit box, may now be deductible and, thus, result in tax savings.

- ◆ **Gifts to Charity** Charitable gifts to qualified organizations are tax deductible. If you're in the 25 percent tax bracket and you give $1,000 to a charitable organization, it really only costs you $750, because you've given away $1,000 and as a result lowered your taxes by $250 (0.25 × $1,000). In effect, Congress is encouraging you to make charitable gifts. The only requirement for this deduction is that the gift goes to a qualified organization and that if you make a single gift of more than $250, you show a receipt for that gift

---

[6]The amount of itemized deductions and personal exemptions you can take are normally phased out for higher income taxpayers. For tax year 2010, however, those income limits were repealed, and the Tax Relief Act of 2010 extended the repeal through 2012.

FACTS OF LIFE

This table shows the average deductions made by different income groups for the most recent year available, based on their adjusted gross income. Use this as a guide to assess how your deductions compare.

Average Deductions by Adjusted Gross Income Level				
	$50–100K	$100–200K	$200–250K	$250K & Up
Charitable Contributions	$2,693	$3,757	$5,895	$20,930
Taxes (Income Taxes, Property Taxes, etc.)	$6,050	$10,798	$18,164	$50,267
Interest (Mortgage Interest, etc.)	$10,659	$13,734	$18,570	$27,865
Medical Expenses	$7,102	$9,269	$21,554	$37,143

Source: Internal Revenue Service, Statistics of Income Bulletin (Washington, DC: IRS, winter 2010).

(a canceled check won't do). Of course, regardless of the size of the gift, you must make sure that you maintain good records. If you can't keep track of your donations, how can you deduct them?

- ◆ **Casualty and Theft Loss** Although you're able to deduct casualty and theft losses, this deduction is rather limited and is of value only to those who suffer huge losses or have very low earnings. The reason for its limited usefulness is that (1) for tax purposes, the first $100 of losses is excluded and (2) you can deduct losses only to the extent that the remaining losses exceed 10 percent of your AGI.

- ◆ **Miscellaneous Deductibles** These deductions include unreimbursed job-related expenses, tax preparation expenses, and investment-related expenses. The problem with these expenses is that they are only deductible to the extent that they are in excess of 2 percent of your AGI. In general, this percentage is a tough hurdle to pass, and, as a result, most taxpayers are not able to benefit from miscellaneous deductions.

The Standard Deduction   The alternative to itemizing deductions is to take the standard deduction. Basically, the standard deduction is the government's best estimate of what the average person would be able to deduct by itemizing. In other words, with the standard deduction, the government has done it for you already. You don't need to figure out your expenses and provide receipts or justification. Unlike itemized deductions, which are limited for higher AGI levels, the standard deduction remains the same regardless of income level. In fact, the level of the standard deduction increases every year to keep up with inflation. Figure 4.2 provides the standard deductions for 2011. Note that additional standard deductions are given to the elderly and the blind.

The Choice: Itemizing or Taking the Standard Deduction   The decision of taking the standard deduction or itemizing may not be particularly difficult if one provides a greater deduction than the other. The choice becomes much more difficult, and also more interesting, when they are close in value. In that case, it may be best to bunch your deductions and alternate each year between taking the standard deduction and itemizing.

FIGURE 4.2 Standard Deduction Amounts

Filing Status	2011
Single	$5,800
Married Filing Jointly or Surviving Spouse	$11,600
Head of Household	$8,500
Married Filing Separately	$5,800

Additional Standard Deductions for the Elderly and Blind: For a taxpayer (and spouse) who is elderly (age 65 or over) or blind, there is an additional deduction allowed.

In effect, you try to avoid incurring deductible expenses in years that you don't itemize. If possible, you postpone them to years when you do itemize and, therefore, get credit for them. For example, you might make 13 monthly mortgage payments in the year you itemize and only 11 in the year you take the standard deduction. There's no question that taking the standard deduction is easier than itemizing, but don't choose to take the standard deduction just because it's simpler—you don't want laziness to cost you money.

Step 4: Claiming Your Exemptions

Once you've subtracted the deductions from the AGI, you're ready to subtract the exemptions. An **exemption** is a deduction that you can make on your return for each person supported by the income on your tax return. The government provides these exemptions so that everyone will have a little bit of untaxed money to spend on necessities. In effect, each exemption allows you to lower your taxable income by $3,700 for the 2011 tax year.[7] Thus, if you're in the 28 percent marginal tax bracket, each exemption you take in 2011 will lower your taxes by $1,036 (that is, $3,700 × 0.28).

Exemption
A deduction you can take on your return for each person supported by the income listed on your tax return.

There are two types of exemptions—personal and dependency. You receive a personal exemption for yourself regardless of your filing status, or yourself and your spouse if filing a joint return, no questions asked. However, qualifying for a dependency exemption is more difficult. To qualify:

♦ Dependents must pass a relationship or household member test. If they're related to you as children, grandchildren, stepchildren, siblings, parents, grandparents, stepparents, uncles, aunts, nieces, nephews, in-laws, and so forth, they're considered to have a qualifying relationship. In fact, almost any relationship short of being a cousin qualifies under the IRS. If they're not related to you, then they must have lived with you over the entire tax year.

♦ The individual being claimed as a dependent generally can't earn more than the exemption amount. However, this income test does not apply to your children under the age of 19 or to children under the age of 24 who are full-time students.

♦ You must provide more than half of the dependent's support.

♦ The dependent must be a U.S. citizen, resident, or national, or a resident of either Mexico or Canada.

Step 5: Calculating Your Taxable Income, and from That, Calculating Your Base Income Tax

Now that you've subtracted your deductions and exemptions from your AGI, you know your taxable income, which is the amount your taxes are based on. Figure 4.3 shows these calculations. For most taxpayers, once you've determined your taxable income, your income tax can be determined directly using the tax tables found in the middle of your federal income tax instructions booklet. The intersection of your taxable income and your filing status determines your taxes due, as shown in Figure 4.4.

If your taxable income is greater than $100,000, you must determine your taxes using the rate schedules because the tax tables don't go that high. The tax rate schedules are found at the end of your federal income tax instructions booklet and were provided earlier in Table 4.1.

---

[7]Exemptions, like standard deductions, are raised each year to match inflation rates, for example, the personal exemption was $3,650 in 2010 and rose to $3,700 in 2011.

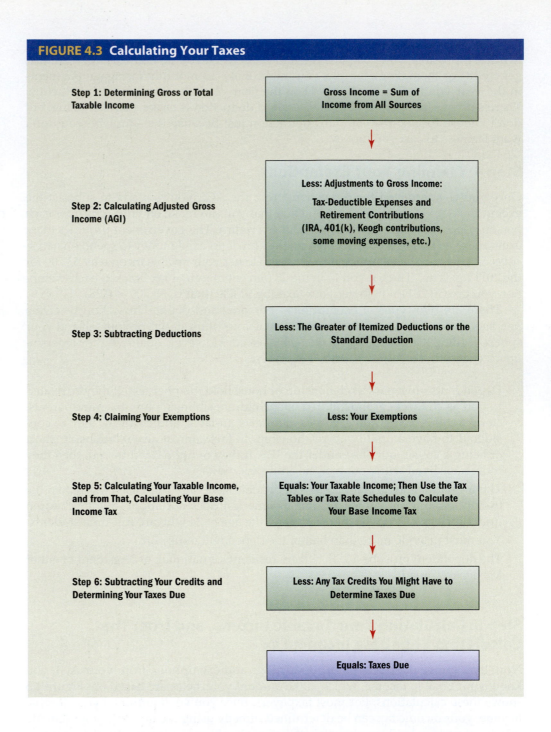

FIGURE 4.3 Calculating Your Taxes

Step 1: Determining Gross or Total Taxable Income	Gross Income = Sum of Income from All Sources
Step 2: Calculating Adjusted Gross Income (AGI)	Less: Adjustments to Gross Income: Tax-Deductible Expenses and Retirement Contributions (IRA, 401(k), Keogh contributions, some moving expenses, etc.)
Step 3: Subtracting Deductions	Less: The Greater of Itemized Deductions or the Standard Deduction
Step 4: Claiming Your Exemptions	Less: Your Exemptions
Step 5: Calculating Your Taxable Income, and from That, Calculating Your Base Income Tax	Equals: Your Taxable Income; Then Use the Tax Tables or Tax Rate Schedules to Calculate Your Base Income Tax
Step 6: Subtracting Your Credits and Determining Your Taxes Due	Less: Any Tax Credits You Might Have to Determine Taxes Due
	Equals: Taxes Due

There's also an alternative minimum tax (AMT) that's aimed at preventing the very wealthy from using tax breaks to the extent that they pay little or nothing. While it is aimed at the very wealthy, every year more and more taxpayers fall prey to it—that's because the AMT brackets aren't adjusted for inflation. Right now, for most people this tax isn't a concern, but if it isn't changed, it has been estimated that by 2015 nearly 50 million filers could be affected by it. The AMT applies different rules in calculating taxable income and then applies a 26 percent and a 28 percent tax rate to all income. It's really Congress's method of ensuring that everyone pays taxes.

FIGURE 4.4 Determining Your Taxes Using the 2011 Tax Tables

Assuming you are married filing jointly with taxable income of $49,423, your taxes would be $6,564.

Each year the amount of taxable income within each bracket is adjusted to reflect inflation.

The filing status is married filing jointly. Thus, you look in this column to calculate your taxes.

The taxable income is $49,423. Thus, you look in this row to determine your taxes.

If line 43 (taxable income) is—		And you are—			
At least	But less than	Single	Married filing jointly	Married filing separately	Head of a household
			Your tax is—		
49,000					
49,000	49,050	8,381	6,504	8,381	7,024
49,050	49,100	8,394	6,511	8,394	7,036
49,100	49,150	8,406	6,519	8,406	7,049
49,150	49,200	8,419	6,526	8,419	7,061
49,200	49,250	8,431	6,534	8,431	7,074
49,250	49,300	8,444	6,541	8,444	7,086
49,300	49,350	8,456	6,549	8,456	7,099
49,350	49,400	8,469	6,556	8,469	7,111
49,400	49,450	8,481	6,564	8,481	7,124
49,450	49,500	8,494	6,571	8,494	7,136
49,500	49,550	8,506	6,579	8,506	7,149
49,550	49,600	8,519	6,586	8,519	7,161
49,600	49,650	8,531	6,594	8,531	7,174
49,650	49,700	8,544	6,601	8,544	7,186
49,700	49,750	8,556	6,609	8,556	7,199
49,750	49,800	8,569	6,616	8,569	7,211
49,800	49,850	8,581	6,624	8,581	7,224
49,850	49,900	8,594	6,631	8,594	7,236
49,900	49,950	8,606	6,639	8,606	7,249
49,950	50,000	8,619	6,646	8,619	7,261

Step 6: Subtract Your Credits and Determine Your Taxes Due

Tax credits reduce your taxes in a direct dollar-for-dollar manner. Whereas deductions merely lower the taxable income from which your taxes are calculated, tax credits are used to reduce the actual taxes that you pay.

There are a number of different tax credits, and they tend to phase out or disappear as your AGI increases. For example, for 2011 and 2012, and possibly in years beyond that if Congress extends it, the **child tax credit** reduces the federal income tax you owe by up to $1,000 for each qualifying child under the age of 17. A qualifying child is an individual for whom the taxpayer can claim a dependency exemption, and is the child, grandchild, stepchild, or eligible foster child of the taxpayer. This child tax credit is given on top of the personal exemption for each child. Again, this is a tax credit, which means it cuts your federal tax bill dollar for dollar. Thus, a family with three children under 17 saves $3,000 in taxes. This tax credit can even become a tax refund for low-income families who don't pay taxes.

However, at the high end of the income scale, this child tax credit begins being phased out after a single parent's adjusted gross income (AGI) reaches $75,000 or a couple's AGI reaches $110,000, regardless of the number of children they have. Once

Child Tax Credit
A tax credit given for each qualifying child under 17.

American Opportunity Credit
A tax credit of up to $2,500 per year per student.

Lifetime Learning Credit
A tax credit for all years of college or graduate school. It also applies to working adults taking classes to improve their work skills.

Child and Dependent Care Credit
A tax credit that offsets your taxes in a direct dollar-for-dollar manner for child and dependent care expenses.

Earned Income Credit
A tax credit available to low-income taxpayers, which effectively serves as a negative income tax.

the phase-out begins, the credit is reduced by $50 for every $1,000 the single parent earns in AGI over $75,000.

Other tax credits include:

◆ The **American Opportunity Credit** is a refundable tax credit for undergraduate college education expenses. This credit provides up to $2,500 in tax credits on the first $4,000 of qualifying educational expenses. At present, the tax credit is scheduled to have a limited life span: It will be available only through 2012, unless Congress decides to extend the credit to other years.

◆ The **Lifetime Learning Credit** provides tax credits up to $2,000 for students during all years of postsecondary education and for courses to acquire or improve job skills; it is also phased out as the taxpayer's earnings rise. While you can claim both the American Opportunity Credit and the Lifetime Learning Credit on the same return, you cannot claim them both for the same student. In addition, you can claim either in the same year that you receive a tax-free distribution from an Education IRA (also called a Coverdell Education Savings Account). Table 4.2 compares the American Opportunity and Lifetime Learning credits.

◆ The **child and dependent care credit** provides a credit to help offset the cost of child care or care for a dependent of any age who is incapacitated due to mental or physical limitations.

◆ The **earned income credit**, which is available to low-income taxpayers, effectively serves as a negative income tax. With the child and dependent care credit, you couldn't get a credit for more than you owed in taxes, but with the earned income credit you could actually get a credit for more than you paid in taxes. In other words, you could pay no taxes and get money back from the IRS. Just as with other tax credits, the earned income credit is phased out for those with higher income levels.

TABLE 4.2 Comparison of Education Credits

	American Opportunity Credit	Lifetime Learning Credit
Maximum credit	Up to $2,500 credit per **eligible student**	Up to $2,000 credit per **return**
Refundable or nonrefundable	40% of credit may be refundable	Credit limited to the amount of tax you must pay on your taxable income
Number of years of post-secondary education	Available **ONLY** for the first **4** years of postsecondary education	Available for all years of postsecondary education and for courses to acquire or improve job skills
Number of tax years credit available	Available **ONLY** for **4** tax years per eligible student	Available for an unlimited number of years
Type of degree required	Student must be pursuing an undergraduate degree or other recognized education credential	Student does not need to be pursuing a degree or other recognized education credential
Number of courses	Student must be enrolled at least half time for at least one academic period beginning during the tax year	Available for one or more courses
Felony drug conviction	No felony drug convictions on student's records	Felony drug convictions are permitted

◆ The **adoption credit** allows for a tax credit for the qualifying cost of adopting a child under the age of 18, or someone who is physically or mentally incapable of self-care.

Adoption Credit
A tax credit of up to $11,390 available for qualifying costs of adopting a child.

In addition, some taxpayers are eligible for additional tax credits, for example:

◆ Totally disabled taxpayers and those over 65 with low incomes.
◆ Taxpayers who pay income tax to another country.
◆ Those who overpay Social Security taxes because they work more than one job.

Although there are not nearly the number of tax credits that there once were, it behooves you to be aware of what qualifies for a tax credit and to take advantage of any credit you qualify for. Once again, *tax credits are subtracted directly from taxes due on a dollar-for-dollar basis.* Your total income tax becomes your base income tax less your tax credits:

Base Income Tax (from tax tables or tax rate calculations)

Less

Tax Credits

Equals

Total Income Tax Due

Other Filing Considerations

4 Choose the tax form that's right for you, file, and survive an audit if necessary.

Before you file you'll have to pick a form and decide if you want to file electronically or not. You'll also want to know how to file an amended return, what to do if you can't make the tax deadline, and where to get help. Fortunately, April 15 only comes once a year.

Choosing a Tax Form

A key to calculating your taxes is deciding which 1040 form to use: 1040EZ, 1040A, or 1040. If the IRS has sent you material, it's already made a guess at what form you'll need and has included it. Still, you have the option of choosing a different form if you prefer.

CHECKLIST 4.1

You Might Be Able to Use Form 1040EZ If . . .

◆ Your filing status is either single or married filing jointly.
◆ You don't itemize deductions.
◆ Your taxable income is below $100,000.
◆ You are under age 65.
◆ Your taxable interest income is less than $1,500.

◆ You have no dependents.
◆ You aren't making a deductible contribution to an IRA or a deduction for student loan interest.
◆ You don't have alimony, taxable pension benefits, or Social Security benefits to report.

CHECKLIST 4.2

You Might Be Able to Use Form 1040A If . . .

- You don't itemize deductions.
- Your taxable income is below $100,000.
- You have capital gain distributions, but no other capital gains or losses.
- Your only tax credits are for child, education, earned income, child and dependent care expenses, elderly, and retirement savings contributions.
- Your only deductions are for IRA contributions or student loan interest.
- Your income was limited to wages, salaries, tips, etc., interest, dividends, capital gain distributions, IRA distributions, pensions and annuities, unemployment compensation, and Social Security benefits.

Form 1040EZ is aimed at those with no dependents, and with taxable income of less than $100,000 per year, who don't itemize. As its name implies, it is an "easy" form to fill out. Form 1040EZ consists of only 12 lines of information, and the instructions fit on the back of the form. In fact, it can even be filled out over the telephone. Checklist 4.1 provides some of the basic requirements you must meet in order to use Form 1040EZ.

Slightly less "EZ" than Form 1040EZ, but still not too complicated, is Form 1040A, the original easy form. Although it still limits total taxable income to $100,000, this income can come from interest, dividends, Social Security benefits, pensions and annuities, scholarships, IRA distributions, and unemployment compensation. In effect, it allows for a much broader range of income sources than is allowed on Form 1040EZ. Form 1040A also allows for dependents and deductible contributions to an IRA. Checklist 4.2 provides some of the basic requirements that must be met in order to use Form 1040A.

Form 1040, which is also called the "1040 long form," is used by everyone else—about 60 percent of all taxpayers—and throws "easy" right out the door. It's longer because it allows for the many complications that can make filing taxes a frustrating experience. On the bright side, though, the 1040 long form allows for the opportunity to avoid paying more in the way of taxes than is legally required. That is, it allows for itemized deductions and adjustments to income that can result in lower taxes. Obviously, your choice of a tax form should not be based on what's easiest to fill out. It should be based on what's financially advantageous to you.

Schedules
Attachments to Form 1040 on which you provide additional information.

Along with Form 1040, there are a number of **schedules**. A schedule is an attachment to Form 1040 on which you provide information regarding income and expenses that flow through to Form 1040. Some of the more common schedules are listed in Table 4.3. If you need an IRS schedule or form, the easiest way to get it is to download it off the IRS Web site at **www.irs.gov** or to call 800-TAX-FORM. The IRS will send it directly to you.

TABLE 4.3 Common Schedules Used with Form 1040

Schedule A: Itemized Deductions	Schedule EIC: Earned Income Credit
Schedule B: Interest and Dividend Income	Schedule F: Profit or Loss from Farming
Schedule C: Profit or Loss from Business	Schedule H: Household Employment Taxes
Schedule D: Capital Gains and Losses	Schedule R: Credit for the Elderly or the Disabled
Schedule E: Supplemental Income and Loss	Schedule SE: Self-Employment Tax

Electronic Filing

While you may not have a choice on paying your taxes, you do have a choice on how to file your tax return. You can file by mail or you can e-file—that is, file your return electronically. In fact, nearly 99 million people used e-file in 2010. The benefits of filing electronically include:

◆ Faster refunds: Direct deposit can speed refunds to e-filers in as few as 10 days.

◆ More accurate returns: IRS computers quickly and automatically check for errors or other missing information, making e-filed returns more accurate and reducing the chance of receiving an error letter from the IRS.

◆ Quick electronic confirmation: Computer e-filers receive an acknowledgment that the IRS has received their returns.

◆ Delete the paperwork with electronic signatures: There is nothing to mail to the IRS.

◆ Federal/state e-filing: Taxpayers in 38 states and the District of Columbia can e-file their federal and state tax returns in one transmission to the IRS. The IRS forwards the state data to the appropriate state tax agency.

Free File   For the 2010 tax year, taxpayers with an adjusted gross income of $58,000 or less were eligible to use Free File. New and repeat users must access Free File only through IRS.gov. Otherwise, the e-file provider might charge them a fee, so be sure to go to IRS.gov to access it. For information, visit **www.irs.gov/efile**.

Filing Late and Amended Returns

Although most returns are filed by April 15, sometimes taxpayers can't make the deadline. In addition, if you discover an error in a prior year's returns, you can file an amended return.

Filing Late   If you're unable to file by April 15, you can request a filing extension from the IRS. You must file Form 4868, Application for Automatic Extension of Time to File U.S. Individual Income Tax Return. If you request a filing extension, the extension is automatic—no questions asked. This extension gives you an additional 6 months to file your return.

As you might expect, a filing extension is a fairly popular request, with over 5 million taxpayers asking for one each year. However, the IRS isn't about to let you off the hook for taxes you owe. In addition to filling out the extension request form, you're asked to enclose a check for any estimated taxes you owe. If you don't enclose a check, you'll be charged interest on the taxes. Moreover, if the amount due is more than 10 percent of your tax bill, you'll also be charged a late penalty of $\frac{1}{2}$ percent per month.

Amending Returns   It's not unusual for someone to make a mistake on a tax return or to realize later that a deduction was omitted. To amend your return use Form 1040X, Amended U.S. Individual Income Tax Return. In fact, you can even amend an amended tax return.

There are some limitations on the use of an amended return. For example, there is a limit on how far back you can go: You can't file an amended return more than 3-years after the original tax due date that you filed. Finally, if you file an amended federal return, make sure you also amend your state and local returns.

Being Audited

Each year the IRS audits the returns of more than 1.5 million taxpayers; in fact, for tax year 2010, about 1.1 percent of returns were audited. What might bring on an **audit**? Unfortunately, you may just have bad luck—the IRS randomly selects a large number of returns each year. You may also be audited because you were audited in the past, particularly if the IRS found some error in your return. In this case, the IRS is merely checking to make sure the error doesn't occur again. You may have been selected because you earn a lot of money. If your itemized deductions are more than 44 percent of your income, your odds of being audited rise even further. In addition, your odds of being audited go up significantly if your return contains a Schedule C for self-employment income. If your expenses on Schedule C amount to more than one-third of your Schedule C income, the odds of an audit rise again.

No one wants to be audited, but unless you've been cheating on your taxes, it's nothing to worry about. Audits come in different forms. Some only ask for additional information and can be handled through the mail. Others require you to meet face-to-face with an IRS representative. In either case, you're given several weeks to prepare your response.

The first step in preparing for an audit is to reexamine the areas in which the IRS has questions. You should gather all supporting data you have—canceled checks, receipts, records—and then try to anticipate any questions the IRS might have and formulate responses to them. The key to winning an audit is good records. If you need help, you can hire a tax accountant or attorney. In fact, this agent can go to the audit in your place, provided you sign a power of attorney form.

MONEY MATTERS

Tips from Marcy Furney, ChFC, Certified Financial Planner™

DO NOT GO GENTLY INTO THAT TAX RETURN

I take in one folder with a few forms, 1099s, my Quicken reports, and one spreadsheet to my CPA in February. My best friend takes in three bulging shoe boxes of paper about April 14. Guess who pays the lower tax preparation fee, and probably saves taxes by having good records of deductions? Organization, as strange as it may sound, is a partial cure for the tax-filing blues.

If you itemize deductions and don't use accounting software, circle any deductible items in your check register. At the end of the year, check off each circled item as you list it, and make sure you have receipts where needed. A list with supporting evidence is a tax preparer's dream and may prevent overlooking deductions. It's also a lifesaver if you get that dreaded audit letter.

Keep a record of all income sources and check each one off as the W-2 or 1099 comes in. It's a bit painful to get your 1040 done and then receive a W-2 from that part-time painting job you had one month last summer. Also, the IRS doesn't accept the "I didn't get a 1099" excuse for excluding interest or dividends. Call any company that hasn't sent you the required forms by the end of January.

Try completing a tax preparer's checklist before beginning your return or heading off to the CPA.

Procrastination can be costly. If you got a refund last year, set a deadline to change your W-4. About the worst investment, besides burying your money in the backyard, is giving the U.S. government an interest-free loan for the year. Also, prepare your return early. If you're expecting a refund, the sooner you get the money back, the sooner it can go to work for you.

One of the biggest time consumers in tax preparation is determining the cost basis of investments that were liquidated during the year. If you don't have records of the original purchase and intervening transactions, you are at the mercy of a brokerage house or investment company to provide the documentation. Prepare a folder when you first set up stock or a mutual fund account and keep every statement. Just a little organization can save time and ensure that the proper amount of tax is paid.

If you're not satisfied with the outcome of the audit, you have the right to appeal. The first step is to see the auditor. Present your argument and see if you can win the appeal with additional information. If you are still not satisfied with the results, you turn to your auditor's manager. If you are still not satisfied, you can file a formal appeal and even go to tax court if necessary.

> ### FACTS OF LIFE
> **1.1 percent** of individuals taxpayers are audited.
> **2.7 percent** of individuals earning between $200,000 and $1 million are audited.
> **8.4 percent** of individuals earning over $1 million are audited.

Unfortunately, an appeal does not guarantee satisfaction. The important point is that you have the right to receive credit for any and all legal deductions, and you should not let fear of being audited interfere with paying the minimum amount of income taxes, provided you do it legally.

Help in Preparing Taxes

Sometimes preparing your taxes is more than you can handle by yourself. The first place to look for help is the IRS. While that may seem akin to consorting with the enemy, the IRS is a good place to start. Information from the IRS is knowledgeable and cheap—in fact, it's free. In addition to the instructions provided with your income tax form, the IRS also has a number of booklets that can be extremely helpful. One of the more informative is IRS Publication 17, *Your Federal Income Tax*, which gives detailed step-by-step instructions to aid you in filing your taxes and is available at **www.irs.gov/pub/irs-pdf/p17.pdf**.

The IRS also provides a phone service, a toll-free "hot line" for tax questions. Although the IRS won't accept any liability for incorrect advice, representatives are generally correct. Moreover, using the IRS hot line as a reference can save you both time and money in getting that answer. The major problem with using the hot line is that it's often busy. The closer you get to April 15, the more difficult it is to connect. The IRS also provides a walk-in service in most areas, where you can meet directly with an IRS employee. Once again, the closer it is to April 15, the harder it is to get an appointment.

In addition to publications from the IRS, there are a number of excellent self-help tax publications, including J. K. Lasser's and Ernst & Young's income tax guides. These tax guides point out areas in which legitimate deductions, which might otherwise be overlooked, can be found. For those with access to a computer and some degree of computer literacy, there are a number of outstanding computer programs for tax preparation. Of course, for those who qualify there is Free File. In addition there is Intuit's TurboTax and TaxCut by H&R Block Financial.

Your final option in preparing your taxes is to hire a tax specialist. Although going to a specialist sounds safe, remember that tax specialists are not licensed or tested—anyone can declare himself or herself to be a tax specialist. There are some rules governing tax specialists, but there's no penalty imposed on your advisor if you pay too much in taxes.

Tax specialists can be divided into those with a national affiliation, such as H&R Block, and independent tax specialists. One advantage of the national affiliation is that employees generally get standardized training, keeping them current with the latest IRS changes and rulings. With independent tax specialists, there's much more variability in terms of training and in the quality of work they do.

> ### FACTS OF LIFE
> Phishing scams often take the form of an e-mail that appears to come from a legitimate source. Some scam e-mails falsely claim to come from the IRS. To date, taxpayers have forwarded more than 33,000 of these scam e-mails, reflecting more than 1,500 different schemes, to the IRS. The IRS never uses e-mail to contact taxpayers about their tax issues.

If you decide to use a tax specialist, you should make sure you avoid the April rush. Because of the volume of tax work that's done near the filing deadline, last-minute returns may not get the attention they deserve. In addition, make sure you get references and inquire about the specialist's background and experience. If your tax specialist does not begin with an extensive interview in which your financial affairs are fully probed, you probably won't get your money's worth.

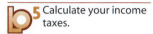 **5** Calculate your income taxes.

Model Taxpayers: The Taylors File Their 2011 Return

Let's take a look at the various steps in calculating taxes for Form 1040. We'll use the Taylors as an example. Chuck and Dianne Taylor have two children: Lindsey, who's 4, and Kathleen, who's 6. Chuck is a repairman for Burlington Industries, where he earned $51,900 in 2011, and Dianne works part-time at a coffee shop, where she earned $6,250 in 2011. On Chuck and Dianne's wages and salaries there was a total of $4,750 in federal tax withheld.

In addition, in 2011 the Taylors also received interest income of $760, $755 in capital gains on stock held for less than 12 months and then sold,[8] and a gift of $10,000 from Chuck's parents. Chuck also contributed $1,668 to his traditional IRA, which is a tax-deferred retirement plan.

The Taylors had another more interesting source of income: They were winners on The Price Is Right. Dianne won a 2011 Honda Accord just by telling Drew Carey the third number in its price. A stunned Dianne Taylor stood on the stage of the CBS studio in Burbank, California, hearing the announcer say "that's right, Dianne, this brand-new Honda Accord comes fully equipped with air, CD Player, automatic windows, and California emission controls. You'll enjoy making heads turn as you drive down the street in this, your new car!" What she didn't hear is that she would have to pay taxes on her prize. What she's taxed on is the fair market price of the car, which is interpreted as what she could realize on an immediate resale. In this case that amount is $20,500, and it becomes part of the Taylors' taxable income.

Because the Taylors had income from a prize (which must be listed on Form 1040 under "other income"), they have no choice but to use the 1040 long form. The first step they must take is to get organized, which means gathering together a copy of last year's return along with all of this year's tax-related information: salary, taxes withheld, mortgage payments, the market price of the car Dianne won, medical expenses, and so on. Fortunately, over the past year the Taylors set aside all their tax-related materials in a folder in Dianne's desk.

One of the first questions asked on Form 1040 is filing status. The best way to determine that is to calculate your taxes filing both jointly and separately and then using the status that gives you the lowest number. For now let's assume that filing a joint return is the best option for the Taylors. The total exemptions claimed by the Taylors were four—one each for Chuck, Dianne, Kathleen, and Lindsey. Figure 4.5 shows the Taylors' 2011 Form 1040. We'll use this figure as a reference as we examine how the Taylors calculated their taxes. All line references correspond to the numbered lines shown on Form 1040.

---

[8]Since the capital gains were realized on stock held for less than 12 months, the entire gain is taxable as ordinary income.

FIGURE 4.5 2011 Federal Income Tax Return for the Taylors, Using Form 1040

Take the time to set up a good tax record-keeping system. Once it's set up, use it!

Married people generally file as married filing jointly (in general, it saves money over filing separately), but for those with widely divergent levels of income and deductions, it might be better to use the married filing separately status.

If you work for yourself, report your income on Schedule C.

If you put money into an IRA or tax-deferred retirement plan and you haven't yet paid taxes on that money, you will have to pay taxes on it when you withdraw it at retirement.

Form **1040** Department of the Treasury—Internal Revenue Service (99)
U.S. Individual Income Tax Return **2011** OMB No. 1545-0074 IRS Use Only—Do not write or staple in this space.

For the year Jan. 1–Dec. 31, 2011, or other tax year beginning , 2011, ending , 20   See separate instructions.

Your first name and initial: **Chuck B.**   Last name: **Taylor**   Your social security number: **111111111**

If a joint return, spouse's first name and initial: **Dianne P.**   Last name: **Taylor**   Spouse's social security number: **222222222**

Home address (number and street). If you have a P.O. box, see instructions. Apt. no.
1969 Yellow Jacket Dr.

▲ Make sure the SSN(s) above and on line 6c are correct.

City, town or post office, state, and ZIP code. If you have a foreign address, also complete spaces below (see instructions).
Ross, GA 12345

Presidential Election Campaign
Check here if you, or your spouse if filing jointly, want $3 to go to this fund. Checking a box below will not change your tax or refund. ☐ You ☐ Spouse

Foreign country name   Foreign province/county   Foreign postal code

Filing Status
Check only one box.
1 ☐ Single
2 ☑ Married filing jointly (even if only one had income)
3 ☐ Married filing separately. Enter spouse's SSN above and full name here. ▶
4 ☐ Head of household (with qualifying person). (See instructions.) If the qualifying person is a child but not your dependent, enter this child's name here. ▶
5 ☐ Qualifying widow(er) with dependent child

Exemptions
6a ☑ Yourself. If someone can claim you as a dependent, **do not** check box 6a .
b ☑ Spouse
Boxes checked on 6a and 6b: **2**

c Dependents:
(1) First name Last name	(2) Dependent's social security number	(3) Dependent's relationship to you	(4) ✓ if child under age 17 qualifying for child tax credit (see instructions)
Kathleen Taylor	333333333	daughter	☑
Lindsey Taylor	444444444	daughter	☑
			☐
			☐

If more than four dependents, see instructions and check here ▶ ☐

No. of children on 6c who:
• lived with you **2**
• did not live with you due to divorce or separation (see instructions)
Dependents on 6c not entered above
Add numbers on lines above ▶ **4**

d Total number of exemptions claimed

Income

Attach Form(s) W-2 here. Also attach Forms W-2G and 1099-R if tax was withheld.

If you did not get a W-2, see instructions.

Enclose, but do not attach, any payment. Also, please use Form 1040-V.

7	Wages, salaries, tips, etc. Attach Form(s) W-2	7	58,150
8a	Taxable interest. Attach Schedule B if required	8a	760
b	Tax-exempt interest. **Do not** include on line 8a	8b	
9a	Ordinary dividends. Attach Schedule B if required	9a	
b	Qualified dividends	9b	
10	Taxable refunds, credits, or offsets of state and local income taxes	10	
11	Alimony received	11	
12	Business income or (loss). Attach Schedule C or C-EZ	12	
13	Capital gain or (loss). Attach Schedule D if required. If not required, check here ▶ ☐	13	755
14	Other gains or (losses). Attach Form 4797	14	
15a	IRA distributions 15a b Taxable amount	15b	
16a	Pensions and annuities 16a b Taxable amount	16b	
17	Rental real estate, royalties, partnerships, S corporations, trusts, etc. Attach Schedule E	17	
18	Farm income or (loss). Attach Schedule F	18	
19	Unemployment compensation	19	
20a	Social security benefits 20a b Taxable amount	20b	
21	Other income. List type and amount	21	20,500
22	Combine the amounts in the far right column for lines 7 through 21. This is your **total income** ▶	22	80,165

Adjusted Gross Income

23	Educator expenses	23	
24	Certain business expenses of reservists, performing artists, and fee-basis government officials. Attach Form 2106 or 2106-EZ	24	
25	Health savings account deduction. Attach Form 8889	25	
26	Moving expenses. Attach Form 3903	26	
27	Deductible part of self-employment tax. Attach Schedule SE	27	
28	Self-employed SEP, SIMPLE, and qualified plans	28	
29	Self-employed health insurance deduction	29	
30	Penalty on early withdrawal of savings	30	
31a	Alimony paid b Recipient's SSN ▶	31a	
32	IRA deduction	32	1,668
33	Student loan interest deduction	33	
34	Tuition and fees. Attach Form 8917	34	
35	Domestic production activities deduction. Attach Form 8903	35	
36	Add lines 23 through 35	36	1,668
37	Subtract line 36 from line 22. This is your **adjusted gross income** ▶	37	78,497

For Disclosure, Privacy Act, and Paperwork Reduction Act Notice, see separate instructions. Cat. No. 11320B Form **1040** (2011)

Determining Gross or Total Income (line 22)

Remember, gross or total income is the sum of all your taxable income from all sources. For the Taylors it includes Chuck and Dianne's wages and salaries of $51,900 + 6,250 = $58,150 (line 7). It also includes taxable interest income of $760 (line 8a), and $755 in capital gains (line 13). In addition, line 21, other income, includes $20,500, the fair market value of the car Dianne won on *The Price Is Right*. All this taxable income is summed to make up total income (line 22).

FIGURE 4.5   2011 Federal Income Tax Return for the Taylors, Using Form 1040 (continued)

Before sitting down to do your taxes, gather up everything you will need, including any tax-related business expenses from the previous year.

If you pay for child or dependent care while you are working, you may be entitled to a tax credit.

Form 1040 (2011) — Page 2

Tax and Credits

Line	Description		Amount
38	Amount from line 37 (adjusted gross income)	38	78,497
39a	Check if: ☐ You were born before January 2, 1947, ☐ Blind. ☐ Spouse was born before January 2, 1947, ☐ Blind. Total boxes checked ▶ 39a		
b	If your spouse itemizes on a separate return or you were a dual-status alien, check here ▶ 39b ☐		

Standard Deduction for—
• People who check any box on line 39a or 39b or who can be claimed as a dependent, see instructions.
• All others:
Single or Married filing separately, $5,800
Married filing jointly or Qualifying widow(er), $11,600
Head of household, $8,500

Line	Description		Amount
40	Itemized deductions (from Schedule A) or your standard deduction (see left margin)	40	14,274
41	Subtract line 40 from line 38	41	64,223
42	Exemptions. Multiply $3,700 by the number on line 6d	42	14,800
43	Taxable income. Subtract line 42 from line 41. If line 42 is more than line 41, enter -0-	43	49,423
44	Tax (see instructions). Check if any from: a ☐ Form(s) 8814 b ☐ Form 4972 c ☐ 962 election	44	6,564
45	Alternative minimum tax (see instructions). Attach Form 6251	45	
46	Add lines 44 and 45 ▶	46	6,564
47	Foreign tax credit. Attach Form 1116 if required	47	
48	Credit for child and dependent care expenses. Attach Form 2441	48	
49	Education credits from Form 8863, line 23	49	
50	Retirement savings contributions credit. Attach Form 8880	50	
51	Child tax credit (see instructions)	51	2,000
52	Residential energy credits. Attach Form 5695	52	
53	Other credits from Form: a ☐ 3800 b ☐ 8801 c ☐	53	
54	Add lines 47 through 53. These are your total credits	54	2,000
55	Subtract line 54 from line 46. If line 54 is more than line 46, enter -0- ▶	55	4,564

Other Taxes

Line	Description		Amount
56	Self-employment tax. Attach Schedule SE	56	
57	Unreported social security and Medicare tax from Form: a ☐ 4137 b ☐ 8919	57	
58	Additional tax on IRAs, other qualified retirement plans, etc. Attach Form 5329 if required	58	
59a	Household employment taxes from Schedule H	59a	
b	First-time homebuyer credit repayment. Attach Form 5405 if required	59b	
60	Other taxes. Enter code(s) from instructions	60	
61	Add lines 55 through 60. This is your total tax ▶	61	4,564

Payments

If you have a qualifying child, attach Schedule EIC.

Line	Description		Amount
62	Federal income tax withheld from Forms W-2 and 1099	62	4,750
63	2011 estimated tax payments and amount applied from 2010 return	63	
64a	Earned income credit (EIC)	64a	
b	Nontaxable combat pay election	64b	
65	Additional child tax credit. Attach Form 8812	65	
66	American opportunity credit from Form 8863, line 14	66	
67	First-time homebuyer credit from Form 5405, line 10	67	
68	Amount paid with request for extension to file	68	
69	Excess social security and tier 1 RRTA tax withheld	69	
70	Credit for federal tax on fuels. Attach Form 4136	70	
71	Credits from Form: a ☐ 2439 b ☐ 8839 c ☐ 8801 d ☐ 8885	71	
72	Add lines 62, 63, 64a, and 65 through 71. These are your total payments ▶	72	4,750

Refund

Line	Description		Amount
73	If line 72 is more than line 61, subtract line 61 from line 72. This is the amount you overpaid	73	186
74a	Amount of line 73 you want refunded to you. If Form 8888 is attached, check here ▶ ☐	74a	186
b	Routing number		
	▶ c Type: ☐ Checking ☐ Savings		
d	Account number		
75	Amount of line 73 you want applied to your 2012 estimated tax ▶ 75		

Direct deposit? See instructions.

Amount You Owe

Line	Description		Amount
76	Amount you owe. Subtract line 72 from line 61. For details on how to pay, see instructions ▶	76	
77	Estimated tax penalty (see instructions)	77	

Third Party Designee

Do you want to allow another person to discuss this return with the IRS (see instructions)? ☐ Yes. Complete below. ☐ No

Designee's name ▶   Phone no. ▶   Personal identification number (PIN) ▶

Sign Here

Under penalties of perjury, I declare that I have examined this return and accompanying schedules and statements, and to the best of my knowledge and belief, they are true, correct, and complete. Declaration of preparer (other than taxpayer) is based on all information of which preparer has any knowledge.

Joint return? See instructions. Keep a copy for your records.

Your signature *Chuck B. Taylor*   Date   Your occupation   Daytime phone number

Spouse's signature. If a joint return, both must sign. *Dianne P. Taylor*   Date   Spouse's occupation   If the IRS sent you an Identity Protection PIN, enter it here (see inst.)

Paid Preparer Use Only

Print/Type preparer's name   Preparer's signature   Date   Check ☐ if self-employed   PTIN

Firm's name ▶   Firm's EIN ▶
Firm's address ▶   Phone no.

Form **1040** (2011)

Chuck and Dianne's salary and wages (line 7)	$58,150
Taxable interest income (line 8a)	760
Capital gains (line 13)	755
Other income (line 21)	20,500
Total income (line 22)	$80,165

Notice that the $10,000 gift from Chuck's parents does not appear as income. This is because gifts are not considered taxable income. Other common sources of income that would not be taxed include interest on state and local debt.

Subtracting Adjustments to Gross or Total Income and Calculating Adjusted Gross Income (line 37)

For the Taylors, the only adjustment to total income is Chuck's IRA deduction of $1,668. Thus, total adjustment made in calculating the Taylors' adjusted gross income is $1,668. Subtracting this adjustment from total income gives the Taylors an AGI, or adjusted gross income, of $78,497.

Subtracting Deductions (line 40)

The Taylors have their choice of taking the standard deduction, which for 2011 was $11,600, or itemizing their deductions. The Taylors' itemized deductions amounted to $14,274, primarily as a result of interest paid on their home mortgage. Figure 4.6 shows the Taylors' deductions. In addition to home mortgage interest payments of $11,079, they paid $2,543 in state and local income taxes and real estate taxes, and made $652 in tax-deductible charitable contributions for a total of $14,274 in deductions. The Taylors were unable to deduct any medical or miscellaneous expenses because neither of these exceeded the AGI limitations set by the IRS. Because the level of the itemized deductions exceeded the standard deduction, they chose to itemize. The itemized deduction of $14,274 is entered in line 40 on Form 1040. Subtracting this amount from their AGI reduces their taxable income to $64,223 (line 41).

Claiming Exemptions (line 42)

The Taylors qualify for four exemptions, with the 2011 exemption amount being $3,700. Thus, the level of total exemptions entered on line 42 is 4 × 3,700 = $14,800. Subtracting this amount further reduces their taxable income to $64,223 − $14,800 = $49,423 (line 43).

Calculating Total Tax (line 61)

For the Taylors, their base income tax can be calculated directly from the tax tables provided in the federal instructions booklet. Their tax comes out to $6,564, which is shown in Figure 4.5 and is entered on line 46. Because the Taylors have dependent children under the age of 17, they qualify for the child tax credit. Remember, a tax credit is subtracted directly from taxes owed. The child tax credit currently (tax year 2011) provides for a tax credit of $1,000 per dependent child. For the tax year 2011, the Taylors received $2,000 in child tax credit. This amount is entered on line 51. Because the total credits entered on line 54 are $2,000, line 55 becomes $4,564.

During 2011 the Taylors had $4,750 in federal income tax withheld thus total tax payments of $4,750 appear in line 72. Because they owed ($4,564) less than they paid ($4,750), they will receive a refund of the difference of $186 from the IRS.

FIGURE 4.6   Schedule A from the Taylors' 2011 Federal Income Tax Return

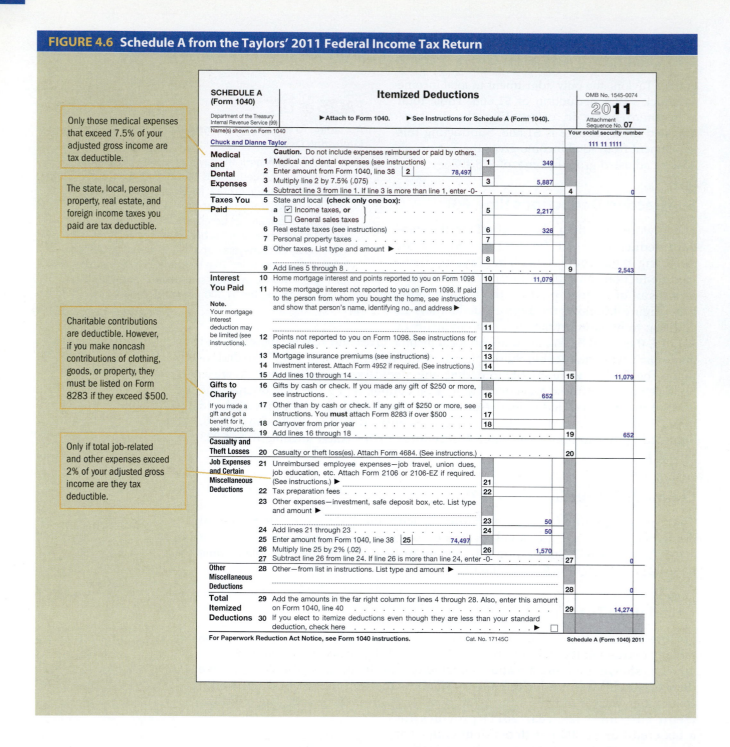

Only those medical expenses that exceed 7.5% of your adjusted gross income are tax deductible.

The state, local, personal property, real estate, and foreign income taxes you paid are tax deductible.

Charitable contributions are deductible. However, if you make noncash contributions of clothing, goods, or property, they must be listed on Form 8283 if they exceed $500.

Only if total job-related and other expenses exceed 2% of your adjusted gross income are they tax deductible.

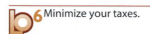

6 Minimize your taxes.

Tax Strategies to Lower Your Taxes

So far we've looked only at preparing your taxes. We now turn to the very important topic of tax planning strategies. Although a tax specialist can help you identify deductions you might otherwise miss, once you begin to prepare your taxes it's probably too late for any strategy that will result in reduced taxes. Tax planning, in general, must be done well ahead of time.

Few people do their tax planning alone. Instead they consult a CPA or even a tax attorney. However, before you see a specialist, you should have a good understanding of how the tax code works so that you can work with a specialist to map out a strategy that suits your needs.

The basic reason for tax planning is to minimize unnecessary tax payments. While the IRS has closed a number of tax loopholes in recent years, there still are many strategies that make sense. Tax strategies should be methods of supplementing a sound investment strategy rather than the focal point of investing.

Keep in mind that Congress and the IRS are continuously tinkering with the tax laws. Your strategy should be to supplement a solid investment strategy with tax considerations.

There are five general tax strategies you can use. They include the following:

◆ Maximize deductions.
◆ Look to capital gains and dividend income.
◆ Shift income to family members in lower tax brackets.
◆ Receive tax-exempt income.
◆ Defer taxes to the future.

Each of these strategies is aimed at avoiding unnecessary taxes, not evading taxes, that is, overstating deductions or not reporting all your income. It's certainly illegal and unwise to evade taxes, but it's foolish to pay more than your fair share.

Maximize Deductions

Strategies for maximizing deductions center on three different tactics: (1) using tax-deferred retirement programs to reduce taxes, (2) using your home as a tax shelter, and (3) shifting and bunching deductions. Each of these three tactics has the same goal: to reduce taxable income to its minimum level.

Using Tax-Deferred Retirement Programs To encourage retirement savings, the government allows several different types of tax-deferred retirement programs. The advantage of these plans is that you (1) don't pay taxes on the money you invest and (2) don't pay interest on the earnings from your retirement account. Let's look at the difference that results from putting your savings in a tax-deferred retirement plan instead of in a normal savings account, both earning a 10 percent return. Let's also assume that you are in the 25 percent marginal tax bracket.

> **STOP & THINK**
>
> It's hard to overstress how valuable tax-deferred retirement plans actually are. Not only do they reduce taxable income but also the contributions grow tax deferred, and many companies match part of your contribution, putting in 50 cents for each dollar that you contribute. Why do you think the government offers tax-deferred retirement plans?

If you took $1,000 of your taxable earnings and decided to invest without using a tax-deferred retirement plan earning 10 percent, you would first pay $250 in taxes, leaving you with only $750 to invest. During the first year you would earn $75 in interest and pay $18.75 in taxes, leaving you with $56.25 of interest after taxes. At the end of the year you would have $806.25 saved. If you let this amount grow at 10 percent before taxes for 25 years, it would accumulate to a total of $4,573.75.

Now let's look at what would happen if you put your money in a tax-deferred account, also earning 10 percent. First, you wouldn't pay taxes on the $1,000, because taxes aren't assessed until you withdraw the money from this account. Thus, you would earn 10 percent interest on $1,000 for a total of $100 interest. In addition, because this is a tax-deferred account, you wouldn't pay taxes on any of this interest, giving you a total of $1,100 after the year. If you left this amount in the tax-deferred account for 25 years, you would have accumulated $10,834.

Of course, you eventually would have to pay taxes on this amount, but even after paying 25 percent taxes on $10,834 you still have about $8,126.03. Why is the difference between the investments so great? Because you've been able to earn interest on money that would have otherwise already been collected by the IRS.

Using Your Home as a Tax Shelter   The tax benefits associated with owning a home are twofold. First, mortgage interest payments are tax deductible and, as such, reduce your taxes. Second, when you eventually sell your house, you are exempt from paying taxes on gains of up to $500,000 for couples filing jointly and $250,000 for those filing singly on the sale of a principal residence.

Just how valuable is the deductibility of your home mortgage interest payments? That depends on several factors. For those in the highest tax brackets, the tax deductibility is much more valuable than it is for those in the lowest bracket. Although if you earn too much, this deduction begins to lose value because of the phase-out of itemized deductions discussed earlier. In addition, if you do not itemize deductions, the tax deductibility of mortgage interest payments is of no value. Moreover, if you had taken the standard deduction without them, and now itemize with them, they would reduce your taxable income only by the difference between the standard deduction and your itemized deductions.

The amount that this reduction in taxable income reduces your taxes is equal to their value. In effect, the tax deductibility of mortgage interest payments reduces the cost of your mortgage by (1 − marginal tax rate). Thus, the after-tax cost of a home mortgage can be determined as follows:

$$\text{after-tax cost of mortgage interest} = \frac{\text{before-tax cost of}}{\text{mortgage interest}} \times (1 - \text{marginal tax rate})$$

In short, the value of the tax deductibility of mortgage interest payments depends on your marginal tax bracket and whether or not you itemize deductions.

In addition, by using your home as collateral, you can take out a home equity loan and deduct your interest payments. This deduction lowers the cost of borrowing. For example, you might consider a home equity loan to finance buying a used car. In 2011 the average cost of a 36-month used car loan was about 5.7 percent, and the average cost of a home equity loan was about 7.2 percent. However, the interest on the home equity loan is generally tax deductible, whereas the interest on the car loan is not.

Recalculating the cost of a home equity loan for an individual in the 25 percent tax bracket on an after-tax basis, it becomes 7.2%(1 − marginal tax rate) or 7.2%(1 − 0.25) = 5.4 percent. Thus, in many cases the cheapest way to borrow money is with a home equity loan.

STOP & THINK

As we'll see in coming chapters, home equity debt, because of the tax deductibility of the interest payments, is the cheapest source of borrowing. Why might it be a good idea to use the money from a home equity loan to consolidate and pay off more costly debt?

Shifting and Bunching Deductions   When we discussed itemizing versus taking the standard deduction, we presented the concept of shifting and bunching deductions. The decision between taking the standard deduction or itemizing becomes difficult when they are close in value. The concept of shifting and bunching deductions involves trying to avoid incurring deductible expenses in years that you don't itemize. Instead, you postpone them to years when you do itemize and, therefore, get credit for them.

Look to Capital Gains and Dividend Income

Recall from our earlier discussion that capital gains refers to the amount by which the selling price of a capital asset—that is, an asset being kept for investment purposes such as stocks, bonds, or real estate—exceeds its purchase price. The example we used was the purchase of 100 shares of Wal-Mart stock for $50 per share and the sale 2 years later of those same shares of Wal-Mart stock for $70 per share. In this case, your capital gains would be $100 \times (\$70 - \$50) = \$2,000$.

If you hold an asset for a year or more, the gain is taxed at a maximum rate of 15 percent for taxpayers whose top tax bracket exceeds 15 percent, and there is no tax for taxpayers in the 10 and 15 percent brackets. At present these rates are set to expire in 2013 unless Congress acts. Thus, if you were in the 35 percent marginal tax bracket, you'd pay less than half your ordinary tax rate.

The other benefit from capital gains is the fact that you don't have to claim it— and, therefore, pay taxes on it—until you sell the asset. In effect, you can postpone paying taxes by not selling the asset. Without question, if you have to pay taxes, it's better to pay 10 years from now than today—that way, you can hold on to your money longer and while you're holding on to it, earn a return on it.

In addition to getting a tax break on capital gains, you also get a tax break on dividend income. Qualified dividends from domestic corporations and qualified foreign corporations are taxed at the same low rates as long-term capital gains. As a result, the maximum rate on qualified dividends is now only 15 percent, and for those in the 10 and 15 percent tax brackets, qualified dividends are tax free.

Shift Income to Family Members in Lower Tax Brackets

Income shifting involves transferring income from family members in high tax brackets to those in lower tax brackets. This process can be complex and involve lawyers and the establishment of **trusts**. A less complicated kind of income shifting involves a relatively simple idea—gifts. You're allowed to give $13,000 per year tax free to as many different people as you like.[9] One of the nice things about annual gifts of less than $13,000 is that the person receiving the gift doesn't pay any taxes either. On annual gifts of $13,000 or less, neither the person who gives nor the person who receives pays any taxes. Best of all, every year you get another gift exclusion that allows you to give $13,000 tax free to as many different people as you like.

Trust
A fiduciary agreement in which one individual holds property for the benefit of another person.

If you're planning on passing your estate on to your children when you die, you might be wise to give some of it away now. That way you can pass on both income and taxes. For example, if Mikel Dimmick is in the 35 percent tax bracket, he might be better off giving his son Izzy, who is in the 10 percent tax bracket, a $13,000 gift rather than keeping the $13,000 for himself. If Mikel gives it as a gift, he doesn't pay taxes on it, and because Izzy is in a lower tax bracket, taxes paid on any future earning on this $13,000 are calculated at a lower rate. As a result, the money grows more than it would otherwise.

Receive Tax-Exempt Income

Interest paid on state and local government debt is tax-exempt for federal income tax purposes. That means if you buy a bond issued by a state or city (a

FACTS OF LIFE

According to a recent *Wall Street Journal* survey, two-fifths of tax-filing adults don't do anything to minimize their taxes.

[9]Based on tax year 2011.

municipal bond), you can collect the interest and not have to pay any taxes on it. For example, in 2011 Newtown, Connecticut, issued $14 million in bonds set to mature in 2024 and 2028. The equivalent taxable yield on a municipal bond is calculated as follows:

$$\text{equivalent taxable yield} = \frac{\text{tax-free yield on the municipal bond}}{(1 - \text{investor's marginal tax bracket})}$$

Thus, if you're in the 28 percent marginal tax bracket, the equivalent taxable yield on a 6 percent municipal bond would be $6\%/(1 - 0.28) = 8.33$ percent. In effect, that means that on an after-tax basis, a taxable bond yielding 8.33 percent and a municipal bond yielding 6 percent are equivalent. The higher your marginal tax bracket, the more beneficial tax-free income is.

Defer Taxes to the Future

401(k) Plan
A tax-deferred retirement plan.

As we've already seen, tax-deferred retirement programs such as traditional IRAs, self-employed retirement or Keogh plans, and **401(k) plans** allow you to defer taxes to the future rather than pay those taxes today. Roth IRAs allow taxes to be paid on the contribution and never again. The idea is to allow you to earn interest on money that would have otherwise already been collected by the IRS.

This concept also applies to capital gains, because you can postpone capital gains taxes until you sell the asset. If you don't recognize all these terms, don't worry. We'll discuss them in depth later in the book. For now, the important point is that saving on a tax-deferred basis has real benefits.

Summary

 Identify and understand the major federal income tax features that affect all taxpayers.

Your taxable income is a function of three numbers—adjusted gross income or AGI, deductions, and exemptions. From there, the tax rates determine how much of the difference between income and deductions will be taken away in taxes. A capital gain is the amount by which the selling price of a capital asset—that is, assets being kept for investment purposes such as stocks or bonds—exceeds its purchase price. Net long-term capital gains less any net short-term capital losses are taxed at a lower maximum rate than ordinary income (short-term gains are treated as ordinary income). In addition to income taxes, you must pay Social Security and Medicare taxes.

 Describe other taxes that you must pay.

In addition to federal income taxes and Social Security, and Medicare taxes, you must pay state and local taxes, excise taxes, sales taxes, property taxes, and gift and estate taxes.

 Understand what is taxable income and how taxes are determined.

To calculate your taxes, you must first determine your total income by summing up your income from all sources. From this amount, adjustments that center on tax-deductible expenses and retirement contributions are subtracted, with the result being adjusted gross income (AGI). From AGI, the deductions (the greater of either the itemized deductions or the standard deduction) and the exemptions are subtracted, with the end result being taxable income.

 4   Choose the tax form that's right for you, file, and survive an audit if necessary.

It is important to understand who must file tax returns, when they must file, what forms to use, electronic filing, and what information is needed to prepare a tax return. Those unable to file by April 15 can request a filing extension from the IRS. In addition, those who discover an error in a prior year's returns can file an amended return.

   Audits can happen to anyone, but are more likely to happen to those with higher incomes or those who are self-employed. The first step in preparing for an audit is to reexamine the areas in which the IRS has questions. Taxpayers who are not satisfied with the outcome of their audit have the right to appeal.

 5   Calculate your income taxes.

For help in filing a tax return, the first place to look is the IRS. There are several good tax books and computer programs that help people prepare their taxes. Tax specialists are people trained—to one degree or another—to help others plan for taxes and prepare their tax returns.

 6   Minimize your taxes.

Five general tax strategies can be used to keep tax bills to a minimum:

- ◆ Maximize deductions.
- ◆ Look to capital gains and dividend income.
- ◆ Shift income to family members in lower tax brackets.
- ◆ Receive tax-exempt income.
- ◆ Defer taxes to the future.

Review Questions

1. How is adjusted gross income different from taxable income?
2. If someone is in the 28 percent marginal tax bracket, is that person's entire income taxed at 28 percent? Why or why not?
3. It can be said that capital gains income is better than interest income because of taxes and timing. Why? Is the same true for dividend income?
4. Briefly explain each filing status. How does filing status affect who must file income taxes? How does filing status affect the standard deduction amount?
5. What is meant by "bracket creep"? What method is employed by the IRS to control "bracket creep"?
6. List the four methods used for collecting income taxes. How is tax withholding affected by the W-4 form?
7. In addition to federal income taxes, what other income-based taxes does the federal government collect? Are these taxes progressive or regressive and how are the taxes calculated?
8. List and describe four non-income-based taxes. Be sure to categorize each tax as either progressive or regressive.

9. What are the three primary types of taxable income, as defined by the IRS?

10. What is taxable income and what is the formula for determining taxable income?

11. What are the major categories of adjustments to gross income? For a taxpayer in the 25 percent marginal tax bracket, how much would adjustments totaling $10,000 save in taxes?

12. List the six most common itemized deductions and describe the limits set on each.

13. What "tests" must be met to qualify as a dependency exemption? As a personal exemption?

14. What is the American Opportunity Credit and what are the eligibility requirements for receiving the credit? How does the credit differ from the Lifetime Learning Credit?

15. What is the maximum allowable taxable income for filing a 1040A or 1040EZ income tax form?

16. Electronic filing of tax returns offers distinct advantages. What are they? What precautions must be taken when using Free File?

17. What federal income tax form is used when filing a late or amended return, and what is the procedure that must be followed?

18. In addition to random selections, what are the four most common "signals" the IRS looks for when selecting taxpayers for audits?

19. What are the three main types of assistance available to the general public for completing their tax forms?

20. What are the five general tax reduction strategies? Give a brief synopsis of each.

Develop Your Skills—Problems and Activities

These problems are available in MyFinanceLab.

1. The Lees, a family of two adults and two dependent children under age 16, had a gross annual income of $68,000 for 2011. Determine their standard deduction, exemption, and child tax credit amounts, as well as their marginal and average tax rates assuming their filing status is married filing jointly.

2. Consider three investors who need to partially liquidate investments to raise cash. In this case, all investments have been held for 3 or more years. Investor A waited for a $1,500 qualified dividend distribution from her mutual fund, and Investor B received $1,500 in interest income from a CD. However, because Investor C could not wait for a distribution, he decided to sell $1,500 of appreciated stock shares. Assuming no commissions, sales charges, or state income tax, and a 25 percent federal marginal tax bracket, which investment will provide the greatest after-tax amount? Would your answer change if all investors were in the 15 percent marginal tax bracket?

3. Sukeeta, a young mother, is preparing to file her 2011 income tax return. Her husband, who was killed in a boating accident in the summer of 2011, always handled the tax filing. Assuming she does not itemize deductions, which filing status should she use? Why? Does she have a choice of status? Which tax form should she use?

4. A couple with three dependent children has an annual adjusted gross income (AGI) of $238,500. Calculate the total dollar amount of personal exemptions that they can claim for the 2011 tax year.

5. Bee and Barney Mayberry have $71,500 in gross income and enough allowable deductions to itemize. Determine the best income tax form for them to use if they are filing jointly. Explain the major reason they can't use the other forms.

6. Calculate the total 2011 tax liability for a single parent of one dependent child with a gross income of $46,250, no salary reductions for employer provided benefits, and no itemized deductions.

7. Using the married filing jointly status and their income and expense statement, calculate the 2011 tax liability for Shameka and Curtis Williams. First use the standard deduction, and then use the following itemized deductions:

Income

| Earned income | $53,000 |
| Interest income | 2,100 |

Expenses

Home mortgage interest	7,900
Real estate and state income taxes	5,850
Miscellaneous deductions	800

Briefly explain to the Williamses which method they should use and why.

8. Given the following information, would it be better for Illinois resident Salem Marcos to itemize her sales tax or her state income tax on her federal tax return?

Federal taxable income	$47,900
Federal marginal income tax rate	25%
State taxable income	$41,250
State marginal income tax rate	3%
Total sales tax paid	$1,300

9. Calculate the Lifetime Learning tax credit available to a single filer earning $40,000 per year if she spent $8,500 on qualified education expenses during 2011.

10. Calculate the 2011 total tax for Gordon Geist, a single taxpayer without dependents and no itemized deductions. He has an active income of $40,000, a short-term capital gain income of $4,000 from the sale of stock, and $7,800 from book royalties.

11. Aliza Grajek is a self-employed nurse with a 2011 gross income of $68,000 and taxable annual income (federal and state) of $55,000 after adjustments, exemptions, and deductions. Calculate her total 2011 income tax liability, including federal, state (5.75 percent), and FICA taxes.

12. Mrs. Hubbard, a mother of two, has been selected for an audit. Advise her on what to do to prepare for the audit and what to do if the audit does not turn out favorably.

13. Harry and Harriet Potter are in their golden years. Discuss the best tax reduction method for them to use in reducing their estate taxes.

Learn by Doing—Suggested Projects

1. Review Figure 4.1 and complete one of the following projects:

   a. Is the advice to "defer income and accelerate deductions" always a good tax planning strategy? Given the projected demands on Social Security and the possibility of rising marginal tax rates, is that good advice for the next few years?

b. As a group, select different dates and research the marginal tax brackets and income ranges for each. What social, political, or economic events were cited to explain the rates? Did specific events trigger changes in the rates? Were presidents applauded or criticized for rate changes that occurred during their administrations? Report your findings to the class.

2. Write a one-page paper discussing why taxes are withheld directly from your pay rather than collected on an annual basis. Also, explain how the amount of taxes withheld is determined.

3. Calculate your income tax liability using two approaches. First, assume that your parents claim you as a dependent. What is your tax liability? Second, assume that you are independent and claim yourself as a dependent. What is your tax liability? Explain the difference.

4. Estimate your non-income-based tax expenditures for the last 6 months. Consider sales taxes, excise taxes, and personal property taxes.

   (*Hints:* To estimate your *personal property taxes*, consult your tax statements or talk with your parents about the taxes on your vehicle (if applicable). To estimate your *sales taxes*, call the applicable state Department of Commerce to determine the tax rates and on what items the taxes are collected. To estimate your *excise taxes*, call the state Department of Commerce to establish the tax rates on items such as tobacco, gasoline, and alcohol. Excise taxes are also collected on phone usage; to get this figure, consult your phone bill.)

5. Save all of your sales receipts for 1 month. At the end of the month calculate the total sales tax paid and annualize the amount by multiplying it by 12. Compare this amount to your total state income tax withheld or paid for the previous year. If everything remained the same and you were able to itemize deductions on your federal taxes, would you be better off itemizing your state income tax or sales tax?

6. Using the information in this chapter, determine which tax form you should use and outline the types of records you will need. Talk with several taxpayers in different socioeconomic groups or stages in the financial life cycle about their tax record-keeping methods. Question them about how their methods have evolved as their situations have changed. Report to your class.

7. Prepare yourself for an audit by collecting all relevant tax records from the last year. Include all pay stubs that verify deductions, credit card bills and their matching receipts that verify tax-deductible expenditures, and all bank account statements. Now grade yourself on how well you are prepared for an audit.

8. Call a certified public accountant (CPA) or enrolled agent and explain that you are a student currently studying taxes. Ask the accountant to explain three of the most commonly recommended tax saving strategies and three of the most commonly audited tax return sections. Prepare a report on your findings.

9. Talk to your parents about their taxes. Do they follow any of the five tax reduction strategies presented in this chapter? Talk to them about the benefit of following one or more of these strategies. Summarize your discussion in a short paper.

Be a Financial Planner—Discussion Case 1

This case is available in MyFinanceLab.

Holly and Zachary Neal, from Dublin, Virginia, are preparing to file their 2011 income taxes. Their children are grown; however, Holly's mother, Martha, has moved in with them so Holly is no longer working. Martha is dependent on their income for support except for her $536 monthly Social Security benefit.

Zachary works for a software company and earns enough to keep their heads above water; however, he had to discontinue participation in his retirement plan so they could pay the bills. Holly is taking this opportunity to work toward her master's degree. They know they will file jointly but need your help preparing their tax return. They have gathered all of the appropriate records, as follows:

1099-DIV, Capital Gains, short-term	$900
Zachary's W-2, Wage and Tax Statement	$54,500
Gambling winnings	$1,500
Inheritance	$35,000
Holly and Zach's aggregate traditional IRA contribution	$5,000
Martha's unreimbursed medical expenses	$5,100
The Neals' unreimbursed medical expenses	$1,700
Martha's total living expenses, excluding medical	$13,000
State taxes withheld and owed	$2,280
Mortgage interest expense	$6,000
Holly's student loan interest payments	$590
Holly's education expense	$5,450

Questions

1. Is Martha's unreimbursed medical expense deductible on the Neals' tax return? Why?
2. Is Martha required to file a tax return? Why or why not?
3. What tax advantage(s), attributable to Holly's education expenses, can the Neals include on their return?
4. How much of the total medical expenses will the Neals be able to deduct on their taxes?
5. Can the Neals' IRA contributions be deducted on their tax return? If so, to what extent?
6. Would the Neals benefit from itemizing their deductions? Why?
7. Calculate the Neals' total 2011 tax liability using the method most advantageous to them.
8. Should Zach have his employer adjust his federal tax withholding amount? Why or why not?

Be a Financial Planner—Discussion Case 2

This case is available in MyFinanceLab.

Austin and Anya Gould are a middle-aged couple with two children, Rusty, age 13 and Sam, age 11, whom they adopted this year. They also bought a new home in the area to give the children a yard in which to play. The Goulds also have an extensive retirement portfolio invested primarily in growth-oriented mutual funds. Their annual investment income is only $500, none of which is attributable to capital gains. Austin works in the banking industry and receives an annual income of $32,500. Anya, who owns the only travel agency in town, makes about $40,000 a year.

The Goulds give extensively to charities. They also have tax deductions from their mortgage interest expense, business expenses, tax expenses, and unreimbursed medical expenses, as follows:

Health insurance (provided by Anya)	$2,200
Rusty's braces	$1,500
Mortgage interest expense	$7,200

Real estate taxes	$900
Investment and tax planning expenses	$1,450
Other medical expenses	$3,600
Charitable contributions	$3,500
Moving expenses	$3,000
Austin's unreimbursed business expenses	$2,300
Qualified adoption expenses	$6,700
State taxes withheld and owed	$4,000

Remember that Anya has some special tax expense deductions because she is self-employed. Be sure to include them when estimating their 2011 taxes.

Questions

1. Calculate Anya's Social Security and Medicare taxes. Calculate how much of the taxes are deductible.
2. Calculate the Goulds' total income and adjusted gross income for the year.
3. Are the moving expenses deductible? Why or why not?
4. Should the Goulds take the standard deduction or should they itemize? What is the amount of their deduction?
5. What tax form will the Goulds use? Why?
6. What credits might the Goulds use to reduce their tax liability?

Be a Financial Planner—Continuing Case: Cory and Tisha Dumont

The objective of the Continuing Case study is to help you synthesize and integrate the various financial planning concepts you have been learning. The case will help you apply your knowledge of constructing financial statements, assessing financial data and resources, calculating taxes, measuring risk exposures, creating specific financial plans for accumulating assets, and analyzing strengths and weaknesses in financial situations.

At the end of each book section you'll be asked to help Cory and Tisha Dumont answer their personal finance questions. By the end of the book you'll know more about Cory and Tisha than you can imagine. Who knows, maybe you will have encountered, or will encounter, the same issues that face the Dumonts. After helping the Dumonts answer their questions, perhaps you will be better equipped to achieve your own financial goals!

Background

Cory and Tisha Dumont recently read an article on personal financial planning in *Money*. The article discussed common financial dilemmas that families face throughout the life cycle. After reading the article, Cory and Tisha realized they have a lot to learn. They are considering enrolling in a personal finance course at their local university, but feel they need more urgent help right now. Based on record-keeping suggestions in the *Money* article, Cory and Tisha have put together the following information to help you answer their personal finance questions.

1. *Family:* Cory and Tisha met in college when they were in their early 20s. They continued to date after graduation, and 6 years ago got married. Cory is 31 years old. Tisha is 30 years old. Their son Chad just turned 4 years old and their daughter, Haley, is 2 years old. They also have a very fat tabby cat named Ms. Cat.

2. *Employment:* Cory works as a store manager and makes $38,000 a year. Tisha works as an accountant and earns $46,000 a year.

3. *Housing:* The Dumonts currently rent a three-bedroom town home for $1,100 per month, but they hope to buy a house. Tisha indicated that she would like to purchase a home within the next 3 to 5 years. The Dumonts are well on their way to achieving their goal. They opted for a small wedding and applied all gifts and family contributions to a market index mutual fund for their "dream" house. When they last checked, the fund account had a balance of $13,000.

Financial Concerns

1. *Taxes:* Cory and Tisha have been surprised at the amount of federal, state, Social Security, and Medicare taxes withheld from their pay. They aren't sure if the tax calculations are correct.

2. *Insurance:* They are also unsure about the amount of automobile, home, health, and life insurance they need. Up until this point, they have always chosen the lowest premiums without much regard to coverage. They were a little amazed to learn recently that the cash value of Tisha's life insurance policy is only $1,800, although they have paid annual premiums of $720 for several years.

3. *Credit and cash management:* Cory and Tisha are also curious about the use of credit. It seems they receive new credit card offers each week that promise a low interest rate and other bonuses. They aren't sure if they should be taking advantage of these offers or keeping their current credit cards. They are often surprised by the amount charged on their monthly credit card statements, and although they make a $100 payment each month, their combined account balances always seem to hover around $1,300. It is common for them to withdraw money from bank ATMs to cover daily expenses, and they usually carry about $100 in cash between them. Even so, it seems they often rely on their credit cards to make ends meet.

4. *Savings:* Cory and Tisha were intrigued by one of the recommendations made in the *Money* article: "Pay yourself first." In fact, it was this statement that prompted the Dumonts to review their finances. They like the concept, but are unsure of how to go about implementing such a goal. They currently have a savings account balance of $2,500 that earns 3 percent in annual interest. The bank where they have their checking account requires them to keep a minimum balance of $1,000 in order to earn annual interest of 0.75 percent. Their current checking account balance is $1,800.

5. *College savings:* Cory and Tisha are concerned about college expenses for Chad and Haley, as they have experienced the impact of long-term student loan payments on their own financial situation.

6. *Retirement savings:* Cory and Tisha both know that they participate in a "qualified retirement plan" at work, but they don't know exactly what that means. They do not currently have an individual retirement arrangement (IRA) or access to profit-sharing plans. A recent statement from Cory's former employer indicated a value of $2,500 in retirement funds that he left with that company.

7. *Risk:* Cory is quick to point out that he doesn't like financial surprises. Tisha, on the other hand, indicated that she is willing to take financial risks when she thinks the returns are worthwhile.

8. *Estate planning issues:* The Dumonts do not have a will or any other estate planning documents.

9. *Recreation and health:* Cory and Tisha enjoy bicycling and hiking with Chad and Haley. They also enjoy playing golf and have considered joining a golf club that charges a $250 monthly fee. The Dumonts are in good health, although they think that Chad will need glasses and braces in the next few years.

Additional Information

Other Estimated Annual Expenditures

Food (at home and dining out)	$6,200
Clothing	$3,100
Auto insurance	$1,800
Transportation (use, maintenance, licensing)	$1,900
Dental and health care	$750
Life insurance for Tisha	$720
Medical insurance (pre-tax employer deduction for a family plan, Tisha)	$2,700
401(k) retirement contribution (pre-tax employer deduction, Cory)	$1,900
401(k) retirement contribution (pre-tax employer deduction, Tisha)	$2,300
Renter's insurance	$200
Utilities (electricity, water/sewer, cable/Internet)	$3,600
Entertainment	$1,500
Telecommunications (cell phones)	$900
Taxes (federal, state, Medicare, Social Security, employer deduction)	$15,000
Property taxes (auto)	$695
Charity donations	$1,200
Day care	$9,700
Savings	$1,000
Miscellaneous	$2,000

Other Assets:

- ◆ Automobile No. 1

  2-year-old, midsize SUV with a fair market value (FMV) of $14,800
  Amount owed: $12,925 (36 months remaining on the loan)
  Monthly payment: $405
- ◆ Automobile No. 2

  4-year-old, 2-door coupe with a FMV of $7,800
  Amount owed: $0
- ◆ Household furniture, electronics, and other personal property worth approximately $12,000
- ◆ Antique jewelry

  Tisha received this as an inheritance from her grandmother and said that she would never part with it. The jewelry has an estimated value of $19,700.
- ◆ When Tisha turned 21 her father gave her 100 shares of the Great Basin Balanced Mutual Fund worth $1,000. Today the fund is worth $2,300.

Other Consumer Debt:

- ◆ Credit card debt (Visa, MasterCard, Discover, American Express, and several store cards)

$1,300 revolving outstanding balance

$50 minimum monthly payments (approximate)

$100 actual monthly payments

◆ Student loan debt (for Cory)

$8,200 balance

$196 monthly payment (48 months remaining on the loan)

$652 interest payment for 2007

◆ Furniture company loan

$5,300 balance

$210 monthly payment (30 months remaining on the loan)

Part I: Financial Planning

Questions

1. Identify the stage of the life cycle that best describes Cory and Tisha today. What important financial planning issues characterize this stage?

2. Based on the issues identified in question 1 and your knowledge of the Dumont household, help Cory and Tisha complete Worksheet 1 to identify their short-term, intermediate-term, and long-term financial goals.

3. Complete Worksheet 5 for the Dumonts. (*Hint:* Data are presented both as background material and as listed annual expenses.)

4. Develop a balance sheet for the Dumonts using Worksheet 4. Do they have a positive or negative net worth?

5. Using information from the income and expense statements and the balance sheet, calculate the following ratios:

a. Current ratio

b. Monthly living expense covered ratio

c. Debt ratio

d. Long-term debt coverage ratio

e. Savings ratio

6. Use the information provided by the ratio analysis to assess the Dumonts' financial health. (*Hint:* Use the recommended ratio limits provided in Chapter 2 as guidelines for measuring the Dumonts' financial flexibility and liquidity.) What recommendations would you make to improve their financial health?

7. Do the Dumonts have an emergency fund? Should they? How much would you recommend that they have in an emergency fund?

8. According to the *Money* article that Cory and Tisha read, they can expect to pay about $100,000 in tuition and related college expenses when Chad enters college and even more for Haley. The Dumonts hope that Chad will receive academic scholarships that will reduce their total college costs to about $40,000. Assuming that the Dumonts started a college savings program today and managed to earn 9 percent a year, ignoring taxes, until Chad was 18, how much would they need to save at the end of each year? How much will the Dumonts need to save each year if Chad does not receive scholarships? See Chapter 3.

9. How much will the Dumonts need to save at the beginning of each year to accumulate $40,000 for Haley to attend college if they can earn 9 percent on their savings? Assuming that the Dumonts need to accumulate $110,000 to fund all of Haley's college expenses, how much do they need to save at the beginning of each year? If, instead, they saved money at the end of each year, how much will

they need to put away every year to meet the $110,000 goal if they can earn 9 percent compounded annually starting today? See Chapter 3.

10. How much will Tisha's Great Basin Balanced Mutual Fund shares (currently valued at $2,300) be worth when Chad enters college, assuming the fund returns 7 percent after taxes on an annualized basis? How much will the shares be worth when Haley turns 18 years old? What will be the value of the shares when Tisha retires at age 67, assuming a 9 percent after-tax return and no deductions from the account? What has been the actual annualized rate of return for the fund since Tisha received it as a gift? See Chapter 3.

11. Recall that the Dumonts set up a savings fund for a future down payment with gifts and contributions from their wedding. How much will this market index fund valued at $13,000 be worth in 3, 5, and 7 years if they can earn a current rate of return of 6 percent? How much will the fund be worth in 3, 5, and 7 years if they could obtain an 8 percent rate of return? See Chapter 3.

12. Assuming an 8 percent return for the current year from their market index fund valued at $13,000, and a 15 percent federal marginal tax rate, how much will the Dumonts pay in taxes on their investment, either from their savings or current income, this year? By how much, after taxes, will their account grow this year? See Chapters 3 and 4.

13. Assuming that Cory does nothing with his 401(k) retirement account from his former employer, and the account grows at a rate of 5 percent annually, how much will Cory have when he retires at 67? If, instead, Cory took control of the money and invested it in a tax-deferred IRA account earning 10 percent annually, how much would he have at age 67? See Chapter 3.

14. Using the income and expense estimates provided by Tisha, calculate the Dumonts' taxable income using the 2011 tax information provided in the text. (*Note*: Ignore unearned taxable income from savings and investments.)

    a. Do the Dumonts have enough tax-deductible expenses to itemize deductions?

    b. Explain the tax ramifications of Cory's student loan interest, estimated to be $652, for 2011.

    c. How much Social Security and Medicare taxes are withheld from Cory and Tisha's income?

    d. What is the Dumonts' total federal income tax liability?

    e. Do the Dumonts qualify for the child tax credit? If so, how will it affect their federal income tax liability? How will a payment or refund be determined?

15. Assume the Dumonts' marginal state income tax rate is 5.75 percent calculated on the basis of the total federal taxable income. Calculate their state tax liability.

16. Based on the total Social Security tax, Medicare tax, federal income tax, and state income tax liabilities calculated above, how close did Tisha come in estimating their tax liability? How does the difference between the estimated and actual tax liabilities change their financial situation? What recommendations would you make?

17. Calculate and interpret for Cory and Tisha the differences between their marginal, average, and effective marginal tax rates. How might these rates change with life events, such as salary increases or the purchase of their home?

PART 2

Managing Your Money

Now that you have an understanding of the financial planning process, it is time to turn to managing your money. This involves not only making sure that you have adequate liquidity, but that your borrowing habits don't keep you from meeting your personal financial goals, and that when you spend money, you do it wisely.

Part 2 begins with an examination of cash and liquidity management with the goal of understanding how to manage your liquid funds effectively. We will then take a look at the use of credit cards and consumer loans. As you may already know, there may not be a more dangerous threat to your financial well-being than credit cards. We will also look at what determines your credit score and how to keep it in good shape. Finally, we will look at smart ways to spend your money, specifically focusing on two of the biggest purchases you will ever make—your car and your home.

In Part 2, we will concentrate on principles 5 and 6:

Principle 5: Stuff Happens, or the Importance of Liquidity—While much of personal financial planning focuses on achieving lifetime goals, it is impossible to reach those goals if you aren't prepared for the unexpected such as the untimely death of a car, the loss of a job, or an injury.

Principle 6: Waste Not, Want Not—Smart Spending Matters—Financial planning and managing your money involves more than just saving and investing; it also involves spending, specifically smart spending. Money isn't easy to come by, so you don't want to waste it.

In addition, we will also touch on these principles:

Principle 1: The Best Protection Is Knowledge

Principle 3: The Time Value of Money

Principle 8: Risk and Return Go Hand in Hand

Principle 10: Just Do It!

5 Cash or Liquid Asset Management

Learning Objectives

 Manage your cash and understand why you need liquid assets.

 Automate your savings.

 Choose from among the different types of financial institutions that provide cash management services.

 Compare the various cash management alternatives.

 Compare rates on the different liquid investment alternatives.

 Establish and use a checking account.

 Transfer funds electronically and understand how electronic funds transfers (EFTs) work.

As we pointed out in Chapter 1, if there's one thing we learned from the recent financial crisis, it's that everyone needs an emergency fund—because let's face it, stuff happens—anyone can lose their job, get sick, or get in an accident. And that was one of the prime messages from the ABC special "Unbroke" which featured a short film where a very nervous Marisa Tomei meets Antonio Banderas on a speed date—and falls for his . . . emergency fund.

"Dating makes a lot of people nervous," Antonio begins as he first meets his speed date.

"No, I'm not nervous about dating; we've only got a few seconds to get to know each other. I'm nervous about money, I'm nervous about the economy, I'm nervous about losing my job. I have a kid, oh; I shouldn't have told you that, do you like kids? Do you have kids? Are you nervous, oh, you're so cute, oh, I shouldn't have said that either."

"I adore children and I'm not nervous about the economy," Antonio replies.

"Oh, why are you rich?"

"No, no, I have relatively modest income, but I always have an emergency fund, 6 months living expenses set aside."

Marisa sits back in her chair, eyes wide, as a slow smile emerges.

"Are you looking for that rich man?" asks Antonio.

"Oh no, no, a man is not a financial plan . . . but an emergency fund, that's a good idea."

We all need an emergency fund—it's definitely a good idea. You've got to plan for the unexpected, that's the whole idea behind **Principle 5: Stuff Happens, or the Importance of Liquidity**.

Unless you're a psychic, you can't predict the unexpected (it wouldn't be unexpected then, would it?), but you can prepare for it. How? By keeping some liquid funds— what most people call an emergency fund—available. Living without an emergency fund is like walking on a high wire without a safety net—it's just something smart people don't do. You've got to plan for the unexpected, and as many people recently learned the hard way, the unexpected sometimes happens. That's why one of your first tasks is to put aside an emergency fund. After all, don't risk financial ruin to an unforeseen expense. Having an emergency fund available is part of good personal financial management, and in this chapter we discuss how to effectively manage the liquid funds that make up your emergency fund. After all, when you think about it, "an emergency fund, that's a good idea."

Managing Liquid Assets

Manage your cash and understand why you need liquid assets.

Cash Management
The management of cash and near cash (liquid) assets.

Cash management is deciding how much to keep in liquid assets and where to keep it. Thirty years ago, cash management meant depositing your cash in a checking or savings account at a local bank. All banks were pretty much the same and their

Liquid Assets
Cash and investments that can easily be converted into cash, such as checking accounts, money market funds, and certificates of deposit (CDs).

services were limited. Today, the situation is very different: Sparked by less regulation and increased competition, banks and other financial institutions offer an array of account types and investments. To understand the underlying logic behind modern cash management, and thus learn how to manage your **liquid assets**, we need to understand the differences in financial institutions and the products and services they offer.

Cash management means not only making choices from among all the alternatives, but also maintaining and managing the results of those choices. Why do you need to keep some of your money in liquid assets? So you can pay your bills and your other normal living expenses, as well as have money to cover unexpected expenses, without having to dip into your long-term investments—that is, so you aren't forced to sell stocks or real estate when you don't want to.

One way to think of liquid assets is as a reservoir, with money moving in as wages are received and moving out as living expenditures. In effect, money moves in and out, and an adequate level of liquid assets keeps this reservoir from running dry. Hey, you don't want your liquid assets to evaporate!

Just as with everything else in personal finance, there are risk-return trade-offs associated with keeping money in the form of liquid assets—it's **Principle 8: Risk and Return Go Hand in Hand** in action. Because liquid assets can be turned into cash quickly and with no loss, they have little risk associated with them. However, because they have little risk, they don't provide a high return. Simply put, liquid assets are characterized by low risk and low expected return. It's really the low risk that's important in cash management.

There's another type of risk associated with keeping liquid assets: The more cash you have, the more you're tempted to spend. Remember your cash budget from Chapter 2? Well, the easiest way to blow your budget is by walking around a mall with your debit card in your wallet or a pocketful of cash. Don't worry, though—even if you lack self-restraint, cash management can help. You see, cash management doesn't just involve deciding where to keep your cash, it involves managing your money and staying on your budget.

FACTS OF LIFE

One problem with carrying cash is that it's easy to spend and many times you can't even recall where you spent it. According to a recent survey, every year about $2,340 in cash "disappears" from Americans' wallets—they simply lose track of that much spending.

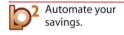
 Automate your savings.

Automating Savings: Pay Yourself First

You can easily use cash management alternatives to automate your savings by having income automatically deducted from your paycheck and placed into savings. It all boils down to paying yourself first. As **Principle 10: Just Do It!** points out, if you don't start, it won't happen. Automating your savings is a great way to make saving less of a chore, and you're less likely to spend money that never becomes part of your liquid assets reservoir. If you have some of your income automatically deducted from your paycheck and placed in savings, you can learn to live within your budget.

Moreover, as you know from **Principle 3: The Time Value of Money**, the earlier you start, the easier it is to achieve your goals. Don't put off financial discipline until you're "making more money"—start today.

Many cash management alternatives lend themselves well to an automated deposit program, and we'll take a look at several of them in this chapter. The advantage of the automated payroll deduction plan is that not only is the money withdrawn from your pay before you get a chance to think about spending it, but it's immediately deposited in an account to earn interest. Thus, your money is immediately put to work.

Financial Institutions

Before we examine the different types of liquid asset accounts, let's take a look at the financial institutions that offer them. As we mentioned earlier, the differences between a traditional bank and other types of financial institutions have narrowed dramatically in the last few decades. Although it's sometimes difficult to differentiate between types of financial institutions, they can be categorized as **deposit-type financial institutions**, which are commonly referred to as "banks," or **nondeposit-type financial institutions** such as mutual funds and brokerage firms. But as you'll see, the distinction between these institutions can be a bit arbitrary.

"Banks" or Deposit-Type Financial Institutions

Financial institutions that provide traditional checking and savings accounts are commonly called "banks" or deposit-type financial institutions. Technically, many of these institutions aren't actually banks but are, in fact, other types of financial institutions that act very similarly to banks. Table 5.1 provides a summary of the different deposit-type financial institutions.

Nondeposit-Type Financial Institutions

Today, mutual fund companies, stockbrokerage firms, insurance companies, and some other firms have moved into what used to be banking territory and have begun offering services that look an awful lot like those offered by banks. For example, you can have a checking account with Merrill Lynch, a consumer loan with General Motors, and a home mortgage with General Electric. This banking competition from outside the traditional banking industry is a relatively recent occurrence, with its roots in the deregulation of the 1980s. However, the competition has been a two-way street. While the deregulation has allowed brokerage firms to offer traditional banking services, it has also let banks offer services traditionally found only at investment companies. Table 5.2 provides a summary of different nondeposit-type financial institutions.

 3 Choose from among the different types of financial institutions that provide cash management services.

Deposit-Type Financial Institutions
Financial institutions that provide traditional checking and savings accounts. Commonly referred to as "banks."

Nondeposit-Type Financial Institutions
Financial institutions such as mutual funds and stock brokerage firms, which don't provide checking and savings accounts.

TABLE 5.1 "Banks" or Deposit-Type Financial Institutions	
Commercial Banks	These offer the widest variety of financial services, including checking and savings accounts, credit cards, safety-deposit boxes, financial consulting, and all types of lending services. They also dominate in terms of the dollar value of the assets they hold and they have more branch offices or locations than any other type of financial institution. They also tend to have neighborhood locations which allow for personal relationships.
Savings and Loan Associations (S&Ls or "thrifts")	Originally established to provide mortgage loans to depositors; today, services offered by S&Ls and commercial banks have become very similar, with both offering almost identical savings alternatives. However, S&Ls often earn one-quarter percent more than savings accounts at competing commercial banks.
Savings Banks	Savings banks are close cousins to savings and loan associations and are generally found in the northeastern United States. Their primary purpose historically has been to provide mortgage funding to their depositors.
Credit Unions	Credit unions are established by a wide variety of organizations such as churches, universities, trade unions, and corporations. They are open only to members of that organization and are quite similar to commercial banks and S&Ls. Because of their tax-exempt status as not-for-profit organizations, they are generally more efficient, often pay higher interest rates, have lower fees, and have more favorable loan rates than commercial banks.

TABLE 5.2 Nondeposit-Type Financial Institutions	
Mutual Funds	A mutual fund is an investment fund that raises money from investors, pools that money, and invests it in a collection of stocks and/or bonds that is managed by a professional investment manager. Mutual funds earn dividends on stocks and interest on bonds, and pay out this income to the fund owners in distributions.
Stockbrokerage Firms	Stockbrokerage firms that have traditionally dealt only with investments such as stocks (hence, their name) have recently introduced a wide variety of cash management tools, including financial counseling, credit cards, and their own money market mutual funds (which we'll talk about later). In effect, they've entered into direct competition with traditional banks.

Online Banking

Online Banking
The ability to perform banking operations through your personal computer.

Online banking—access to your accounts, and the ability to conduct business transactions, through the Internet, a mobile phone, or some other online device—is a service offered by banks, S&Ls, credit unions, and other financial institutions. With online banking you may be able to:

◆ Access your accounts at any time of day.
◆ Check your balances and see when checks have cleared and when deposits have been made.
◆ Transfer funds between accounts.
◆ Download your financial information directly into your personal financial or tax software.
◆ Pay bills and receive payments online.

Online banking also allows you to choose an Internet-only bank if you wish. An Internet-only bank is one that does not have physical branches, and as a result, you can only access it through the Internet. Because of the cost savings that Internet-only banks experience, many times they provide higher interest rates and lower fees than traditional banks. Table 5.3 provides a listing of the advantages and disadvantages of online banking.

What to Look for in a Financial Institution

So how do you choose among all these alternatives? Well, in order to know, you need answers to these questions:

◆ Which financial institution offers the kind of services you want and need? Let's say you want to open a checking account, a money market account, and you need a $5,000 home equity loan. Look to institutions that offer these products.
◆ Is your investment safe? Is your investment insured? Is this financial institution sound?
◆ What are all the costs and returns associated with the services you want? Find out whether there are minimum deposit requirements or hidden fees. Look for the lowest costs and highest returns.

Once you've answered these questions, look at the personal service offered. You want a financial institution that will work for you—one where you can talk to and get to know the manager. The more personal the relationship you have with your financial institution, the more you'll be able to adapt its services to your needs, and

TABLE 5.3 Online Banking

Advantages of Online Banking

- **Personal financial management support:** You can import data into a personal finance program such as Mini.com, Quicken, Microsoft Money, or TurboTax.
- **Convenience:** View and track your accounts, pay bills, view up-to-the minute credit card activity anytime, from anywhere.
- **Efficiency:** You can access and manage all of your bank accounts, including IRAs, CDs, even securities, from one secure site, and transfer funds between your checking and savings accounts, or to another customer's account.
- **Effectiveness:** Many online banking sites provide stock quotes, rate alerts, and personal financial management support that allows you to import data into a personal finance program such as Mint.com.

Disadvantages of Online Banking

- **Start-up time:** It takes time and some effort to register for your bank's online program. If you are setting up an account together with a spouse, you may have to sign a durable power of attorney before the bank will display all of your holdings together.
- **Adapting to online banking:** Banking sites can be difficult to navigate at first, so expect to spend some time working through the tutorial. In addition, these sites periodically change, which may require re-entering data.
- **Feeling comfortable:** Many people just don't feel comfortable banking online, and regardless of how comfortable you feel, you should always print the transaction receipt and keep it with your bank records until it shows up on your bank statement.
- **Customer service:** The potential for poor customer service is a downside to online banking.

the better you'll feel about your investment. Also consider convenience. You want an institution with a convenient location and convenient hours.

Finally, there's no reason why you should limit yourself to one institution. In fact, financial institutions have different strengths and offer different services at different costs. Feel free to mix and match to take advantage of their different strengths and rates, and to get the best and most appropriate services you can.

Cash Management Alternatives

 4 Compare the various cash management alternatives.

Now that we know what kinds of financial institutions exist, let's take a look at the cash management alternatives they offer.

Checking Accounts

A checking account is a federally protected account in which you deposit your liquid funds so you can withdraw them quickly and easily by means of a written check or debit card.

> **Advantages:** Liquid
> Safe—federally insured
> Low minimum balance
> Convenient

Many people use checking accounts as a convenient way of paying bills, which is so much better than carrying around a wad of cash or, worse yet, putting that cash in the mail! Checking accounts are easy to open, often requiring a low minimum balance. In deciding among the available types of checking accounts, it may seem as though there are countless choices, but really there are just two basic types: interest bearing and non-interest bearing. A non-interest-bearing checking account is actually a **demand deposit**. Usually, with a demand deposit account the customer pays for the checking privilege by maintaining a minimum balance or being charged per check.

Demand Deposit
A type of checking account on which no interest is paid.

As you can guess from the name, an interest-bearing checking account pays interest. Another name for an interest-bearing checking account is a **NOW (negotiable order of withdrawal) account**. NOW accounts are simply checking accounts on which you earn interest on your balance.

Everyone knows that an account that pays interest is more desirable from a financial standpoint than an account that doesn't pay interest, right? Not necessarily.

NOW (Negotiable Order of Withdrawal) Account

A checking account on which you earn interest on your balance.

Disadvantages:	Minimum balance required
	Monthly fee
	Opportunity cost
	Pays less than some other alternatives for your money

Receiving interest on your "money in waiting" is good, but read the fine print: If you must maintain a minimum balance and you happen to dip below it, you might not get any interest on your account for that month and you might even have to pay a penalty in addition to your monthly fee.

The monthly fee, of course, represents a cost, but so does the minimum balance, which forces you to hold more money in your checking account than you otherwise would (this is called the forced balance) and it represents what we call the opportunity cost, or the cost of something in terms of the opportunity you forgo to have it. In this case, you could use that minimum balance to pay down your school loan, or to take a trip to the Bahamas.

Even though an interest-bearing checking account pays interest, it generally pays less than other cash management alternatives which we will discuss shortly. Given this and the additional costs, an interest-bearing checking account is not always preferable.

To determine which type of account is better for you, compare the interest you earn on the interest-bearing checking account against any monthly fees that you incur plus any lost interest resulting from holding more money in your checking account than you otherwise would.

Because a checking account is one of the most important liquid assets you'll ever have, we take a much closer look at the mechanics of opening one later in this chapter.

Savings Accounts

Savings Account

A deposit account that pays interest.

A **savings account** allows you to keep your money in a safe, federally insured financial institution while it earns a guaranteed fixed return or interest.

Advantages:	Liquid
	Safe—federally insured
	Earns higher interest than a checking account

A savings account is extremely liquid and gives you relatively quick access to your money. It is also very easy to set up and maintain your account. In the past, withdrawals and other transactions would have been registered in a passbook, which is why many savings accounts used to be called "passbook" accounts. Today, although passbook accounts still exist, statement accounts—where the customer receives a monthly statement of the account's balance and activities—are replacing passbook accounts as the dominant type of savings account.

Disadvantages:	Minimum holding time and/or balance
	Charges/fees
	Low interest rate
	Inconvenient

A savings account is also called a time deposit because you may be required to keep your money deposited for a minimum time period before you can withdraw it. There may be charges if your account dips below a certain balance and there may even be fees charged for inquires on an account balance.

Because savings accounts are extremely liquid, they don't have a high yield. It is important to check the current rate offered by your bank as the going interest rates for a savings account are often much lower than that limit.

Finally, when you want to withdraw your money, you must go to the bank to do so or have the bank mail you a check. No weekend or holiday hours may make it difficult to have access to your funds as quickly as you may need them. Your funds are liquid, but not as accessible as just writing that check.

Money Market Deposit Accounts

A **money market deposit account (MMDA)** is an alternative to the savings accounts offered by commercial banks. It works about the same way a savings account works—you deposit your money in a bank and have access to it through an ATM or by writing a limited number of checks.

> **Money Market Deposit Account (MMDA)**
> A bank account that provides a rate of interest that varies with the current market rate of interest.

    Advantages: Safe—federally insured
                        Earns interest
                        Check-writing privileges

With an MMDA you receive a rate of interest that varies with the current market rate of interest, but it is not a guaranteed fixed rate. The primary advantage of an MMDA over a savings account is that although this rate fluctuates on a weekly basis, it is, in general, higher than the fixed rate paid on savings accounts. In addition, some MMDAs also offer a limited check-writing service, generally six checks per month.

    Disadvantages: High minimum balance/penalties
                            Interest rates below alternatives

When comparing an MMDA to a typical savings account, you might find that it generally requires a higher minimum balance, sometimes as much as $1,000, and imposes penalties if your balance drops below this level. When compared to other investment alternatives such as CDs and mutual funds, which we will look at next, it sometimes pays less interest and suffers from its relative return in addition to the minimum balance required.

Therefore, when considering investing funds in an MMDA, compare all the associated costs with the return, and then compare it to other investment alternatives.

> ### STOP & THINK
>
> You shouldn't be enticed to put your savings in an MMDA just because it pays a bit more than a standard savings account. You must also look carefully at the minimum required balance. Many times this minimum balance forces you to keep more in the MMDA than you would otherwise. If you have a MMDA, what is the minimum balance?

Certificates of Deposit

A **certificate of deposit (CD)** is a savings alternative that pays a fixed rate of interest while keeping your funds on deposit for a set period of time, which can range from 30 days to several years.

> **Certificates of Deposit (CDs)**
> Savings alternatives that pay a fixed rate of interest while keeping your funds on deposit for a set period of time that can range from 30 days to several years.

    Advantages: Safe—federally insured
                        Fixed interest rate (beneficial if interest rates drop)
                        Convenient—buy through payroll deduction plan

CDs are a good place to hold your money until you want to do something else with it. The longer the time period for which the funds are tied up in the CD, the higher the interest rate paid on the CD. Because the interest rate is usually fixed, if interest rates drop you still receive the promised rate. In addition, the rate your CD earns depends on its size; the higher the deposit in the CD, the higher the interest rate. CDs are for money that you have in hand now and want to keep safe. They are generally considered liquid assets because their maturity lengths are fairly short. Maybe you have money now from your summer job with College Pro Painters that you plan to use for *next* year's tuition. A CD will hold that money out of temptation's way and return more than will a general savings account.

>**Disadvantages:** Penalty for early withdrawal
>Fixed interest rate (bad if interest rates rise)
>Minimum deposit required

With a CD, one of the trade-offs is loss of liquidity versus higher return. If you need your money before the CD matures or comes due, you may face an early withdrawal penalty. Knowing how much money you will receive at maturity is a good thing, but with the locked-in rate of interest, if interest rates rise the interest you receive on your CD stays fixed at its lower rate.

The rate you can earn on a CD varies from bank to bank and between banks and other institutions that offer them, such as brokerage firms. Interestingly, banks use CDs as a marketing tool to lure new customers by offering high interest rates. To find the best interest rate, you may need to look a little further than just your neighborhood. The interest rate offered on CDs can vary dramatically from region to region—in fact, in the past differences of 2 percent or more have been common. To research rates offered by institutions both inside and outside your local area, try BankRate.com (**www.bankrate.com**) where you can find the best rates in the country. The bottom line is that if you're considering investing in a CD, search nationally. Purchasing a CD from a financial institution in another geographic region usually entails simply wiring or mailing your funds to the target bank, and sometimes your local bank will match those rates found elsewhere. It's certainly worth a try!

Money Market Mutual Funds

Money Market Mutual Funds (MMMFs)
Mutual funds that invest in short-term (generally with a maturity of less than 90 days) notes of very high denomination.

Money market mutual funds (MMMFs) provide an interesting alternative to traditional liquid investments offered by financial institutions. Investors in MMMFs receive interest on a pool of investments less an administrative fee, which is usually less than 1 percent of the total investment. An MMMF draws together the savings of many individuals and invests those funds in very large, credit worthy debt issued by the government or by large corporations.

>**Advantages:** High interest rates
>Check-writing privileges
>Limited risk due to short maturity of investments
>Convenient—buy through payroll deduction plan

By pooling investments, investors can purchase higher-priced investments and, thus, earn a higher rate of return than they could get individually. MMMFs almost always have a higher yield than do bank money market deposit accounts or traditional savings accounts.

The interest rate earned on an MMMF varies daily as interest rates change. Exactly how much more they yield than MMDAs depends of course on the level of interest rates. When rates are low, the difference can drop to less than one-half percent, but when rates are high, it can be several percentage points. When you invest in an MMMF, you purchase shares at the price of $1 per share. You then earn interest on your shares daily, although interest is posted to your account monthly.

One nice feature of MMMFs is that they allow limited check-writing privileges, although there's generally a minimum amount for which the check must be written. However, in an attempt to lure funds away from bank checking accounts, many MMMFs have lifted limits on both the number of checks written and check amounts.

Disadvantages: Administrative fees
Minimum initial investment
Not federally insured
Minimum check amount

For most MMMFs there is a minimum initial investment of between $500 and $2,000, after which there may be a minimum level for subsequent deposits. Remember, too, that MMMFs carry administrative costs.

Although MMMFs are not perfect substitutes for checking accounts, they do provide an attractive place to put excess funds awaiting more permanent investment. They also compare very favorably with savings accounts; the only differences are that money is deposited by mail, withdrawn by writing a check, and is not federally insured.

> **FACTS OF LIFE**
>
> According to a recent survey, 48 percent of Americans suffer from "mystery spending"—that is, they can't identify where they spend cash. Seven percent of those surveyed said they lose track of $100 or more each month.

Asset Management Accounts

An **asset management account** is a comprehensive financial services package offered by a brokerage firm and, recently, some investment banking institutions. It can include banking services such as a checking account, credit card, debit card, an MMMF, loans, automatic payment of any fixed debt such as mortgages, and brokerage services such as buying and selling stocks or bonds, and a system for the direct payment of interest, dividends, and proceeds from security sales into the MMMF.

Advantages: Monthly summary statements
Automatic coordination of money management
Unlimited check writing
High return
Convenient—buy through payroll deduction plan

The parent brokerage firm provides the customer with a monthly statement summarizing all financial activities. These all-purpose accounts were established by brokerage firms primarily to bring new accounts to the firm, but as a result of their comprehensive nature they provide investors with a number of advantages over other cash management alternatives.

The major advantage of an asset management account is that it automatically coordinates the flow of funds into and out of your MMMF. The parent brokerage firm does this with a computer program that "sweeps" funds into and out of the MMMF. For example, interest and dividends received from securities owned are automatically "swept" into the MMMF. Check-writing privileges are unlimited and if you write a check for an amount greater than what is held in your MMMF, securities from the investment portion of your asset management account are automatically sold and the proceeds "swept" into the money market fund to cover the check. Similarly, a deposit into the MMMF automatically goes toward reducing any loans outstanding and thereafter automatically goes into the MMMF.

Although many different variations of the asset management account are offered by different brokers, they really don't involve any management of assets. The only automatic management of assets occurs when stocks are sold to cover checks that exceed the MMMF. For those with numerous security holdings and somewhat complicated financial dealings, an asset management account may be of value. The single, consolidated monthly financial statement is great for tax purposes.

Asset Management Accounts
Comprehensive financial services packages offered by a brokerage firm, which can include a checking account; credit and debit cards; an MMMF; loans; automatic payment of fixed payments such as mortgages; brokerage services (buying and selling stocks or bonds); and a system for the direct payment of interest, dividends, and proceeds from security sales into the MMMF.

Disadvantages: Costly—monthly/quarterly fees and commissions
Minimum initial investment
Not federally insured

In addition to monthly, quarterly, or annual service charges of $50 to $125, there is generally a rather large minimum balance required, ranging upward of $10,000 in stocks and cash. Also, brokerage firms charge commissions on any stock transactions they perform. Thus, although the benefits of an asset management account may be great, they come with a fairly steep price *and no guarantee of return*. The commissions paid on the sale of stocks associated with an asset management account may be much higher than you might have paid if there had been the opportunity to shop around and sell the stock through the least expensive broker.

In short, although these accounts are an interesting alternative cash management tool, you must weigh the service charge, the high minimum balance, and the relatively high commissions on any stock sales against their returns in making your decision. You will find that the benefits and services offered as well as the costs will differ greatly. The theory is that your money is constantly working for you, but there are no guarantees. As with everything else, a bit of research can *possibly* save you a lot of money.

U.S. Treasury Bills, or T-Bills

U.S. Treasury Bills or T-Bills
Short-term notes of debt issued by the federal government, with maturities ranging from 4 weeks to 12 months.

U.S. Treasury bills, or **T-bills**, are short-term notes of debt issued by the federal government, with maturities ranging from 4 weeks to 12 months.

Advantages: Risk-free—guaranteed by federal government
Exempt from state and local taxes
Federal taxes vary with current rates

Denomination
The face value or amount that's returned to the bondholder at maturity. It's also referred to as the bond's par value.

The minimum **denomination** or face value is $1,000. When you purchase a T-bill you don't receive any interest payment. Instead, your interest comes in the form of appreciation. That is, you pay less than its face value, and when the T-bill matures you receive its full face value.

With a T-bill, when you need cash, all you do is sell the T-bill through a broker, which while easy, is less convenient than going to an ATM or writing a check. They are also extremely safe, having been issued by the federal government. In terms of returns, the interest rate carried on T-bills is similar to that on MMMFs. In addition, your return, although subject to federal taxes, isn't subject to state or local taxes.

Disadvantage: Low rate of return because they are risk-free

The only negative associated with T-bills is the fact that you won't get a great return because they are exceptionally safe. Generally, CDs and money market mutual funds will give you a higher rate of interest.

U.S. Savings Bonds

U.S. Savings Bond
A type of security that's actually a loan on which you receive interest, generally every 6 months for the life of the bond. When the bond matures, or comes due, you get back your investment, or "loan." What you get back at maturity is usually the face value of the loan, although the amount you get could be more or less than what you paid for the bond originally.

U.S. Savings Bonds are safe, low-risk savings products issued by the U.S. Treasury Department. When you buy them, you are making a loan to the federal government. They offer a safe place for your money.

Advantages: Safe—return guaranteed by federal government
Affordable—available in low denominations
Taxes—no state or local taxes, exempt from federal taxes if used
for education
Convenient—buy through payroll deduction plan, online, or at
most financial institutions
Redeem at any bank
No sales commissions or fees

During times of stock market uncertainty, many investors look for safer, more conservative investments. We will compare and contrast the traditional Series EE bond with the relatively new Series I bond, which was first issued in September, 1998.

Series EE and Series I bonds are safe investment vehicles because they are backed by the federal government; they can be purchased for as little as $25; they have interest rates that vary over the life of the bonds with no interest due until they are redeemed; they are local and state tax-exempt with federal tax exemption if used for educational purposes; and they recognize the interest income on an accrual or cash basis. They have a 12-month minimum holding period (neither can be cashed in during the first year); they will have a penalty of the last 3 months accumulated interest if redeemed within 5 years of issue (after that time there is no penalty); they can be purchased quite easily through **www.TreasuryDirect.gov**, your local financial institution, or through payroll deduction plans; and they are effortless to redeem at any bank and never have any commissions or fees.

There is a slight difference in how they are sold and issued. Although they both come in paper and electronic formats, the Series EE paper bonds are sold at 50 percent of face value (buy a $50 Series EE bond for $25) whereas the electronic Series EE, and both the paper and electronic Series I, are all sold at face value (the $50 bonds will cost you $50). As of January 1, 2008, an individual can invest a maximum of $5,000 in each category of paper and electronic Series EE and Series I bonds for a total purchase of $20,000 per person.

The other, perhaps more significant, difference is that EE bonds are guaranteed to reach their maturity at face value in 20 years, and continue to pay interest for an additional 10 years. There is no such guarantee for I bonds. All EE bonds sold on or after May 1, 2005, pay a fixed interest rate. I bonds, on the other hand, grow with inflation-indexed earnings for up to 30 years. They usually increase in value every month and their interest is compounded semiannually. The I bond earnings rate is set by a combination of two separate rates: a fixed rate of return and a semiannual inflation rate, which are combined to determine the bond's earnings rate for the next 6 months. The only certainty with I bonds is that the bonds will not fall below the most recent redemption value during any 6-month period.

To get the current rate on Series EE and Series I bonds you can call 800-US-BONDS or check the Web site at **www.savingsbond.gov**.

STOP & THINK

As we saw in the recent economic downturn, one of the mistakes many people made was not having a large enough emergency fund. On the other hand, another common mistake many people make is keeping too much in very liquid assets. They view investments in CDs and MMMFs as "safe." In reality, they're not safe in the sense that they'll have a difficult time keeping pace with inflation, let alone growing in terms of purchasing power. In short, just as too little in liquid assets is dangerous and can be costly when an emergency occurs, too much in liquid assets is dangerous in that you may tie up too much of your savings in low-return investments. As a result, you may not be able to achieve your future goals like retirement. Striking a balance is the key. Why is striking a balance between liquidity and returns so important?

Disadvantages: Low liquidity—must hold for 12 months; penalty if redeemed before 5 years
Long maturity
Interest compounds only semiannually
Limits on how many you can buy per year
Other investments may earn more

Both Series EE and I bonds have features that can make them an attractive investment alternative. But how do they stack up against the other cash management alternatives? In terms of liquidity, not bad; but in terms of liquidity, not that good. Remember, if you cash them in before maturity, you may receive a reduced return. However, if you're using them to save money for a long-term goal such as your child's college tuition, liquidity is not so important. After all, the money is for college, not for emergencies!

Note that although Series HH bonds were discontinued in August 2004, the outstanding ones are secure. You can find out about the rates and terms that apply to those bonds at **www.TreasuryDirect.gov**.

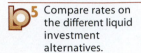

5 Compare rates on the different liquid investment alternatives.

Comparing Cash Management Alternatives

Now that you know what cash management alternatives are available to you, how do you compare them to determine what's best for you? First, you consider service and convenience, but then to decide between them you need to (1) examine returns using comparable interest rates, (2) take into account their tax status, and (3) consider their safety or risk. Table 5.4 provides a summary comparison of the different types of cash management alternatives that we have looked at in this chapter.

TABLE 5.4 Different Cash Management Alternatives

Cash Management Technique	Advantages	Disadvantages
Checking or Demand Deposit Account	Liquid Safe—federally insured Low minimum balance Convenient	Minimum balance required Monthly fee Opportunity cost Pays less than some other alternatives for your money
Savings or Time Deposit Account	Liquid Safe—federally insured Earns higher interest than a checking account	Minimum holding time and/or balance Charges/fees Low interest rate Inconvenient
Money Market Deposit Account	Safe—federally insured Earns interest Check-writing privileges	High minimum balance/penalties Interest rates below alternatives
Certificate of Deposit (CD)	Safe—federally Insured Fixed interest rate (beneficial if interest rates drop) Convenient (buy through payroll deduction plan)	Penalty for early withdrawal Fixed interest rate (bad if interest rates rise) Minimum deposit required
Money Market Mutual Fund	High interest rates Check-writing privileges Limited risk due to short maturity of investments Convenient—buy through payroll deduction plan	Administrative fees Minimum initial investment Not federally insured Minimum check amount
Asset Management Account	Monthly summary statements Automatic coordination of money management Unlimited check writing High return Convenient—buy through payroll deduction plan	Costly—monthly/quarterly fees and commissions Minimum initial investment Not federally insured
U.S. Treasury Bills, or T-Bills	Risk-free—guaranteed by federal government Exempt from state and local taxes Federal taxes vary with current rates	Low rate of return because they are risk-free
U.S. Savings Bonds	Safe—return guaranteed by federal government Affordable—available in low denominations Taxes—no state or local taxes, exempt from federal taxes if used for education Convenient—buy through payroll deduction plan, online, or at most financial institutions Redeem at any bank No sales commissions or fees	Low liquidity—must hold 12 months; penalty if redeemed before 5 years Long maturity Interest compounds only semiannually Limits on how many you can buy per year Other investments may earn more

Comparable Interest Rates

To make intelligent decisions on where to invest your money, you need to compare interest rates. Unfortunately, comparing interest rates is difficult because some rates are quoted as compounded annually, and others are quoted as compounded quarterly or even daily. The only way interest rates can logically be compared is to convert them to some common compounding period. That's what the **annual percentage yield (APY)** is all about.

The Truth in Savings Act of 1993 requires financial institutions to report the rate of interest using the APY so that it's easier for the consumer to make comparisons. The APY converts interest rates compounded for different periods into comparable annual rates, allowing you to compare interest rates easily. However, make sure that you're comparing APYs and not "quoted rates," which may assume different compounding periods.

Once you understand differences in rates, make sure you understand the method used to determine the account balance on which interest will be paid. Is it your actual balance, your lowest monthly balance, or what? The method that's the best for you, the saver, bases interest on your money from the day you deposit it until the day you withdraw it. Fortunately, this is the method most institutions use, but it's still good to make sure.

Annual Percentage Yield (APY)
The simple annual percentage yield that converts interest rates compounded for different periods into comparable annual rates. It allows you to easily compare interest rates.

Tax Considerations

As we saw in Chapter 4, taxes can affect the real rate of return on investments. In comparing the returns on cash management investment alternatives, you must also make sure that the rates you compare are all on the same tax basis—that is, they are all either before- or after-tax calculations. On some investments part of the return is taxable and part is tax-exempt, making these calculations a bit tricky.

As you recall from Chapter 4, calculation of the after-tax return begins with a determination of your marginal tax bracket, the tax rate at which any additional income you receive will be taxed. This marginal tax rate combines the federal and state tax rates that you pay on the investment that you're considering. The **after-tax return** can then be determined as follows:

After-Tax Return
The actual return you earn on taxable investments once taxes have been paid. It is equal to the taxable return (1 − marginal tax rate) + the nontaxable return.

$$\text{after-tax return} = \text{taxable return}(1 - \text{marginal tax rate}) + \text{nontaxable return}$$

Here's an example: Assume you're considering two MMMFs. Fund A is tax-exempt and pays 5 percent, and fund B is taxable and pays 6.5 percent. Further assume that your top tax bracket is 25 percent and you live in a state that doesn't impose income taxes. Which of these two alternatives is better? To compare them, you must put both on an after-tax basis:

$$\text{Fund A's after-tax return} = 5\%$$
(Remember, it's a tax-exempt fund, so it's all nontaxable.)
$$\text{Fund B's after-tax return} = 6.5\% \times (1 - 0.25) = 4.875\%$$

Thus, given your marginal tax bracket, Fund A, which provides a tax-exempt return of 5 percent, is the better of the two alternatives.

Keep in mind that although Fund A may be the better alternative for you, it's not the best alternative for everyone. For example, the after-tax return on Fund B for a person with a marginal tax rate of 10 percent is:

$$\text{Fund B's after-tax return given a 10\% marginal tax bracket}$$
$$= 6.5\% \times (1 - 0.10) = 5.85\%$$

STOP & THINK

The idea behind cash management is to keep money, but not too much, set aside in case there is an emergency. The more you keep set aside, the safer you are, but the money you set aside will be lucky to keep pace with inflation. For example, if you can earn 2 percent on an MMMF, but you are in the 30 percent marginal tax bracket, your after-tax return would be 2%(1 − 0.30) = 1.4%. If inflation were 3 percent, your real return would be −1.6%. Should you be more concerned with your before- or after-tax real return?

Thus, the higher your marginal tax bracket, the more you benefit from a tax-exempt investment.

In calculating the after-tax return, keep in mind that you are interested in the return after *both* federal and state taxes. When calculating the after-tax return on a Treasury bond, which is taxed at the federal but not the state level, you must adjust for federal taxes. Likewise, when calculating the after-tax return on a municipal bond that is tax exempt at the federal but not the state level, you must adjust for state taxes.

Safety

You might think that any deposit in any financial institution is safe. Not so. Some banks and S&Ls take more risk than they should. Sometimes that risk catches up with them, and it's your money that's lost. However, some deposits at financial institutions are insured, and some cash management alternatives are safer than others. To understand how safe your investments are, it's necessary to understand how federal insurance works and how MMMFs operate.

Federal Deposit Insurance Corporation (FDIC)
The federal agency that insures deposits at commercial banks.

National Credit Union Association
The federal agency that insures accounts at credit unions.

Federal Deposit Insurance   Although most liquid investments are quite safe, federal deposit insurance eliminates any questions and worries you might have about safety. The **Federal Deposit Insurance Corporation (FDIC)** insures deposits at commercial banks and S&Ls, and the **National Credit Union Association** insures credit unions. These are federal agencies established to protect you against failures involving financial institutions.

Today, if your account is with a federally insured institution, it's insured for up to $250,000 per depositor (not per account). For example, you may have $190,000 in a savings account and $80,000 in a checking account, both in your name at the same institution. Your combined money ($270,000) will be insured for only $250,000. However, if these accounts were held with one in your name and one in your spouse's name, or if the accounts are in different ownership categories (single accounts, joint accounts, directed retirement accounts, or revocable trust accounts), all would be fully insured. If you would like more coverage, you can simply spread your accounts among different federally insured banks, and each account at each separate bank receives the $250,000 insurance. This insurance guarantees that you'll get back your money, up to the insured limit, if the financial institution goes bust.

Money Market Mutual Funds   Although funds in MMMFs aren't insured, they're invested in a diversified portfolio of government bonds guaranteed by the government and short-term corporate bonds that are virtually risk-free. The safety of an investment in an MMMF comes from the fact that it is well diversified and that investments are limited to very short-term government and corporate debt. Because it takes time for a corporation's problems to become so severe that it defaults on its debt, it's relatively easy to predict whether debt is risky if it has only a 90-day maturity.

Thus, MMMFs are essentially risk-free. The only risk they might have would be associated with possible criminal activity on the part of the fund managers. This risk is eliminated through effective monitoring of the fund's activities, which occurs in the larger funds. Investing in a large, high-quality MMMF is pretty much risk-free.

FACTS OF LIFE

American men under the age of 34 are the biggest "mystery spenders"; that is, they can't identify where they spend cash. Their cash mystery spending averages $59 per week, or $3,078 per year, with more than half saying their cash tends to disappear most often during a night out.

Establishing and Using a Checking Account

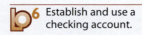
6 Establish and use a checking account.

There are a lot of alternatives available for cash management, but it would be almost impossible to function in today's economy without a checking account. Most people write checks to cover the rent, utility bills, and tuition. Carrying cash to cover these sizable bills would be too dangerous—checks are convenient and simple. In fact, each year approximately 60 billion checks are written.

Let's look at how to open and maintain a checking account. Keep in mind that checking accounts can be set up at all types of financial institutions, not just commercial banks.

Choosing a Financial Institution

The first step in opening a checking account is choosing a financial institution. In deciding where to open a checking account, you should consider the three Cs—cost, convenience, and consideration—in addition to the safety of the financial institution. Remember, in picking a checking account you're also picking a financial institution with which you'll have a financial relationship. Thus, you should consider not only cost, but also convenience and how comfortable you are with the manager and employees. Checklist 5.1 provides some specific items that make up the three Cs.

The Cost Factor

The cost of the account is probably the basic factor in determining what type of account to open and where to open it. If you meet a minimum balance level, some financial institutions provide you with free checking privileges. This minimum balance can vary dramatically, going all the way up to $10,000. If the minimum isn't met, one of a number of alternative fee structures will be imposed. Let's take a moment to examine the fee arrangements for checking accounts.

Monthly Fee   With a monthly fee arrangement, you pay a set fee regardless of your average balance and how many checks you write.

Minimum Balance   Under a minimum balance arrangement, your monthly fee depends upon how much cash you maintain in your account. If your average balance exceeds a set level, the monthly fee is waived; if not, you pay the monthly fee. Even if the fee is waived, you still pay the opportunity cost of having your funds tied up in the minimum balance, where they either do not earn interest or earn a very low rate.

Charge Per Check   At some financial institutions, in addition to paying a small fixed monthly fee, there's also a charge per check. The trade-off here is that if you don't use many checks, the total cost of this type of account may be considerably less than an account with a higher monthly fee and no per check charge.

Balance-Dependent Scaled Fees   Under balance-dependent scaled fees, the fee declines depending on the average balance held. That is, for accounts with small average balances, there is a relatively high monthly fee. However, for accounts with larger average balances, the monthly fee declines and is eventually eliminated for accounts with very large average balances.

When opening a NOW account, which you recall is a checking account on which you earn interest, remember that any interest you earn helps offset fees and minimum balance requirements.

<table>
<tr><td>

CHECKLIST 5.1

The Three Cs of Choosing a Financial Institution

</td><td>

Cost
- Fees
- Rates
- Minimum balances
- Per check charges

Convenience
- Location
- Access to ATMs
- Availability of safety-deposit boxes

</td><td>

- Availability of direct deposit services
- Availability of overdraft protection

Consideration
- Personal attention provided
- Financial advice that you are comfortable accessing

Safety—The Final Consideration
- Federal deposit insurance

</td></tr>
</table>

Convenience Factor

Direct Deposit
The depositing of payments, such as payroll checks, directly into your checking account. This is done electronically.

Safety-Deposit Box
A storage unit at a bank or other financial institution in which valuables and important documents are stored for safekeeping.

Overdraft Protection
Provision of an automatic loan to your checking account whenever sufficient funds are not available to cover checks that have been written against the account.

In addition to low cost, your financial institution should offer services that make it easy to use. Obviously, you want an institution located near your home—the closer you are to the bank and if the bank offers plenty of ATMs, the easier it is to make financial transactions. In addition, safety-deposit boxes, **direct deposit** services, and overdraft protection are other conveniences.

Safety-Deposit Boxes   **Safety-deposit boxes** serve as important storage places for financial documents and valuables. Smaller safety-deposit boxes can cost as little as $25 to $50 per year, with the costs varying by location and increasing as the size of the box increases. There are two keys to every safety-deposit box. You're given one key, and the financial institution retains the second key. Both keys are needed to open the box.

Overdraft Protection   **Overdraft protection** is an automatic loan made to your checking account whenever your account doesn't contain enough cash to cover the checks that you've written against it. Checks drawn against a checking account with overdraft protection will not bounce. Given the charges for bounced checks and the hassle of dealing with them, you probably want some type of protection. Unfortunately, overdraft protection can be very expensive. Overdraft loans generally come in $100 increments, so if your checking account is $5 overdrawn, you receive an automatic loan of $100 and now have a checking account balance of $95. The problem is that there may be a hefty fee along with a high interest rate charged on the overdraft loan. Less expensive solutions include an overdraft line of credit, a link to your credit card, or a link to your savings account—you might want to see if your bank provides any of these alternatives. Although overdraft protection is desirable, it's still an expensive convenience that should be viewed as a safety net against errors you may make, not as a device to rely on regularly. In fact, overdraft protection on debit and ATM cards had become so costly for consumers that the Federal Reserve recently put in place new rules to protect consumers. These new rules are provided in Table 5.5.

STOP & THINK

Why all the concern over overdraft protection on debit and ATM cards? The way it worked before the new Fed rules was you might be automatically enrolled in overdraft protection, and then when you make a debit card or ATM transaction without sufficient funds, your bank would spot you the money and charge you a fee. Unfortunately, only later when you got home and logged into your account would you realize you've been charged a $35 overdraft fee for that $5 Caramel Macchiato at Starbucks. Under the new Fed rules you have to opt into this kind of coverage—and if you don't the bank will reject your transaction when there aren't sufficient funds and there won't be any charges. How much money were U.S. banks making off debit and ATM overdraft fees? In 2009, they made over $20 billion on them! Do you understand why banks were so upset at this new Fed rule?

TABLE 5.5 Overdraft Protection and New Rules for Debit and ATM Cards

Overdraft Protection	Generally, banks can cover your overdrafts in one of two ways.
	• **Standard overdraft practices.** Your bank will cover your transaction for a flat fee of about $20–30 **each** time you overdraw your account. For example, if you make a purchase with your debit card for $150 but only have $100 in your account, your account will be overdrawn by $50 and your bank will charge you a fee. If you then make an ATM withdrawal for $50, your account will be overdrawn by $100 and you will be charged another fee. In this example, if the fee your bank charges for its standard overdraft practices is $30, you will pay a total of $60 in fees.
	• **Overdraft protection plans.** Your bank may offer a line of credit or a link to your savings account to cover transactions when you overdraw your account. Banks typically charge a fee each time you overdraw your account, but these overdraft protection plans may be less expensive than their standard overdraft practices.
The New Rules	One of the changes that came out of the recent financial crisis dealt with new rules for debit and ATM card overdrafts.
	• **You choose.** In the past, some banks automatically enrolled you in their standard overdraft practices for all types of transactions when you opened an account. Under the new rules, your bank must first get your permission to apply its standard overdraft practices to *everyday debit card and ATM transactions before* you can be charged overdraft fees. To grant this permission, you will need to respond to the notice and opt in (agree).
	• **Existing accounts.** If you do not opt in (agree), your bank's standard overdraft practices won't apply to your everyday debit card and ATM transactions. These transactions typically will be declined when you don't have enough money in your account, but you will not be charged overdraft fees.
	• **New accounts.** If you open a new account, your bank cannot charge you overdraft fees for everyday debit card and ATM transactions unless you opt in.
	• **Flexibility.** Whatever your decision, the new overdraft rules give you flexibility. If you opt in, you can cancel at any time. If you do not opt in, you can do so later.
	• **Checks and automatic bill payments.** The new rules *do not cover checks or automatic bill payments* that you may have set up for paying bills such as your mortgage, rent, or utilities. Your bank may still automatically enroll you in their standard overdraft practices for these types of transactions. If you do not want your bank's standard overdraft practices in these instances, talk to your bank; you may or may not have the option to cancel.

Source: www.federalreserve.gov/consumerinfo/wyntk_overdraft.htm, accessed June 28, 2011.

Another convenience is the ability to **stop payment** on a check. If you want to cancel a check you've already written, you can go online or call your financial institution and ask that payment on this check be stopped. You'll generally have to follow up with a written authorization, and the service involves a cost of between $5 and $20.

Stop Payment
An order you can give your financial institution to stop payment on a check you've written.

Consideration Factor

In choosing a financial institution, you want one that gives personal attention. If you have a problem, you want to feel comfortable in approaching a teller with it. And in case you need financial advice, you want a knowledgeable, approachable person at your branch. Although ATMs are extremely convenient, they don't answer questions, correct whatever's wrong, or work with you when you need a loan.

Balancing Your Checking Account

Anyone who's ever tried to build anything with blocks knows that unbalanced objects tend to fall over. Checking accounts can be the same way. If the records you keep in your check register produce the same numbers that appear in your statement, your checking account is balanced. If not, well, you'd better hope that you have overdraft protection. Although it's not essential that your checking account be perfectly balanced at all times, you're a lot less likely to accidentally bounce a check if your account is balanced.

The basics of balancing a checkbook are relatively simple. First, keep track of every transaction—every check you write, every deposit, every ATM transaction—and enter it in your check register. Obviously, if you don't keep track of the checks you've written and the ATM withdrawals you've made, you can't balance your checkbook. Then, when your monthly statement arrives, compare it to your check register to make sure that no mistakes have been made. Your checks clear electronically, which means fast, and you will receive an electronic image of your canceled check or simply a notation of it in your checking account statement. That means when you write a check, you have to make sure you have enough money in your account to cover that check on the day you write it, not on the day you *think* it will clear your bank. If you've received interest on your account or incurred any bank charges, enter them. Then, reconcile your register balance with the bank balance.

By reconciling your balance with the monthly statement you receive from the bank, you can locate any errors you or the bank has made. Figures 5.1 and 5.2 show you how to balance a checking account. Many banks provide a reconciliation form on the back of the monthly statement. To determine your balance, begin with the ending statement balance shown on your monthly statement. To this you add any deposits or credits you've made since the statement date. Then subtract any outstanding checks or debits issued by you but not yet paid as of the date of the statement. The difference should be the ending balance on your current statement. If this number doesn't agree with the account register balance, check your math and make sure that all transactions are correct and entered into your register.

Other Types of Checks

If the price of something you wish to purchase is very large or you are buying abroad, a personal check isn't an acceptable form of payment. After all, what guarantee do sellers have that you've got enough money in your account to cover the check? In that case, you can guarantee payment through the use of a cashier's check, a certified check, a money order, or a traveler's check.

Cashier's Check

A check drawn on a bank or financial institution's account.

Cashier's Check   A **cashier's check** is a check drawn on the bank or financial institution's account. These checks can be used by people with no checking account. Because it's really a check from a bank, it can bounce only if the bank doesn't have funds to cover it—which isn't too likely. A cashier's check usually costs you a fee of around $10, as well as the amount of the check. The bank then writes a check from its own account to a specific payee.

Certified Check

A personal check that's been certified as being good by the financial institution on which it's drawn.

Certified Check   A **certified check** is a personal check that has been certified as being good by the financial institution on which it's drawn. To certify a check, the bank first makes sure there are sufficient funds in the individual's account to cover the check. Funds equal to the amount of the check are then immediately frozen, and the check is certified. The cost for this service generally runs around $10 per certified check.

Money Order

A check similar to a cashier's check except that it is generally issued by the U.S. Postal Service or some other nonbanking institution.

Money Order   A **money order** is a variation of the cashier's check, except that it's generally issued by the U.S. Postal Service or many other nonbanking institutions. For example, money orders can be purchased at many 7-Eleven stores! The fee

FIGURE 5.1 Worksheet for Balancing Your Checking Account

1. Record in your check register all items that appear on the monthly statement received from the bank that have not previously been entered, for example, cash withdrawals from an ATM, automatic transfers, service charges, and any other transactions.
2. In your checking account register, check off any deposits or credits and checks or debits shown on the monthly statement.
3. In Section A: Deposits and Credits below, list any deposits that have been made since the date of the statement.

Section A: Deposits and Credits

Date	Amount
1.	
2.	
3.	
4.	
5.	
6.	
Total Amount:	_____

4. In Section B: Outstanding Checks and Debits below, list any checks and debits issued by you that have not yet been reported on your account statement.

Section B: Outstanding Checks and Debits

Check Number	Amount
1.	
2.	
3.	
4.	
5.	
6.	
7.	
Total Amount:	_____

5. Write in the ending statement balance provided in the monthly statement that you received from your bank. .... _____
6. Write in the total amount of the deposits and credits you have made since the statement date (total of Section A above). .... + _____
7. Total the amounts in lines 5 and 6. .... = _____
8. Write in the total amounts of outstanding checks and debits (total of Section B above). .... − _____
9. Subtract the amount in line 8 from the amount in line 7. This is your **adjusted statement balance.** .... = _____

If your adjusted statement balance as calculated above does not agree with your account register balance:

A. Review last month's statement to reconcilement to make sure any differences were corrected.
B. Check to make sure that all deposits, interest earned, and service charges shown on the monthly statement from your bank are included in your account register.
C. Check your addition and subtraction in both your account register and in this month's checking account balance reconcilement above.

associated with a money order generally varies, depending on the size of the money order.

Traveler's Checks   **Traveler's checks** are similar to cashier's checks except that they don't specify a specific payee, and they come in specific denominations ($20, $50, and $100). They're issued by large financial institutions, such as Citibank, Visa, and American Express, and are sold through local banking institutions. The advantage of traveler's checks is that they're accepted almost anywhere in the world because they are viewed as riskless checks. Also, if lost or stolen, they're generally replaced quickly, without charge. The cost to purchase traveler's checks is generally 1 percent. Thus, $500 worth of traveler's checks would carry a $5 purchase fee.

Traveler's Checks
Checks issued by large financial institutions, such as Citibank, Visa, and American Express, that are sold through local banking institutions and are similar to cashier's checks except that they don't specify a specific payee and they come in specific denominations ($20, $50, and $100).

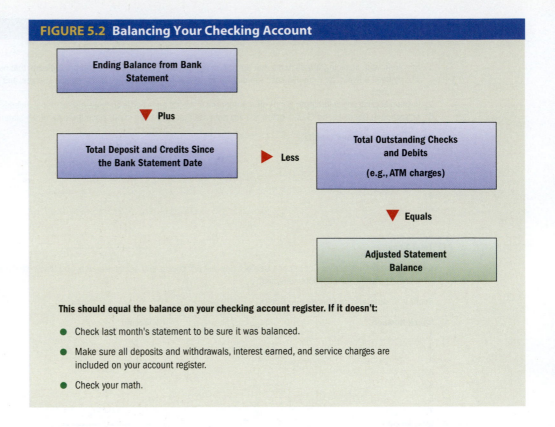

FIGURE 5.2 Balancing Your Checking Account

Ending Balance from Bank Statement

▼ Plus

Total Deposit and Credits Since the Bank Statement Date

▶ Less

Total Outstanding Checks and Debits

(e.g., ATM charges)

▼ Equals

Adjusted Statement Balance

This should equal the balance on your checking account register. If it doesn't:

- Check last month's statement to be sure it was balanced.
- Make sure all deposits and withdrawals, interest earned, and service charges are included on your account register.
- Check your math.

LO7 Transfer funds electronically and understand how electronic funds transfers (EFTs) work.

Electronic Funds Transfer (EFT)

Any financial transaction that takes place electronically.

Electronic Funds Transfers

Electronic funds transfer (EFT), which refers to any financial transaction that takes place electronically, is the most rapidly changing area of cash management today. With an EFT, funds move between accounts instantly and without paper. Examples of EFTs are paying for groceries with a debit card, withdrawing cash from an ATM, or having your paycheck directly deposited at your bank.

The advantages of EFTs are that the transactions take place immediately, and the consumer doesn't have to carry cash or write a check. They're great for things like paying all kinds of charges from insurance premiums, to mortgage payments, to phone and utilities bills. EFTs can tighten up your cash management habits by ensuring that you never carry cash. It's ironic, but you might be better able to manage your cash by not using cash.

To give you a better understanding of EFT and how it affects you, we discuss ATMs, debit cards, and smart cards in the following sections. You'll notice that there's no mention of credit cards here. Why? Because credit cards don't involve the electronic transfer of money—they involve the electronic *borrowing* of money. Don't worry, we deal with them in detail in the next chapter.

Automated Teller Machines

Automated Teller Machine (ATM) or Cash Machine

Machines found at most financial institutions that can be used to make withdrawals, deposits, transfers, and account inquiries.

An **automated teller machine (ATM)** or **cash machine** provides cash instantly and can be accessed through a credit or debit card. If you use a credit card to access the ATM, then the cash is "borrowed" from the line of credit you have with the financial institution that issued your credit card. Because these funds are borrowed, you begin paying usually very high interest on them immediately. The ATM can also be used to access funds held in an account—for example, funds can be withdrawn from your checking account using a debit card.

MONEY MATTERS

Tips from Marcy Furney, ChFC, Certified Financial Planner™

CHECK IT OUT

Balance your checkbook immediately after receiving your statement every month. You'll avoid possible charges for letting your balance get too low or bouncing checks. Mark off each canceled check in your register and compare your balance to the balance on the statement. Don't just take the bank's word for it.

Enter into your check register any automatic EFTs or bank drafts for next month when you do your reconciliation. This avoids the possibility of overdraft. EFTs are a great time and postage saver for bills like insurance premiums, mortgages, and car payments, but you must keep up with them. A $20 insufficient funds fee for each returned check can cancel out much of the benefit.

If you have a computer, consider purchasing personal bookkeeping software. Most programs are very easy to use and are excellent sources of information for budgeting, cash flow analysis, and even tracking debt and investments.

If you need to get a handle on your spending or are watching your budget, include in your check register what each check was written for. Many registers provide a shaded line below each check entry for that purpose. If yours doesn't, just record checks on every other line and fill in the reason below each one. At the end of each month, take a few minutes to analyze your outflows. Caution: Entries such as "misc." or "household item" aren't very useful.

Examine your bank statement for any charges or maintenance fees and make sure they're actually due. Ideally you should find a bank that charges no monthly fees if the balance is kept at a reasonably low level. Be aware that minimum balances may be calculated in different ways. Some may charge a fee if your balance ever goes below a given amount, while others use an average daily balance calculation.

Read the inserts in your monthly bank statement. Even though they may appear to be "junk mail," they're your bank's means of notifying you regarding important procedural and charging changes.

Investigate the costs and values of other services the bank may offer in association with your checking account before using them. For example, check printing through a bank is normally higher than through outside companies. Also, investments the bank offers may be limited and carry relatively high loads without giving you the service and level of advice provided by a personal advisor.

The obvious appeal of ATMs is their convenience. ATMs never close and are available in many parts of the world. To use an ATM, you insert or swipe your card, punch in your **personal identification number**, or **PIN**, which is a four- to seven-digit number assigned to your account, and indicate how much cash you'd like. Easy, right? But, as with everything else in finance, there's a cost to convenience. In the case of ATMs, most banks charge an access fee for any transaction. If you're using an ATM not owned by the bank that issued your card, this charge can range up to $3 per transaction. The bank that owns the ATM can also charge you up to $2 for using its machine. At a grand total of up to $5 per transaction, using an ATM can be quite expensive.

The big problem with an ATM transaction is crime. Since most people who walk away from an ATM have money on them, ATMs tend to attract criminals. This doesn't mean that you shouldn't use them, but you should be careful. Don't use them late at night, don't use them in isolated areas, don't be the only person at the ATM, and don't drive up to an ATM in an unlocked car.

In addition, take care that no one has access to your PIN. Although your liability for unauthorized transactions on an ATM is only $50 provided you notify the bank immediately, it jumps to $500 if a delay of 2 days in reporting occurs and becomes unlimited if the delay exceeds 60 days. You should choose a PIN different from your birthday, Social Security number, street address, or any other number a criminal might logically guess. Checklist 5.2 provides a number of steps to follow to ensure ATM security.

Personal Identification Number (PIN)
A four- to seven-digit personal identification number assigned to your account.

CHECKLIST 5.2
ATM Security

Keep Your Card Secure

♦ Treat your ATM card like cash. Always keep your card in a safe place. It's a good idea to store your card in a card sleeve. The sleeve protects the card's magnetic strip and helps ensure that the card functions properly.

♦ Keep your PIN a secret. Memorize your code. Never write it on your card or store it with the card. Never tell your code to anyone. And never let someone else enter your code for you.

♦ Report a lost or stolen card at once. Even though your ATM card cannot be used without your PIN, promptly report a lost or stolen card.

♦ Check your receipts against your monthly statement to guard against ATM fraud.

Security at ATMs

♦ Always observe your surroundings before conducting an ATM transaction.

♦ If an ATM is obstructed from view or poorly lit, go to another ATM.

♦ If you are using a walk-up ATM, take a companion along if possible—especially at night.

♦ Minimize time spent at the ATM by having your card out and ready to use.

♦ If you see anyone or anything suspicious while conducting a transaction, cancel your transaction and leave.

♦ If you are followed after making an ATM transaction, go immediately to a heavily populated, well-lighted area and call the police.

♦ If you are at a drive-up ATM, keep your engine running, the doors locked, and the windows up at all times when waiting in line. Before rolling down the windows to use the ATM, check the entire area for anything or anyone suspicious.

Debit Cards

Debit Card
A card that allows you to access the money in your accounts electronically.

A **debit card** is something of a cross between a credit card and a checking account. It's like a credit card in that it's a plastic card you can use instead of cash, but it works more like a checking account. When you write a check, you're spending money that you have in your checking account. Unless you have overdraft protection, you can't write a check for more than what is in your account. A debit card is linked to an account, and when you use it, you're spending the money in that account. It's kind of like writing an electronic check, only there's no paper involved, and the check gets "cashed" instantly. When the money in your account runs out, you can't use your debit card again until you make another deposit.

Debit cards, like credit cards, allow you to avoid carrying cash, but make it impossible to rack up a big credit card balance. With a debit card, you're spending your own money, as opposed to borrowing money. You probably have a debit card now: Your ATM card is actually a type of debit card in that it gives you access to your checking account, but many ATM cards do even more. They also give you access to your savings account and allow you to transfer money between your different accounts. Debit cards are gaining more popularity with financial institutions, and some predict that debit cards will soon replace checking accounts.

While you can keep using your debit card as long as you have money in your account, card "blocking" can leave some of your money inaccessible. Card blocking occurs when you use a debit card (or credit card) to check into a hotel or rent a car and the anticipated expenses are blocked, in effect, placing a hold on the money. For example, if you check into a $100 a day hotel for 4 days, the hotel would likely block $400 on your debit (or credit) card. If you pay your bill when you check out using the same card, the block will be lifted in a day or two. However, if you use another card to pay the bill it is likely that the $400 block will remain on your account for up to 15 days. If you don't have a big balance, this can be a problem. To avoid it, use the same card to pay the bill as you did at the beginning of the transaction. In addition, blocking policies vary quite a bit from one card issuer to another, so you might want to shop around and ask what the blocking policies are when you're looking for a new card.

Smart Cards

Smart cards, sometimes called memory cards or electronic wallets, are a variation on debit cards, but instead of withdrawing funds from a designated account with a bank, you withdraw them from an account that's actually stored magnetically in the smart card. In fact, your smart card may include more than just money, it may include your ID—perhaps a driver's license or your student ID—along with insurance information, medical history, or any other type of information that would be handy to have. At Virginia Tech the student ID, called the Hokie Passport, also serves as a smart card and can be used at dining services, vending machines, and many merchants in town; similarly, James Madison University's smart card is called the JAC card and works just like the one at Virginia Tech. In fact, smart cards have become very common at colleges and universities.

The advantages to the issuing agency are that it receives use of the funds in the smart cards before the transactions are completed and smart cards can reduce paperwork considerably. The advantages to the user are that smart cards are convenient and reduce the need to carry cash.

Gift or Stored Value Cards

If you've made a purchase with a merchant gift card, placed phone calls with a prepaid telephone card, or bought something using a prepaid debit card, you've used a gift or stored value card. These cards are becoming more and more common, and for some individuals they are taking the place of checking accounts.

There are actually two different types of gift or stored value cards: The first is the single-purpose or "closed-loop" card, which can only be used at one store for one purpose; the second is the multipurpose or "open-loop" card, which can be used all over, just like a credit card. It is the multipurpose stored value card that is replacing checking accounts for many individuals. In fact, it's becoming more and more common to receive your paycheck on a stored value card, with more than 1,000 companies, including Wal-Mart, FedEx, McDonald's, U-Haul, UPS, Coca-Cola, Blockbuster Video, and Denny's offering to pay employees with Visa Payroll cards, which are a form of stored value cards, instead of checks.

Beware, however, because stored value cards come with a wide range of features and fee structures. For example, many have activation fees, maintenance fees, and ATM transaction fees. On top of these common fees, some also have reload fees, transaction limit fees, inactivity fees, dispute fees, and money transfer fees.

FACTS OF LIFE
Electronic payments account for over three-quarters of all noncash payments.

Number of Noncash Payments

- Prepaid Cards 5.5%
- Checks (paid) 22.4%
- Debit Card 34.8%
- Direct Electronic Transfer 17.5%
- Credit Card 19.8%

Source: Board of Governors of the Federal Reserve System, *The 2010 Federal Reserve Payments Study* (Washington, DC: Federal Reserve System, 2010).

Smart Cards
Similar to debit cards, but these cards actually magnetically store their own accounts. Funds are transferred into the cards, which are then used the same way you'd use a debit card. When the funds run out, the card is useless until more funds are magnetically transferred in.

Fixing Mistakes—Theirs, Not Yours

How can errors occur in EFTs? Sometimes they're human errors—not getting full credit for deposits—and sometimes they're computer errors. The first step in dealing with errors is to avoid letting them occur. You may not have much control with computer errors, but you can avoid human errors.

Perhaps the most common human error involves deposits, with most problems stemming from cash deposits made directly in ATMs. To avoid this type of error, never deposit cash in an ATM. If an error occurs and you aren't credited for what you deposited, it's very difficult to prove that you're right.

If an error does occur, report it immediately. Call the bank, and if it's closed, try to leave a message. By law you must write to the bank within 60 days of receiving your statement. If you can't settle the dispute with the bank, write to the Federal Reserve Board's Division of Consumer and Community Affairs, 20th and C Streets NW, Washington, DC 20551.

Summary

 Manage your cash and understand why you need liquid assets.

Cash management is the control of your cash and liquid assets. Liquid assets allow you to invest your money while still keeping it available to pay bills or to cover an emergency. Although liquid asset investments are low risk and provide you with emergency funds, they don't provide you with a very good return. The basic idea behind cash management is balancing the risk of not having enough in the way of liquid assets with the potential for greater return on other investments.

 Automate your savings.

The key to meeting long-term goals is to make saving a part of your everyday life. Having some of your income automatically placed in savings forces you to learn to live at your take-home salary level.

 Choose from among the different types of financial institutions that provide cash management services.

In recent years there have been many changes in the field of cash management, and nowhere is this more evident than in financial institutions themselves. Industry changes and increased competition have resulted in a vast reshaping of many institutions. However, we can still divide them into deposit-type institutions (banks) and nondeposit-type institutions. Recently, nondeposit institutions have been offering traditional banking services, resulting in more choices than ever for managing cash.

 Compare the various cash management alternatives.

Given the number of different financial institutions vying for your liquid funds, it's no surprise that there are a variety of different cash management alternatives. These include checking accounts, savings accounts, money market deposit accounts, certificates of deposit, money market mutual funds, asset management accounts, T-bills, and savings bonds.

 Compare rates on the different liquid investment alternatives.

When comparing different liquid investment alternatives, you must look not only at their return but also at how safe they are. In addition, you must remember that the only valid rate comparisons are ones that use similar compounding methods (annual, semiannual, and so on) and have similar tax treatment.

Establish and use a checking account.
Your checking account is your most essential cash management tool. When deciding where to open a checking account, you should give consideration to the three Cs: cost, convenience, and consideration. You should also keep an eye out for safety—are your funds federally insured?

Transfer funds electronically and understand how electronic funds transfers (EFTs) work.
"Electronic funds transfer" refers to any financial transaction that takes place electronically, for example, paying for dinner with a debit card or having your paycheck deposited directly. The advantage of an electronic funds transfer is that the transaction takes place immediately and the consumer does not have to carry cash or write a check.

Review Questions

1. What are liquid assets? How does this category of assets relate to **Principles 5: Stuff Happens, or the Importance of Liquidity** and **Principle 8: Risk and Return Go Hand in Hand**?

2. Name three characteristics of liquid assets. What are the disadvantages of having too much or too little money held as liquid assets?

3. What factors have affected the alternatives available to consumers for cash management?

4. What is the primary advantage of automating your savings?

5. Give two examples of both deposit-type and nondeposit-type financial institutions. Describe their similarities.

6. What are three advantages and two disadvantages to online banking?

7. What is a credit union and what are some of its distinguishing features?

8. What is a NOW account? What are its advantages and disadvantages?

9. List three characteristics of certificates of deposit (CDs).

10. Describe and compare a money market deposit account (MMDA) and a money market mutual fund (MMMF).

11. Describe how an asset management account works and what financial services are included. What are the disadvantages associated with this type of account?

12. Describe and compare two common federal government debt instruments: Treasury bills and U.S. Series EE savings bonds.

13. Who would benefit the most from investing in tax-exempt securities? Why?

14. What factors should you consider when choosing a financial institution?

15. What is overdraft protection? How do the new federal rules affect the way overdraft protection works?

16. What are electronic funds transfers (EFTs)? Describe and compare three different types of EFTs.

17. Describe the function of a smart card. Why is it important to protect your smart card?

Develop Your Skills—Problems and Activities

These problems are available in MyFinanceLab.

1. Use Worksheet 1 to list three short-term goals and/or expenses for which a savings account, money market mutual fund, or other liquid assets vehicle would be the appropriate place for your money.

2. After reading the new account insert in his monthly statement, Tony Mercadante determined that the FDIC considers a joint account as a separate depositor. He and his wife, Cynthia, have three accounts at ABC Bank & Trust, one joint account with a balance of $60,000 and two individual accounts—his has a $150,000 balance and hers has a $254,000 balance. What amounts of FDIC coverage do they each have?

3. Your friend Ed has a money market mutual fund account, with automatic deposit of his paycheck into an interest-bearing checking account at the company credit union, and a CD from the local branch of a bank that advertises "coast-to-coast" banking. What is the benefit of "mixing and matching" financial institutions and their services?

4. Calculate the percentage return on a 1-year Treasury bill with a face value of $10,000 if you pay $9,600 to purchase it and receive its full face value at maturity.

5. Calculate the after-tax return of a 6.65 percent, 20-year, A-rated corporate bond for an investor in the 15 percent marginal tax bracket. Compare this yield to a 5.25 percent, 20-year, A-rated, tax-exempt municipal bond and explain which alternative is better. Repeat the calculations and comparison for an investor in the 33 percent marginal tax bracket.

6. Assuming a 1-year, money market account investment at 3.5 percent (APY), a 2.5 percent inflation rate, a 28 percent marginal tax bracket, and a constant $50,000 balance calculate the after-tax rate of return, the real rate of return, and the total monetary return. What are the implications of this result for cash management decisions?

7. Based on the after-tax returns, at what federal tax rate (as shown in Chapter 4 on page 96) is an investor better off choosing a tax-exempt 2.78 percent municipal bond over a taxable 4.03 percent corporate bond?

8. Describe the online banking features that you have used or would use in the future. Would you consider using an Internet-only bank? Why or why not? What could be the primary advantages and disadvantages of an Internet-only bank?

Learn by Doing—Suggested Projects

1. Compare your current bank or credit union checking account to at least two others according to the "three Cs" criteria. Be sure to include one Internet-only bank in the comparison. Describe which is the best account for you and why.

2. Consult the Web site **www.imoneynet.com** or **www.bankrate.com** for a comparison of current earnings on different taxable and tax-exempt retail money market mutual funds. Visit the Web sites for at least three of the funds to compare their features. For example, what is the minimum initial amount required to open an account? The minimum amount required for subsequent deposits? The minimum allowable amount for a check written on the account?

3. Shop for a new liquid asset account appropriate for your needs (e.g., bank account, CD, money market mutual fund). Describe the purchase process (e.g., dollar cost, "paperwork") and your anticipated future use(s) for this money.

4. Interview a stockbroker about the characteristics of cash or liquid asset management alternatives sold by brokerage firms. Inquire about the fees charged for purchasing these products and the interest rates that they can earn. Request and read available product literature.

5. Review your latest savings account statement. Find the annual percentage yield (APY) paid on your account and compare it to the "quoted rate." What method is used to determine the account balance in which interest is credited? What was your after-tax and real (after inflation) rate of return?

6. Use Worksheet 8 to reconcile the balance in a bank or credit union checking account.

7. Banks charge billions of dollars per year in overdraft, insufficient funds, or "bounced" check fees. As a group project, survey several local financial institutions to determine their fees and overdraft protection charges. Now try to determine the effective interest rate for each bank on a $100 check that causes an account to be overdrawn for 1 week.

8. As a group project, develop a chart noting the cost of making a transaction at an ATM machine owned by your bank and at a machine owned by another bank. Compare the costs reported by the members of the group. How can these fees be avoided? How do they relate to the "three Cs" criteria for choosing a financial institution?

Be a Financial Planner—Discussion Case 1

This case is available in MyFinanceLab.

Shu Chang, 22, has just moved to Denver to begin her first professional job. She is concerned about her finances and, specifically, wants to save for "a rainy day" and a new car purchase in 2 years. Su's new job pays $30,500, of which she keeps $24,000 after taxes. Her monthly expenses total $1,600. Shu's new employer offers a 401(k) plan and matches employees' contributions up to 6 percent of their salary. The employer also provides a credit union and a U.S. Savings Bond purchase program. Shu also just inherited $5,000.

Shu's older brother, Wen, has urged Shu to start saving from "day one" on the job. Wen has lost a job twice in the last 5 years through company downsizing and now keeps $35,000 in a 4 percent money market mutual fund in case it happens again. Wen's annual take-home pay is $48,000.

Shu has started shopping around for accounts to hold her liquid assets. She'd like to earn the highest rate possible and avoid paying fees for falling below a specified minimum balance. She plans to open two accounts: one for paying monthly bills and another for short-term savings.

Questions

1. Name at least three ways that Shu could automate her asset management. Suggest at least one option for retirement savings, general savings, and general convenience.

2. What major factors should Shu consider when selecting a checking and/or savings account?

3. Why does Shu need an emergency fund? Assuming she wants to follow her brother's lead, how much emergency savings should she try to set aside? What type of account would you recommend for her emergency fund?

4. Comment on Wen's use of liquid assets. How is his savings philosophy both risky and conservative? What is the real, after-tax rate of return, assuming a 3 percent inflation rate and 25 percent marginal tax bracket?

5. Shu has narrowed her "savings" account choices to a standard checking account paying 1.25 percent, a money market deposit account (MMDA) paying 3 percent, and a money market mutual fund (MMMF) earning 3.75 percent. Which liquid asset vehicle would you recommend for paying monthly expenses, and which would you recommend for saving for the car down payment? Explain the advantages and disadvantages associated with each choice.

6. Shu has heard that some local auto dealerships may require a cashier's check for the down payment. Why is a cashier's check preferable to a certified check?

Be a Financial Planner—Discussion Case 2

This case is available in MyFinanceLab.

Jarod Douglas Jones is a young professional just getting started in the world. He has been having some difficulty getting his checkbook to match his bank statement. Last month all he had to do was subtract the service charge from his checkbook register and the amounts matched. This month is different. He would like your help reconciling the problem. Help him find his mistake(s) and learn the procedures for balancing his checkbook each month.

    Hint: Use Figure 5.1 or Worksheet 8.

Big USA Bank

Summary

Beginning balance	6/27	$1,964.17
Total deposits		$2,823.46
Total withdrawals		$2,982.74
Service charge		$4.50
ATM fees		$3.00
Ending balance	7/29	$1,797.39

Deposits and Electronic Credits

Automatic payroll	6/30	$1,161.73
Automatic payroll	7/15	$1,161.73
Branch deposit	7/23	$500.00

Withdrawals and Electronic Debits

Auto Insurance Draft	7/1	$70.50
Visa—Check 1074	7/5	$45.20
Big Al's All-U-Care-To-Eat	7/7	$39.00
ATM	7/10	$30.00
A Cut Above Hair Salon	7/19	$23.00
ATM	7/21	$50.00

Checks

1071	7/01	$30.00
1072	7/03	$50.00
1073	7/08	$100.00
1074	7/06	See above
1075	7/09	$147.11
1076	7/16	$69.75
1077	7/10	$27.81
1078	7/12	$302.20
1080*	7/20	$350.00
1081	7/21	$20.50
1082	7/22	$1,599.11
1084*	7/23	$28.56

*Break in Sequence

Date	Number	Payee/Description	Credit	Debit	Balance
					$2,005.98
24-Jun	1070	Dinner out		$41.81	($41.81)
					$1,964.17
26-Jun	1071	Cash		$30.00	($30.00)
					$1,934.17
29-Jun	1072	Video game		$50.00	($50.00)
					$1,884.17
30-Jun		Payroll	$1,161.73		$1,161.73
					$3,045.90
1-Jul		Auto Insurance		$70.50	($70.50)
					$2,975.40
1-Jul	1073	Cash		$100.00	($100.00)
					$2,875.40
3-Jul	1074	Visa		$45.20	($45.20)
					$2,830.20
3-Jul	1075	Store card		$147.11	($147.11)
					$2,683.09
8-Jul	1076	Gas card		$69.75	($69.75)
					$2,623.34
8-Jul	1077	Cell phone		$27.81	($27.81)
					$2,595.53
9-Jul	1078	Owed to parents		$302.20	($320.20)
					$2,275.33
12-Jul	1079	Dinner out		$37.87	($37.87)
					$2,237.46
15-Jul		Payroll	$1,161.73		$1,161.73
					$3,399.19
15-Jul	1080	Auto payment		$350.00	($350.00)
					$3,049.19
15-Jul	1081	Master Card		$20.50	($20.50)
					$3,028.69
18-Jul	1082	Discover Card		$1,599.11	($1,599.11)
					$1,429.58
18-Jul	1083	Cash		$125.00	($125.00)
					$1,304.58
19-Jul		Hair Cut		$23.00	($23.00)
					$1,281.58
23-Jul	1084	Cell phone		$28.56	($28.56)
					$1,253.02
23-Jul		Gift	$500.00		$500.00
					$1,753.02
21-Jul		ATM withdrawal		$51.50	($51.50)
					$1,701.52
28-Jul	1085	Cheap Food Store		$47.25	($47.25)
					$1,654.27
29-Jul	1086	Sears		$9.16	($9.16)
					$1,645.11

Using Credit Cards: The Role of Open Credit

Learning Objectives

 Know how credit cards work.

 Understand the costs of credit.

 Describe the different types of credit cards.

 Know what determines your credit card worthiness and how to secure a credit card.

 Manage your credit cards and open credit.

We've all said those three little words, and lived to regret it . . . "just charge it." Credit cards are easy to get and, for many of us, much too easy to use. How tough is it to get one? You probably know by now—not tough at all. In fact, about two-thirds of all college freshmen have credit cards, and by their senior year, over 90 percent of all students have at least one.

Be it in real life or in TV land, you can find countless stories revolving around the perils of plastic. And if you want a credit card, you can surely get one—after all, students are prime customers for credit card companies. In the world of TV, even Bart Simpson got one. It all happened after complaining that he never gets any mail. Marge gave him the family's junk mail, and one piece of that junk mail was a credit card application. It didn't take Bart long to fill it out—giving his occupation as a "butt doctor," his income as "whatever I find I keep," and his name as "Santa's Little Helper," which also happens to be the name of Bart's dog on TV—that's all it took, and in real life, it doesn't take much more. Then, 6 to 8 weeks later it arrives, a credit card issued by the Money Bank to Santos L. Helper. As you can imagine, things get a bit out of control from there, as Bart goes on a spending spree ordering gifts for all the family from the "Covet House" catalog—a Vancouver smoked salmon and a radio-frying pan for Marge, a golf shirt with corporate logo for Homer, "Trucker's Choice Stay-Alert Capsules" for Lisa, and all kinds of stuff for himself including a "limited edition" Collie.

Debt isn't a bad thing, in fact, some debt is good. But it's dangerous—it's easy to take on more debt than you should. And, the most dangerous debt is right in your pocket—your credit card. Still, it's necessary.

If you've ever had to make hotel reservations or buy concert tickets over the phone or the Internet, you understand that in today's economy, you really need to have a credit card. And almost everyone has one. In fact, Americans hold more than 1.4 billion credit cards of all types—that's over four and a half cards for each man, woman, and child and almost half of those are Visa and MasterCard, with the remainder being department store, oil company, and other merchants' charge cards. There's just no denying that having and using credit cards has become part of our financial culture.

You can't beat them for convenience, but if you're not careful, credit cards will cost you. They can be mighty expensive; some charge over 20 percent interest on unpaid balances. Because most people don't consider these interest charges when they're buying whatever it is they've just got to have, bank credit card debt (excluding store and gas credit cards) in the United States is estimated to be around $800 billion. If the interest rate on this sum were 20 percent, that would mean America is paying $160 billion each year in credit card charges. Unless you want to be one of the people paying a share of that $160 billion, you need to manage your credit cards wisely.

1 Know how credit cards work.

Credit
Receiving cash, goods, or services with an obligation to pay later.

Consumer Credit
Credit purchases for personal needs other than for home mortgages—this can include anything from an auto loan to credit card debt.

Open Credit or Revolving Credit
A line of credit that you can use and then pay back at whatever pace you like so long as you pay a minimum balance each month, paying interest on the unpaid balance.

A First Look at Credit Cards and Open Credit

Credit involves receiving cash, goods, or services with an obligation to pay later. In shopper's language, "Charge it," "Put it on my account," and "I'll pay for it with plastic," are all opening lines to the use of credit. Credit purchases made for personal needs other than for home mortgages are referred to collectively as **consumer credit**—this can include anything from an auto loan to credit card debt.

Open credit or revolving credit is a line of consumer credit extended before you make a purchase. Once you use open credit, you can pay back your debt at whatever pace you like so long as you pay a specified minimum balance each month. Today, most open credit comes in the form of credit card purchases, but open credit is actually any type of charge or credit account, because with a charge or credit account you've been extended a line of credit before you make a purchase. Examples of open credit range from the charge account you have at a local hardware store, to an Exxon charge card, to a credit account you have with your broker, to your Austin Power's Titanium Visa card. However, credit cards dominate, which isn't that surprising, given that there are around 7,000 different kinds of Visas, MasterCards, and other cards to choose from. Because of the predominance of credit cards, most of our discussion focuses on them, but the same basic principles apply to all credit and charge accounts.

When buying on credit, you can charge whatever you want, as long as you stay under the credit limit. Each month you'll receive a statement that shows both the outstanding balance on your account and the minimum payment due. You can then pay anywhere between the minimum payment and the balance. Any unpaid balance plus interest on that unpaid balance carries over and becomes part of next month's outstanding balance. As long as you pay the minimum balance every month, the credit issuer will continue to extend you a credit limit or line of credit, which is a preapproved amount of credit given in advance of any purchase.

As you probably already know, the higher the balance you maintain on your credit lines, the higher your costs will be. But other factors, too, determine your costs. The following sections discuss the basic factors that affect the costs of credit cards and other forms of open credit, including the interest rate, the balance calculation method, the cost of cash advances, the grace period, the annual fee, and other additional or penalty fees.

> ## FACTS of LIFE
>
> According to a study by Nellie Mae, 76 percent of **undergraduates** begin each school year with credit cards.

Interest Rates

Annual Percentage Rate (APR)
The true simple interest rate paid over the life of the loan. It's a reasonable approximation for the true cost of borrowing, and the Truth in Lending Act requires that all consumer loan agreements disclose the APR in bold print.

The main factor that determines the cost of a line of credit is the **annual percentage rate (APR)**, which is the true simple interest rate paid over the life of the loan. It takes most of the costs into account, including interest on the balance, the loan processing fee, and document preparation fee, but it only sometimes includes the loan application fee, and normally does not include the cost of credit reports. The importance of the APR is that while there can be differences in what's included in it, it's calculated the same way by all lenders, and the federal Truth in Lending Act requires that all consumer loan agreements disclose the APR in bold print. As a result, it's a good place to start to compare competing lines of credit.

Some credit cards have fixed APRs and some have variable APRs. With a variable-rate credit card, the rate you pay is tied to another interest rate. For example, many credit cards are tied to the prime rate of interest, which is the rate banks charge their best customers. Variable APR credit cards typically charge the prime rate plus a percentage. So if the interest rate that variable-rate credit cards charge varies, a fixed-rate card means the rate it charges is fixed and *doesn't* vary, right? No! The interest rate a fixed rate credit card charges may indeed change. All the credit card company needs to do is to inform you in writing at least 15 days before changing its rates.

APRs vary dramatically from one credit account to another. In 2011 when the national average APR on standard variable rate credit cards was 14.44 percent Chase had credit cards with rates from below 10 percent all the way up to 23 percent! Rates vary not only from one credit account to another, but can also vary over time on the same card. Some rates stay fixed, but others change based on market factors, for example, when interest rates in general change.

Some credit cards also offer low introductory rates called "teaser rates." These initial rates, which last 6 months to a year, can run as low as 0 percent, but can jump to 17 to 18 percent after the introductory period is over. About two-thirds of the credit card offers sent out in the mail each year have some type of teaser rate.

Also keep in mind that most credit accounts compound interest—that is, you end up paying interest on interest. So, if your credit card compounds interest on a monthly basis and you carry a balance, you could end up paying a rate of 21.7 percent on a credit card with a 19.8 percent APR.

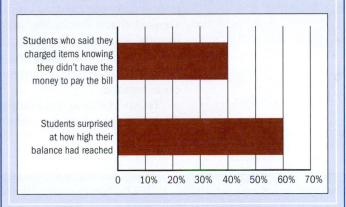
Calculating the Balance Owed

Once you know your APR, it's easy to calculate the cost of your credit account. You simply multiply your APR by your outstanding balance. That's easy enough, right? Wrong. The **method of determining the balance** (or **balance calculation method**) varies from one credit account to another. Before we get into the nitty gritty of the different ways that balances are calculated, remember this: If you don't carry a balance—if you pay off your outstanding balance each month—there is no unpaid balance and therefore no interest charge! Paying off your balance each month will make selecting a credit card easier (because you won't have to be concerned with interest rates) and will almost certainly make you richer. Unfortunately, not everyone does; in fact, according to the Federal Reserve Survey of Consumer Finances, 71 percent of cardholders ages 25 to 34 don't pay off their credit cards every month—they're still making someone rich, but unfortunately, not themselves.

The three primary methods used to determine interest charges on an unpaid credit balance are (1) the average daily balance method, (2) the previous balance method, and (3) the adjusted balance method.

The most commonly used method for calculating interest payments is the **average daily balance method**; in fact, according to the Bankcard Holders Association of America, this method is used by about 95 percent of all bank card issuers. This method adds up your daily balances for each day during the billing period and then divides this sum by the number of days in the billing period to calculate your average balance. Your interest payments are then based on this balance.

An alternative to this method is the **previous balance method**, in which interest payments are charged against what you owed at the end of the previous billing period, with no credit given for this month's payments. This method is relatively simple, but it's also expensive.

Method of Determining the Balance (or Balance Calculation Method)
The method by which a credit card balance is determined. The finance charges are then based on the level of this balance.

Average Daily Balance Method
A method of calculating the balance on which interest is paid by summing the outstanding balances owed each day during the billing period and dividing by the number of days in the period.

Previous Balance Method
A method of calculating interest payments on outstanding credit using the balance at the end of the previous billing period.

Adjusted Balance Method
A method of calculating interest payments on outstanding credit in which interest payments are charged against the balance at the end of the previous billing period less any payments and returns made.

A third method used by lenders is the **adjusted balance method**, which is a favorable variation of the previous balance method. Under this method, interest is charged against the previous month's balance only after any payments have been subtracted. Because interest isn't charged on payments, this method results in lower interest charges than the previous balance method. An example of interest calculations using these three methods is given in Figure 6.1.

There are numerous variations to these three methods. For example, some lenders calculate the average daily balance *including* new purchases; others *exclude* them. There's been a recent trend toward using a two-cycle average daily balance. Interest is calculated over the past two billing periods whenever the entire balance isn't completely paid off. Actually, the interest payments are the same under the two-cycle and one-cycle average daily balance methods for anyone who pays off the balance each month or who carries a balance from month to month.

The big losers under a two-cycle average daily balance method are those who periodically pay off their entire balance. A study by the Bankcard Holders of America showed that a cardholder with a 19.8 percent interest rate who charged $1,000 per month, paid only the minimum payment except for every third month when the entire balance was paid, and continued this pattern for the entire year, would pay $132 in finance charges under the one-cycle method and over $196 under the two-cycle method.

To say the least, calculating the charges on your balance is extremely confusing. There's one surefire way around this problem: Pay off your balance every month.

FIGURE 6.1   Calculation of Interest on Outstanding Balances

Example: Your credit card's annual interest rate is 18 percent and you begin the month with a previous balance of $1,000. In addition, your payments against your credit card balance this month are $900, which are made on the 15th of the month. You make no additional purchases during the month.

Calculate your average daily balance by summing the daily balances and dividing by the number of days in the period.

Average Daily Balance Method

Monthly Interest Rate	1.5%
Sum of All Daily Balances	
During the Billing Period	$16,500
Days in Billing Period	30 days
Average Daily Balance	$550
Interest Charged	$8.25
	($550 × 1.5%)

Under the previous balance method, interest payments are charged against the balance at the end of the previous billing period. In effect, interest is charged on the entire closing balance regardless of whether or not payments and returns are made. Thus, regardless of the size of any partial credit repayment during the month, you will still pay interest on the total unpaid balance you had at the end of the previous billing period.

Previous Balance Method

Monthly Interest Rate	1.5%
Previous Balance	$1,000
Payments	$900
Interest Charged	$15.00
	($1,000 × 1.5%)

The adjusted balance method is a favorable variation of the previous balance method in which interest payments are charged against the balance at the end of the previous billing period less any payments and returns made. Because interest is not charged on payments, this method results in lower interest charges than does the previous balance method.

Adjusted Balance Method

Monthly Interest Rate	1.5%
Previous Balance	$1,000
Payments	$900
Interest Charged	$1.50
	($100 × 1.5%)

Buying Money: The Cash Advance

Many credit cards allow you to get cash advances at automated teller machines (ATMs). In effect, you're taking out a loan when you get a cash advance—and it's an extremely expensive way to borrow money. When you withdraw cash from an ATM using your credit card, you begin paying interest *immediately*, as opposed to when you purchase an item with a credit card, when interest is not charged until after the date the payment is due. Also, many credit cards charge a higher rate on cash advances than they do on normal purchases.

In addition, cash advances generally carry an up-front fee of 2 to 4 percent of the amount advanced. Finally, many cards require you to pay down the balance for purchases before you pay down the higher interest rate cash advance balance. Keep in mind that although you can give yourself a big, fat, immediate cash loan using your credit card, that loan comes with some big, fat, immediate charges.

> ### FACTS OF LIFE
>
> According to a study of **undergraduates** by Nellie Mae, the average outstanding balance on **undergraduate** credit cards was $2,169, while the average outstanding balance on **graduate** student credit cards is $8,612. Moreover, on average, the older the **graduate** student the greater the credit card balance they hold. Nellie Mae found that older **graduate** students (age 30–59) carry $12,593 in credit card debt, almost twice as much as their younger counterparts (age 22–29) who carry an average debt of $6,479.

Grace Period

Typically, the lender allows you a **grace period** before charging interest on an outstanding balance. For most credit cards, there's a 20- to 25-day grace period from the date of the bill. Once the grace period has passed, you're charged the APR on the balance as determined by the credit card issuer.

As a result of the grace period, finance charges might not be assessed against credit card purchases for almost 2 months. For example, if the credit card issuer mails out bills on the first of the month, a purchase made on the second of the month would not appear until the next month's bill and not have to be paid until the end of the grace period—22 to 25 days after that—a total of almost 2 months. Although most credit cards allow a grace period on normal purchases, it's a general rule that with cash advances there is no grace period, meaning that finance charges are assessed against the cash advance from the date it is received.

Beware! Some credit cards don't have a grace period—that is, you start paying interest when you make the purchase. If your credit card doesn't provide for a grace period, that means you pay a finance charge on every purchase you make with your credit card!

The most confusing aspect of grace periods is this: With most credit cards, if you don't completely pay off all your previous month's borrowing, then the grace period doesn't apply and you begin paying interest immediately on new purchases. In fact, the size of your unpaid balance doesn't matter—it could be only one penny. The result is the same: On most credit cards the grace period is canceled if you carry an unpaid balance from the previous month.

Grace Period
The length of time given to make a payment before interest is charged against the outstanding balance on a credit card.

Annual Fee

Some credit card issuers also impose an **annual fee** for the privilege of using their card. Typically the charge ranges from $10 to $100, but the American Express Centurion Card charges a $2,500 annual fee. These fees add up quickly if you have several cards. However, over 70 percent of the 25 biggest credit card issuers don't charge an annual fee, and others don't charge one as long as you use their card at least once per year.

Annual Fee
A fixed annual charge imposed by a credit card.

Merchant's Discount Fee
The percentage of the sale that the merchant pays to the credit card issuer.

Cash Advance Fee
A charge for making a cash advance, paid as either a fixed amount or a percentage of the cash advance.

Late Fee
A fee imposed as a result of not paying your credit card bill on time.

Over-the-Limit Fee
A fee imposed whenever you go over your credit limit.

Penalty Rate
The rate you pay if you don't make your minimum payments on time.

How do these card issuers make money? Well, there's the rate of interest they charge on outstanding balances, plus they charge a fee to the merchants that accept their card. Typically, when you charge a purchase against your credit card, the merchant pays a percentage of the sale, called the **merchant's discount fee**, to the credit card issuer. This fee typically ranges from 1.5 to 5 percent (and in some cases up to 10 percent) of the amount charged.

Additional Fees

If credit card issuers make money from merchant discount fees every time you use their cards, you'd think that paying your annual fee and the sometimes exorbitant interest on your balance would be enough to keep them happy. Of course, you'd be wrong. There are still plenty of additional and penalty fees.

First, there's a **cash advance fee**, which we talked about earlier. It is either a fixed amount—for example, $5 per transaction—or a percentage—usually around 3 percent—of the cash advance. Remember, that's on top of the interest you are charged from the date of the advance. Remember, too, that some credit card issuers charge a higher interest rate on cash advances than they do on normal charges to the card. Bottom line? A small cash advance can wind up being a big financial setback.

Another fee you might get stuck paying is a **late fee**, which results from not paying your credit card bill on time. As a result of the new CARD Act, credit card late fees are capped at $25 for occasional late payments; however, if the cardholder is late more than once in a 6-month period the fees can be higher. By "on time," the credit card company may not just mean a specific date, but also a certain time may be specified, say, 1 P.M. On top of the late fee, you might also get hit with an **over-the-limit fee** for charging more than your credit limit allows. In 2010, the average over-the-limit fee was more than $39, and these fees are on the rise.

Finally, there are **penalty rates**. This is the interest rate you pay on your balance if you don't make your minimum payments on time. For example, the rate you pay on your balance could rise by 10 percent or more if you don't make your minimum payment on time. Considering that if you don't make your minimum payment on time you will also be paying a late fee, it is clear that to avoid being crushed by credit card costs, always make your minimum payment by the date the payment is due!

Lastly, watch closely for changes in policies and rates. These are usually announced via "bill stuffers"—notices enclosed with your bill. Be alert for the words: "Important Notice of Change in Terms," which may signal a higher interest rate, a bigger late fee, or a shorter grace period.

When choosing a credit card the bottom line is this: Beware! Before you sign up for that N'SyncUltraTitanium card with a $100,000 line of credit and an introductory 0.0 percent APR, read the fine print.

> ## STOP & THINK
>
> If you pay only your minimum balance, you might be paying for a long time. If you have a balance of $3,900 on a card with an 18 percent APR, and you pay only the minimum amount required by some cards each month, paying off your bill would take 35 years. Moreover, you'd end up paying $10,096 in interest in addition to the principal of $3,900. What to do? Answer: Avoid carrying a balance; pay off your credit card balance each month. If you do carry a balance, pay it off as quickly as possible. If you've ever carried a balance, what's the highest its been?

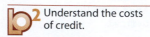 Understand the costs of credit.

The Pros and Cons of Credit Cards

Now that you know how expensive credit can be, why would you ever want to use it? Well, there are some good reasons. Let's take a look at them. (Then, we'll look at some of the disadvantages of using credit cards.)

The Advantages of Credit Cards

Without question, it would be difficult to function in society today without some kind of credit card or open credit. Simple tasks such as making hotel reservations would be nearly impossible without a credit card. Credit cards can be used as identification when cashing checks, for video rental memberships, and almost anywhere else multiple pieces of identification are needed. And using credit extends your shopping opportunities—it's nearly impossible to make a purchase over the phone or the Internet without a credit card.

> **FACTS OF LIFE**
>
> The new CARD Act reduced fees.
>
> ◆ Late Fees (pre-reform average): $39
> ◆ Maximum today: $25

Consider, too, that it's more convenient to purchase items with credit cards. Not only do you receive an itemized billing of exactly how much you spent and where you spent it, but you also reduce the risk of theft associated with carrying around large amounts of cash. Open credit also is a source of temporary emergency funds. If you have enough open credit to cover emergency expenses, you don't need to keep as much in liquid emergency funds. Credit, then, frees you to put your money in higher-yielding investments.

P5 Principle Stuff Happens, or the Importance of Liquidity

By purchasing an item on credit, you get to use it before you actually pay for it. Thus when you buy an Aeropostale shirt or a Glee Cast CD and charge it, you can wear the shirt or play the CD as much as you like in spite of the fact that you won't really pay for it until you pay your credit card bill. And by using a single credit card to make purchases from a variety of sources, you consolidate your bills. You can also use credit to consolidate your debt. Many individuals with numerous outstanding bills transfer all these debts to a single credit card in an effort to get better control over their borrowing.

If the price of an item that you intend to purchase is about to go up, buying the item on credit today lets you pay less than you'd have to pay tomorrow. In addition, if you pay your full credit card balance each month, a credit card allows you to earn interest on money you would not have if you paid cash from the date of the purchase until the payment date.

Many cards offer "free" extended product warranties and travel insurance. Some give you frequent flier miles on your favorite airline or credit toward the purchase of anything from Shell gasoline and GM cars to *Rolling Stone* magazine or toys at Toys "R" Us. These benefits, while valuable, may not actually be free, because the cards that offer them are more likely to carry an annual fee.

> **FACTS OF LIFE**
>
> According to a study of **undergraduates** by Nellie Mae, college students from the Northeast had the lowest outstanding average balances while students from the Midwest had the highest balances.

The Drawbacks of Credit Cards

Although credit cards are indispensable in today's economy, they've also caused enormous problems for many individuals. There are many reasons to be wary of credit cards and open credit. While there are more advantages to credit cards than there are disadvantages, the disadvantages are significant.

First, it's simply too easy to spend money with a credit card because it seems as if you haven't really spent money. Moreover, it's too easy to lose track of exactly how much you've spent because what you've charged doesn't appear until your monthly statement shows up. If you've overspent, your only recourse may be to pay off your purchases over time, paying hefty amounts of interest and spending much more than you'd bargained for.

It's not just that you pay interest on an unpaid credit card balance; it's the high rate of interest that you pay that makes credit card borrowing so unappealing. For example, in 2011 the average 15-year fixed-rate home mortgage charged 4.15 percent,

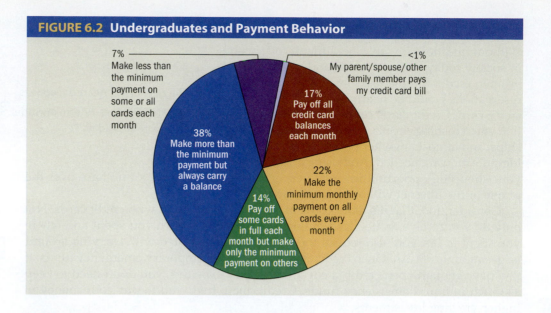

FIGURE 6.2 Undergraduates and Payment Behavior

the average home equity line of credit charged 7.20 percent, and the average credit card charged 14.44 percent. At the same time, 1-year CDs paid only 1.06 percent. Banks are effectively borrowing money at 1.06 percent and lending it out—by issuing credit cards—at 14.44 percent. That's quite a tidy profit, and it explains why you keep getting credit card applications in the mail.

Any time you use a credit card, you're obligating future income. That is, in the future you'll have less budget flexibility because a portion of your take-home pay will have to be used to pay off credit card expenditures plus any interest on your unpaid balance. If you don't control your spending, you can wind up with some heavy budgetary problems as a larger and larger portion of your income goes toward paying off past debt and interest owed. If this problem sounds familiar, look no further than our national debt.

Just how well do undergraduates do at paying off their credit card bills? Not that well at all according to a study by Nellie Mae. As shown in Figure 6.2, only 17 percent of undergraduates pay off their credit cards each month, while 38 percent make more than the minimum payment but always carry a balance on their credit cards.

What the CARD Act Means for You—The New Credit Card Rules

With the passage of the Credit Card Accountability, Responsibility, and Disclosure (CARD) Act of 2009 came sweeping reform resulting in new credit card rules. Let's take a look at them.[1]

1. **Notification of rate increase.** Your credit card company has to tell you when they plan to increase your rate or other fees. Your credit card company must send you a notice 45 days before they can

   ◆ increase your interest rate;
   ◆ change certain fees (such as annual fees, cash advance fees, and late fees) that apply to your account; or
   ◆ make other significant changes to the terms of your card.

---

[1] *Source:* Board of Governors of the Federal Reserve System, accessed March 9, 2011, www.federalreserve .gov/consumerinfo/wyntk_creditcardrules.htm and www.federalreserve.gov/consumerinfo/wyntk_ creditcardrules2.htm.

The company does **not** have to send you a 45-day advance notice if

- ◆ you have a variable interest rate tied to an index (if the index goes up, the company does not have to provide notice before your rate goes up);
- ◆ your introductory rate expires and reverts to the previously disclosed "go-to" rate;
- ◆ your rate increases because you are in a workout agreement and you haven't made your payments as agreed.

2. **Notification of schedule for pay off.** Your credit card company has to tell you how long it will take to pay off your balance. Your monthly credit card bill will include information on how long it will take you to pay off your balance if you only make minimum payments. It will also tell you how much you would need to pay each month in order to pay off your balance in 3 years.

3. **No interest rate increases for the first year.** Your credit card company cannot increase your rate for the first 12 months after you open an account. There are some exceptions:

- ◆ If your card has a variable interest rate tied to an index (your rate can go up whenever the index goes up).
- ◆ If there is an introductory rate, it must be in place for at least 6 months; after that your rate can revert to the "go-to" rate the company disclosed when you got the card.
- ◆ If you are more than 60 days late in paying your bill, your rate can go up.
- ◆ If you are in a workout agreement and you don't make your payments as agreed, your rate can go up.

4. **Increased rates apply only to new charges.** If your credit card company does raise your interest rate after the first year, the new rate will apply only to new charges you make. If you have a balance, your old interest rate will apply to that balance.

5. **Restrictions on over-the-limit transactions.** You must tell your credit card company that you want it to allow transactions that will take you over your credit limit. Otherwise, if a transaction would take you over your limit, it may be turned down. If you do not opt in to over-the-limit transactions and your credit card company allows one to go through, it cannot charge you an over-the-limit fee.

6. **Caps on high-fee cards.** If your credit card company requires you to pay fees (such as an annual fee or application fee), those fees cannot total more than 25 percent of the initial credit limit. For example, if your initial credit limit is $500, the fees for the first year cannot be more than $125. This limit does not apply to penalty fees, such as penalties for late payments.

7. **Protections for underage consumers.** If you are under 21, you will need to show that you are able to make payments, or you will need a cosigner, in order to open a credit card account.

8. **Standard payment dates and times.** Your credit card company must mail or deliver your credit card bill at least 21 days before your payment is due.

9. **Payments directed to highest interest balances first.** If you make more than the minimum payment on your credit card bill, your credit card company must in general apply the excess amount to the balance with the highest interest rate.

10. **Fee limits.** Your credit card company cannot charge you a fee of more than $25 unless:

- ◆ one of your last six payments was late, in which case your fee may be up to $35; or
- ◆ your credit card company can show that the costs it incurs as a result of late payments justify a higher fee.

In addition, your credit card company cannot charge a late payment fee that is greater than your minimum payment. So, if your minimum payment is $20, your late payment fee can't be more than $20. Similarly, if you exceed your credit limit by $5, you can't be charged an over-the-limit fee of more than $5.

11. No inactivity fees. Your credit card company can't charge you inactivity fees, such as fees for not using your card.

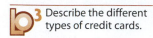 **3** Describe the different types of credit cards.

Choosing a Source of Open Credit

There are several different types of open credit available today including some credit card variations along with the traditional charge account. Let's take a look at these options, and then discuss how to choose which one is best for you.

Bank Credit Cards

Bank Credit Card
A credit card issued by a bank or large corporation, generally as a Visa or MasterCard.

Most credit card purchases are made on bank credit cards. A **bank credit card** is a credit card issued by a bank or large corporation, for example, AT&T and Quicken both issue credit cards, generally as a Visa or MasterCard. Visa and MasterCard don't actually issue cards themselves; rather, they act as franchise organizations that provide credit authorization systems, accounting-statement record keeping, and advertising services, and allow banks and large corporations to issue the cards with the Visa or MasterCard name. Within certain broad limits, banks can establish their own policies with respect to interest, grace periods, fees, and services, so there are dramatic differences among bank credit cards.

Visa and MasterCard are so popular because they provide an efficient system of credit authorization. Being able to check a customer's credit at the time of purchase provides merchants with an assurance that there is no problem with the credit card or line of credit. It has led to the wide acceptance of these bank credit cards both in the United States and abroad. Today there are over 7,000 to choose from.

Today many bank cards also offer benefits such as rental-car damage coverage, extended warranties, and travel accident insurance, as well as frequent flier miles and rebates of all kinds. Generally, bank cards that provide rebates are "co-branded" or "rebate cards." They have a "brand name" listed on the card, such as GM or Disney, and provide rebates and discounts on GM cars, airline tickets, and Disney vacations.

Many bank cards come with reward programs in which you earn points that may be redeemed for travel, merchandise, and cash rebates. But once again, the terms on reward cards can vary dramatically. To check for rewards programs and compare annual fees and interest rates visit **www.bankrate.com**. Obviously, reward programs are great as long as you pay off your credit card every month. But you don't want the potential for airline miles or bonus points to cause you to charge more than you would otherwise. You want to make sure the benefits are worth more than the card's costs, including the annual fee.

The one card that is a bit different is the Discover card. Although Visa and MasterCard license their services to the banks that in turn issue the credit cards, the Discover card is issued by a single bank. Not only is the Discover bank card different in that it has a single issuer, it also contains some unusual features: It carries no annual fee and returns to cardholders a small percentage of their annual purchases.

STOP & THINK

Even if you're "preapproved" for a card at a certain interest rate with a specific fee structure, it doesn't mean that that's the card you'll actually get. After the credit card company reviews your credit history and the facts you disclose in the application, you may be sent a card with less favorable terms than the one originally offered to you. Do you think you might activate the new card before you looked closely at the terms? Do you think this practice is ethical? Why or why not?

Bank Card Variations

There are several different card classes of bank credit cards. A card class refers to the credit level of the cardholder. At the low end is the standard with credit limits from $500 to $3,000. Above that are Gold cards, such as the Visa Gold card, which offer a bigger line of credit, generally $5,000 and up, and provide extra perks or incentives. Finally, there are **premium** or **prestige credit cards**, such as the MasterCard Platinum card, which offer credit limits as high as $100,000 or more and benefits beyond a standard credit card, such as emergency medical and legal services, travel insurance and services, rebates, and warranties on new purchases. Now, Visa and MasterCard even offer Titanium cards, with higher credit limits and even more benefits.

Another variation of the bank credit card is the **affinity card**, which is a credit card issued in conjunction with a specific charity or organization such as the Sierra Club, Mothers Against Drunk Driving (MADD), the National Rifle Association (NRA), and many colleges and universities. The card bears the sponsoring group's name, logo, or picture. These cards send a portion of their annual fee or a percentage of the purchases back to the sponsoring organization.

Although the fees and annual interest rates on affinity cards vary from card to card, in general affinity cards are expensive: Their annual fees start at $20 and their interest rates are higher than most bank cards. Still, many individuals use them, seeing them as an easy way to support their favorite charity or organization. Actually, it can be an expensive way to make charitable donations, particularly if you ever maintain an unpaid balance. Also, a large part of your charitable donation actually gets "donated" to the issuing bank, and you can't take a tax deduction for that donation!

The final variation on the bank credit card is the **secured credit card**. A secured credit card is a regular bank credit card backed by the pledge of some collateralized asset. If you can't pay what you've charged to your credit card, the issuing bank has a specific asset it can lay claim to. For example, your credit card may be linked to a CD you hold in the issuing bank. If you can't pay off your charges—so long, CD. For the bank, no customer is a bad risk if they are able to put up collateral. But what's the benefit to you? Why would you want a secured credit card? Well, you likely wouldn't, but you may not have a choice. If you're a bad credit risk, it may be the only credit card you can get.

Premium or Prestige Credit Card

A bank or travel and entertainment (T&E) credit card that offers credit limits as high as $100,000 or more in addition to numerous added perks, including emergency medical and legal services, travel services, rebates, and insurance on new purchases.

Affinity Card

A credit card issued in conjunction with a specific charity or organization. It carries the sponsoring group's name and/or picture on the credit card itself and sends a portion of the annual fee or a percentage of the purchases back to the sponsoring organization.

Secured Credit Card

A credit card backed by the pledge of some collateralized asset.

FACTS OF LIFE

The typical consumer has access to approximately $19,000 on all of his or her credit cards combined. More than half of all people with credit cards are using less than 30 percent of their total credit limit, and just 1 in 7 are using 80 percent or more of their credit card limit.

Travel and Entertainment Cards

Travel and entertainment (T&E) cards, such as the American Express Corporate card, were initially aimed at providing business customers with a means of paying for travel, business entertainment, and other business expenses, while keeping these charges separate from personal expenditures. Over time, however, T&E cards have come to be used similarly to traditional bank credit cards. The major difference between T&E cards and bank credit cards is that T&E cards *do not* offer revolving credit and require full payment of the balance each month. Aside from the prestige that they may afford holders, their only advantage is their interest-free grace period.

The issuer's only income from these cards is the annual fee, which can run as high as $2,500 per year, and the merchant's discount fee on each purchase. The three primary issuers of T&E cards are American Express, Diners Club, and Carte Blanche, with American Express dominating this market. There are also T&E premium or prestige cards.

Travel and Entertainment (T&E) Card

A credit card initially meant for business customers to allow them to pay for travel and entertainment expenses, keeping them separate from their other expenditures.

Single-Purpose Cards

Single-Purpose Card
A credit card that can be used only at a specific company.

A **single-purpose card** is a credit card that can be used only at a specific company. For example, a Texaco credit card can be used only to charge purchases at a Texaco service station. These companies issue their own cards and avoid merchant's discount fees. The terms associated with single-purpose cards vary dramatically from card to card: Some allow for revolving credit and others do not, but in general, they don't require an annual fee.

If you can use your US Airways Visa card at the Texaco station, why do you need a Texaco charge card? The answer is, you don't, and if you're trying to get enough miles for that free flight to San Francisco, you'd be better off using your Visa. However, these cards do limit credit access to a single company, which may be an advantage. For example, a mother may want her 16-year-old daughter to have a Texaco credit card in case she needs to buy gas, but may not want her to have a Visa card that she can take to the mall.

Traditional Charge Account

Traditional Charge Account
A charge account, as opposed to a credit card, that can be used to make purchases only at the issuing company.

A **traditional charge account** is a charge account offered by a business. For example, phone and utility companies and even doctors and dentists provide services and bill you later, usually giving you a grace period to pay up. This payment system is a type of open credit account—one in which no cards are involved. After you receive your monthly bill, you're expected to pay it in full. If payment is not received by the due date, an interest penalty is generally tacked on.

The major advantage of a charge account is convenience. Just think how tedious it would be to have to pay for each long-distance phone call, or to pay for your electricity on a daily basis. In addition, there's the benefit of an interest-free grace period and the use of services before having to pay for them. For the billing company, a traditional charge account is primarily a matter of convenience—it's just an easy and efficient way to collect bills.

The Choice: What's Best for You

In evaluating the many kinds of credit cards available, you'll find that different cards have different strong points. Some cards have low fees and extended grace periods but high interest rates. Although this may be the best combination for some, it may be the worst for others. You have to understand how you're going to use the card before you can decide which one to choose. Most individuals use credit cards for convenience, for credit, or both.

A *credit user* generally carries an unpaid balance from month to month. Most credit users don't use the grace period, and the annual fee pales relative to the amount of interest they pay annually. If you're a credit user, the most important decision factor is the APR or interest rate on the unpaid balance, because it will be the largest credit expense you face. Should the issuing bank's location be a concern in choosing a credit card? No: Regardless of where your credit card issuer is located, your card works essentially the same. A credit user should search as far and wide as necessary to get the card with the lowest possible interest rate.

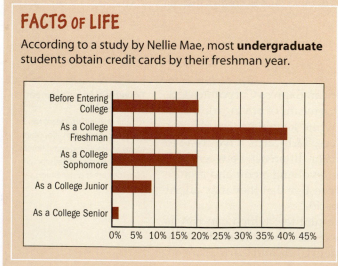

FACTS of LIFE

According to a study by Nellie Mae, most **undergraduate** students obtain credit cards by their freshman year.

MONEY MATTERS

Tips from Marcy Furney, ChFC, Certified Financial Planner™

CREDIT LINES

One of my clients told me she finally got control of her impulse purchasing on credit by putting her cards in a zipper bag and freezing them in a bucket of water. That way she has some time to think things through while she waits for them to thaw. If this sounds too bizarre to you, or your freezer is too full of TV dinners and ice cream, here are some more ideas.

Carry one credit card and use it only for convenience. That means you can use it only if there's money in the bank to cover the amount of the charge.

Subtract the charge from your check register when you make it. Negative balance? Then no charging!

Pay your entire balance each month.

If you have large balances on high-interest cards, look for one with lower interest and transfer the debt. Don't use that card for any new charges. Set a date for clearing the balance, calculate how much you have to pay each month to meet the deadline, and pay it off. Most cards offer the lower rate for only a year or so and some charge higher interest on new charges than the published rate for the transferred amount.

Protect yourself from fraud and temptation by shredding those "you have already been approved" credit card applications and the "convenience checks" sent by your credit card company. Though you can't do much about stopping the applications, you can request that your current credit providers discontinue sending the checks. Normally they are part of planned marketing campaigns, and it takes 2 to 3 months for the mailings to stop.

If you are in too deep but have an excellent payment record, call the credit card company to discuss lowering your interest rate. Some won't consider such a request if you have current charges on that card. Check into a home equity loan to pay off the debt. Be aware, though, that you must have your spending under control and be willing to pay off that loan quickly, or you jeopardize the roof over your head.

Don't even consider investing money if you have consumer debt. No investment can guarantee you a return equal to the 18 to 21 percent cost of credit.

If you're paying off a large balance, make that payment a fixed expense in your budget. Never pay just the minimum amount on your statement. You may have to forgo entertainment or "brown bag" your lunch for a while.

Take control. An excellent credit history is a true asset, and a large line of credit could be very important in case of emergency.

For a *convenience user*—someone who pays off the credit card balance each month—the interest rate is irrelevant. Convenience users should look for a credit card with a low annual fee and an interest-free grace period. The interest-free grace period is especially important because it allows convenience users to pay off their balance each month without incurring any interest payments. Beyond a low annual fee and an interest-free grace period, a convenience user might consider a card that carries benefits, such as a Marriott credit card or one that gives frequent flier miles.

A *convenience and credit user* is someone who generally, but not always, pays off all of the balance. For this type of credit user, the ideal card is one with no annual fee, an interest-free grace period, and a low interest rate on the unpaid balance. Unfortunately, finding all of this in one card is next to impossible. Convenience and credit users, therefore, must simply look for the combination of features they think will result in the lowest total cost, considering both the interest rate and the annual fee. Figure 6.3 shows what features different types of credit card users find important.

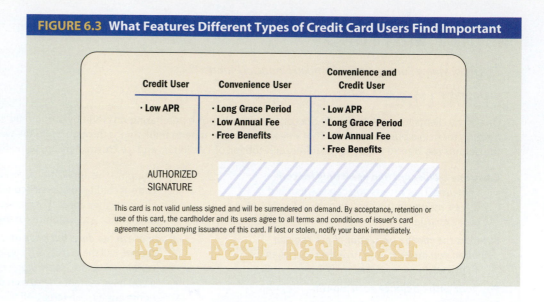

FIGURE 6.3 What Features Different Types of Credit Card Users Find Important

Credit User	Convenience User	Convenience and Credit User
· Low APR	· Long Grace Period · Low Annual Fee · Free Benefits	· Low APR · Long Grace Period · Low Annual Fee · Free Benefits

AUTHORIZED SIGNATURE

This card is not valid unless signed and will be surrendered on demand. By acceptance, retention or use of this card, the cardholder and its users agree to all terms and conditions of issuer's card agreement accompanying issuance of this card. If lost or stolen, notify your bank immediately.

1234 1234 1234 1234

4 Know what determines your credit card worthiness and how to secure a credit card.

Getting a Credit Card

For a college student today, getting a credit card is generally not a problem. Credit card issuers see college students as excellent prospects. They may not be earning much now, but their future earning prospects are bright. Also, some lenders try to ensure themselves of payment by requiring parents to cosign on the credit cards; others simply assume that the student's parents will step in if there are problems paying off any debt. Credit card issuers many times set up shop near large campuses and offer free gifts—anything from free or discount flights to free Frisbees—for those who apply. In addition, if you have a mailbox, there's a good chance you'll get a credit card offer. Fortunately, the CARD Act of 2009 has toned down the actions of credit card issuers by banning offers of freebies (pizzas and T-shirts, for example) if students sign up for credit cards on or near campus (where "near campus" is defined as within 1,000 feet) or at college-sponsored events. In addition, credit card issuers are now banned from issuing credit cards to anyone under 21—unless they can show proof that they can repay the credit card loans independently or someone over 21 cosigns on the account with them. But once you're 21, you're fair game. And there are plenty of credit card offers to go around. In fact, credit card companies send out a whopping 6 billion credit card offers annually, or roughly 60 per U.S. household! As for the average college student, prior to the new law they received about eight solicitations each year. However, the 2009 CARD Act does not allow for prescreened credit card offers for those under 21 unless they opt in. Still, if you're a typical college student, by your senior year you'll probably be carrying four or more credit cards as shown in Figure 6.4.

For a student, getting a credit card is an excellent idea. First, it can be used for emergency funds while away from home. Second, by using a credit card prudently, a student can build up a solid credit history. Is your credit history important? Well, yes, if you ever want to do such things as buy a house, rent an apartment, or get a job.

The first step in obtaining a credit card is applying. The application focuses on factors that determine your creditworthiness, or your ability and willingness to repay any charges incurred. Sometimes the lender may insist on an interview. You've absolutely got to be honest and consistent in the application process. If your answers are inconsistent or don't conform to what the lender has found out independently, your application will be turned down. Let's find out what makes you creditworthy.

FIGURE 6.4 Undergraduates Carrying Four or More Credit Cards

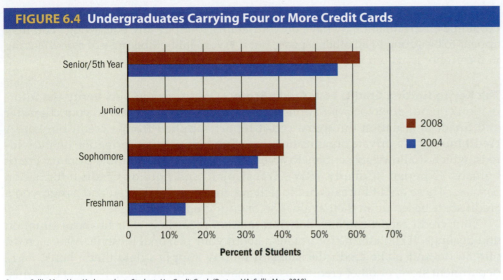

Source: Sallie Mae, *How Undergraduate Students Use Credit Cards* (Reston, VA: Sallie Mae, 2010).

Credit Evaluation: The Five Cs of Credit

In determining what makes an individual creditworthy, most lenders refer to the "five Cs" of credit: character, capacity, capital, collateral, and conditions. *Character* refers to your sense of responsibility with respect to debt payment. Have you established a record of timely repayment of past debts, such as student loans? Keep in mind that exhibiting good character involves not overextending yourself with respect to credit—not taking on too much debt given your income level. In assessing your character, lenders also look at how long you've lived at one address and how long you've held your current job. In effect, stability often passes for character.

Capacity and *capital* work together in determining your ability to repay any credit card charges. In assessing your *capacity*, lenders look to both your current income level and your current level of borrowing—that is, lenders are concerned with your level of nonobligated income. Most financial advisors suggest that your total debt payments, including mortgage payments, should account for less than 36 percent of your gross pay.

Capital refers to the size of your financial holdings or investment portfolio. Obviously, the more you have in savings, the more creditworthy you are. By looking at your capital, lenders want to know whether your income is sufficient to provide for the debt you've already incurred. The larger your nonobligated annual income (capacity) and the value of your investment portfolio (capital), the more creditworthy you are.

Collateral refers to assets or property offered as security to obtain credit. If you were to default on a loan, the collateral—perhaps a car or a piece of land—would be sold and the proceeds from the sale would go to repay the debt. The more your collateral is worth, the more creditworthy you are.

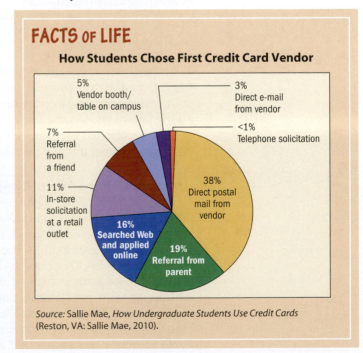

FACTS of LIFE

How Students Chose First Credit Card Vendor

5% Vendor booth/table on campus

3% Direct e-mail from vendor

<1% Telephone solicitation

7% Referral from a friend

11% In-store solicitation at a retail outlet

16% Searched Web and applied online

19% Referral from parent

38% Direct postal mail from vendor

Source: Sallie Mae, *How Undergraduate Students Use Credit Cards* (Reston, VA: Sallie Mae, 2010).

The last of the five Cs is *conditions*. Conditions refers to the impact the current economic environment may have on your ability to repay any borrowing. You may appear to be strong in all other aspects, but if you're laid off because of a downswing in the economy, you might not be able to meet your obligations.

The Key to Getting Credit: Your Credit Score

Credit card issuers verify the information you put down on your application and get information about your character and financial situation through a credit report supplied from a credit bureau. A **credit bureau** is a private organization that maintains credit information on individuals, which it allows subscribers to access for a fee. There are three primary credit bureaus: Experian (formerly TRW), TransUnion, and Equifax Credit Information Services. These credit bureaus put together a credit report on you and assign you a credit score based upon their evaluation of your creditworthiness.

Your credit report contains only information regarding your financial situation and dealings. It contains no information about your personal lifestyle. Also, a credit bureau doesn't make credit decisions: It merely supplies data that a bank, S&L, department store, or other creditor uses to make a credit decision. But make no mistake, your credit information not only plays a big role in whether you get that loan, it also helps determine how high your interest rate will be.

Determining Creditworthiness

Once your credit information has been assembled, it is translated into a three-digit number—your credit score—which measures your creditworthiness. Although some lenders look at each application individually and make a judgment call, it's more common that your credit application will be evaluated using credit scoring. **Credit scoring** involves the numerical evaluation or "scoring" of applicants. This score is then evaluated according to a predetermined standard. If your score is up to the acceptance standard, you are approved for credit. Credit scoring is efficient and relatively inexpensive for the lender. Its benefit to the borrower is that because it reduces the lender's uncertainty, the lender is more often able to make credit available to good risk customers at lower interest rates. However, credit scoring is not a flawless method of evaluating creditworthiness.

Your Credit Score

Your credit score has an enormous effect on your financial life, influencing everything from the rate you pay on your credit cards, to the size of your credit line, to your insurance rates, to your mortgage rate, to the amount of junk mail you receive asking you to take on one more credit card. In short, when it comes to lending money, you'll be evaluated by your credit score. With a strong credit score you'll also be paying a much lower interest rate on any money you borrow.

How Your Credit Score Is Computed—FICO and VantageScore

There are two primary credit scoring systems—FICO and VantageScore—with FICO being the dominant one. Although FICO scores go by a number of different names depending upon which credit bureau is calculating the credit score, they are calculated using models developed by the Fair Isaac Corporation. VantageScores are a new alternative to FICO scores and were initially aimed at helping lenders better evaluate those with poor, or subprime, credit. Both models begin with the information on your credit report and use this information to calculate a score that can run from 300 all the way to 850 for FICO and 500 to 990 for VantageScore. Figure 6.5 provides the distribution of the percent of the population with different FICO scores. You can also get an estimate of what your credit score is online at

Credit Bureau
A company that gathers information on consumers' financial history, including how quickly they have paid bills and whether they have been delinquent on bills in the past. The company summarizes this information and sells it to customers.

Credit Scoring
The numerical evaluation or "scoring" of credit applicants based on their credit history.

FIGURE 6.5 National Distribution of FICO Scores

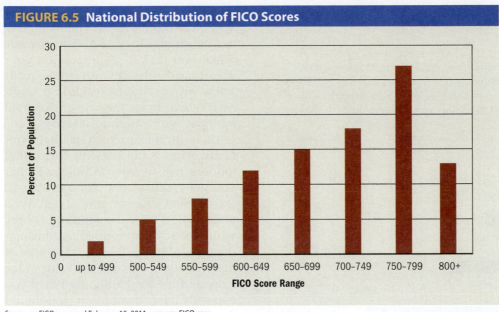

Source: myFICO, accessed February 15, 2011, www.myFICO.com.

www.myfico.com/ficocreditscoreestimator. You'll also find that your credit score may vary from credit bureau to credit bureau because while the different credit bureaus may be using the same credit scoring model to come up with a score, they may have different credit data in your file or use slightly different calculation methods. These FICO scores and VantageScores are then provided to lenders by the different credit bureaus.

What's a good credit score? In 2011, the national average FICO score was 693, but the cutoff to get the best mortgage rate generally requires a score of 760 or higher, with a score of around 620 often times serving as a cutoff point for receiving credit for many lenders. In effect, a good credit score doesn't just mean that you'll get a loan, it also means that you'll be paying less for it. For example, a person with a 760 score will be offered an interest rate of about 1.59 percent less on a loan than a person with a 639 score. Table 6.1 gives representative rates for different FICO scores along with what the monthly interest payments would be on a $300,000, 30-year fixed mortgage loan in 2011. As you can see in Table 6.1, the savings from a good FICO score also hold true for auto loans.

TABLE 6.1 Representative Rates and Monthly Payments for Different FICO Scores

30-Year Fixed Mortgage			36-Month Auto Loan		
FICO Score	APR	Monthly Payment	FICO Score	APR	Monthly Payment
760–850	4.571%	$1,533	720–850	4.811%	$747
700–759	4.793%	$1,573	690–719	6.331%	$764
680–699	4.970%	$1,605	660–689	8.210%	$786
660–679	5.184%	$1,644	620–659	11.797%	$828
640–659	5.614%	$1,725	590–619	17.656%	$900
620–639	6.160%	$1,830	500–589	18.663%	$912
Mortgage loan amount: $300,000			Auto loan amount: $25,000		

FACTS OF LIFE

Between fall 2004 and spring 2008, there was a dramatic decrease in students carrying zero balances on their credit cards. Moreover, it was the freshman class where this change was most pronounced. In fall 2004, 69 percent of freshmen had a zero balance on their credit cards while in spring 2008, the percentage of freshmen with a zero balance dropped to only 15 percent.

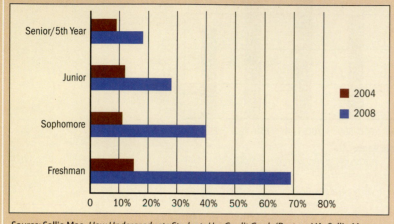

Source: Sallie Mae, *How Undergraduate Students Use Credit Cards* (Reston, VA: Sallie Mae, 2010).

While a low FICO score will cost you quite a bit when it comes time to get a mortgage loan, it costs even more when you look at its impact on your credit card rate. It's not unusual for a low FICO score to result in a credit card rate of twice the rate of that paid by those with a high FICO score.

It is important to note that your credit score is not the only factor that lenders use in determining whether you get credit or not. For example, in the decision whether or not to give you a mortgage loan the lending agency will look at your employment history, the type of job you have, the value of the property relative to the value of the loan, and the total amount of debt you currently have. In addition, you should know that the lending agency can't even calculate a FICO score for you unless you have had at least one credit account open for at least 6 months and have used that credit card in that time. In effect, if you haven't been using credit over the past 6 months they can't calculate your FICO score. Before looking at how your credit score is calculated, let's take a look at what is in your credit report.

What's in Your Credit Report   While each credit reporting agency uses a different format, all credit reports contain the same basic information. In your credit report you'll find:

◆ **Identifying Information** This includes your name, address, Social Security number, date of birth, and employment information; this information is used to identify you and is not used in determining your credit score.

◆ **Trade Lines or Credit Accounts** Lenders report on each account you have established with them. This information includes the type of account (credit cards, student loans, auto loan, mortgage, etc.) along with creditor and account number, balance, date opened, payment history, and current status, such as "OK," "Closed by customer," or "30 days late payment."

◆ **Inquiries** When you apply for a loan, you authorize your lender to ask for a copy of your credit report. This results in inquiries appearing on your credit report. Everyone who accessed your credit report within the last 2 years appears in this list in this section of your credit report. Your credit report also lists both "voluntary" inquiries, spurred by your own requests for credit, and "involuntary" inquiries, such as when lenders order your report so as to make you a preapproved credit offer in the mail.

◆ **Public Record and Collection Items** Your credit report also includes public record information collected from state and county courts, and information on overdue debt from collection agencies. Public record information includes bankruptcies, foreclosures, suits, wage attachments, liens, and judgments.

The Factors That Determine Your Credit Score   Now let's look at the five factors that determine your credit score, with Figure 6.6 illustrating this breakdown.

FIGURE 6.6 Factors That Determine Your Credit Score

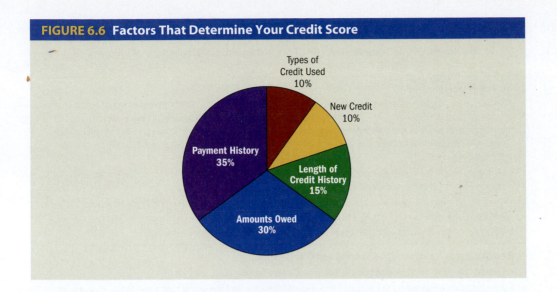

1. **Your Payment History (35 percent of your score)** Typically, your payment history makes up about 35 percent of your score. Since a lender is considering extending credit to you, it only makes sense that they want to know how you've handled your credit payments in the past.

2. **The Amount You Owe and Your Available Credit (30 percent of your score)** The amount you owe on your credit cards, your mortgage, your car loans, and any other outstanding debt, along with your total available credit account for about 30 percent of your FICO score. The amount of debt you have outstanding is not the only factor; whether you are close to or at your credit limit is also important.

3. **Length of Credit History (15 percent of your score)** The longer your credit accounts have been open and the longer you have had accounts with the same creditors, the higher will be your credit score, with these factors accounting for 15 percent of your score.

4. **Types of Credit Used (10 percent of your score)** The wider the variety of credit that you have accounts for 10 percent of your credit score. If you have several different types of credit outstanding, for example, credit cards, retail accounts, installment loans, an auto loan, and a mortgage loan, that is seen as an indication that you know how to handle your money.

5. **New Credit (10 percent of your score)** If you have recently made a lot of applications for credit, you will lose points on your FICO score. This is because individuals who are moving toward bankruptcy generally take one last grasp at credit, hoping it will keep them afloat.

Monitoring Your Credit Score   It's important to monitor your credit score. First, you must ensure that there are no errors in your credit report, since that's what is used to calculate your credit score. To do this you'll need to get a copy of your credit report annually. Some experts recommend getting a copy every few months to monitor for identity theft. The Fair and Accurate Credit Transactions Act (FACT Act) allows you to request one free copy of your credit report each year from the three major credit bureaus: Experian, Equifax, and TransUnion. If you'd like more information on how to request your report, log into **www.annualcreditreport .com**. Take care to ensure that you reach the FACT Act supported site, as imposter Web sites are on the rise. Table 6.2 provides additional information on the FACT Act.

TABLE 6.2 The Fair and Accurate Credit Transactions Act (FACT Act)
The Fair and Accurate Credit Transactions Act (FACT Act) was signed in 2003 with many of its provisions becoming active in 2004 and 2005. It provided:
Greater Protection Against Identity Theft   • You can now request one free copy of your credit report each year from each of the three major credit bureaus: Experian, Equifax, and TransUnion. You can get information about the availability of credit reports by logging on to **www.annualcreditreport.com** or calling 1–877–322–8228. It may be safer to call for your credit report using the toll free number because of all the imposter Web sites—as of mid-2005 there were some 98 of them!   • With just one phone call to a single credit bureau you can place a fraud alert on your credit record and improve the security of your credit rating.   • Once you've placed a fraud alert on your credit record, anyone who uses your credit report is required to take additional measures to confirm your identity before opening an account.   • Only the last five digits of your credit card number will be printed on electronic receipts.
New Standards for Information Sharing and Credit Reporting   • Federal law governing credit reporting will override inconsistent state laws.   • New limits are imposed on the sharing of medical information and the use of customer information among affiliated companies.

If you've already used up your one free report from each of the three credit bureaus this year and would like another, you can either order online (**www.MyFico.com**) or contact the credit bureaus directly. Once you have your credit report, you should make sure that the information in it is correct. Look at all the credit accounts listed and make sure they are yours and that they're correct. Do mistakes appear often in credit reports? The National Association of Public Interest Research Groups says that 79 percent of the credit reports it surveyed contained either serious errors or other mistakes of some kind. Moreover, it found that 25 percent of the credit reports it surveyed contained errors that were significant enough to result in the denial of credit, errors such as false delinquencies, and accounts that did not belong to the consumer.

Consumer Credit Rights

The easiest way to resolve a credit complaint is to take it directly to the creditor. However, if that doesn't work, there are a number of federal laws aimed at protecting you if you have a complaint about credit.

The Credit Bureau and Your Rights   Because your credit report is so important, Congress passed the Fair and Accurate Credit Transactions Act (FACT Act) in 2003, which we discussed earlier. This act allows you to request one free copy of your credit report each year from the three major credit bureaus: Experian, Equifax, and TransUnion.

If the information in your file isn't accurate or complete, contact the credit bureaus; their contact information is given in Table 6.3. They must investigate any errors you point out and make corrections. For example, your file may inadvertently contain information about someone with a name very similar to yours, or it may contain incorrect or incomplete credit information, perhaps listing accounts that are closed or that you never had. If there are any mistakes, you should notify your credit bureau so it can investigate and make the corrections.

If the credit bureau investigates and determines that the information in your report is inaccurate, you have the right to have in your file a statement presenting your view of the issue. This statement gives you the chance to dispute the accuracy of information in your file. In any case, if you do find inaccuracies, they should be pointed out immediately.

TABLE 6.3 National Credit Bureaus			
	Equifax Credit Information Services www.equifax.com	**Experian (formerly TRW) www.experian.com**	**TransUnion www.tuc.com**
To Report Fraud	800–525–6285	Experian Consumer Assistance P.O. Box 949 Allen, TX 75013 888–397–3742	800–916–8800
To Dispute Something in Your Report	P.O. Box 740256 Atlanta, GA 30374–0256 800–216–1035 800–685–5000	P.O. Box 949 Allen, TX 75013–0949 888–397–3742	P.O. Box 34012 Fullerton, CA 92634 800–916–8800

The Fair Credit Reporting Act (FCRA) also limits the length of time damaging information can remain in your file. Bankruptcy information can remain in your file for only 10 years, and other negative information must be removed from your file after 7 years.

The FCRA also limits access to your credit file to those who have a legitimate right to view it, such as a financial institution considering extending you credit, an employer, or a company doing business with you. You also have the right to know who has seen your credit report.

If Your Credit Card Application Is Rejected If your credit card application is rejected, you have two choices. First, you can apply for a card with another financial institution. Getting rejected at one bank doesn't necessarily mean you'll get rejected at another. Second, find out why you've been rejected. Set up an appointment with the credit card manager and find out what caused your rejection. Once you know the reason, address the problem. You might have to correct inaccurate information on your credit report, or you might have to start doing some things differently.

Resolving Billing Errors Your credit card statement may contain a math error, it may include billing for an item you never received, it may include double billing for an item you purchased—the possible errors are many. Fortunately, the Fair Credit Billing Act (FCBA) provides a procedure for correcting billing errors. Under the FCBA you're allowed to withhold payment for the item in question while you petition the card issuer to investigate the matter. Table 6.4 provides a summary of the major laws governing consumer credit.

To begin an investigation of a billing problem, the FCBA requires that you notify your card issuer *in writing within 60 days* of the statement date. In your inquiry you must include your name, address, and account number in addition to a description of the error, including its date, the dollar amount of the billing error, and the reason you feel it's in error. You should also note in your letter that you're making this billing inquiry under the FCBA.

This letter should then be sent to the "billing inquiry" or "billing error" address given on your credit card bill. Because most bill payments are handled automatically, including your complaint with your payment will likely ensure that it'll be lost forever. Moreover, the FCBA requires that an

FACTS OF LIFE

Graduate school is expensive. According to a study of graduate students by Nellie Mae, whereas 93 percent of the graduate student survey respondents make at least the required minimum monthly payments, only 20 percent said they pay off their cards in full each month.

TABLE 6.4 Major Provisions of Consumer Credit Laws

Truth in Lending Act of 1968: Requires lenders to disclose the true cost of consumer credit, explaining all charges, terms, and conditions involved. It requires that the consumer be provided with the total finance charge and annual percentage rate on the loan.

Truth in Lending Act (amended 1971): Prohibits lenders from sending unauthorized credit cards and limits cardholders' liability to $50 for unauthorized use.

Fair Credit Billing Act of 1975: Sets procedures for correcting billing errors on open credit accounts. It also allows consumers to withhold payment for defective goods purchased with a credit card. In addition, it sets limits on the time some information can be kept in your credit file.

Equal Credit Opportunity Act of 1975: Prohibits credit discrimination on the basis of sex and marital status. It also requires lenders to provide a written statement explaining any adverse action taken.

Equal Credit Opportunity Act (amended 1977): Prohibits credit discrimination based on race, national origin, religion, age, or receipt of public assistance.

Fair Debt Collection Practices Act of 1978: Prohibits unfair, abusive, and deceptive practices by debt collectors, and establishes procedures for debt collection.

Truth in Lending Act (amended 1982): Requires installment credit contracts to be written in plain English.

Fair Credit Reporting Reform Act of 1996 (updated version of the Fair Credit Reporting Act of 1971): Requires that consumers be provided with the name of any credit agency supplying a credit report that leads to the denial of credit. It gives consumers the right to know what is in their credit reports and challenge incorrect information. It also requires that employers get written permission from current or prospective employees before reviewing their credit files. In addition, it allows consumers to sue creditors if reporting errors are not corrected.

Fair and Accurate Credit Transactions Act (FACT Act) of 2003: It allows you to request one free copy of your credit report each year from the three major credit bureaus.

Credit Card Accountability, Responsibility, and Disclosure (CARD) Act of 2009: Bans unfair rate increases by banning retroactive rate increases and providing first-year protection; prevents unfair fee traps (for example, late fee traps); requires cardholders to opt in to over-the-limit fees, restrains unfair subprime fees, and limits fees on gift and stored-value cards; requires plain sight and plain language disclosures; adds new accountability measures for regulators; and provides new protections for college students and young adults, including a requirement that card issuers and universities disclose agreements with respect to the marketing or distribution of credit cards to students.

Dodd-Frank Wall Street Reform and Consumer Protection Act (Dodd-Frank Act) of 2010: Created the Consumer Financial Protection Bureau (CFPB) with the purpose of educating consumers, enforcing federal consumer laws, and gathering and analyzing information to lead to a better understanding of consumers, financial services providers, and consumer markets.

address to which billing questions should be directed be included on your statement. Make sure you keep a copy of your letter for future reference.

Within 30 days you should receive notice that an investigation of your complaint has been initiated. The card issuer has 90 days or two billing cycles to complete the investigation. On completion of the investigation, either your account will be credited the disputed amount or you'll receive an explanation from the card issuer as to why it feels your complaint isn't legitimate.

You can continue to dispute your billing charges by notifying the card issuer within your grace period, but the process of correcting it becomes more complicated. If you don't pay, you can be reported delinquent to your credit agency, and you risk the chance of being sued by the card issuer and having your credit rating go down the tubes. Still, if you feel the bank isn't handling your inquiry in an appropriate manner, contact the regulatory agency that oversees the card. Alternatively, you could contact an attorney or consider filing a claim in small claims court.

Creating the Consumer Financial Protection Bureau (CFPB)   The role of the CFPB is to educate the consumer, to enforce federal consumer laws, and to gather and analyze information leading to a better understanding of consumers, financial services providers, and consumer markets. What exactly does all this mean? It means that the CFPB will provide a single location for financial protection and oversight—and its job will be to help consumers make better decisions. For example, when you shop for a financial product, be it a home loan, a credit card, or a student loan, how do you know it's the best deal? You can wade through all the advertising and page after page of fine print, but once you've done that it is still difficult to make side-by-side comparisons and it is all too easy to end up with a deal that doesn't work for you and your family. As we saw in the recent financial crisis, this has real-life consequences—for you and for the whole economy. We saw consumers take on more and more dangerous loans including millions of risky and unaffordable mortgages, and we know how all that turned out. What was our government doing during all this? Many government agencies supervised different parts of the system, and these parts did not interact. As a result, it was nearly impossible for people to hold any one agency accountable.

In July 2010 Congress passed the Dodd-Frank Wall Street Reform and Consumer Protection Act (Dodd-Frank Act), and President Obama signed it into law. Instead of important consumer protection powers being scattered across the federal government, this law put them under one roof with a single entity, the CFPB, given the oversight authority to make sure that consumer financial markets work. Its job is to make credit products and other consumer financial services easier to understand by making sure that prices are clear up-front and risks are easy to see. The new CFPB will also work to cut down on the fine print and make the prices and risks clear for mortgages, credit cards, and other kinds of financial products and services. That way, it will be easier to do some comparison shopping and choose the products that are the best for you and your situation.

What's the CFPB up to right now? It's in the process of inventing itself. But we do have a pretty good idea what it wants to do and that is to help consumers make good financial decisions. In so doing, the CFPB has been given the job of implementing and enforcing new protections under the Dodd-Frank Act that will:

◆ require mortgage lenders to determine that a borrower has the ability to repay a loan by verifying income and making sure borrowers can afford loans even after teaser rates expire and payments rise;

◆ prohibit prepayment penalties, which can make it expensive to refinance, for high-cost loans and adjustable-rate mortgages;

◆ put an end to practices like paying bonuses to mortgage brokers and loan officers who steer borrowers into higher-cost loans than they otherwise qualify for; and

◆ require clearer and simpler disclosures about international money transfers.

Identity Theft

Identity theft occurs when someone uses your name, address, Social Security number (SSN), bank or credit card account number, or other identifying information without your knowledge to commit fraud or other crimes.

In general, identity fraud tends to be a "low-tech" crime. Typically, personal identifying information is stolen from a purse or wallet, or from a person's mail or trash. Sometimes it is garnered from a change of address form the thieves filled out to divert your mail. Less often, it is obtained from hacking into a computer, or could be a result of "pretexting" which involves getting your personal information under false pretenses. For example, a pretexter calls you on the telephone, claiming to be

Identity Theft
The use of your name, address, Social Security number (SSN), bank or credit card account number, or other identifying information by someone other than you without your knowledge to commit fraud or other crimes.

from a survey firm and asks you a few questions; or he may send an e-mail claiming to be from eBay or Citibank stating that unless you respond to the e-mail and provide personal information, your account will be closed.

Once an identity thief has the information he needs, he can go on a spending spree with your credit card, open new credit cards, take out loans, and even establish phone service in your name—in short, these thieves can make your life miserable. Granted, you aren't liable for these charges, but getting things straightened out can be a royal pain.

How Do You Know If You're a Victim of Identity Theft?   The following are signs that identity theft may have happened to you:

◆ You receive a credit card that you didn't apply for.

◆ You are denied credit, or you are offered less than favorable credit terms, such as a high interest rate, for no apparent reason.

◆ You receive calls or letters from debt collectors or businesses about merchandise or services you didn't buy.

◆ You fail to receive bills or other mail.

If you think your identity has been stolen, here's what to do:

STEP 1: Contact the fraud department of any one of the three major credit bureaus to place a fraud alert on your credit file.

STEP 2: Close the accounts that you know or that you believe have been tampered with or opened fraudulently.

STEP 3: File a police report.

STEP 4: File a complaint with the FTC at the government's consumer information Web site (**www.consumer.gov**).

Controlling and Managing Your Credit Cards and Open Credit

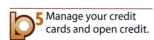
5 Manage your credit cards and open credit.

The first step in managing your credit is knowing what you have charged. It's far too easy to charge a pizza here, a gas fill-up there, and so forth until all control is lost. Remember, a lot of personal finance is about control. If you don't keep track of what you spend, it's hard to control what you spend.

Reducing Your Balance

In addition to knowing exactly what the interest charge is on your credit card, it's important to understand how long it takes to pay off debt if you don't make meaningful payments—that is, payments well above the required minimum monthly payment. First, most credit cards require that you pay about 4 percent of your outstanding balance monthly. This means that if you're paying 18 percent interest on that balance, you're getting almost nowhere.

To get an idea of how long it takes to get rid of credit card debt, let's look at an example. If your initial balance is $3,000 and you pay off 4 percent each month, you'd be paying off $120 a month. In addition to your beginning balance and the amount you pay off each month, your credit card interest rate also plays a role in

TABLE 6.5 How Long It Can Take to Eliminate Credit Card Debt

Each Month Pay This Percentage of the Initial Outstanding Balance	Annual Credit Card Interest Rate			
	9%	12%	15%	18%
4%	28 months	29 months	30 months	32 months
5%	22 months	22 months	23 months	24 months
10%	10 months	11 months	11 months	11 months
15%	7 months	7 months	7 months	7 months

Step 1: Find the row that corresponds to the percentage of your initial balance that you intend to pay off each month. If you have an initial outstanding balance of $5,000 and you intend to pay off $200 each month, you would be paying off $200/$5,000 = 4% each month. Thus, you should look in the 4% row.

Step 2: Find the column that corresponds to the annual percentage that you pay on your credit card. If your credit card charges 15%, look in the 15% column.

Step 3: The intersection of the payments row and the credit card interest column shows how many months it would take to pay off your initial balance. If you pay off 4% of your initial balance each month and the card charges 15%, it would take 30 months to pay off your initial balance.

If you pay off only 2 percent of your initial balance per month, and the credit card interest rate is 15 percent, it would take 79 months or over 6½ years before your credit card debt is paid. Keep in mind that this time frame assumes you don't charge anything more on your card. If you have a substantial balance and keep charging, you may never get out of debt.

determining how long it takes to eliminate your debt. Table 6.5 shows you how to calculate how long it would take to pay off your balance. Simply find the intersection of the percentage of your initial balance that you are paying off and the interest rate on your credit card.

Protecting Against Fraud

What happens if your credit card is stolen? If you report the loss before any fraudulent charges occur, you owe nothing. However, if charges are made before you report it missing, your liability is limited to $50 per card. (This liability limit makes credit card insurance unnecessary.) Still, it is the inconvenience associated with the loss of your credit card that makes it important to guard against fraud.

Most steps to guard against credit card fraud are obvious. First, save all your credit card receipts and compare them against your credit card bill to make sure there are no false charges. After you've compared them with your billings, destroy these receipts, because they contain your credit card number.

Second, do not give out your credit card number over the telephone unless you're purchasing an item, you initiated the sale, and the telephone you're using is a private land line. A thief can easily eavesdrop on a conversation taking place at a public phone, and cell phones are not as secure as land lines. Finally, never leave a store without your card. One way of ensuring you never leave your card behind is to hold your wallet in your hand until you receive your credit card back. Table 6.6 provides some tips on avoiding identity theft.

FACTS OF LIFE

According to a study by Nellie Mae of graduate students, 93 percent would have liked more information on financial management topics before they started school and would like financial management education made available to them now. Lucky you—you'll be ahead of the game!

TABLE 6.6　How to Prevent Identity Theft

- In a safe place at home, keep a detailed list of all your credit and debit cards and other accounts, including the 24-hour customer service phone numbers for each. This information will help you cancel your accounts quickly and minimize the danger to your finances.
- Don't carry documents that include your Social Security number or any PIN numbers, passwords, or access codes for bank or credit cards.
- Keep your birth certificate, passport, and Social Security card in a fireproof strong box in your home, or in a safety deposit box. If you lose your driver's license, these will be your only official forms of identification.
- Check your credit reports with the three national credit bureaus—TransUnion, Experian and Equifax—for suspicious activity at least once a year. Federal law entitles you to a free annual report; to get it, call (877) 322-8228.

Trouble Signs in Credit Card Spending

The next step in controlling credit card borrowing is to examine your credit card habits and determine whether you have a problem. Although there's no simple formula for highlighting problems, many financial planners use a credit card habits quiz that forces you to look at your behavior and recognize any weaknesses you might have.

Checklist 6.1 provides sample questions that are used in a credit card habits quiz. The questions are intended to make you think about and reevaluate your credit card habits. If you answer yes to any question, you may have a problem.

If You Can't Pay Your Credit Card Bills

Once you've gotten into trouble through the overuse of credit cards, getting out is a real hassle. The first step is, of course, putting in place a budget that brings in more money than you spend. This involves self-control—making sure you act your wage. Within this budget, paying off your credit card must come off the top—that is, before you get a chance to spend any money at all, you take care of your planned contribution toward paying off your credit card debt. Along with this remedy there are other options you might consider. First, you should make sure you have the least expensive credit card possible, given your habits. You should have a credit card that fits your usage habits.

CHECKLIST 5.1
The Credit Card Habits Quiz

If you answer yes to any of these questions, you may have problems controlling your credit card spending.
- Do you make only the minimum payment on your credit card each month?
- Have you reached your spending limit on one or more credit cards?
- When out to dinner with a group of friends, do you pay the entire bill with your credit card and have them reimburse you for their share with cash?
- Do you wait for your monthly bill to determine how much you have charged on your credit card rather than keep track of all your credit card spending as it occurs?
- Do you get cash advances because you do not have enough money in your checking account?
- Have you been turned down for credit or had one of your credit cards canceled?
- Have you used some of your savings to pay off credit card bills?
- Do you know how much of your credit card bill is from interest?
- Does your stomach start churning when you get your credit card bill?

You might also consider using savings to pay off current credit card debt. However, don't make a habit of dipping into your savings to pay debt. If it has to happen at all, it should happen only once—when you are reevaluating spending behavior and making a permanent change in the way you use credit cards. Using savings may be a good one-time solution because the interest rate on the unpaid balance on an average credit card is approximately 16 percent. If you're only earning 4 percent after taxes on your savings, then by using savings to pay off credit card borrowing, you'll save 12 percent. Another alternative that you might consider to lower the cost of your outstanding debt is to use a secured loan or a home equity loan to pay off your high-cost credit card debt. We'll look at consumer loans and debt of this type in Chapter 7.

Summary

Know how credit cards work.

Open credit is a running line of credit that you can use to make charges up to a certain point as long as you pay off a minimum amount of your debt each month. The main form of open credit is the credit card, which has become an essential part of our personal finances.

Understand the costs of credit.

Basic factors that affect the cost of open credit are the interest rate, the balance calculation method, the cost of cash advances, the grace period, the annual fee, and other additional or penalty fees including the over-the-limit fee and penalty rates. The advantages of using credit cards or open credit include (1) convenience or ease of shopping, (2) emergency use, (3) the ability to consume before you pay, (4) consolidation of bills, (5) buying in anticipation of price increases, (6) as a source of interest-free credit, (7) to make reservations, (8) as identification, and (9) may be a source of free benefits.

The reasons you should be wary of credit cards and open credit are that it's possible to lose control of spending, they are expensive, and you'll have less income to spend in the future.

Describe the different types of credit cards.

There are many choices of open credit lines, including different types of credit cards, as well as charge accounts. There are three basic types of credit cards: bank credit cards, travel and entertainment cards, and single-purpose cards.

Know what determines your credit card worthiness and how to secure a credit card.

In determining what makes an individual creditworthy, most lenders refer to the "five Cs" of credit—character, capacity, capital, collateral, and conditions. The credit card issuer verifies the information you put down on your application against your credit report from a credit bureau. A credit bureau is a private organization that maintains credit information on individuals. The three national credit bureaus are Experian, TransUnion, and Equifax Credit Information Services. Under the Fair Credit Reporting Act (FCRA) passed by Congress in 1971 (and subsequently amended to help ensure that credit reports are accurate), you have the right to view your credit report.

Manage your credit cards and open credit.
Different credit cards charge different annual percentage rates (APRs), and they also calculate the finance charges imposed in different ways. It is important to know how the unpaid balance is calculated. To control credit card use, focus on controlling credit card spending and look for signs of trouble.

Review Questions

1. Define the term *credit*. How is credit different from open credit? What is revolving credit?

2. Paying a $30 annual fee for the privilege of using a credit card can be thought of as adding $2.50 to your monthly bill. What other card features and fees affect the cost of credit?

3. Describe how a lender calculates the annual percentage rate (APR) when issuing credit. Why is the APR such an important tool when shopping for credit?

4. Explain the differences in the three balance calculation methods used by credit card issuers. Given similar account activity, which will result in the lowest monthly interest charge and the highest monthly interest charge?

5. What is a grace period? Why would a grace period be canceled or eliminated?

6. List and briefly describe the most common fees and penalties imposed by credit card issuers.

7. List five benefits, or advantages, associated with credit card or open credit use. What is the major disadvantage?

8. List and briefly describe the 11 credit card rules resulting from the CARD Act of 2009.

9. Explain the differences in a bank credit card, a premium or prestige credit card, an affinity credit card, and a secured credit card. What are credit card classes?

10. Although they are called "credit cards," T&E cards and single-purpose cards are uniquely different from bank credit cards. What are the differences? What do they have in common with a traditional charge account?

11. What is (are) the most important decision factor(s) in choosing a credit card for a credit user, a convenience user, and convenience and credit user?

12. Explain how the CARD Act of 2009 has changed the way college students apply for and access credit cards.

13. Explain the five Cs of credit and how they relate to individual creditworthiness.

14. What is a credit (FICO or VantageScore) score? How does a credit score affect the availability and cost of credit?

15. What factors are considered in the calculation of the FICO score? Briefly explain each.

16. List the protections against identity theft offered by the FACT Act. How does **Principle 10: Just Do It!** apply to these protections?

17. What other protection to your credit information does the Fair Credit Reporting Act provide?

18. Describe the steps involved when attempting to resolve a billing error.

19. What are the warning signs of identity theft? What steps can you take to avoid it?

20. List four ways to avoid credit card fraud.

21. Develop a list of five to eight warning signs that someone may be having trouble with credit or may be a credit card abuser.

22. Aside from paying more by increasing income and reducing spending, list three other strategies for dealing with overuse of credit cards.

Develop Your Skills—Problems and Activities

These problems are available in MyFinanceLab.

1. Ted and Tiffany are meeting Mitch and Amber at the Green Turtle Club later in the evening. Wanting to set some limits on what could be an expensive evening, Ted stops at the ATM and uses his credit card to get a cash advance. When the two couples meet for dinner, Tiffany tells Amber that she is going to splurge and get lobster because Ted is rolling in cash. Mitch overhears this and begins to laugh at Ted for making such a financial blunder. Ted argues that Mitch is blind to the convenience and control offered by cash advances, as research shows that people tend to spend more when using credit cards. Tiffany and Amber ask you to determine who is right, but you must thoroughly defend your answer to settle the argument.

2. Assume the following: Melita carried an average daily balance of $550 on her credit card this month. Her previous balance last month was $1,000, compared to a balance of $100 this month. There are 30 days in this billing cycle and Melita always makes a payment on the fifteenth of the month. Based on this information, calculate the monthly interest charges for credit card accounts charging 14 percent, 16 percent, and 18 percent interest. Complete the following chart. Since the average daily balance is the most commonly used balance calculation method, is shopping for a lower interest rate really that important?

	14%	16%	18%
Average Daily Balance	$6.42		
Previous Balance		$13.33	
Adjusted Balance			$1.50

3. Credit card issuers often use credit bureau data to "preselect" consumers who will be sent marketing materials and application forms. Describe the profile of a consumer who might be sent an application for a bank credit card, a premium or prestige credit card, an affinity credit card, and a secured credit card.

4. With the availability of free credit reports, consumers are encouraged to check their report every 4 months—one report from each of the three major bureaus. In the past, consumers also were encouraged to check their report before applying for credit, after being denied credit, and before applying for a job. Is this still good advice? Should you add a statement to your report each time? Of the situations described above, which will require the purchase of a report?

5. With only a part-time job and the need for a professional wardrobe, Rachel quickly maxed out her credit card the summer after graduation. With her first full-time paycheck in August, she vowed not to use the card and to pay $240 each month toward paying down her $8,000 outstanding balance. The card has an annual interest rate of 18 percent. How long will it take Rachel to pay for her wardrobe? Should she shop for a new card? Why or why not?

6. Consumer credit laws have been implemented over the years to protect consumers against creditor abuses. Match the following consumer credit issues with the appropriate consumer credit law:

- ◆ Controls debt collection procedures and practice
- ◆ Prohibits credit discrimination because of race, age, or national origin
- ◆ Establishes the APR and requires the disclosure of all credit-related costs
- ◆ Requires credit contracts to be written in plain English
- ◆ Requires a "rejection letter" or written explanation of any adverse action taken
- ◆ Limits marketing of credit cards to the mailing of application packets and prohibits the mailing of unrequested credit cards
- ◆ Payment for defective goods purchased with a credit card can legally be withheld
- ◆ Limits fraudulent card use to $50 payment by the cardholder
- ◆ Ensures that divorced individuals can receive credit
- ◆ Provides annual access to one free credit report from each of the major credit bureaus
- ◆ Reduces credit card late fees to $25
- ◆ Limits the issuance of credit cards to consumers under age 21
- ◆ Requires clear and simple disclosures related to international money transfers

7. A leading financial publication reported that the average baby boomer credit user will pay approximately $1,200 in interest annually. If, instead of paying interest, this amount was saved every year, how much would one of these credit users accumulate in a tax-deferred account earning 8 percent over 10, 15, or 20 years?

Learn by Doing—Suggested Projects

1. Working in a small group, collect credit card marketing information or the summary of account information sent to cardholders for three to five different cards. Be sure to protect the identity of the recipients. Or, use selected card information from one or more categories reported on **www.cardtrak.com**. Use the information to complete one or more of the following activities.

   a. Summarize the card information into a chart showing the purchase balance calculation method, annual percentage rate (APR) of interest for purchases, grace period, annual fee, and minimum finance charge. Compare the results.

   b. Summarize the card information pertaining to cash advances into a chart showing grace period, interest rate, and transaction fee for cash advances. Compare the results.

   c. Summarize the card information pertaining to additional or penalty fees into a chart. Consider the penalty APR as well as fees for late payment, exceeding the credit limit, or a bounced check. Compare the results.

   d. Summarize the additional benefits, or "perks," that are available, such as insurance programs, car rental discounts, traveler assistance, and so on. Compare the results.

   e. Select the card that would be most appropriate for a credit user. Justify your choice.

   f. Select the card that would be most appropriate for a convenience user. Justify your choice.

   g. Review the information requested on the application. Explain how the information relates to the "five Cs of credit."

2. Some credit card issuers are beginning to assess fees and other charges on convenience users. Ask your friends and peers if they think a convenience credit card user (*Note*: you may need to define this term for them) should be charged for the privilege of using a credit card. Place their specific responses and group responses into categories. Use this information to create a short report for class.

3. Interview individuals who represent the three stages of the financial life cycle about their credit card usage. How many cards do they have? What kind or class of cards (rebate, premium, affinity, T&E, or single purpose) do they have? How often do they use their cards and typically for what purchases? What is their available line of credit? Classify them as convenience users, credit users, or convenience and credit users. Summarize your findings in an oral or written report, noting differences in credit card use across the financial life cycle. Be sure to protect the identity of the recipients, and insure them that all responses are confidential.

4. Break into two or three groups to research the use of affinity cards. First, develop a list of affinity cards and their sponsors. Does your university sponsor a card? Next, each group should choose a card(s) to research the benefits offered to the sponsor and the user. What disadvantages are associated with affinity cards? In general, does the group think that using an affinity card makes a personality statement about the user?

5. Review the factors, and their weightings, used by Fair Isaac to calculate a credit score. Ask 10 to 20 people what factors they think should be considered in the score calculation. Be prepared to record factors identified, and to compare the response to the actual list. Did your respondents identify the correct factors, or were their responses significantly different? Were they surprised by the factors and weightings actually used? Did the factors identified vary with the age and credit experience of the respondent?

6. Visit the FACT Act–supported Web site at **www.annualcreditreport.com** to determine how to check your credit report and the information needed. For fun, see if you can locate some of the imposter Web sites. What information suggested that the imposter site was a legitimate FACT Act–supported site? What information suggested that it was a fake?

7. Some students are strongly opposed to having a credit card. Sometimes this opposition is based on family values and sometimes on fear. Other students argue that in today's world it is almost impossible to live without a credit card and that credit is often better than cash. Ask a group of students their opinions on the use of credit. What percentage of the students fall into the credit card avoidance category, and what percentage think a credit card is essential? What is your opinion on this issue? Use this information as the basis for a short class discussion and debate.

8. This chapter reports findings from a recent study by Nellie Mae. To learn more about Nellie Mae and other research findings, visit **www.nelliemae.com**.

9. Research the background and passage of one of the consumer credit laws discussed in the chapter. Explain why this protection was needed, and describe what practices prompted the passage of this legislation. What changes resulted?

10. Credit card fraud is considered almost incidental to the potentially more damaging and costly problem of identity theft. Check the Internet for recent statistics on the number of consumers affected, the potential costs involved, and the personal impact of this crime.

11. Visit the Consumer Financial Protection Bureau Web site (**www.consumerfinance .gov**). Based on the public information available, describe what role the bureau plays in providing consumer education, federal consumer law enforcement, and supervision of the consumer financial marketplace.

Be a Financial Planner—Discussion Case 1

This case is available in MyFinanceLab.

Maria will be a college sophomore next year and she is determined to have her own credit card. She will not be employed during the school year but is convinced that she can pay for credit card expenses based on her summer earnings. Maria's parents have read a number of articles about the problems of credit cards and college students, including examples of students leaving school after a downward spiral of credit cards, overspending, working to pay bills, worrying about bills, working more hours to pay bills, and eventually withdrawing from school. When Maria showed up with a handful of applications including Visa, a Gold MasterCard, Discover, a Visa sponsored by her university, an American Express, a secured MasterCard, and a gas company card her parents were overwhelmed. Maria admitted she didn't want them *all*. "I'm not stupid," she declared. Since Maria obviously needed to learn about credit cards, her parents agreed to cosign her application on one condition. She had to approach her choice just as she would a class project and research the following questions.

Questions

1. Assuming Maria does not really care about her parents' approval and ignores their assignment, will she be able to receive a credit card without their help? Would your answer change if Maria was a graduating senior?

2. Why would an unemployed college student need a credit card? What are the advantages of having a credit card? What are the disadvantages?

3. Should Maria have more than one card? What is the recommended number of credit cards for the average consumer?

4. Shopping for credit can be compared to shopping for any other consumer product—consider the product's cost, features, advantages, and disadvantages. In other words, does the product meet the user's needs? Help Maria compare her credit choices given the applications she has collected.

5. Based on the analysis in question 4, what class(es) of credit cards, if any, should Maria seriously consider? What other products, if any, might she consider applying for?

6. List and summarize the basic factors that affect credit card costs. Rank these factors in terms of importance and relevance based on Maria's situation.

7. While comparing the applications she had collected, Maria was thrilled to receive a "preapproved" offer for a standard card. What precautions should Maria be alert to when considering this offer?

8. If she uses her card only for her books this fall and next fall, how will these purchases affect her monthly payments if she still wants to eliminate her balance and be debt free in 24 months? (Assume that her book purchases are for $600 and are 3 months and 15 months away.)

9. To avoid credit abuse problems, what do you consider to be the most important rules for Maria to follow when using a credit card?

10. How might Maria's credit card use impact her future job search? What should she do to avoid any problems?

11. To avoid credit card fraud or identity theft problems, what do you consider to be the most important rules for Maria to follow when using a credit card?

Be a Financial Planner—Discussion Case 2

This case is available in MyFinanceLab.

Garth was amazed to hear that his friend Lindsey always pays off her credit card balance each month. Garth just assumed that everyone used credit cards the same way—buy now, pay later—only in his case, months later. He buys almost everything he needs or wants, including clothes, food, and entertainment with his card. When Lindsey asked him about the balance calculation method, APR, grace period, or other fees and features of his card, Garth was clueless. He reasoned that his credit card was a safe and convenient way to shop and it allowed him to buy expensive items by paying minimum monthly payments. Overall, Garth thought of himself as a responsible credit user, despite the fact he had been late making a few monthly payments and, once or twice, had gone over his credit limit. He also uses his card regularly to obtain cash advances. After hearing all of this, Lindsey is worried about her friend. She has come to you for help in answering the following questions.

Questions

1. What type of credit user is Garth? Based on your answer, what is the number one factor that should influence Garth's choice of a credit card?

2. Lindsey insisted that Garth request a free credit report. List and briefly explain the information that Lindsey will need to help Garth decipher his report.

3. Nathaniel, another friend, suggested that Garth should obtain a secured credit card, or better yet a Titanium card. Do you agree? Why or why not?

4. Based on what you know about Garth, what kind of additional fees and penalties is he most likely to encounter? What is the impact of these fees and penalties on Garth?

5. Explain the differences in credit card interest rates when described as a fixed, variable, teaser, or penalty rate. How do these different rates affect the cost of using a credit card?

6. What factors should Garth consider if he decides to transfer his current card balance to another card?

7. Much to his surprise, Garth was rejected on his last credit card application. What actions, if any, should he take? Why should he be concerned about this rejection if he still has his other cards?

8. Use Table 6.5 to determine how many months Garth will need to pay off a $3,000 outstanding balance if he pays $150 per month with an APR of 15 percent and he does not make any additional purchases. Tell Garth how much his monthly payment needs to be in order to eliminate his debt in 12 months, assuming no additional purchases.

9. After Lindsey's crash course on credit education, Garth decided to discipline himself by closing a couple of his older accounts. Is this a good strategy?

10. What advice would you give Garth if he has trouble paying his credit card bill in the future?

7 Using Consumer Loans: The Role of Planned Borrowing

Learning Objectives

 Understand the various consumer loans.

 Calculate the cost of a consumer loan.

 Pick an appropriate source for your loan.

 Control your debt.

Debt and credit aren't necessarily bad things, but similar to everything else, moderation and control are important.

It's all too easy to end up with more debt than you can comfortably handle, and just how much debt that is depends on your financial status. In 1999, Elton John took borrowing to his limit when he had to secure a $40 million loan from a London bank to consolidate and pay off the debts he had accumulated while racking up as much as $400,000 a week in credit card bills . . . that's a lot of boas. He was blowing through money like a candle in the wind, accumulating over 3,000 pairs of glasses and a wardrobe unparalleled by any other rock star. He simply had the gift to spend . . . and, as his spending peaked, he had the need to borrow.

Sure, Elton John could spend $1 million in a day, but he could also write a song in 15 minutes that would make him another million. Most of us, thank goodness, don't have much in common with Elton John's spending habits, but one thing we do have in common with Elton is the ability to let debt and borrowing get out of control. To achieve the truly good life, it's vital to maintain control of your finances and live within your means. Chapter 6 examined credit cards and other sources of open credit. We now turn our attention to **consumer loans**. You can think of consumer loans as the next step up in debt. They're stricter and more formal than credit cards and other open credit. Instead of giving you a limited, borrow-when-you-want open line of credit, they involve formal contracts detailing exactly how much you're borrowing and exactly when and how you're going to pay it back. Open credit is for making convenience purchases—tonight's dinner or a new *Gnomeo and Juliet II* DVD. Consumer loans are usually used for bigger purchases. With consumer loans, you can borrow more and pay it back at a slower pace than you can with open credit, but you have to lock yourself into a set repayment schedule. Because it forces you to plan your purchase and your repayment, consumer loans are sometimes called "planned borrowing."

Consumer Loan
A loan involving a formal contract detailing exactly how much you're borrowing and when and how you're going to pay it back.

It would be ideal to have enough cash on hand to buy everything you need or want. Hey, no one likes owing someone else money. However, sometimes purchases are too big or the timing is such that you have to borrow money to finance a particular goal and pay for it later. Consumer loans allow you to do just that. However, consumer loans carry a price. While they let you consume more now, they create a financial obligation that can be a burden later. Control is the key—without it even the Rocket Man, with all his wealth, couldn't stay in flight.

Consumer Loans—Your Choices

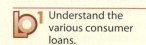

Understand the various consumer loans.

Not all consumer loans look the same. They can range from single-payment, unsecured fixed-rate loans to secured, variable-rate installment loans. What does all that mean? Let's take a look at the characteristics and associated terminology of consumer loans.

First Decision: Single-Payment Versus Installment Loans

Single-Payment or Balloon Loan
A loan that is paid back in a single lump-sum payment at maturity, or the due date of the loan, which is usually specified in the loan contract. At that date you pay back the amount you borrowed plus all interest charges.

Bridge or Interim Loan
A short-term loan that provides funding until a longer-term source can be secured or until additional financing is found.

Installment Loan
A loan that calls for repayment of both the interest and the principal at regular intervals, with the payment levels set in such a way that the loan expires at a preset date.

Loan Amortization
The repayment of a loan using equal monthly payments that cover a portion of the principal and the interest on the declining balance. The amount of the monthly payment going toward interest payment starts off large and steadily declines, while the amount going toward the principal starts off small and steadily increases.

Secured Loan
A loan that's guaranteed by a specific asset.

Unsecured Loan
A loan that's not guaranteed by a specific asset.

Fixed Interest Rate Loan
A loan with an interest rate that stays fixed for the entire duration of the loan.

Variable or Adjustable Interest Rate Loan
A loan in which the interest rate does not stay fixed but varies based on the market interest rate.

Prime Rate
The interest rate banks charge to their most creditworthy, or "prime," customers.

Consumer loans can be either single-payment loans or installment loans. A **single-payment or balloon loan** is a loan that's paid back in a single lump-sum payment at maturity, or the due date of the loan, which is usually specified in the loan contract. At that date you pay back the amount you borrowed plus all interest charges. Single-payment loans generally have a relatively short maturity of less than 1 year. Needless to say, paying off a loan of this kind is generally quite difficult if you don't have access to a large amount of money when it matures. As a result, they're generally used as **bridge or interim loans** to provide short-term funding until longer-term or additional financing is found. A bridge loan might be used in financing the building of a house, with the mortgage loan being used to pay off the bridge loan and provide more permanent funding.

An **installment loan** calls for repayment of both interest and principal at regular intervals, with the payment levels set so that the loan expires at a preset date. The amount of the monthly payment going toward interest starts off large and steadily decreases, while the amount going toward the principal starts off small and steadily increases. In effect, as you pay off more of the loan each month, your interest expenses decline, and your principal payment increases. This process is commonly referred to as **loan amortization**. Installment loans are very common and are used to finance cars, appliances, and other big-ticket items.

Second Decision: Secured Versus Unsecured Loans

Consumer loans are either secured or unsecured. A **secured loan** is guaranteed by a specific asset. If you can't meet the loan payments, that asset can be seized and sold to cover the amount due. Many times the asset purchased with the funds from the loan is used for security. For example, if you borrow money to buy a car, that car is generally used as collateral for the loan. If you don't make your car payment, your car may be repossessed.

Repossessed collateral, though, may or may not cover what you owe. That is, after the collateral is repossessed, you could still owe money. For example, if you owed $40,000 on your house, but the bank could only get $35,000 for it, you'd still owe another $5,000. That means you'd have your home repossessed and still owe money on it! Other assets commonly used as security for a loan are certificates of deposit (CDs), stocks, jewelry, land, and bank accounts. Securities reduce lender risk, so lenders charge a lower rate on a secured loan than they would on a comparable unsecured loan.

An **unsecured loan** requires no collateral. In general, larger unsecured loans are given only to borrowers with excellent credit histories, because the only security the lender has is the individual's promise to pay. The big disadvantage of unsecured loans is that they're quite expensive.

Third Decision: Variable-Rate Versus Fixed-Rate Loans

The interest payments associated with a consumer loan can either be fixed or variable. A **fixed interest rate loan** isn't tied to market interest rates. It maintains a single interest rate for the entire duration of the loan. Regardless of whether market interest rates swing up or down, the interest rate you pay remains fixed. The vast majority of consumer loans have fixed rates.

A **variable** or **adjustable interest rate loan** *is* tied to a market interest rate, such as the prime rate or the 6-month Treasury bill rate. The interest rate you pay varies as that market rate changes. The **prime rate** is the interest rate banks charge to their most creditworthy customers. Most consumer loans are set above the prime rate or the Treasury bill rate. For example, your loan might be set at 4 percent over prime.

In this case, if the prime rate is 5 percent at the moment, the rate you pay on your variable-rate loan would be 9 percent. If the prime jumps to 8 percent, your rate would change to 12 percent.

Not all variable-rate loans are the same. For example, rates may be adjusted at different, but fixed, intervals. Some loans adjust every month, others every year. The less frequently the loan adjusts, the less you have to worry about rate changes. You should also know the volatility of the interest rate to which the loan is pegged. In general, short-term market rates tend to change more than long-term market rates. Therefore, variable-rate loans tied to the 6-month Treasury bill rate expose you to more risk of rate changes than do loans tied to, say, the 20-year Treasury bond rate.

Of course, variable-rate loans usually have rate caps that prevent interest rates from varying too much. The periodic cap limits the maximum the interest rate can jump during one adjustment. The lifetime cap limits the amount that the interest rate can jump over the life of the loan. The larger the fluctuations allowed by the caps, the greater the risk. The bottom line on a variable interest rate loan is that if interest rates drop, you win, and if interest rates rise, you lose.

> ### FACTS of LIFE
> In 2006, for the first time since the 1950s when the Federal Reserve began keeping record, household debt levels surpassed household income—and they surpassed it by more than 8 percent.

So which is better, a fixed-rate loan or a variable-rate loan? Neither one necessarily. The choice between a variable- and a fixed-rate loan is another example of **Principle 8: Risk and Return Go Hand in Hand**. With a variable-rate loan, the borrower bears the risk that interest rates will go up and the payments will increase accordingly. With a fixed-rate loan, the lender bears the risk that interest rates will go up and—because the interest rate of the loan is fixed—that they will lose interest income. Because the lender bears more risk, fixed-rate loans generally cost more than variable-rate loans.

An alternative to a fixed- or variable-rate loan is a convertible loan. A **convertible loan** is a variable-rate loan that can be converted into a fixed-rate loan at the borrower's option at specified dates in the future. Although convertible loans are much less common than variable- or fixed-rate loans, they do offer the advantage of the lower cost of a variable-rate loan along with the ability to lock into the savings of a fixed-rate loan.

P8 Principle

Convertible Loan
A variable-rate loan that can be converted into a fixed-rate loan at the borrower's option at specified dates in the future.

Fourth Decision: The Loan's Maturity—Shorter Versus Longer Term Loans

With a shorter term loan, the monthly payments are larger because you are paying off more of the amount that you've borrowed each month. For example, if you borrow $10,000 at 8 percent, with a 3-year loan, your monthly payments would be $313, but if the loan was for 10 years rather than 3 years, the payments would drop to $121 per month. However, even though your monthly interest payments are smaller with the 10-year loan, the total amount of interest you pay over the life of the loan is more.

However, agreeing to a shorter term loan, often results in a lower interest rate on your loan. Why is that the case? Lenders generally charge a lower interest rate on shorter term loans because the shorter the term, the lower the probability that you will experience a financial disaster such as the loss of your job or a medical emergency.

Understand the Terms of the Loan: The Loan Contract

The loan contract spells out all the conditions of the loan in exhaustive detail. If the item being purchased is to be used as collateral for the loan, then the contract will

FIGURE 7.1 An Installment Purchase Contract

Keep in mind when taking out an installment purchase contract that, similar to a product such as a television or an automobile, the loan you are taking out is also a product. You should make sure it's something you can afford and that you understand what you're signing.

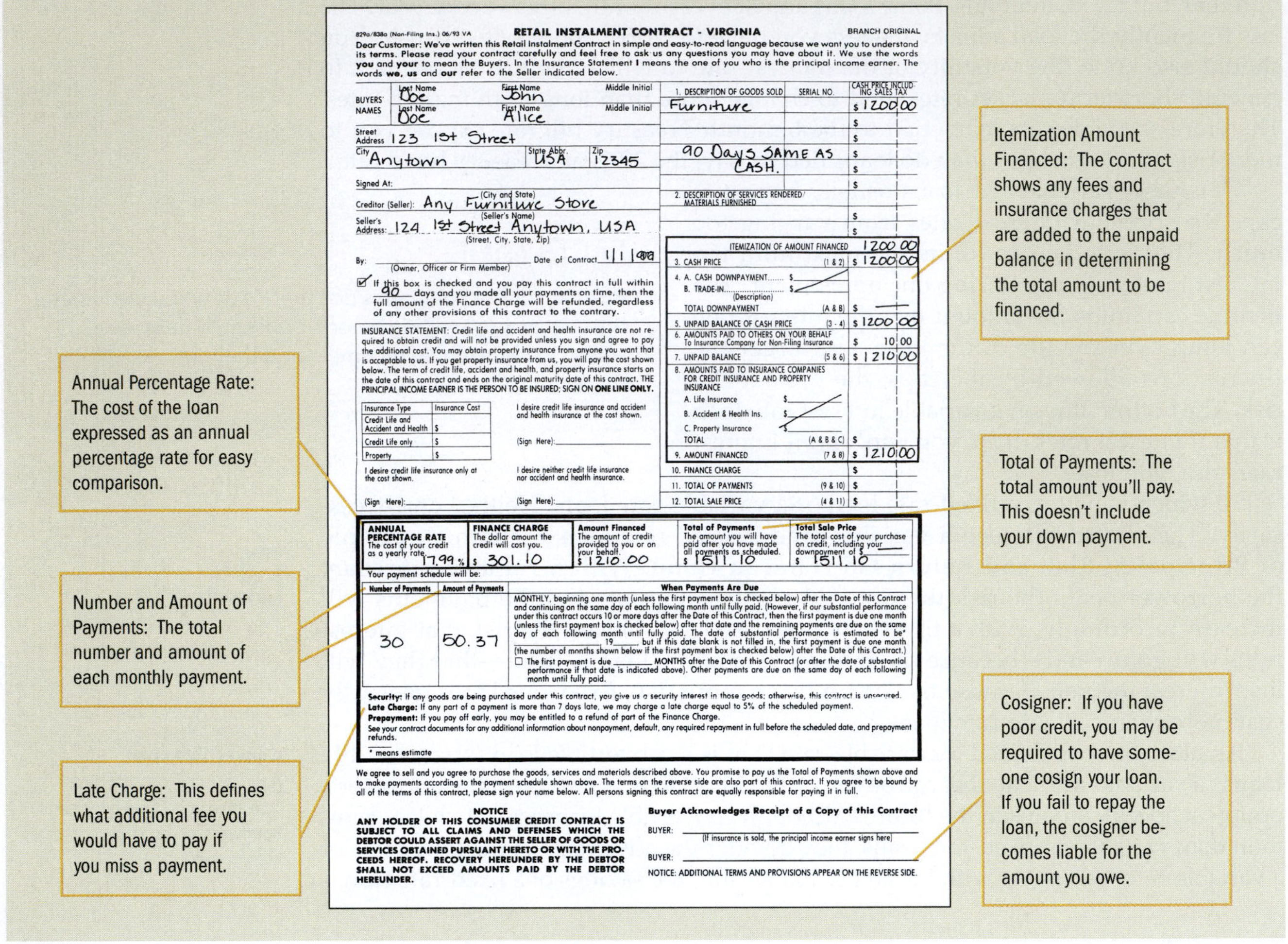

Itemization Amount Financed: The contract shows any fees and insurance charges that are added to the unpaid balance in determining the total amount to be financed.

Annual Percentage Rate: The cost of the loan expressed as an annual percentage rate for easy comparison.

Number and Amount of Payments: The total number and amount of each monthly payment.

Late Charge: This defines what additional fee you would have to pay if you miss a payment.

Total of Payments: The total amount you'll pay. This doesn't include your down payment.

Cosigner: If you have poor credit, you may be required to have someone cosign your loan. If you fail to repay the loan, the cosigner becomes liable for the amount you owe.

Security Agreement

An agreement that identifies whether the lender or borrower retains control over the item being purchased.

Default

The failure of a borrower to make a scheduled interest or principal payment.

Note

The formal document that outlines the legal obligations of both the lender and the borrower.

Insurance Agreement Clause

A loan requirement of a borrower to purchase credit life insurance that would pay off the loan in the event of the borrower's death.

contain a **security agreement** saying so. The security agreement identifies whether the lender or borrower retains control over the item being purchased. The formal agreement stating the payment schedule and the rights of both lender and borrower in the case of **default** are outlined in the **note**.

The note is standard on all loans, and the security agreement is standard on secured loans. Other clauses are sometimes included in a loan contract, including an insurance agreement clause, an acceleration clause, a deficiency payment clause, and a recourse clause. An example of an installment purchase contract is given in Figure 7.1.

Insurance Agreement Clause

With an **insurance agreement clause** you're required to purchase credit life insurance to pay off the loan in the event of your death. For you, credit life insurance adds nothing to the loan other than cost. It's really the lender who benefits. If an insurance agreement clause is included, its cost should justifiably be included as a cost of the loan.

Acceleration Clause

An **acceleration clause** states that if you miss one payment, the entire loan comes due immediately. If at that time you can't pay off the entire loan, the collateral will be repossessed and sold to pay off the balance due. Acceleration clauses are standard in most loans. However, lenders usually won't immediately invoke the acceleration clause but instead will allow you a chance to make good on the overdue payments.

Deficiency Payments Clause

A **deficiency payments clause** states that if you default on a secured loan, not only can the lender repossess whatever is secured, but if the sale of that asset doesn't cover what you owe, you can also be billed for the difference.

To make sense out of this clause, let's say you missed some car payments and had your car repossessed. If you owed a balance of $10,000, and the car was sold at auction by the lender for only $9,000, you'd still owe $1,000. In addition, under the deficiency payments clause you would also be responsible for collection costs, say $150; selling costs, perhaps another $150; and attorney fees of, say, $100. As a result, you'd not only lose your car, but would also be billed for $1,400 ($1,000 + $150 + $150 + $100).

Recourse Clause

A **recourse clause** defines what actions a lender can take to claim money from you in case you default. The recourse clause may allow the lender to attach your wages, which means that a certain portion of your salary would go directly to the lender to pay off your debt.

Special Types of Consumer Loans

Although consumer loans are used for almost anything, several special-purpose consumer loans deserve close attention. It's important to look at these loans not only because they are extremely common, but also because they include unique advantages and disadvantages you should be aware of.

Home Equity Loans

A **home equity loan or second mortgage** is special type of secured loan that uses the built-up equity in your home as collateral against the loan. Generally, you can borrow from 50 to 85 percent of your equity—that is, your home value minus your first mortgage balance. For example, if you own a home with a market value of $200,000 and have an outstanding balance on your first mortgage of $80,000, your home equity would be $120,000. With this much equity, you would be able to get a home equity loan of between $60,000 and $102,000 (0.50 × $120,000, and 0.85 × $120,000, respectively). In this case, your home is security on a loan that can be used for any purpose (it needn't be home related).

Advantages of Home Equity Loans   The primary advantage of a home equity loan over an alternative loan is cost. The first cost advantage arises because the interest on a home equity loan is generally tax deductible up to a maximum of $100,000, provided the loan doesn't exceed your home's market value. So, for every dollar of interest you pay on your home equity loan, your taxable income is lowered by $1. If you're in a 25 percent marginal tax bracket, paying $1 of interest on a home equity loan will save you 25¢ in taxes. The after-tax cost of paying $1 of interest on this home equity loan would be only 75¢, or $1 (1 − 0.25). Hey, don't scoff at a 25¢ savings. That change adds up:

Acceleration Clause
A loan requirement stating that if the borrower misses one payment, the entire loan comes due immediately.

Deficiency Payments Clause
A loan requirement stating that if you default on a secured loan, not only can the lender repossess whatever is secured, but if the sale of that asset doesn't cover what is owed, you can also be billed for the difference.

Recourse Clause
A clause in a loan contract defining what actions a lender can take to claim money from a borrower in the case of default.

Home Equity Loan or Second Mortgage
A loan that uses a borrower's built-up equity in his or her home as collateral against the loan.

A person in a 25 percent marginal tax bracket borrowing $33,333 at 12 percent would save $1,000 a year if the interest is tax-deductible.

You can also calculate the after-tax cost of the home equity loan by taking the before-tax cost of the home equity loan and multiplying it by $[1 - (\text{marginal tax rate})]$:

$$\text{after-tax cost of a home equity loan} = \text{before-tax cost}\,(1 - \text{marginal tax rate})$$

As you recall from Chapter 4, you have to determine your marginal tax bracket before you can calculate the after-tax cost. This marginal tax rate is the rate at which any additional income you receive will be taxed, and it combines the federal and state tax rates that you pay on the investment you're considering. If the before-tax interest rate on the home equity loan is 9 percent and you're in the 25 percent marginal tax bracket, then the after-tax cost of the loan would be 6.75 percent, calculated as follows:

$$6.75\% = 9\%(1 - 0.25)$$

Thus, you might pay 9 percent on this loan, but the cost to you, after taking into account the fact that interest on this loan lowers your taxes, is only 6.75 percent.

The second cost advantage of home equity loans is that they generally carry a lower interest rate than do other consumer loans. Because home equity loans are secured loans, lenders consider them less risky and charge a lower interest rate on them.

Disadvantages and Dangers of Home Equity Loans   The major disadvantage of a home equity loan is that it puts your home at risk. When you decide on a home equity loan, use caution and make sure that you aren't taking on more debt than you can support.

The use of a home equity loan also limits future financing flexibility. Although it's an excellent source of emergency funding, you can have only one home equity loan outstanding at a time. And don't forget that any borrowing places an obligation on future earnings and reduces future disposable income.

In the mid-2000s, before the housing bust, many people believed that real estate could only go up in value—constantly appreciating in price. In hindsight, it's pretty clear that's not always the case, and when it goes down, it can go a long way down. Much of the sales pitch of home equity loans was that they were an easy way to capture some of the price appreciation in your home. The problem was that the price appreciation might not be around for long if housing prices dropped.

Prior to the 1980s, home equity loans were referred to as "second mortgages," which gave consumers the feeling that they were taking on more debt than they should—as a result, second mortgages weren't that popular. In order to make them more appealing, second mortgages became home equity loans and their popularity soared—after all, it was the home owner's equity, why not tap into it? In fact, one advertisement declared, "Now, when the value of your home goes up, you can take credit for it."[1] The end result was that many consumers used their homes as an ATM machine, and when the housing crash came, they lost their homes.

Student Loans

Student Loan
A loan with low, federally subsidized interest rate given to students based on financial need.

Student loans are federally subsidized loans with low interest rates given to students making satisfactory progress in their degree program, based on financial need. If you're like most students, you may already know more about this subject than you'd care to. In fact, as Figure 7.2 shows, few students can afford to pay for college without some form of education loan, with about two-thirds of 4-year undergraduate students taking on some

---

[1] Louise Story, "Home Equity Frenzy Was a Bank Ad Come True," *New York Times*, August 14, 2008.

FIGURE 7.2 Percent of Students at a 4-Year College Who Borrow

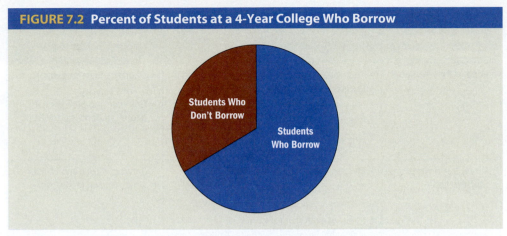

Source: FinAid! accessed March 11, 2011, www.finaid.org/loans/.

debt. How much did they borrow? Just looking at the borrowers, and including the money their parents borrowed for their education, the average cumulative debt is $27,708. It's a bit lower for students who go to public colleges and higher for those who go to private colleges.

Just so you don't feel alone, let's ask, "How much student debt is there?" Well, in 2010 the amount of student loan debt actually exceeded the total amount of credit card debt. And we all know how much credit card debt there is—lots! In fact, while credit card debt stood at about $800 billion at the beginning of 2011, student loan debt had climbed to $830 billion as shown in Figure 7.3. That's an amazing number, particularly given the fact that total student loan debt was only $200 billion in 2000. In recent years, student loans have grown tremendously. In fact, in 2010 alone, new federal student loan volume exceeded $100 billion.

FACTS OF LIFE

How do you think you'll stack up against the average when you graduate? Keep in mind about a third of all students don't borrow at all.

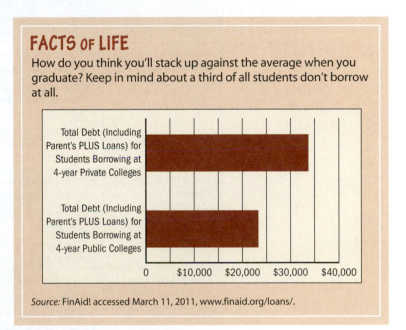

Source: FinAid! accessed March 11, 2011, www.finaid.org/loans/.

FIGURE 7.3 The Rise of Student Loan Debt

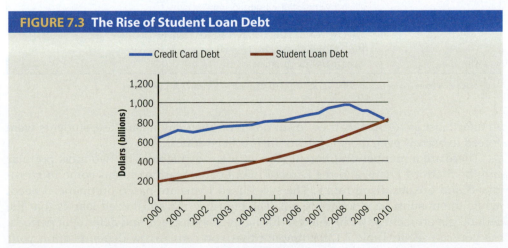

Source: Federal Reserve Bank, Statistical Release G.18, January 2011.

TABLE 7.1 Student Loan Comparisons

Federal Student Loan Program	Program Details	Annual Award Limits (subject to change)
Federal Perkins Loan	• Your college is the lender; payment is owed to the college that made the loan • For undergraduate and graduate students • Interest charged on this loan is 5% • Funds depend on student's financial need and availability of funds at the college	• Undergraduate students: up to $5,500 • Graduate and professional degree students: up to $8,000
Direct Subsidized Stafford Loan	• Must be at least a half-time student • Must have financial need • For undergraduate and graduate students • Borrower is not charged interest while in college and during grace and deferment periods • Interest charged on this loan is 4.5% for undergraduates and 6.8% for graduate students • The U.S. government is the lender; payment is owed to the U.S. government	• Between $3,500 and $8,500 depending on grade level
Direct Unsubsidized Stafford Loan	• Must be at least a half-time student • For undergraduate and graduate students • Borrower is responsible for all interest on the loan including while in college and during grace and deferment periods • Interest charged on this loan is 6.8% • The U.S. government is the lender; payment is owed to the U.S. government	• Between $5,500 to $20,500 (less any subsidized amount received for the same period) depending on grade level and dependency status
Direct PLUS Loans for Parents	• For parents of dependent students • Borrower is responsible for all the interest • Interest charged on this loan is 7.9% • Must not have negative credit history • The U.S. government is the lender: payment is owed to the U.S. government	• Maximum amount is cost of attendance minus any other financial aid the student receives
Direct PLUS Loans for Graduate and Professional Students	• For graduate and professional degree students • Borrower is responsible for all the interest • Interest charged on this loan is 7.9% • Must not have a negative credit history • Must have applied for annual loan maximum eligibility under the Subsidized and Unsubsidized Stafford Loan Programs before applying for a Graduate/Professional PLUS Loan • The U.S. government is the lender: payment is owed to the U.S. government	• Maximum amount is *cost of attendance* minus any other financial aid the student receives

Note: For additional information on federal student aid, call 1-800-4-FED-AID or visit www.studentaid.ed.gov/funding.

In effect, just as consumers tried to cut down on their credit card use, students were forced to borrow even more to pay for their college education.

There are a number of different student loans available. The two most popular are the Stafford Loans and the Direct PLUS Loans. Stafford Loans come in subsidized and unsubsidized forms. The subsidized loans are based on financial need, while the unsubsidized loans are not. The big plus of a subsidized loan is that the federal government pays the interest during in-school, grace, and deferment periods. As you can see in Table 7.1, the amount that you can borrow depends upon your grade level and whether or not you are a dependent.

While Stafford Loans are for students, Direct PLUS Loans are for parents. With PLUS Loans you may borrow up to your full cost of attendance, minus any other financial aid you receive (including Direct Subsidized Loans, Direct Unsubsidized Loans, scholarships, and certain fellowships), and they come with an interest rate of 7.9 percent.

The process of applying for one of these loans begins at the financial aid office of your school. You fill out the financial aid form, and your school helps you find a lender. One nice thing about student loans is that, as was noted in Chapter 4, you can deduct up to $2,500 from your taxes regardless of whether you itemize or not. Eligibility for this deduction is phased out for single filers with AGI between $60,000 and $75,000, and from $120,000 to $150,000 for joint filers.

Obviously, an education is an excellent investment in your future, one worth going into debt over. The student loan program offers a way to borrow at a below-market rate, regardless of your credit situation. Still, you must keep in mind that when taking out a student loan, you're sacrificing future financing flexibility. The increased income you get as a result of completing your education should more than offset this cost. Of course, nothing may offset the hassle of dealing with student loan officers, but that's just life.

> ## STOP & THINK
>
> For some people, it's a race between running out of money and running out of month. Everything you do in personal finance finds its roots in your budget. While there is a place in your budget for consumer debt, it should be planned rather than result from "running out of money." The key, of course, is to spend less than you bring in—that means living below your means. Obvious, but not always easy. What spending do you think you might be able to eliminate?

Automobile Loans

An **automobile loan** is a secured loan made specifically for the purchase of an automobile, with the automobile being purchased used as the collateral. These loans are generally short term, often only 24, 36, or 48 months, although they can be as long as 5 or 6 years. In recent years automobile loans have been used as a marketing tool to sell cars. Very low-cost loans of 3 percent or less are used to lure customers, or the low rates are used to sell slow-moving models. The rate on auto loans is also quite low because lenders know that if you don't pay, they'll repossess your car and sell it to someone else to pay off the loan.

Auto companies also use low-cost auto loan rates to push cars when they produce more than they can sell or when they're trying to get rid of last year's models because new ones are coming out soon. As a result, in 2011, while the national average auto loan rate was at 4.91% percent Ford was offering a 0.0 percent rate on the 2011 Ford Focus Sedan.

Automobile Loan
A loan made specifically for the purchase of an automobile, which uses the automobile as collateral against the loan.

Cost and Early Payment of Consumer Loans

 Calculate the cost of a consumer loan.

Before deciding whether to borrow money, you should know exactly what the loan costs and what flexibility you have in terms of paying it off early. Fortunately, this information is readily available. In fact, under the Truth in Lending Act, you must be informed in writing of the total finance charges and the APR of the loan before you sign a loan agreement.

The finance charges include all the costs associated with the loan—for example, interest payments, loan-processing fees, fees for a credit check, and any required insurance fees. The **APR, or annual percentage rate**, is the simple percentage cost of all finance charges over the life of the loan on an annual basis. Keep in mind that this includes noninterest finance charges.

As noted earlier, consumer loans fall into two categories: (1) single-payment or balloon loans, and (2) installment loans.

APR or Annual Percentage Rate
The true simple interest rate paid over the life of a loan. It's a reasonable approximation for the true cost of borrowing, and the Truth in Lending Act requires that all consumer loan agreements disclose the APR in bold print.

Cost of Single-Payment Loans

The Truth in Lending Act requires lenders to provide you with the finance charges and APR associated with a loan, but it's a good idea to be familiar with the two different ways loans are made—one that removes interest at the beginning (the discount method) and one that doesn't (the simple interest method). The APR and finance charges are given to you in the form of a **loan disclosure statement** similar to the one shown in Figure 7.4.

Loan Disclosure Statement
A statement that provides the APR and interest charges associated with a loan.

Simple Interest Method   The calculation of interest under the simple interest loan method is as follows:

$$\text{interest} = \text{principal} \times \text{interest rate} \times \text{time}$$

The principal is the amount borrowed, the interest rate is exactly what you think it is, and the time is the period over which the funds are borrowed. For example, if $10,000 were borrowed for 6 months at an annual rate of 12 percent, the interest charges would be calculated as $600, as follows:

$$\$600 = \$10,000 \times 0.12 \times \frac{1}{2}$$

Note that the value for time is ½ because the money is borrowed for half of a year. If we're talking about single-payment loans, both the interest and the principal are due at maturity. Thus, in the loan we've just described, you'd receive $10,000 when you take out the loan, and 6 months later you'd repay $10,600.

For single-payment loans, the stated interest rate and the APR are always the same if there are no noninterest finance charges. The APR can be calculated as follows:

$$\text{APR} = \frac{\text{average annual finance charges}}{\text{average loan balance outstanding}}$$

In this case, it's calculated as follows:

$$\text{APR} = \frac{(\$600/0.5)}{\$10,000} = \frac{\$1,200}{\$10,000} = 0.12, \text{ or } 12\%$$

Notice that the annual finance charges are equal to the total finance charges divided by the number of periods the loan continues. In this case, it's a 6-month loan, and because we paid $600 to have the loan for 6 months, we'd have had to pay $1,200 if the loan were outstanding for a full year. Therefore, $1,200 is the annual finance charge. Keep in mind that if there had been noninterest finance charges, they would be included as part of the finance charges.

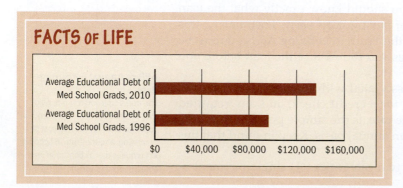
Discount Method   With a discount method single-payment loan, the entire interest charge is subtracted from the loan principal before you receive the money, and at maturity you

FIGURE 7.4   A Loan Disclosure Statement

A loan disclosure statement is required by the Truth in Lending Act and provides the APR, the finance charge, and the total of payments associated with the loan.

Annual Percentage Rate: The APR, or annual percentage rate, is the true simple interest rate paid over the life of the loan. It is calculated by dividing the average annual finance charge by the average loan balance outstanding.

Finance Charge: The finance charge includes all the costs associated with the loan, for example, interest payments, loan processing fees, fees for a credit check, and any required insurance fees.

Amount Financed: This is the amount you are borrowing, or the principal.

Total of Payments: This is the sum of your finance charge and the amount that you are borrowing.

ANNUAL PERCENTAGE RATE The cost of my credit as a yearly rate.	FINANCE CHARGE The dollar amount the credit will cost me.	Amount Financed. The amount of credit provided to me or on my behalf.	Total of Payments. The amount I will have paid after I have made all payments as scheduled.

I have the right to receive at this time an itemization of the Amount Financed: (_____) I want an itemization. (_____) I do not want an itemization.

My payment schedule will be: (Initials)   (Initials)

No. of Payments	Payment Amount	Frequency	Due Date	No. of Payments	Payment Amount	Frequency	Due Date

Variable Rate.
If my loan, as indicated above, has a variable rate, my interest rate may increase during the term of my loan based on movement of the WSJ Prime Rate. My interest rate will not increase more than once each month. If my loan is secured by a principal dwelling for a term greater than one year, disclosures about the variable rate have been provided to me earlier.

____   If indicated, my loan has multiple payments for a term of more than 60 months. Any increase in my interest rate will increase the number of payments and may increase the payment amounts. If my loan were for $10,000 for 144 months at 12% and the interest rate increased to 12.50% in three months, my regular payment would increase by $7.30 beginning with my Sixty-First payment.

____   MAXIMUM RATE. If indicated, the maximum interest rate will not exceed:

____   If indicated, my loan has multiple payments for a term of 60 months or less. Any increase in my interest rate will increase the number of payments. If my loan were for $10,000 for 60 months at 12% and the interest rate increased to 12.50% in three months I would have to make one additional payment of $196.56.

____   If indicated, my loan has a single payment. Any increase in my interest rate will increase the amount due at maturity. If my loan were for $10,000 at 12% for 90 days, and my interest rate increased to 12.25% in 20 days, then my final payment would increase by $4.80.

Security. I am giving a security interest in:

____   the goods or property being purchased.   ____   other (describe):

Collateral securing other loans with you may also secure this loan, except my principal dwelling or household goods.

Filing Fees.   **Prepayment.** If I pay off early, I may have to pay a penalty and I will not be entitled to a refund of part of any prepaid finance charge.

Late charges. If you receive any payment 8 days or more after the due date, I agree to pay you a late charge of 5% of my payment.

____   If indicated, this loan is for the purchase of property used as my principal dwelling and someone buying my principal dwelling cannot assume the remainder of my loan on the original terms.

____   If indicated, the Annual Percentage Rate does not take into account my required deposit.

I may see my contract documents for any additional information about nonpayment, default, any required repayment in full before the scheduled due date, and prepayment refunds and penalties.

I understand that credit life and credit disability insurance are not required to get this loan. **You will not provide it unless I sign the NOTICE OF PROPOSED GROUP CREDIT INSURANCE form and agree to pay the cost.** If I want any of these insurance coverages, I must be sure that the insurance coverage I want is indicated, that the amount of the premium is filled in, and that I have signed below. If I request credit life insurance or credit disability insurance, I have the right to rescind the insurance policy or certificate of insurance by giving written notice to the insurance company within 15 days from the date I received the policy or certificate. The term of any insurance I request is for the stated term of this loan unless shown otherwise.

INSURED		TYPE	PREMIUM
#1	#2		
____	____	Credit Life	
____		Credit Disability	

If this loan is secured, I may obtain property insurance from any insurer I choose.

I request coverage(s) checked for the premiums shown above

_____
Signature of Insured #1 (Life only or Life and Disability)

I request coverage(s) checked for the premiums shown above

_____
Signature of Insured #2 (Life only)

repay the principal. For example, if you borrow $10,000 for 1 year and the interest rate is 11 percent, your finance charges would be $1,100 ($10,000 × 0.11). Under the discount method, you'd receive only $8,900 ($10,000 less the interest of $1,100), and in 1 year you'd have to repay the entire principal of $10,000. In effect, you'd really have a loan of only $8,900, because the interest is prepaid. The APR for this example is 12.36 percent, calculated as follows:

$$\text{APR} = \frac{\$1,100}{\$8,900} = 0.1236, \text{ or } 12.36\%$$

Again, you'll notice that we have assumed there are no noninterest finance charges. If our earlier example of a $10,000 loan at 12 percent for 6 months had been lent using the discount method, the APR would be calculated to be 13.64 percent, as follows:

$$\text{APR} = \frac{(\$600/0.5)}{\$8,800} = \frac{\$1,200}{\$8,800} = 0.1364, \text{ or } 13.64\%$$

Notice that the APR is larger when money is lent under the discounted method than when it's lent under the simple interest method. Why? Because under the discount method, with the interest taken out before you receive the loan, you actually receive less than the stated principal of the loan.

Payday Loans—A Dangerous Kind of Single-Payment Loans

Be wary of "payday loans." Payday loans, generally given by check cashing companies, are aimed at people with jobs and checking accounts, but who need some money (usually $100 to $500) to tide them over for 1 or 2 weeks, or until their next "payday." Lately, these loans have even surfaced on college campuses where students may not even have a job or a paycheck, just an allowance from home. The cost on these loans comes in the form of a fee, which generally runs from $15 to $30 for the 1- or 2-week loan.

How bad are payday loans? Lisa Engelkins, a single mom raising a 5-year-old and making less than $8 an hour, was struggling to keep up with her bills and saw an ad on the TV for a "payday loan" and decided to try it. She wrote a check for $300 and got back $255, and then to keep the check from bouncing, she repeatedly took out $300 loans—she did that 35 times. The bottom line on that payday loan was $1,575 in interest to extend the $255 loan—that's an annual rate of 390 percent.

The loans work like this: You need $100 to cover you until your next paycheck or money from home. So you go to a payday lender and borrow $100. The payday lender gets a check from you for $115 drawn on your empty bank account. Then 2 weeks later, when you get paid, or you get that check from home, the lender either cashes the check or lets you "flip" the loan, or pay another fee to renew the loan for another 2 weeks. If you annualized the interest rate, you'd find that you're borrowing at

FACTS OF LIFE

Research from the Center for Responsible Lending (CRL) shows that the payday lenders do not make money by providing one-time assistance during a time of financial need, but instead make money by keeping borrowers in debt. According to CRL's research, borrowers who receive five or more loans a year account for 83 percent of the lenders' business.

FACTS OF LIFE

Here's a true story: Sandra Harris, an accounting technician, from Wilmington, NC, found herself in a cash crunch after her husband had lost his job as an executive chef. Her car insurance was due, and she didn't have the money, so she turned to Payday Loans Direct, paid the $50 fee for a $200 loan, and was able to pay her insurance bill on time. When the loan came due she was ready to pay it off, but instead renewed it, and then renewed it again, raised it, and took out more payday loans. At the end of 6 months she was paying over $600 per month in fees, none of which applied to her debt, and paid a total $8,000 in fees for six payday loans. As with many payday loans, this one came with a sad ending as she was evicted and her car was repossessed.

TABLE 7.2 Payday Loan Facts
Ninety-nine percent of payday loans go to repeat borrowers.
The average payday borrower is flipped eight times by a single lender.
African American neighborhoods have three times as many payday loan shops per capita as white neighborhoods in North Carolina, even when income is taken into account.
The average payday borrower pays $800 to borrow $325.
The Center for Responsible Lending has estimated that predatory payday lending costs American families $4.8 billion annually. That cost is increasing rapidly, as the size of the market explodes.

Source: Center for Responsible Lending, Payday Lending, accessed June 21, 2011, www.responsiblelending.org/payday-lending.

an interest rate of close to 400 percent. Even worse, if your fee was $30 (that is, you borrowed $100 and gave the payday lender a check for $130 to cover your $100 loan), you'd have paid close to 800 percent interest. Not a very wise way to borrow money, is it? Remember **Principle 1: The Best Protection Is Knowledge**, along with the old saying, "A fool and his money are soon parted."

These things are awful—if you're thinking about getting a payday loan, "just say no." They don't benefit borrowers, but instead trap them into a cycle of borrowing. How bad are they? Just look to Table 7.2 for an answer.

Certainly, there have been attempts to eliminate these loans. In 2006, Congress acted to protect military families by prohibiting payday and title lenders from charging higher than 36 percent APR, but this just protected service men and women. On a broader front, 17 states and the District of Columbia have enacted strong payday loan laws. For example, in Georgia payday lending is explicitly prohibited and a violation of racketeering laws, while in New York and New Jersey payday lending is prohibited through their criminal usury statutes, limiting loans to 25 percent and 30 percent annual interest, respectively. On the other hand, payday loans are legal in the other 33 states. However, even where there are payday loan laws, payday lenders find ways around them. One of those ways is to reach out through the Internet, and today over 21 percent of all payday loans take place over the Internet. You would think this would still be illegal, but to circumvent these laws, a number of payday lenders have partnered up with American Indian tribes, and as arms of American Indian tribes they are protected from enforcement action. The result is that if there isn't a payday loan tempting you around the corner, there is a lender looking for you online.

Cost of Installment Loans

With an installment loan, repayment of both the interest and the principal occurs at regular intervals, with payment levels set so that the loan expires at a preset date. Installment loans use either the simple interest or the add-on method to determine what the payments will be.

Simple Interest Method   The simple interest method is the most common method of calculating payments on an installment loan. Recall that the monthly payments on an installment loan remain the same each month, but the portion of your monthly payment that goes toward interest declines each month, while the portion going toward the principal increases. In effect, you pay interest only on the unpaid balance of the loan, which declines as it's gradually paid off.

We can determine your monthly payment on an installment loan using either a financial calculator (using the present value of an annuity calculation to determine *PMT*, the payment) or financial tables to determine the monthly payment. The trick here, as you learned in Chapter 3, is to input the number of months into *N* and convert the annual interest rate into a monthly interest rate. To convert the annual interest rate into its monthly equivalent we simply divide the annual interest rate by 12. Let's look at the example of a 12-month installment loan for $5,000 at 18 percent.

Calculator Clues

Since it is a loan with 12 monthly payments, N is expressed as the number of months, which is 12; and I/Y becomes the interest rate per month. To calculate the interest rate per month we simply divide the annual rate by 12, which is 14/12. Once you've input the values, you solve for PMT by entering CPT PMT:

Enter:	12	14/12	5,000		0
	N	I/Y	PV	PMT	FV
Solve for:				−448.94	

The answer in the output row is shown as a negative number. Remember, with a financial calculator, each problem will have two cash flows, and one will be a positive number and one a negative number. The idea is that you borrow money from the bank (a positive number, because "you receive the money"), and at some other point in time you pay the money back to the bank (a negative number, because "you pay it back").

Thus, a 12-month installment loan of $5,000 at 14 percent would result in monthly payments of $448.94.

We can also determine the monthly payment using installment loan tables, which appear in Appendix E in the back of the book and in an abbreviated form in Table 7.3. Looking in the interest rate equals 14% row and the 12-month column, we find that the monthly payment on a similar $1,000 installment loan would be $89.79. To determine the monthly payment on a $5,000 loan, we need only multiply this amount by 5 because this loan is for $5,000, not $1,000. Thus, using the tables we find that the monthly payment would be $448.95 (the difference between this and what we determined using a calculator, $448.94, is simply a rounding error). Remember, your loan payments remain

TABLE 7.3 Monthly Installment Loan Tables ($1,000 loan with interest payments compounded monthly)

Interest	Loan Maturity (in months)				
	6	**12**	**18**	**24**	**30**
13.00%	173.04	89.32	61.45	47.54	39.22
13.25%	173.17	89.43	61.56	47.66	39.34
13.50%	173.29	89.55	61.68	47.78	39.46
13.75%	173.41	89.67	61.80	47.89	39.58
14.00%	173.54	89.79	61.92	48.01	39.70
14.25%	173.66	89.80	62.03	48.13	39.82
14.50%	173.79	90.02	62.15	48.25	39.94
14.75%	173.91	90.14	62.27	48.37	40.06
15.00%	174.03	90.26	62.38	48.49	40.18

Example: Determine the monthly payment on a 12-month, 14% installment loan for $5,000.

Step 1: Looking at the intersection of the 14% row and the 12-month column, we find that the monthly payment on a similar $1,000 installment loan would be $89.79.

Step 2: To determine the monthly payment on a $5,000 loan, we need only multiply $89.79 by 5 because this loan is for $5,000 rather than $1,000.

TABLE 7.4 Illustration of a 12-Month Installment Loan for $5,000 at 14%

Month	Starting Balance	Total Monthly Payment	Interest Monthly Payment	Principal Monthly Payment	Ending Balance
1	$5,000.00	$448.94	$58.33	$390.61	$4,609.39
2	4,609.39	448.94	53.78	395.16	4,214.23
3	4,214.23	448.94	49.17	399.77	3,814.46
4	3,814.46	448.94	44.50	404.44	3,410.02
5	3,410.02	448.94	39.78	409.16	3,000.86
6	3,000.86	448.94	35.01	413.93	2,586.93
7	2,586.93	448.94	30.18	418.76	2,168.17
8	2,168.17	448.94	25.30	423.64	1,744.53
9	1,744.53	448.94	20.35	428.59	1,315.94
10	1,315.94	448.94	15.35	433.59	882.35
11	882.35	448.94	10.29	438.65	443.70
12	443.70	448.94	5.18	443.76	0.00*
Total		$5,387.28	$387.22	$5,000.06	

*Actually, you've overpaid by 6¢.

constant, and as you pay off more of the loan each month, your interest expenses decline. Therefore, your principal payment increases, as shown in Table 7.4.

Because you're paying interest only on the unpaid balance, if there are nonfinance charges, the stated interest rate is equal to the APR. In effect, there's no trickery here, you just pay interest on what you owe.

Add-On Method   With an add-on interest installment loan, interest charges are calculated using the original balance. These charges are then added to the loan, and this amount is paid off over the life of the loan. Loans using the add-on method can be quite costly and, in general, should be avoided. Look back at our example of a 12-month, $5,000 loan at 14 percent. You'd first calculate the total interest payments to be $700, as follows:

$$\text{interest} = \text{principal} \times \text{interest rate} \times \text{time}$$
$$\text{interest} = \$5,000 \times 0.14 \times 1 = \$700$$

You'd then add this interest payment to the principal to determine your total repayment amount. To determine your monthly payments, just divide this figure by the number of months over which the loan is to be repaid. In this case, the loan is to be repaid over 12 months; thus, the monthly payments would be $475.

$$\frac{\$700 + \$5,000}{12} = \$475$$

This results in an APR of close to 25 percent. As you can see, there's a very big difference between the stated interest rate, which was 14 percent, and the APR. In fact, the add-on method generally results in an APR of close to twice the level of the stated interest rate. That's because you're paying interest on the original principal over the entire life of the loan.

TABLE 7.5	Calculating the APR for an Add-On Loan
Situation	You are considering a 12-month add-on loan for $5,000 at 14% with a total finance charge of $700. This loan has 12 monthly payments of $475. What is the loan's APR?
Solution	Use the *N*-ratio method to approximate the loan's APR. The *N*-ratio method approximates an add-on loan's APR using the following formula: $$APR = \frac{M \times (95N + 9) \times F}{12N \times (N + 1) \times (4P + F)}$$ Where: *M* = number of payments in a year *N* = number of payments over life of the loan *F* = total finance charge *P* = loan principal (amount borrowed) In this example, *M* = 12, *N* = 12, *F* = $700, and *P* = $5,000. Substituting these numbers into the *N*-ratio method approximation formula, you get: $$APR = \frac{12 \times \left[(95 \times 12) + 9\right] \times \$700}{(12 \times 12) \times (12+1) \times \left[(4 \times \$5,000) + \$700\right]}$$ $$= \frac{12 \times 1,149 \times \$700}{144 \times 13 \times \$20,000}$$ $$= \frac{\$9,651,600}{\$38,750,400}$$ $$= 0.2491 \text{ or } 24.91\%$$ Thus, the APR on this 12-month, 14% add-on loan is actually 24.91%.

Even though the amount of outstanding principal keeps decreasing as you pay back the loan, you still pay interest on the amount you originally borrowed. That's why there was such a big difference between the advertised rate of 14 percent and the actual APR of close to 25 percent in the example. Fortunately, the Truth in Lending Act requires lenders to disclose the loan's APR, thereby giving you a more accurate read on the cost of the loan regardless of the method used to calculate interest payments.

N-Ratio Method
A method of approximating the APR.

The calculation of the APR for add-on loans is extremely complicated. However, an approximation can be calculated using the **N-ratio method,** which is shown in Table 7.5.

Early Payment of an Add-On Loan

With an installment loan, if you decide to pay off your loan before its maturity you must first determine how much principal you still owe. Under the simple interest method, interest is paid only on the remaining balance or principal, and it's relatively easy to figure out how much principal remains to be paid.

Rule of 78s or Sum of the Year's Digits
A rule to determine what proportion of each loan payment goes toward paying the interest and what proportion goes toward paying the principal.

If you want to repay an add-on interest installment early, things get a little tougher. There is usually a provision in the loan contract for calculating the unpaid principal and the amount of interest that you would no longer owe if the loan was repaid early. The most common method for determining how much interest you have paid on an add-on installment loan is the **rule of 78s or the sum of the year's digits**.

The rule of 78s determines what proportion of each payment goes toward paying the principal. Table 7.6 looks at our earlier example of a 12-month, $5,000 loan at 14 percent. According to the rule of 78s, more interest is paid in the early periods because you owe more money in the early periods since the loan hasn't been paid down yet. In the example in Table 7.6, in the first month it is assumed that 12/78 of the total interest is paid, while in the last month, only 1/78 of the total interest is paid.

What is the bottom line with respect to add-on loans? First, they are very expensive and should be avoided if at all possible. Moreover, if you decide to pay off your loan early, you could be in for a surprise—there may be a penalty imposed on an early pay off. In fact, it's not uncommon for lenders to keep 20 percent of your prepaid interest as a prepayment penalty. In addition, most add-on loans of a year or less don't allow for any rebate of prepaid interest if you decide to pay the loan off early.

> ### STOP & THINK
>
> In ancient India and Nepal, creditors would "fast on" debtors to collect what was owed them. This involved the creditor sitting at the debtor's front door and fasting until the debt was collected. If the creditor died of starvation, the locals would drag the debtor from his house and beat him to death. Do you think this was an effective approach? Why or why not?

TABLE 7.6 Early Payoff of an Add-On Loan—the Rule of 78s	
Situation	You have a 12-month add-on loan for $5,000 at 14%. You have been paying $475 a month for the past 6 months. You would like to pay off this loan. How much do you still owe?
Solution	Use the rule of 78s to determine what you still owe. **Step 1: Sum up all the months' digits.** First, number each month in descending order down to 1, that is, if it is a 12-month loan, the first month would be assigned 12, the second month 11, and so forth, and then add up all these numbers. One shortcut is to calculate the sum of the months' digits using the following formula: $$\text{Sum of digits} = \left(\frac{N}{2}\right) \times (N + 1)$$ where N is the number of months in the original loan. $$\text{Sum of digits} = \left(\frac{12}{2}\right) \times (12 + 1) = 78$$ **Step 2: Sum the remaining months' digits.** In this case you will sum the numbers of the remaining months: $$6 + 5 + 4 + 3 + 2 + 1 = 21$$ **Step 3: Determine the portion of the interest that will be avoided if the loan is repaid early.** Divide the result in Step 1 by the result in Step 2. $$\text{Portion of Interest Avoided} = \frac{21}{78}$$ **Step 4: Determine the dollar interest charge avoided by an early payment.** Multiply the result in Step 3 times the total dollar interest charge on the loan to determine how much interest will be avoided by an early payment. Total dollar interest is ($0.14 \times \$5,000 \times 1$). Thus, the dollar interest charge avoided by an early repayment is: $$\left(\frac{21}{78}\right) \times (0.14 \times \$5,000 \times 1 \text{ year}) = \$188.46.$$ **Step 5: Calculate the payoff for the loan.** Subtract the result from Step 4 (the interest charges avoided) from total amount due to the lender for the remaining payments. In this case, there are 6 payments of $475 for a total of $2,850 ($6 \times \$475 = \$2,850$). Subtracting $188.46 from this amount yields $2,661.54.

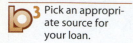

3 Pick an appropriate source for your loan.

Getting the Best Rate on Your Consumer Loans

You should approach applying for a consumer loan in the same way you approach any other consumer purchase. Shop around for the best deal and be prepared to negotiate. Remember, you're the customer.

Where should you shop for a loan? Well, that depends. There's no one perfect lender for everyone. Table 7.7 lists a number of possible credit sources along with the types of loans they make and the advantages and limitations of borrowing from those institutions. Let's take a look at some, starting with the least expensive sources.

Inexpensive Sources

In general, the least expensive source of funds is your family. You don't usually pay the market rate on a family loan; instead you may pay what your family would have earned had they kept this money in a savings account. The obvious downside to a family loan is that if you can't repay it, your family suffers. Also, many people feel uncomfortable borrowing money from their families.

TABLE 7.7 Possible Sources of Credit

Lenders	Types of Loans	Advantages	Limitations
Commercial banks	Home mortgage Home improvement Education Personal Auto, mobile home	Widely available Financial counseling may be offered	Generally competitive Do not take credit risks Primarily larger loans
Savings and loans	Home mortgage Home improvement Education* Personal* Auto, mobile home*	Low costs May provide financial counseling	Selective in lending, only lend to good risks
Credit unions	Home mortgage Home improvement Education Personal Auto, mobile home	Easy to arrange for member in good standing Lowest rates Excellent service	Lend to members only
Sales financing companies (financing where you made the purchase)	Auto Appliance (major) Boat Mobile home	Very convenient Good terms during special promotions Easy to get Processed quickly	High rates Because loan is secured, defaulting can mean loss of item and payments already made
Small loan companies (personal finance companies)	Auto Personal	Easy to get Good credit rating not required Processed quickly	High rates Cosigner often required Maximum size limited by law
Insurance companies	General purpose	Easy to arrange low rates Can borrow up to 95% of policy's surrender value No obligation to repay	Outstanding loan and accumulated interest reduces payment to survivors Policy ownership is required
Brokerage firms	Margin account General purpose loans, using investments as security	Easy to arrange Little delay in getting money Flexible repayment	Changing value of investments can require payment of additional security Margin requirements can change

*In some states only.

Home equity loans and other types of secured loans are also relatively inexpensive because the lending agency has an asset to claim if you can't pay up. The downside of loans of this type is the fact that while assets are tied up as collateral, you can't take out additional first loans on them, so you lose some financing flexibility. Also, if you can't make your payments, you lose your assets. Where do you look for home equity loans? Almost all lending agencies offer them.

Insurance companies that lend on the cash value of life insurance policies also offer relatively low rates. Their rates are low because they're really not taking on any risk—you're borrowing against the cash value of an insurance policy you have with them.

> ### STOP & THINK
>
> When your borrowing isn't tax deductible, which is the case when it's not your mortgage or a home equity loan, the cost of borrowing is actually higher than it appears. If you're in the 30 percent marginal tax bracket, in order to pay $70 of interest you must actually earn $100, with Uncle Sam taking the first $30 out for taxes and leaving you $70 for your interest payment. Given your marginal tax rate, how much would you need to earn to pay $70 of interest if your borrowing wasn't tax deductible?

More Expensive Sources

Credit unions, S&Ls, and commercial banks are also good sources of funds. The precise cost of borrowing from each of these institutions depends on the type of loan—secured versus unsecured—the length of the loan, and whether it's a variable- or fixed-rate loan. More important is the fact that the same loan may have a significantly different interest rate from one lender to another. Remember, you've got to shop around for your loan. Although these three sources offer loans that are quite similar in nature, credit unions generally offer the most favorable terms.

Most Expensive Sources

In general, financing from retail stores on purchases you make in them is quite expensive. Borrowing from a finance company or small loan company is also extremely expensive. Unfortunately, to borrow from other sources, you generally need a solid credit rating. In effect, those who are in the most desperate financial shape generally have to pay the most for credit, which in turn keeps them in desperate financial shape.

Keys to Getting the Best Rate

How do you get the most favorable interest rate on a loan? The primary key is a strong credit rating. The other keys to securing a favorable rate all involve **Principle 8: Risk and Return Go Hand in Hand**. To get a low rate, the loan must be relatively risk free to the lender. Other than improving your credit rating, there are four ways to reduce the lender's risk. First, use a variable-rate loan. With a variable-rate loan you, rather than your bank, will suffer if interest rates rise. A variable-rate loan allows a lender to charge you an interest rate that goes up and down with market interest rates, so the lender then gives you a lower interest rate. If you can't afford the payments if interest rates rise, stay away from variable rate loans. Second, keep the length, or term, of the loan as short as possible. Interest rates decrease as the length of the loan decreases. As we mentioned earlier, the shorter the term, the lower the probability that you will experience a financial disaster before you pay off your loan and the less risk you have of defaulting. Third, provide collateral for the loan. Secured loans are less risky because the lender has an asset designated as collateral in the event of default by the borrower. Finally, put a large down payment toward anything you finance. The larger your down payment, the less you have to borrow and the larger your ownership stake in the asset you are financing. Having a large ownership stake in something is seen as increasing the borrower's desire to pay off the loan.

> ### FACTS OF LIFE
> According to the College Board, the median debt for 4-year college graduates is $19,300.

Should You Borrow or Pay Cash?

In any debt decision, control and planning are the key words. Overriding all your personal finance decisions is the act of setting a budget, living within that budget, and understanding the consequences of your actions.

Debt is, in general, quite expensive. Before you borrow to spend, STOP! Remember, not only do you pay more for what you purchase because of the interest on your loans, but making indebtedness a permanent feature in your financial portfolio tends to impair your future financial flexibility.

Don't borrow to spend if you can avoid it. Decide whether or not you really need to buy that new item. Does it fit into your personal financial planning program? If the answer is no, the process stops there. If the answer is yes, the question becomes whether or not to borrow. In deciding to use cash rather than credit, you must be sure that using cash doesn't materially affect your goal of having sufficient liquidity to carry you through a financial emergency. The answer to this question may leave you with no choice but to borrow. If not, you then have to ask whether the cost of borrowing to purchase the item is greater or less than what you are earning on your savings. Sometimes the interest rate you would be charged on the funds you borrow may be so low that you are better off borrowing at that low rate than using your savings. For example, if Ford is offering 0.9 percent financing on a new car, you might be better off keeping your money in a money market account where it is earning 3 percent, and borrowing the money for the car at 0.9 percent from Ford. On the other hand, if Ford is charging 7 percent financing, and you are only earning 3 percent on your savings, you are better off using your savings. In short, if the benefits outweigh the costs, borrowing makes sense.

MONEY MATTERS

Tips from Marcy Furney, ChFC, Certified Financial Planner™

AND NOW, A FEW WORDS FROM THE "LOAN RANGER"

When most people apply for a mortgage or other large loan, they often go into the process totally unprepared. This can result in delays, repeated trips, numerous phone calls, and possibly denial of credit if your situation is marginal. Make yourself as creditworthy as possible.

If you have no credit history, obtain a credit card or a small loan and make payments on time. You may need a cosigner to obtain a large loan, even if you have an excellent income. Ability to pay isn't the same as demonstrated willingness to pay.

Pay off all the debt you can before you apply. A relatively small credit card balance could cause your ratios to be too high to qualify.

Order your own credit reports and examine them for any errors. Make sure they're in good order before you proceed. If there's been a payment problem, write out the reason for the problem and the resolution. Also document thoroughly any reports that are being contested.

List all your investments and cash, show the name and address of the firm where they're being held, and include account numbers. Make copies of your current statement on each and attach them to the list. Do the same with all debt.

If you're applying for a mortgage be sure to provide the lenders' names, their addresses, and your loan numbers for any previous home loans.

Make copies of your last W-2 and most recent pay stub. If you're self-employed, take copies of your proof of income, for example, Schedule C and Form 1040 from your most recent tax return.

Fill out applications neatly and concisely. Provide copies of all supporting documents. Don't try to hide anything and don't volunteer personal information that isn't requested and isn't directly related to your creditworthiness.

The more complete and organized the information you provide, the less the loan processor will have to do. That could give you a slight edge.

Once you've provided the lender with all the information needed to process the loan, take the initiative to check on your application's progress periodically.

Controlling Your Use of Debt

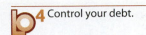

The first step in controlling debt is to determine how much debt you can comfortably handle. The debt level with which you're comfortable and which you may need changes as you pass through different stages of the financial life cycle. Early on, housing and family demands coupled with a relatively low income level make it natural for individuals to build up debt. In later years, as income rises, debt as a portion of income tends to decline.

The bottom line is that you must use your common sense in analyzing your commitments. However, there are several measures that you can use to control your commitments. They include the debt limit ratio and the debt resolution rule.

Debt Limit Ratio

The debt limit ratio is a measure of the percentage of your take-home pay or income taken up by nonmortgage debt payments.

$$\text{debt limit ratio} = \frac{\text{total monthly nonmortgage debt payments}}{\text{total monthly take-home pay}}$$

An individual's total debt can be divided into consumer debt and mortgage debt. Mortgage payments aren't included in the debt limit ratio because this ratio measures your commitment to consumer credit, which tends to be a more expensive type of debt. In order to maintain a reasonable degree of flexibility, ideally you should strive to keep this ratio below 15 percent. At that debt level, you still have a borrowing reserve for emergencies and the unexpected. That is, because of your low level of debt commitment, you should easily be able to secure additional borrowing without stretching your debt commitment to an uncomfortable level.

Once this ratio reaches 20 percent, most financial planners would advise you to limit the use of any additional consumer debt. One problem when consumer debt payments reach this level is the lack of access to additional debt in an emergency. The importance of maintaining an adequate degree of financial flexibility can't be overemphasized. Obviously, as this ratio increases, your future financial flexibility declines.

Many lenders use what is called the 28/36 rule in evaluating mortgage applicants. That is, if your total projected mortgage payments (including insurance and real estate taxes) fall below 28 percent of your gross monthly income, and your total debt payments including these mortgage payments plus any consumer credit payments fall below 36 percent, you're considered a good credit risk. If you don't meet this minimum standard, you may be required to come up with an additional down payment, or you may simply be rejected.

Debt Resolution Rule

The debt resolution rule is used by financial planners to help control debt obligations, excluding borrowing associated with education and home financing, by forcing you to repay all your outstanding debt obligations every 4 years. The logic behind this rule is that consumer credit should be short-term in nature. If it lasts over 4 years, it's not short term. Unfortunately, it's all too easy to rely on consumer credit as a long-term source of funding. Given its relative costs, this type of funding should be used sparingly.

Controlling Consumer Debt

The key to controlling consumer debt is to make sure it fits with the goals you've set and the budget you've developed to achieve these goals. This was the process

CHECKLIST 7.1
Financial Danger Quiz

If you answer yes to any of these questions, you might be in financial trouble.

◆ Do you have little or no savings?
◆ Do you know what to expect when you get your bank or credit card statement?
◆ Have you been turned down for a loan?
◆ Do you carry credit card debt from month to month?
◆ Do your fixed expenses seem to eat up most or all of your income?
◆ Do you have insufficient health insurance?
◆ Do you live without a budget?
◆ Are you borrowing from one lender to pay another?
◆ Are you uncertain about the kind of mortgage you have?
◆ Have you ever taken out a payday loan?
◆ Do creditors call you about payments?
◆ Are you uncertain about the total amount of your debts?
◆ Have you had more than one check returned because of insufficient funds?
◆ Does the trip to the mailbox terrify you because you aren't sure what you'll find in the way of bills?
◆ Are your debts impacting your home life?
◆ Do you find your financial problems seem overwhelming?

discussed in Chapter 2. What we're talking about here is control. As you know, control is a major issue in personal finance.

The inspiration for financial discipline must come with an understanding of how costly and potentially painful the alternative is. It's easy to walk out of college with a good deal of consumer debt. However, keep in mind the costs of borrowing and how borrowing limits your future financial flexibility.

What might tip you off that you might be in financial trouble? In the previous chapter we looked at some signs that you might have problems with your credit cards, now let's take a look at Checklist 7.1 for some clues that you might be in financial trouble.

What to Do if You Can't Pay Your Bills

Once you have gotten into trouble through the overuse of credit, getting out becomes a difficult and painful task. The first step is, of course, putting in place a budget that brings in more money than goes out. The second step involves self-control in the use of credit.

Go to Your Creditor   The first place to go if you can't pay a bill is to the one to whom you owe the money. If you owe money to a bank, go there first. The bank may be willing to restructure the loan.

Credit or Debt Counselor
A trained professional specializing in developing personal budgets and debt repayment programs.

Go to a Credit Counselor   If your creditors are unable or unwilling to help you resolve your dilemma, consider seeking help from a **credit or debt counselor**, a trained professional specializing in developing personal budgets and debt repayment programs. A credit counselor helps you organize your finances and develop a workable plan to pay off your debts. However, you must be careful when choosing a credit or debt counselor. One good place to find a reliable credit counselor is the Consumer Credit Counseling Service (800-388-2227 or on the Web at **www.nfcc.org**), which is a nonprofit agency affiliated with the National Foundation for Consumer Credit. Before you sign on with a credit counselor, make sure you investigate his or her qualifications by checking with your local Better Business Bureau and state consumer protection office to see if there have been any complaints registered against him or her.

Other Options   In addition, there are other options, which we looked at in the previous chapter, that you might consider. First, you should make sure you're borrowing as inexpensively as possible. Small loan companies sometimes charge as much as 40 percent on loans. Avoid them and see if there's a cheaper way to get the funds you need.

A second option to consider is using savings to pay off current debt. You shouldn't do so more than once—when you're reevaluating and changing your spending and credit use patterns in a permanent manner. If you are only earning 4 percent after taxes on your savings, then using savings to pay off consumer debt at 10 or 12 percent may be a good idea. However, your borrowing should be controlled in such a way that it doesn't get out of hand and doesn't warrant this remedy on a regular basis. This is an emergency measure to be taken only in the extreme situation.

> **FACTS OF LIFE**
>
> There are now over 20,000 payday loan shops in the United States.

Another alternative is to use a debt consolidation loan to stretch out your payments and possibly reduce your interest. A **debt consolidation loan** is a loan used to pay off all your current debts. The purpose of a loan of this kind is to lower your monthly payment. A debt consolidation loan doesn't eliminate your debt problems, it merely restructures the payments associated with paying off that debt. Before you sign on with a debt consolidation company, make sure you know what you're getting into—make sure you check it out with the Better Business Bureau and the state consumer protection office—that should tell you something about whether or not this is a company you'd like to assist you. Again, this isn't the optimum solution. The best solution is to take control of your borrowing from the onset.

Debt Consolidation Loan
A loan used to pay off all your current debts.

Bankruptcy as the Last Resort   A final alternative in the most extreme case of debt is personal **bankruptcy**. This is not a step to be taken lightly. It doesn't wipe out all your obligations—for example, student loans, alimony, and tax liabilities remain—but it relieves some of the financial pressure.

Bankruptcy
The inability to pay off your debts.

The primary contributing factor to bankruptcies is major illnesses and the costs and loss of income associated with them. Another factor contributing to the large number of bankruptcies is the easy availability of credit that leads to living beyond your means. Divorce and job loss are also major contributors to bankruptcy.

The two most commonly used types of personal bankruptcy are Chapter 13 bankruptcy, the wage earner plan, and Chapter 7 bankruptcy, straight bankruptcy. There are several other types of bankruptcy, but because they are so specialized, we discuss only Chapter 13 and Chapter 7 in detail. The primary difference between Chapter 13 and Chapter 7 bankruptcy is that under Chapter 13 you design a plan that will allow you to repay the majority of your debts, while under Chapter 7 bankruptcy, most of your debts are discharged. But in order to qualify for Chapter 7 bankruptcy as opposed to Chapter 13 bankruptcy, you have to meet a Chapter 7 means test that compares your income to the median income in your state. If your income falls below the median income in your state, you can file for Chapter 7 bankruptcy. However, if it's greater than the median income in your state, you'll have to do other calculations regarding your income and allowable expenses to determine if you can file for Chapter 7 bankruptcy. This means test went into place as the result of legislation signed into effect in 2005 and resulted in a sharp drop in the number of bankruptcies—it also resulted in a lot of people filing for bankruptcy just prior to the new law taking effect as shown in

> **STOP & THINK**
>
> Debt consolidation loans are very appealing because they offer hope to those who can't keep up with their current payment schedules. Before taking out a debt consolidation loan, however, keep in mind that you may be paying a higher interest rate on the consolidation loan than you are on your current debt. If the problems that led you into this dilemma in the first place aren't solved, do you think a debt consolidation loan will result in a permanent solution? What would you need to do to solve your debt problems?

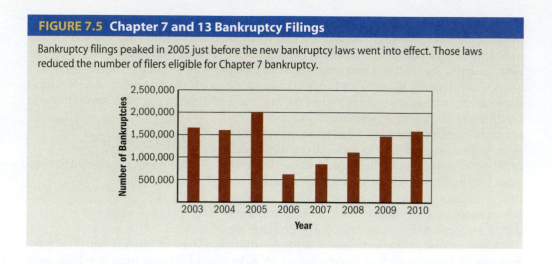

FIGURE 7.5 Chapter 7 and 13 Bankruptcy Filings

Bankruptcy filings peaked in 2005 just before the new bankruptcy laws went into effect. Those laws reduced the number of filers eligible for Chapter 7 bankruptcy.

Figure 7.5. Prior to the new legislation, in 2005, there were over 2 million bankruptcies nationwide. That's about one in every 53 U.S. households. In 2006 that number had dropped to around 600,000, but since then has been creeping up as shown in Figure 7.5. Figure 7.6 provides a comparison of the two primary personal bankruptcy options.

Chapter 13: The Wage Earner's Plan

To file for Chapter 13 bankruptcy, you must have a regular income, secured debts of less than $1,081,400, and unsecured debts of less than $360,475 (these are figures accessed in March 2011 and are adjusted each year for inflation). Under Chapter 13,

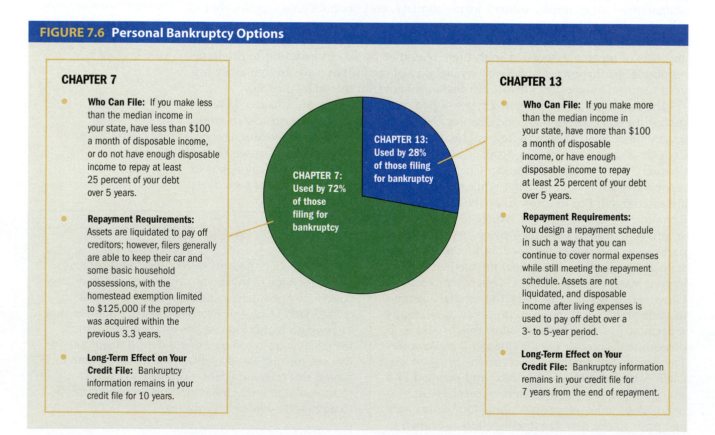

FIGURE 7.6 Personal Bankruptcy Options

CHAPTER 7

- **Who Can File:** If you make less than the median income in your state, have less than $100 a month of disposable income, or do not have enough disposable income to repay at least 25 percent of your debt over 5 years.

- **Repayment Requirements:** Assets are liquidated to pay off creditors; however, filers generally are able to keep their car and some basic household possessions, with the homestead exemption limited to $125,000 if the property was acquired within the previous 3.3 years.

- **Long-Term Effect on Your Credit File:** Bankruptcy information remains in your credit file for 10 years.

CHAPTER 7: Used by 72% of those filing for bankruptcy

CHAPTER 13: Used by 28% of those filing for bankruptcy

CHAPTER 13

- **Who Can File:** If you make more than the median income in your state, have more than $100 a month of disposable income, or have enough disposable income to repay at least 25 percent of your debt over 5 years.

- **Repayment Requirements:** You design a repayment schedule in such a way that you can continue to cover normal expenses while still meeting the repayment schedule. Assets are not liquidated, and disposable income after living expenses is used to pay off debt over a 3- to 5-year period.

- **Long-Term Effect on Your Credit File:** Bankruptcy information remains in your credit file for 7 years from the end of repayment.

you design a plan that will allow you to repay the majority of your debts, whereas under Chapter 7 bankruptcy, most of your debts are discharged. The repayment schedule under Chapter 13 is designed so that you can continue to cover normal expenses while still meeting the repayment obligation. You maintain title and possession of your assets and, other than the new debt repayment schedule, continue on with life as before. For your creditors, it means a controlled repayment of debt obligations with the court's supervision. For the individual, it may mean relief from the harassment of bill collectors and the pressure of never knowing how future obligations will be met.

FACTS OF LIFE

Bankruptcies went up dramatically in the last century. Before then people didn't live as long, and when they did get sick, they died—in effect, death kept them out of financial trouble. Today, medicine can do wonders, but it can also put you in a financial predicament that is hard to recover from.

Bankruptcy happens to all kinds of good people, and it can provide breathing room to start over when there's no hope. Burt Reynolds, Hollywood's number 1 box office draw from 1978 through 1982, along with Kim Basinger, Toni Braxton, Marion "Suge" Knight, and Antonio Tarver (the WBC light heavyweight boxing champ) have all filed for bankruptcy. Although Burt Reynolds made a ton of money in movies such as *Smokey and the Bandit* and *Cannonball Run*, he also lost around $15 million in Po-Folks restaurants. When he finally filed for bankruptcy he had $11.2 million in debts and assets worth only $6.65 million. Because he exceeded the debt limits of Chapter 13 bankruptcy, he was forced to file under Chapter 11. Among his debts were a loan from CBS of $3.7 million plus interest and $121,797 to his custom wigmaker. Chapter 11 bankruptcy gave him the breathing room to begin again and regain control of his finances.

Chapter 7: Straight Bankruptcy

Chapter 7 bankruptcy, or straight bankruptcy, is a more severe type of bankruptcy. Under Chapter 7, the individual who doesn't have any possibility of repaying debts is given the opportunity to eliminate them and begin again. Exactly what assets you can keep varies from state to state, but your home equity exemption is limited to $125,000 if the property was acquired within the previous $3\frac{1}{3}$ years.

To qualify for Chapter 7 bankruptcy as opposed to Chapter 13 you must pass a "means test" that attempts to determine if you are earning enough to be able to pay off at least some of your debt. In effect, the major intent of bankruptcy reform is to require people who can afford to make some payments toward their debt to make these payments, while still affording them the right to have the rest of their debt erased. These people must file Chapter 13 as opposed to Chapter 7. If you make more than the median income in your state, have more than $100 a month of disposable income, or have enough disposable income to repay at least 25 percent of your debt over 5 years, then you may have to do a Chapter 13 bankruptcy. In addition, within 6 months of when you can file for bankruptcy you must complete a credit counseling course, the purpose of which is to inform consumers of the consequences of bankruptcy. Then, before any debts are discharged, you must also take a course in personal financial management.

The bottom line is that while you will not lose everything, you will have to sell a good portion of your assets in order to satisfy Chapter 7 requirements. Most of your debts will be wiped out, but some will remain, such as child support, alimony, student loans, and taxes. A trustee arranges to

FACTS OF LIFE

According to Elizabeth Warren, a professor of law at Harvard, and the individual initially in charge of setting up the Consumer Financial Protection Bureau, over half of the families that file for bankruptcy do so in the aftermath of an illness or accident.

collect and sell all of your nonexempt property, with the proceeds divided among the creditors. In short, the courts confiscate and sell most of your assets to pay off creditors and, in return, eliminate most of your debts. Needless to say, Chapter 7 bankruptcy is a drastic step and should be taken only after consultation with a financial advisor and your lawyer.

Summary

 Understand the various consumer loans.
A single-payment loan is a loan that's paid back in a single lump-sum payment at maturity. In general, these loans have a stated maturity date. An installment loan calls for repayment of both interest and principal at regular intervals, with the payment levels set in such a way that the loan expires at a preset date.

Consumer loans are either secured or unsecured. A secured loan is a loan that is guaranteed by a specific asset. With an unsecured loan, no collateral is required.

With a fixed interest rate loan, the interest rate is fixed for the entire duration of the loan, but with a variable interest rate loan, the interest rate is tied to a market interest rate and periodically adjusts to reflect movements in that market interest rate. A home equity loan, or second mortgage, is a loan that uses a borrower's built-up equity in his or her home as collateral against the loan.

 Calculate the cost of a consumer loan.
It's important to know exactly what a loan costs. The finance charges include all the costs associated with the loan—interest payments, loan processing fees, fees for a credit check, and any required insurance fees. The APR is the simple percentage cost of the credit paid over the life of the loan on an annual basis.

 Pick an appropriate source for your loan.
There are numerous sources of consumer loans, which vary dramatically in terms of cost, including family, insurance companies, credit unions, savings and loan associations, commercial banks, small loan companies, retail stores, and credit cards.

The key to getting a favorable rate on a loan, or even qualifying for a loan in the first place, is a strong credit rating. In addition, there are four other ways that you can reduce the lender's risk and thereby secure a favorable rate: (1) use a variable-rate loan, (2) keep the term of the loan as short as possible, (3) provide collateral for the loan, and (4) put a large down payment toward the item being financed.

 Control your debt.
Before borrowing, you must make sure that borrowing fits within your financial plan, including living within your budget, and that you understand all the consequences of your actions. You must also determine how much debt you can afford. Not only should you use your common sense in analyzing your debt commitments, but you should also measure the severity of your credit commitments using the ratio of the nonmortgage debt service to take-home pay and the debt resolution rule.

Review Questions

1. How does a single-payment or balloon loan differ from an installment loan? What is a bridge loan?

2. Describe the differences between a secured and unsecured loan. How does **Principle 8: Risk and Return Go Hand in Hand** apply?

3. Describe a variable- or adjustable-rate loan. List four features that should be compared when shopping for this type of loan. What is a convertible loan?

4. Are the initial rates lower on a fixed-rate loan or a variable-rate loan? Why?

5. Credit contracts often include the acceleration clause, the deficiency payments clause, and the recourse clause to give the lender options for collecting the debt. Explain each clause. What is the purpose of the insurance agreement clause?

6. Home equity credit loans and credit lines are very popular sources of consumer credit. List the advantages and disadvantages of borrowing against home equity.

7. Student loan programs are available to students and parents to finance college-related expenses. Compare and contrast the programs available to students and parents. How are the interest rates determined?

8. Home equity, student, and auto loans are special-purpose consumer loans. Which ones offer the unique benefit of tax deductibility for interest paid?

9. What loan costs are included in the determination of finance charges? What is APR? How is it used?

10. What are payday loans? Besides the high interest rates, what are some of the dangers associated with this type of loan?

11. What methods are used to calculate interest on a single-payment loan? Which method is preferable to the consumer?

12. Why are loans based on the simple interest method a better option than loans using the add-on method? Is this true even if the consumer decides to repay the loan early?

13. Loan costs vary significantly with the lender. Identify at least two inexpensive loan sources, two more expensive loan sources, and two most expensive loan sources.

14. Based on **Principle 8: Risk and Return Go Hand in Hand**, name five ways you can reduce the risk for the lender thereby reducing the return for the lender and saving yourself money.

15. Why are mortgage payments not included in the debt limit ratio?

16. According to the debt resolution rule, what is the time frame for repayment of short-term debt? What types of borrowing are not considered in the debt resolution rule?

17. Remedies for overcoming excessive credit use can impact your present and future financial situation. Name eight remedies to consider when you are having trouble paying your bills. List the advantages and disadvantages of each.

18. What is the fundamental difference between Chapter 7 and Chapter 13 bankruptcy? What three major criteria differentiate a filer's eligibility for each chapter? What debts cannot be discharged in a Chapter 7 bankruptcy?

Develop Your Skills—Problems and Activities

These problems are available in MyFinanceLab.

1. Rico needs approximately $2,500 to buy a new computer. A 2-year unsecured loan through the credit union is available for 12 percent interest. The current rate on his revolving home equity line is 8.75 percent, although he is reluctant to

use it. Rico is in the 15 percent federal tax bracket and the 5.75 percent state tax bracket. Which loan should he choose? Why? Regardless of the loan chosen, Rico wants to pay off the loan in 24 months. Calculate the payments for him, assuming both loans use the simple interest calculation method.

2. Shirley, a recent college graduate, excitedly described to her older sister the $1,500 sofa, chair, and tables she found today. However, when asked she could not tell her sister which interest calculation method was to be used on her credit-based purchase. Calculate the monthly payments and total cost for a bank loan assuming a 1-year repayment period and 14 percent interest. Now assume the store uses the add-on method of interest calculation. Calculate the monthly payment and total cost with a 1-year repayment period and 12 percent interest. Explain why the bank payment and total cost are lower even though the stated interest rate is higher.

3. Using the information on the two loans described in problem 2, how much interest would Shirley have "saved" or been rebated if she could have repaid the loans after 6 months?

4. Which results in a lower total interest charge, borrowing $1,000 to be repaid 12 months later as a single-payment loan or borrowing $1,000 to be repaid as a 12-month installment loan? Assume a simple interest method of calculation at 12 percent interest. Defend your answer.

5. Consumers should comparison shop for credit just as they would for any other consumer good or service. How might a consumer's stage of the financial life cycle, income, net worth, or credit score affect the availability of loan sources and the associated cost of the loans offered?

6. Camerin wants a new big screen TV and home theater surround sound system, which he thinks will cost $4,000. The store will finance up to $3,500 for 2 years at 19.5 percent interest rate. Assuming Camerin accepts the store's financing, what will his monthly payment be? If he increases his down payment to $1,000, how much will his monthly payment be?

7. Antonio would like to replace his golf clubs with a custom measured set. A local sporting goods megastore is advertising custom clubs for $800, including a new bag. In-store financing is available at 2 percent or he can choose not to renew his $500 certificate of deposit (CD), which just matured. The advertised CD renewal rate is 2 percent. Antonio knows the in-store financing costs would not affect his taxes, but he knows he'll pay taxes (25 percent federal taxes and 5.75 percent state taxes) on the CD interest earnings. Should he cash the CD or use the in-store financing? Why?

8. Noel and Herman need to replace Noel's car. But with the furniture and appliance payments, the credit card bills, and Herman's car payment, they are uncertain if they can afford another payment. The auto-financing representative has asked, "What size payments are you thinking of?" Current payments total $475 of their $3,250 combined monthly take-home pay. Calculate the debt limit ratio to help them decide about the car purchase and answer the question, "What size payments are you thinking of?" by first assuming a 15 percent limit and then "stretching" it to a 20 percent limit.

Learn by Doing—Suggested Projects

1. Visit a bank, a credit union, and a retail outlet that offer credit. Ask for a copy of the contract for a consumer installment loan or purchase. Compare the contracts for an explanation of the credit terms as well as the various contract clauses identified in this chapter. How do interest rates vary for secured and unsecured

loans? Do they offer fixed- and adjustable-rate loans? What method(s) of interest calculation do they use? Prepare a report of your findings.

2. Visit the FAFSA Web site (**www.fafsa.ed.gov**) to learn about the different student loans available through the government. How do you qualify for federal loans? Using FAFSA's online calculator, determine how much your monthly payment will be if you borrow $10,000 and use the standard repayment period of 10 years with an interest rate of 6.8 percent.

3. Visit several payday lenders to learn about their lending process, limits, and fees. Do the lenders compete on cost or convenience? Do they serve college students with little or no income? Prepare a report of your findings.

4. Interview the financial manager at an auto dealership to learn about the available financing options. Since the auto purchased will serve as collateral, and the vehicle trade-in value can be the down payment, how does the interest rate and term of the loan affect, or reduce, the lender's risk? How can the consumer get the best auto financing deal? Discuss the debt resolution rule in light of the increasing length of auto loans.

5. Using your anticipated entry-level take-home pay, calculate the maximum non-mortgage debt payment that you can safely handle. What are the implications given your actual or anticipated debt for credit cards, auto loan, or school loans? Can you afford additional borrowing for furniture, appliances, travel, or other needs? (Assume that take-home pay would be 75 percent of projected gross salary.)

6. Schedule an interview with a representative of the local branch of the National Foundation for Consumer Credit debt counseling service or use their Web site (**www.nfcc.org**). Identify the services offered to consumers and creditors, as well as the factors that commonly contribute to problems in repaying debts. What strategies are used to remedy different situations? Which remedies seem to be the most effective?

7. To learn more about personal bankruptcy, interview an attorney (or other knowledgeable bankruptcy professional) who often handles bankruptcy proceedings. Ask about spending trends and household events that contribute to bankruptcy, typical costs for filing bankruptcy, and the effect of filing on the consumer's financial future. Report your findings.

8. Ask your parents or other family members to describe their feelings about, and their use of, credit. Use Checklist 7.1 as a framework to guide your discussion by having your family members honestly answer the questions. (If you are discussing with two or more members, consider having them answer the questions separately.)

9. Talk with a loan officer at a local bank or credit union. Discuss the approval qualifications for unsecured, secured, and home equity loans and the range of interest rates available with each. Also, discuss the effect of the debt limit ratio and the credit score on loan approval and interest rate. Write a brief synopsis of the information.

10. Go to **www.paydayloaninfo.org** to see how payday loans are regulated in your state. Write a brief report detailing the maximum loan amount and annual percentage rate allowed in your state. Explain the different restrictions that apply to members of the military.

Be a Financial Planner—Discussion Case 1

This case is available in MyFinanceLab.

Karou is considering different options for financing the $12,000 balance on her planned new car purchase. The cheapest advertised rate among the local banks is 7 percent for a 48-month car loan. The current rate on her revolving home equity line is 8.5 percent. Karou is in the 25 percent federal tax bracket and the 5.75 percent state tax bracket.

Questions

1. Calculate Karou's monthly car payment using your financial calculator. Compare the payment amount if she uses the 48-month car loan through her local bank versus her home equity line of credit. Assume both loans will amortize over 48 months and use the simple interest method.

2. What is Karou's income tax savings over the life of the loan if she chooses to use her home equity line of credit to finance the purchase of her new car?

3. Which loan offers the lower payment? Which loan has the lower after-tax cost? Use this information to determine which loan she should choose.

4. In a discussion with her father about financing her new car, Karou was surprised to hear that he once financed a car with the add-on method of interest calculation. He planned to repay the $2,000 loan within 1 year but was able to do so after 9 months because of a bonus he earned at work. The interest rate was 5 percent. Calculate the monthly payments, as well as the final payment to pay off the loan. How much interest was "saved," or rebated, using this method of financing and the rule of 78s?

5. Assume Karou's father could finance $2,000 today at 5 percent using the simple interest method of calculation. How much would the payments be? Calculate the final payment to pay off the loan after 9 months. How much interest was "saved"?

6. Considering the information in questions 4 and 5, calculate the difference in finance charges assuming neither loan was paid off early.

7. Assuming Karou did not have access to a home equity line, what factors might she consider to reduce the lender's risk and, therefore, "buy" herself a lower-cost loan? (*Hint:* Consider **Principle 8: Risk and Return Go Hand in Hand**).

8. What is the collateral for each of the loans Karou is considering? If the bank repossessed her car, would she still have to repay her loan?

Be a Financial Planner—Discussion Case 2

This case is available in MyFinanceLab.

You work in the financial aid office and Mary Lou Hennings, a junior, has come to you for advice. She just found out that her father has been "downsized" from his job. To ensure that she has sufficient funding for her senior year, she needs to apply for a loan to help with expenses. She has a part-time job with take-home pay of $375 per month. She expects her annual net earnings to be approximately $30,000 after graduation, although she plans to continue living at home for another year or two. Her parents have told her she can use up to $10,000 of their home equity line of credit; however, she is not sure she wants to do that. She does not have any debt, except for 3 more years of monthly auto payments of $189. She is worried about trying to pay for an additional loan while still in school although her dad is convinced he will find another job soon and be able to make the payments.

Questions

1. What types of student loans are available to Mary Lou and what lending limits apply?

2. Assume her student loan will have an interest rate of 8 percent and her parents' home equity line has a rate of 9.25 percent. If both loans have a 10-year maturity, what will her monthly payment be on $5,000, ignoring any possible deferments?

3. Explain the tax consequences of the two options, assuming Mary Lou is in the 25 percent marginal federal tax bracket and her parents are in the 28 percent tax bracket. No state income tax is assessed.

4. Using her current income, calculate her debt limit ratio for the most expensive school loan and her auto loan during school. Using her projected income, calculate her debt limit ratio for the loans after graduation.

5. Considering all available information, which loan would you suggest to Mary Lou? Why? Are there other options for financing her education?

CHAPTER

8 The Home and Automobile Decision

Learning Objectives

 Make good buying decisions.

 Choose a vehicle that suits your needs and budget.

 Choose housing that meets your needs.

 Decide whether to rent or buy housing.

 Calculate the costs of buying a home.

 Get the most out of your mortgage.

Most of us look for a home that fits our family and our lifestyle. You know, enough bedrooms, maybe a playroom for the kids, a kitchen that allows us to cook with ease. But not Johnny Depp. A few years ago, after he starred in *Ed Wood*, a film featuring famous movie star Bela Lugosi, Depp became so fascinated with Lugosi, that he bought his former home. Beautiful and secluded, this house is truly a castle, built of gray stone with turrets and iron trim. And it's big—7,430 square feet in all, with 28 rooms, including 8 bedrooms and 10 bathrooms. Even for a mega-star like Johnny Depp, the house was a major purchase, costing roughly $2 million.

Depp also owns a $2 million villa in the south of France, near the Riviera, where he spends time with his family. In addition, perhaps inspired by the movie *The Pirates of the Caribbean*, he purchased a 35-acre island in the Bahamas for $3.6 million. The island, Little Hall's Pond Cay, has six white sandy beaches and a central lagoon surrounded by palm trees—perfect for Depp, who brought the role of Captain Jack Sparrow to life.

What would make a home "perfect" for you? As you might imagine—or perhaps already know—buying a house isn't just a financial decision, it's also a personal and emotional one, so it has to fit both your lifestyle and your wallet. For most people, buying a home is the single biggest investment they'll ever make, which is why it's so important to understand all the complexities and financial implications of this purchase.

Buying a car is another major purchasing decision. Although a car isn't considered an investment, it *is* an expenditure, and a huge one at that. In either case—buying a house or a car—you're probably going to need a loan and are thus committing a large portion of your future earnings over a long period of time. Because both of these purchases have a dramatic impact on your personal finances, you need to consider each carefully.

Smart Buying

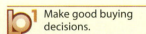

Make good buying decisions.

In this chapter, we talk about spending money rather than saving it. Just as you work hard to save money, you should also work hard when spending it, taking the time to make well-thought-out and well-researched buying decisions. To help you do this, we'll look at four steps in a smart buying process. You can apply this process to any major purchasing decision. It is a way to place some control on your purchasing, a way to ensure that your final selection isn't only the best product for the best price, but a product that you need at a cost that fits your budget. One of the big benefits of this approach is that it eliminates impulse buying, a sure budget blower if there ever was one.

Let's look at each of the four steps to smart buying in general. Then, we'll apply these steps, first to an automobile purchase, and then to a home purchase.

Step 1: Differentiate Want from Need

Before even deciding to make a purchase, smart buying requires that you separate your wants from your needs. This doesn't mean never buying anything you simply want, it just means recognizing such a purchase for what it is, and making sure you can afford it. For most of us, "want" purchases often carry a tradeoff. A new iPod, for example, may mean sacrificing other material wants—such as foregoing your daily latte for the next 6 months. The important thing to determine before buying a "want" is whether the purchase will interfere with your ability to pay for your needs. It's one thing to give up Starbucks, it's another not be able to pay your rent!

Step 2: Do Your Homework

After deciding to make a purchase, you need to make sure to do it wisely. Let's say you are in the market for a new flat screen TV. The first thing you need to know is how much you can you afford to spend on one. After you determine what your budget will allow, take the time to research the details. What is the price range for flat screen TVs? What are the differences in quality? What are the features of each brand?

Do some comparison shopping. For many purchases you can start your research with *Consumer Reports*, a publication that provides unbiased ratings and recommendations for a host of products and services. It's available at your library or bookstore. Another informative guide on smart buying, the *Consumer Action Handbook*, downloadable from the Internet at **www.consumeraction.gov/viewpdf.shtml**.

Step 3: Make Your Purchase

When you're ready to make your purchase, it is sometimes just a matter of going to the cheapest source and buying the product. However, with some products, such as a car, there may be negotiation involved. In purchases that require haggling, you increase your chances of getting the best deal possible by first doing all the research you can. One key to negotiating a good price is knowing the markup on the product—the price the dealer adds on above what he or she paid for the product. (This is part of Step 2: Do Your Homework.) Knowing the markup gives you an idea of how much room there is for negotiation. You also want to make sure that you're dealing with someone with the authority to lower the price. And be sure to consider the various financing alternatives, determining not only which is the best deal, but which alternative best fits your monthly budget. Checklist 8.1 gives some tips on smart buying.

Step 4: Maintain Your Purchase

Smart buying means getting the best product or service at the best price with financing that's right for you. Smart buying also means maintaining your purchase after the deal is done, which includes physically maintaining what you've bought, as well as resolving any complaints or issues about the purchase or the product. If you have a problem, the first thing to do is contact the seller. If that doesn't do it, contact the headquarters of the company that made or sold the product. Most large companies have a toll-free 800 number. It's generally on the product's instructions; if not, you can usually get it on the company's Web site or by calling the directory of 800 telephone numbers at 800-555-1212.

You can also write to the company. Make sure to address your letter to the consumer office or the company president. In your correspondence, describe the problem, what you've done so far to try to resolve it, and what action you'd like taken. Do you want your money back, or do you want the product exchanged? Keep in mind that your problem may not be resolved immediately. When dealing

---

CHECKLIST 8.1
Before You Buy

◆ Decide in advance exactly what you want and what you can afford. Don't buy on impulse or because a salesperson is pressuring you.

◆ Take advantage of sales, but compare prices. Do not assume an item is a bargain just because it is advertised as one.

◆ Don't rush into a large purchase because the "price is only good today."

◆ Be aware of such extra charges as delivery fees, installation charges, service costs, and postage and handling fees. Add them into the total cost.

◆ Ask about the seller's refund or exchange policy.

◆ Don't sign a contract without reading it, if you don't understand it, or if there are any blank spaces in it.

◆ Before buying a product or service, contact your consumer protection office to see if there are automatic cancellation periods for the purchase you are making. In some states, there are cancellation periods for dating clubs, health clubs, and time-share and campground memberships. Federal law gives you cancellation rights for certain door-to-door sales.

◆ Walk out or hang up on high-pressure sales tactics. Don't allow yourself to feel forced or pressured into buying something.

◆ Don't do business over the telephone with companies you do not know.

◆ Be suspicious of post office box addresses. If you have a complaint, you might have trouble locating the company.

◆ Do not respond to any prize or gift offer that requires you to pay even a small amount of money.

◆ Don't rely on a salesperson's verbal promises. Get everything in writing.

Source: U.S. Office of Consumer Affairs, *Consumer's Resource Handbook,* 2011.

---

with a company directly, keep notes, including the name of the person with whom you spoke, the date, and what was done. Save copies of all letters to and from the company.

If your problem still isn't resolved, it's time to work through such organizations as the Better Business Bureau, along with other local, state, and federal organizations that might provide help. Checklist 8.2 gives some tips on making a complaint, while Figure 8.1 provides a sample complaint letter.

Smart Buying in Action: Buying a Vehicle

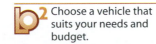 Choose a vehicle that suits your needs and budget.

Next to buying a house, your vehicle is probably your largest investment. Although there are major differences between buying a stereo and a car or truck—the price, for one thing—the process is essentially the same.

Ten years ago the only decision to be made in the purchase of a new car was whether to buy a new one or a used one. Today you can also consider leasing. What brought on this new method of vehicle financing? Sticker shock. Today the cost of a new vehicle is beyond the financial means of many Americans. Leasing, which is becoming increasingly popular, offers an affordable alternative. In effect, leasing is renting a vehicle for an extended period, with a small or no down payment and low monthly payments. To understand the process of purchasing or leasing a vehicle, we'll follow the basic smart buying process, adapting it to fit the vehicle decision.

CHECKLIST 8.2
Making a Complaint

- Keep a record of your efforts to resolve the problem.
- First contact the business that sold you the item or performed the service. If that doesn't work, go directly to the company or the manufacturer.
- When you write to the company, describe the problem, what you have done so far to resolve it, and what solution you want. Address letters, faxes, or e-mails to the company consumer affairs department or to the president if there is no consumer affairs office. Use the sample consumer complaint letter in Figure 8.1 as a guide.
- Type your letter. Include copies, not originals, of all documents. Include the date and place you made the purchase, who performed the service, information about the product (such as the serial or model number and warranty terms), what went wrong, with whom you have tried to resolve the problem, and what you want done to correct the problem.
- Consider sending letters with a return receipt requested. This will cost more, but it will give you proof that the letter was received and will tell you who signed for it.
- If you make your complaint by telephone, be reasonable, not angry or threatening.
- Allow time for the person you contacted to resolve your problem. Keep notes of the date, with whom you spoke, what was agreed on, and the next steps to be taken. Save copies of all letters to and from the company.
- If you believe you have given the company enough time to resolve the problem, file a complaint with your state or local consumer protection office, the Better Business Bureau, or the regulatory agency that has jurisdiction over the business.
- Don't give up until you are satisfied.

Source: U.S. Office of Consumer Affairs, *Consumer's Resource Handbook*, 2011.

Step 1: Differentiate Want from Need

Very few decisions pit needs against wants as directly as which car to buy. For most people, choosing a car is more than deciding what best suits their lifestyle and what they can afford; people want a car that reflects who they are. A new Dodge Caravan minivan may be the most practical choice for you, your husband, and your three kids, but you may still really *want* a MINI Cooper convertible, which costs about the same. In making this decision, as with any major purchase decision, you'll first have to decide which features and qualities you need, and which features and qualities you just want. The facts of your life will dictate many of the features that you need. Does your work require that you do a lot of hauling? Do you have two black labs that you take with you everywhere? What about the kids—do you have enough room for them to be comfortable during the 3-hour drive to your vacation spot? Or do you need a car just to tool around town with your best friend? (If this is the case, buy the MINI Cooper.)

After you determine which features you need—a flatbed for your work, a "way back" for the dogs, or a car that seats five with room for suitcases—make a list of features you want. If you're on the road for work 3 hours a day, a CD player may seem vital to you. Or you may really crave a portable DVD player knowing that if the kids can watch *Puss in Boots* on the long drive to Grandma's you'll get a bit more peace and quiet.

Now that you have a list of what you need and what you want, how do you know what you can afford? Let's find out.

FIGURE 8.1   Sample Complaint Letter

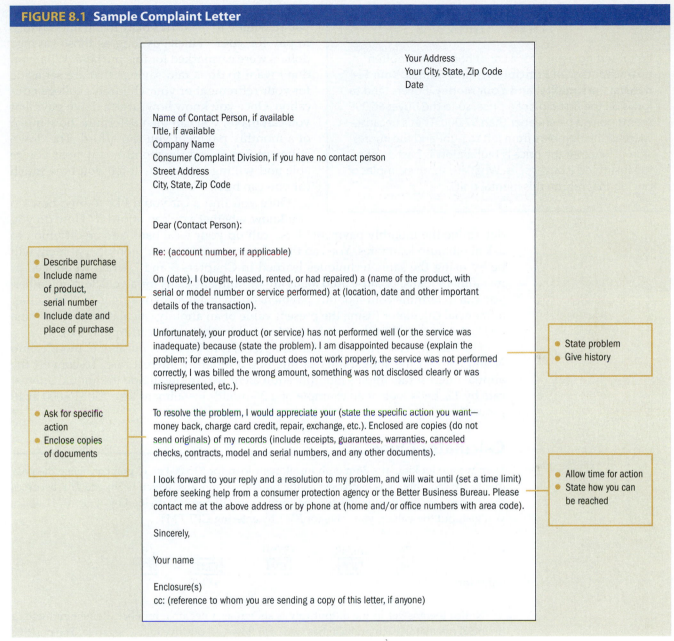

Describe purchase
- Include name of product, serial number
- Include date and place of purchase

Ask for specific action
- Enclose copies of documents

> Your Address
> Your City, State, Zip Code
> Date
>
> Name of Contact Person, if available
> Title, if available
> Company Name
> Consumer Complaint Division, if you have no contact person
> Street Address
> City, State, Zip Code
>
> Dear (Contact Person):
>
> Re: (account number, if applicable)
>
> On (date), I (bought, leased, rented, or had repaired) a (name of the product, with serial or model number or service performed) at (location, date and other important details of the transaction).
>
> Unfortunately, your product (or service) has not performed well (or the service was inadequate) because (state the problem). I am disappointed because (explain the problem; for example, the product does not work properly, the service was not performed correctly, I was billed the wrong amount, something was not disclosed clearly or was misrepresented, etc.).
>
> To resolve the problem, I would appreciate your (state the specific action you want—money back, charge card credit, repair, exchange, etc.). Enclosed are copies (do not send originals) of my records (include receipts, guarantees, warranties, canceled checks, contracts, model and serial numbers, and any other documents).
>
> I look forward to your reply and a resolution to my problem, and will wait until (set a time limit) before seeking help from a consumer protection agency or the Better Business Bureau. Please contact me at the above address or by phone at (home and/or office numbers with area code).
>
> Sincerely,
>
> Your name
>
> Enclosure(s)
> cc: (reference to whom you are sending a copy of this letter, if anyone)

State problem
- Give history

Allow time for action
- State how you can be reached

Source: U.S. Office of Consumer Affairs, *Consumer Resource Handbook,* 2011.

Step 2: Do Your Homework

When considering purchasing or leasing a car, doing your homework involves not only determining what kind of car you want, but how much you can afford. Let's look at the issue of money first.

How Much Can You Afford?   Vehicles are expensive. What can you realistically afford? It makes no sense to purchase a vehicle that will put such financial strain on you that either other goals or your lifestyle must be compromised. While it's interesting to note that a typical family spends between 4 and 6 months' worth of its annual income when it buys a new car, the most important thing to remember is that your purchase must fit into your budget.

STOP & THINK

When setting a price for a car or home, sellers often take advantage of **Principle 9: Mind Games, Your Financial Personality, and Your Money**. Buyers tend to focus on the first digit of a price, so to the buyer $6,999 seems quite a bit cheaper than $7,000. That's because we read the numbers from left to right and the impression of whether the price is high or low is based upon the first thing a buyer sees. What are some examples of pricing that rely on this mental trait?

First determine the size of the down payment you're willing to make. It's okay to tap into savings to pay for your vehicle, as long as those savings dollars were earmarked for this purpose. What you don't want to do is raid savings that are set aside for your retirement or your children's college education. Once you know how large a down payment you can make, you can then determine how much of a monthly payment you can afford. The down payment figure and the monthly payment you're able and willing to make will tell you how much car you can buy.

Once you find a car you'd like to buy, how do you know whether you can afford it? How do you determine the monthly payment? First, call up your local bank and credit union to ask about auto loan rates. You can then determine what your monthly payment will be by using the same techniques learned in Chapters 3 and 7 when we looked at installment loans, because auto loans are installment loans for a vehicle. Remember, you can determine your monthly payment on an installment or auto loan using either a financial calculator (using the present value of an annuity calculation to determine *PMT*, the payment) or the installment loan tables that appear in Appendix E.

The trick here, as you learned in Chapter 3, is to input the number of months into *N* and convert the annual interest rate into a monthly interest rate. To convert the annual interest rate into its monthly equivalent we simply divide the annual interest rate by 12. Let's look at an example of a 36-month installment loan for $15,000 at 10 percent.

Calculator Clues

Here we are looking at a 36-month installment loan for $15,000 at 10 percent. Since the payments are monthly, *N* is expressed as the number of months, which is 36; and *I/Y* becomes the interest rate per month which is the annual rate (10 percent) divided by 12 or 10/12. Once you've input the values, you solve for *PMT* by entering CPT PMT:

Enter:	36	10/12	15,000		0
	N	I/Y	PV	PMT	FV
Solve for:				−484.01	

Notice the answer in the output row is shown as a negative number. Remember, with a financial calculator, each problem has two cash flows—a positive and a negative: The positive because you "receive money from the bank" and the negative because you "pay the money back."

The answer as shown in the output row is −$484.01. Thus, a 36-month installment loan of $15,000 at 10 percent would result in monthly payments of $484.01.

Using the installment loan tables that appear in Appendix E and in an abbreviated form in Table 7.3 is just as easy as using a financial calculator. Looking in the interest row and the 36-month column, we find that the monthly payment on a similar $1,000 installment loan would be $32.27. To determine the monthly payment on a $15,000 loan, we need only multiply this amount by 15. Using the tables, we find that the monthly payments would be $484.05.

So, if you buy a vehicle and finance $15,000 of its price over 36 months, your monthly payment will be approximately $484. Can you come up with this much every month for 3 years? Only you can decide. If in order to make that kind of monthly payment you will have to change your lifestyle considerably, perhaps it's time to think about a different, more affordable vehicle. Or, you might investigate a used vehicle of the same model.

Today, with all the formerly leased vehicles coming back on the market as used vehicles, a reasonable alternative to help you align what you want with what you can afford may be a used vehicle. In general, a used vehicle costs less and requires less in the way of a down payment. In fact, the savings from buying a used vehicle instead of a new vehicle every 3 years have been estimated to be between $1,500 and $2,000 per year. Moreover, a used vehicle tends to decline in value much more slowly than a new vehicle. The downside of purchasing a used vehicle is that it is more likely to have mechanical problems and may not be under warranty.

Which Vehicle Is Right for You?   Now let's turn to the decision of what vehicle is best for you. Start by comparison shopping, which means looking at the choices and trading off the price against product attributes and quality. Use all resources available to do your comparison shopping—read magazines, go on the Web, and take the time to visit several auto dealers in person. Remember, buying a vehicle is a personal decision. Every vehicle drives a bit differently, and your choice should fit you financially as well as physically, so be sure to take any vehicle you're considering for a test drive before you purchase it.

> ### STOP & THINK
>
> When selling your car, take advantage of **Principle 9: Mind Games, Your Financial Personality, and Your Money** and get the best price possible. If your car has a favorable book value, tell the potential buyer what it is. In doing so, you can affect what the buyer thinks the car is actually worth. If you saw the book value of a car you were considering, how would it impact what you thought the car was worth?

Also make sure you consider differences in operating and insurance costs. For example, due to increased repairs, a used vehicle generally costs more to operate than a new vehicle. You'll also want to consider the vehicle's warranty—the better the warranty, the lower the future costs. In addition, insurance costs on different cars vary dramatically. That Mercedes SL65 AMG is going to have much higher insurance, about $3,500, than a Ford Taurus, at only $1,270.

Step 3: Make Your Purchase

Once you've decided what vehicle is best for you, the next hurdle is getting it for a fair price. To determine a fair price, you must first know what the dealer cost or invoice price is. This is a relatively easy number to come by. It can be found in *Edmund's Car Buying Guide*, which is available at most libraries and bookstores; on the Internet at Edmund's site at **www.edmunds.com**; or at Kelley Blue Book, **www.kbb.com**, which provides the manufacturer's suggested retail price, the dealer's invoice, any rebates and financing incentives, projected resale values, and insurance premium information, along with reviews and evaluations.

The factory invoice price is important in determining how much the dealer pays for the car, but it isn't the whole story, because when most cars are sold the dealer receives a **holdback** from the manufacturer. Generally, the holdback amounts to 2 to 3 percent of the price of the vehicle. For example, in 2011 a new Ford Explorer had a sticker price of $28,190. The dealer cost or invoice price was $26,730. So the markup appears to be only 5.5 percent. However, if the dealer sold that Explorer, he or she would receive a 3 percent holdback amounting to $845.70. Including the holdback, the markup would actually be 8.6 percent. In addition, Ford was offering a $1,500 rebate, so you'd actually pay even less, but keep in mind that the rebate from Ford doesn't impact what your dealer receives, so the price shouldn't be impacted by it. Also keep in mind that the average markup on a new vehicle is just over 6 percent. In addition to the holdback, some cars also have rebates or additional dealer incentives.

Holdback
In auto sales, an amount of money, generally in the 2 to 3 percent range, that the manufacturer gives the dealer on the sale of an automobile.

CHECKLIST 8.3
Tips on Buying a New Vehicle

◆ Evaluate your needs and financial situation. Read consumer magazines and test-drive several models before you make a final choice. Check out Web sites such as Consumer Reports (**www.consumerreports.org**), Motor Trend (**www.motortrend.com**), Car and Driver (**www.caranddriver.com**), and Edmunds automotive books and network (**www.edmunds.com**) to evaluate the latest models and options.

◆ Find out the dealer's invoice price for the car and options. This is what the manufacturer charged the dealer for the car. You can order this information for a small fee from consumer publications you can find at your local library, or get it for free on the Internet at Kelley Blue Book (**www.kbb.com**). From there, negotiate from the dealer's cost up, not from the sticker price down.

◆ Find out if the manufacturer is offering rebates. Two Web sites that offer this information are **www.carsdirect.com** and **www.autopedia.com/html/Rebate.html**.

◆ Get price quotes from several dealers. Make sure you know whether the prices quoted are the prices before or after the rebates are deducted.

◆ Compare financing from different sources (e.g., banks, credit unions, and other dealers) before you sign the contract.

◆ Read and understand every document you are asked to sign. Do not sign anything until you have made a final decision to buy.

◆ Think twice about adding expensive extras you probably don't need to your purchase (e.g., credit insurance service contracts, or rust proofing).

◆ Inspect and test-drive the vehicle you plan to buy, but do not take possession of the car until the whole deal, including financing, is finalized.

◆ Don't make a hasty decision—leave your checkbook at home.

◆ Don't buy because the salesperson is pressuring you to make a decision.

◆ Don't be afraid to walk away. It's not uncommon to get the best deal when you're in your car ready to leave.

◆ Shop at the end of the month: This is when dealers are trying to meet quotas so they may be willing to take less now than at other times of the month.

Source: U.S. Office of Consumer Affairs, *Consumer's Resource Handbook,* 2011.

Now you're ready to approach several dealers and get quotes on the vehicle you want. You want to be prepared when you're ready to negotiate. Checklist 8.3 provides a list of buying tips.

In general, you shouldn't have to pay more than $100 to $500 after rebates over the invoice price on the vehicle if it's an American-made vehicle and a bit more over this price for a foreign-built vehicle. However, what you'll pay depends on the demand for the car and the size of the holdbacks that the dealer receives from the manufacturer. Getting quotes is the best way to determine what a good price is.

If you're considering a used car, the negotiating process is a bit more complicated. Again, when you find the car you want, you must determine a fair price. Used-car prices can be found in the *National Automobile Dealers Association (NADA) Official Used Car Guide* and in *Edmund's Used Car Prices*, both of which are generally available at local libraries or from the Kelley Blue Book, which can be found on the Internet at **www.kbb.com**. Checklist 8.4 provides a list of things to consider when purchasing a pre-owned vehicle.

CHECKLIST 8.4
Buying a Used Vehicle

◆ Check newspaper ads and used-car guides at a local library so you know the fair price of the car you want.

◆ Look up repair recalls for car models you are considering. Call the Auto Safety Hotline at 800-424-9393 to get recall information on a car.

◆ Negotiate!

◆ Shop during daylight hours so that you can thoroughly inspect the car and take a test drive. Don't forget to check all the lights, air conditioner, heater, and other parts of the electrical system.

◆ Do not agree to buy a car unless you've had it inspected by an independent mechanic of your choice.

◆ Ask questions about the previous ownership and mechanical history of the car. If possible, contact the former owner to find out if the car was in an accident or had any other problems.

◆ Ask the previous owner or the manufacturer for a copy of the original manufacturer's warranty. It still might be in effect and transferable to you.

◆ Don't sign anything that you don't understand. Read all the documents carefully. Negotiate the changes you want and get them written into the contract.

Source: U.S. Office of Consumer Affairs, *Consumer's Resource Handbook*, 2011.

Financing Alternatives   In general, the cheapest way to buy a car is with cash. Unfortunately, the high price of a new car or truck often makes this an unrealistic alternative. While most auto dealerships offer financing on both new and pre-owned vehicles, it's vital to investigate all the financing options before you buy. Check out the alternatives offered by your bank and your credit union. Investigate the possibility of a home equity loan and its tax advantages. When you're negotiating the price of a new vehicle, keep the question of financing out of the negotiations; retain the flexibility to borrow money where it's cheapest. Remember though, that the auto dealer may offer the best deal in financing. In Chapter 7, we noted that an auto loan is simply a short-term secured loan made to finance the purchase of a vehicle, with that vehicle serving as the collateral for the loan. Often, very low-cost loans, even down to 0.0 percent, are offered by automakers as a marketing tool, sometimes to sell models that are not in high demand.

As you might expect, the shorter the term you borrow for, the higher the monthly payments. For example, if you borrow $15,000 at 9 percent for 24 months, your monthly payment will be $685.27, but if your payments were spread out over 48 months, they would drop to $373.28 per month.

And don't forget about the option to lease. Leasing usually appeals to those who are financially stable, prefer to get a new vehicle every few years, drive less than 15,000 miles annually, and would rather not put up with the hassle of trade-in and maintenance. It's also popular with those who have good credit but don't have the up-front money needed to buy a new vehicle.

Checklist 8.5 provides a brief profile of those who might want to give leasing serious consideration. It covers a lot of people. In fact, almost one-third of all new vehicles are leased instead of purchased, and this figure rises to over 50 percent for the more expensive models. However, because leasing is so different from buying, many people don't fully understand the process.

There are two basic types of leases: closed-end leases and open-end leases. About 80 percent of all new vehicle leases are **closed-end leases, or walk-away leases,** in

Closed-End Lease or Walk-Away Lease
A vehicle lease in which you return the vehicle at the end of the lease and literally walk away from any further responsibilities. You need merely bring the vehicle back in good condition with normal wear and tear, and the vehicle dealer assumes the responsibility for reselling the vehicle.

<table>
<tr><td>

CHECKLIST 8.5
Leasing May Make Sense if...

</td><td>

- The lease under consideration is a closed-end, not an open-end, lease.
- You are financially stable.
- It is important to you that you have a new car every 2 to 4 years.
- You do not drive over 15,000 miles annually.
- You take good care of your car and it ages with only normal wear and tear.

</td><td>

- You are not bothered by the thought of monthly payments that never end.
- You use your vehicle for business travel.
- You do not modify your car (e.g., add superchargers or after-market suspension components).
- The manufacturer of the vehicle you are interested in is offering very low-priced leasing options.

</td></tr>
</table>

Purchase Option
An automobile lease option that allows you to buy the car at the end of the lease for either its residual value or a fixed price that is specified in the lease.

Open-End Lease
An automobile lease stating that when the lease expires, the current market value of the car will be compared to the residual value of the car as specified in the lease.

which you return the vehicle at the end of the lease and literally walk away from any further responsibilities. You need merely bring the vehicle back in good condition with normal wear and tear, and the vehicle dealer assumes the responsibility for reselling the vehicle. Many closed-end leases also contain a **purchase option**, which allows you to buy the vehicle at the end of the lease for its residual value or a fixed price specified in the lease.

With an **open-end lease**, when the lease expires, the current market value of the vehicle is compared to what the value of the vehicle was estimated to be as specified in the lease contract. If the vehicle is worth less at the end of the lease than was estimated originally, the open-end lease requires you to pay the difference. That difference can mean an awful lot of money to you; without question, you don't want an open-end lease.

Exactly how is the cost of your lease determined? Whether you have a walk-away lease or an open-end lease, the amount you pay for the lease is determined by two factors. The first is how much the value of the vehicle you're leasing is expected to decline while you're leasing it. For example, if you took out a 2-year lease on a vehicle that was worth $25,000 new and was expected to drop in value to $16,000 after 2 years, you'd pay the difference ($25,000 − $16,000 = $9,000) plus finance charges. In addition to the depreciation charge, there's a rent charge, which is actually the finance charge built into the lease and is like the total interest charged on a loan. Your monthly lease payment depends on the following criteria:

- The agreed-upon price of the vehicle
- Any other up-front fees, such as taxes, insurance, or service contracts
- Your down payment plus any trade-in allowance or rebate
- The value of the vehicle at the end of the lease
- The rent or finance charges
- The length of the lease

Because of all the difficulties consumers have had in evaluating vehicle leases, the Federal Reserve Board requires dealers and other leasing companies to provide customers with a leasing worksheet explaining the charges. A copy of such a worksheet is provided in Figure 8.2.

Keys to getting a good lease include:

- Negotiate a fair, agreed-upon value for the car before you sign the lease.
  - Don't express your interest in leasing until you negotiate the vehicle's price.
- Down payment—try to keep to a minimum.

FIGURE 8.2 Federal Consumer Leasing Act Lease Disclosure Form

Be very wary of any "other charges." If there are any, ask about them and check with other dealers to see if they impose similar charges.

The gross capitalized cost is the negotiated "selling price." It should be less than the manufacturer's suggested retail price.

The residual value is the projected market value of the car at the end of the lease. This is negotiated. The difference between this value and the gross capitalized cost (less any down payment, trade-in, rebate, or noncash credit) is what you're charged for over the lease period.

While it's difficult to define, normal wear and tear generally refers to normal dings, dents, small scratches, stone chips, and tire wear over the period of the lease. Excessive wear and use would refer to missing parts, damaged body panels, cuts, tears, and burns in the upholstery, broken glass, and other damage beyond what might be expected. Because it's so difficult to define, you should insist that it be defined in the lease contract.

Date _____

Lessor(s) _____   Lessee(s) _____

| Amount Due at Lease Signing (Itemized below)* $ _____ | Monthly Payments Your first monthly payment of $ _____ is due on _____, followed by _____ payments of $ _____ due on the _____ of each month. The total of your monthly payments is $ _____. | Other Charges (not part of your monthly payment) Disposition fee (if you do not purchase the vehicle) $ _____ [Annual tax] _____ Total $ _____ | Total of Payments (The amount you will have paid by the end of the lease) $ _____ |

Itemization of Amount Due at Lease Signing

Amount Due at Lease Signing:
- Capitalized cost reduction $ _____
- First monthly payment _____
- Refundable security deposit _____
- Title fees _____
- Registration fees _____

Total $ _____

How the Amount Due at Lease Signing will be paid:
- Net trade-in allowance $ _____
- Rebates and noncash credits _____
- Amount to be paid in cash _____

Total $ _____

Your monthly payment is determined as shown below:

Gross capitalized cost. The agreed upon value of the vehicle ($ _____) and any items you pay over the lease term (such as service contracts, insurance, and any outstanding prior loan or lease balance) .... $ _____

If you want an itemization of this amount, please check this box. ☐

Capitalized cost reduction. The amount of any net trade-in allowance, rebate, noncash credit, or cash you pay that reduces the gross capitalized cost .... – _____
Adjusted capitalized cost. The amount used in calculating your base monthly payment .... = _____
Residual value. The value of the vehicle at the end of the lease used in calculating your base monthly payment .... – _____
Depreciation and any amortized amounts. The amount charged for the vehicle's decline in value through normal use and for other items paid over the lease term .... = _____
Rent charge. The amount charged in addition to the depreciation and any amortized amounts .... + _____
Total of base monthly payments. The depreciation and any amortized amounts plus the rent charge .... = _____
Lease term. The number of months in your lease .... ÷ _____
Base monthly payment .... = _____
Monthly sales/use tax .... + _____
_____ .... = $ _____
Total monthly payment ....

Early Termination. You may have to pay a substantial charge if you end this lease early. The charge may be up to several thousand dollars. The actual charge will depend on when the lease is terminated. The earlier you end the lease, the greater this charge is likely to be.

Excessive Wear and Use. You may be charged for excessive wear based on our standards for normal use [and for mileage in excess of _____ miles per year at the rate of _____ per mile].

Purchase Option at End of Lease Term. [You have an option to purchase the vehicle at the end of the lease term for $ _____ [and a purchase option fee of $ _____].] [You do not have an option to purchase the vehicle at the end of the lease term.]

Other Important Terms. See your lease documents for additional information on early termination, purchase options and maintenance responsibilities, warranties, late and default charges, insurance, and any security interest, if applicable.

◆ Warranty—make sure it covers the entire lease period for all major repairs.
  • Define "normal wear and tear."
◆ Termination fee (for ending the lease early)—know what it is!
  • Have insurance protection to cover an early termination policy in case of an accident.
◆ Depreciation factor—since the lease payment is based on what the vehicle is worth at the end of the lease, you might pay less on a more expensive car that depreciates slowly.

STOP & THINK

What's in a price? The answer is quite a bit, and that's because of **Principle 9: Mind Games, Your Financial Personality, and Your Money**. You'll find that the price you set for your car or house will impact the price a buyer is willing to pay. When you set a high price, buyers use that information when they determine how much they think the car or house is actually worth. However, if you set the price ridiculously high, the impact of the price will be much less than if you set a high, but realistic price.

◆ Rent or finance charge—you want the lowest possible. You can find a listing of subsidized leases on Edmund's Web site.

To determine whether it's better to lease or to buy, you simply need to compare the costs of each over the *same* time frame. That is, you need to compare a 2-year lease with buying and financing a vehicle over 2 years. In addition, as the market for leasing previously leased, 2-year-old vehicles expands, there may be new opportunities, provided you understand the mechanics of leasing.

Figure 8.3 provides a comparative analysis for a lease-versus-purchase decision. In this figure, the cost of purchasing is $13,504.32, whereas the cost of leasing is $14,328.42. Thus, it's cheaper to purchase the Lexus in this example than it is to lease it.

FIGURE 8.3 Worksheet for the Lease-Versus-Purchase Decision

ASSUMPTIONS: Lexus IS-250—2 years

Purchase	Lease
Price = $34,000	Capitalized cost = $34,000
Down payment = $6,800*	Capitalized cost reduction = $2,950*
2-year loan for $27,500 at 8% = monthly payment of $1,230.18	Monthly lease payments = $459.83
5% opportunity cost of down payment	Security deposit = $475
	5% opportunity cost of down payment

Expected market value of car at the end of 2 years = $23,500. (This value is subtracted in the "Purchase" situation, and is used to negotiate the monthly lease payment in the "Lease" situation.)

COST OF PURCHASING

			Your Numbers
a.	Agreed-upon purchase price	$34,000	_____
b.	Down payment	$6,800	_____
c.	Total loan payments (monthly loan payment of $1,230.18 × 24 months)	$29,524.32	_____
d.	Opportunity cost on down payment (5% opportunity cost × 2 years × line b)	$680	_____
e.	Less: Expected market value of the car at the end of the loan	−$23,500	_____
f.	**Total cost of purchasing (lines b + c + d − e)**	**$13,504.32**	_____

COST OF LEASING

g.	Down payment (capitalized cost reduction) of $2,950 plus security deposit of $475	$3,425	_____
h.	Total lease payments (monthly lease payments of $459.83 × 24 months)	$11,035.92	_____
i.	Opportunity cost of total initial payment (5% opportunity cost × 2 years × line g)	$342.50	_____
j.	Any end-of-lease charges (perhaps for excess miles), if applicable	$0	_____
k.	Less: Refund of security deposit	−$475.00	_____
l.	**Total cost of leasing (lines g + h + i + j − k)**	**$14,328.42**	_____

*We ignore taxes, title, and registration in this example because they are generally the same whether you lease or purchase the car.

Step 4: Maintain Your Purchase

Given the size of the investment you make in a vehicle, it only makes sense to keep the vehicle in the best running order possible. The place to start is by reading the owner's manual, and following it's regular maintenance instructions.

And don't ignore signs of trouble. You drive your car every day and you know how it feels and sounds. Listen for unusual sounds, look for drips, leaks, smoke, warning lights, and pay attention to gauge readings. Also, watch for any changes in acceleration, engine performance, gas mileage, or fluid levels. If you notice any changes in your car's performance, take it for servicing as soon as possible, and be prepared to describe the symptoms accurately.

With a new car purchase, and with some pre-owned purchases, your first line of protection is the warranty, which provides coverage for the basic parts against manufacturer's defects for a set period of time or miles. In addition, corrosion coverage is provided along with coverage of the engine, transmission, and drive train. For most cars this coverage extends through the first 3 years of ownership or 36,000 miles, whichever comes first. However, some cars come with warranties that cover up to 7 years or 70,000 miles.

It's a good idea to choose a repair facility before you need one. To find the best, ask friends and associates for recommendations. Even in this high-tech era, old-fashioned word-of-mouth recommendations are still most valuable. At the repair shop, look for evidence of qualified technicians, such as trade school diplomas, certificates of advanced course work, and ASE certifications (that is, certified by the National Institute for Automotive Service Excellence)—a national standard of technician competence. If the service was not all you expected, don't rush to another shop. Discuss the problem with the manager or owner. Give the business a chance to resolve the problem. Reputable shops value customer feedback and will make a sincere effort to keep your business.

But what happens if a repair shop or the dealer just can't fix your problems? The answer is *lemon laws*. All states and the District of Columbia provide for a refund if the manufacturer can't seem to fix your problem. Generally, these laws require that you make at least four attempts to fix the problem and that your car is out of service for at least 30 days during the first year after purchase or the first 12,000 miles. If that's the case, you're entitled to a refund on your purchase.

Smart Buying in Action: Housing

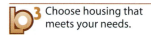 **3** Choose housing that meets your needs.

Why is owning our own home so important to so many of us? Well, it's part of the American dream. At least in the United States, many people equate owning your own home with financial success: You've made it, at least in part, if you own your own home. Also it's just kind of neat to own something large enough to walk around in.

Buying something as large as a house takes a lot of money. In fact, as you saw in Figure 2.6, a typical household spends $16,895 on housing, which makes up about 34.4 percent of their total expenditures. Of that $16,895, about $10,075, or 20.5 percent of their total expenditures, is spent on shelter with utilities, fuels, and public services making up another $3,645, household operations costing $1,011, housekeeping supplies at $659, and household furnishings and equipment at $1,506. Home ownership is also an investment—the biggest investment you're likely to make. So it's important that you approach buying a house not only as the attainment of your dream, but also as the investment that it is. If you don't, your dream could quickly become a nightmare.

How do you go about making a smart housing decision? Using the smart buying approach. Let's take a closer look at the process when it's applied to buying a home.

Your Housing Options

For most people, lifestyle is a major player in their housing choice. Kids, schools, pets, privacy, sociability, space, and other lifestyle concerns tend to point people toward one type of housing or another. The needs-versus-wants issue also plays a major role. Many people would like to live in a mansion, but that kind of housing just doesn't fit into many monthly budgets. Together, your lifestyle, wants, and needs, constrained by your monthly budget, provide focus on a realistic housing alternative for you.

You know what kind of lifestyle you have, but you might not know what type of housing will best suit it. In fact, you might not even know what types of housing are available. Let's take a minute to examine the basic choices.

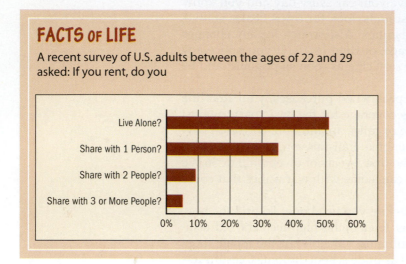

FACTS of LIFE

A recent survey of U.S. adults between the ages of 22 and 29 asked: If you rent, do you

- Live Alone?
- Share with 1 Person?
- Share with 2 People?
- Share with 3 or More People?

(0% 10% 20% 30% 40% 50% 60%)

House   A house is the popular choice for most individuals because it offers space and privacy. It also offers greater control over style, decoration, and home improvement. If you want your home to build equity or wealth, buying a house may be a good choice. However, home ownership carries with it more work than do other housing choices. If you own the house, you're responsible for maintenance, repair, and renovations.

Cooperative or Co-op
An apartment building or group of apartments owned by a corporation in which the residents of the building are the stockholders.

Cooperatives and Condominiums   A **cooperative**, or **co-op**, is an apartment building or group of apartments owned by a corporation in which the residents of the building are the stockholders. The residents buy stock in the corporation, which in turn gives them the right to occupy a unit in the building. Although the residents don't own their units, they do have a right to occupy their units for as long as they own stock in the cooperative.

When you "buy into" a co-op, you buy shares of the corporation that reflect the dollar value of your "space." The larger the size of your space and the more desirable its location, the more shares you have to buy. One problem with co-ops is that you may have a tough time getting a mortgage because many banks and other financial institutions may be uncomfortable using the stock as collateral. In addition to purchasing stock in the corporation, shareholders also have to pay a monthly **homeowner's fee** to the cooperative corporation, which in turn is responsible for paying taxes and maintaining the building and grounds. There can also be special assessments in addition to the normal maintenance fees to take care of large maintenance items.

Homeowner's Fee
A monthly fee paid by shareholders to the cooperative corporation for paying property taxes and maintaining the building and grounds.

Whether or not a co-op is for you depends on your lifestyle. If you're looking for an affordable, low-maintenance situation with a good helping of shared amenities such as swimming pools, tennis courts, health centers, and security guards, a co-op may be a good alternative. However, if you're more interested in privacy and control over style and decoration, a co-op may be a poor choice. In addition, co-ops generally have less potential than houses for capital appreciation, and they can be difficult to sell.

Condominium (Condo)
A type of apartment building or apartment complex that allows for the individual ownership of the apartment units but joint ownership of the land, common areas, and facilities.

A **condominium (condo)** is a type of apartment or apartment complex that allows for individual ownership of the dwelling units but joint ownership of the land, common areas, and facilities, including swimming pools, tennis courts, health facilities, parking lots, and grounds. In effect, you pay for and own your apartment, and you have a proportionate share of the land and common areas. As with a co-op, you still have to pay a maintenance fee, which generally covers interest, taxes, groundskeeping, water, and utilities.

The form that condos take can vary greatly—from apartment buildings or townhouses to office buildings or high-rises on the oceanfront. The advantages and disadvantages of living in a condo are similar to those of living in co-ops. However, condos allow for the direct ownership of a specific unit, not just shares in a corporation.

A more recent variation on cooperatives and condominiums are **planned unit developments (PUDs)**. These enjoy most of their popularity on the West Coast. With a planned unit development, you own your own home and the land it sits on, but you share ownership of the development with your neighbors and pay a homeowner's fee for common expenses and maintenance.

> **Planned Unit Developments (PUDs)**
> A development where you own your own home and the land it sits on, but you share ownership of the development with your neighbors and pay a homeowner's fee for common expenses and maintenance.

Apartments and Other Rental Housing These types of housing appeal to those who are interested in an affordable, low-maintenance situation with little financial commitment, from which it is possible to move with minimum inconvenience. This description often fits young, single people, since when they start out they may not have the funds available to buy a home, or may not yet be committed to a geographical area. For others, rental housing may simply be a lifestyle decision. You may want limited upkeep and no long-term commitment, or you may want to be free to change to jobs that may take you away from the area. Most of us, at some point, live in rental housing. The downside of apartment life generally involves a lack of choice. For example, you may not be allowed to have a pet, or you may have limited ability to remodel the apartment to fit your taste.

> **FACTS OF LIFE**
>
> House sizes have increased while family sizes have decreased:
>
> | **1970, Median Single Family Home** | **2010, Median Single Family Home** |
> | --- | --- |
> | 1,385 square feet | 2,321 square feet |
> | 3.14 people | 2.5 people |

Step 1: Differentiate Want from Need

Just as with any other major buying decision, the first step in purchasing housing is to determine what it is you want versus what it is you need. Begin by determining what is most important to you about a new home. Is the quality of the schools that your children will attend top priority? Or, is it more important that you're free to take that big promotion when it comes your way—the one that will require you to move across the country? You also need to examine your budget and determine how much you can and are willing to spend on housing costs.

Generally, house hunting and apartment shopping is exciting, although it may also be exhausting, frustrating, and confusing. One way to make the experience as pleasant as possible is to know as much about what you want before you begin to look. First, consider location. Life in the country is a lot different from life in the suburbs, which is a lot different from life in the city. Determine what's most important to you: solitude, community, or the action that the city life promises? Once you're convinced which setting suits you, consider the neighborhood. Is it safe? Is it convenient to your job, to shopping, to schools? And what about the schools? How does the school district in the neighborhood you're considering compare to other districts in the state and across the country?

Step 2: Do Your Homework

When you first consider buying a home, you must—as with any major purchase—do your homework. Your homework regarding home ownership is twofold. First, you must investigate the potential home and all that goes with it—the neighborhood, the lifestyle of the community, and to what degree the home fits your needs. The second part of your homework includes understanding how much you can afford to pay for a home. Let's first talk about how to research the kind of neighborhood and lifestyle of the community that best suits you.

Without question, the place to start, if you're trying to find out about a new community, is the Internet—and you'll want to visit more than one Web site. There are some great Web sites devoted to providing you help in choosing a place to live. One of the best is the Neighborhood Scout (**www.neighborhoodscout.com**). Unfortunately, Neighborhood Scout is a bit expensive, running about $40 for a 1-month subscription, but it provides a wealth of information on schools, home appreciation rates by neighborhood, and crime rates. Considering the amount you'll be investing in a new home, this may be information you'll want to have. Another great Web site is Homefair.com (**www.homefair.com**), which is free. This Web site provides cost of living comparisons between cities, city reports, crime statistics, school reports, along with information on choosing the right school for your children.

But of course, one of the biggest elements that will help decide where to live is money. How do you even know what buying a home costs? Let's get to work on answering this important question.

To make a sound decision about what to buy, where to buy, or whether to buy at all, you need to understand the costs that come with home ownership. The costs of home ownership can be divided into (1) one-time, or initial, costs, (2) recurring costs, and (3) maintenance and operating costs. Let's look at each of them.

One-Time Costs   Houses cost a lot of money! As a result, almost no one can afford to pay for a house all at once. For anyone who can, the entire price of the house is a one-time cost. For the rest of us, our one-time cost includes the **down payment**, which is the up-front money due at the time of the sale when buying a home.

The down payment is the buyer's equity, or ownership share, in the house, and lenders like to see a large down payment. Why? Because if a borrower stops paying back a loan, he or she loses the title to the house as well as the equity. The more equity—that is, the larger the down payment—the more the borrower stands to lose by not paying, and thus the more likely the borrower is to pay.

Down Payment
The amount of money outside of or not covered by mortgage funds that the homebuyer puts down on a home at the time of sale.

Your down payment will vary according to the type of financing you receive. For traditional mortgage loans, the typical down payment is 20 percent. Thus, for a $150,000 home, a typical down payment is $30,000. Needless to say, that's an awful lot of money. Fortunately, for those who cannot come up with a 20 percent down payment, there are alternatives. For example, you can buy private mortgage insurance, which is insurance that covers the lender if you default. This will allow you to pay as little as 5 percent down.

Closing or Settlement Costs
Expenses associated with finalizing the transfer of ownership of the house.

Another one-time expense for homebuyers is **closing or settlement costs**. Although they vary quite a bit from house to house, depending on the size of the loan, the local costs, and the loan arrangements made, they typically range from 3 to 7 percent of the cost of the house.

Several of the more important components of closing costs include:

Points or Discount Points
Charges used to raise the effective cost of the mortgage loan, which must be paid in full at the time of the closing.

◆ **Points or discount points:** Points are a one-time additional interest charge by the lender, due at closing—that is, when the sale is final. Each point is equal to 1 percent of the mortgage loan. Thus, if you get a $120,000 loan with two points, the two points would be $2,400, or $1,200 each. Lenders use these points to raise the effective cost of the loan, but points can also be used as a bargaining chip.

Many times you'll see trade-offs between interest rates and points—you can get a lower rate with high points or a higher rate with no points.

The longer you plan on staying in a home, the more important a low-interest rate is. You pay points only once, at closing, but you pay interest over the life of the loan. If you're planning on staying in your home for a long time, you might be better off taking a few points to get a lower rate. If you don't expect to be there too long, it's important to keep the points you pay to a minimum. The only virtue of points is that they're tax deductible when associated with the financing of the purchase of a home.

♦ **Loan origination fee:** A loan origination fee is generally one point, or 1 percent of the loan amount. Its purpose is to compensate the lender for the cost of reviewing and finalizing the loan. Unfortunately, because it's not considered an interest payment, it's not tax deductible.

♦ **Loan application fee:** The loan application fee, also paid to the lender, is generally in the $200 to $300 range and covers some of the processing costs associated with the loan.

♦ **Appraisal fee:** An appraisal is an estimate of what your home and property are worth. Lenders require an appraisal before a mortgage loan is approved so they can be sure that they aren't lending you more money than the value of the property. Although the costs for an appraisal vary depending on the size and location of the house, an appraisal fee usually runs between $200 and $300.

♦ **Other fees and costs:** There are many other fees and charges you'll pay when buying a home. For example, a **title search** fee is paid to an attorney for searching public land records to make sure the person selling you the property really owns it. Title insurance must be purchased to protect you against challenges to the title, perhaps due to a forged deed. There's also an attorney's fee for work on the sales contract; a notary fee; a fee for recording the deed at the courthouse; the cost of your credit report; and the cost of termite and radon inspection to make sure the house is in good shape.

Figure 8.4 gives a summary of typical one-time costs on a $120,000 mortgage loan—buying a $150,000 house with 20 percent down. You'll notice in the example that one-time costs amount to almost 24 percent of the cost of the house. Keep in

Loan Origination Fee
A fee of generally one point, or 1 percent of the loan amount. Its purpose is to compensate the lender for the cost of reviewing and finalizing the loan.

Loan Application Fee
A fee, generally in the $200 to $300 range, that is meant to defer some of the processing costs associated with the loan.

Appraisal Fee
A fee for an appraisal of the house, which is generally required before a mortgage loan is approved. Although the cost varies depending on the size and location of the house, it can easily run between $200 and $300.

Title Search
An investigation of the public land records to determine the legal ownership rights to property or a home.

FIGURE 8.4 Estimated Initial Costs of Buying a Home: The Down Payment, Points, and Closing Costs on the Purchase of a $150,000 House, Borrowing $120,000, with 20% Down at a Rate of 6% with 2 Points

Down Payment	$30,000
Points	2,400
Loan Origination Fee	1,200
Loan Application Fee	300
Appraisal Fee	300
Title Search Fee	200
Title Insurance	500
Attorney's Fee	400
Recording Fee	20
Credit Report	50
Termite and Radon Inspection Fee	150
Notary Fee	50
Total Initial Costs	**$35,570**

TABLE 8.1 Monthly Mortgage Payments Required to Repay a $10,000 Loan with Different Interest Rates and Different Maturities

Rate of Interest (%)	Loan Maturity					
	10 Years	15 Years	20 Years	25 Years	30 Years	40 Years
4.0	$101.25	$73.97	$60.60	$52.78	$47.74	$41.79
4.5	103.64	76.50	63.26	55.58	50.67	44.96
5.0	106.07	79.08	66.00	58.46	53.68	48.22
5.5	108.53	81.71	68.79	61.41	56.79	51.58
6.0	111.02	84.39	71.64	64.43	59.96	50.22
6.5	113.55	87.11	74.56	67.52	63.21	58.55
7.0	116.11	89.88	77.53	70.68	66.53	62.14
7.5	118.71	92.71	80.56	73.90	69.93	65.81
8.0	121.33	95.57	83.65	77.19	73.38	69.53
8.5	123.99	98.48	86.79	80.53	76.90	73.31
9.0	126.68	101.43	89.98	83.92	80.47	77.14
9.5	129.40	104.43	93.22	87.37	84.09	81.01
10.0	132.16	107.47	96.51	90.88	87.76	84.91
10.5	134.94	110.54	99.84	94.42	91.48	88.86
11.0	137.76	113.66	103.22	98.02	95.24	92.83
11.5	140.60	116.82	106.65	101.65	99.03	96.83
12.0	143.48	120.02	110.11	105.33	102.86	100.85
12.5	146.38	123.26	113.62	109.04	106.73	104.89
13.0	149.32	126.53	117.16	112.79	110.62	108.95
13.5	152.27	129.83	120.74	116.56	114.54	113.03
14.0	155.27	133.17	124.35	120.38	118.49	117.11
14.5	158.29	136.55	128.00	124.22	122.46	121.21
15.0	161.33	139.96	131.68	128.08	126.44	125.32

Calculating monthly payments on a loan:

Step 1: Divide the amount borrowed by $10,000. For example, for a $100,000 loan, the Step 1 value would be $100,000/$10,000 = 10.

Step 2: Find the monthly payment for a $10,000 loan at the appropriate interest rate and maturity in the table above. For a 15-year mortgage at 9%, the value would be $101.43.

Step 3: Multiply the Step 1 value by the Step 2 value. In the example, this is 10 × $101.43 = $1,014.30.

mind that the law requires that the annual percentage rate (APR) on a mortgage be disclosed to the borrower. Although points must be included in the calculations, fees for taking out the loan application, doing an appraisal, and the credit check are not. In addition, the lender can change the APR by as much as one-eighth of a percent before settlement without notifying the buyer.

Recurring Costs   The majority of recurring costs generally consists of monthly mortgage payments, the size of which depends on how much you borrow, at what interest rate, and for how long. Basically, the higher the interest rate, and the shorter the length of the loan, the higher your monthly payments.

Table 8.1 shows the level of monthly payments to repay a $10,000 loan at various combinations of interest rates and maturities. From Table 8.1, you can see that on a

15-year 6.0 percent, $10,000 mortgage, the monthly payments would be $84.39. If you increased the maturity to 30 years, though, the monthly payment drops to $59.96. Thus, if you are considering a $130,000, 15-year mortgage loan at 6.0 percent, the payments would be $1,097.07 ($130,000/$10,000 × $84.39 = $1,097.07). Similarly, the monthly payments on a $130,000, 30-year mortgage loan at 6.0 percent would be $779.48 ($130,000/$10,000 × $59.96 = $779.48).

Mortgage payments are the primary recurring cost, but they're actually made up of four costs, generally referred to as **PITI**, which stands for principal, interest, taxes, and insurance. In addition to paying off the loan principal and interest charges, you'll need to pay property taxes and insurance premiums. These monthly property taxes and insurance payments are generally made along with your loan principal and interest payments, and are held for you in a special reserve account, called an **escrow account**. Funds accumulate over time until they are drawn out to pay property taxes and insurance.

The logic behind an escrow account is this: Paying your insurance and taxes regularly, in small amounts, is less painful than paying them in one large, annual lump sum. Lenders often use the total PITI level to measure an individual's financial capacity. As a rule of thumb, your PITI costs shouldn't exceed 28 percent of your pretax monthly income.

PITI
An acronym standing for the total of your monthly principal, interest, taxes, and insurance.

Escrow Account
A reserve account in which funds are deposited, generally on a monthly basis, and accumulate over time until they are drawn out to pay property taxes and insurance.

Maintenance and Operating Costs   Whether the house you buy is old or new, big or small, in the country or in the city, you'll have maintenance and operating costs. Examples of these costs are roof repairs, new refrigerators, and landscaping. Don't forget to plan for these expenses when buying a home. Even homebuyers who budget for maintenance and operating costs are still often shocked by their first repair bill or the cost of a Japanese maple sapling!

> ### STOP & THINK
>
> Remodeling is not as good an investment as purchasing the house in the first place. A recent survey showed that you can expect to recoup 95 percent of the cost of kitchen remodeling, 83 percent of a family room addition, 77 percent of a bathroom remodeling, and 72 percent from the addition of a deck. That means if you remodel your bathroom you'll lose 23 percent—without question, a bad investment. What rooms have you or your parents remodeled?

Renting Versus Buying

For most people, the rent-versus-buy decision is not based on finances but on lifestyle. Perhaps you want to rent an apartment because you want the freedom to be able to take a promotion that comes your way, or you may want to buy a house because you want to live in a particular neighborhood. Let's examine Figure 8.5, which provides a

4 Decide whether to rent or buy housing.

FIGURE 8.5 Renting Versus Buying

Renting		Buying
• Mobility; can relocate without incurring real estate selling costs		• Allows you to build up equity over time
• No down payment required		• Possibility of property's appreciation
• May involve a lower monthly cash flow—you only pay rent; a homeowner pays the mortgage, taxes, insurance, and upkeep	**VS.**	• Allows for a good deal of personal freedom to remodel, landscape, and redecorate to suit your taste
• Avoids the risk of falling housing prices		• Significant tax advantages, including deduction of interest and property taxes
• Many times extensive amenities such as swimming pools, tennis courts, and health clubs are provided		• No chance of rent rising over time
• No home repair and maintenance		• Your home is a potential source of cash in the form of home equity loans
• No groundskeeping		
• No property taxes		
• You are immune to losses due to housing price depreciation		

listing of advantages to both renting and buying. As you can see, many of the reasons for renting center on flexibility—both financial flexibility, because renting generally involves lower monthly payments, and lifestyle flexibility, because you can avoid the responsibilities associated with ownership.

Although the rent or buy decision is usually less about money than about life choices, before making this decision it's a good idea to understand its financial implications. First, compare the costs associated with each alternative. Interestingly, the results that you get often depend mainly on how long you're planning to live in the place. Why? Well, when you buy a house or apartment, you experience a lot of up-front, one-time costs. However, the major financial advantages—price appreciation and the tax benefits—occur gradually over time, taking a number of years of price appreciation and tax benefits to offset those initial up-front costs. With renting, you don't have those large, one-time costs—in fact, you generally just have a security deposit that you get back when you move out.

Figure 8.6 presents the financial aspects of the rent-versus-buy decision.[1] In the example, the alternatives compared are renting an apartment for $900 per month versus buying a house for $100,000 with 20 percent down and a 30-year mortgage at 8 percent, which would include monthly payments of $587.01. (Calculated using a financial calculator. If calculated using Table 8.1, the monthly payment becomes $587.04; the difference is a rounding error.) You'll notice in this example we've ignored the time value of money to simplify the analysis.

The primary cost of renting is the rent itself. The total cost of renting for 7 years is simply seven times the cost of renting for 1 year, although rent will probably increase over those 7 years. Other costs of renting include renter's insurance and the opportunity cost of lost interest due to having funds tied up in the security deposit.

The costs of buying are more complex. Although we have discussed most of the costs associated with owning a home, one cost we haven't looked at yet is the opportunity cost of having money tied up in a down payment. Because the money used for your down payment can no longer be invested to earn a profit, you should consider the after-tax return you'd have earned on this money as a cost of buying. Another cost of ownership comes when you may eventually sell—that's the one-time selling cost resulting from the sales commission to a real estate broker when the owner moves and sells the house.

Notice that the down payment itself isn't a cost; only the opportunity cost represents a cost. That's because you still have that money; it's still yours. In fact, it's your equity in your house or apartment.

These costs are partially offset by the benefits of ownership, which include the accumulation of equity resulting from a portion of the mortgage payment going toward the loan principal and the appreciation in the value of the home. Further, substantial savings are available to those who itemize. These savings result from the tax deductibility of the interest portion of mortgage payments, property taxes, and any points paid in the closing costs. If you don't itemize your tax deductions, you don't reap the tax benefits from these deductions.

Look at Figure 8.6 and notice two major points. First, buying a home generally isn't financially desirable if you don't intend to stay in it for more than 2 or 3 years. The longer you stay in the home, the more it hopefully appreciates in value, and the more financially advantageous buying (and selling) is. Second, the benefits of buying instead of renting are substantially greater for those who itemize their taxes than for those who don't itemize. In fact, the advantage to buying over renting is more than twice as large for those who itemize ($31,420.48) than for those who don't itemize ($14,539.00) when looking at the 7-year time frame.

---

[1]The detailed calculations for Figure 8.6 are provided in the appendix to this chapter.

FIGURE 8.6 Worksheet for the Rent-Versus-Buy Decision

ASSUMPTIONS: Buying option: $20,000 down and an $80,000, 30-year mortgage at 8%. Rental option: $900 per month. Time frames: 1 year and 7 years; 28% marginal tax rate; after-tax rate of return = 5%; house appreciates in value at 3% per year; sales commission is 5% of the price of the house; closing costs = $5,000, which includes 2 points.

COST OF RENTING

		1 Year		7 Years
a. Total rent payments	a.	$10,800	a.	$75,600
b. Total renter's insurance payments	+ b.	$250	+ b.	$1,750
c. Interest lost as a result of making a security deposit (security deposit times after-tax interest rate)	+ c.	$90	+ c.	$630
d. **Total cost of renting (lines a + b + c)**	= d.	$11,140	= d.	$77,980

COST OF BUYING

e. Total mortgage payments	e.	$7,044	e.	$49,309
f. Property taxes (annual)	+ f.	$2,200	+ f.	$15,400
g. Homeowner's insurance (annual)	+ g.	$600	+ g.	$4,200
h. Maintenance, repairs, and any additional utilities	+ h.	$500	+ h.	$3,500
i. After-tax cost of interest lost due to down payment	+ i.	$1,000	+ i.	$7,000
j. Closing costs	+ j.	$5,000	+ j.	$5,000
k. Less: mortgage payments going toward principal	− k.	$668	− k.	$6,018
l. Less: home appreciation less sales commission when sold	− l.	−$2,150*	− l.	$14,950
m. **Equals: cost of buying a home for those who don't itemize** (lines e + f + g + h + i + j − k − l)	= m.	$17,826	= m.	$63,441
Additional savings to home buyers who itemize				
n. Less tax savings from deductibility of interest payments	− n.	$1,785	− n.	$12,121
o. Less tax savings from deductibility of property taxes	− o.	$616	− o.	$4,312
p. Less tax savings from deductibility of points	− p.	$448	− p.	$448
q. **Total cost of buying a home to those who itemize (line m minus lines n through p)**	= q.	$14,977	= q.	$46,560
Advantage of buying to those who do not itemize = Total cost of renting − total cost of buying for those who do not itemize: if negative, rent; if positive, buy (line d − line m)	−	$6,686	+	$14,539
Advantage of buying to those who itemize = Total cost of renting − total cost of buying for those who itemize: if negative, rent; if positive, buy (line d − line q)	−	$3,837	+	$31,420

*Note: If you only own the home for 1 year, the value here is negative, meaning the sales commission is greater than the appreciation in home value. Thus, this is an additional cost, not a savings, and we are subtracting a negative—in effect, adding the $2,150 to the cost of buying the house.

Finally, for many people, buying a home is a good means of "forced savings." Because some of your mortgage payment goes toward paying off the loan principal, a mortgage forces you to save in a sense. Although you're really buying something rather than saving, you are buying something that not only doesn't get "used up," but may appreciate in value over time.

Determining What You Can Afford

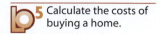
5 Calculate the costs of buying a home.

We've looked at all the costs associated with buying a home, and compared the advantages of renting versus buying. Let's say you decide to buy a home. Before you begin your house hunt in earnest you have to know one thing: How much can you afford to spend? In order to know the answer to this question, you must first know the answer to three others: (1) What is the maximum amount that a bank will lend me? (2) Should I borrow up to this maximum? (3) How big a down payment can I afford?

Let's look at Question 1. Regardless of what you think you can afford, banks and other lenders impose a maximum amount that they want to lend you based on your income and current debt levels. Specifically, they look at three things: (1) your financial history, (2) your ability to pay, and (3) the appraised value of the home.

Financial History   In evaluating your financial history, lenders generally focus on the steadiness of your income, your credit report, and your FICO credit score. If you're self-employed, you may have to provide proof that you've maintained steady income for the past several years. Lenders also examine your credit report. It's wise to check out your FICO score and get a copy of your credit report several months before applying for a loan to allow time for the correction of any errors that may appear on it. If a lender doesn't like the look of your financial history, you'll have a tough time obtaining a mortgage.

Calculating Your Mortgage Limit: Method 1—Ability to Pay—PITI to Monthly Gross Income   Lenders generally measure your ability to pay through the use of ratios. In particular, they look at the percentage of your income that goes to housing costs. The ratio lenders look at is that of your PITI compared to your monthly gross income. In general, lenders would like to see this ratio at a maximum of 28 percent.

Calculating Your Mortgage Limit: Method 2—Ability to Pay—PITI Plus Other Debt Payments to Monthly Gross Income   Lenders also look at the ratio of your PITI plus any other debt payments that will take over 10 months to pay off, compared to your monthly gross income. This ratio is used to account for the fact that many individuals have a sizable amount of outstanding debt, including student loans, car loans, and credit card debt. In general, lenders would like to see this ratio at a maximum of 36 percent. Note that different lenders may calculate these and other ratios a bit differently. They may also have different acceptable maximums.

Calculating Your Mortgage Limit: Method 3—Appraised Home Value   Regardless of your financial history and ability to pay ratios, most lenders limit mortgage loans to 80 percent of the appraised value of the house. This limitation protects lenders by forcing the borrower to put up a substantial down payment. Lenders assume that the larger a borrower's down payment, the less likely he or she will default on the loan.

If a borrower does default, the lender assumes possession of the home, and the 80 percent limitation protects the lender in another way. The lender will sell the home to recoup its losses on the loan, and with the 80 percent rule in effect, the asking price of the home could fall by a full 20 percent—the same amount the borrower initially had to pay out—and the lender would still be able to recover the full amount it loaned out.

Calculating Your Mortgage Limit   The maximum loan size you'll qualify for is determined by the financial picture that develops as the lender reviews these three measures of your ability to pay. The lowest amount wins. Figure 8.7 shows the basic methods lenders use to determine how much they'll loan you.

How Much Should You Borrow?   Although a bank may be willing to lend you $150,000, you might not want to borrow that much. Taking on a mortgage means a large commitment of future earnings. Before deciding how much to borrow, look at your overall financial plan. Will a $150,000 mortgage keep you from meeting your other goals—in particular, your retirement goals? Moreover, will it put such a strain on your monthly budget that you can no longer maintain the lifestyle you want? Don't let your mortgage payments, or any other debt payments, control your life. Only you can decide just how much you're interested in borrowing. Just because a

FIGURE 8.7 Worksheet for Calculating the Maximum Mortgage Loan for Which You Qualify

ASSUMPTIONS: Annual gross income = $65,000
Estimated monthly real estate taxes and insurance = $200
Anticipated interest rate on the mortgage loan = 8%
Mortgage maturity = 30 years
Current nonmortgage debt payments = $400
Funds available for down payment and closing costs = $56,000
Closing costs are estimated to be $10,000
Minimum acceptable down payment = 20%

METHOD 1—The Ability to Pay PITI Ratio (PI = Principal and Interest, TI = Taxes and Insurance)

(Lenders limit your monthly housing costs, as measured by PITI, to 28% of your gross monthly income.)

			Your Numbers
a.	Monthly income (annual income divided by 12)	$5,417	
b.	Times 28% ($5,417 × 0.28) = PITI limit	× 0.28 = $1,517	
c.	Less: estimated monthly real estate taxes and insurance payments of $200 per month (TI)	− $200	
d.	Equals your **maximum monthly mortgage payment** (PI)	= $1,317	

Steps to determine the **maximum mortgage loan level:**

STEP 1: Using Table 8.1, determine monthly mortgage payment
with a 30-year maturity and an 8% interest) = $73.38

STEP 2: Divide the maximum monthly mortgage payment (line d) by
the monthly mortgage payment (Step 1) and multiply by the amount
of the mortgage ($10,000)
($1,317/$73.78) × $10,000 = $179,477

METHOD 2—The Ability to Pay PITI (Principal, Interest, Taxes and Insurance)
Plus Other Fixed Monthly Payments, Ratio.

(Lenders use 36% of your total current monthly fixed payments to determine the amount of your loan.)

			Your Numbers
e.	Monthly income (annual income divided by 12)	$5,417	
f.	Times 36% ($5,417 × 0.36) = PITI limit	× 0.36 = $1,950	
g.	Less current nonmortgage debt payments	− $400	
h.	Less estimated monthly real estate tax and insurance payments of $200 per month (TI)	− $200	
i.	Equals your **maximum monthly mortgage payment** (PI)	= $1,350	

Steps to determine the **maximum mortgage loan level:**

STEP 1: Using Table 8.1, determine monthly mortgage payment
with a 30-year maturity and an 8% interest) = $73.38

STEP 2: Divide the maximum monthly mortgage payment (line i) by
the monthly mortgage payment (Step 1) and multiply by the amount
of the mortgage ($10,000)
($1,350/$73.78) × $10,000 = $183,974

METHOD 3—The "80 Percent of the Appraised Value of the House" Rule

(You pay 20% of the appraised value and can borrow 80% of the appraised value of the house.)

			Your Numbers
j.	Funds available for down payment and closing costs	$56,000	
k.	Less closing costs	− $10,000	
l.	Equals funds available for the down payment (the 20%)	= $46,000	
m.	Times 4 equals the maximum mortgage level (the 80%)	× 4.0 = $184,000	

Conclusion: maximum mortgage level for which you will qualify
(the lower of the amounts using Methods 1, 2, or 3): = $179,477

bank will loan you $150K doesn't mean you have to borrow that much! Look at your own financial situation, monthly budget, goals, and lifestyle, and decide for yourself how much you want to take on.

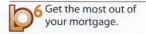

6 Get the most out of your mortgage.

Financing the Purchase—The Mortgage

Just as a home is the biggest purchase you will likely ever make, a mortgage is the biggest loan you will likely ever take on. To say the least, not all mortgages are the same. In fact, whether or not you can afford to buy a house doesn't just depend on how much the house costs, but also on the specifics of the mortgage, such as how long it lasts, whether the interest rate changes over time, and whether it's insured by the government. Let's take a closer look at mortgages, where you get them, and how they work.

Sources of Mortgages   Savings and loan institutions (S&Ls) and commercial banks are the primary sources of mortgage loans, but they certainly aren't the only sources. Other traditional lenders, such as credit unions and mutual savings banks, offer mortgage loans, in addition to specialized lenders such as mortgage bankers and mortgage brokers.

Mortgage bankers originate mortgage loans, sell them to banks, pension funds, and insurance companies, and service or collect the monthly payments. Their only business is making mortgage loans, and in general, they deal only in fixed-rate mortgage loans. There's really no advantage or disadvantage to using a mortgage banker instead of a traditional source of mortgage loans, such as an S&L. Hey, if the mortgage banker's got the more favorable rate or the better deal, go for it.

Mortgage brokers are middlemen whose job is to place mortgage loans with lenders for a fee, but not to originate those loans. The advantage of using mortgage brokers is that they do the comparison shopping for you. That is, they work with a number of lenders and choose the best terms and rates available.

Mortgage Banker
Someone who originates mortgage loans with funds from other investors, such as pension funds and insurance companies, and services the monthly payments.

Mortgage Broker
A middleman who, for a fee, secures mortgage loans for borrowers but doesn't actually make those mortgage loans. Mortgage brokers will find the best loan available for the borrower.

Conventional Mortgage Loan
A loan from a bank or S&L that is secured by the property being purchased.

Government-Backed Mortgage Loan
A mortgage loan made by a traditional lender, but insured by the government.

Conventional and Government-Backed Mortgages

Once you find the right lender and get your mortgage, it can be categorized as **conventional** or **government-backed**. Conventional mortgage loans are simply loans from a bank or S&L secured by the property being purchased. If you default on a mortgage loan, the lender seizes the property, sells it, and recovers the funds owed.

With government-backed mortgage loans, the traditional lender still makes the loan, but the government insures it. Veteran's Administration (VA) and Federal Housing Administration (FHA) loans are the two primary types of government-backed loans, and have accounted for an increasing percentage of new mortgages in recent years. In fact, in 2009 they accounted for over 35 percent of new mortgages. Traditionally, FHA and VA loans have been a favorite for first-time buyers who do not have the 10- or 20-percent down payments traditionally required for other mortgages. However, during the housing bubble of the mid-2000s, they fell out of favor as private lenders entered the housing market with low- and no-down payment mortgages for applicants with almost no income.

The FHA and VA programs are quite similar, and they both share the same basic advantages and disadvantages. The primary advantages of VA and FHA loans include the following:

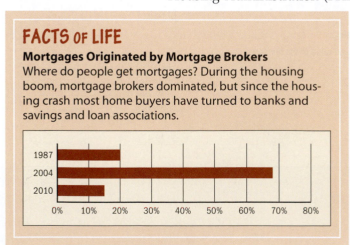

FACTS OF LIFE

Mortgages Originated by Mortgage Brokers
Where do people get mortgages? During the housing boom, mortgage brokers dominated, but since the housing crash most home buyers have turned to banks and savings and loan associations.

◆ An interest rate 0.5 to 1 percent below that of conventional mortgage loans

◆ A smaller down payment requirement

◆ Less strict financial requirements

The primary disadvantages of VA and FHA loans include the following:

◆ Increased paperwork required to qualify for the loan

◆ Higher closing costs due to mortgage insurance premiums required with FHA loans; guarantee fees required with VA loans.

◆ Limits on the amount of funding that can be obtained

Although the FHA guarantees the entire loan, it doesn't assume all the costs for the required mortgage default insurance. In fact, with an FHA loan you're expected to pay for a portion of the cost, which is generally 3.8 percent of the loan. However, because FHA loans are guaranteed, the interest rate charged on them is generally below the rate charged on conventional loans, so you can still wind up saving money.

VA mortgages are much more limited in access: Only veterans and their unmarried surviving spouses are eligible for them. In addition, FHA loans allow for both fixed- and variable-rate loans, but VA loans must be fixed-rate loans with the rate generally being between 0.5 and 1 percentage point below that of conventional loans. VA loans don't require anything in the way of a down payment, but they do require a 1.25 percent VA funding fee payable at closing.

Fixed-Rate Mortgages

Although conventional and government-backed are broad classifications for mortgages, there are also more refined classifications, such as fixed versus variable rate. A fixed-rate mortgage is one on which the monthly payment doesn't change, regardless of what happens to market interest rates. If mortgage interest rates are low, a fixed-rate mortgage allows you to lock in those low rates for the rest of the loan. The term or length of fixed-rate mortgages is generally either 15 or 30 years, with 30-year fixed-rate mortgage loans being the most popular. Many mortgages also come with assumability and prepayment privileges.

An **assumable loan** is one that can be transferred to a new buyer, who simply assumes or takes over the mortgage obligations. As a result, the new buyer doesn't incur the costs of obtaining a new loan. Moreover, if interest rates have gone up since the original assumable mortgage was taken out, the buyer can assume the mortgage at the lower rate. For example, if the mortgage was originally issued at 7.5 percent and rates have now gone up to 9 percent, the buyer could assume the mortgage at 7.5 percent. These advantages make it easier to sell a home with an assumable mortgage, particularly when interest rates have gone up since the mortgage was issued. The assumability privilege is common to all FHA loans and is also common to many conventional mortgage loans.

The **prepayment privilege** allows the borrower to make early cash payments that are applied toward the principal, thus reducing the amount of interest due or, if interest rates fall, to simply refinance. Many mortgages restrict prepayment by limiting the amount that can be prepaid or charging a penalty for prepayment.

Adjustable-Rate Mortgages

With an **adjustable-rate mortgage (ARM)**, the interest rate fluctuates according to the level of current market interest rates within limits at specific intervals. From the lender's point of view, ARMs are wonderful because they allow for a match between the rate the lender pays on savings accounts to fund the loan and the income from

Assumable Loan
A mortgage loan that can be transferred to a new buyer, who simply assumes or takes over the mortgage obligations. Such a mortgage saves the new buyer the costs of obtaining a new mortgage loan.

Prepayment Privilege
A clause in a mortgage allowing the borrower to make early cash payments that are applied toward the principal.

Adjustable-Rate Mortgage (ARM)
A mortgage in which the interest rate charged fluctuates with the level of current interest rates. The loan fluctuates, or is adjusted, at set intervals (say, every year) and only within set limits.

MONEY MATTERS

Tips from Marcy Furney, ChFC, Certified Financial Planner"

HOME SWEET HOME

A home isn't necessarily a money-making investment. *Make sure your reasons for purchasing reach beyond intending to resell at a profit. The real estate market is intricate, and many factors are at play in determining resale value.*

Beware of the "hidden costs" of homeownership. *Decorating and landscaping can be major expenses in a new home. Utilities, maintenance, and repairs are ongoing budget items. If you're buying a preowned home, ask to see utility bills for different seasons.*

Whenever possible, prequalify for your loan so that you'll know approximately how much you can spend. *You may want to stay below the maximum you can finance so that you will have some buffer for other expenses.*

Make sure the lender locks in the interest rate quoted you and find out how long it will be guaranteed. *Be sure to get to the closing before that period runs out or take the initiative to renegotiate the rate.*

Keep good records of any improvements, not repairs, you make on your home. *Include the cost, what was done, and when. These improvements can be useful in boosting the market value of your home when you sell it.*

On high-dollar houses with potential capital gains tax, improvements will also serve to increase your cost basis.

When you shop for your home, be sure to do detailed investigation of the neighborhood, schools, pending zoning issues, and so on. *Once you have found just the right place, consider hiring an engineer to check out the structure itself.*

If you handle your money responsibly, you may want to get a loan without an escrow account. *You will have to pay your own tax and insurance bills, but you'll have the flexibility to make some interest on the money you set aside for those expenses. To some extent, you can also time those payments to fit your cash flow and tax situation. Different states and lenders have varying requirements for such a loan.*

Remember that paying off your mortgage doesn't mean that you have free housing. *Besides maintenance, you'll have tax and insurance expenses forever. People who are retiring now are finding that their housing costs from these items are almost equal to the original mortgage payment made 30 or so years ago.*

---

the loan. Because lenders like ARMs so much, they generally charge a lower rate of interest on them—that's the appeal of ARMs to borrowers.

From the borrower's perspective, you're better off with an ARM if interest rates drop, because your interest rate drops accordingly and you won't have to refinance, which costs money. On the other hand, if interest rates rise, you're better off with a fixed-rate loan, because you will have locked in at a low rate.

To understand ARMs you need to understand the terminology that surrounds them, including the initial rate, index, margin, adjustment interval, rate cap, payment cap, and negative amortization.

Initial Rate

The initial rate charged on an ARM, sometimes called the teaser rate. This rate holds only for a short period, generally between 3 and 24 months, before being adjusted upward.

Initial Rate   The **initial rate** is sometimes called the teaser rate for a reason. This rate holds only for a short period, generally between 3 and 24 months. In some cases, it's set deceptively low. Once the rate is allowed to move up and down, or float, it generally rises. In evaluating the cost of the ARM, you should focus on the ARM's real rate, that is, what the rate would be today if it wasn't for the teaser rate.

Interest Rate Index   The rate on ARMs is tied to an interest rate index that's not controlled by the lender. As that interest rate index rises and falls, so does the ARM rate. The following are some of the more common indexes:

◆ The rate on 6- or 12-month U.S. Treasury securities
◆ The Federal Housing Finance Board's National Average Contract Mortgage rate, which is the national average mortgage loan rate
◆ The average cost of funds as measured by either the average rate paid on CDs or the 11th Federal Home Loan Bank District Cost of Funds

Which index is the best is debatable. However, stable indexes are better because they won't produce radical rate shifts. When shopping for an ARM, be sure to ask for some historical data on the index from your lender.

Margin   Your ARM may be set at the 6-month U.S. Treasury bill rate plus 2 percent. The amount over the index rate that the rate on the ARM is set at is called the margin. Thus:

$$\text{ARM rate} = \text{index rate} + \text{margin}$$

If the index rate is 5.0 percent and the margin is 2.5 percent, then the ARM rate is 7.5 percent.

Adjustment Interval   The adjustment interval defines how frequently the rate on the ARM will be reset. One year is the most common adjustment period, although some ARMs have adjustment intervals as low as 3 months and some as long as 7 years.

An adjustment interval of 1 year means that every year—generally on the anniversary of the loan—the rate on the ARM is reset to the index rate plus the margin. In general, it's better to have a longer adjustment interval, because the shorter the adjustment interval, the more volatile the mortgage payments.

Rate Cap   The rate cap limits how much the interest rate on an ARM can change. Most ARMs have both periodic caps and lifetime caps. A *periodic cap* limits the amount by which the interest rate can change during any adjustment. Normally, the ARM rate will go up 3 percent if the index goes up 3 percent. However, if the periodic cap is 2 percent and the index rate increases by 3 percent, the rate on the ARM would still only increase by 2 percent. Most conventional ARM loans have periodic caps of 2 percent. FHA loans have 1 percent periodic caps.

The *lifetime cap* limits the amount by which the interest rate can change during the life of the ARM. Thus, for an ARM with an initial rate of 6 percent and a lifetime cap of 5 percent, the highest and lowest this ARM could go would be down to 1 percent or up to 11 percent. Borrowers love lifetime caps because they limit the ARM rate to a specific range. In evaluating a lifetime cap, be sure that you know whether the cap is linked to the initial or the real rate.

Payment Cap   A payment cap sets a dollar limit on how much your monthly payment can increase during any adjustment period. A payment cap limits the change in the monthly mortgage payment, but it doesn't limit changes in the interest rate being charged on the borrowed money. If the payments are capped, and the interest rate isn't capped, when interest rates go up, more of your mortgage payment could end up going toward interest and not principal.

In fact, if interest rates keep going up, it's possible that the monthly payment amount will be too small to even cover the interest due and you end up owing more than you borrowed. In this case, **negative amortization** occurs. When this happens, the unpaid interest is added to the unpaid balance on the loan. In effect, the size of the mortgage balance can grow over time, and you can end up owing more than the original amount of the loan. You pay interest on your unpaid interest, and the term of the loan can drag out. Because negative amortization is something to avoid, and can only occur when there's a payment cap limit but not an interest rate cap, you should avoid mortgages with payment but not interest rate caps.

Negative Amortization
A situation in which the monthly payments are less than the interest that's due on the loan. As a result, the unpaid interest is added to the principal, and you end up owing more at the end of the month than you did at the beginning of the month.

ARM Innovations   Over the years, several variations of the standard ARM have been introduced, including:

◆ **Convertible ARM:** Offers the borrower the option to convert the ARM loan to a fixed-rate loan before a designated time. There is a nominal fee involved.

◆ **Reduction-Option ARM:** Offers the borrower a one time opportunity to adjust the interest rate on the loan. This offer generally occurs in years 2 through 6 and you choose if and when you will use it.

◆ **Two-Step ARM:** Combines the aspects of fixed-rate and adjustable-rate mortgages. It starts off with a lower rate than the current market fixed-rate loan and, after a certain period, the interest rate changes and remains at the current market rate for the life of the loan. The two most common types of two-step mortgages are the 5/25 and 7/23, offering the lower interest rate for the first 5 or 7 years and then adjusting the rate for the remaining 25 or 23 years.

Adjustable-Rate Versus Fixed-Rate Mortgages

For the homebuyer, the primary advantage of an ARM is that the initial rate charged is lower than that on fixed-rate loans. Initial ARM rates are lower because the borrower assumes the risk that interest rates will rise. Thus, the rate gap between 1-year adjustable-rate mortgages and 30-year fixed-rate mortgages is generally between 0.5 and 2 percent. For example, in mid-2011, the rate gap was about 1.46 percent.

One commonly stated advantage of this low initial rate is that you may qualify for a larger loan because your monthly payment, PITI, is lower. However, if interest rates rise, pushing your monthly ARM payment upward, you may find yourself overcommitted.

Don't choose an ARM in the hope that interest rates will fall and your payments will be lower. Predicting future interest rates certainly isn't something on which you want to gamble your house and financial future. You can be sure that interest rates will never fall below zero (which would mean that lenders would owe *you* money!), but you can never be sure just how high they'll rise. If you have a lifetime cap on your mortgage, you know just how high your rates can rise, but this knowledge doesn't help if you're hoping never to have to pay that much. In short, if you can't afford the maximum payment you might have to make on an ARM should interest rates rise, you probably shouldn't take it on.

In general, a fixed-rate mortgage is better than an adjustable-rate mortgage. With a fixed-rate mortgage, you know your payments, and, as a result, can plan for them in advance. Don't forget that the basis of personal financial management is control and planning, and a fixed-rate mortgage allows for both. ARMs allow for neither. If you don't like financial risk and have difficulty handling financial stress, ARMs are dangerous.

Still, if you intend to stay in the house only a few years, or if current interest rates are extremely high, you may want to consider an ARM. Remember, much of the advantage of an ARM comes in the early years when you're guaranteed a low rate.

Specialty Mortgage Options

Most of the alternative mortgage options serve the same purpose: to keep the initial mortgage payments as low as possible to make buying a house more affordable to first-time and cash-strapped buyers. Unfortunately, keeping the payments down in the early years generally means larger payments in later years, or some other concession.

Balloon Payment Mortgage
A mortgage with relatively small monthly payments for several years (generally 5 or 7 years), after which the loan must be paid off in one large balloon payment.

Balloon Payment Mortgage With a **balloon payment mortgage**, you make relatively small monthly payments for several years (generally 5 or 7 years), after which the loan comes due and you must pay it off in one large payment. Exactly how large the initial payments are varies. In some cases, the initial mortgage payments are only large enough to cover the interest on the loan, and in other cases, the payments may be equivalent to the loan's amortized value over 30 years. However, what balloon payment mortgage loans all have in common is that the payments are constant for a few years and then the loan comes due and is paid off with a very large, final payment.

Some traditional lenders don't offer balloon payment mortgages. In fact, most of these mortgages are offered by the sellers themselves, who are anxious to sell the house but don't need the funds from the sale immediately. Watch out for balloon mortgages, because they come with serious potential problems. For many individuals, coming up with the final balloon payment is difficult at best. It generally means they will have to take out a new mortgage just to pay off the old one. If interest rates have risen, the homeowner will be forced to refinance at a higher rate.

In addition, when the balloon payment comes due, the homeowner may have very little in the way of equity in the home if the monthly payments have included only interest. In fact, if the market value of the home has declined, the balloon payment that's due could be greater than the house is worth.

Graduated Payment Mortgages   With a **graduated payment mortgage**, the payments are set in advance in such a way that they rise steadily for a specified period of time, generally 5 to 10 years, and then level off. The selling point behind graduated payment mortgages is that the initial payments are relatively low, so you'll be able to afford a house sooner. The assumption is that, as your earning power increases over time, you'll be able to afford the rising payments. In effect, you're assuming that your income will grow into the level of future payments. Unfortunately, you might be assuming incorrectly, and you might be putting an obligation on your future income that you can't handle.

Graduated Payment Mortgage
A mortgage in which payments are arranged to steadily rise for a specified period of time, generally 5 to 10 years, and then level off.

Growing Equity Mortgage
A conventional 30-year mortgage in which prepayment is automatic and planned for. Payments begin at the same level as those for a 30-year fixed-rate mortgage and then rise annually—generally increasing at between 2 and 9 percent per year—allowing the mortgage to be paid off early.

Growing Equity Mortgages   A **growing equity mortgage** is designed to let the homebuyer pay off the mortgage early, which is done by paying a little extra each year. It doesn't really help the cash-strapped buyer. Payments on a growing equity mortgage begin at the same level as on a conventional 30-year fixed-rate mortgage. Each year the payments increase, and this increase goes toward paying off the principal.

With a growing equity mortgage, you know how your payments are going to increase ahead of time. Generally, they increase by between 2 and 9 percent each year. The result is that a 30-year mortgage is paid off in less than 20 years. While a growing equity mortgage forces a disciplined prepayment of your mortgage, there is no advantage, and less flexibility, over a fixed-rate mortgage loan with a prepayment clause.

> ## STOP & THINK
>
> When setting a price for your home, take advantage of **Principle 9: Mind Games, Your Financial Personality, and Your Money** and use it to send a message to a potential buyer. If you think your house will fetch $498,000, a round figure such as $495,000 sends buyers the message of quality, while a precise figure such as $495,765 sends the message of a bargain and that you've given the price a lot of thought. Mentally, if you're trying to give the impression of prestige, use a round number, if you're trying to give the impression of a bargain, use a precise number. Do you think you, as a buyer, might react this way?

Shared Appreciation Mortgages   With a **shared appreciation mortgage**, the borrower receives a below-market interest rate. In return, the lender receives a portion of the future appreciation (usually between 30 and 50 percent) in the value of the home. Thus, if you purchase a $100,000 home with a shared appreciation mortgage that promises the lender 50 percent of any price appreciation, and 10 years later sell the home for $180,000, the lender would receive one-half of the $80,000 price appreciation. Generally, mortgages of this type are not issued by traditional mortgage lenders, but by family members or investors.

Shared Appreciation Mortgage
A mortgage in which the borrower receives a below-market interest rate in return for which the lender receives a portion of the future appreciation (generally between 30 and 50 percent) in the value of the home.

Interest Only Mortgage
A mortgage with interest only payments for an initial set period (e.g., for 5 years on a 30-year loan) and after this period the borrower pays interest and principal with payments adjusted upward to reflect full amortization over the remaining years of the loan.

Interest Only Mortgages   This term can be a bit misleading since there's no such thing as an interest only mortgage, because eventually you pay the loan principal as well. An **interest only mortgage** is actually a combination of an interest only payment scheme for an initial set period combined with a traditional mortgage. As a result, you make only interest payments for an initial set period, after which you make both interest and principal payments. Once the interest only period ends, your monthly payments are adjusted upward to reflect full amortization over the remaining years of the loan.

Option Payment ARM Mortgages   With an option payment ARM mortgage, you have the option of making different types of mortgage payments each month. Your options might include:

◆ An amount less than the interest due on the loan.
◆ Interest only on the loan.
◆ The payment amount that would be required on a 15- or 30-year fixed rate loan.

Risks Associated with Specialty Mortgages   Because specialty mortgages are adjustable rate loans, there can be a big jump in monthly payments if interest rates rise, and with some types of specialty mortgages the amount you owe can actually climb over time. As such, you should think twice before taking on a specialty mortgage. Be sure to read the fine print. Make sure you know exactly how much your monthly payment could increase, when this might happen, and whether you could afford it. You should also look very closely at any penalties that you might incur if you try to refinance your mortgage.

A Word of Warning: Beware of Subprime Mortgages and Predatory Lending

"Bad Credit, No Problem!" With that come-on, lenders have targeted subprime borrowers and unscrupulous lenders have used it as a lead in to abusive lending practices, often referred to as predatory lending. Subprime, or nonprime, mortgages are simply mortgages, 80 percent of which are adjustable rate, taken out by borrowers with low credit scores. Although there is nothing wrong with individuals with less-than-perfect credit borrowing to buy a house, in recent years this market has been flooded with predatory lenders who have taken advantage of these borrowers, steering them into high-cost loans they have little chance of paying off when they could have qualified for lower cost, more affordable financing.

Over the past few years, the number of subprime mortgages has increased dramatically. Between 2001 and 2003, less than 10 percent of all new mortgages came from subprime lending, but by 2005 and 2006, this number climbed to over 20 percent of all new mortgages before dropping to about 8 percent of all new mortgages in 2007.

How have nonprime mortgages fared? According to the U.S. Government Accountability Office (GAO), of the 4.59 million nonprime loans that remained at the end of 2009, about 16 percent were in default (that is, 90 or more days late) and about 14 percent were in the foreclosure process, for a total serious delinquency rate of 30 percent as shown in Figure 8.8. Another 11.5 percent were delinquent at 30 to 89 days late. Thus, the good news was that 58.5 percent were current, and the bad news was that 41.5 percent were either delinquent or in the foreclosure process.

 How do you avoid predatory lending? The answer is with knowledge—just think back to **Principle 1: The Best Protection Is Knowledge**. Take a look at some common predatory mortgage lending practices shown in Figure 8.9.

Mortgage Decisions: Length or Term of the Loan

Another decision faced by homebuyers is whether to go for a 15- or 30-year maturity on their mortgage. Three things to consider when making this decision are: (1)

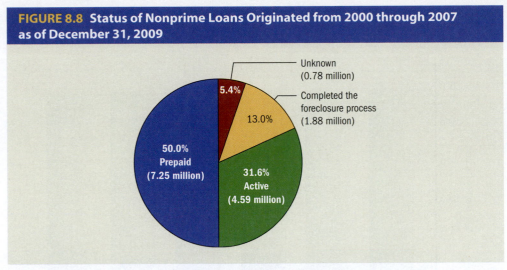

FIGURE 8.8 Status of Nonprime Loans Originated from 2000 through 2007 as of December 31, 2009

Source: GAO, Nonprime Mortgages, Analysis of Loan Performance, Factors Associated with Defaults, and Data Sources, August 2010.

prepayment opportunities; (2) the size of the monthly payments; and (3) the interest rate.

If you can secure a 30-year mortgage with a prepayment privilege, you could easily pay it off in 15 years by making additional payments every month. Why not just take out a 15-year loan if you're planning on paying it off within 15 years anyway?

With a 30-year loan, you wouldn't be locked in to paying the higher monthly rates of a 15-year loan, and you'd have the flexibility of being able to skip making your additional payments and pay a much lower amount per month if an emergency arose. Thus, at first glance, for those with financial discipline, the 30-year mortgage is preferable. However, there is one additional variable that needs to be added into the equation: the interest rate.

In general, the interest rate on 15-year mortgages is lower than the rate on 30-year mortgages. For example, in 2011 the average rate on a 30-year fixed-rate mortgage was

FIGURE 8.9 Common Predatory Mortgage Lending Practices

Common Predatory Mortgage Lending Practices

- **Steering** Charging high interest rates (9 to 20 percent) on subprime mortgages for borrowers who have good enough credit to qualify for prime-rate loans.
- **Excessive Points and Broker Fees** These are costs not directly reflected in interest rates. With predatory loans, these fees can be over 5 percent.
- **Not Considering the Borrower's Ability to Pay** Predatory mortgage lenders often loan more than the borrower can afford to repay. In fact, predatory mortgage lenders have been known to encourage borrowers to lie about their income to borrow more than they can afford.
- **Yield-Spread Premiums or Kickbacks to Brokers** With many predatory mortgages, the mortgage broker gets a kickback from the lender for delivering loans with excessively high interest rates.
- **Balloon Loans** Loans with an unreasonably high payment due at the end of or during the loan's term. In many cases, the balloon payment is hidden and is almost the size of the original loan. The end result is that these loans force foreclosure or refinancing.
- **Loan Flipping** With predatory mortgage lending, lenders may "flip" a loan by unnecessarily refinancing it with no benefit to the borrower.
- **Prepayment Penalties** Excessive fees that the borrower must pay if the loan is paid off early or refinanced. The purpose of these prepayment penalties is to lock the borrower into the high-interest loan.
- **Upward Only Adjustable Rate Mortgages (ARMs)** These are ARMs that only adjust up, with the borrower's interest rate and monthly payment climbing as often as every 6 months.
- **Bait and Switch Costs** The cost or loan terms at closing are not what the borrower agreed to.

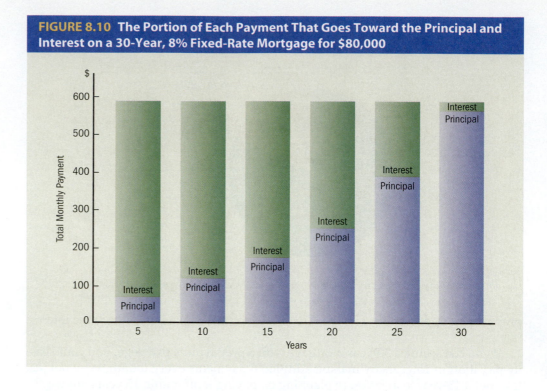

FIGURE 8.10 The Portion of Each Payment That Goes Toward the Principal and Interest on a 30-Year, 8% Fixed-Rate Mortgage for $80,000

4.82 percent and the average rate on a 15-year fixed-rate mortgage was 4.08 percent. Interest also comes into play when you consider your overall payments. A longer term means you pay interest over a longer period. For example, let's look at a 30-year, 8 percent fixed-rate mortgage for $80,000. The monthly payments on such a mortgage are $587.01.

Figure 8.10 illustrates the portion of each payment that goes toward the principal on a 30-year, 8 percent fixed-rate mortgage. As you can see, initially less than 10 percent of the first monthly payment, only $53.68, goes toward paying off the loan balance. The result is that over the life of a longer-term mortgage, total interest payments are much larger.

Table 8.2 shows the impact of the loan term on total interest paid. Keep in mind that these calculations are for an 8 percent mortgage. If the mortgage rate were higher, the total interest payments for the longer-term loan would be proportionately greater. In effect, as interest rates increase, this relationship becomes even more dramatic. Also, keep in mind that this relationship is amplified by the fact that you would pay a lower interest rate on the shorter-term mortgage.

Unfortunately, the total level of interest paid doesn't tell the whole story. There are two other complications: the time value of money and the effect of taxes. Remember, with a longer-term mortgage, your payments are lower but are stretched

TABLE 8.2   Impact of the Loan Term on the Total Interest Paid and Monthly Payment for an $80,000 Fixed-Rate Mortgage at 8%

Length of Mortgage Loan	Monthly Payment	Total Interest
15 years	$764.52	$ 57,614.13
20 years	669.15	80,597.38
25 years	617.45	105,237.47
30 years	587.01	131,326.30

FIGURE 8.11 Comparing a Shorter- Versus Longer-Term Loan

Advantages to a 15-Year Mortgage	Advantages to a 30-Year Mortgage
• Lower interest rate. • Provides a discipline to force savings. • Saves quite a bit of interest over the life of the mortgage. • Equity is built up at a faster pace. • Increased equity may allow you to trade up to a more expensive house.	• Lower payments give you more financial flexibility—if a financial emergency arises, the payments are lower and, as such, you have more uncommitted money to address the emergency. • Provides affordability—you may not be able to buy the house you want with a 15-year mortgage. • If the mortgage contains a prepayment provision, you can mimic the payment pattern on a 15-year mortgage while maintaining financial flexibility. • If you are borrowing on credit cards, which are a much more expensive form of debt than mortgages, you would be better off paying off your credit card debt before you took on higher mortgage payments. • If your investment alternative earns returns well above the mortgage interest rate, and you are a disciplined saver, that, along with the tax advantage associated with mortgage debt, makes a longer-term mortgage more attractive.

out longer. As a result, you're paying back your loan with future dollars that are worth less because of inflation.

In other words, when you make the smaller, 30-year payment, you can take the difference in payments and invest it until the end of the 30-year period. Of course, with a 15-year mortgage, when the 15-year period ends, you can invest the amount you were paying each month until the end of the 30-year period. Exactly what you have at the end of 30 years depends on what assumptions you make about what you could earn on these investments. Also, don't forget that interest on home mortgages is tax deductible and lowers taxes. As a result, the tax effect favors the longer-term mortgage.

Figure 8.11 provides a listing of some of the advantages of different length mortgages. When deciding on a term length for your mortgage, make sure you weigh all these factors. You've also got to make sure that what you do fits into your grand financial plan. You certainly don't want to be making extra payments to pay off an 8 percent mortgage while you're borrowing money on your credit card at 18 or 20 percent. Also, don't let repaying your mortgage get in the way of your other financial goals.

Coming Up with the Down Payment

For many people, especially those buying their first home, the real challenge is getting together a down payment. The most obvious and best way of coming up with a down payment is to save. If owning a home is one of your financial goals, saving for it should have a place in your financial budget. For most homebuyers, saving enough for a down payment takes a few years.

In addition to saving, many first-time homebuyers also rely on gifts and funds from parents or relatives. In fact, approximately 30 percent of all first-time homebuyers receive some financial aid from parents or relatives. But for conventional—that is, non-federally backed loans, at least 5 percent of the closing costs have to come from the homebuyer rather than from gifts. Actually, most lenders require a "gift letter" stating that any funds contributed by relatives don't have to be repaid.

If you're having trouble raising enough money for a down payment, you might consider trying to reduce the size of the down payment you need. Federally backed loans—Federal Housing Administration (FHA), the Department of Veteran Affairs (VA), and the Farmers Home Administration (FmHA) loans—don't require as large a down payment as conventional loans. In fact, FHA allows a minimum down payment of as little as 5 percent on older homes and 10 percent on new homes.

If all else fails, consider **private mortgage insurance**. This type of insurance protects the lender in the event that the borrower is unable to make the mortgage payments. It is paid for by the borrower and generally runs from 0.3 percent to 2.0 percent of the loan amount, depending on the down payment level. With private mortgage insurance, many lenders will allow you to borrow more than 80 percent of the appraised value of the home.

A final source of funds for your down payment is your IRA. First-time homebuyers can withdraw up to $10,000 from their IRAs without penalty before age 59½. While this is a possible source, it's also one that you should try to avoid. Remember, taking money out of your IRA is just trading off one goal (financial security at retirement) for another (home ownership). The problem is that your IRA grows tax free, and once you take the money out, you can't get it back in. Moreover, if it is a traditional (as opposed to Roth) IRA, you will have to pay income tax on the distribution. That means if you are in the 25 percent marginal tax bracket, you'll withdraw $10,000 and pay $2,500 in taxes on the withdrawal, leaving you with $7,500 for your down payment.

Prequalifying

Although your ability to pay, in addition to the level of funds you have available for a down payment, should give you a realistic idea of how large a mortgage loan you'll qualify for, it's a good idea to have this amount confirmed by seeing a lender and prequalifying for a loan. To do this, ask a lender to determine how large a mortgage it will lend you, and provide you with a letter stating its willingness to lend you this sum. Prequalification lessens the uncertainty surrounding what you can and can't spend, making you a more attractive buyer to potential sellers.

Step 3: Make Your Purchase

Just as with any other major purchase, buying a home involves comparison shopping with an eye on price, product attributes (in this case, location, schools, number of rooms, and so forth), and quality (in this case, the quality of the house or apartment). Finding the right house or apartment is both involved and important. Our discussion of the search process focuses primarily on buying a house, but the same search principles also apply to buying a condo or renting an apartment.

Once you know what you're looking for, it's time to start looking. Most homebuyers enlist the aid of a real estate agent. These agents can provide buyers with a lot of help in searching for homes and deciding on good neighborhoods, but you should note that the traditional real estate agent is really working for the seller: It's the seller who pays the real estate agent's commission. As a result, your best interests and the agent's best interests may be in conflict. Thus, although the agent may be your friend, you should make your own decisions based on a thorough understanding of the alternatives. Differentiating between advice and a sales pitch, and protecting yourself with knowledge, relate to **Principle 1: The Best Protection Is Knowledge**.

The traditional real estate agent has a bit of a conflict of interest, and it's the buyer's interests that lose out. In addition, real estate agents can sell only listed property—that is, property on which a real estate firm has a contract to sell.

Although this conflict of interest doesn't negate the benefits of using a real estate agent, you should definitely take some precautions. For example, you should never let your agent know your top price. If you tell the agent your top price, he or she may share that information with the seller, in which case your negotiating power will go out the window. You should also let the broker know that you intend to stay within your budget. If you don't get a particular house because it's more than you're able or willing to pay, let it go. There are always others.

An alternative to the traditional real estate agent is the **independent** or **exclusive buyer-broker**. This type of broker is a real estate agent hired by the prospective buyer, who represents the buyer exclusively and is obligated to get the buyer the best possible deal. In general, the broker is paid by splitting the commission with the seller's agent. Buyer-brokers aren't limited in their search to properties that have been listed through real estate firms. They show both unlisted—that is, homes being sold directly by the owner—and listed homes.

Moreover, because buyer-brokers work for the buyer, they tend to be more objective and critical in examining a house. Although exclusive buyer-brokers have gained popularity, they still aren't that common in many areas of the country. If you're interested in using a buyer-broker and can't find one, you can obtain a referral from the National Association of Exclusive Buyer Agents at **www.naeba.org/**. A recent survey showed that individuals who used buyer-brokers saved an average of 9 percent off the home's asking price versus only 3 percent for all buyers.

There is also a wealth of information to help with the selection of a home and making the purchase on the Internet. One of the first places to explore is HUD's Buying a Home Web site at **www.hud.gov/buying/index.cfm**. It has a section on your rights as a homebuyer, how much mortgage can you afford, finding a real estate broker, shopping for a home, building a home, and more. Another great source of information on the Web is Homefair.com at **www.homefair.com/**, which provides information on picking the right city, school reports, finding an apartment, finding a home, and organizing your move. Also take a look at Checklist 8.6.

FACTS OF LIFE

The number of individuals selling their homes without the help of a realtor had been steadily rising up until the housing crash, but has dropped since then as sellers have looked for all the help they can get in selling their homes.

12% of sellers sold their homes without a realtor in 2005.
20% of sellers sold their homes without a realtor in 2006.
13% of sellers sold their homes without a realtor in 2010.

Independent or Exclusive Buyer-Broker
A real estate agent hired by the prospective homebuyer who exclusively represents the homebuyer. Such brokers are obligated to get the buyer the best possible deal and, in general, are paid by splitting the commission with the seller's agent.

CHECKLIST 8.6

A Housing Checklist for Buyers and Sellers

If you're selling your house and decide to work with a realtor:

◆ Look for a realtor that works full-time and has at least 3 years' experience. Ask how many transactions the realtor made during the previous year and the year before that—a good realtor sells at least 30 homes per year.

◆ Make sure that there is an "out clause" in the contract, which allows you to terminate the contact whenever you want—you don't want to lock in a bad agent for 6 months.

◆ Pick a realtor who works and lives in your area.

If you're buying a house:

◆ When you're deciding what you can afford, remember, those numbers are meant as a ceiling, not a floor.

◆ If at all possible, try to avoid the need for private mortgage insurance by putting down at least 20 percent of a home's cost.

◆ When you're looking at what to borrow, borrow what you need, not what you can. Many times lenders will often offer you the maximum you can borrow—just go for what you need.

◆ Understand how your real estate agent is being compensated. Generally, it is through a commission, which means the more you pay, the more they make.

Real Estate Short Sale
A sale of property where the proceeds from the sale fall short of the balance owed on the property.

What about short sales? A **real estate short sale** occurs when the proceeds from the sale of the property fall short of the balance owed on the property. First, let's try to gain an understanding of why a short sale might occur. Let's assume that you aren't able to make your mortgage payments, but because real estate is in a slump your house is now worth less than the amount you still owe the bank. For example, you still owe $250,000 on the house you bought 2 years ago for $350,000, but the house is now valued at $175,000. If it goes into foreclosure, you'll not only lose your home, but you'll also have difficulty buying another house for years to come because of a poor credit record. Your bank would like to move the property, because it's not receiving any mortgage payments, and it would also like to avoid foreclosure, which is costly for banks. Through a short sale, your house is sold for less than you still owe, but, since there is no foreclosure, there is less damage to your credit standing. In general, the bank loses the difference between what is owed and what they receive from the sale of the house. How common are short sales? As a result of the housing crash, they are quite common. In fact, in 2010, about 19 percent of all real estate transactions were short sales, 28 percent were on foreclosed homes, and the remaining 53 percent were on nondistressed homes.

When you find a house you like, you need to have it inspected. The house might be falling apart. Hey, it might even be haunted! A good home should be structurally sound, and its heating, air-conditioning, plumbing, and electrical systems should be free from problems. Unfortunately, very few homebuyers are truly qualified to inspect and evaluate these aspects of a home. If you're not one of the lucky few, you should enlist the aid of a professional building inspector. You should be able to get the name of an inspector from your real estate agent or the local chamber of commerce.

Once you've decided which house you'd like to live in, the next step is making the purchase. Traditionally, negotiating a price for a house involves a good deal of bargaining. The home is "listed" at a certain selling price by the seller, meaning the seller would like to receive that price. However, all prices are open to negotiation. Many times the buyer will offer a price below what the home is listed at. The offer can also include conditions or contingencies to be met as part of the contract. For example, you may want appliances or draperies to remain in the home, or your offer may be contingent on being able to close by a certain date.

When the sellers receive an offer from a potential buyer, they can accept the offer, counter the offer, or refuse the offer. The counteroffer is carried between the buyer and the seller by the real estate agent—you may never see the seller face-to-face. In some cases, the haggling can go on for some time until a final price and other conditions are set. However, know that while the negotiating is taking place, another potential buyer may come in, make an offer, and the seller can accept that offer, leaving you flat!

The Contract   Once the price is agreed upon, an attorney or the real estate agent can draw up a contract to buy the home. Real estate contracts are relatively standard but make sure your contract has all of the following elements:

♦ The price, method of payment, buyer and seller, date on which the buyer will take possession, and a legal description of the property should all be stated clearly.

♦ The legal title to the home must be free and clear of all liens and encumbrances. Whether the buyer or the seller pays for the title search should be stated in the contract.

♦ A house must be certified to be free of termite or radon problems.

♦ A contingent on suitable funding clause should be included, stating that if you're unable to secure suitable financing (where you specifically state the amount, rate, and terms), the contract will be voided and you'll receive your deposit back in full.

◆ Because the home will change ownership during, rather than at the end of, the year, the contract should state what portion of the utilities, insurance, taxes, and interest on mortgage payments will be paid by the buyer and what portion will be paid by the seller.

◆ The condition the home will be in at the date of transfer should be stated, and a final walk-through should be provided to assure the buyer that the home is in the contracted condition.

◆ Any other contingencies that have been agreed upon should be included.

If the contract is accepted, the buyer will give the seller some **earnest money**, which is a deposit on the purchase assuring the seller that the buyer is serious about buying.

At **closing**, the title is transferred, the seller is paid in full, and the buyer takes possession of the home. At this point, the buyer must pay the balance of the down payment. For example, if you're buying a home for $150,000 with 20 percent down, at closing you must pay $30,000 less any earnest money you paid when the contract was signed.

In addition to the remaining down payment, you'll also have to pay the closing costs with a cashier's or certified check. You don't have to worry about figuring out exactly what you have to pay at closing. The lender will give you a **settlement** or **closing statement** at least one business day before closing. Finally, the legal documents are examined and signed, for which you may want to consult your lawyer, and the keys are passed. You now own a home!

Step 4: Maintain Your Purchase

Once you've purchased a home, you're then in charge of upkeep and maintenance. To say the least, owning a home can take up a good deal of time. In addition, you should always keep an eye out toward making sure that you have financed your home in the least expensive way possible. That leads us to a discussion of refinancing your mortgage.

Refinancing is simply taking out a new mortgage, usually at a lower rate, to pay off your old one. Whenever mortgage interest rates drop, people refinance. No one wants to be paying 12 percent on a mortgage when the going rate is now 8 percent. The typical rule of thumb states that you should refinance when mortgage interest rates fall by 2 percent. However, there's more to refinancing than just interest rates.

When you refinance, you again incur most of the closing costs already discussed, including points, the loan application fee, the termite and radon inspection fee, and so on. The refinancing decision really rides on whether or not the lower rate you could get will compensate for these additional costs in a reasonable amount of time.

Let's look at an example: You currently have a 15-year-old, 30-year mortgage at 11 percent and are considering refinancing it with a 15-year mortgage at 8 percent. When you bought your home, you took out a $100,000 mortgage with a monthly payment of $952.32. Today, 15 years later, you still have a balance on your mortgage of $83,789.07. If you refinanced this loan over 15 years at 8 percent, your payments would drop to $800.73.

Earnest Money
A deposit on the home purchase to assure the seller that the buyer is serious about buying the house.

Closing
The time at which the title is transferred and the seller is paid in full for the house. At this time, the buyer takes possession of the house.

Settlement or Closing Statement
A statement listing the funds required at closing, which should be furnished to the buyer by the real estate broker at least 1 business day before closing for review.

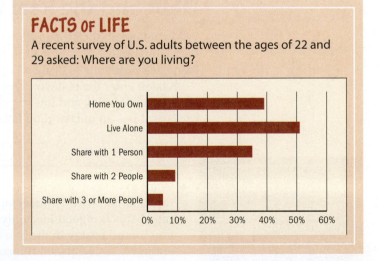

FACTS OF LIFE
A recent survey of U.S. adults between the ages of 22 and 29 asked: Where are you living?

FIGURE 8.12 Worksheet for Refinancing Analysis

Monthly Benefits from Refinancing	Example	Your Numbers
a. Present monthly mortgage payments	$952.32	
b. Mortgage payments after refinancing	$800.73	
c. Monthly savings, pretax (line a − line b)	$151.59	
d. Additional tax on monthly savings (line c × 28% tax rate)	$42.45	
e. Monthly savings on an after-tax basis (line c − line d)	$109.14	

Cost of Refinancing

	Example	Your Numbers
f. Total after-tax closing costs, including any prepayment penalty incurred	$2,600	

Number of Months Needed to Break Even

	Example	Your Numbers
g. Months needed for interest saved to equal the refinancing costs incurred as a result of taking out a new mortgage loan (line f ÷ line e)	23.8 months	

If you estimate that your total after-tax closing costs would be $2,600, it would take you 23.8 months for the savings from the decrease in monthly payments to cover the closing costs incurred as a result of refinancing, as shown in Figure 8.12. Thus, if you expect to continue to live in your home for over 2 years, you should consider refinancing at the lower rate. Checklist 8.7 provides a number of reasons why refinancing might be a good idea.

Tying Things Together: Debt and the Real World

We've talked about debt a number of times in this book. We talked about credit card debt, consumer loans, home mortgages, home equity loans, auto loans, and student loans. It's now time to bring all of this together.

As you enter the real world, you take with you some college education, unlimited hope and potential, and lots of debt. In fact, the typical college student has 4.6 credit cards and has an outstanding balance on those credit cards of $3,173, according to a

---

CHECKLIST 8.7

Refinancing Might Be a Good Idea if You . . .

◆ Want to get out of a high-interest-rate loan to take advantage of lower rates. This is a good idea only if you intend to stay in the house long enough to make the additional fees worthwhile.

◆ Have an adjustable-rate mortgage (ARM) and want a fixed-rate loan to have the certainty of knowing exactly what the mortgage payment will be for the life of the loan.

◆ Want to convert to an ARM with a lower interest rate or more protective features (such as a better rate and payment caps) than the ARM you currently have.

◆ Want to build up equity more quickly by converting to a loan with a shorter term.

◆ Want to draw on the equity built up in your home to get cash for a major purchase or for your children's education.

Source: A Consumers Guide to Mortgage Refinancing (Washington, DC: Federal Reserve Board, 2011).

2009 study of undergraduates by Nellie Mae, a subsidiary of Sallie Mae, a leading provider of federal loans to students. Moreover, it's been estimated that the typical grad with loans—and that's about half of all college students—will leave college with both a diploma and about $27,800 in debts. Some of that debt will be from credit cards and some—on average, about $17,900 of it—will be from student loans.

The Trap of Too Much Debt

Today, debt is being marketed to adults the same way toys are marketed to children—and for many, it's just too hard to resist. Here are some of the results.

◆ Students and those with little capacity to repay are being given the opportunity to ring up debts at will. Look at Cal Duncan, 24, of Blacksburg, Virginia. He got his first credit card (along with a free Frisbee) as a sophomore at Virginia Tech. "All I needed to get that credit card," Cal recalls, "was my college ID and a pulse." After 4 years at Virginia Tech, Cal graduated with a degree in business and eight credit cards. These cards came with all kinds of free goodies, including phone calling cards, a savings bond, thermos coffee cups for the car, and meals at Burger King and Taco Bell. "It was like getting something for nothing. All I had to do was sign my name and I'd get a free gift along with a credit card. And, once I had the cards, it was hard not to use them."

Most of Cal's charging during his college days came in his senior year. "I figured I'd be earning the big bucks next year, so there was no reason to deprive myself of that pizza, or CD, or that night out." That same attitude stayed with Cal during his first year on the job. When reality finally set in, Cal had amassed credit card debt which, along with his outstanding student loans, more than equalled his annual salary. As Cal says, "It was all too easy. It just didn't seem like I was spending real money. I remember heading to Kroger to buy a box of macaroni and cheese and partway there thinking of all the money I was going to make the next year. I turned around and headed home where I called Papa John's Pizza because they take Visa and MasterCard—why suffer when I was planning on making the big bucks in the future? Never did I imagine that it would be anything but easy to pay it off."

◆ People are encouraged to borrow more than they should; in fact, borrowing is becoming part of our culture. As long as you make your credit card payments, regardless of how painful those payments are, you'll be tempted by increased borrowing limits and you'll receive more credit card offers. Now that Cal is in the real world, working to pay off his debts, he still receives "a weekly offer" of a new credit card. It's the youngest group of consumers who are most at risk here. They're the ones who grew up on plastic and seem to have the biggest problem controlling its usage. In fact, according to a recent survey, of those aged 30 and under, almost 60 percent do not pay off their credit card bills every month—for those 60 or older, this number falls to less than 15 percent.

◆ Bankruptcies have been on the rise. As a result of the ease of borrowing, the typical American is taking on much more debt than ever before. In fact, debt as a percent of annual disposable income has nearly doubled over the past 40 years. Unfortunately, that's more debt than many of us can accommodate. The result in 2010 was that almost 1.59 million Americans filed for bankruptcy.

With all this bad debt and low teaser rates, it would seem that banks wouldn't be making any money, but that's not the case. Today, banks make mortgage, credit card, and auto loans; package them; and sell them as collateralized securities. That means that an investor, rather than the bank that issued your credit card, may be holding your credit card debt. What this does is make it easier for banks to make more credit card loans, and if you don't pay, it's not their problem. It's now the problem of whoever bought the credit card loans from your bank. The result: a never-ending stream of credit card debt offers, regardless of the borrower's ability to repay.

Successful Debt Management

After hearing all the stories of doom associated with people taking on too much debt, you should keep in mind that debt isn't all bad. In fact, without it, it would be impossible for most people to ever buy a home. The bottom line is that debt and borrowing are pretty complicated, and as a result, you'll want to understand the keys to successful debt management.

Key 1: The Obvious: Spend Less Than You Earn and Budget Your Money   The key to controlling debt is both obvious and simple: Spend less than you earn, and if you can't afford it, don't charge it. This all goes back to living below your means. Of course, that may mean some changes in your lifestyle, but no matter what else you do with your financial plan, its success depends on your ability to spend less than you earn.

This also means that you've got to have an active budget, and you've got to stick to it. Of course, the budget has to be flexible enough to work, but it also means you can't borrow to make spending match up with money that comes in. Even more important, it means control. That is, not letting lenders decide where and when you're going to borrow. A budget simply doesn't make sense if it relies on borrowing to pay for day-to-day expenditures. A budget also doesn't make sense if it doesn't have any savings built into it. Let's face it, apart from saving for retirement and your children's education, you're going to run into some emergencies along the way—perhaps medical needs, unemployment, or divorce—that will force you to dip into your reserves.

Key 2: Know the Costs   Perhaps the best deterrent against unnecessary borrowing is to know the costs. You should know your credit card interest rate, your statement due date, and your credit limit. You should also know that if you don't pay your bill in full, you'll also be paying interest.

When economists talk about borrowing, they talk about "forgoing future consumption opportunities in lieu of present consumption," that is, spending money that you haven't yet earned and paying it back with future earnings. In fact, there's an old saying that "spending money you haven't earned yet is like using up years you haven't lived yet." What all this means, of course, is that you won't be able to spend as much in the future—most people understand that—but they don't understand how *much* future consumption they have given up when they put that pizza on their credit card. If you put that pizza on a credit card that charges 18 percent and you don't pay off your balance each month, you bought one expensive pizza. Moreover, as shown in Table 6.5, if you only pay off the minimum, you may be paying interest on that pizza for 32 months! Things are even worse with payday loans, as we saw earlier in Chapter 7. The annual interest rate can get up in the 400 percent range. Just knowing what you're paying may be enough to control that need to spend.

If you do end up borrowing money, make sure you do it from a quality lender. Checklist 8.8 provides some early warning signs on lenders.

Key 3: Understand the Difference Between Good and Bad Debt   Not all borrowing is a bad idea. When does borrowing make sense? Whenever the item fulfills one of your goals. It should outlive the financing, and it should provide a return that is greater than the cost. For example, borrowing to finance your education makes

---

CHECKLIST 8.8

Lenders: Early Warning Signs

Avoid Any Lender Who . . .

◆ Tells you to falsify information on the loan application. For example, the lender tells you to say your loan is primarily for business purposes when it's not.

◆ Pressures you into applying for a loan or applying for more money than you need.

◆ Pressures you into accepting monthly payments you can't make.

◆ Fails to provide required loan disclosures or tells you not to read them.

◆ Misrepresents the kind of credit you're getting. For example, calling a one-time loan a line of credit.

◆ Promises one set of terms when you apply, and gives you another set of terms to sign—with no legitimate explanation for the change.

◆ Tells you to sign blank forms—the lender says they'll fill them in later.

◆ Says you can't have copies of documents that you've signed.

Source: "Don't Sign on the Bottom Line," Federal Reserve Board, 2011, and "Early Warning Signs," Federal Trade Commission, January 2004.

---

sense because you will use that education long after you've paid off your student loans, and your education should more than pay for itself in terms of employment opportunities. The same is true for a home mortgage. Your house should be standing long after you've paid off your mortgage. In addition, you'll no longer have to pay rent, and hopefully, your home will appreciate in value. An auto loan may also fit this definition of good debt because your car should still be running when your loan is paid off.

But auto loans aren't always good debt. In order for them to qualify as good debt, you must have a sufficient down payment and make sure the payments are large enough to pay the car off as opposed to rolling unpaid debt from this car to the next one. With 6-year auto loans now available, you may really be "renting" your car, because it may not be worth anything by the time it's paid off. If that's the case, try a less expensive car or consider the used car market.

How about that big screen TV? It should last longer than the payments. Having a big screen TV may be one of your goals, but it won't provide a return greater than the cost. Once that TV is in your home, its value is only a fraction of what it was originally. Try saving up to pay for this type of expenditure and not letting the seller decide how you're going to finance it. What about normal day-to-day operating expenses—food, rent, and clothes? Borrowing to finance these expenses will set you up for future problems that only winning the lottery can solve.

Unfortunately, sometimes there isn't a real choice, such as when an emergency comes up. If that happens you should know that you are going to have to adjust your lifestyle so you can undo the financial damage that you've done as soon as possible.

Key 4: Make Sure You Can Repay What You Borrow—Set Your Own Standards Just because someone is willing to lend you money is no reason to accept the loan. For example, as discussed in this and the next chapter, most mortgage lenders set a limit to the amount that they will lend you based on the ratio of your mortgage payments (along with taxes and insurance plus other debt payments) to your monthly gross income, and it is generally limited to 36 percent or less. What if you find a lender who is willing to lend you up to the point where your mortgage payments along with taxes and insurance plus other debt payments reach 40 percent of your gross monthly income? Should you go with that loan and buy a bigger house? The answer is you have to determine your own borrowing capacity and stick to it. Your mortgage broker may be more interested with you taking out a mortgage so that he or she can collect his or her fee than he or she is with whether or not you can make the payments. You are the one that suffers if you have problems making your debt payments, and let's face it, getting in debt over your head is easy to do if you aren't careful.

One way to avoid it is to apply the standards a bank would to yourself. Don't let someone else dictate how much you borrow. Remember, you are the one that has to make the payments. If you think the loan obligates too much of your monthly income, lower the amount that you are borrowing. The problem many people run into is that once they get the home mortgage, they take on even more debt. They buy furniture, appliances, and electronics to fill the house, and a car to fill the garage. Also keep an eye on your debt limit ratio and the debt resolution rule that we just introduced.

The bottom line is that regardless of how you decide to do it, you have to manage your own debt. You have to limit yourself because with all the competition in the lending industry, you may get the opportunity to borrow more than you can afford.

Key 5: Keep Your Credit Score Strong—It Keeps Costs Down and Is a Source of Emergency Money

A poor credit score can hurt you in getting a car loan, an apartment, and even a job. That, by itself, should be enough inspiration to keep your credit score strong. However, one thing many people don't realize is that your credit score also determines what rate you're going to pay when you borrow. Those who have the greatest need for low borrowing rates end up paying the highest rates. This holds true for the interest rate on credit cards all the way to the rate on home mortgages. Is the rate differential significant? You bet. In fact, the interest rate on mortgage home loans can be up to 6 percent more for individuals with poor credit ratings—that's about twice as high.

You can also look at your borrowing capacity as an emergency account. If and when an emergency comes, having untapped borrowing capacity will allow you to borrow money when you most need it. A habit of borrowing up to your limit only sets up problems in the future. It also forces you to keep a larger emergency fund than you would otherwise have to. And because less liquid investments generally have a higher return than do highly liquid investments, you will be able to earn more on your investments.

The way to avoid these problems is to avoid borrowing up to your full capacity, to pay your bills on time, and to make sure no errors pop up in your credit reports. You'll want to review your credit report every year—remember, you can get them free. If you look back to Table 6.3, you'll find the location of the major credit bureaus. If you find an error, make sure it gets corrected.

> **STOP & THINK**
>
> In an emergency, the best asset you have is good credit.

Key 6: Don't Live with Bad (and Expensive) Debt

In 2010, according to **CreditCards.com** and **Cardweb.com**, average credit card debt per household with at least one credit card was $15,788, up from $2,985 in 1990. Unless it's paid off every month, that's a lot of what we have called "bad" debt. It's debt that often is a result of buying without forethought. Because in early 2011 the average interest rate on a credit card then was around 14.73 percent—that's expensive borrowing.

The strategy many credit card borrowers use is to jump to a teaser rate—a low rate that lasts, in general, for 6 months. After the 6-month period is over, the rate jumps to the postpromotional level, generally somewhere around 15 to 18 percent. The idea is to then jump again. Unfortunately, credit card companies have strategies to counter this ploy. On some cards, a balance cannot be transferred for an entire year, or on the new card the low rate may only apply to new purchases. One alternative is to try to negotiate down your rate on your current card. A better alternative is to get rid of your bad debt entirely.

If you want to rid yourself of bad debt, the first thing that must be done is to eliminate the lifestyle pattern that led to the debt in the first place. You've got to start living below your means. Once you've made the necessary lifestyle adjustments, you've got to attack your debt with dogged determination. First, you've got to pay much more than the minimum. Table 6.5 will give you an idea of how long it will take to eliminate your debt. This is no fun, but the alternative is no hope.

If you're paying 15 percent on your debt and it doesn't look like an end is in sight, you might consider liquidating some investments that pay less than that. For example, if you have money in a savings account that pays 1 percent, you'd be much better off using your savings account to pay off your debt. In fact, you'll save more than the differential of 14 percent (eliminating 15 percent debt payments but losing 1 percent income from your savings account), because you'd have to pay taxes on that 1 percent return from your savings.

If you don't have an investment to liquidate, you might consider borrowing at a lower rate to pay off your 15 percent debt. For example, you might want to get a home equity loan. One advantage of such a loan is that the interest you pay is tax deductible. You could also consider borrowing against your life insurance if it has cash value, or borrowing from friends and family. Of course, these are desperate measures, and they can be taken only once. That means you've got to make a serious lifestyle change if you're going to take this path. This should also make clear the crippling effect bad debt can have on your financial future.

Summary

 ### Make good buying decisions.

The first step in smart buying is to separate your wants from your needs. Once you've determined the alternatives, it's time to compare the different products and make trade-offs between their quality, features, and price. The key to success in negotiating is knowing as much as possible about the markup on the product. The final step is the postpurchase process, involving maintenance and the resolution of any complaints that might arise. This smart buying process works for just about any purchase decision you make.

 ### Choose a vehicle that suits your needs and budget.

While your home may be your largest investment, your automobile is your largest frequent expense. Choose a car that fits both your personal and financial needs.

Once you have decided what is best for you, the next hurdle is getting it for a fair price. The place to start is to find out what the dealer cost or invoice price is. Next, you must make the financing decision. Should you buy or lease? Leasing a car is similar to renting. About 80 percent of all new car leases are closed-end or walk-away leases. With this type of lease you return the car at the end of the lease and literally walk away from any further responsibilities.

 ### Choose housing that meets your needs.

No single type of housing is right for everyone. A single-family house is the traditional choice, and it is the most popular choice for most people because it offers more space, privacy, and owner control. A cooperative or co-op is an apartment building or group of apartments owned by a corporation where the residents of the building are the stockholders of the corporation.

Decide whether to rent or buy housing.

There are a number of reasons renting may be preferable to buying. In order to make a logical decision about whether to rent or buy, or what is truly affordable, you need to have a basic understanding of the costs that come with home ownership. These include one-time or initial costs such as the down payment, points, and closing costs; recurring costs associated with financing, including mortgage payments, property taxes, and insurance; and recurring costs associated with upkeep and maintenance.

Calculate the costs of buying a home.

The first step in the housing decision involves preshopping, in which you focus on the rent-versus-buy decision and determine what is affordable. Just as with any other major purchase, the second step involves comparison shopping with an eye on price, product attributes, and the quality of the house or apartment.

Once you decide which house or apartment you'd like to live in, the next step is purchasing the house, or in the case of renting an apartment, signing the lease. Once again, the process is essentially the same as with any other major purchase—negotiate a price and evaluate the financing alternatives. Once you've purchased a home, you're in charge of upkeep and maintenance.

Get the most out of your mortgage.

Mortgages can be categorized as conventional or government-backed. Conventional mortgages are simply loans from a bank or S&L secured by the property being purchased. With government-backed loans, the bank or S&L still makes the loan, but the government insures the loan. S&Ls and commercial banks are the primary sources of mortgage loans, but they certainly are not the only sources. Mortgage loans are also available from other traditional lenders such as credit unions and mutual savings banks, as well as from specialized lenders such as mortgage bankers and mortgage brokers.

Mortgages also come with fixed or adjustable rates. A fixed-rate mortgage is one on which the monthly payment does not change regardless of what happens to interest rates. With an adjustable-rate mortgage (ARM), the interest rate fluctuates up and down with the level of current interest rates, within limits at specific intervals. If interest rates drop, you may want to refinance your mortgage, which is simply taking out a new mortgage to pay off your old one.

Review Questions

1. What issues, or factors, does the "smart buyer" process attempt to control?
2. Summarize the four-step process for smart buying. How does **Principle 9: Mind Games, Your Financial Personality, and Your Money** play a role in this process?
3. Effective complaints do not reflect anger or include threats. List five key points to remember when making an effective complaint.
4. What factors should you consider when trying to determine what vehicle to buy?
5. What three factors determine the monthly payment on an automobile loan?

6. What is the holdback on a new car? Why are the holdback, rebates, dealer incentive, and markup important when negotiating a new car price?

7. What is the purpose of an auto lease? What are the two types of leases? What is the major difference between the two?

8. Identify the characteristics of a consumer who should seriously consider auto leasing. What are the six factors that determine the monthly lease payment?

9. Whether it is for a new or used vehicle, why is auto maintenance so important? List five maintenance tips to remember.

10. What is the difference between a condo and a co-op? What are the advantages and disadvantages of each compared to living in a single-family house?

11. What is a Planned Unit Development? How does it differ from a condominium?

12. What three major categories of expenses make up the costs of homeownership? Give two examples of each.

13. What are the initial, or one-time, costs associated with financing a home?

14. What four separate expenses make up the mortgage payment? What acronym is used to describe a mortgage payment?

15. What are the advantages and disadvantages of buying versus renting a home?

16. What two primary lifestyle and financial factors should you consider in the buy or rent decision?

17. From a financial point of view, over a 7-year period, why is it better to own than to rent? Consider costs, return, and taxes in your answer. (*Hint:* Use Figure 8.6.)

18. What three factors determine the maximum amount a bank will finance for a home mortgage?

19. What are the advantages and disadvantages of using IRA savings as a down payment?

20. What is the difference between a traditional real estate agent and an independent buyer-broker? Is there an advantage to either for someone buying a home?

21. What factors should be considered before signing a lease or rental agreement?

22. What provisions should be outlined in a real estate contract?

23. What is the difference between mortgage bankers and mortgage brokers? Does either offer prospective homeowners an advantage? If so, what?

24. What are the advantages and disadvantages of government-backed loans, such as VA or FHA loans?

25. What are some of the advantages and disadvantages of "option" ARM mortgages? How have these loans been abused recently?

26. What two factors determine the interest rate for an ARM? How might this differ from the initial rate? Why are the factors of rate caps and adjustment intervals important?

27. The interest rate index is an important consideration when shopping for an ARM. What factor(s) should you always consider when comparing indexes?

28. List the advantages of a fixed-rate mortgage. In contrast, what are the advantages of an adjustable-rate mortgage, or ARM?

29. How do the time value of money and taxes complicate the decision on the term of a mortgage?

30. What are some factors that determine whether or not a homeowner should refinance?

31. Define what is meant by the term "short sale." Provide an example of when this type of sale is typically used.

32. List and describe six keys to successful debt management. How do you differentiate good and bad debt?

33. What are at least three early warning signs to watch for when working with a lender?

Develop Your Skills—Problems and Activities

These problems are available in MyFinanceLab.

1. Determine the total first-year cost of car ownership for Milagros. She just purchased a vehicle valued for $15,000 with the following costs:

Auto Loan: Amount—$15,000, Duration—4 years, APR—8.65 percent

Property Taxes: 2 percent of vehicle value/year

Sales Taxes: 3 percent of the sales price

Title and Tags: $40/year

Maintenance and Usage Costs: $1,500/year

Insurance: $2,000/year

2. Use your financial calculator to compute the monthly payment and the total amount spent if you financed $20,000 for 5 years at 8 percent per year. Also calculate the payment if you financed the car for only 4 years. Finally, calculate the payment for 3 years. What do you notice about the payment under the different time assumptions?

3. Use Appendix E, the *Monthly Installment Loan Tables*, to calculate the monthly payments for a vehicle that costs $15,000 if you financed the entire purchase over 4 years at an annual interest rate of 7 percent. Also calculate the loan payments assuming rates of 8 percent and 9 percent. Compare the total amount spent on the vehicle under each assumption. Use the Auto Loan Calculator to calculate the monthly payments for a vehicle that costs $15,000 if you financed the entire purchase over 4 years at an annual interest rate of 7 percent. Also calculate the loan payments assuming rates of 8 percent and 9 percent. Compare the total amount spent on the vehicle under each assumption.

4. Annie's mortgage statement shows a total payment of $699.12 with $604.60 paid toward principal and interest and $94.52 paid for taxes and insurance. Taxes and insurance for 3 months were collected at closing. Now after 6 months of payments, she is curious about the total in her escrow account. Calculate the amount for her and explain the account.

5. Calculate the monthly payments of a 30-year fixed-rate mortgage at 6.25 percent for $100,000. How much interest is paid over the life of the loan?

6. Calculate how much money a prospective homeowner would need for closing costs on a house that costs $100,000. Calculate based on a 20 percent down payment, 2 discount points on the loan, a 1-point origination fee, and $1,400 in miscellaneous other fees.

7. Use your financial calculator to determine the monthly payments for each of the following $100,000 mortgage loans. Assume no prepayments.

a. 30-year fixed at 8.5 percent

b. 15-year fixed at 7.5 percent

c. 20-year fixed at 8.0 percent

8. Use your calculator to determine (1) the current mortgage payment, (2) the total interest paid, (3) the payment after the first adjustment, and (4) the maximum payment for each of the following $150,000, 30-year mortgages. Assume that the initial interest rate is 6 percent.

a. Annually adjustable, 1 percent per year, 5 percent lifetime cap
b. Fixed for 3 years then annually adjustable, 2 percent per year, 5 percent lifetime cap
c. Fixed for 5 years then annually adjustable, 2 percent per year, 6 percent lifetime cap
d. Fixed for 5 years then adjustable every 5 years, 3 percent per period, 6 percent lifetime cap

9. Kalid is purchasing a home but expects interest rates to fall, so he is choosing an 8.375 percent adjustable-rate mortgage with a 1-year adjustment interval. During the first 3 years of his mortgage, he got lucky and the interest rate fell 2½ percent per year but unfortunately his floor rate was 5.5 percent. Calculate his average interest rate for years 1–3 for his 30-year 2/6 ARM assuming the maximum allowable adjustments for the time period.

10. Determine the maximum 30-year fixed-rate mortgage amount for which a couple could qualify if the rate is 9.5 percent. Assume they have other debt payments totaling $500 per month and a combined annual income of $45,500. Monthly escrow payments for real estate taxes and homeowner's insurance are estimated to be $125.

Learn by Doing—Suggested Projects

1. Your friend recently completed a home addition that included a new laundry room and larger master bath. There appears to be a problem with the plumbing drain. If the master bath commode is flushed while the washer is draining, the commode backs up. So far, it has not overflowed onto the floor. Help your friend write a complaint letter to the construction company.

2. Research several automotive Web sites (e.g., manufacturers, dealers, **Edmunds .com**, **autotrader.com**, etc.) and write a one-page report on your findings.

3. List your needs (including budget) and your wants for a new automobile. Consult sources such as Web sites, magazines, and dealership literature, and make a financially and personally wise decision about which vehicle to buy. Include your lists and discuss your reasoning in a short report.

4. List the pros and cons, from both a financial and personal perspective, of leasing and financing a vehicle. Now visit an auto dealership and ask for a copy of their purchase and lease agreements. Evaluate the agreements and associated fees in a one-page report.

5. Write a one- or two-page summary of the possible advantages and disadvantages, both financial and personal, of renting and owning a home.

6. Talk with your parents, another homeowner, or consult your own records to determine the amount of money that was paid in up-front closing costs for a recent closing on a home. Write a report outlining the costs.

7. Consult the real estate section in your local paper, a real estate listings booklet, or real estate listings on the Web. Choose two homes that you might actually consider within the next 5 to 10 years. Calculate the down payment and the principal and interest portion of the mortgage payment if you financed 80 percent of the sales price over 30 years at a rate of 6.5 percent. With that limited insight on the one-time and recurring costs, also consider the maintenance and operating

costs for each home. Write a report outlining your wants and needs, your calculations, and the reasoning behind your choice.

8. As a group project, visit a local bank, mortgage company, and a credit union. Speak with a representative about the different mortgages available through each institution. Collect the information and then write a report discussing the features of each and which mortgage you might choose.

9. Assume you are buying a new $175,000 home in your area. Find the mortgage rate information in the newspaper or on the Internet and compare several loans—make sure that you consider one adjustable-rate option. Consider the rate, duration, type, initial and *future* monthly payments, closing costs, and points (if applicable). Calculate the monthly payment based on financing 80 percent and calculate the total amount paid over the life of the loan including up-front costs. Assume that closing costs equal 2.5 percent of the selling price of the house plus the down payment and discount points.

10. Talk with a realtor or mortgage lender about either FHA or VA mortgages. Ask them to describe their likes, dislikes, and experiences with the programs, as well as the advantages and disadvantages for the home purchaser. If eligible, would you consider these government-backed loans? Why or why not?

11. Talk with your parents or other close family relative(s) to determine if they have ever encountered an unethical lender. Use Checklist 8.8 as a guide when asking your family questions. If someone has come across an unethical lender, what did the relative do in response? Share your story with others in class.

Be a Financial Planner—Discussion Case 1

This case is available in MyFinanceLab.

Samuel and Grace Paganelli want to replace their 1996 pickup, which Samuel drives for work. They already own two vehicles, but they need to replace Samuel's truck because it has nearly 225,000 miles on the odometer. The replacement must be a vehicle that fits his job as a self-employed electrician.

Samuel knows that he drives a lot on the job and is worried about the high-mileage penalty on many leases, as well as the fees for excessive wear and tear. However, Grace is more concerned about the depreciation loss on a new truck purchase than the mileage penalty and would rather lease the new vehicle. She also likes the idea of having a new, safer truck every few years without the hassle of resale. Samuel also does not like the fact that, if they lease, they would not own the vehicle he will use for work. Warranty protection to insure the truck remains in service is very important.

They feel that they can afford to spend $550 per month over 4 years for a new vehicle, as long as their other associated expenses such as insurance, gas, and maintenance are not too high. The Paganellis also do not know where to start looking for a vehicle without the hassle of negotiating with dealerships.

Questions

1. Identify seven sources of vehicle purchasing information and the type of information available in each source.

2. For all the information available, what specific information about the different makes and models is the most relevant to Samuel and Grace in making their purchasing decision?

3. What is the highest price they can pay on the new vehicle if they can afford a down payment of $4,000? Assume they finance their purchase for 48 months at 7.5 percent. (*Hint:* This is a present value of an annuity problem.)

4. According to the National Automotive Dealer Association (NADA) guide found at **www .nadaguides.com**, are the Paganellis better off to sell their pickup or use it as a trade-in? Consider both price and time in your answer.

5. If they were to lease, what key factors are important in a good lease?

6. Explain to Grace and Samuel the guidelines of leasing and whether or not it is a smart financial move for them to consider. Would they be better off with a closed-end or open-end lease? From a purely financial perspective, would you recommend leasing or financing? Complete Worksheet 9 to substantiate your recommendation.

7. If Samuel purchases a "lemon," what alternatives are available to prevent the truck from "short-circuiting" his business?

Be a Financial Planner—Discussion Case 2

This case is available in MyFinanceLab.

With a raise from his investment firm, Seyed Abdallah, 31, is inspired to look for a new home. Buying a home will allow Seyed, who is single and in the 25 percent marginal tax bracket, to itemize taxes. He has come to you for help.

Financially he is fairly secure but he is also very risk averse. His salary is $63,000 a year but he does not know how much he should spend on housing. His current housing expenditures include rent of $900 per month and renter's insurance premiums totaling $150 per year. His monthly bills include a $450-per-month lease payment for his 2010 Acura TL and a $150-per-month student loan payment. He also paid a security deposit of 2 months' rent from which he could be earning 8 percent after taxes.

Seyed has researched the recurring costs of homeownership. He has found that the real estate tax rate is $0.91 per $100 of assessed value and homeowner's insurance policies cost approximately $275 per year. He is unsure of the maintenance costs but estimates them at $350 per year.

He likes the idea of owning his own home because as real estate values increase the value of his home will increase instead of his rent payment. Local property values have been increasing at 5 percent per year over the last 7 years even with the recent economic downturn, and real estate sales commissions equal 6 percent of the purchase price. One of his concerns about buying a home is the immediate cost of the down payment and closing costs. These closing costs, he has found, include a 1 percent origination fee, 2 discount points on the mortgage, and 3 percent of the home purchase price in various other fees due at closing. He also knows that he would pay a 20 percent down payment up front to qualify for financing. Another concern is the lost investment income on this money that is currently earning an 8 percent after-tax return.

Questions

1. Write a short description of the four types of housing generally available for Seyed.

2. List several sources of information applicable to any real estate purchase that might be helpful to Seyed in making a decision. Should he consider prequalifying?

3. Use the lending guidelines to determine the maximum dollar amount that he could spend per month on his home payment (PITI).

4. Calculate Seyed's monthly PITI payment. To calculate principal and interest (PI) assume he has purchased a home for $140,000 and has a $112,000, 30-year, 7.625 percent fixed-rate mortgage. To calculate the local real estate taxes (T) use the real estate tax rate as given in the case, assuming the property has an assessed value of $128,000. Also include Seyed's projected homeowner's insurance (I) cost as given in the case.

5. Complete Worksheet 10 to determine if Seyed should buy or continue renting. To purchase the house considered in question 4, Seyed would pay $6,000 in closing costs including $2,500 in discount points. Consider a 1- and 7-year time horizon.

6. Seyed is now considering a house that is selling for $180,000. Estimate the dollar amount Seyed should be prepared to pay on the day of closing. Assume an interest rate of 8.625 percent, closing costs of 5 percent of the sales price, and a 20 percent down payment.

7. Assuming the house in question 6 is appraised for $180,000 and the information in the case concerning the taxes and insurance holds true, can Seyed afford the home if he finances it for 15 years? 20 years? 30 years? Why or why not? Use Worksheet 11 to guide your answer. (*Hint:* Remember the qualification amount will be the lowest of the three values on the worksheet—not the highest.)

8. Will Seyed need private mortgage insurance? Will he need a gift letter?

9. Given his risk tolerance, what type of mortgage would you recommend to Seyed? Should he consider an interest-only mortgage?

Be a Financial Planner—Continuing Case: Cory and Tisha Dumont

Part II: Managing Your Money

Cory and Tisha are back asking for your help, only this time the topics are cash management, credit use, and major purchases. Tempting credit card offers continue to come in the mail. Recall that they have Visa, MasterCard, Discover, and American Express credit cards as well as several other store cards, with a combined average balance of $1,300. Minimum monthly payments equal approximately $50 although they typically pay $100 per month.

Tisha's sister and her husband just bought their first home, making Tisha even more anxious to move from their rented house. Cory wants to wait awhile longer before buying a home and has suggested that they should replace their older high-mileage car. Cory and Tisha realize that funds for another payment are limited, not to mention money for a house payment. Their options are to reduce payments on their credit cards or to reduce other expenses. At any rate, $300 a month seems to be the maximum amount available for an auto loan, not to mention any likely increase in their auto insurance premium associated with the new vehicle. Help them answer the following questions.

Questions

1. As a result of a recent corporate merger, Tisha is eligible to join a credit union. What are the advantages and disadvantages of doing so instead of remaining with a commercial bank?

2. Should they consider online banking? What are the advantages and disadvantages when compared to traditional banking services?

3. The Dumonts' commercial bank was recently bought by a large, out-of-state bank. Because required minimum balances and bank fees have increased, the Dumonts have considered shopping for a new bank. What factors should they consider?

4. When considering the credit union, online, and bank alternatives, what three general factors should the Dumonts review for each? How might debit card services and costs vary with each?

5. The Dumonts have asked your advice on using a CD, money market mutual fund or asset management account for their emergency fund. What is the best choice? Why? Is there another type of account they should consider? Why is the balance between liquidity and return so important with an emergency fund?

6. The newsletter enclosed with their bank statement had articles on blocking as well as the safety and convenience of stored value cards. Briefly explain how the Dumonts can avoid problems with blocking. What cautions should they consider with stored value cards?

7. Which provides the higher after-tax yield: the Dumonts' 3 percent bank savings account or a federal and state tax-free money market fund yielding 2.25 percent? The Dumonts are in the 15 percent federal marginal tax bracket.

8. The *Money* article recommended that you "pay yourself first." Tisha is not sure how to do this but likes the idea of "saving money without having to think about it." Give her some advice about ways to "automate" her savings.

9. Because of his concern over "financial surprises," Cory wants to learn more about identity theft. What practices should he and Tisha follow to protect themselves?

10. The Dumonts' take-home pay (after deductions for taxes and benefits) is approximately $5,175 monthly. Current nonmortgage debt payments equal $911 (i.e., $405 auto, $100 miscellaneous credit, $196 student loan, and $210 furniture). Calculate and interpret their debt limit ratio. Assume they could purchase another auto with a $300 monthly payment. Calculate and interpret their revised debt limit ratio. What advice would you give the Dumonts about purchasing another vehicle?

11. Concerned that they might depend on credit too much, Tisha and Cory have asked you about the typical warning signs of excessive credit use. List five to eight of those signs. What alternatives should they consider if they occasionally can't pay their bills on time?

12. What is the maximum number of credit cards recommended? Given what you know about the typical characteristics of the cards Cory and Tisha carry, what recommendations would you make about keeping or canceling their cards? Consider the advantages and disadvantages of each type and class of card. How does the FICO score calculation affect your recommendation? Also, what card features are important to "credit users" as opposed to "convenience users"?

13. In anticipation of purchasing a home, Cory and Tisha have been advised to check their credit report. Why? What is the role of the credit bureau, the credit report, and the FICO score in the determination of creditworthiness and the cost of credit? How can they get their credit report? What are the Dumonts' alternatives if they find erroneous information in their credit report?

14. What are the "five Cs" of credit? Define and explain each, based on the information provided about the Dumont household.

15. Cory and Tisha are convinced that "good debt" means "cheap debt." Help them identify one or two sources of credit that would be categorized as inexpensive, more expensive, or most expensive. Where would payday loans fit? Why?

16. Discussions over lunch where Tisha works often turn to "making ends meet." One coworker has been to a credit counselor, while another is currently processing a debt consolidation loan application. Are these alternatives helpful for those who can't pay their bills? What two fundamental strategies are imperative for someone recovering from credit overuse?

17. Help Cory and Tisha apply the four steps of the smart buying process to decide whether or not to replace their car. What sources of consumer information might be useful to them?

18. A recent TV advertisement offered a lease option for $259 a month on a car that both Tisha and Cory like. It fits their budget, but they are unsure of the contract obligations. What criteria should they consider to determine if leasing is their best alternative? What cautions would you give them about an open-end lease compared to a closed-end lease?

19. If Cory and Tisha decide to purchase rather than lease another car, what factors must they consider when comparing a new or used car purchase? What factors should they consider in determining whether to sell their car outright or trade it in toward their next purchase?

20. Cory and Tisha found a used car that costs $12,000. They can finance through their bank for 8.75 percent interest for a maximum of 48 months. The rate for new car financing is 7.50 percent for 60 months or 7.35 percent for 48 months. If they could find a comparably priced new vehicle, how much would they save per month in interest charges if they finance the vehicle for 48 months?

21. Considering the information in question 20, how much interest would be saved if the Dumonts financed the used vehicle for 36 months, instead of 48 months, if the rate remains the same?

22. In reviewing the sample auto loan contract, Cory and Tisha questioned the term "secured loan." They also were unsure of the terms "default," "repossession," and "deficiency payment clause." Explain these terms. What can they do to avoid repossession?

23. In a few years Tisha and Cory might want to consider a home equity loan to finance a car purchase or to help pay for Chad's or Haley's college costs. What are the advantages and disadvantages of using this credit source as opposed to the typical auto or student loan? Specifically, what are the tax consequences?

24. Last week, the local newspaper mortgage rate column reported that a 30-year fixed-rate mortgage was 6.5 percent, while the rate for a 7-year balloon payment mortgage was 5.75 percent (payments calculated on the basis of 30-year amortization). A 1-year ARM was available for 5.5 percent (payments calculated on the basis of 30-year amortization). Assuming a loan amount of $120,000, calculate the payment for each mortgage. Aside from the significant differences in the mortgage payment amounts, what other factors should the Dumonts consider when choosing their mortgage? What are the advantages and disadvantages of an interest-only mortgage?

25. Based on their gross monthly income of $7,000 and monthly debt repayments of $911, what is the maximum mortgage amount for which Cory and Tisha could currently qualify? Monthly real estate tax (T) and homeowners insurance (I) are estimated at $170 per month. Calculate the mortgage amount using both the 28 percent qualification rule and the 36 percent qualification rule. (*Hint:* Refer to Figure 8.7 or use Worksheet 11.) Use 7 percent as the current rate of interest and assume a 30-year, fixed-rate mortgage.

26. How has Cory's student loan affected his creditworthiness in applying for a mortgage? What is the relationship between PITI and consumer credit when calculating the 36 percent qualification rule?

27. Compare the Dumonts' monthly mortgage payment for PITI in question 25 with their current monthly rent and renter's insurance cost of $1,300. Should Cory and Tisha consider purchasing a house that would require their maximum qualification mortgage loan amount? Defend your answer.

28. Given the maximum mortgage qualification amount determined in question 25, calculate a 20 percent down payment. If closing costs average 5 percent of the cost of the house, how much will they need on the day of closing? How does this compare with the $13,000 in the stock market index mutual fund account for their house down payment?

29. Using the monthly PI payment for the maximum mortgage qualification amount in question 25, calculate the total cost of the Dumonts' home if the mortgage is not paid off early. How much of this cost is interest?

30. Tisha would like to consider a 15-year mortgage so that the house would be paid for before Haley enters college. Explain how the factors of monthly payment, total interest paid, time value of money, and the effect of taxes impact this decision.

31. Briefly explain the concepts of one-time, recurring, and maintenance and operating costs to Cory and Tisha. How should they consider these three categories of costs when shopping for their home?

Appendix

Crunchin' the Numbers— Calculations for Figure 8.6

FIGURE 8A.1 Worksheet for the Rent-Versus-Buy Decision Calculations

ASSUMPTIONS: Buying option: $20,000 down and an $80,000, 30-year mortgage at 8%. Rental option: $900 per month. Time Frames: 1 year and 7 years; 28% marginal tax rate; after-tax rate of return = 5%; house appreciates in value at 3% per year; sales commission is 5% of the price of the house; closing costs = $5,000, which includes 2 points.

COST OF RENTING

	1 Year	7 Years	Your Numbers
a. Total monthly rent costs (monthly rent $900 × 12 months × no. years)	a. $10,800	a. $75,600	_____
b. Total renter's insurance (annual renter's insurance $250 × no. years)	+ b. $250	+ b. $1,750	_____
c. After-tax opportunity cost of interest lost because of having to make a security deposit (security deposit of $1,800 × after-tax rate of return of 5% × no. years)	+ c. $90	+ c. $630	_____
d. **Total cost of renting (lines a + b + c)**	= d. $11,140	= d. $77,980	_____

COST OF BUYING

e. Total mortgage payments (monthly payments $587.01 × 12 months × no. years)	e. $7,044.12	e. $49,308.84	_____
f. Property taxes on the new house (property taxes of $2,200 × no. years)	+ f. $2,200	+ f. $15,400	_____
g. Homeowner's insurance (annual homeowner's insurance $600 × no. years)	+ g. $600	+ g. $4,200	_____
h. Additional operating costs beyond those of renting. Maintenance, repairs, and any additional utilities and heating costs (additional annual operating costs $500 × no. years)	+ h. $500	+ h. $3,500	_____
i. After-tax opportunity cost of interest lost because of having to make a down payment (down payment of $20,000 × after-tax rate of return of 5% × no. years)	+ i. $1,000	+ i. $7,000	_____
j. Closing costs, including points (closing costs of $5,000)	+ j. $5,000	+ j. $5,000	_____
k. Less savings: Total mortgage payments going toward the loan principal*	− k. $668.26	− k. $6,017.84	_____
l. Less savings: Estimated appreciation in the value of the home less sales commission at the end of the period (current market value of house $100,000 × annual growth in house value of 3% × no. years − sales commission at end of the period of 5% × future value of house)	− l. −($2,150)†	− l. $14,950	_____
m. **Equals: Total cost of buying a home for those who do not itemize (lines e + f + g + h + i + j − k − l)**	= m. $17,825.86	= m. $63,441.00	_____
Additional savings to home buyers who itemize			
n. Less savings: Tax savings from the tax-deductibility of the interest portion of the mortgage payments (total amount of interest payments made × marginal tax rate of 28%)	− n. $1,785.24	− n. $12,121.48	_____
o. Less savings: Tax savings from the tax-deductibility of the property taxes on the new house (property taxes of $2,200 × marginal tax rate of 28% × no. years)	− o. $616	− o. $4,312	_____
p. Less savings: Tax savings from the tax-deductibility of the points portion of the closing costs (total points paid of $1,600 × marginal tax rate of 28%)	− p. $448	− p. $448	_____
q. **Total cost of buying a home to homebuyers who itemize (line m minus lines n through p)**	= q. $14,976.62	− q. $46,559.52	_____
Advantage of buying to those who *do not itemize* = Total cost of renting − total cost of buying for those who *do not itemize*: if negative, rent; if positive, buy (line d − line m)	− $6,685.86	− $14,539.00	_____
Advantage of buying to those who *itemize* = Total cost of renting − total cost of buying for those who *itemize*: if negative, rent; if positive, buy (line d − line q)	− $3,836.62	− $31,420.48	_____

*The total interest and principal payments can be calculated directly or approximated. To approximate the total annual interest payments, multiply the outstanding size of the loan by the interest rate, in this case $80,000 × 0.08 = $6,400, then multiply this by the number of years. In the case of the 1-year time horizon, the approximation method yields $6,400 of total interest while a direct calculation yields $6,375.86. While the approximation method works well for short time horizons, it is less accurate for longer time horizons.

†Note: If you only own the home for 1 year, the value here is negative, meaning the sales commission is greater than the appreciation in home value. Thus, this is an additional cost, not a savings, and we are subtracting a negative—in effect, adding the $2,150 to the cost of buying the house.

PART 3
Protecting Yourself with Insurance

Now that you have an understanding of the financial planning process and managing your money, it's time to turn your attention to protecting yourself with insurance. In putting together your financial plan, insurance is an extremely important topic. After all, the unexpected can happen, and when it does you want to make sure that your financial plan, and the chance to achieve your financial goals, don't vanish.

Part 3: Protecting Yourself with Insurance begins with an examination of life and health insurance. We will gain an understanding of your needs for life insurance, and whether you even need it. We will also look at health care and what provisions in a health care plan might be important to you. We will then turn our attention to property and liability insurance, both homeowner's and automobile insurance, and look at how to file an insurance claim.

In Part 3, we will specifically focus on:

Principle 7: Protect Yourself Against Major Catastrophes—Without question, the worst time to find out that you don't have the right amount or right kind of insurance is just after a tragedy occurs. What makes purchasing insurance a problem is that it is extremely difficult to compare policies because of the many subtle differences they contain. Remember, the focus of this book is on planning and control, and while we can't control the unexpected, we can plan in such a way that it does not prevent us from achieving our lifetime goals.

In addition, in Part 3 we will also touch on Principle 8: Risk and Return Go Hand in Hand.

Life and Health Insurance

Learning Objectives

 Understand the importance of insurance.

 Determine your life insurance needs and design a life insurance program.

 Describe the major types of coverage available and the typical provisions that are included.

 Design a health care insurance program and understand what provisions are important to you.

 Describe disability insurance and the choices available to you.

Explain the purpose of long-term care insurance and the provisions that might be important to you.

I f you were asked who you felt had the greatest need for life insurance—who would you pick, Batman or Fred Flintstone? In a recent survey, 1,000 Americans were asked that question and the winner, by an almost 2-to-1 margin, was Batman! Well, as you will learn in this chapter—they got it wrong. There's no question that Batman lives a dangerous life, but he is unmarried and wealthy, and as a result doesn't need life insurance. How about Fred Flintstone? Well, he's the primary breadwinner for the Flintstones and if something were to happen to him, life insurance would allow Wilma and Pebbles to maintain their standard of living.

How about Jack Bauer, who lives in the TV world of *24*? If you don't know, Jack Bauer, played by Kiefer Sutherland, works out of the Counter Terrorist Unit (CTU) in

Los Angeles where he has prevented a number of terrorist attacks on the United States. Jack probably needs both life and health insurance. Similar to Batman, he lives a dangerous life, but unlike Batman, Jack has a daughter, Kim, who was left by her husband at a time when she didn't have a job (in season 5), has a daughter, and lives in a world of danger. While Jack's life insurance as a government employee is his annual salary plus $2,000, Jack should probably get some additional life insurance. How much will that life insurance policy cost Jack? Judging by his job, and the fact that there's always a terrorist trying to kill him, it will most likely be pretty expensive. After all, the higher the probability that you'll someday use your life insurance policy, the more expensive it tends to be.

How about health insurance for Jack? Fortunately, he's covered through his job at CTU, but he'll want to make sure that his daughter Kim has health insurance, even if he has to pay for it himself. One other type of insurance we'll look at in this chapter is disability insurance. Because Jack has such a dangerous job, he might want some additional coverage to supplement what the government provides him. But once again, because he has such a dangerous job, his disability insurance will be quite expensive.

No one likes to think about illness or disability, let alone put a lot of effort or money into insuring against it. However, health insurance is an issue none of us can afford to dismiss. Similarly, most of us would prefer to avoid thinking about and planning for our deaths. As a result, when the time is right to get our first life insurance policy, most of us do not seek it out—instead, someone approaches us, convinces us it's important, and then we buy it. Because insurance has a language all its own, it is often difficult to understand all the differences between one policy and another, and to know how much to buy.

Life insurance is also an odd thing to purchase—it's not meant to benefit you. Hey, you're dead—you no longer have any needs. When you consider your need for life insurance, you must keep in mind its purpose: to protect your dependents in the event of your death. Life insurance can give you peace of mind by ensuring that your dependents will have the financial resources to pay off your debts and keep their home, and that your children will be able to go to college and live comfortably.

Most college students, as a rule, don't have a need for life insurance—they tend to be single and have no dependents. That doesn't mean they won't buy life insurance, especially if a persuasive salesperson comes to call. It is still vital to have a basic understanding of both life insurance and health insurance. In this chapter, we will examine the types of coverage available and the process of buying insurance. After all, the unexpected can happen—and it can happen to you.

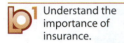 Understand the importance of insurance.

The Importance of Insurance

The need for both life and health insurance arises from **Principle 7: Protect Yourself Against Major Catastrophes.** The key concepts here are *planning* and *control*. After all, this whole book is based on controlling your financial situation through careful planning. If you plan carefully enough, you can control your finances even after your death.

An insurance policy is a contract with an insurance company that spells out what losses are covered, what the policy costs, and who receives payments if a loss occurs. Whether or not to take out an insurance policy is a matter of risk–return trade-offs. Are you willing to pay for an insurance policy to cover your risks? To start you on the road to understanding insurance, let's take a look at some of the basic ideas behind it, beginning with the relationship of insurance to risk.

Why Are Health and Life Insurance So Important?

Health insurance provides protection for you and your family against financially devastating medical bills. Life insurance protects your family in case you die. If you haven't planned wisely, your death could be a financial catastrophe for your dependents.

Why Is It So Costly?

Today, health care is costly, primarily because there is a lack of incentive to economize. Presently, over 50 percent of Americans receive some government health care entitlements, such as Medicare or Medicaid, and most Americans have medical insurance. As a result, there simply isn't any incentive for patients, doctors, or hospitals to exercise restraint in medical billing. If you aren't paying out of your own pocket, why should you care what your bills are? And if these bills are certain to be paid, why should doctors or hospitals care how much they charge?

A second reason that health care is so costly is that today's medical care has become extremely sophisticated. For example, it now takes 12 years and costs over $230 million to develop, test, and certify a new drug, and drug companies are passing these costs on to patients. Finally, the cost of litigation from malpractice suits has skyrocketed. It's not uncommon for doctors to pay malpractice insurance premiums of $150,000 or $250,000 per year. These costs, too, are then passed directly on to patients.

What Do These High Costs Mean for You?

First, medical care and medical insurance must become more efficient if we're to continue to be able to afford quality health care. This change may mean that your doctor joins an HMO, or your company's insurance policy no longer covers all your health care expenses. It also means that many companies will try to cut down on their health care costs by providing only limited insurance coverage or hiring temporary workers who don't get a full benefits package.

What About Those Who Have No Health Insurance?

That's one of the things the **Patient Protection and Affordable Care Act,**[1] which was signed into law in 2010, tries to address. The Congressional Budget Office (CBO) estimates that by the time the new law, much of which goes into effect in 2014, is fully implemented, it will provide health coverage to over 32 million Americans who are currently without health insurance, and as a result over 95 percent of Americans will then have health care insurance. Still, that means that 5 percent of Americans will not have health insurance.

Insurance is important—that's why Congress passed the Affordable Care Act. In putting together your personal financial plan, insurance needs to be a top priority. As medical costs go through the roof, so does your risk of having your financial roof cave in due to health-related problems. Without appropriate insurance, one accident or one illness can ruin your whole financial plan.

Later in the chapter we will take a close look at all the ins and outs of health insurance. First, however, let's look in detail at life insurance. We'll find out all we need to know, so that your dependents are taken care of in case of your death, and so that you can rest easy, knowing that this is the case.

Patient Protection and Affordable Care Act
Commonly referred to as the Affordable Care Act, this major health care act was signed into law in 2010 and put in place comprehensive health insurance reforms to take effect over the following 4 years and beyond, with most changes taking place by 2014.

Determining Your Life Insurance Needs

 2 Determine your life insurance needs and design a life insurance program.

Unless medical science comes up with something mighty impressive in the next few years, we all have to die sometime. Life insurance allows you to eliminate or at least substantially reduce the financial consequences of your death for your dependents.

Do You Need Life Insurance?

Insurance is based on the concept of **risk pooling**, which means that individuals share the financial risks they face. The logic behind risk pooling is drawn from the idea of diversification. Life insurance allows individuals to pool the financial risks associated with death. In effect, everyone pays something into the "pool." When an insured person dies, his or her family receives some of the money from the pot, which offsets the lost income due to death.

The amount that everyone puts into the pot is called a **premium**, and the size of the premium depends on the probability of when you will die. To determine your chance of death, insurance companies employ **actuaries**, statisticians who specialize in estimating the probability of death based on personal characteristics, such as your age and your general health, as well as lifestyle specifics such as whether or not you exercise. Insurance companies are able to predict with a good deal of accuracy the number of deaths that will occur in a given population of policyholders and charge each policyholder a fair premium. Smokers stand a much higher risk of dying than do nonsmokers, for example, so smokers are charged higher premiums.

Risk Pooling
Sharing the financial consequences associated with risk.

Premium
A life insurance payment.

Actuaries
Statisticians who specialize in estimating the probability of death based on personal characteristics.

---

[1]At the time of writing, the Affordable Care Act was being challenged in court by more than two dozen states that joined a lawsuit stating the health care law was unconstitutional.

Face Amount or Face of Policy
The amount of insurance provided by the policy at death.

Insured
The person whose life is insured by the life insurance policy.

Policyholder or Policy Owner
The individual or business that owns the life insurance policy.

Beneficiary
The individual designated to receive the insurance policy's proceeds upon the death of the insured.

The amount of insurance provided by the policy at death is called the **face amount** or **face of policy**. The **insured** is the person whose life is insured by the life insurance policy. Sometimes the policy is owned (or "held") by an individual, and other times it's held by a business. In either case, the owner is referred to as the **policyholder** or **policy owner**. The individual designated by the owner of the life insurance policy to receive the insurance policy's proceeds upon the death of the insured is called the **beneficiary**.

How do you know whether you need life insurance? Well, as we said, the purpose of life insurance is to provide for your dependents in the event of your death. If you're single and have no dependents, you generally don't need life insurance. However, you still might want to buy life insurance if you're at a higher risk of contracting a terminal illness, such as cancer or AIDS, or an uninsurable condition that could prevent later purchases of insurance, such as diabetes or heart disease. Although insurance policies don't pay off until you are dead, if you're terminally ill it's possible to receive a reduced settlement, similar to borrowing against your policy, or to sell your insurance policy at a discount before you die. For those with a high risk of serious health problems, a life insurance policy can be viewed as a form of health insurance. For anyone without a spouse or dependents, life insurance simply doesn't make sense.

If you do have a spouse or dependents, then life insurance can help make up for the wages lost as a result of your death. In addition to replacing lost income, it can cover burial expenses, medical and hospital expenses not covered by your health insurance, outstanding bills and loans, and attorney's fees related to estate settlement. Life insurance can also be used to provide funds for housing and for your children's education.

In determining whether or not you need life insurance, think back to what we said about the purpose of life insurance at the opening of this chapter—it's not meant to benefit the insured but those left behind. Table 9.1 provides a list of who might need life insurance.

How Much Life Insurance Do You Need?

Let's say you need life insurance. The question then becomes *how much* do you need? The first step is deciding what your priorities and goals are. Do you want to provide

---

TABLE 9.1 Should You Buy Life Insurance?

Life insurance is not necessary if:

You're single and don't have any dependents.

You're married, a double-income couple, with no children. Consider life insurance only if you're concerned that your surviving spouse's lifestyle will suffer if you die.

You're married but aren't employed. Consider life insurance only if you have young children and your spouse would have financial problems with day care and housekeeping if you die.

You're retired. Consider life insurance only if your spouse couldn't live on your savings, including Social Security and your pension, if you die.

Consider life insurance if:

You have children. You should have coverage for raising and educating your children until they are financially self-sufficient.

You're married, a single-income couple, with no children. You should have insurance to allow your surviving spouse to maintain his or her lifestyle until he or she can become self-sufficient.

You own your own business. A life insurance policy can allow your family to pay off any business debt if you die.

The value of your estate is over the estate tax-free transfer threshold, which was $3.5 million in 2009. Life insurance can be an effective tool for passing on an estate without incurring taxes.

enough money for your kids to go to college? Do you want to leave enough money for your wife to buy her own home? Do you want to provide your husband with enough money to live on for the next few years while he takes care of the kids? Different people are going to have different philosophies about providing for their survivors, and none of those philosophies is right or wrong.

After deciding your goals, the next step in figuring out how much insurance you need involves some numbers. Start with your net worth, because the larger your net worth, the more you have in the way of wealth to support your dependents, and consequently the less life insurance you need. Don't forget to throw in numbers to compensate for inflation and the earnings on possible future investments.

Is the process starting to sound complicated? Luckily, there are two basic approaches you can use to crunch the numbers that will tell you how much life insurance you need: (1) the earnings multiple approach and (2) the needs approach.

Earnings Multiple Approach   Some financial planners suggest that you purchase life insurance that covers from 5 to 15 times your annual gross income. The **earnings multiple approach** is used to figure out exactly how much insurance this amounts to. This method doesn't take into account your individual level of savings or your financial well-being.

Earnings Multiple Approach
A method of determining exactly how much life insurance you need by using a multiple of your yearly earnings.

The earnings multiple approach is based on the notion that you want to replace a stream of annual income that's lost due to the death of a breadwinner. That is, you want to replace one stream of annual income with another. What this approach does is tell you how big a lump-sum settlement you would need to replace that stream of annual income.

Actually, a stream of annual income for a set number of years is just like the annuities we looked at in Chapter 3. The earnings multiple approach works the same way present value of annuity problems work. To determine the lump-sum settlement you need, simply multiply your present annual gross income by the appropriate earnings multiple.

Table 9.2 provides an abbreviated table of earnings multiples. To simplify the presentation (and speed the sale), many insurance agents present the earnings multiple numbers without explaining the logic behind them. You need to keep in mind,

TABLE 9.2 Earnings Multiples for Life Insurance

Number of Years You Want the Lost Earnings Stream Replaced	After-Tax, After-Inflation Return Assumed on the Insurance Settlement		
	3%	**4%**	**5%**
3 years	2.83	2.76	2.73
5 years	4.58	4.45	4.33
7 years	6.23	6.00	5.79
10 years	8.53	8.11	7.72
15 years	11.94	11.12	10.38
20 years	14.88	13.59	12.46
25 years	17.41	15.62	14.09
30 years	19.06	17.29	15.37
40 years	23.12	19.79	17.16
50 years	25.73	21.48	18.26

then, that the earnings multiple that applies to your situation depends entirely on the number of years you need the lost income stream and the rate of return that you assume you can earn on the insurance settlement. The longer you need to replace the income stream, the greater the multiple. The higher the return you believe you can earn on the settlement, the lower the multiple.

Let's examine how this approach might be applied to Leonard and Nancy Cohen. Leonard is the breadwinner, making a cool $80,000 per year. The Cohens currently have two young children, ages 2 and 4, and they don't plan to have any more. The kids won't be self-supporting for another 20 years, and Leonard and Nancy want to make sure they're provided for if something happens to Leonard. Nancy's a good investor and is sure she could get a 5 percent return, after taxes and inflation, on an invested insurance settlement.

How much life insurance do the Cohens need? Rather than simply multiply Leonard's salary times the earnings multiple, we need to first adjust his salary downward to compensate for the fact that the family's living expenses will drop slightly with Leonard's death. Generally, family living expenses fall by about 30 percent with the loss of an adult family member if there's only one surviving family member. The larger the size of the surviving family, the less the living expenses drop as a percentage of total family expenses. For example, expenses drop by only 26 percent for a surviving family of two, or 22 percent for a surviving family of three, and they continue to drop another 2 percent for each additional surviving family member. To calculate the Cohens' target replacement salary, we adjust Leonard's present salary downward by multiplying it by a factor of (1 − 0.22), or 0.78. The target replacement salary thus becomes $80,000 × 0.78 = $62,400.

Now we're ready to use the earnings multiples. Remember, we need to measure these amounts in today's dollars. In this case, $n = 20$ years and $i = 5$ percent. Looking in the earnings multiples in Table 9.2, we find an earnings multiple of 12.46. Multiplying Leonard's adjusted salary by this factor, we get $777,504. That is, under the earnings multiple approach, the level of life insurance needed becomes:

$$\begin{matrix} \text{life insurance} \\ \text{needs} \end{matrix} = \begin{matrix} \text{income stream} \\ \text{to be replaced} \end{matrix} \times \left[1 - \begin{matrix} \text{percentage of family income} \\ \text{spent on deceased's needs} \end{matrix} \right] \times \begin{matrix} \text{earnings} \\ \text{multiple} \end{matrix}$$

$$= \$80,000 \times (1 - 0.22) \times 12.46$$

$$= \$777,504$$

Calculator Clues

Life Insurance Needs—The Present Value of an Annuity

Let's solve the problem above using a financial calculator. In this example, we're trying to find out how much life insurance we'd need to generate a 20-year $62,400 annuity, given a discount rate of 5 percent (we expect to earn 5 percent after inflation and taxes). That's the same as solving for the present value of an annuity.

Enter: 20   5   62,400   0
              [N]   [I/Y]   [PV]   [PMT]   [FV]

Solve for: −777,642

Aside from a bit of rounding error, this is what we got using the tables. As expected, you get a negative sign on the PV.

Keep in mind, though, that this method isn't very useful unless it considers the effects of taxes and inflation. Also, remember that this method considers only your income replacement needs, not your need to eliminate debt or save for specific goals. Most important, you've got to remember that your insurance needs are going to change over time. That means that your earnings multiple is going to change over time and that you're going to need to update your insurance coverage from time to time.

Needs Approach   The **needs approach** attempts to determine the funds necessary to meet the needs of a family after the death of the primary breadwinner. You can think of the earnings multiple as a "one size fits all" method and the needs approach as a customized method. It is a bit more complicated than the earnings multiplier, but it allows you to account for the fact that your family's needs may be different from the average. Let's look at some of those needs:

Needs Approach
A method of determining how much life insurance you need based on funds your family would require to maintain their lifestyle after your death.

- ◆ **Immediate needs at the time of death:** Sometimes called **cleanup funds**, these include final health costs, burial costs, inheritance taxes, estate taxes, and legal fees.

Cleanup Funds
Funds needed to cover immediate expenses at the time of your death.

- ◆ **Debt elimination funds:** Funds to cover outstanding debts, including credit card and consumer debt, car loans, and mortgage debt. For example, you may wish to reduce the financial burden on your spouse by paying off half of your outstanding mortgage principal.

- ◆ **Immediate transitional funds:** Funds needed to cover expenses such as new job training or a college degree for the surviving spouse and child care during this period. For spouses who are already employed, transitional funds may be used to cover a leave of absence.

> ## FACTS OF LIFE
> According to a recent study by LIMRA, 30 percent of U.S. households have no life insurance coverage—this compares to 22 percent without coverage in 2004. While not everyone needs life insurance, the study found that 11 million households with children younger than 18 have no life insurance.

- ◆ **Dependency expenses:** These are family expenses incurred while children are in school and dependent upon family support. One approach to determining current total household expenses is to use the deceased's income less annual savings as an estimate. Some of this amount may come from the surviving spouse's income as well as Social Security and the deceased's pension from his or her job.

- ◆ **Spousal life income:** Supplemental income for the surviving spouse after the children have left home and are self-supporting, but before the surviving spouse retires from whatever job he or she has.

- ◆ **Educational expenses for the children.**

- ◆ **Retirement income:** This would include any additional income stream that might be needed for the surviving spouse after retirement. It would make up for any shortfall after taking into account Social Security and pension benefits.

To use the needs approach, you must determine the dollar amount that would be needed by your family in each category. Fortunately, most people have assets or some existing insurance that will partially meet their life insurance needs. To calculate additional life insurance needs, you would take the total funds needed and subtract your available assets and insurance.

As you make your calculations, keep in mind that the time value of money is going to come into play if this approach is to have any meaning. For instance, your family will receive the insurance settlement when you die, but some of the uses for that settlement may be far off in the future—perhaps funding your children's college education. Sometimes insurance salespeople simply add up all the needs, regardless of how far off they are, and use that as a target level for life insurance. What that does is overestimate the amount of insurance you need.

Once you know how much life insurance you need, it's time to figure out what kind of insurance is available.

3 Describe the major types of coverage available and the typical provisions that are included.

Term Insurance
A type of insurance that pays your beneficiary a specific amount of money if you die while covered by the policy.

Cash-Value Insurance
A type of insurance that has two components: life insurance and a savings plan.

Major Types of Life Insurance

There are two major types of life insurance: term insurance and cash-value insurance. **Term insurance** is pure life insurance. You pay a set premium that's based on the probability of when you'll die. For that premium, you receive a set amount of coverage for a set number of years. Term insurance covers only a very specific period, or "term." If you die, your beneficiary receives your death benefits.

Cash-value insurance is more than simple life insurance. It has two components: life insurance and a savings plan. Some of your premiums go toward life insurance and some go toward savings. With cash-value insurance, when you die, your beneficiary is paid those savings as part of your death benefit. There's an almost infinite number of variations of cash-value insurance, and there are several different categories of term insurance. Table 9.3 summarizes them all, and we now examine them in detail.

Term Insurance and Its Features

As we mentioned earlier, term life insurance is pure life insurance that pays the beneficiary the death benefit of the policy if the insured dies during the coverage period. In effect, term insurance has no face value. Its sole purpose is to provide death benefits to the policyholder's beneficiaries.

The primary advantage of term insurance is its affordability. It's an inexpensive way of protecting your loved ones. The big disadvantage with term insurance is that

TABLE 9.3 What's What in Life Insurance				
Type of Policy	**Coverage Period**	**Annual Premium**	**Death Benefit**	**Cash Value**
Term Life Insurance	Provides protection for a specified time period, typically 1 to 30 years.	Least expensive form of life insurance. Low initial premium, with the premium increasing as the insured gets older.	Fixed death benefit.	No cash value.
Whole Life Insurance	Provides permanent protection.	The premium is fixed.	Fixed death benefit.	The cash value is fixed. The investment portion of the policy grows on a tax-deferred basis while the policy is in force.
Universal Life Insurance	Provides permanent protection.	Allows for flexible premium payments so that policyholders can vary the amount and timing of their payments as their financial needs change.	Death benefits are flexible, although proof of insurability may be required if you want to raise them.	The cash value of the policy depends on the level of payments made and the investment results of the insurance company. The investment portion of the policy grows on a tax-deferred basis while the policy is in force.
Variable Life Insurance	Provides permanent protection.	Allows for either fixed or flexible premium.	Death benefits are flexible, reflecting the performance of the mutual funds (subaccounts) in the death benefits account.	The cash value of the policy depends on the performance of the mutual funds (subaccounts) in the cash value account. The policyholder controls the investment risk, choosing the investment strategy for the policy.

the cost rises each time your policy is renewed. To counter that complaint, the insurance industry has recently begun to offer 30-year level-term policies. For example, in 2011, a 25-year-old nonsmoking male could lock in an annual rate of $503 for a policy with a $500,000 death benefit for 30 years from Genworth Financial.

Renewable Term Insurance   The "term" of the term life insurance contract can be 1, 5, 10, 20, or 30 years. Coverage terminates at the end of this period unless it's renewed. In general, most term insurance is **renewable term insurance**, which allows it to be continually renewed for an agreed-upon period or up to a specified age, often 65, 70, or 75 (and in some cases up to 94), regardless of the insured's health. Even if your health declines after you buy the policy, you're still able to renew your coverage.

The ability to renew term insurance is critical. After all, if you're basing your family's security on a life insurance policy that you suddenly can't renew, you've got a big problem. You shouldn't consider taking on term insurance that isn't renewable. Each time your contract is renewed, the premium is increased to reflect your increased age and the accompanying increase in the chance of mortality. Without proof of insurability (taking and passing another medical exam), most premiums increase dramatically at the end of the term period. Once an individual reaches the age of 55, the premiums increase rather rapidly, as can be seen in Figure 9.1.

Decreasing Term Insurance   Each time renewable term insurance is renewed, the premium increases. With **decreasing term insurance**, the premiums remain constant, but the face amount of the policy declines. If you purchase decreasing term insurance, you decide on a premium level, and the face amount—the amount of the death benefit to be paid—declines each year to reflect the increased probability that you'll die.

Decreasing term insurance is based on the assumption that your wealth will increase when your children leave home and become self-sufficient, and thus you will need less insurance. However, just because some individuals' insurance needs decline as they get older doesn't mean yours will. In addition, not all declining term

Renewable Term Insurance
A type of term insurance that can be renewed for an agreed-upon period or up to a specified age (usually 65 or 70) regardless of the insured's health.

Decreasing Term Insurance
Term insurance in which the annual premium remains constant but the face amount of the policy declines each year.

FIGURE 9.1 The Rising Cost of Yearly Renewable Term Insurance—Annual Premiums for $100,000 Coverage on a 35-Year-Old Nonsmoking Male

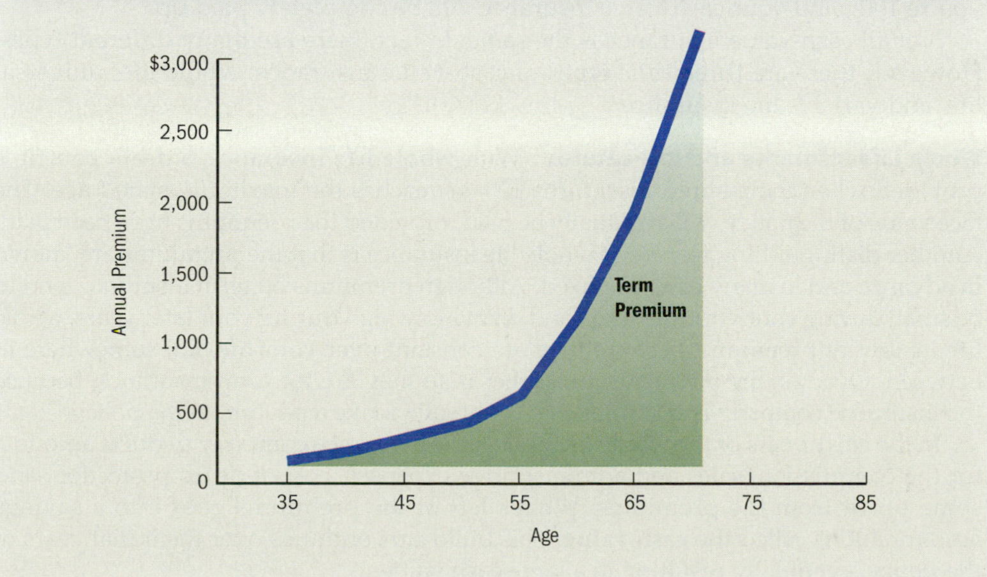

Group Term Insurance
Term insurance provided, usually without a medical exam, to a specific group of individuals, such as company employees, who are associated for some purpose other than to buy insurance.

Credit or Mortgage Group Life Insurance
Group life insurance that's provided by a lender for its debtors.

insurance policies decline the same way. Some decline at a constant, steady rate, and others decline at accelerating rates. What's important here is that you choose a policy that's going to cover your future needs completely.

Group Term Insurance   This type of insurance refers to the way the insurance is sold rather than to any unusual traits of the policy itself. **Group term insurance** is term insurance provided, usually without a medical exam, to a specific group of individuals who are associated for some purpose other than to buy insurance. The group may be employees of the same company or members of a common association or professional group. If it's an association or professional group, the members might be required to take a medical exam; most employee term insurance doesn't require an exam.

STOP & THINK

If, for example, you have a very low interest rate on your home mortgage, you may rather have your insurance proceeds go toward paying off some other more expensive debt. However, with mortgage group life insurance, you have no choice—it goes to pay off your mortgage. Who do you think mortgage insurance benefits the most?

Credit or Mortgage Group Life Insurance   One variation of group life insurance that's promoted by lending agencies is **credit** or **mortgage group life insurance**, which is simply group life insurance provided by a lender for its debtors. The level of coverage is enough to cover the individual's outstanding debt. If the debtor dies while the policy is in effect, the proceeds are used to pay off the debt.

Convertible Term Life Insurance
Term life insurance that can be converted into cash-value life insurance at the insured's discretion regardless of his or her medical condition and without a medical exam.

Convertible Term Life Insurance   Another category is **convertible term life insurance**, which refers to term life insurance that you can convert into cash-value life insurance (we'll look at this in detail next) at your discretion regardless of your medical condition and without a medical exam. Many times this conversion feature is only offered during the first years of the policy. The conversion may be accompanied by a corresponding increase in the premium.

Cash-Value Insurance and Its Features

Cash-value insurance is any insurance policy that provides both a death benefit and an opportunity to accumulate cash value. It's a permanent type of insurance—if you make the premium payments, eventually you'll get paid. At some point, you'll have made all the required premium payments (which in the extreme case could last until you're 100), and your cash-value insurance will be completely paid up.

Not all cash-value insurance is the same. In fact, there are many different types. However, there are three *basic* types of cash-value insurance: whole life, universal life, and variable life insurance.

Whole Life Insurance
Cash-value insurance that provides permanent coverage and a death benefit when the insured dies. If the insured turns 100, the policy pays off, even though the insured hasn't died.

Whole Life Insurance and Its Features   With **whole life insurance**, a death benefit is provided when the insured dies, turns 100, or reaches the maximum stated age. The face value of the policy will eventually be paid, provided the premiums have been paid. Another distinguishing feature of whole life insurance is that the premiums are known in advance and in many cases are fixed. Although premiums on term insurance tend to be small during your younger years and dizzyingly high during your later years, whole life insurance premiums, because they are constant over your life, fall somewhere in between. Over all, the payments are higher than they are for term insurance, because the insurance company is guaranteed to eventually make a payout on the policy.

In the early years of the whole life policy, the insurance company deducts amounts for the commission, sales and administrative expenses, cost of death protection, and some profit from the premiums. What's left of the premiums goes into a savings account and is called the **cash value**. This build-up continues over the initial years of the policy, eventually resulting in a large cash value.

Cash Value
The money that the policyholder is entitled to if the policy is terminated.

As time goes by and the policyholder ages, the premium, which remains constant, is no longer large enough to cover the death claim. Thus, in the later years the cash value is used to supplement the level premiums and provide the desired level of death coverage.

The cash value of the insurance policy is really the policyholder's savings. The policyholder can borrow against the policy's cash value or, alternatively, the policyholder can gain access to the cash value by terminating the policy. Access is gained by exercising the policyholder's nonforfeiture right. The **nonforfeiture right** gives the policyholder the policy's cash value in exchange for the policyholder giving up his or her right to a death benefit.

If the policyholder doesn't want cash, but instead wants insurance, the cash value can be used to purchase paid-up insurance—that is, insurance that doesn't have any additional payments due—or to buy extended term insurance. Many people see the nonforfeiture right as a major advantage to whole life—at least you get something back when you terminate the policy.

There are a number of different premium payment patterns available to whole life policyholders. *Continuous-*, *level-*, or *straight-premium whole life* requires the policyholder to pay a constant premium until the insured turns 100 or dies. With a *single-premium* or *single-payment whole life* policy, the policyholder makes only one very large initial payment. A hybrid of these two patterns is the *limited-premium whole life* policy, in which large premiums are required for a specified number of years, after which the policy is considered paid up.

For example, you may pay until you are 65, after which the policy is paid up. As with all whole life insurance, it then provides insurance protection for the insured's entire life or until the policy is terminated and the cash value is claimed. The size of the premiums depends, of course, on the number of premiums to be paid and the age of the insured. The popularity of the limited-payment plan stems from the fact that the payments will cease when retirement approaches, and at that point the policy has built up a significant cash value.

As with all else in the life insurance area, there are almost an unlimited number of variations on the whole life theme. One such variation worth noting is *modified whole life*. The premiums begin at a level below comparable whole life and gradually rise in steps until the final premiums are above those of comparable whole life. There are also *combination whole life* policies, which include elements of whole life and decreasing term insurance. The change in coverage is done in such a way that the face amount of the policy remains constant, with the coverage gradually shifting from term to whole life.

What are the primary disadvantages of whole life insurance? First, it doesn't provide nearly the level of death protection that term insurance does for the same price. Second, the yield on the cash value investment portion of the policy generally isn't competitive with yields on alternative investments.

However, whole life insurance does provide for both savings and permanent insurance needs. If you have a need for permanent insurance protection—perhaps you have a child or spouse who'll never be financially independent and for whom you must provide—then you should seriously consider whole life insurance.

Universal Life Insurance and Its Features

A **universal life insurance** policy is a type of cash-value insurance combining term insurance with a tax-deferred savings feature in a package in which both the premiums and benefits are flexible. Premiums can vary between the insurance company's minimum and the maximum premium level as set by the IRS.

Nonforfeiture Right
The right of a policyholder to choose to receive the policy's cash value in exchange for the policyholder giving up his or her right to a death benefit.

> **FACTS OF LIFE**
>
> Every year Taiwan has a Ghost Month, where tradition states that ghosts return to roam the earth—for the believers, this is pretty scary stuff. To ease people's minds, the Taiwan Central Insurance Company sells Ghost Month supplemental insurance that only covers that month. This insurance covers accidents on public transportation, fires, and earthquakes, whether or not the damage was caused by ghosts.

Universal Life Insurance
A type of cash value insurance that's much more flexible than whole life. It allows you to vary the premium payments and the level of protection.

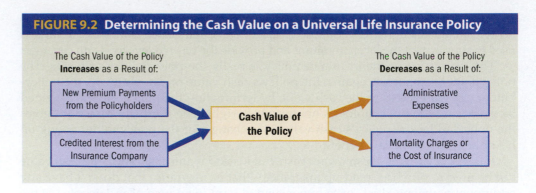

FIGURE 9.2 Determining the Cash Value on a Universal Life Insurance Policy

You start out by paying a premium dictated by the insurance company. After the company subtracts expenses and mortality charges to pay for the life insurance protection, the remainder of the premium plus interest is added to the cash value. Premium payments may then be increased or decreased by the policyholder, which will increase or decrease the cash value of the policy. You can also increase or decrease the death benefit. In effect, a universal life policy is much like a term insurance policy, with any additional premium going toward savings.

An important feature of universal life insurance is that the funds are broken down into three separate parts: the mortality charge or term insurance, the cash value or savings, and the administrative expenses. This unbundling is what gives the policyholder the flexibility to vary the premium payments. If you skip a payment or don't make one large enough to cover your mortality charge and the administrative expenses, the rest will simply be subtracted from the cash value. If the cash value isn't enough to cover the premium, the policy will lapse!

Although there are limits, if you make a huge payment, the amount greater than that needed to cover the mortality charge and the administrative expenses is credited to your cash value or savings. The relationship that determines the cash value is shown in Figure 9.2.

One of the shortcomings of universal life is that the returns fluctuate dramatically. Moreover, for many policyholders the flexibility to pass on making premium payments is just too tempting, and as a result many policies simply lapse. Finally, given fluctuating returns and high expense charges, you may not end up with as much in the way of savings as you had anticipated.

Variable Life Insurance
Insurance that provides permanent insurance coverage as whole life does; however, the policyholder, rather than the insurance company, takes on the investment risk.

The value of universal life is its flexibility. If you have uneven and fluctuating income and need to be able to skip premium payments, this form of insurance might appeal to you. Still, universal life should be approached with caution. Insurance policies should be purchased mainly for their insurance protection. With universal life, the insurance and administrative portions of the policy are very expensive.

STOP & THINK

Seeing a computer printout that shows with precision exactly what your cash-value life insurance policy will be worth in the future is impressive, but it may be meaningless. As with any other financial analysis, the results are all based on assumptions—if it's "garbage in," it's also "garbage out." Why do you think a salesperson might want to assume very high, unrealistic returns in the future?

Variable Life Insurance and Its Features   Another category is **variable life insurance**, which is aimed at individuals who want to manage their own investments and are willing to take risks. It's a type of whole life in which the cash value and death benefit are tied to and vary according to the performance of a set of investments chosen by the policyholder. The policyholder, rather than the insurance company, takes on the investment risk—that is, you decide how the cash value or savings portion of your policy is invested. If it does well, you benefit; if it bombs, you lose.

There are two basic forms of variable life: (1) straight variable life, which has fixed premiums; and (2) variable universal life, on which the premiums are flexible. The array of investment funds from which the policyholder chooses is quite large, including money market, bond, and stock funds. The returns are earned on a tax-deferred basis just as they are on other cash-value insurance forms. In fact, you can switch between different types of investment funds without suffering any tax consequences.

The cash value of a variable life insurance policy results from fixed premiums minus company expenses and the mortality charges (the cost of the term insurance). There is no guarantee of a minimum cash value, and what happens to the cash value doesn't affect the insurance company. In effect, variable life is similar to buying term insurance and investing money in mutual funds.

Term Versus Cash-Value Life Insurance

With all these different types of insurance, it can be pretty hard comparing policies and figuring out what you need. You could spend way too much of your waking hours—and even some of your sleeping hours if you're a vivid dreamer—trying to figure out what's best for you. We suggest starting off slowly. The basic question you need to ask yourself is whether you want term insurance or cash-value insurance.

For most individuals, term insurance is the better alternative. It provides for your life insurance needs at a relatively low cost, which is the real purpose of insurance. It allows for affordable coverage during the years in which you need life insurance most.

With cash-value insurance, the premiums are so high that you may be tempted to carry less insurance than you actually need. The only true advantages of cash-value insurance are tax advantages—the growth of the cash value on a deferred tax basis and the fact that life insurance isn't considered part of your estate. However, these advantages generally don't make cash-value insurance a good investment in a relative sense—other tax-deferred investment plans are better.

Fine-Tuning Your Policy: Contract Clauses, Riders, and Settlement Options

It's important to know that in the world of insurance there is really no "standard policy." In fact, there are actually hundreds of provisions that you can use to individualize your policy. Be sure that you carefully read this legal document before you sign on the dotted line. We will introduce some common features that appear in almost all insurance contracts.

Contract Clauses

Contract clauses are the particular provisions or stipulations that appear in your insurance policy.

Beneficiary Provision The primary beneficiary is the person designated to receive the death benefits when you die. This beneficiary can be a person, a business, or a trust. You will also name one or more contingent beneficiaries who will receive the death benefits only if the primary beneficiary dies before the benefits have been distributed.

Coverage Grace Period The **coverage grace period** gives you an extension of generally 30 days in which to make your premium payments without canceling your policy. During this period, the policy remains in force and you can make payments without penalty.

Coverage Grace Period
The late-payment period for premiums during which time the policy stays in effect and no interest is charged. If payments still aren't made, the policy can be canceled after the grace period.

FACTS OF LIFE

You can also insure specific body parts. Keith Richards, the Rolling Stones guitarist, has insured his hands.

Loan Clause   Cash-value policies include a **loan clause** that allows you to borrow against the cash value of the policy. The rate is usually quite favorable, there are no fees or carrying charges, and there is no maturity date on the policy loan. However, if you die with an outstanding policy loan, the death benefit will be reduced by the outstanding amount due. This would probably be contrary to your goals, and there might also be tax penalties associated with policy withdrawals.

Nonforfeiture Clause   The nonforfeiture clause defines the choices available to policyholders who miss premium payments, causing the policy to lapse. It protects the cash value of the policy. Options generally include receiving the policy's cash value, exchanging the policy's cash value for a paid-up policy with a reduced face value, and exchanging the policy's face value for a paid-up term policy. While no one should plan on letting a policy lapse, this clause can be very valuable if you should ever "just forget" or be unable to pay your premiums for an extended period.

Policy Reinstatement Clause   The **policy reinstatement clause** deals with the conditions necessary to restore a lapsed policy to its full force and effect, generally within 3 to 5 years after the policy has expired. You must pay all past-due premiums, interest, and policy loans.

Change of Policy Clause   The **change of policy clause** allows you to change the form of your policy. For example, you may want to convert your continuous-premium whole life policy to a limited-premium whole life so that your premium payments will cease. You might have to pass a physical examination first.

Suicide Clause   Virtually all insurance contracts include a suicide clause which states that the insurance company won't pay off for suicide deaths that occur within the first 2 years of the contract.

Payment Premium Clause   This clause defines how you will pay your premiums. Options include annual, semiannual, quarterly, or monthly. Annual payments are generally the cheapest.

Incontestability Clause   The incontestability clause states that the insurance company cannot dispute the validity of the contract after a specified period of time, usually 2 years. This clause is crucial. It protects your beneficiary against policy cancellations due to error, concealment, or innocent misstatement made by the insured on the original application.

Riders

Riders are special provisions that may be added to your policy, often at an additional cost, to provide extra benefits or features to a policy in order to meet your specific needs.

Waiver of Premium for Disability Rider   This type of rider allows your insurance protection to stay in place by paying your premium if you become disabled before you reach a certain age, usually 65. Because your need for insurance certainly doesn't diminish if you become disabled, this is a pretty good rider to have if it doesn't cost too much. Shop around—you might be able to cover your insurance expenses with a personal disability insurance plan for less.

Accidental Death Benefit Rider or Multiple Indemnity   An accidental death benefit rider increases the death benefit—doubling it in the case of "double indemnity" or tripling it in "triple indemnity"—if you die in an accident rather than from natural causes. It is usually an inexpensive rider because of the slim chance that the insurance company will ever have to pay it off.

Guaranteed Insurability Rider   A guaranteed insurability rider gives you the right to increase your life insurance protection in the future without a medical exam regardless of your health. It allows you to purchase additional coverage at specified times such as after the birth of a child, when you buy a house, or if you increase your business. It is insurance against future uninsurability and is a relatively inexpensive way to insure that you can get the additional coverage that you might need.

Cost-of-Living Adjustment (COLA) Rider   This rider increases your death benefits at the same rate as inflation without forcing you to pass a new medical exam, allowing you to keep up with expected increases in the cost of living.

Living Benefits Rider   Some cash-value policies allow for "living benefits" that grant an early payout of a percentage of the anticipated death benefits to the terminally ill insured. It usually requires a doctor's statement saying that you have 6 months to a year to live. These payments are made to the policyholder, not the beneficiary. This rider can often be added to a policy at any time, generally with no extra fee, and can offer peace of mind at a critical time by helping to offset medical costs.

Settlement or Payout Options

Settlement or payout options are alternative ways a beneficiary can choose to receive the policy benefits upon the death of the insured. It is important to keep in mind any possible tax implications regarding payout. In general, life insurance death benefits are not subject to income taxes.

Settlement or Payout Options
The alternative ways that a beneficiary can choose to receive the policy benefits upon the death of the insured.

Lump-Sum Settlement   A lump-sum settlement pays the entire death benefit, tax-free, to the beneficiary at one time. It allows the beneficiary to withdraw, use, and/or invest the funds in any way that he or she wishes. The primary drawback of a lump-sum settlement is that it requires the beneficiary to have the self-control and knowledge to manage it. The funds that you imagined would put your children through college might be sending them off on a trip to Disneyland in a new motor home. A single lump-sum payment may be an appropriate option, but if you choose it, it's wise to also work out a long-run financial plan with a professional financial planner.

Interest-Only Settlement   With an interest-only settlement, instead of receiving the death benefits immediately, they are left on deposit with the insurance company for a specified length of time earning interest that is tied to the market interest rate, with a guaranteed minimum rate. Your beneficiary will pay taxes on the interest earned after your death. There are many variations of this settlement method, including the option of partial or complete withdrawal of the cash value.

> ### STOP & THINK
>
> Why do you think medical bills are squeezing more families? While there are a number of reasons, part of the problem is that we all live longer than we did in the past. The life expectancy for a woman born in 1900 was 49; however, for a woman born in 2000, the life expectancy was 80. Medical costs rise as you live longer.

Installment-Payments Settlement   The cash value, including both interest and principal, is completely distributed over a fixed period or in fixed payments. When proceeds are taken in installments, the portion of each payment attributable to the basic death benefit is tax-free, but the portion attributable to interest earned on the proceeds is taxable. If you choose the fixed-period option, the size of the policy settlement, the number of payment periods, and the interest rate work together to determine the size of the payments.

Instead of choosing a fixed period for the distribution of the settlement, you can actually choose the specific amount of the fixed payments. In this case, the size of the policy settlement, the interest rate credited to the policy settlement, and the desired size of the payments work together to determine the number of periods over which payments will be received.

Calculator Clues

Calculating an Installment Payment Settlement

You can either calculate how much each payment would be, or if you have a certain amount you'd like to receive each year, you can determine the number of payments you will get.

Calculating the payment size is simply a matter of solving for the payment size (PMT), where PV is the policy settlement, I/Y is the interest rate credited to the policy settlement, and N is the number of periods over which the payments are to be made. Let's assume you want to receive annual payments for 20 years, the policy settlement is for $500,000, and the interest credited to the policy settlement is 8 percent. What is the payment's size?

Enter:	20	8	500,000		0
	N	I/Y	PV	PMT	FV
Solve for:				−50,926.10	

As expected, PMT takes on a negative sign, and you would receive annual payments of $50,926.10.

Solve for the number of payments—let's now assume you'd like your annual payments to be $75,000. How many annual payments would you receive?

Enter:		8	−500,000	75,000	0
	N	I/Y	PV	PMT	FV
Solve for:	9.9				

You'll notice we gave the present value, $500,000, a negative sign and the payment, $75,000, a positive sign. Why? Because a calculator looks at cash flows like it's a bank—we deposit our money in the bank (and the sign is negative because the money "leaves our hands"), and later we take our money out of the bank (and the sign is positive because the money "returns to our hands"). As a result, every problem will have a positive and negative sign on the cash flows.

Life Annuity Settlement   With a life annuity, the beneficiary receives income for life. Here are several of the variations that provide monthly income:

- ◆ **Straight Life Annuity:** Beneficiaries receive monthly payments regardless of how long they live. The insurance company's obligation ends when the beneficiary dies—even if it has been only 1 month! The insurance company keeps the remaining cash value. A young beneficiary receives a much smaller monthly payment than an older beneficiary, but the payments arrive for life.
- ◆ **Period Certain Annuity:** Payments are guaranteed for a certain period of time (e.g., 10–20 years). If the beneficiary dies before this certain period ends, the payments go to a secondary beneficiary.
- ◆ **Refund Annuity:** A refund annuity provides the beneficiary with income for life as well as bestowing any remaining death benefit on a secondary beneficiary if the primary beneficiary dies. The monthly payments will be smaller than those received under a straight life annuity because the insurance company will have to pay out more money over time.
- ◆ **Joint Life and Survivorship Annuity:** This option provides fixed monthly payments as long as one of two named beneficiaries remains alive. Generally, the

two beneficiaries are husband and wife, with the annuity providing them with income as long as one survives. Again, because the insurance company will have to pay out for a longer time, the monthly annuity payments are less than they would be for a straight life annuity.

Buying Life Insurance

Not all insurance *companies* are the same. When you put money in a bank, the government guarantees your account through the FDIC. There are no guarantees with life insurance. Although each state has a guarantee association to protect policyholders if an insurance company goes out of business, generally these state funds have no assets. If an insurance company goes under, the other insurance companies doing business in that state are "taxed" and the funds are used to take care of any claims.[2] As you can imagine, delays and confusion are common.

It's essential to choose an efficiently run life insurance company that will be around when your policy matures. Fortunately, the selection process is made much easier by a number of insurance rating services including A.M. Best, Fitch, Moody's, Standard & Poor's, and Weiss, which all rate the ability of insurance companies to pay off claims. Because you'll be charged a small fee for rating information if you call one of the rating agencies, the simplest way to get ratings is to go to your local library. Table 9.4 provides a listing of the insurance company ratings from each service and what they mean.

Selecting an Agent

Before you deal with an insurance agent, you should know a bit about how insurance sales work. First, keep in mind that most insurance agents make their living through commissions, so they're understandably eager to make a sale. Don't feel obligated to purchase your policy from an agent just because he or she did some research and put together a plan for you—that's the agent's job.

Because it's difficult to know all you might like to know about insurance, selecting your agent is extremely important. So how do you find a good agent? Well, it helps to be aware of the agent's professional designation. Is the agent simply licensed to sell insurance, or is he or she a chartered life underwriter (CLU), the most rigorous of all life insurance designations? To obtain this title, a life insurance salesperson must master both technical information on insurance and also show mastery in the related areas of finance, accounting, taxation, business law, and economics.

To begin the agent search process, make a list of prospects from good companies. This list can come from friends, colleagues, and relatives in addition to recommendations from bankers, accountants, and lawyers who specialize in personal financial planning. Next, interview the agents to find out which ones you feel comfortable with and whether they're full-time insurance agents with some degree of experience. Once you've selected several agents you feel comfortable with, have them give you a quote on your desired insurance plan.

> ### STOP & THINK
>
> It's not unusual for cash-value life insurance policies to have commissions of 80 to 100 percent of the first year's premium. The only way you can find out is to ask. Because this information may help you determine why one policy is being pushed instead of another, the size of the commission is good information to know. Why don't people ask?

---

[2]In addition, most states impose a limit on the amount of coverage they'll honor. These limits are generally $100,000 for cash value for an individual life policy, and $300,000 in death benefits, or $300,000 for all claims combined for an individual or family. These limits may be well below your desired coverage level.

TABLE 9.4 Insurance Company Ratings

Rating Description	A.M. Best	Fitch	Moody's	Standard & Poor's	Weiss
Superior Minimal risk of financial instability.	A++ A+	AAA	Aaa	AAA	A+
Excellent Financially strong with excellent ability to pay claims.	A A−	AA+ AA AA−	Aa1 Aa2 Aa3	AA+ AA AA−	A A−
Good Good ability to pay claims—stronger than the average company.	B++ B+	A+ A A−	A1 A2 A3	A+ A A−	B+ B B−
Adequate More risk than "good" rating.	B B−	BBB+ BBB BBB−	Baa1 Baa2 Baa3	BBB+ BBB BBB−	C+ C C−
Below Average Below average claims-paying ability and financial strength.	C++ C+	BB+ BB BB−	Ba1 Ba2 Ba3	BB+ BB BB−	D+ D D−
Financially Weak High degree of risk and vulnerable to default.	C C− D	B+ B B−	B1 B2 B3 D	B+ B B−	E+ E E−
Nonviable Extremely risky, in or near default.	E F	CCC CC DDD DD D	Caa Ca C	CCC CC R	F

To get further rating information, visit the rating companies' Web sites:

A.M. Best—www.ambest.com

Fitch—www.fitchratings.com

Moody's—www.moodys.com

Standard & Poor's—www.standardandpoors.com

Weiss—www.weissratings.com

Comparing Costs

Now it's time to compare the costs of the competing policies. There are several comparison methods you can use, the most common of which are the traditional net cost (TNC) method and the interest-adjusted net cost method (IANC), or surrender cost index.

The **traditional net cost (TNC) method** is calculated by summing the premiums over a stated period (usually 10 or 20 years) and from this subtracting the sum of all dividends over that same period. The policy's cash value at the end of the stated period is then subtracted from this amount. The final result is divided by the number of years in the stated period and presented as total net cost per some level of coverage.

What's important here isn't what's included in the calculations, but what's excluded. The traditional net cost method doesn't take into consideration the time value of money. As a result, it's virtually meaningless. If an agent presents it to you as a reasonable means of analyzing the costs of a policy, you might want to consider another insurance agent.

Traditional Net Cost (TNC) Method

A method of comparing insurance costs that sums the premiums over a stated period (usually 10 or 20 years) and subtracts from this the sum of all dividends over that same period.

A more widely accepted means of comparing similar but competing policies is the **interest-adjusted net cost (IANC) method**, which is also called the **surrender cost index**. Although this method has its own shortcomings, it does incorporate the time value of money into its calculations and has gained a good deal of acceptance in the insurance industry.

This method is just like the TNC method except that it recognizes the time value of money. However, this method depends on the choice of the appropriate discount rate and the estimate of the dividends and cash value from the policy. The agent's estimates may be high and not realistic. To be safe, take the results of every comparative analysis method with a hefty grain of salt. Note, though, that there are almost as many methods for comparing insurance costs as there are different types of policies, and they all involve making assumptions.

Interest-Adjusted Net Cost (IANC) Method or Surrender Cost Index
A method of comparing insurance costs that incorporates the time value of money into its calculations.

> ### FACTS OF LIFE
> One way to pay on life insurance is to pay annually rather than monthly. For example, according to AccuQuote, a healthy 35-year-old man can get a $250,000, 20-year term policy for just $14.44 per month. The same policy costs $165 if premiums are paid annually versus $173 when you add up the monthly premiums.

Making a Purchase: The Net or an Advisor

Once you've decided whether you need life insurance or not, and if so, how much is right for you, the decision becomes term versus cash-value insurance. If you decide on term insurance, consider shopping on the Web. There you can find instant quotes and excellent rates. This is because you can receive instant quotes from over 300 companies, and with that many alternatives, you'll end up with a great rate.

Where do you find this help on the Web? Several instant quote services compile databases of life insurance quotes and provide you with the costs and the companies offering the lowest cost policies that fit your needs. QuoteSmith has a continually updated database that contains 375 insurance companies. All you have to do is enter some basic information and you'll get a quote.

Does it pay to shop around? You bet it does! Insurance rates vary dramatically from one company to another. In fact, the annual premiums found on the Internet on a 20-year term policy for $500,000 for a 25-year-old male with preferred rates varied from a low of $260 to a high of $1,465. Take a look at these Web quote services:

Insure.com	**www.insure.com**
AccuQuote	**www.accuquote.com**

Once you decide on a policy, the insurance company will, at its expense, send a nurse or technician to your house to give you a basic physical: He or she will ask questions on your medical history, take blood, and give you an EKG. It's just that simple. To make sure you've gotten the best deal, check at least two of the Web quote services and give an independent insurance agent a call.

If you've decided on cash-value insurance, things get a bit more complicated. That's because it's almost impossible to compare different policies, all with different features and different assumptions. Still, you can go to the Web to get quotes on different policies.

Health Insurance

Design a health care insurance program and understand what provisions are important to you.

Now let's turn our attention to health insurance. You've probably heard of the Patient Protection and Affordable Care Act that was signed into law in 2010—it represents a major shift in health care in America. Much of what it does is aimed at making sure that almost everyone has health insurance. However, it doesn't replace the old system—just as before, there will be health care options, your insurance will still come from a private

MONEY MATTERS

Tips from Marcy Furney, ChFC, Certified Financial Planner™

WHAT THEY NEVER TOLD YOU ABOUT LIFE INSURANCE

Your primary concern should be a sufficient death benefit to cover your dependents' needs. Accidental death coverage doesn't count in the calculation unless you are 100 percent sure you will die by accident.

Take your beneficiary designation seriously. It allows money to go to your dependents without the delay of probate. If your beneficiary can't handle money, consider a periodic payment settlement option or designate a trust with a reliable trustee to receive the proceeds. Small children cannot receive life insurance payments directly. To avoid red tape, you should use some type of trust or guardian arrangement.

Consider a common disaster clause in your beneficiary designation. It will guarantee that your death benefit goes to your contingent beneficiary if the primary beneficiary dies within a stated number of days of your death. Otherwise, the proceeds could be tied up in the primary beneficiary's estate and go to someone you wouldn't have chosen.

Never count on group life insurance as your total program. You could leave your job at a time when your medical condition would prevent obtaining replacement coverage. Although great strides have been made in making group health insurance "portable," the same is not true

for group life insurance. Some group life policies are convertible to personal policies, but the rates can be three to ten times higher than the group rate. Also, investigate the rates for group supplemental life programs, which allow you to purchase coverage amounts above what your employer provides. If you are in good health, you may find lower premiums through a personal policy.

Put some thought into ownership of your policies. Though death benefits are free of income tax, they are normally included in your estate. Certain ownership arrangements can avoid some or all estate taxes. Also, in cases of divorce, it seems best for spouses to own and control each other's policies. This is especially true if there are children relying on potential benefits.

Familiarize yourself with riders such as waiver of premium, waiver of charges (on universal policies), and living benefits. Know when they pay and under what conditions. Evaluate the cost of riders versus their benefits.

Good intentions without complete information could result in tremendous headaches for those you are trying to protect. Don't forgo the assistance and knowledge of a competent independent agent for fear of paying higher premiums. Many use the same products with the same prices as Internet and telephone services.

insurance company, and that insurance company will still reimburse your doctors for your care.

There are plenty of health care options available, but most people rely on their employer for health insurance coverage, which is an employee benefit for many workers. If your employer provides you with health insurance benefits, your choices are limited to what they offer. And employer-sponsored health care coverage usually isn't free. Employees often have to pay for co-payments associated with visits to the doctor, prescriptions, and monthly premiums. In effect, you pay a portion of the premium, and your employer pays the rest. Some employers offer you a variety of choices, but usually if you want additional or better coverage, you will have to make additional payments. Each year you are generally given an opportunity to switch between the different types of coverage that are offered.

If you're not getting insurance through your employer, you have more options, and beginning in 2014, as a result of the Affordable Care Act, if you're self-employed or if your employer doesn't offer coverage, you'll be able to obtain a plan through a health insurance exchange. The exchanges are modeled on the federal employee health program that is available to members of Congress and contains a range of private plans to choose from. All in all, it is expected that about 25 million people will buy coverage through exchanges, and nearly 6 in 10 will be eligible for help with their premiums.

We live in a world of choices, so of course there are several different types of health insurance coverage available. Hey, if you've got 31 choices when buying such a thing as ice cream, you should at least have a few choices when it comes to buying something as important as health insurance. As with buying ice cream, though, it's easy to get carried away with health insurance and want everything you can get. Even though you could obtain insurance to cover just about everything down to a common sneeze (bless you), the purpose of health insurance isn't to cover all the costs of health care—it's to prevent financial ruin—remember **Principle 5: Stuff Happens, or the Importance of Liquidity**. You're going to have to pay a doctor's bill every now and again, and you'll need to spring for that bottle of Tylenol when you get a headache. Of course, if you've got chronic headaches and go through a bottle of Tylenol every day, you're going to want someone to pick up that cost. Everyone's needs are different, and the key to selecting insurance is to choose only the types of coverage you need.

2010 Health Care Reform

Before we jump in and look at all the different forms of health care insurance, let's take a look at the health care reform bill that President Obama signed into law in March 2010 that commonly goes by the name the Affordable Care Act. The reforms within this act go into effect over time, with portions of the new law being effective immediately and the final portions of the law going into effect in 2018. However, in early 2011, more than two dozen states joined a lawsuit stating the health care law was unconstitutional. Those states won two key federal cases, with the argument the federal government can't force Americans to buy health insurance being the one that has carried the most weight. The different measures in the law can be classified as:

◆ Providing New Consumer Protections
◆ Improving Quality and Lowering Costs
◆ Increasing Access to Affordable Care
◆ Holding Insurance Companies Accountable

However, even though the Affordable Care Act makes major changes in health care, your interaction with the U.S. medical system will remain more or less the same—you'll pay a private insurance company and they'll reimburse your doctors for care. In addition, while there was much talk of a public health insurance option, there isn't one; instead, you'll still deal with one of many insurance companies. In effect, this bill tinkers with the way the current system works rather than scrapping it and replacing it with a new one.

Still, it does some important things that may affect you. For example, one provision that takes effect in 2014 prohibits insurance companies from denying coverage to those with preexisting health conditions. Other provisions aimed at increasing the number of people with insurance help set up insurance exchanges, where insurance could be purchased, and provide tax credits for insurance purchases to small businesses and the poor and middle class. In addition, employers with more than 50 workers would be required to offer insurance, and those that don't would face a fine of $2,000 per employee if any of their employees got federal subsidies to buy their own coverage. There are also other reforms to the insurance market, such as allowing children to stay on their parent's insurance policy until they turn 26, keeping insurance companies from dropping people who get sick, and restricting annual and lifetime limits on what your insurer will pay. In addition, for seniors, it works at closing the gap in Medicare prescription drug coverage, known as the "donut hole."

The easiest way of understanding this law and its major provisions is to look at the changes it makes as they relate to these different categories and by when they are put in place. Take a look at Table 9.5, which presents the major provisions in this act.

TABLE 9.5 Major Provisions of the Affordable Care Act[a]

Providing New Consumer Protections

- Prohibits insurance companies from denying coverage to children under the age of 19 due to a preexisting condition—begins 2010
- Prohibits insurance companies from rescinding coverage due to an error or other technical mistake on a customer's application—begins 2010
- Eliminates lifetime dollar limits on essential benefits—begins 2010
- Prohibits insurance companies from refusing to sell coverage or renew policies because of an individual's preexisting conditions—begins 2014
- Prohibits new plans and existing group plans from imposing annual dollar limits on the amount of coverage an individual may receive—begins 2014
- Prohibits dropping or limiting coverage because an individual chooses to participate in a clinical trial—begins 2014

Improving Quality and Lowering Costs

- Provides some small businesses with tax credits to help them provide insurance benefits to their workers—begins 2010
- Provides a $250 rebate to Medicare drug beneficiaries who fall into the "donut hole" coverage gap. The bill eventually closes that gap, which currently begins after $2,700 is spent on drugs—begins 2010
- Requires that all new plans must cover certain preventive services such as mammograms and colonoscopies without charging a deductible, co-pay, or coinsurance—begins 2010
- Provides certain free preventive services, such as annual wellness visits and personalized prevention plans for seniors on Medicare—begins 2011
- Provides new funding to state Medicaid programs that choose to cover preventive services for patients at little or no cost—begins 2013
- To make coverage affordable, provides tax credits for insurance coverage for people with income between 100 percent and 400 percent of the poverty line who are not eligible for other affordable coverage (in 2010, 400 percent of the poverty line comes out to about $43,000 for an individual or $88,000 for a family of four)—begins 2014
- Establishes health insurance exchanges, so that if your employer doesn't offer insurance you will be able to buy insurance directly in an exchange where you will be offered a choice of health plans that meet certain benefits and cost standards—begins 2014
- Increases the size of the small business tax credits that began in 2010—begins 2014
- Requires most individuals who can afford it to obtain basic health insurance coverage or pay a $695 annual fee to help offset the costs of caring for uninsured Americans—begins 2014

Increasing Access to Affordable Care

- Ensures children will be allowed to stay on their parents' plan until they turn 26 years old—begins 2010
- Increases access to Medicaid by allowing those who earn less than 133 percent of the poverty level (approximately $14,000 for an individual and $29,000 for a family of four) to be eligible to enroll in Medicaid
- To help fund health care, imposes an excise tax on high-cost employer-provided plans. The first $27,500 of a family plan and $10,200 for individual coverage is exempt from the tax—begins 2018

Holding Insurance Companies Accountable

- Requires that at least 85 percent of all premium dollars collected by insurance companies for large employer plans are spent on health care services and health care quality improvement—begins 2011
- Provides a new option called CLASS for long-term health care insurance—begins 2012

[a]For a more inclusive look at the provisions of the Affordable Care Act, go to www.healthcare.gov/law/introduction/index.html.

Basic Health Insurance

Basic Health Insurance
A term used to describe most health insurance, which includes a combination of hospital, surgical, and physician expense insurance.

Most health insurance includes a combination of hospital, surgical, and physician expense insurance. These three types of insurance are generally sold in a combination called **basic health insurance**. Many policies provide basic health insurance and then allow the policyholder to choose from a long list of policy options. Although each additional option provides additional coverage, it also involves an additional premium.

Hospital Insurance   Hospital insurance is generally part of every insurance plan. It covers the costs associated with a hospital stay, including room charges, nursing costs, operating room fees, and drugs supplied by the hospital. Depending on the policy, hospital insurance may reimburse the policyholder for specific charges, give the policyholder a set amount of money for each day he or she is hospitalized, or pay the hospital directly for the policyholder's expenses.

If the policyholder receives a set amount of money per day of hospitalization, he or she must make up the difference between what is charged and what is received from the insurance company. Almost all plans, regardless of their type, impose limits on both the daily hospital costs and the number of days covered.

Hospital Insurance
Insurance that covers the costs associated with a hospital stay, including room charges, nursing costs, operating room fees, and drugs supplied by the hospital.

Surgical Insurance   Surgical insurance covers the cost of surgery. A surgical policy generally lists the specific operations it covers and cites either a maximum dollar amount for each operation, or reimbursement to the surgeon for what is considered reasonable and customary based on typical charges in that region. You'll have to cover any charges above what the policy will cover, and you also might have to pay a deductible. Although surgical insurance may not completely cover surgery charges, it should reduce them to a manageable level.

One complaint with surgical insurance policies is that many times they don't cover what might be considered "experimental" treatment. Insurance companies have refused to pay for bone marrow transplants to combat cancer and some experimental treatments for AIDS patients. Although the companies look at these coverage limitations as an attempt to keep costs down (experimental surgery tends to be painfully expensive), if you're facing cancer or AIDS you're going to look at things differently. Remember, though, that surgical insurance has its limits. If you're considering a treatment not specified in your policy, you should see a lawyer to help you convince your insurance company ahead of time that the procedure should be covered.

Surgical Insurance
Insurance that covers the cost of surgery.

Physician Expense Insurance   Physician expense insurance covers physicians' fees outside of surgery, including office or home visits, lab fees, and x-ray costs when they're not performed in a hospital.

Physician Expense Insurance
Insurance that covers physicians' fees outside of surgery.

Major Medical Expense Insurance   Major medical expense insurance is aimed at covering medical costs beyond those covered by basic health insurance. It's meant to offset all the financial effects of a catastrophic illness. Where basic health insurance leaves off, major medical expense insurance takes over.

It generally doesn't provide complete coverage, but instead allows for deductibles and coinsurance payments in order to keep costs down. For example, the deductible may require the policyholder to pay for the first two office visits beyond what's covered by the basic insurance policy. It may then cover only 80 percent of the costs, with the policyholder responsible for making up the difference.

It's also not uncommon for such a policy to allow for **stop-loss provision**, which limits the total dollar amount the policyholder is responsible for. When deductibles and coinsurance payments by the policyholder reach a set limit, the insurance company takes full financial responsibility for any additional medical expenses.

Major Medical Expense Insurance
Insurance that covers medical costs beyond those covered by basic health insurance.

Stop-Loss Provision
A medical insurance feature that limits the total dollar amount that the policyholder is responsible for paying.

> **FACTS OF LIFE**
>
> Twenty-one percent of Americans smoke, and smoking is expensive. The extra lifetime medical cost of smoking is $17,500, and the average hospital bill for lung cancer is $45,500.

Dental and Eye Insurance

As the names imply, dental insurance provides dental coverage and eye insurance provides coverage for eye examinations, glasses, and contact lenses. Although these are certainly nice to have, don't bother buying them if they're not provided by your employer. Dental and eye insurance pay for expenses that are relatively minor and regular—that is, they can be planned for.

Dread Disease and Accident Insurance

Dread disease and accident insurance are sold to provide additional protection if you're struck by a specific disease or if you're in an accident. An example of dread disease insurance is cancer insurance, which is generally sold on television or through the mail. This insurance provides additional coverage for the costs associated with this one specific disease. This kind of policy is not a great idea. In fact, one state has banned its sale and other state insurance regulators have posted advisories cautioning people about these policies. In addition, most dread disease policies aren't guaranteed renewable. A much better idea is a comprehensive policy, and starting in 2014 as a result of the Affordable Care Act, all new health insurance plans sold to individuals and small businesses must include a range of essential health benefits.

Accident insurance works about the same way. If you're in an accident, an accident insurance policy will provide a specific amount for every day you must stay in the hospital and a certain amount for the loss of any body parts.

Once again, the idea is to provide protection against major catastrophes while ignoring the small stuff. Because you don't know ahead of time what might bring on a catastrophe, your health insurance must be comprehensive. Avoid the accident and dread disease insurance, and instead make sure your policy is comprehensive.

Basic Health Care Choices

Fee-for-Service or Traditional Indemnity Plan
An insurance plan that provides reimbursement for all or part of your medical expenditures. In general, it gives you a good deal of freedom to choose your doctor and hospital.

Managed Health Care or Prepaid Care Plan
An insurance plan that entitles you to the health care provided by a specified group of participating doctors, hospitals, and clinics. These plans are generally offered by health maintenance organizations or variations of them.

There are two basic types of plans available: (1) traditional fee-for-service plans and (2) managed health care, or prepaid care. Under a **fee-for-service or traditional indemnity plan**, you are reimbursed for all or part of your medical expenditures, and in general, you have a good deal of freedom to choose your doctor and hospital. Under a **managed health care or prepaid care plan**, most of your expenses are already covered and don't need to be reimbursed, but you're limited to receiving health care from a specified group of participating doctors, hospitals, and clinics.

Where do we go to get health care coverage? Well, we basically have two choices: private health care or government-sponsored health care Let's look at each of these options.

Private Health Care Plans

There are more than 800 private insurance companies whose main business comes from selling health insurance policies to individuals and to employers to be offered as part of a benefits package. These companies offer a variety of traditional fee-for-service and managed health care plans.

Of note is Blue Cross and Blue Shield, which provides coverage to approximately 70 million individuals through prepaid health care plans rather than insurance policies. The company contracts with hospitals and doctors to provide specified health care coverage to members for a contracted payment or fee.

FACTS OF LIFE

In 2009, almost 60 percent of those in employer health insurance plans had lifetime limits on coverage running from below $1 million to $2 million or more. The new law eliminates these limits.

Fee-for-Service or Traditional Indemnity Plans   With a fee-for-service plan, the doctor or hospital bills you directly for the cost of services, and the insurance company reimburses you. Although there may be some restrictions on which doctors and hospitals you can use, these plans provide the greatest degree of health provider choice.

Most fee-for-service plans include a coinsurance provision. A **coinsurance or percentage participation provision** defines the percentage of each claim that the insurance company will pay. For example, if there's an 80 percent participation premium on hospital claims up to $2,000 and 100 percent participation thereafter, then you'd pay 20 percent of the first $2,000 of your hospital insurance claim, and the insurance company would pay the remainder.

Most fee-for-service plans also include a co-payment or deductible. A **co-payment or deductible** is the amount of your medical expenses that you must pay before the insurance company will reimburse you on a claim. A deductible can be set up in several different ways. For example, there may be a $10 deductible on all prescriptions. The insured pays the first $10 of the prescription, and the insurance company will cover the remainder. There might be an overall deductible of $250 or $500 on all health care. In this case, you'd pay the first $250 or $500 of any medical care costs you might have, and the insurance company will then cover any additional medical care costs up to a certain point.

Overall, fee-for-service plans are very desirable. Their big advantage is complete choice over doctors, hospitals, and clinics. Unfortunately, these plans are relatively expensive and involve a good deal of paperwork. While many employers still provide fee-for-service plans for their workers, they are dropping quickly in terms of popularity in favor of the less expensive managed health care. If you're considering a fee-for-service plan, Checklist 9.1 will lead you through some questions to ask.

Managed Health Care   Managed health care plans are offered by health maintenance organizations and allow members access to needed services from specified doctors and hospitals. Managed health care plans both pay for and provide health

Coinsurance or Percentage Participation Provision
An insurance provision that defines the percentage of each claim that the insurance company will pay.

Co-Payment or Deductible
The amount of expenses that the insured must pay before the insurance company will pay any insurance benefits.

CHECKLIST 9.1
Fee-for-Service Plans

In choosing a fee-for-service plan, ask . . .

◆ How much is the monthly premium? What will your total cost be each year? There are individual rates and family rates.

◆ What does the policy cover? Does it cover prescription drugs, out-of-hospital care, or home care? Are there limits on the amount or the number of days the company will pay for these services? The best plans cover a broad range of services.

◆ Are you currently being treated for a medical condition that may not be covered under your new plan? Are there limitations or a waiting period involved in the coverage?

◆ What is the deductible? Often you can lower your monthly health insurance premium by buying a policy with a higher yearly deductible amount.

◆ What is the coinsurance rate? What percent of your bills for allowable services will you have to pay?

◆ What is the maximum you would pay out of pocket per year? How much would it cost you directly before the insurance company would pay everything else?

◆ Is there a lifetime maximum cap the insurer will pay? The cap is an amount after which the insurance company won't pay anymore. This is important to know if you or someone in your family has an illness that requires expensive treatments.

Source: Agency for Health Care Policy and Research and the National Council on Patient Information and Education, Rockville, MD, 2011.

care services. For example, under a managed health care plan you may receive all your health services at one location. Under some plans you may not be guaranteed that you'll see the same doctor each time, just that you'll get the health care you need at low or no cost. However, most managed care plans provide you with a primary care physician, and many plans allow that physician to be one of your own choosing (for a slight fee).

Just as with the fee-for-service plans, it's quite common for there to be a visit fee or co-payment of around $20, and a typical co-payment for an emergency room visit is $50. There is also generally a co-payment on prescriptions. The purpose of co-payments is to keep insurance costs down. Not only do they serve as a deductible, forcing the patient to pay the first portion of the health care bill, but they also serve as a disincentive to seek care.

The big advantage of a managed health care plan is its efficiency. Because it offers you health care directly, there's considerably less in the way of paperwork and its associated costs. Moreover, because most managed health care plans involve a number of doctors, the entire facility can provide extended office hours, whereas each individual doctor is responsible for staffing the facility for a limited period. In fact, in many managed health care facilities, doctors work at that facility in addition to carrying on a private practice. There are two basic types of managed health care: (1) health maintenance organizations, or HMOs, and (2) preferred provider organizations, or PPOs.

FACTS of LIFE

Insurance keeps you healthy. You're much more likely to get preventive screening if you have insurance. The percentage of women age 50–64 who had a mammogram in the past 2 years is shown below.

Uninsured All Year	(bar ≈ 20%)
Insured All Year	(bar ≈ 47%)

Scale: 0% 10% 20% 30% 40% 50% 60%

Source: Commonwealth Fund Biennial Health Insurance Survey.

Managed Health Care: HMOs   The most popular form of managed health care is the **health maintenance organization, or HMO**, which is a prepaid insurance plan that entitles members to the services of participating doctors, hospitals, and clinics. Members pay a flat fee for this privilege and then can select a managing physician who is responsible for the care of that member. There may also be a co-payment required with each visit to the doctor or each prescription filled. There are three basic types of HMOs: (1) individual practice association plans, (2) group practice plans, and (3) point-of-service plans.

An **individual practice association plan, or IPA**, is an HMO made up of independent doctors. The patients go to the doctors' offices and receive their medical treatment there. In fact, many IPA doctors also maintain a regular practice. With a **group practice plan**, doctors are generally employed directly by the HMO and work out of a central, shared facility. Members of the HMO can receive their medical treatment only from these doctors and only at these central facilities. A **point-of-service plan** allows its members to seek medical treatment from both affiliated and nonaffiliated doctors. Coverage by HMO-affiliated doctors tends to be free or at least covered at a very low co-payment rate. Co-payments for nonaffiliated doctors tend to be much higher.

Although there are some individual differences, most HMOs have very broad coverage, and include doctor, hospital, laboratory, and emergency costs. Prescription costs are often covered, too. Of course, this coverage also requires co-payments.

Most HMOs are associated with an employer's group coverage. That is, the plans are offered through an employer as a part of the employee benefits package. Still, private individuals can join an HMO—and there are plenty to choose from. There are over 600 HMOs operating in the United States. Because each has its own

---

Health Maintenance Organization (HMO)

A prepaid insurance plan that entitles members to the services of participating doctors, hospitals, and clinics.

Individual Practice Association Plan (IPA)

An HMO made up of independent doctors, in which the patients visit the doctors and receive their medical treatment in the doctors' regular offices.

Group Practice Plan

An insurance plan in which doctors are generally employed directly by an HMO, and members of the HMO must receive their medical treatment from these doctors at a central facility.

Point-of-Service Plan

An insurance plan that allows its members to seek medical treatment from both HMO-affiliated doctors and non-HMO-affiliated doctors.

participating doctors and hospitals, each serves a limited geographic area. In order to use health facilities elsewhere, you usually need a referral.

Because members receive comprehensive health care services, HMOs emphasize preventive medicine because preventing an illness is an awful lot cheaper than curing it. As a result, many HMOs provide regular physical examinations. In contrast, most fee-for-service plans only cover illness-related health care claims.

Finally, HMOs are efficient, costing as little as 60 percent of what a comparable fee-for-service insurance plan would cost. The preventive care, coupled with minimized paperwork and efficient handling of patients, allows for the cost savings. It's no wonder that employers prefer to offer HMO coverage. If HMOs are cheaper for you, they're also cheaper for your employer, who covers a good deal of your insurance premium each month.

There are, of course, some major drawbacks to HMOs. Service can be too quick or cursory, and waits can be long. If you need a service not provided by your HMO, receiving a referral, especially one outside of the HMO's geographic area, can be a hassle. Many members feel the lack of choice is far too restricting, and that having to choose from a small, fixed list of doctors, or not being able to choose at all, means they are not getting the kind of care they want. They do not like that they're unable to establish a personal relationship with a doctor, and they are also concerned that the available doctors might not be the best or most qualified. More questions about the quality of care stem from some of the incentive systems HMOs use. Doctors often receive bonuses based on the number of patients seen or based on the amount of money saved, leading some to wonder if certain doctors don't cut corners to earn bigger bonuses.

If you're choosing an HMO, take a look at Checklist 9.2 for some guidance.

Managed Health Care: PPOs
A **preferred provider organization (PPO)** is a bit like a cross between a traditional fee-for-service plan and an HMO. Under a PPO, an employer or insurer negotiates with a group of doctors and hospitals to provide health care for its employees or members at reduced rates. Doctors and hospitals that agree to the pricing system become members of the PPO. In fact, a doctor or hospital can be a member of a number of different PPOs. To encourage use of member doctors, PPOs generally have an additional, or penalty, co-payment requirement for service from nonmembers. The big advantage of the PPO is that it allows for health care at a discount, with the negotiating power of the insurer or employer determining how great a discount is achieved.

Preferred Provider Organization (PPO)
An insurance plan under which an employer or insurer negotiates with a group of doctors and hospitals to provide health care for its employees or members at reduced rates.

Group Versus Individual Health Insurance
Group health insurance refers to the way the health insurance is sold rather than to the characteristics of the insurance policy. This insurance is provided to a specific group of individuals who are associated for some purpose other than to buy insurance. Usually this group of individuals all work for the same employer or all belong to a common association or professional group.

Group Health Insurance
Health insurance that's sold, usually without a medical exam, to a specific group of individuals who are associated for some purpose other than to buy insurance.

Most employee health insurance doesn't require subscribers to pass a medical exam, but group insurance offered through an association or professional group does. In general, the cost of group health insurance is about 15 to 40 percent less than that of a comparable individual health insurance policy. Why? Because an individual simply doesn't have the bargaining power that a group has.

CHECKLIST 9.2
Choosing an HMO

Here are some things to consider when choosing an HMO:

◆ Are there many doctors to choose from? Do you select from a list of contract physicians or from the available staff of a group practice? Which doctors are accepting new patients? How hard is it to change doctors if you decide you want someone else?

◆ How are referrals to specialists handled?

◆ Is it easy to get appointments? How far in advance must routine visits be scheduled? What arrangements does the HMO have for handling emergency care?

◆ Does the HMO offer the services you want? What preventive services are provided? Are there limits on medical tests, surgery, mental health care, home care, or other

support offered? What if you need special service not provided by the HMO?

◆ What is the service area of the HMO? Where are the facilities located in your community that serve HMO members? How convenient to your home and workplace are the doctors, hospitals, and emergency care centers that make up the HMO network? What happens if you or a family member are out of town and need medical treatment?

◆ What will the HMO plan cost? What is the yearly total for monthly fees? In addition, are there co-payments for office visits, emergency care, prescribed drugs, or other services? How much?

Source: Agency for Health Care Policy and Research and the National Council on Patient Information and Education, Rockville, MD, 2011.

Individual Insurance Policy
An insurance policy that is tailor-made for you, reflecting your age, health (as determined by an examination), and chosen deductible size.

An **individual insurance policy** is one tailor-made for you that reflects your age, health (as determined by an examination), geographic location, and chosen deductible amount. Are there any advantages to individual policies? In general, other than the ability to tailor the policy to meet your specific needs, there are none. Group and individual policies tend to offer the same coverage, so the only major difference between them is cost. Individual policies tend to be more expensive in most, but not all, cases, so you should almost always try to get group insurance.

Just as with life insurance companies, it's important to get insurance from a company that's in sound financial condition, that is, one that could absorb higher-than-expected losses and continue to provide coverage. How do you go about selecting such a company? Your insurance company should receive either an A++ or an A+ rating from A.M. Best. Claim service provided by your company should be fast, fair, and courteous. Don't select a company that raises premiums based on claims. Finally, select only a company that's prohibited from canceling policies. You should be able to determine how well a particular company fares in these areas from an interview with your insurance agent. And once you file a health insurance claim, don't give up if your claim is initially denied. Table 9.6 provides a step-by-step approach to appealing your claim.

STOP & THINK

What do you do if you don't qualify for group coverage? You might want to consider joining a group that has coverage. Trade groups, alumni, political, and religious organizations are a few groups to check out. You'll probably end up saving much more in insurance than you pay in group dues. Where do you think you could get group coverage?

TABLE 9.6 Appealing Health Insurance Claim Decisions
If your health insurer has denied coverage for medical care you received, you have a right to appeal the claim and ask that the company reverse its decision. You can be your own health care advocate. Here's what you can do:
Step 1: Review your policy and explanation of benefits.
Step 2: Contact your insurer and keep detailed records of your contacts (copies of letters, time and date of conversations).
Step 3: Request documentation from your doctor or employer to support your case.
Step 4: Write a formal complaint letter explaining what care was denied and why you are appealing via the company's internal review process.
Step 5: If the internal appeal is not granted through step 4, file a claim with your state's insurance department.
For more information: visit **nclnet.org** or **statehealthfacts.org**.

Source: U.S. General Services Administration, Consumer Action Handbook, 2011, www.consumeraction.gov/.

Government-Sponsored Health Care Plans

Government-sponsored plans fall into two categories: (1) state plans, which provide for work-related accidents and illness under state **workers' compensation laws**, and (2) federal plans, such as Medicare and Medicaid.

Workers' Compensation Laws
State laws that provide payment for work-related accidents and illness.

Workers' Compensation Workers' compensation laws date from the early 1900s, when our economy changed from predominantly agricultural to industrial. At that time, workers put in long hours in unsafe conditions, and work-related accidents were all too common. Fueled by the public outcry to Upton Sinclair's 1906 book *The Jungle*, states passed a series of laws aimed at providing work-related accident and illness insurance to workers.

Because these are state laws, each state determines the benefits level for workers. Some states provide broad coverage and others exclude some workers. For example, some states exclude workers for small businesses. Given the variability in coverage from state to state, you should contact your benefits office to see exactly what coverage you have. For workers without enough workers' compensation coverage, or for those with no coverage at all, some private insurance companies offer a type of workers' compensation insurance.

Medicare
A government insurance program enacted in 1968 to provide medical benefits to the disabled and those over 65. It is divided into two parts: Part A, which provides hospital insurance benefits, and Part B, which allows for voluntary supplemental insurance.

Medicare The **Medicare** program was enacted in 1968 to provide medical benefits to the disabled and to persons 65 and older who qualify for Social Security benefits. The cost of this insurance is covered by Social Security, with the individual patient paying an annual deductible. The Medicare program is way too complicated for us to explain here—but we'll try anyway. For a complete listing of Medicare benefits, you'll want to go to *Medicare and You*, which is available at any Social Security Administration office or downloadable from the Web at **www.medicare.gov**. Coverage is divided into the following parts:

◆ **Medicare Part A—Hospital Insurance:** Part A provides basic hospital insurance benefits. Participation in Part A is compulsory and covers most hospital costs, including operating room costs, nursing care, a semiprivate room, and prescription drugs furnished by the hospital. Part A also helps cover a skilled nursing facility, hospice, and home health care if you meet certain conditions. You or your supplemental insurance company pay set dollar amounts or percentages of the cost depending on services used. Table 9.7 provides an abbreviated breakdown of benefits and charges.

TABLE 9.7   Medicare Benefits and Services

Medicare Part A: 2011

Services	Benefit	Medicare Pays	You Pay[a]
Hospitalization Semiprivate room and board, general nursing, and other hospital services and supplies (payments based on benefit periods)	First 60 days 61st to 90th day 91st to 150th day[b] Beyond 150 days	All but $1,132 All but $283 a day All but $566 a day Nothing	$1,132 $283 a day $566 a day All costs
Skilled Nursing Facility Care Semiprivate room and board, skilled nursing and rehabilitative services, and other services and supplies (payments based on benefit periods)	First 20 days Additional 80 days Beyond 100 days	100% of approved amount All but $141.50 a day Nothing	Nothing Up to $141.50 a day All costs
Home Health Care Part-time or intermittent skilled care, home health aide services, durable medical equipment and supplies, and other services	Unlimited as long as you meet Medicare conditions	100% of approved amount; 80% of approved amount for durable medical equipment	Nothing for services; 20% of approved amount for durable medical equipment
Hospice Care Pain relief, symptom management, and support services for the terminally ill	For as long as doctor certifies need	All but limited costs (up to $5) for outpatient drugs and inpatient respite care (up to 5% of the Medicare-approved amount)	Limited costs for outpatient drugs (up to $5) and inpatient respite care (up to 5% of the Medicare-approved amount)
Blood When furnished by a hospital or skilled nursing facility during a covered stay	Unlimited if medically necessary	If the hospital has to buy blood for you, you must either pay the hospital costs for the first 3 units of blood you get in a calendar year or have the blood donated.	If the hospital has to buy blood for you, you must either pay the hospital costs for the first 3 units of blood you get in a calendar year or have the blood donated.[c]

[a]Either you or your insurance company is responsible for paying the amounts listed in the "You Pay" column.

[b]This 60-reserve-days benefit may be used only once in a lifetime.

[c]Blood paid for or replaced under Part B of Medicare during the calendar year does not have to be paid for or replaced under Part A.

◆ **Medicare Part B—Supplemental Medical Insurance:** Part B of the Medicare plan is voluntary and provides coverage for doctors' fees and a wide range of medical services and supplies. The medically necessary services of a doctor are covered no matter where you receive them—at home, in the doctor's office, in a clinic, in a nursing home, or in a hospital.

With Part B, there is a monthly premium, which for most people (individuals earning less than $85,000 and couples earning less than $170,000) was $115.40 in 2011, with a $162 annual deductible, after which Medicare pays 80 percent of the charges for covered medical services. Again, Table 9.7 provides an abbreviated breakdown of benefits and charges.

◆ **Medicare Part C—Medicare Advantage Plans:** Medicare Advantage Plans bring more choices to Medicare by offering a variety of private plans with comprehensive care, combining Medicare health coverage with a drug benefit. In addition, some offer benefits not covered by traditional Medicare, such as vision and dental care and more preventive services.

TABLE 9.7 *(continued)*

	Medicare Part B: 2011		
Services	**Benefit**	**Medicare Pays**	**You Pay**[a]
Medical and Other Services The Medicare-approved amount for most doctor services (including most doctor services while you're a hospital inpatient), outpatient therapy, and durable medical equipment	Unlimited if medically necessary	80% of approved amount (after $162 deductible); reduced to 55% for most outpatient mental health services	$162 deductible, plus 20% of approved amount and limited charges above approved amount
Clinical Laboratory Services Blood tests, urinalyses, and more	Unlimited if medically necessary	Generally 100% of approved amount	Nothing for services
Home Health Care Part-time or intermittent skilled care, home health aide services, durable medical equipment and supplies, and other services	Unlimited as long as you meet Medicare conditions	100% of approved amount; 80% of approved amount for durable medical equipment	Nothing for services; 20% of approved amount for durable medical equipment
Outpatient Hospital Treatment Services for the diagnosis or treatment of illness or injury	Unlimited if medically necessary	Medicare payment to hospital based on hospital cost	20% of whatever the hospital charges (after $162 deductible)
Blood	Unlimited if medically necessary	80% of approved amount (after $162 deductible and starting with 4th unit)	First 3 units plus 20% of approved amount for additional units (after $162 deductible)[b]

[a]Either you or your insurance company is responsible for paying the amounts in the "You Pay" column.

[b]Blood paid for or replaced under Part A of Medicare during the calendar year does not have to be paid for or replaced under Part B.

Source: U.S. Department of Health and Human Services, *Medicare and You*, 2011.

◆ **Medicare Part D—Medicare Prescription Drug Coverage:** These plans are available through private companies that work with and are approved by Medicare to provide prescription drug coverage, and are available for everyone with Medicare. To get Medicare drug coverage, you must join a Medicare drug plan. You pay a separate premium in addition to your Part B premium.

You must enroll in a Medicare drug plan when you are first eligible to avoid a late-enrollment penalty. Every year between November 15–December 31, you can switch to a different Medicare drug plan (switch companies) if your plan coverage changes or your needs change.

After you join a Medicare drug plan, the plan will mail you membership materials, including a card to use when you get your prescriptions filled. When you use the card, you may have to provide a co-payment, coinsurance, and/or deductible if any are charged by the plan.

Medicare prescription drug plans vary widely in cost and drugs covered. As a result, when you compare plans, you'll want to look closely at:

- Coverage—check to see if the plan covers your prescription drugs.
- Cost—check to see how much your prescription drugs cost in each plan.
- Convenience—make sure the plan's pharmacies include the ones you want to use.

Medigap Insurance
Insurance sold by private insurance companies aimed at bridging gaps in Medicare coverage.

Medigap Plans   A **Medigap insurance** policy is health insurance sold by private insurance companies to fill the "gaps" in original Medicare plan coverage. Insurance companies can only sell you a "standardized" Medigap policy. These standardized policies (Medigap Plans A through L) all have specific benefits so you can compare them easily. While the different Medigap plans have the same benefits, it is important to compare Medigap policies because their costs can vary.

Medicaid
A government medical insurance plan for the needy.

Medicaid   **Medicaid** was enacted in 1965 and is a medical assistance program aimed at the needy. It's a joint program operated by the federal and state governments, with the benefits varying from state to state. The purpose of Medicaid is to provide medical care for the aged, blind, and disabled as well as to needy families with dependent children. Because some of those covered by Medicaid are also covered by Medicare, Medicaid payments go toward Medicare premiums, deductibles, and co-payments. Again, this program is very limited in scope, with no guarantee that it will be in its present form at a later point if and when you might need it.

Controlling Health Care Costs

Without question the first step in controlling health care costs is to stay healthy. Not only is health care insurance cheaper and more accessible if you're healthy, but your out-of-pocket health care expenditures decline, along with lost wages associated with missed work. In fact, a good part of staying healthy doesn't cost anything.

To gain an idea of the benefits of being healthy, let's look at the savings experienced by a "two-pack-a-day" smoker who quits smoking. First, depending on how high your state's cigarette taxes are, the immediate savings could be up to $1,600 a year. If you're in the 28 percent tax bracket, this figure translates to $2,222 of before-tax earnings. Now let's add the savings from not getting lung cancer and not having a baby born with smoking-related illnesses. (Of course, you'll have more expenses from living longer than you would if you kept on smoking and died younger.) In addition to staying healthy, you can also help to control medical costs by using medical reimbursement accounts and, in some cases, opting out of your company's health care plan.

> **FACTS of LIFE**
>
> A recent study reports that 85 percent of companies with 500 or more employees offer flexible spending accounts for health care expenses; however, only 27 percent of eligible employees use them. They also determined that the average annual amount contributed is about $1,400.

Flexible Spending Accounts

Flexible Spending Account (FSA)
An employer-sponsored medical plan that allows each employee to have pre-tax earnings deposited into a specially designated account for the purposes of paying health care bills. The employee can withdraw funds from this account to offset unreimbursed medical or dental expenses or qualified child care expenses.

A **flexible spending account (FSA)** is a savings plan established by an employer that allows each employee to have pre-tax earnings deposited into a specially designated account. Employees can withdraw funds from their accounts to offset unreimbursed medical or dental expenses, for example, co-pays to doctors, or qualified child care. There's a cap set on the maximum an employee can deposit into this account.

The biggest drawback to this plan is that any contributions to the flexible spending account not used by the end of the year are lost. In effect, it's a "use it or lose it" system. Generally, it's a good idea to set aside only 80 percent of anticipated health care expenditures in order to avoid any forfeit of funds at year's end. The advantage of such a plan is that health care expenditures that are otherwise uncovered are made on a before-tax basis. For example, many people use their medical reimbursement accounts to cover the deductible from their insurance plan. Thus, for every $100 set aside into this account, taxable income is reduced by $100. Beginning in 2014, as the result of the Affordable Care Act, there will be a $2,500 cap on FSA contributions.

TABLE 9.8 A Sampling of What Flexible Spending Accounts Can and Cannot Be Used For

Can be used for:	Cannot be used for:
Ambulance service	Baby sitting and child care (may be reimbursed through flexible spending accounts for dependent care)
Acupuncture	
Artificial limb	Cosmetic surgery to improve appearance
Birth control pills	Diapers
Braille books and magazines	Funeral expenses
Co-pays to doctors	Health club dues
Cosmetic surgery (relating to congenital deformity or disfigurement from disease or injury)	Housekeeper
Dental fees	Insurance premiums
Guide dogs	Maternity clothes
Nursing home care	Over-the-counter medical supplies (if not prescribed by a doctor)
Oxygen equipment	Swimming lessons
Psychoanalysis	Weight-loss program (for general health)
Special school for learning-disabled child	
Wheelchairs	

A flexible spending plan not only provides tax savings on unreimbursed health care expenditures, but also allows for pre-tax dollars to pay for other medical expenses that many health care plans do not cover, such as eyeglasses and orthodontia expenses. In fact, there is a good deal of flexibility with respect to how funds from a flexible spending plan can be used, as can be seen in Table 9.8.

Health Savings Accounts

Health Savings Accounts (HSAs) are another option to help people pay for medical expenses. Those who may take advantage of HSAs include the self-employed, small business owners, employees of small to medium-sized businesses that offer only bare-bones health benefits, and those under age 65 who pay for health care on their own. For 2011, almost anyone *with* a qualified high-deductible health plan (which is a health insurance plan with a minimum deductible of $1,200 if it's self-only coverage or $2,400 if it's family coverage) can also have a Health Savings Account. A Health Savings Account allows individuals to pay for current health expenses and save for future qualified medical and retiree health expenses on a *tax-free basis*. You can use your HSA funds to pay for expenses before you meet your deductible as well as for services not covered by your health plan, such as medical expenses after retirement and long-term care expenses. One nice thing about HSAs is that you don't lose HSA funds at the end of the year. Unspent balances remain in your account earning interest until you spend them on medical care.

COBRA and Changing Jobs

Under COBRA, which stands for the Consolidated Omnibus Budget Reconciliation Act, if you work for a company with 20 employees or more, you will be given the opportunity to continue your health insurance coverage for 18 months to 3 years after you leave the company, depending on why you left.

You are, of course, responsible for the cost of this insurance, but it will probably be less expensive than purchasing individual insurance. If you wish to

FACTS OF LIFE

The most common wellness benefits are smoke cessation classes, health risk assessments, and company gyms. Unfortunately, over 75 percent of workers don't take advantage of these free offers.

continue your coverage, you must notify your employer of your intent to make payment on your insurance within 60 days of leaving the company.

Choosing No Coverage—or "Opting Out"

As the cost of health care plans has skyrocketed, many firms have begun to look for ways to reduce health care costs as a means of increasing profitability. More and more firms now offer cash incentives to workers to opt out of the firm's health care plan or to elect not to cover their families. In fact, about half of all companies allow for "opting out," and it's been estimated that up to 20 percent of those who can opt out do, receiving $300 and upward in cash or other benefits for doing so. For example, at Avon Products, Inc., about one-quarter of the 6,700 full-time workers opt out of the health care plan, freeing up $1,450 each in benefit credits. These workers can use these savings to buy other benefits or take the money in cash.

> **FACTS OF LIFE**
>
> What do you think the cost of a 4-day hospital stay is? According to Harris Interactive, the average guess is $7,762, but the answer is over $20,000!

If your spouse also has health care coverage where he or she works, opting out may be reasonable. However, you must first consider what might happen if your spouse lost his or her job or if the company discontinues health care coverage, perhaps in a downsizing move. The question becomes, can you get back in your plan whenever you want?

The answer depends on your company. Some plans require a medical examination or only allow sign-up during an annual reenrollment period. One exception is a change in family or dependent status—perhaps marriage, birth, or adoption. These individuals are given special enrollment rights, which allow them to enroll without waiting until the plan's next regular enrollment period. If, however, opting out of your company's health care coverage means being left uncovered, then opting out probably doesn't make any sense at all. It's important not to get lured into trading your financial security for the "easy money" of opting out of coverage. In fact, starting in 2014, the Affordable Care Act states that employees must be automatically enrolled in their employer-sponsored health care plans.

Finding the Perfect Plan

What should you look for in a health insurance policy? First, it should include the full cost of basic services (minus your deductible). As Milton Berle once said, "The problem with a policy is that the big print giveth and the small print taketh away." Second, it should be noncancelable or guaranteed renewable. Don't understand what we just said? That's OK. You'll figure it out as we look at some of the important provisions in health insurance policies.

Important Provisions in Health Insurance Policies

Who's Covered?   Health insurance policies can cover individuals, families, or groups. If you have family coverage, you should have an understanding of (1) the age to which your children are covered and what happens if they're still dependents after this age, (2) what happens if you get divorced, and (3) whether stepchildren are covered. The point here is that you should understand exactly who's covered under your plan.

Terms of Payment   The terms of payment define your financial obligation on a health care claim, including any deductibles, coinsurance payments, limits on claims, and stop-loss provisions specified in your policy.

Deductibles or co-payments identify the amount of a claim that the policyholder pays on a claim. The higher the deductible, the lower the premium. It's a good idea to take the highest deductible, because you get more coverage per dollar that way. The insurance coverage is more efficient and you accomplish your goal of providing protection against catastrophes.

There may also be limits set on specific claims. For example, there may be a maximum dollar amount the policy will pay for specific operations. Alternatively, the limit may be set at what is customary in a particular geographic area. In addition, a stop-loss provision may also be included in the policy.

Preexisting Conditions   In 2011, most policies contained some type of preexisting condition provision, which excludes coverage for a specified length of time or forever for any preexisting illness that the policyholder may have. Obviously, this provision is meant to protect the insurance company and keep individuals from waiting until they identify health problems to sign up for health insurance. For those changing jobs, it's less of a problem. If you have had group health coverage for 2 years, and you switch jobs and go to another group coverage plan, the new health plan cannot impose another preexisting condition exclusion period. However, all that will change soon as the provisions of the Affordable Care Act kick in. One change already in place is that insurance companies can no longer deny children coverage based on a preexisting condition. In addition, starting in 2014, insurance companies will no longer be able to deny coverage to anyone with preexisting conditions.

Although it probably goes without saying, don't lie on your application—it could make the policy null and void. In addition, make sure you read your entire policy—don't assume the salesperson told you everything. Also, read all the updates that are sent to you—things can change.

Guaranteed Renewability   A **guaranteed renewability** provision allows you to renew your health insurance policy regardless of your health until you reach some preset age, generally 65. Although you can't be singled out for a rate increase, your premiums may rise if you are deemed more risky than before. Obviously, you want a health insurance plan you can always renew so that you don't get cut off if you get sick. Fortunately, in 2014, the guaranteed renewability becomes law for all insurance contracts other than student insurance—there's an exception for that because you can't keep your student insurance when you aren't a student.

Guaranteed Renewability
A health insurance provision that allows you to renew your policy regardless of your health until you reach some preset age, generally 65.

Exclusions   Some policies contain provisions that exclude certain injuries and illnesses. For example, costs associated with certain cosmetic dental procedures and cosmetic surgery are commonly excluded.

Emotional and Mental Disorders   Policies vary greatly with respect to the degree to which they allow for coverage of emotional and mental disorders. Today, stress-related disorders and depression, many times brought on by chemical imbalances in the brain, are extremely common. Although some policies provide full coverage, others don't cover any of these costs, and still others provide only partial or limited coverage for a relatively short time period.

STOP & THINK

Don't try to save money by buying less health insurance than you actually need—that only defeats the purpose of insurance, which is protection. You should also make sure your policy benefits keep up with inflation and your life circumstances. Review your policy every few years and whenever there's a major change, such as the birth of children, marriage, or divorce. How do you expect your health insurance needs to change in the coming years?

FACTS OF LIFE

The best insurance is living a healthy, safe life. For young adults, this means driving safely. Auto accidents are the number one killer of teenagers. In fact, across the country teens make up 5 percent of the driving population, but account for 14 percent of the country's auto fatalities. Nearly half of all 16- to 19-year-old female deaths occur as a result of automobile accidents. Among boys of the same age, 36 percent of deaths are due to crashes. More than one-quarter of drivers under 21 killed on the roadways have a blood alcohol content of 0.10 or higher. The likelihood of fatal crashes for teenagers is highest between 9 P.M. and 6 A.M.

In fact, costs from these disorders have risen so sharply in recent years that most policies require large co-payments or limit the number of annual visits to a psychiatrist or counselor. Fortunately, in 2014, mental health and substance use disorder services will become part of the essential benefits package, a set of health care service categories that must be covered by the plans offered through the exchanges and Medicaid. Given the very high costs that can be associated with emotional and mental disorders, it's a good idea to make sure your health insurance policy provides adequate coverage. Hey, you don't want insurance worries to drive you crazy.

 5 Describe disability insurance and the choices available to you.

Disability Insurance
Health insurance that provides payments to the insured in the event that income is interrupted by illness, sickness, or accident.

Disability Insurance

Disability insurance is related to health insurance, but it's more like earning-power insurance. When a disability occurs, life, along with all its expenses, goes on. What stops is your income. Your house payments continue, your children's educational costs continue, food and utility costs continue, and your medical expenses generally rise—all while your income stops.

Who needs disability insurance? Anyone who relies on income from a job. In fact, for individuals between the ages of 35 and 65, your chance of incurring a disability that would cause you to miss 90 or more days of work is equal to your chance of dying. A 30-year-old has about a 47 percent chance of incurring a 90-day disability before the age of 65. You need disability insurance, even if you're single and without dependents. If you have dependents who rely on your earning power, this insurance is a must. Remember, disability insurance kicks in only if there's a financial catastrophe in the offing. Therefore, it fits in perfectly with our view of necessary insurance.

Given its importance, why are so many people without it? The answer is, the price. Although the price varies greatly depending on age, health, and occupation, in addition to the dollar amount of coverage and how long you're disabled before the policy kicks in, it's easy to spend over $1,000 per year on disability insurance.

Your occupation may have the biggest impact on coverage costs. Insurers generally classify customers into one of five risk classes, depending on occupation. A college professor is generally classified as a class 5 risk, and a construction worker is classified as a class 1 risk. These ratings, in turn, are reflected in the rates charged, with the college professor being given a lower rate than a construction worker because the college professor has a lower probability of becoming disabled.

Sources of Disability Insurance

Many employers provide some level of disability insurance as part of a benefits package. Employers who don't include it in the benefits package may make group disability insurance available at favorable prices. If you're self-employed, you'll have to find a group plan or purchase an individual policy. Most individuals have some degree of coverage from Social Security or workers' compensation.

Although most workers are covered by some form of workers' compensation, these benefits apply only if the disability is work-related. The degree of coverage is determined by the individual states and, as a result, there's a good deal of variability from state to state. You shouldn't assume that you're covered or that your coverage is comprehensive.

For those covered by Social Security, disability benefits vary according to the number of years you've been in the Social Security system and your salary. However, if you qualify, you don't receive any payments until you've been disabled for 5 months, and then you receive benefits only if your disability is expected to last for at least 1 year or until death. Moreover, in order to qualify for benefits, you must not be able to work at any job, not just the job you were trained for.

How Much Disability Coverage Should You Have?

You should have enough disability insurance to maintain your living standard at an acceptable level if you are no longer able to work. Remember, your investment income won't stop with a disability, it's your income from working that will stop, and it's the portion of your income from working that you rely on to maintain your current standard of living that must be replaced. If you've accumulated some investments and are earning more than you need to live on—that is, saving a good portion of your earnings—you may need to replace only 30 percent of your after-tax income. However, someone with little savings who's living hand-to-mouth may need disability insurance that covers 80 percent of after-tax income.

Most insurance companies don't write disability policies that cover over 67 to 80 percent of a person's after-tax salary. They figure that if too much of your income is covered, you won't have an incentive to go back to work. Notice that the discussion focuses on the replacement of after-tax income. Although the insurance premiums that you pay on disability income aren't tax deductible, disability income is generally treated as tax-free income. Figure 9.3 provides a worksheet you can use to get an estimate of how much disability insurance coverage you might want or need.

Disability Features That Make Sense

Disability insurance policies vary more from insurance company to insurance company than do health insurance policies. Therefore, you really need to have an idea of what's desirable in a disability plan. The following sections discuss a few key features to look for.

Definition of Disability   What exactly does your policy consider a disability? In general, most policies define people as disabled if they can't perform the duties of their "own occupation" or perform the duties of "any occupation for which they are reasonably suited." Unfortunately, deciding what occupation for which you are "reasonably suited" may be difficult. It's wise to stick with a policy that defines you as disabled if you can't perform your normal job.

An alternative is the combination definition. Under the combination definition, you're covered if you can't perform your "own occupation" for the first 2 years of your disability. Thereafter, you're covered if you can't perform "any occupation for which

---

FIGURE 9.3 Worksheet for Estimating How Much Disability Insurance Coverage You Need

1. Current monthly after-tax job-related income   _____
2. Existing disability coverage on an *after-tax basis*
    - Social Security benefits   _____
    - Disability insurance from employer   + _____
    - Veterans' benefits and other federal and state
      disability insurance   + _____
    - Other disability coverage in place   + _____

    Total Existing Coverage   =   _____
3. Added disability coverage needed to maintain
    current level of after-tax job-related income
    in the event of a disability (subtract 2 from 1)   _____

Note: We haven't included workers' compensation disability benefits because they accompany only work-related injuries.

you're reasonably suited." Defining "disability" in this way promotes retraining during the first 2 years. Policies using this definition tend to be less expensive than those that use only the "own occupation" definition. Given the cost trade-offs, you might want to give serious consideration to policies that use a combination definition.

Residual or Partial Payments When Returning to Work Part-Time   Some policies offer partial disability payments that allow workers to return to work on a part-time basis and still receive benefits. These payments make up the difference between what workers would make if working full-time and their part-time earnings. Partial disability payments are a desirable feature, especially for the self-employed.

Short-Term Disability (STD)
A disability policy that provides benefits over a given period, generally from 6 months to 2 years.

Long-Term Disability (LTD)
A disability policy that provides benefits until the individual reaches an age specified in the contract, generally 65 or 70, or for the insured's lifetime.

Benefit Duration   Disability policies generally provide benefits for a maximum period, or until the disability ends (or the disabled person reaches 65 or 70 years of age). A **short-term disability (STD)** policy generally provides benefits on disabilities from 6 months to 2 years after a short wait of 8 to 30 days. A **long-term disability (LTD)** policy generally provides benefits until the individual reaches an age specified in the contract, or for the insured's lifetime. Only a long-term disability policy makes any sense, because only a long-term disability policy protects against financial catastrophe.

Waiting or Elimination Period
The period after the disability during which no benefits occur.

Waiting (or Elimination) Period   The **waiting or elimination period** refers to the period after the disability during which no benefits occur. The waiting period is equivalent to a deductible in a health care insurance policy. Most disability policies have waiting periods that range from 1 month to 6 months. Of course, the longer the waiting period, the less expensive the contract. In fact, a contract with a 3-month waiting period might lower costs by almost 30 percent from a contract with a 1-month waiting period.

> ## FACTS OF LIFE
>
> According to the American Council of Life Insurers, by the time you turn 85, you have a 50 percent chance of needing long-term care, and by 2040, when today's college graduates are turning 50, the cost of nursing homes is expected to run about $200,000 a year.

What disability insurance must protect you against is the loss of income associated with longer-term illnesses. Thus, in light of the cost differences, you should give serious consideration to a 3-month waiting period.

Waiver of Premium Provision
A disability insurance provision that allows your insurance to stay in force should you become unable to work because of disability or illness.

Waiver of Premium   In general, it's a good idea to have a **waiver of premium provision**, which waives premium payments if you become disabled. But be sure to look closely at the costs.

Noncancelable   You should also insist on a policy that's noncancelable. This provision protects you against having your policy canceled if, for whatever reason, your risk of becoming disabled increases, and it guarantees that the policy is renewable. It also protects you against rate increases.

Rehabilitation Coverage
A disability insurance provision that allows payments for vocational rehabilitation, allowing the policyholder to be retrained for employment.

Rehabilitation Coverage   A **rehabilitation coverage** provision provides for vocational rehabilitation, allowing the policyholder to be retrained for employment. This coverage generally provides for employment-related educational or job-training programs.

Long-Term Care Insurance
Insurance that's aimed at covering the costs associated with long-term nursing home care, commonly associated with victims of stroke, chronic illness, or Alzheimer's disease, or those who can simply no longer manage to live on their own.

Long-Term Care Insurance

6   Explain the purpose of long-term care insurance and the provisions that might be important to you.

Long-term care insurance pays for nursing home expenses as well as home health care. When first introduced some 25 years ago, it was marketed strictly as "nursing home insurance." Now it has evolved to meet the needs of individuals who need care but still can stay in their own home. The insurance is meant to cover the costs associated with long-term care for those who have had strokes, chronic diseases, or Alzheimer's disease, as well as those who can simply no longer manage to live on their own. In effect, it's another form of disability insurance. Its downside is that it's expensive.

It would seem that long-term health care should either be a part of major medical insurance or covered under Medicare. It isn't. This is actually a relatively new area of coverage for insurance. It's been partially inspired by our increasing life expectancies and the resultant increase in the chance that you may eventually need some level of care. The interest in long-term health care coverage has also been inspired by the high cost of such care.

Long-term health care insurance is meant to protect you against the financial consequences of these costs. These policies are generally set up to provide a daily dollar benefit over the time the policyholder requires nursing home care. With most policies, these benefits are not subject to federal taxes. The payments are generally sent directly to the nursing home to cover charges. They're often not available to individuals under 40 years of age, with the premiums rising for older policyholders. Unfortunately, many long-term care insurance policies come laden with exceptions and conditions. Moreover, the lack of understanding and uniformity associated with some policies allows them to be sold not as a part of a financial plan, but through the use of fear tactics.

If you're going to purchase long-term health care insurance, make sure you do so while you're healthy. You'll also want to look for good health and marital discounts. In fact, if you're in good health you can save up to 10 percent from John Hancock and up to 20 percent from Unum. In addition, most companies offer discounts from 10 percent to 20 percent for married couples who purchase two policies. As with other types of health care insurance, it's available only when you don't need it. It should also only be purchased from high-quality insurance companies. Table 9.9 provides a listing of some of the provisions you might want to have included in a long-term health care policy, while Table 9.10 provides some questions to ask when considering a long-term health care policy.

TABLE 9.9 Long-Term Health Care Provisions

Necessary

Selection of Company Consider only high-quality insurance companies with either an A11 or an A1 rating from A.M. Best. Never consider TV-celebrity-advertised insurance.

Qualifying for Benefits The insured is unable to perform at most two "activities of daily living" (ADLs) without assistance.

Qualifying for Benefits Policy includes coverage for Alzheimer's and Parkinson's disease.

Qualifying for Benefits Hospital stay not required for benefits.

Benefit Period A minimum 3- to 6-year benefit period.

Inflation Adjustment The policy should give you the option of purchasing inflation coverage.

Noncancelability The policy should not be cancelable.

Desirable, but Not Necessary—Cost–Benefit Trade-Offs

Waiver of Premium While desirable, it may be too expensive to warrant serious consideration.

Type of Care Home care, adult day care, and hospice care for the terminally ill.

Benefit Period Women should consider longer benefit periods.

Cost-Reducing Provision to Consider

Waiting Period Consider a waiting period of 100 days or more—if affordable.

Provisions to Avoid—Not Worth the Cost

Nonforfeiture Clause or Provision Simply too expensive.

TABLE 9.10 Long -Term Care Insurance
Medical advances have resulted in an increased need for nursing home care and assisted living. Most health insurance plans and Medicare severely limit or exclude long-term care. Here are some questions to ask when considering a separate long-term care insurance policy:
• **What qualifies you for benefits?** Some insurers say you must be unable to perform a specific number of the following activities of daily living: eating, walking, getting from bed to a chair, dressing, bathing, using the restroom, and remaining continent.
• **What type of care is covered?** Does the policy cover nursing home care? What about coverage for assisted-living facilities that provide less client care than a nursing home? If you want to stay in your home, will it pay for care provided by visiting nurses and therapists? What about help with food preparation and housecleaning?
• **What will the benefit amount be?** Most plans are written to provide a specific dollar benefit per day. The benefit for home care is usually about half the nursing home benefit, but some policies pay the same for both forms of care. Other plans pay only for your actual expenses.
• **What is the benefit period?** It is possible to get a policy with lifetime benefits, but this can be very expensive. Other options for coverage are from 1 to 6 years. The average nursing home stay is about 2.5 years.
• **Is the benefit adjusted for inflation?** If you buy a policy prior to age 60, you face the risk that a fixed daily benefit will not be enough by the time you need it.
• **Is there a waiting period before benefits begin?** A 20- to 100-day period is not unusual.

Source: U.S. General Services Administration, Consumer Action Handbook, 2011, www.consumeraction.gov/.

Those who have a history of long-term disabilities, Alzheimer's, or Parkinson's disease in the family and those who have savings they want to protect should consider long-term health care insurance. If you don't have funds to cover nursing home care, Medicaid, which is aimed at the needy, will cover your costs. If you have money but don't have dependents, you probably don't need long-term health care insurance. If you need nursing home care, pay for it out of your savings. After all, you saved that money to provide for you in retirement.

Most policies require the insured to be unable to perform at most two "activities of daily living" (ADLs) without assistance. These ADLs include such tasks as walking, dressing, and eating. Some plans also allow cognitive impairment, such as the short-term memory loss suffered by Alzheimer's and Parkinson's disease patients, to be sufficient for benefits. You should consider only policies that include coverage for Alzheimer's and Parkinson's disease. The following sections discuss some provisions to consider.

> **FACTS OF LIFE**
>
> According to the Health Institute Association of America, approximately 10 million Americans age 65 or older needed long-term care in 2011 and that number is expected to increase to 12 million by 2020. And according to a survey by John Hancock, the average annual cost of 1 year in a nursing home in a private room reached just over $85,775 in 2011.

Type of Care   Policies vary with respect to the coverage of home care. Some policies provide only nursing home care, while others provide for adult day care and hospice care for the terminally ill. In fact, a number of long-term care policies recently have provided for reimbursement for nonlicensed caregivers, including family and friends, rather than requiring care to be provided only by licensed caregivers. It's a good idea to seek a policy with flexible coverage provisions and a home care option.

Benefit Period   Benefit periods on long-term health care insurance can range all the way from 1 year to lifetime. Unfortunately, lifetime coverage provisions tend to be very expensive. Because the average stay in a nursing home is under 2 years, you should make sure your coverage has a minimum 3- to 6-year benefit period. In addition, because women tend to spend longer periods in nursing care than men, women should consider a longer benefit period.

Waiting Period   Just as with disability insurance, the waiting period on long-term care insurance can be thought of as a deductible—you have to absorb the expense of nursing home care during the waiting period. This waiting period can run anywhere from 0 days up to a full year—but the most common is a waiting period of from 20 to 100 days. As you might expect, the longer the waiting period, the less the cost of the insurance.

For example, at age 65 simply by raising the waiting period from 20 days to 100 days you can cut the cost of a long-term care policy to just over 10 percent of what it would cost otherwise. That's a pretty hefty savings, but if you do require care, that difference of 80 days in the waiting period would cost you $12,000 the first year and even more as the level of your protection rises with the inflation protection. For that reason, many financial advisors recommend that you go with a 20-day waiting period.

Inflation Adjustment   There's no telling what the cost of nursing home care will be when you need it. If nursing home costs increase by 5 percent per year, they will double in only 15 years. Without some inflation protection, your policy may not be of much help when you need it. Make sure to include an inflation protection provision if you buy long-term health care insurance.

Waiver of Premium   A waiver of premium provision allows your insurance to stay in force while you are receiving benefits. This is an area that has undergone a good deal of change recently. Most policies waive premiums once you begin receiving benefits. Recently, many companies have begun to offer dual waiver of premium riders: Both spouses' premiums are waived when either one of them meets the waiver of premium conditions. However, you should be careful in selecting this option because the costs associated with it can vary dramatically from policy to policy.

Summary

Understand the importance of insurance.
The purpose of life insurance is to control the financial effect your dependents experience when you die. Life insurance can replace the lost income that results from the death of the wage earner. Insurance is based on the concept of risk pooling. With life insurance, everyone pays a premium, determined by the probability of your dying, and no one suffers a big loss.

Determine your life insurance needs and design a life insurance program.
The first step in determining how much life insurance you need is to review your net worth. The larger your net worth, the more you have in the way of wealth to support your family, and consequently the less life insurance you need. The earnings multiple approach provides a rough estimate of your needs by using a multiple of your yearly income. An alternative method of determining how much insurance you need is the needs approach.

Describe the major types of coverage available and the typical provisions that are included.
There are two very different categories of life insurance—term and cash-value. Term life insurance is pure life insurance that pays the beneficiary the face value of the policy if the insured individual dies during the coverage

period. Cash-value insurance is any policy that provides both a death benefit and an opportunity to accumulate cash value.

One way of fine-tuning your insurance policy is through riders. A rider is a special provision that may be added to your policy. In general, life insurance death benefits are income tax free. Thus, if there's a single lump-sum settlement, there are generally no taxes due on the full face value of the contract.

Once you've determined your needs, the first order of business is selecting an insurance company and an agent. The final step is to compare the costs of the competing policies.

 Design a health care insurance program and understand what provisions are important to you.

In March 2010 President Obama signed into law the Affordable Care Act. The reforms within this act go into effect over time, with portions of the new law being effective immediately and the final portions of the law going into effect in 2018. The Affordable Care Act makes major changes in health care, but your interaction with the U.S. medical system will remain more or less the same—you'll pay a private insurance company and they'll reimburse your doctors for care. The law is aimed at providing new consumer protections, improving quality and lowering costs, increasing access to affordable care, and holding insurance companies accountable.

Health insurance serves the same purpose as other forms of insurance— to protect you and your dependents from financial catastrophe. Most health insurance includes a combination of hospital, surgical, and physician expense insurance, which is generally sold in a combination called basic health insurance. Major medical expense insurance is aimed at covering medical costs beyond those covered by basic health insurance.

The choices of health care providers are traditional fee-for-service plans and managed health care or prepaid care. Many times under a fee-for-service plan, there's a deductible or coinsurance fee. A deductible is the amount the insured must pay before the insurance company will begin paying benefits, and a coinsurance or percentage participation provision defines the percentage of each claim that the insurance company will pay.

 Describe disability insurance and the choices available to you.

Disability insurance provides income in the event of a disability. Anyone who relies on income from a job for financial support needs disability insurance. Many employers provide some level of disability insurance as part of their benefits package.

 Explain the purpose of long-term care insurance and the provisions that might be important to you.

Long-term care insurance is another form of disability insurance that covers the cost of long-term nursing home care. Provisions to consider include the type of care, the benefit period, the waiting period, inflation adjustment, and a waiver of premium.

Review Questions

1. How are the concepts of the risk–return trade-off, risk pooling, and the work of actuaries a foundation for the logic of insurance as well as the premium you will ultimately pay?

2. Define the following life insurance terms: *beneficiary, face amount, insured, policy-holder,* and *policy owner.* How are these terms related?

3. How does the Affordable Care Act address the issue of individuals with no health insurance? What percentage of Americans are expected to have health insurance by the time the act is fully implemented?

4. What is the main purpose of life insurance? Describe the types of households that need life insurance and those that do not. Summarize the underlying factors that determine the need for life insurance.

5. Compare and contrast the two basic approaches used to determine the amount of life insurance needed. What are the primary factors considered?

6. Briefly describe five common types of term life insurance.

7. Briefly describe the three major categories of cash-value life insurance.

8. Describe the major differences between term and cash-value life insurance. What are the primary advantages and disadvantages of each?

9. Define the following life insurance policy features: coverage grace period, loan clause, nonforfeiture clause, policy reinstatement clause, suicide clause, and incontestability clause.

10. What is a policy rider? Describe five commonly available life insurance policy riders.

11. Explain the four primary life insurance policy settlement options available to the beneficiary.

12. When a beneficiary chooses income for life, what monthly income options are available?

13. When shopping for life insurance, what key factors should you consider when comparing companies, agents, and cash-value and term policies? How could the Internet assist you?

14. Explain the new health insurance exchange system as outlined in the Affordable Care Act. How does this benefit self-employed individuals?

15. The Affordable Care Act has four major provisions. List these and explain at least two changes that are associated with the provision.

16. Define *coinsurance* and *deductible.*

17. Why are dental and eye insurance, dread disease insurance, and accident insurance typically not recommended? What's the best alternative for meeting these expenses?

18. What are the fundamental differences between a fee-for-service health care plan and a managed health care plan? Beyond the method of paying for services, what is the other fundamental difference?

19. Both an HMO and a PPO health plan are examples of managed health care. Describe the similarities and differences between these two plans.

20. Describe the major differences between group health insurance and individual health insurance. Which is likely to be cheaper?

21. When shopping for an individual health insurance policy, what factors should you compare?

22. What steps should you take if your health insurance claim is denied?

23. Briefly describe the target recipients and the benefits provided by the government-sponsored health care plans of workers' compensation, Medicare, and Medicaid. Who is eligible for coverage under each plan?

24. How do Medicare Parts B, C, and D, and Medigap policies expand the health care coverage available to persons 65 and older who qualify for Social Security?

25. Summarize the advantages and disadvantages of using a flexible spending account to help control health care costs. What is the cap on how much you can contribute to a flexible spending account?

26. How does the combination of a qualified high-deductible health insurance plan and a Health Savings Account offer a cost-effective approach to paying for health care? Who might find this option beneficial?

27. What health care protection does the COBRA law provide?

28. Summarize the advantages and disadvantages of "opting out" of employer-sponsored health insurance. If you opt out of coverage, what exceptions will allow you to enroll in your employer-sponsored health care plan without having to wait until the next open enrollment period?

29. Define the following health care policy terms: *guaranteed renewable* and *exclusions*. How has the Affordable Care Act changed the coverage for preexisting conditions and mental disorders?

30. What protection does disability insurance provide? Who provides disability insurance coverage and why is it important? How much coverage should consumers purchase?

31. Define the following disability insurance terms: *definition of disability*, *residual (partial) payments*, and *benefit duration*. Why is the definition of disability so critical to the availability of benefits?

32. Describe long-term care insurance. What policy features should a person look for when shopping for a long-term care policy?

33. Why are the waiting (elimination) period and the waiver of premium important provisions when purchasing disability *and* long-term care insurance?

Develop Your Skills—Problems and Activities

These problems are available in MyFinanceLab.

1. Joetta Hernandez is a single parent with two children and she earns $45,000 a year. Her employer's group life insurance policy would pay 2.5 times her salary. She also has $60,000 saved in a 401(k) plan, $5,000 in mutual funds, and a $3,000 CD. She wants to purchase term life insurance for 15 years until her youngest child is self-supporting. She is not concerned about her outstanding mortgage, as the children would live with her sister in the event of Joetta's death. Assuming she can receive a 3 percent after-tax, after-inflation return on insurance proceeds, use the earnings multiple method to calculate her insurance need. How much more insurance does Joetta need to buy? What other information would you need to know to use the needs approach to calculate Joetta's insurance coverage?

2. Virgil Cronk wants to purchase a life insurance policy where he can increase his future coverage without having to take another medical exam. Virgil's family has a history of cardiac problems. Name at least two policy riders that he should consider adding to his policy. Virgil's friend Roy, who has been diagnosed with advanced AIDS, is being treated with a number of experimental drugs. What rider would benefit a terminally ill person such as Roy?

3. The Baulding family has a basic health insurance plan that pays 80 percent of out-of-hospital expenses up to $3,000 a year after a deductible of $250 per person. If three family members have doctor and prescription drug expenses of $980, $1,840, and $220, respectively, how much will the Bauldings family and the insurance company each pay? How could they benefit from a flexible spending account established through Mr. Baulding's employer? What are the advantages and disadvantages of establishing such an account?

4. Latesha Moore has a choice at work between a traditional health insurance plan that pays 80 percent of the cost of doctor visits after a $250 deductible and an HMO that charges a $10 co-payment per visit plus a $20 monthly premium deduction from her paycheck. Latesha anticipates seeing a doctor once a month for her high blood pressure. The cost of each office visit is $50. She normally sees the doctor an average of three times a year for other health concerns. Comment on the difference in costs between the two health care plans and the advantages and disadvantages of each.

5. Julie Rios has take-home pay of $3,200 per month and a disability insurance policy that replaces 60 percent of earnings after a 90-day (3-month) waiting period. She has accumulated 80 sick days at work. Julie was involved in an auto accident and was out of work for 4 months. How much income did she lose and how much would be replaced by her disability policy? How else could she replace her lost earnings? If after 4 months Julie could only return to work half-time for an additional 3 months due to continuing physical therapy, how might she benefit from a residual benefits clause? How much will she receive in disability benefits for this period?

6. Bobbi Hilton, 62, is considering the purchase of a 5-year long-term care policy. If nursing home costs average $5,000 per month in her area, how much could she have to pay out-of-pocket for 5 years without long-term care insurance? What can Bobbi do to reduce the cost of this coverage?

Learn by Doing—Suggested Projects

1. Interview at least three people from different stages of the life cycle to determine if they own one or more of the following: life insurance, health insurance, dental or eye care insurance, dread disease insurance, accident insurance, disability insurance, or long-term care insurance. What factors influenced their decision to buy or not buy the insurance coverage? Also inquire about the amount of coverage, type of policy, and premium cost. Prepare a report of your findings.

2. Use an Internet quote service and obtain life insurance premium quotes for $100,000 of term, whole life, and universal life insurance. Base your request on your own age, gender, and health characteristics (e.g., nonsmoker). How would the costs change if your health characteristics changed (e.g., smoker or non-smoker)? What if you waited 10 years? How do your characteristics or the projected changes relate to the concept of risk pooling? Prepare a one-page report of your findings.

3. Interview a friend employed in your career field or interview a benefits representative from a company/agency in your career field. Discuss the benefits that you might expect to receive as an employee (e.g., life, health, dental, eye care, accident, or disability insurance) and the out-of-pocket premium costs. Share your findings within the group; summarize the differences in the benefit packages identified in different industries or sectors of the economy.

4. Read your parents' life insurance policy, or that of a friend or relative, cover to cover. Prepare a one-page report of key policy features including beneficiary designation, policy clauses, settlement options, nonforfeiture options, and riders. Interpret the nonforfeiture options if the policy owner ceased premium payments.

5. Follow the systematic process of shopping for life insurance by comparing information on the company, the agent (if applicable), and the policy for at least two different term policies. Base the purchase on your own personal characteristics and a face amount of $100,000. Be sure to include the guaranteed insurability rider as well as any other riders appropriate to your situation. Document your findings and defend your policy choice.

6. Many college students lose health insurance coverage through their parents' policy on the day of graduation or a specified birthday (e.g., age 26). If you are covered through your parents' policy, determine when your coverage will end. Then determine available options for purchasing health insurance through your parents' group coverage using COBRA, your university, or other independent or group options. Determine your best alternative; report on the coverage and the premium.

7. Begin or increase an activity associated with maintaining a healthy lifestyle (e.g., diet, exercise, and not smoking). Change your habit and maintain this activity for at least a month. Did the lifestyle change increase or decrease spending in the short term? What insurance costs might be affected in the long term? Report on your experience.

8. Talk to one or more senior citizens about their experiences with Medicare and/or supplemental Medigap health insurance. How does this coverage and the processing of claims compare with the coverage available prior to retirement? Did those you interviewed have the option to continue their company-provided benefits in retirement? Report your findings.

9. As a part of a group project, interview a representative from a nursing home, extended care facility, or other assisted living facility and discuss the costs and payment methods used. Are residents using Medicare, Medigap, Medicaid, long-term care insurance, or personal funds to pay for the facility's services? Tour the facility and note your impressions of the facility and the resident activities. Report your findings to the group and compare the results from different care facilities.

Be a Financial Planner—Discussion Case 1

This case is available in MyFinanceLab.

Adam and Cassie Porterfield, a healthy couple in their mid-30s, were delighted when Adam landed a new job with a promotion and increased salary. But, they were disappointed to learn that he would not be eligible for benefits for 90 days. The company offers a comprehensive package of health insurance, vision insurance, dental insurance, life insurance (1.5 times salary at no premium charge), short- and long-term disability insurance, and long-term care insurance. An employee can choose how to spend the employer-provided premium dollars to purchase any combination of insurance or additional life insurance.

Questions

1. In the mix of premiums the Porterfields can spend, how should Adam and Cassie rank Adam's insurance needs for the seven types of coverage offered? What factors should they consider?

2. Should Adam consider purchasing more life insurance than the company-provided free benefit? What two methods could he use to assess his needs relative to his total life insurance coverage?

3. Adam has heard that his employer offers a health insurance "opt out" option with a $75-per-month payment to the employee. Assuming Cassie's employer offers very similar coverage limits, should Adam and Cassie consider the opt out option? Discuss the pros and cons of opting out.

4. Name two or three important factors to consider when purchasing disability insurance. Should Adam first consider short-term or long-term disability?

5. Should the Porterfields consider changing their company-provided insurance benefits if they become parents? Defend your answer.

Be a Financial Planner—Discussion Case 2

This case is available in MyFinanceLab.

Wendy and Frank Kampe, 30 and 35, are considering the purchase of life insurance. Wendy doesn't have any coverage whereas Frank has a $150,000 group policy at work. The Kampes have two young children, ages 3 and 5. Wendy earns $28,000 annually from a part-time, home-based business. Frank's annual salary is $55,000. From their income, they save $7,500 a year. The rest goes for expenses. The couple estimates that the children will be financially dependent, except for college costs, for about another 15 years. Once the children are in college, Wendy assumes their annual expenses will be $60,000.

In preparation for a visit with their insurance agent, the Kampes have estimated the following expenses if Frank were to die:

Immediate needs at death	$25,000
Outstanding debt (including mortgage repayment)	$90,000
Transitional funds for Wendy to expand her business to fully support the family	$15,000
College expenses for their two children	$205,000

They also anticipate, should Frank die, receiving $8,000 a year in Social Security survivor's benefits until the youngest child turns 18, and $5,000 annually in pension benefits, until Wendy turns 80. Wendy projects her gross annual income to be $40,000 after her business expansion. Once the children are self-supporting, Wendy wants to plan a spousal life income for 15 more years, from age 45 to age 60. Lastly, she wants to plan on $30,000 a year in retirement income for another 20 years from age 60 to age 80. She anticipates receiving a 5 percent after-tax, after-inflation return on their investments.

To date, the Kampes have accumulated a total of $107,000 of assets, not including $45,000 of home equity. Their assets include $10,000 in an emergency fund, $12,000 in IRA funds for Wendy, $35,000 in other investments, and $50,000 in Frank's employer 401(k) plan.

Questions

1. Using Worksheet 12, determine the amount of additional life insurance, if any, that the Kampes should purchase to protect Wendy if Frank should die. (*Hint:* Wendy's IRA balance is included in the total available assets on line ff. This is an assumption that would not be right for every situation given that access to the money would be limited by IRS withdrawal taxes and penalties.)

2. Should Wendy purchase an insurance policy? Why or why not? If so, what type of policy would you recommend for Wendy?

3. What type of life insurance policy would you recommend that Frank purchase?

4. What would happen to Frank's group life insurance if he leaves his present job?

5. What could happen to the Kampes' children if Frank or Wendy should die without adequate life insurance coverage?

6. Should the Kampes name the children as life insurance beneficiaries?

7. Which life insurance riders might the Kampes select when purchasing a policy?

8. Since they will make a concerted effort to become informed about life insurance, should the Kampes also purchase life insurance on the children, rather than waiting until later when they would have to reeducate themselves for life insurance shopping?

9. The Kampes save $7,500 a year for an emergency fund, retirement, and other investments, with the remainder spent to support their lifestyle. How might the concept of mental accounting and **Principle 9: Mind Games, Your Financial Personality, and Your Money** affect their decision to purchase life insurance?

10 Property and Liability Insurance

Learning Objectives

 Understand, buy, and maintain homeowner's insurance in a cost-effective way.

 Recover on a liability or a loss to your property.

 Buy the automobile insurance policy that's right for you.

 File a claim on your automobile insurance.

Roseanne Dore was no stranger to hard luck. Her husband died about 10 years ago and left her alone to raise their three daughters who were 12, 7, and 3 at the time. But she rose to the occasion, taking a job as a cafeteria server at the local elementary school and did her best, even serving as a Girl Scout leader. Fortunately, she did have a house to raise her children in, a house that she and her late husband built together. But tragedy struck again; her home on Kiwi Lane in Kingston, Washington, burned to the ground. For most people, insurance would have saved the day. But when Dore filed a claim on her insurance policy, she found out that her home insurance policy had lapsed when her agent retired. The house was completely uninhabitable and Roseanne was forced to move with her three daughters into a half-built, backyard storage shed that had no plumbing, electricity, or running water.

Fortunately for the Dores, things turned out in the end. Just after sunup on an early November morning, six strangers snuck across the pasture adjacent to their house and ran up to the door. Prime time television had come to Kiwi Lane. From in front of their makeshift shelter, Rosanne Dore and her three daughters were summoned to the

door with a "Good morning, Dore family!"—the signature line of Ty Pennington, host of ABC TV's *Extreme Makeover: Home Edition.* What followed was high-ratings television at its best. The Dores were whisked away in a limousine and flown to Disney World in Florida for a 1-week vacation and returned to a new two-story, 3,200-square-foot house worth an estimated $500,000, with six bedrooms and seven bathrooms, stocked with food, dishes, linens, and furniture.

People don't like to think about tragedy. Mulling over fire, floods, and car accidents just doesn't make for much fun. However, unless you're the Dore family, you need to prepare for these unlikely, unlucky events. How? Insurance. Let's face it, if you haven't prepared ahead of time with insurance, the experience becomes much worse. In the end, the Dores were lucky, but you probably won't have their luck so you'd better have insurance.

As with health and life insurance, the logic behind property insurance and is drawn from the idea of diversification in **Principle 8: Risk and Return Go Hand in Hand**. Property insurance allows individuals to pool the financial risks associated with property losses—a fire, burglary, or auto accident—to eliminate catastrophic losses. Everyone shares in everyone else's property losses by paying the average cost. As a result, no one experiences a catastrophic loss.

The purpose of homeowner's insurance, automobile insurance, and other types of insurance, is the same: to guard against financial catastrophe. The need for property insurance rises from **Principle 7: Protect Yourself Against Major Catastrophes**. In the case of property insurance, our philosophy continues to be to provide protection against major catastrophes while ignoring the small stuff. It's not the $60 broken window that you should be concerned about—it's the $60,000 damage to your kitchen from an oven fire. The $60,000 expense could wipe out your entire savings if you don't have homeowner's insurance.

The insurance discussed in this chapter protects you against the financial risks of loss of or damage to your home or automobile, and the legal liabilities associated with injuries or property damage to others. Unfortunately, homeowner's and automobile insurance policies, similar to life and health policies, are filled with their own jargon. Deciding how much and exactly what kind of insurance to buy is a challenge. Don't worry, though. This chapter teaches you what you need to know to manage your homeowner's and automobile insurance like a pro.

The Dores got their second chance, and you can bet this time through they've got insurance.

1 Understand, buy, and maintain homeowner's insurance in a cost-effective way.

Peril
An event or happening, whether natural or man-made, that causes a financial loss.

Protecting Your Home

In the United States, the first type of homeowner's insurance was fire insurance, offered in 1735 by a small company in Charleston, South Carolina. It wasn't until 1958 that the first modern "homeowner's" policy was sold.

Before homeowner's insurance, separate insurance policies were needed for every **peril**—that is, there was an insurance policy to cover fire, theft, windstorm damage, and so forth. Homeowner's insurance simplified the process by offering protection against multiple perils in one overarching policy. This new type of policy gave families peace of mind. It also helped them keep better track of their coverage by consolidating what would have previously been numerous different policies, probably with numerous different companies.

Today's homeowner's policies are sold in six basic versions. While you can add extra forms of coverage and individualize your insurance, the standardization makes comparison shopping easy—much easier than shopping for any other type of insurance. Unfortunately, standardization has actually stifled competition a bit. As a result, the homeowner's insurance industry is dominated by the five largest insurers, who insure about half of all homes. Let's take a look at these six standardized policies.

Packaged Policies: HOs

HOs
The six standardized "homeowner's" insurance policies available to homeowners and renters.

Named Perils
A type of insurance that covers a specific set of named perils. If a peril isn't specifically named, it isn't covered.

Open Perils
A type of insurance that covers all perils except those specifically noted as excluded.

Property Insurance
Insurance that protects you against the loss of your property or possessions.

Personal Liability Insurance
Insurance covering all liabilities other than those resulting from the negligent operation of an automobile or those associated with business or professional causes.

Today's six basic homeowner's policies are known as **HOs**, which stands for Home Owners. Although they're called homeowner's insurance, they cover more than the home. They also provide liability insurance and cover renters. Three of them, HO-1, HO-2, and HO-3, provide basic, broad policies specifically for homeowners with HO-1 and HO-2 offering **named perils** insurance, while HO-3 offers **open perils** insurance. Policy HO-4 is actually renter's insurance, HO-6 is for condominium owners, and HO-8 is for older homes.

Table 10.1 summarizes the basic coverage provided under each of these policies. Although each packaged policy provides a different type and level of insurance, all six HOs are divided into two sections. Section I addresses **property insurance**, which protects you against the loss of your property or possessions due to various perils. Section II provides for **personal liability insurance**, which protects you from the financial losses incurred if someone is injured on your property or as a result of your actions.

Section I: Property Coverage   Property covered under homeowner's insurance is covered for a certain dollar amount. This is the maximum amount the insurance company will pay out for a given claim. If an item is insured for $100,000, the insurance company will pay out claims of up to $100,000.

TABLE 10.1 Comparing Homeowner's Insurance Policies

HO-1 (Basic Form)—Provides such very narrow coverage that it isn't available in most states.

A. Dwelling: Based on structure's replacement value; minimum $15,000

B. Other structures: 10% of insurance on house

C. Personal property: 50% of insurance on house

D. Loss of use: 10% of insurance on house

Covered Perils:

- Fire or lightning
- Vandalism or malicious mischief
- Riot or civil commotion
- Volcanic eruption

- Smoke
- Explosion
- Glass breakage
- Vehicles

- Windstorm or hail
- Theft
- Aircraft

E. Personal liability: $100,000

F. Medical payments to others: $1,000 per person

HO-2 (Broad Form)—A named perils form of insurance. That is, it covers a set of named perils, such as fire, lightning, windstorm, and so on. If a peril isn't specifically named in this policy, it isn't covered. Typically costs 5 to 10 percent more than HO-1 coverage.

Coverage A, B, C, E, and F same as HO-1

D. Loss of use: 20% of insurance on house

Covered Perils: Same as HO-1, plus:

- Falling objects
- Weight of ice, snow, or sleet
- Accidental discharge of water or steam
- Accidental tearing apart or cracking of heating system, air-conditioning, fire sprinkler, or appliance

- Freezing of plumbing, heating, air-conditioning, fire sprinkler, or appliance
- Accidental damage from electrical current

HO-3 (All-Risk Form)—Covers all direct physical losses to your home. It offers open perils protection, meaning it covers all perils except those specifically excluded. Excluded perils might include flood, earthquake, war, and nuclear accident. Typically costs 10 to 15 percent more than an HO-1 policy.

Coverage B, C, D, E, and F same as HO-2

A. Dwelling: Based on structure's replacement value; minimum $20,000

Covered Perils: Same perils for personal property as HO-2

- Dwelling and other structures are covered against risk of direct loss to property. All losses are covered except those losses specifically excluded.

HO-4 (Renter's Form)—Aimed at renters or tenants and covers personal belongings, but does not include liability insurance.

Coverage E and F same as HO-1 and HO-2

A. Dwelling: Not applicable

B. Other structures: Not applicable

C. Personal property: Minimum varies by company

D. Loss of use: 20% of insurance on personal property

Covered Perils: Same perils for personal property as HO-2

HO-6 (Condominium Form)—Provides personal property and liability insurance for co-op or condominium owners.

Coverage E and F same as HO-1 and HO-2

A. Dwelling: $1,000 minimum on the unit

B. Other structures: Included in Coverage A

C. Personal property: Minimum varies by company

D. Loss of use: 40% of insurance on personal property

Covered Perils: Same perils for personal property as HO-2

(continued)

TABLE 10.1   Comparing Homeowner's Insurance Policies (*continued*)

HO-8 (Older Homes Insurance)—Designed for older homes, insuring them for repair costs or actual cash value rather than replacement cost.

Coverage E and F same as HO-1 and HO-2

A. Dwelling: Based on structure's market value
B. Other structures: 10% of insurance on house
C. Personal property: 50% of insurance on house
D. Loss of use: 10% of insurance on house

Covered Perils: Same as HO-1

Within Section I of all HO policies, except HO-4, there are four basic coverages:

- ◆ Coverage A: Dwelling
- ◆ Coverage B: Other structures
- ◆ Coverage C: Personal property
- ◆ Coverage D: Loss of use

Coverage A protects the house and any attachments to it—for example, an attached garage. However, if the land surrounding the house is destroyed by an explosion, this coverage won't pay to repair or restore it.

Coverage B protects other structures on the premises that aren't attached to the house—for example, your landscaping, a detached garage, or an outhouse. The level of this coverage is limited to 10 percent of the home's coverage. For example, if the home carries $200,000 of insurance, the other structures would carry $20,000 insurance. Still, at $20,000, that's one valuable outhouse! Again, the land isn't covered, and if the additional structure is used for business purposes, it's not covered.

> **FACTS OF LIFE**
>
> When you apply for homeowner's insurance, don't add the cost of the land. After all, your land will still be there no matter what happens. If you add in the land value you'll be buying more insurance than you need, and you'll be spending more than is necessary.

Coverage C protects any personal property that's owned or used by the policyholder, regardless of the location of this property. In other words, if you're on a vacation in Hawaii and someone hits you with a pineapple and steals your suitcase, your personal property is still covered. In addition, the personal property of your guests is covered while that property is in your home. So, if your home burns down during a party, any personal property losses of guests would be covered.

The amount of this coverage is equal to 50 percent of the home's coverage. Thus, if the home carries $200,000 of insurance, the personal property insurance would be $100,000. Within this coverage there are limits on some types of losses. For example, there's a $200 limit on money, bank notes, gold, and silver. There's also a $1,000 limit on securities, valuable papers, manuscripts, tickets, and stamps, and a $2,500 limit on the theft of silverware, goldware, and pewterware. In addition, certain property is excluded from coverage—for example, animals, birds, and fish. Before buying any policy, be aware of all of its limitations.

Coverage D provides benefits if your home can't be used because of an insured loss. The amount of loss of use coverage is limited to 20 percent of the amount of insurance on the house. Under this coverage, three benefits are provided: additional living expenses, fair rental value, and prohibited use. The additional living expenses benefits reimburse you for the cost of living in a temporary location until your home is repaired. The fair rental value benefit covers any rental losses you might experience. For example, if you rent a room in your home for $300 per month, and because of a fire it's uninhabitable for 2 months, you'd receive $600 for the loss of rent. Prohibited use coverage provides living expenses for up to 2 weeks if a civil authority declares your home to be uninhabitable, perhaps because of a gas leak in a neighbor's home.

Section II: Personal Liability Coverage   Section II of a homeowner's insurance policy covers personal liability, which protects policyholders and their family members from financial loss if someone is injured on their property or as a result of their actions. It's extremely important because of the protection it provides against potentially catastrophic losses from liability suits. This protection covers all liabilities other than business and professional liability, and liabilities resulting from the negligent operation of an automobile. The minimum level of liability coverage per accident is $100,000.

Personal liability also covers the medical expenses of anyone injured by the policyholders, their family, or by an animal they own. These days, when everyone wants to sue everyone else for outrageous settlements, it's good to have your liabilities covered. You never know when your close friends or dear Aunt Edith might slip on your stairs, scrape a shin, and sue you for several million dollars in damages.

This portion of Section II is really a small medical insurance policy. It covers payments up to $1,000 for medical expenses to nonfamily members who are injured in your home. For example, if someone falls down your stairs and breaks a leg, this coverage would take care of up to $1,000 worth of their medical expenses.

Supplemental Coverage

Coverage C of Section I of an HO provides protection for your personal property. However, depending on the type and dollar value of your assets, or the perils that you face, you might want to consider supplemental coverage. There are dozens of types of supplemental coverage to choose from. Some of the more common types that we will look at in detail next include personal articles floaters, earthquake protection, flood protection, inflation guard, and replacement cost. In general, the additional coverage can be added through an **endorsement**, which is a written attachment to an insurance policy to add or subtract coverage.

Personal Articles Floaters   **Personal articles floaters** provide extended coverage for all personal property, regardless of where the property is located, for the policyholder and all household residents except children away at school. This coverage is generally sold as an extension to the homeowner's policy on an "all-risk" basis; it covers losses of any kind other than specifically excluded perils, which generally include war, wear and tear, mechanical breakdown, vermin, and nuclear disaster.

There are a number of variations of the personal articles floater, but they all perform the same task: They provide extended coverage to personal property. Recall the limit on personal property coverage is set at 50 percent of the dwelling coverage, but within this coverage there are also limits on some specific types of losses. For example, there's a $2,500 limit on the theft of silverware, goldware, and pewterware, so if the value of your silverware is $25,000, you might want a personal articles floater to cover your silverware to its market value.

Earthquake Coverage   Because damage from earthquakes is specifically excluded from coverage in the standardized packaged HO policies, supplemental earthquake coverage is an important addition in high-risk areas. In fact, in California,

Endorsement
A written attachment to an insurance policy to add or subtract coverage.

Personal Articles Floater
An extension to a homeowner's insurance policy that provides coverage for all personal property regardless of where it's located. This coverage applies to the policyholder and all household residents except children away at school.

insurers are required to offer earthquake coverage as an add-on. Of course, not all Californians elect to buy such coverage—only about 20 percent of those affected by the 1989 San Francisco earthquake had earthquake coverage. The rates on this coverage vary depending on the earthquake risk. Rates near the San Andreas fault cost up to $4 per $1,000 of coverage, which means coverage on a $200,000 home would run $800 per year.

Flood Protection   Flood protection includes coverage not only from flood, but from water damage due to hurricanes, mudslides, and unusual erosion along the Great Lakes and the Great Salt Lake. It's also a bit different from other coverage in that it's generally administered and subsidized by the federal government through the Department of Housing and Urban Development (HUD).

To be eligible for flood insurance, your community must comply with HUD requirements, which involve floodplain studies and planning. Once a community receives approval from HUD, you can purchase up to $250,000 of coverage on your dwelling and an additional $100,000 on its contents.

Inflation Guard

An endorsement that automatically updates the level of property coverage based on an index of replacement costs that continually updates the cost of building a home.

Inflation Guard   An **inflation guard** endorsement automatically updates your property coverage based on an index of replacement costs that continually updates the cost of building a home. In effect, the coverage—along with the premiums—automatically increase each year.

Actual Cash Value

The replacement value of the house less accumulated depreciation (which is the decline in value over time due to wear and tear).

Personal Property Replacement Cost Coverage   Homeowner's insurance is set up to pay the policyholder the **actual cash value** of the loss. Unfortunately, when you're talking about personal property, the actual cash value, which is the replacement cost minus estimated depreciation (wear-and-tear costs), can be well below the cost of replacing the asset. For example, if the property could be replaced for $500, and it's been used for half its expected life, it would have an actual cash value of $250. Moreover, under the actual cash value, you're responsible for maintaining detailed records of the date of purchase, purchase price, and estimated depreciation of all your property.

Replacement Cost Coverage

Additional homeowner's coverage that provides for the actual replacement cost of a stolen or destroyed item as opposed to the actual cash value.

As an alternative, most homeowner's policies come with optional **replacement cost coverage**, which provides for the actual replacement cost of a stolen or destroyed item as opposed to the actual cash value. Replacement cost coverage can generally be added for an additional 5 to 15 percent over the cost of the homeowner's insurance without this option. Although replacement cost coverage doesn't mean that you no longer have to keep track of your possessions, it does mean that you'll be able to replace them in the event of a loss.

Added Liability Insurance   Basic policies generally provide $100,000 of liability coverage. Although this figure may sound like a lot, it's no longer uncommon for court judgments to climb well above this amount. Also, if you've accumulated a relatively sizable net worth, you need increased liability insurance to protect your assets. Fortunately, for a relatively small fee, most insurance companies will allow you to raise your level of liability coverage to $300,000 or $500,000.

Personal Umbrella Policy

A homeowner's policy that provides excess liability insurance with protection against lawsuits and judgments generally ranging from $1 million to $10 million.

Alternatively, you might want to buy a **personal umbrella policy**, which, for a reasonable cost, provides protection ranging from $1 million to $10 million against lawsuits and judgments. An umbrella policy provides excess liability insurance over basic underlying contracts. It doesn't go into effect until you've exhausted your automobile or homeowner's liability coverage.

It's also quite broad in coverage, generally covering most losses. However, it does exclude acts committed with intent to cause injury, activities associated with aircraft and some watercraft, and most business and professional activities. Business owner and professional policies must be purchased separately.

Your Insurance Needs

How much insurance do you need? Answering this question is easy. In fact, we've already started answering it. We've discussed both the need for inflation guard coverage to make sure inflation doesn't negate insurance coverage and the need for replacement cost coverage on possessions.

What about replacement cost coverage on your house? This coverage actually provides us with the final answer to our question: You need enough insurance to allow for full replacement in the event of a loss—a total loss.

Coinsurance and the "80 Percent Rule"

Insurance companies have a way of encouraging you to be covered for a total loss. It's called a **coinsurance provision**, and it requires that you pay a portion of your own losses if you don't purchase what they consider an adequate level of insurance. Many companies follow the **80 percent rule** and require you to carry at least 80 percent of your home's full replacement cost. This 80 percent rule relates to losses on your dwelling only—not those on your personal property.

There are some restrictions to this coverage, though. First, the amount paid is limited to the limits of the policy—that is, a $100,000 insurance policy will pay only up to its $100,000 limit. Second, you usually have to rebuild your home on the same location. Third, if you don't rebuild your home, the insurer is liable only for the actual cash-value loss, which is generally quite a bit less than the replacement cost. Finally, the replacement cost coverage is in effect only if your home is insured for at least 80 percent of its replacement cost.

This 80 percent rule makes insuring your home for less than at least 80 percent of its replacement cost seem unattractive. If your home currently has a replacement value of $100,000 and is insured for $80,000 and a fire causes damages of $50,000, you would be paid the full $50,000 with no deduction for depreciation (wear and tear). However, if the fire destroyed your home, you would collect only $80,000, the face value of your policy.

If the 80 percent rule isn't met, the homeowner must pay for part of any losses. This is commonly referred to as the coinsurance provision. If your house is insured for less than 80 percent of its replacement value, in the event of a loss you'll receive the greater of the following:

◆ The actual cash value of the portion of your house that was destroyed (remember that the actual cash value is the replacement cost minus depreciation)

or

◆ The amount of insurance purchased (80% of replacement cost × the amount of loss)

What does all this mean? It means that it would be a grave mistake not to insure your home for at least 80 percent of its replacement cost. If you satisfy the 80 percent rule and your house is destroyed or damaged, your policy will pay to fully repair or replace your home up to the amount of insurance purchased. If you don't satisfy the 80 percent rule, you probably won't get enough to replace it. You may want more insurance, but certainly not less.

Coinsurance Provision

A provision or requirement of homeowner's insurance requiring the insured to pay a portion of the claim if he or she purchased an inadequate amount of insurance (in this case, less than 80 percent of the replacement cost).

80 Percent Rule

A homeowner's insurance rule stating that the replacement cost coverage is in effect only if the home is insured for at least 80 percent of its replacement cost. This rule is intended to discourage homeowners from insuring for less than the replacement cost of their homes.

FACTS of LIFE

The CBS *Sunday Morning* show aired a segment titled "Check the Fine Print." That segment highlighted the plight of Marcy and Gerald Stanton of San Bernardino, CA. In 2003, their house, which they had lived in for 40 years, was ravaged by a firestorm that burned down 3,700 houses. Their house was insured for $250,000. Unfortunately, the cost to rebuild would run $400,000. With 64 percent of U.S. homes considered underinsured, according to CBS, millions of Americans could face the same plight.

The Bottom Line

Unfortunately, there's no neat, tidy formula to tell you exactly how much homeowner's insurance you need. Determining the amount of coverage you need is a procedure that requires some thought and foresight on your part. Because the amount of assets and possessions you've managed to acquire is always changing, so are your insurance needs. As has been the case for just about every personal finance matter we've examined so far, you need to revisit your insurance needs from time to time, just to make sure those needs are being met.

When determining how much homeowner's insurance you need, you should look at Checklist 10.1 for direction.

Keeping Your Costs Down—Insurance Credit Scoring

Insurance Credit Score
A credit score, based on the same information as your traditional credit score, which is used in determining what your home and auto insurance rates will be.

In recent years, insurance companies have turned to credit scoring models to help them identify customers who are most likely to make claims. In effect, insurers are using credit scoring system data to create a new scale—the **insurance credit score**—based on the same information as your credit score that we looked at in Chapter 6. That's right, not only do you have a credit score to determine whether you can get credit and what rate you'll be paying when you borrow, but you also have an insurance credit score that helps determine what your home and auto insurance rates will be.

How do insurers justify using your credit score to determine what they should charge you for insurance? For whatever reason, there appears to be a link between your credit score and your insurance loss ratio, which is a measure that includes both claim frequency and cost for both homeowner's and auto insurance. This

CHECKLIST 10.1

How Much Insurance Do You Need?

◆ You need enough insurance to cover the replacement of your home in the event of a complete loss. This coverage will need to reflect any changes in increased costs due to changing building codes.

◆ You should have protection against inflation eroding your coverage.

◆ If you're in a flood or earthquake area, you need special protection against these disasters—just think about Hurricane Katrina in New Orleans.

◆ If you have detached structures or elaborate landscaping, you should determine whether or not they're adequately covered under a standard policy.

◆ If you have a home office, you should consider additional coverage. Remember, your homeowner's policy doesn't provide business liability coverage.

◆ You need adequate coverage for personal property. For most people, replacement cost property insurance is a good idea.

◆ If you have possessions that need special protection—for example, a valuable coin collection or jewelry—you should consider a floater policy.

◆ If your assets are much greater than the liability limits on your homeowner's policy, you should consider additional liability coverage.

◆ If you're renting, you need adequate insurance for your personal property.

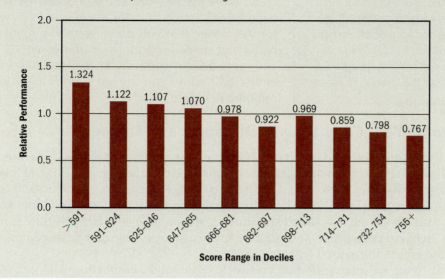

FIGURE 10.1 The Relationship Between Your Credit Score and the Cost of Your Homeowner's Insurance Policy to Your Insurance Company

Individuals with the lowest scores have losses that are 32.4 percent above average; those with the best scores have losses that are 33.3 percent below average.

Source: Insurance Information Institute, with original data source: Tillinghast Towers-Perrin.www.iii.org

relationship is shown in Figure 10.1. Once this relationship was uncovered in the late 1980s, insurance companies jumped on it to set rates. In fact, a majority of home insurers use insurance credit scores in setting their homeowner's policy rates.[1] After all, insurance companies try to set rates that reflect the cost of claims. They've done this for years using age and gender; for example men and teenagers generally pay higher rates. Why? Because according to the National Safety Council, men are 69 percent more likely to be driving in fatal automobile accidents than are women. As a result, men pay more for automobile insurance. Similarly, drivers aged 16 to 20 are 2 to 3 times more likely to have an automobile accident than older drivers and, therefore, they pay quite a bit more for their automobile insurance.

The bottom line is the lower your insurance credit score, the higher your home-owner's insurance rate will be. While there isn't much controversy as to whether there is a relationship between credit standing and insurance claims, no one has yet to come up with a definitive answer as to why this relationship exists. Regardless of the reason, the courts have ruled that it's legal to use credit scoring in setting insurance rates, and the Fair Credit Reporting Act (FCRA) allows for insurance companies to obtain credit reports and use them in setting insurance rates. However, some states have set restrictions as to the use of insurance credit scoring. For example, it is illegal in Hawaii.

Your insurance credit score is calculated in a manner very similar to your normal credit score. Once again, just as Fair Isaac provides information as to how your credit score is calculated, it also provides information as to how it calculates your insurance credit score. In this case the weightings are slightly different, with a slightly greater weight given to your payment history and a slightly lower weight given to the types of credit used.

---

[1] Federal Trade Commission, "Need Credit on Insurance? Your Credit Score Helps Determine What You'll Pay," accessed April 27 , 2011, www.ftc.gov/bcp/edu/pubs/consumer/credit/cre24.shtm.

STOP & THINK

Getting insurance quotes online is a good idea. It only takes a minute, and you'll get three to five quotes from insurance companies. But there are a lot more than five insurance companies in your state, and you'll want as many quotes as you can get. That means you'll want to visit as many insurance quote sites as possible. What things have you saved money on by buying over the Internet?

What does this mean for you? It means that your normal credit score and your insurance credit score are going to be very closely related. As a result, you've got to be very serious about managing your credit score because if it is low, not only will you have a hard time borrowing money and pay more for the money that you do borrow, but you'll also be paying more for both your homeowner's and your automobile insurance. To manage your insurance credit score, you'll want to follow the steps outlined in Figure 10.2.

Keeping Your Costs Down—Discounts and Savings

What determines the cost of your homeowner's policy? Three basic factors are involved: (1) the location of your home, (2) the type of structure, and (3) your level of coverage and policy type. Location affects coverage because of differences in crime levels and regional perils (such as earthquakes in California and tornadoes in the Midwest). Older and less sound structures cost more to insure because they're more likely to have problems. In addition, the greater the coverage and more comprehensive the policy, the more it costs.

Still, there are some ways that you can keep down the cost of homeowner's insurance. Start by selecting a financially sound insurer with low comparative costs. Then take advantage of as many discounts as possible. Here are some potential discounts and savings methods:

Deductible
The amount that you are responsible for paying before insurance coverage kicks in.

◆ **High deductible discounts. The deductible**, which is the amount you agree to pay before insurance coverage kicks in, can be thought of as coinsurance. The larger the deductible you are willing to accept, the less you pay for insurance

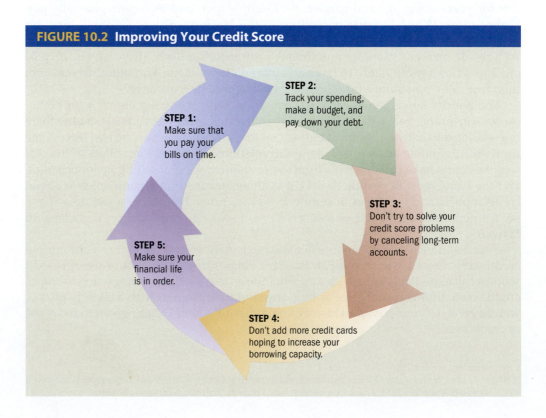

FIGURE 10.2 Improving Your Credit Score

STEP 1: Make sure that you pay your bills on time.

STEP 2: Track your spending, make a budget, and pay down your debt.

STEP 3: Don't try to solve your credit score problems by canceling long-term accounts.

STEP 4: Don't add more credit cards hoping to increase your borrowing capacity.

STEP 5: Make sure your financial life is in order.

coverage. Typically, insurance companies require a $250 deductible and provide discounts if you're willing to accept a higher deductible.

Keep in mind that the purpose of insurance is not to offset all costs, only catastrophic ones. To keep the costs of homeowner's insurance under control, you'll have to share some of the risks with the insurance company. In other words, you should be responsible for all minor expenses, and the insurance company should cover all large expenses. Give serious consideration to taking as large a deductible as you can afford. Here are some other things to keep in mind that might save you money:

◆ **Security system/smoke detector discounts.** Many insurance companies also offer discounts of from 2 to 5 percent if you install security and smoke detector systems. Larger discounts are available if you install in-home sprinkler systems.

◆ **Multiple policy discounts.** Insurance companies often provide discounts to customers who have more than one policy with them; for example, their automobile *and* homeowner's coverage.

◆ **Pay your insurance premiums annually.** If you pay your insurance premiums annually in one lump sum rather than quarterly, or extended over several months, most insurance companies will offer you a discount.

◆ **Other discounts.** Some companies offer a discount for homes made with fire-resistant materials, for homeowners over the age of 55, and for individuals who've had homeowner's insurance with a single company for an extended number of years.

◆ **Consider a direct writer.** A **direct writer** is an insurance company that distributes its products to customers without the use of agents. Companies that don't use agents don't have to pay salaries or commissions, so they can afford to offer lower prices.

◆ **Shop around.** Compare costs among high-quality insurers. Premiums for similar coverage can vary by as much as 25 percent. Checklist 10.2 reviews the process of shopping for homeowner's insurance.

◆ **Double-check your policy.** Make sure the policy you receive is what you ordered. Check the type and level of coverage, and any endorsements that you requested. It'll be too late to correct any errors once you file a claim.

W14 Worksheet

Direct Writer
An insurance company that distributes its products directly to customers, without the use of agents.

FACTS OF LIFE

One healthy way to reduce your insurance premiums is to quit smoking. Smoking accounts for about 23,000 residential fires a year. As a result, many insurance companies offer discounts to nonsmoking families.

Making Your Coverage Work

Recover on a liability or a loss to your property.

By now you should be able to go out and buy the policy that's just right for you. However, is that policy enough to protect you from losing your possessions and assets? Nope. How can your insurance company make good on your policy and pay you for a loss if it doesn't know what possessions you've lost or what they were worth?

For your homeowner's insurance to provide effective protection against loss, you need to establish proof of ownership and value your assets using a detailed inventory of everything you own. If you can't prove that you owned a stereo worth $2,000, your insurance company isn't going to reimburse you for it if it gets stolen.

CHECKLIST 10.2

A Checklist for Homeowner's Insurance

◆ Determine the amount and type of homeowner's insurance you need.

◆ Put together a list of top-quality insurance agents (as listed in *A.M. Best's Key Rating Guide on Property and Casualty Insurers*, also located on their Web site at **www.ambest .com**) with a good local reputation who carry these insurers.

◆ Consult with agents, letting them know what you are looking for. Give consideration to any recommendations or modifications they might suggest.

◆ If you already have an auto insurance policy, you'll want to contact that agent or insurer—you may get a discount by purchasing both coverages through one company.

◆ In addition to contacting your auto insurance agent, you'll want to make at least three more calls for quotes, including one to a direct writer—an insurance company that uses an 800-number-based sales force, such as Amica (800-242-6422); or, if you have a military connection, call USAA (800-531-8100). One call should also be to an insurer with its own sales force, such as State Farm or Allstate, and one call should be to an independent agent, who can quote you a variety of prices.

◆ Get several bids on the total package, including all modifications, floaters, and extensions.

◆ Conduct an annual review of your homeowner's insurance coverage.

FACTS OF LIFE

Why don't renters have renter's insurance? Twenty-six percent said they felt it was too expensive, while 17 percent said they didn't know they needed it, and 8 percent said they never heard of it. Is it too expensive? According to a recent study, the average cost of renter's insurance is $195 a year.

Fortunately, the inventory process isn't all that difficult. Begin by putting together a list of household items. To aid you in this process, most insurance agents should be able to provide you with an inventory worksheet, or you can get one on the Web at **www.c21amhomes.com/inventory worksheet.htm**. If you have access to a video recorder, walk through your home or apartment videotaping and describing the contents. Ideally, your inventory should be as detailed as possible and include the date of purchase, the cost, the model and serial number, and the brand name for each item. Note the original cost and date of purchase of major items whenever possible. In addition, make sure each room is taped from a number of different angles, with all closet doors open. Be sure to videotape the contents of drawers and cabinets. When taping valuables such as jewelry and silverware, take a careful shot of them.

Once you've finished your video or written inventory, you should keep it in a safety-deposit box, with a family member living elsewhere, or with your insurance agent. Why not keep it yourself? Well, if your house burns down, your inventory would burn, too, and all your efforts would quickly go up in smoke.

OK, now you've got a good insurance policy and an inventory of your possessions. Now you're effectively covered, right? Not exactly. To collect on a loss, you must follow a few basic steps outlined in Checklist 10.3.

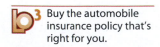
3 Buy the automobile insurance policy that's right for you.

Automobile Insurance

At this point, you should be pretty safe at home, thanks to your homeowner's insurance and your newfound knowledge of how to manage it and file claims. You need to leave home at least every now and again, though. What happens when you get in your car? Are you safe there, too? Not unless you have automobile insurance.

◆ Report your loss immediately. In the case of a burglary or theft, report the incident immediately to the police. If a credit or ATM card has been stolen, you should also notify the issuing company. In addition, you should notify your insurance agent.

◆ Make temporary repairs to protect your property. If your house has sustained damage and your insurance agent hasn't had time to inspect it, don't let the damage sit untouched. Board up broken windows and holes in the roof or walls to prevent any further damage and to protect your home against burglary.

◆ Make a detailed list of everything lost or damaged. Using your inventory—now you'll be glad you made one—put together a detailed list describing the items that were lost or damaged and their value. Present this list to your insurance agent and the police.

◆ Maintain records of the insurance settlement process. Keep records of all your expenses.

◆ Confirm the adjuster's estimate. Your insurance company will send an adjuster to evaluate the claim and recommend to the insurance company a dollar amount for the settlement. Before settling, get an estimate from a local contractor as to how much the repairs will cost. Don't agree to anything less than a fair settlement.

There are around 30 million accidents each year in the United States alone. That works out to about one accident for every five licensed drivers, which is why most states require by law that all licensed drivers must be covered by auto insurance. Let's start our discussion by taking a look at the standardized personal automobile policy.

Personal Automobile Policy

Fortunately, automobile insurance is relatively standard, with all policies following a similar package format called the **personal automobile policy (PAP)**. Each policy contains both liability and property damage coverage, and each package of insurance includes four basic parts:

Personal Automobile Policy (PAP)
A standardized insurance policy for an individual or family.

◆ **Part A: Liability coverage.** This coverage provides protection for you if you're legally liable for bodily injury and property damage caused by your automobile. It includes payment for any judgment awarded, court costs, and legal defense fees.

◆ **Part B: Medical expense coverage.** This coverage pays medical bills and funeral expenses, with limits per person for you and your passengers.

◆ **Part C: Uninsured motorist's protection coverage.** This coverage is required in many states and protects you by covering bodily injury (and property damage in a few states) caused by drivers without liability insurance.

◆ **Part D: Damage to your automobile coverage.** This coverage is also known as collision or comprehensive insurance, and provides coverage for theft of your auto or for damage from almost any peril other than collision.

Figure 10.3 illustrates the typical policy parts as they relate to the liability and property coverage. Now let's look at each coverage part in greater detail.

PAP Part A: Liability Coverage   Part A of a personal automobile policy involves liability coverage, which provides protection from loss resulting from lawsuits that might arise because of an auto accident.

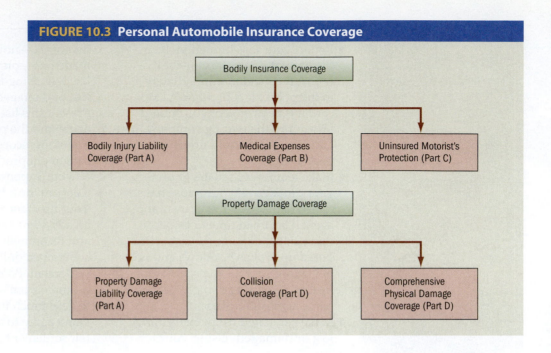

FIGURE 10.3 Personal Automobile Insurance Coverage

Combined Single Limit
Auto insurance liability coverage that combines both bodily injury and property damage liability.

Split-Limit Coverage
Auto insurance liability coverage that allows for either separate coverage limits for bodily injury and property damage, split-coverage limits per person, or both.

Liability coverage can be presented as a **combined single limit**, meaning that the coverage applies to a combination of both bodily injury and property damage liability, without a separate limit for each person, or as **split-limit coverage**, which allows for either separate coverage limits for bodily injury and property damage, split-coverage limits per person, or both. Figure 10.4 provides an example of how this works.

Considering the enormous sums of money judges are handing out in settlements of lawsuits over automobile accidents, it's important to carry adequate liability insurance. Although most states require minimum levels of coverage, this is generally well below what is needed by most people who are involved in auto accidents. In fact, most professional financial planners recommend that you carry at least $100,000 of bodily injury liability coverage per person and $300,000 of bodily injury liability coverage for all persons, and if you have sizable assets, you should consider raising this to $250,000 per person and $500,000 per accident—making that change will increase your premiums by about 10 percent. Also, they recommend that you carry at least $100,000 of property damage liability insurance coverage.

Of course, these are general recommendations and what you carry should reflect your net worth and annual income—the greater your assets, the more coverage you should carry.

In addition to paying the policy limits for the damages you caused, the insurer also agrees under Part A to defend you in any civil cases arising from the accident and to pay all legal costs. These legal costs are paid *in addition* to your policy limits. However, the insurance company won't defend you against any criminal charges brought against you as a result of a charge such as drunk driving.

PAP Part B: Medical Expenses Coverage   The medical expenses coverage pays all reasonable medical and funeral expenses incurred within 3 years of an accident by the policyholder, his or her family members, and other persons injured in an accident involving a covered automobile. In fact, it covers the policyholder and his or her family regardless of whether they're in an automobile or walking along the street, just as long as they're not injured by a vehicle that wasn't designed for use on public roads, such as a snowmobile or farm tractor.

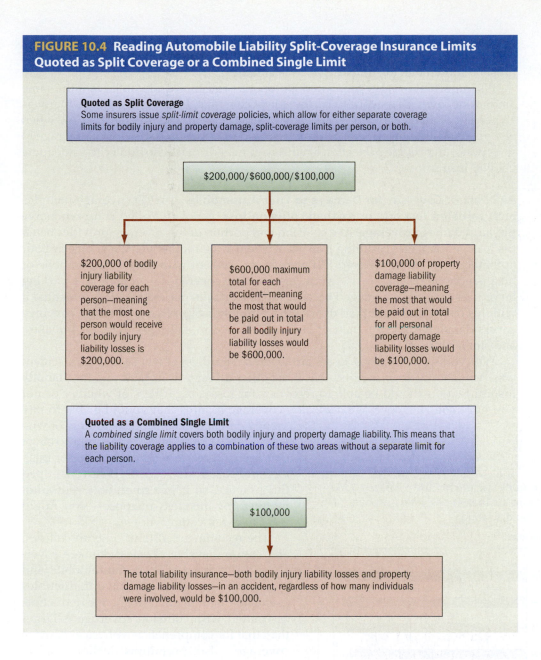

FIGURE 10.4 Reading Automobile Liability Split-Coverage Insurance Limits Quoted as Split Coverage or a Combined Single Limit

Quoted as Split Coverage
Some insurers issue *split-limit coverage* policies, which allow for either separate coverage limits for bodily injury and property damage, split-coverage limits per person, or both.

$200,000/$600,000/$100,000

$200,000 of bodily injury liability coverage for each person—meaning that the most one person would receive for bodily injury liability losses is $200,000.

$600,000 maximum total for each accident—meaning the most that would be paid out in total for all bodily injury liability losses would be $600,000.

$100,000 of property damage liability coverage—meaning the most that would be paid out in total for all personal property damage liability losses would be $100,000.

Quoted as a Combined Single Limit
A *combined single limit* covers both bodily injury and property damage liability. This means that the liability coverage applies to a combination of these two areas without a separate limit for each person.

$100,000

The total liability insurance—both bodily injury liability losses and property damage liability losses—in an accident, regardless of how many individuals were involved, would be $100,000.

If you're driving a car you don't own, your medical expenses will be covered, but not those of other passengers in the car or pedestrians who are injured—the owner of the car would be responsible for that insurance. In addition, your PAP medical expense coverage doesn't specify fault. That is, you're not insured based upon who is at fault in an accident. As a result, you receive payment for any medical expenses faster because the insurance company doesn't need to waste time establishing fault.

FACTS OF LIFE

Almost anything can cause an accident. According to an MSNBC report, two of the weirdest claims involved a motorist who said a frozen squirrel fell out of a tree and crashed through the windshield. Another involved a motorist who stated, "As I was driving around a bend, one of the doors opened and a frozen kebab flew out, hitting and damaging a passing car."

PAP Part C: Uninsured Motorist's Protection Coverage   Coverage for injuries caused by an uninsured motorist, a negligent driver whose insurance company is insolvent,

Uninsured Motorist's Protection Coverage
Coverage against injuries caused by a hit-and-run driver or by an uninsured motorist or a negligent driver whose insurance company is insolvent.

or a hit-and-run driver is provided by **uninsured motorist's protection coverage**. To collect on a claim, not only must the other driver not have available insurance, but it must be shown that the other driver was at fault.

It's important to carry uninsured motorist's protection and you'll want the same amount of coverage as you do bodily injury coverage, because roughly as many as 15 percent of all drivers don't carry any insurance at all, and you never know when one might slam into your car. You can also add underinsured motorist's coverage to your policy to provide protection against negligent drivers who don't carry adequate liability insurance.

PAP Part D: Coverage for Damage to Your Automobile   Part D coverage includes both **collision loss** and **other than collision loss**, generally called **comprehensive physical damage coverage**. The collision loss portion of the coverage provides benefits to cover damages resulting from an accident with another vehicle or object. Your automobile would be covered if it were in an accident with another automobile or hit a telephone pole. Likewise, your car would be covered if it were hit in a parking lot or if its door were damaged because the person who parked next to you dented it with his or her door and then drove off. Comprehensive physical damage coverage covers damage from fire, theft or larceny, windstorm, falling objects, earthquakes, and similar causes.

Collision Loss
The portion of auto insurance coverage that provides benefits to cover damages resulting from an accident with another vehicle or object.

Other Than Collision Loss or Comprehensive Physical Damage Coverage
Auto insurance coverage for noncollision losses. For example, it would cover damage if the car were hit in a parking lot or if the door were damaged as a result of banging it into a parked car next to it.

With collision insurance, losses are covered regardless of whose fault the accident was. You should keep in mind that if the other driver was at fault and has liability insurance, you should be able to recover your losses regardless of whether or not you have collision coverage. Collision coverage assures that you'll be able to pay for any damage to your car regardless of who was at fault. Collision coverage used to cover damage suffered to rental cars used for business purposes. Many insurers have stopped this practice, so if you commonly rent automobiles for business purposes, you might want to check your coverage.

The recommended limit on both collision and comprehensive physical damage coverage is the cash value of your automobile, and both coverages generally have deductibles associated with them. Usually, the deductible associated with collision coverage is larger than that for comprehensive physical damage coverage. Also, premiums decline sharply as deductibles are raised. As a result, you'll want to choose the highest deductible you can afford to pay out of pocket, and you'll want to make the deductible at least $500.

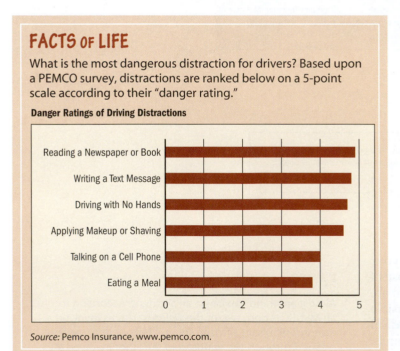

FACTS OF LIFE

What is the most dangerous distraction for drivers? Based upon a PEMCO survey, distractions are ranked below on a 5-point scale according to their "danger rating."

Danger Ratings of Driving Distractions

Source: Pemco Insurance, www.pemco.com.

For example, one major insurance company charges an annual premium of $488 on comprehensive insurance on a new Ford Focus for a youthful operator based on a deductible of $50. If the deductible is raised to $100, the premium drops to $420. By raising the deductible by $50, you can save $68 in annual premiums. In effect, a premium of $68 is being charged for $50 of additional coverage. If you have less than one accident per year, you're better off with the $100 deductible. If you have more than one accident per year, you should probably pay some attention to improving your driving skills. Table 10.2 provides a summary of the different parts of the PAP.

TABLE 10.2 The Personal Automobile Policy (PAP)		
Coverage Description	**Individuals Covered**	**Recommended Policy Limits**
Liability Coverage—Part A Part A of a PAP involves liability coverage and provides coverage against lawsuits that might arise from negligent ownership or operation of an automobile.	Nonexcluded relatives who live with the insured, regardless of whether the automobile is owned or not.	$100,000 bodily injury liability coverage per person and $300,000 of bodily injury coverage for all persons, and if you have sizable assets, raise this to $250,000 per person and $500,000 per accident. $100,000 property damage liability coverage.
Medical Expenses Coverage—Part B Your medical expenses coverage includes all reasonable medical and funeral expenses incurred by the policyholder and family members in addition to other persons injured while occupying a covered automobile.	The policyholder and his or her family, regardless of whether they are in an automobile or walking, as long as they are injured by a vehicle that was designed for use on public roads.	$50,000 of coverage per person.
Uninsured Motorist's Protection Coverage—Part C Uninsured motorist's protection coverage provides benefits for injuries caused by an uninsured motorist, a negligent driver whose insurance company is insolvent, or a hit-and-run driver.	Insured family members driving non-owned automobile with permission, and anyone driving an insured car with permission.	$250,000 of coverage per person and $500,000 of coverage per accident.
Coverage for Damage to Your Automobile—Part D Protection against damage to or theft of your automobile is provided in Part D coverage. This coverage includes both collision loss and loss resulting from other than collision loss, generally called comprehensive physical damage coverage.	Anyone driving an insured automobile with permission.	Actual cash value of your automobile. In addition, you'll want to choose the highest deductible you can afford to pay out of pocket, and you'll want to make the deductible at least $500.

Exclusions The PAP provides broad coverage, but there are a number of standard exclusions. Although there may be others, standard exclusions generally include the following:

♦ You're not covered in the case of intentional injury or damage.
♦ You're not covered if you're using a vehicle without the permission of the owner.
♦ You're not covered if you're using a vehicle with fewer than four wheels.
♦ You're not covered if you're driving another person's car that is provided for you on a regular basis.
♦ You're not covered if you own the automobile but don't have it listed on your insurance policy.
♦ You're not covered if you're carrying passengers for a fee.
♦ You're not covered while driving in a race or other speed contest.

No-Fault Insurance

In an attempt to keep insurance costs down—in particular, those costs associated with settling claims—many states have turned to the concept of **no-fault insurance**. Today, over half of all states have some variation of a no-fault system.

> **FACTS OF LIFE**
>
> According to a study in the journal *Human Factors*, driving while talking on a cell phone results in 2,600 deaths and 330,000 injuries every year. Why? Because a 20-year-old driver on a cell phone has the same reaction time as a 70-year-old driver not using one.

No-Fault Insurance
A type of auto insurance in which your insurance company protects you in the case of an accident regardless of who is at fault.

STOP & THINK

Just having home and auto insurance may not be enough. Too often things happen that are unrelated to your home or car. What if you're riding your bike and you bump into an elderly man who falls and fractures his spine? Also, keep in mind that the liability coverage on your homeowner's insurance generally runs about $100,000 to $300,000, while the liability coverage on your auto insurance often is only $100,000. In a lawsuit today, that's peanuts. Don't take the risk: Consider an **umbrella liability insurance policy** or **umbrella policy**—they aren't that expensive. An umbrella policy supplements the liability coverage you already have through your home and auto insurance and provides an extra layer of protection. These policies kick in after the liability insurance in your homeowner's and auto policy runs out and provide coverage for claims that are not covered under your homeowner's insurance. What types of claims do you think this type of policy might cover?

Umbrella Liability Insurance or Umbrella Policy
An insurance policy that supplements liability coverage on a homeowner's and/or automobile insurance policy. This insurance kicks in after the homeowner's and/or automobile policy coverage run(s) out and provides coverage for claims not covered under homeowner's insurance such as libel, slander, and invasion of privacy.

No-fault insurance is based on the idea that your insurance company should pay for your losses, regardless of who's at fault. All the legal expenses associated with attaching blame would then be lifted, and insurance coverage should prove to be less costly.

Under no-fault insurance, if you were in an accident, your insurance company would pay for your losses and the losses suffered by your passengers, and the other driver's insurance company would pay for his or her losses. Sounds like a good idea, right? Well, no-fault insurance has its problems. The biggest problem is that no-fault insurance imposes limits on medical expenses and other claims. In some states, the limited coverage may not be enough to cover all legitimate medical expenses.

You can still sue for "pain and suffering," but only if the other driver was at fault.

Buying Automobile Insurance

Now that you know about the basic types of coverage in automobile insurance, you can make an informed choice in buying some. How much will you need to spend? Well, that depends on how good a comparison shopper you are. It also depends on some factors that are pretty much beyond your control. Let's take a look at these factors, and then at what you can do to get the best possible deal.

Determinants of the Cost of Automobile Insurance   The following are the major determinants of the cost of automobile insurance:

- **The type of automobile.** The sportier and more high-powered your car is, the more your insurance will cost. In fact, in buying an automobile, the cost of insurance should be factored into the purchase decision.
- **The use of your automobile.** The less you use your car, the less you'll have to pay in insurance premiums.
- **The driver's personal characteristics.** Young unmarried males generally pay the most for their insurance, because they have a statistically greater chance of having an accident. Age, sex, and marital status all go into determining how much you pay for insurance.
- **The driver's driving record.** If you've received traffic tickets or had traffic accidents, you'll probably have to pay more for your insurance. Exactly how much your premiums go up depends on the nature of your violations. If you receive a driving-under-the-influence-of-alcohol (DUI) citation, you can expect a hefty increase in your premiums.
- **Where you live.** In general, because of a higher incidence of accidents and theft, insurance is more expensive for those who live in urban areas.
- **Discounts that you qualify for.** A wide variety of discounts are available for cars that have certain safety features and for individuals who have characteristics identified with safe drivers. Table 10.3 lists some of the most common automobile insurance discounts.
- **Your insurance credit score.** Just as with homeowner's insurance, your insurance credit score goes a long way in determining what you pay for auto insurance. In

FACTS OF LIFE

Why are the automobile insurance rates so much higher for a male under the age of 25 than for a female of the same age? One of the major reasons is that males in that age group drive much more than do females.

TABLE 10.3 Common Automobile Insurance Discounts

You can reduce your auto insurance premiums significantly by taking advantage of discounts. Listed below are the most common automobile insurance discounts.

Accident Free. Ten percent discounts on most coverage after 3 years without a chargeable accident. After 6 years, the discount rises to 15 percent.

Multiple Automobiles. Fifteen percent discount for insuring more than one car with the same company.

Low Annual Mileage. Fifteen percent discount if you drive fewer than 7,500 miles per year.

Automobile and Homeowner's Together. Five to 15 percent off both policies if with the same company.

Low "Damageability." Ten to 30 percent off collision and comprehensive premiums if the car is statistically less likely to result in an expensive claim because it is cheaper to repair or less appealing to thieves.

Good Student. Up to 25 percent discount for unmarried drivers under 25 who rank in the top 20 percent of their class, have a B average, or are on the honor roll.

Over 50. Ten percent discount off the usual adult rate if you are over 50.

Defensive Driving Course. Five percent discount if you complete a defensive driving course (many times only applies to drivers 55 or older).

Passive Restraints. Up to 40 percent discount on some coverages if you have airbags or automatic seatbelts. Antilock brakes also add a 5 percent discount.

Noncommuter or Carpooler. Fifteen percent discount if you drive less than 30 miles to and from work each day.

Antitheft Devices. Fifteen percent discount depending on where you live and the type of device.

fact, insurance credit scoring is even more common with automobile insurance than it is with homeowner's insurance, with about 92 of the 100 largest personal automobile insurers using some sort of insurance credit scoring. How do insurance companies justify this? They have found that drivers with poorer insurance credit scores incurred much higher losses than did those with stronger insurance credit scores. In fact, as can be seen in Figure 10.5, those in the lowest 10 percent of insurance credit scores generated losses that were nearly twice as large for property damage liability claims and more than twice as large for bodily injury, collision, and comprehensive claims than those in the highest 10 percent. As a result, many insurers use insurance credit scoring to set rates.

Keeping Your Costs Down   There are several general ways you can keep your automobile insurance rates down while ensuring complete coverage. They include the following:

◆ **Shop comparatively.** Different insurers don't charge identical prices for identical coverage. In fact, rates can vary by as much as 100 percent from carrier to carrier, and that's why you'll want to get a minimum of three different quotes on your automobile insurance. In addition, make sure you get quotes with different size deductibles.

◆ **Consider only high-quality insurers.** You should check *A.M. Best Reports* (**www .ambest.com**)—considering only insurers earning one of Best's two highest rankings—to assess the quality of the insurer before purchasing insurance.

◆ **Take advantage of discounts.** You can lower your premiums considerably by taking available discounts. Those in driver's education courses, over 50, graduates of defensive driving courses, students with good grades, and carpool participants all have the potential for discounts.

◆ **Buy a car that's relatively inexpensive to insure.** In making your purchase decision, factor in the cost of insurance on your new car.

FIGURE 10.5 Estimated Average Amount Paid Out on Claims, Relative to Highest Score Decile (lowest score = 1; high score = 10)

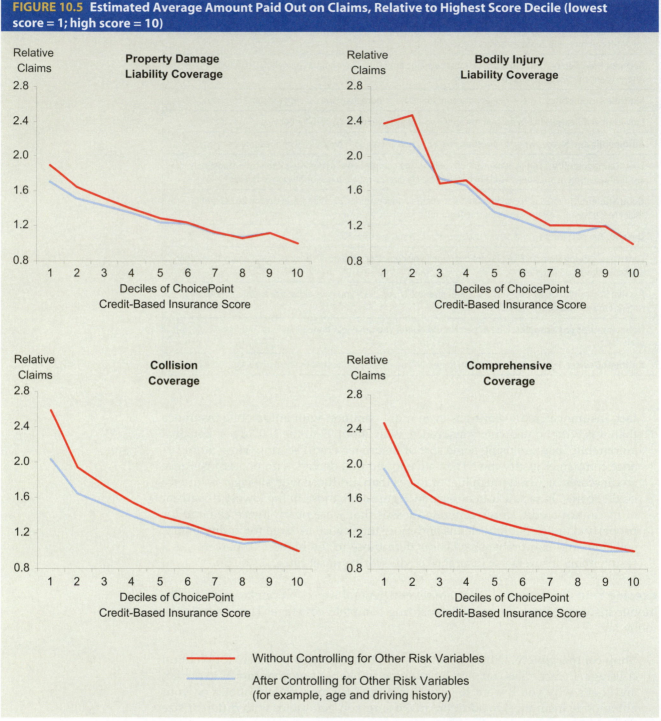

Source: Federal Trade Commission, *Credit-Based Insurance Scores: Impacts on Consumers of Automobile Insurance, A Report to Congress by the Federal Trade Commission,* July 2007, p. 127.

◆ **Improve your driving record.** You have control over your driving record, and it goes a long way toward determining your premiums.

◆ **Raise your deductibles.** As with homeowner's insurance, raising your deductibles can significantly lower your premiums.

◆ **Keep adequate liability insurance.** With increasing medical and hospital expenses, damage awards have increased dramatically in recent years.

Filing a Claim

There are a number of steps that you should take if you're involved in an automobile accident. It's a good idea to keep a list of these steps in your glove compartment, because after an accident you may be too shaken up to recall them. Your "to do" list should include the following actions:

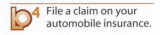 File a claim on your automobile insurance.

1. Get help for anyone injured. Because it's a felony to leave the scene of an accident, you should have someone call the police and an ambulance.
2. Move your car to a safe place or put up flares to prevent further accidents.
3. Get the names and addresses of any witnesses. Get their license plate numbers if you can't get their names. Also get the names of those in the other car (or cars) involved in the accident.
4. Cooperate with the police.
5. If you think the other driver may have been driving under the influence, insist that you both take a test for alcohol.
6. Write down your recollection of what happened. If you have a camera, take pictures of the scene.
7. Don't sign anything, don't admit guilt, and don't comment on how much insurance you have.

 15
Worksheet

MONEY MATTERS

Tips from Marcy Furney, ChFC, Certified Financial Planner™

GOTCHA COVERED

Adopt the mind-set that insurance is to protect you from major losses; it isn't a maintenance plan. Understand that the basis of insurance is pooling of risk. If all policyholders pay $100, and all make a $5,000 claim, the system won't work. Fraudulent and frivolous claims result in costs going up for everyone.

If you must lower the bill for auto or home insurance, consider increasing the deductible, not decreasing the amount of coverage. Also, make sure you're taking advantage of any discounts.

Keep the deductible on property insurance high enough to help avoid the temptation to file claims for small losses. A history of multiple claims may result in your policy being canceled or your coverage being moved to a higher-risk, higher-cost company. Claims experience may also prevent you from shopping around for lower rates.

Check with your insurance company regarding requirements to insure valuables such as furs, jewelry, antiques, or collections. Most require fairly recent appraisals (2 years old or less). Appraisals can be expensive, so do it right the first time. Don't assume that all items you own are fully covered by your homeowner's or renter's policy.

Don't be lulled into a sense of security with the basic limits on your auto and home policies. Protect your assets with a personal umbrella policy, which increases your coverage to a million dollars or more.

If you're a professional, be sure to obtain liability insurance to cover your particular activities. Doctors are not the only practitioners subject to malpractice claims.

When obtaining car insurance, disclose all information regarding the use of your auto. If you drive your vehicle in the course of doing business, you may need business-class coverage on your personal auto policy or a special commercial policy. Driving under the wrong class or coverage could subject you to denial of any claims.

Many discounts are governed by the type of car you drive, how many cars you have, your age, or the features of your home. In the states that allow defensive driving course discounts without age restrictions, almost anyone can get a 5 to 10 percent reduction on a policy. One course can qualify you for up to 3 years of rate reduction and would probably pay for itself in 6 months to 1 year. Some states will allow you to take defensive driving for the insurance discount and then take it again in the same year to remove a ticket from your driving record.

8. Get a copy of the police report and make sure it's accurate.
9. Call your insurance agent as soon as possible.
10. Cooperate with your insurer. Remember, if there is a lawsuit, your insurer will defend you.
11. Keep records of all your expenditures associated with the accident.
12. In the case of a serious accident, meet with a lawyer so that you know what your rights are and what you can do to protect them.

Summary

Understand, buy, and maintain homeowner's insurance in a cost-effective way.

There are six standardized, packaged homeowner's policies, each with a different type and level of insurance, available to homeowners and renters. All policies are identified as HOs. Three of them, HO-1, HO-2, and HO-3, are basic, broad policies specifically for homeowners. Policy HO-4 is renter's insurance, HO-6 is for condominium owners, and HO-8 is for older homes. Each of these HO policies is divided into sections that provide property insurance (Section I), and liability coverage (Section II).

Because there are some gaps in coverage, many homeowners purchase supplemental coverage. Some of the more common types of added coverage include personal articles floaters, earthquake protection, flood protection, inflation guard, and replacement cost.

You need enough homeowner's insurance to cover the replacement of your home in the event of a complete loss. This coverage needs to reflect any changes in increased costs due to changing building codes. As your assets grow in value, it's important that you continuously review your homeowner's coverage to make sure that it reflects these changes.

How do you keep costs down? There are several ways, including taking a high deductible, installing a security system and smoke detector, having multiple policies with the same company, paying premiums annually, not smoking, considering a direct writer, and shopping around.

Recover on a liability or a loss to your property.

For your homeowner's insurance to provide effective protection, you must be able to verify your loss by establishing proof of ownership and the value of your assets with a detailed asset inventory. In the event of a loss, you should report your loss immediately, make temporary repairs to protect your property, make a detailed list of everything lost or damaged, maintain records of the settlement process, and confirm the adjuster's estimate.

Buy the automobile insurance policy that's right for you.

With automobile insurance, the various sections of the policy are divided up into "parts." There are two primary areas of automobile protection, which are detailed in the first four parts of your policy. First, there's protection against bodily injury, which includes bodily injury liability coverage (Part A), medical expenses coverage (Part B), and uninsured motorist's protection (Part C). Second, there's protection against property damage, which includes property damage liability coverage (Part A), collision coverage (Part D), and comprehensive physical damage coverage (Part D); see Figure 10.3.

The five major determinants of the cost of automobile insurance are (1) the type of automobile and its use; (2) the driver's age, sex, marital status, and driving record characteristics; (3) where the policyholder lives; (4) the discounts the policyholder qualifies for; and (5) the policyholder's insurance credit score.

There are several general ways you can keep your automobile insurance rates down while ensuring complete coverage. They include comparison shopping, considering only high-quality insurers, taking advantage of discounts, improving your driving record, raising your deductibles, and keeping adequate liability insurance.

 4   File a claim on your automobile insurance.
Once you have your auto insurance, you need to be able to file a claim. A listing of what to do is given in the section titled "Filing a Claim"—you might want to xerox that and keep it in the glove compartment of your car.

Review Questions

1. Itemize and describe the differences among the six basic types of standardized homeowner's policies. Which of the first three policy types is the most comprehensive?

2. List and describe the four parts of Section I and the two parts of Section II of a homeowner's insurance policy.

3. What types of personal property have additional, more restrictive limits under Coverage C of Section I? What are they? What can you do to protect yourself from these losses?

4. List and describe at least five examples of supplemental coverage available as an addition to homeowner's policies. Which two supplemental coverages are the most important? Why?

5. Should homeowners consider purchasing an umbrella policy? Why or why not? What exclusions apply?

6. What is meant by the 80 percent rule as it applies to the purchase of homeowner's insurance to protect the dwelling?

7. Develop a list of guidelines that homeowners should consider when purchasing a homeowner's policy.

8. Explain why insurance companies use a consumer's insurance credit score when calculating insurance premiums. What are the five steps you can take to improve your score and keep premiums down?

9. Describe at least five ways, other than increasing your insurance credit score, to reduce the cost of homeowner's insurance.

10. How do you establish proof of ownership and value of assets? What are the key pieces of information that should be included? Why is this important?

11. List the duties that a homeowner has after a loss to make an insurance claim.

12. Describe the four parts of a standardized personal auto policy (PAP).

13. Explain the difference between split-limit auto liability coverage and combined single limit liability coverage.

14. What coverage and limitations apply to legal costs resulting from an auto accident?

15. What is the difference between uninsured motorist's coverage and underinsured motorist's coverage?

16. What is the difference between collision loss and comprehensive physical damage coverage?

17. Explain the fundamental concept of no-fault auto insurance. What problems exist with this system? Can you sue for damages?

18. Name several standard exclusions that would limit the amount of coverage available in a personal automobile policy.

19. Describe the factors that are major determinants of the cost of auto insurance.

20. List and describe the different types of auto insurance discounts that are commonly available. Which ones provide the greatest saving?

21. List and briefly describe the ways a consumer can reduce the cost of auto insurance premiums.

22. If involved in an accident, what should you do at the scene and after the accident?

23. Explain why it is almost always best to choose the highest liability coverage limits and deductible you can afford when purchasing automobile insurance.

Develop Your Skills—Problems and Activities

These problems are available in MyFinanceLab.

1. Jody Solan currently insures her home for 100 percent of its replacement value with an HO-3 policy. For Jody this works out to $140,000 in dwelling (Part A) coverage. What are the maximum dollar coverage amounts for Parts B, C, and D of her homeowner's policy?

2. Keith and Nancy Diem have personal property coverage with a $250 limit on currency, a $1,000 limit on jewelry, and a $2,500 limit on gold, silver, and pewter. They do not have a personal property floater. If $500 cash, $2,400 of jewelry, and $1,500 of pewterware were stolen from their home, what amount of loss would be covered by their homeowner's policy? If the Diems' deductible is $250, how much will they receive on their claim?

3. How much would a homeowner receive with actual cash-value coverage and replacement cost coverage for a 3-year old sofa destroyed by a fire? The sofa would cost $1,000 to replace today, whereas it cost $850 3 years ago, and it has an estimated life of 6 years.

4. Carmella Estevez has a homeowner's insurance policy with $100,000 of liability insurance. She is concerned about the risk of lawsuits because her property borders a neighborhood park. What can she do to increase her liability coverage? How much will Carmella's yearly premiums change as a result of increasing her liability coverage?

5. Jerry Carter's home is currently valued, on a replacement cost basis, at $315,000. The last time he checked his home was insured for $235,000 and he did not have an inflation guard endorsement. If he has a $25,500 claim due to a kitchen fire, how much will his homeowner's insurance policy pay? How much would be paid if his home were totally destroyed? In order to obtain full replacement coverage, how much insurance should Jerry carry on his house?

6. Carmen Viers lost everything to a fire and has spent the last 8 weeks living in a motel room at a cost of $4,500. Her dwelling, which was destroyed as a result of a lighting strike, was insured with an HO-2 policy for $280,000. Prior to the loss, her home was valued at $300,000, her detached garage and poolhouse were valued at $38,000, and her personal property had an actual cash value of $91,000. To make matters worse she sustained $10,000 in injuries while trying, unsuccessfully, to save her three Greyhound dogs valued at $6,000 each. How much of her total losses and expenses will be reimbursed if she has a $1,000 deductible?

7. Larry Simmons has split-limit 100/300/50 automobile liability insurance. Several months ago Larry was in an accident in which he was found to be at fault. Four passengers hurt in the accident were seriously injured and were awarded $100,000 each because of Larry's negligence. How much of this judgment will Larry's insurance policy cover? What amount will Larry have to pay out of pocket?

8. Bill Buckely has split-limit 25/50/10 auto insurance coverage on his 2008 Subaru. Driving home from work in a snowstorm, he hit a Mercedes, slid into a guardrail, and knocked down a telephone pole. Damages to the Mercedes, the guardrail, and the telephone pole were $8,500, $2,000, and $4,500, respectively. How much will Bill's insurance company pay? How much will Bill be required to pay directly?

9. Jessica Railes is purchasing a condo and is shopping for an HO-6 policy. Her auto insurer quoted her an annual rate of $550. However, if she were to insure both the condo and her car with the same company, the insurer would give her an 8 percent discount on her HO-6 policy and a 10 percent discount on her $1,200 annual auto premium. By how much will this reduce Jessica's premium? In addition to the discount, what are other advantages of purchasing both auto and homeowner's insurance with the same company?

10. The Superior Insurance Company of Maine recently advertised the following discounts for qualified drivers:

   ◆ 10 percent discount to drivers who have not had an accident in the past 7 years
   ◆ 15 percent discount for those with two or more cars; 5 percent for insuring both home and car
   ◆ 10 percent discount for those who drive less than 10,000 miles a year
   ◆ 25 percent discount if driver is a good student (student with a B average or above)
   ◆ 10 percent discount for someone aged 50 or older; 5 percent for drivers aged 24 to 49
   ◆ 5 percent discount for someone who has taken a defensive driving course
   ◆ 15 percent discount for noncommuters (less than 30 miles round-trip)
   ◆ 15 percent discount for cars with antitheft devices

   Jana, 25 years old, currently pays $1,200 for a PAP a year for her 2009 Pontiac GT. She uses her car to commute 40 miles round-trip to work and for her biannual cross-country trips to visit relatives. Last year she received a speeding ticket but took a defensive driving course in order to remove the ticket from her record; she has never had an accident. When she purchased her car she had an alarm installed. Jana is sure that she qualifies for at least one or more discounts. Calculate her new premium if she transfers to the Superior Insurance Company.

Learn by Doing—Suggested Projects

1. Unless you are Dorothy in the *Wizard of Oz*, it may be hard to imagine how you could need homeowner's or renter's liability insurance to protect yourself from damages caused to others. Auto accidents happen all the time, but house accidents? Research examples of typical or atypical liability claims covered by personal liability coverage or an umbrella policy; prepare a written or oral report to share with the class.

2. Prepare a detailed inventory of your personal property. Take photographs or make a videotape to provide additional evidence of property ownership. List the

brand, model number, and serial number of valuable items such as appliances, stereo equipment, and computers.

3. Interview an insurance agent about the differences in cost on a homeowner's or auto insurance policy based on changes in the amount of the deductible that is selected. Write a one-page report of your findings.

4. Interview at least ten people and ask the following questions:

   ◆ What are your auto liability insurance limits and deductibles?
   ◆ If you own your own home, do you have an all-risk or named perils coverage on the structure?
   ◆ If you own your own home, do you have replacement cost or actual cash-value coverage on the contents?
   ◆ If you are a renter, do you have a renter's insurance policy?
   ◆ Do you have an umbrella policy?

   Report the findings from your interviews. Did you find that the majority of respondents knew a little or a great deal about their current insurance coverages? Did many of the renters whom you interviewed have insurance? Why or why not? How many respondents knew what an umbrella policy was? Based on your interviews, what conclusions can you draw about the public's level of insurance knowledge?

5. Select three vehicles of similar style, price, and age (e.g., Toyota Camry, Hyundai Sonata, and Ford Fusion) and compare the insurance premiums (by interviewing an agent, visiting a Web site, or calling a toll-free information line) for a given amount of coverage (e.g., 100/300/100) for each vehicle, holding other factors such as driver, location, and annual mileage constant. Write a one-page report of your findings.

6. Compare the rates for a given amount of auto insurance (by interviewing an agent, visiting a Web site, or calling a toll-free information line) for:

   a. An unmarried male and an unmarried female of the same age

   b. A driver under age 25 and a driver over 25

   c. A city dweller and a driver living in a suburban/rural area

   d. A married driver and an unmarried driver of the same age

   In all situations assume the drivers have clean driving records and have been continuously insured for the previous 2 years.

7. Obtain two or three quotes on the costs of renter's insurance in your area. (This can be done in about 10 minutes at **www.answerfinancial.com**, **www.insure. com**, or similar Web site.) Report on the price differences among different insurance carriers and the differences in coverages. If possible, also obtain price quotes for insuring both a car and a rental with the same insurance company. Describe any pricing differences that you might have found.

8. Interview a property and casualty insurance agent to find out what type of homeowner's and auto insurance policies are most commonly purchased in your area and which policy features are most often recommended to clients. Why do you think coverages and recommendations might be different in your area of the country versus other areas?

Be a Financial Planner—Discussion Case 1

This case is available in MyFinanceLab.

Graham and Eustacia Leyland are planning to buy a $185,000 home near Bethel Corners, NY. The home is in "snow country" about a mile from Lake Ontario and is situated on the Salmon River that overflows its banks about every 2 years. They estimate that their personal property is worth $165,000, but they really aren't sure. This includes nearly $30,000 of computer and other electronic equipment, a $15,000 coin collection inherited from Graham's father, and $25,000 in irreplaceable artwork. The Leylands' net worth, including their current $120,000 home, is about $600,000. The Leylands asked their insurance agent to find them the best coverage, taking advantage of all possible cost-saving measures. They do not want a lot of out-of-pocket expenses if their home or personal property is damaged or lost and they want their insurance to keep pace with increasing costs.

Questions

1. What type of homeowner's insurance policy is best for the Leylands? Which covered perils would be of greatest interest living in their location?

2. What is the minimum amount of Part A coverage that the Leylands should purchase on their new home? What risks do they face if they purchase only the minimum required coverage? How much insurance should they purchase in order to reduce their financial risks?

3. Given the value and nature of their personal property and the restrictive Coverage C limits, what other supplemental coverages would you recommend that the Leylands purchase? Document your recommendations both in terms of the protection offered and the cost of coverage.

4. Given the winter snow and ice common to upstate New York, what recommendations would you make for their Section II coverage?

5. Should the Leylands buy flood insurance? If so, how do they go about purchasing it?

6. Should the Leylands consider purchasing an umbrella policy? Why or why not?

Be a Financial Planner—Discussion Case 2

This case is available in MyFinanceLab.

Bronwyn Lipper, a 2009 graduate with a degree in biochemistry, has a promising career ahead of her. Already, her employer has offered to pay for graduate school, and in the past 2 years she has been promoted three times. Three years ago she purchased a townhouse for $210,000 in Laurel, Maryland. Today, her townhouse is valued at over $270,000. More recently, Bronwyn purchased a new Ford Escape hybrid. She appreciates the energy savings and the safety the SUV gives her on her 45-mile round-trip commute into Baltimore. Overall, Bronwyn feels economically secure. She has over $35,000 in savings and growing retirement accounts. On her drive home from work last night she heard a radio report of a person who lost everything when he caused an auto accident and was underinsured. Bronwyn certainly does not want this to happen to her. Help her consider the following questions and issues.

Questions

1. After reviewing her personal automobile policy, Bronwyn realized that she had $75,000, single limit, Part A coverage; $15,000 Part B coverage; $75,000 Part C coverage; and "full" Part D coverage. Is Bronwyn adequately insured? Explain your answer.

2. Bronwyn was quoted $1,400 a year for a split-coverage policy with the following limits: $75,000/$150,000/$50,000, assuming a $100 deductible. Are these limits adequate given Bronwyn's financial situation and potential liability? What would you recommend as a minimum split-coverage limit? What will be the impact of your recommendation on her policy premium?

3. The insurance company that quoted her a split-coverage policy also indicated that she could choose a $100, $250, $500, or $1,000 deductible. If Bronwyn wants to reduce her premium costs, what deductible should she choose? Why?

4. If she decides not to boost her liability limits, how will others be compensated for their losses—property, medical, or funeral—if she is involved in a serious accident and found liable for expenses that exceed her policy limits? Would others be compensated by Bronwyn's policy for their injuries if she is not liable? If so, under what part of the policy?

5. Should Bronwyn continue to purchase Part C and D coverage? Why or why not?

6. What type of discounts might be available for Bronwyn that will help reduce her annual insurance premium?

7. How does **Principle 5: Stuff Happens, or the Importance of Liquidity** address Bronwyn's concerns about balancing adequate coverage, a reasonably high deductible to reduce the premium, and the need for emergency savings?

8. Bronwyn has heard about an umbrella policy but is unsure if it is needed. Would you recommend that she purchase such a policy? Explain your answer. Approximately how much will such a policy cost, assuming that she insures her townhouse and car with the same insurance company?

9. If Bronwyn were to get in an accident in her daily commute, why should she never admit guilt, sign anything, or comment on how much insurance she has?

Be a Financial Planner—Continuing Case: Cory and Tisha Dumont

Cory and Tisha read a recent newspaper article stating that personal bankruptcy and other financial problems often result from uninsured losses. This made them curious about their own insurance coverage, so Cory and Tisha have come back to you for assistance. Because they want to buy their home very soon, they are also interested in homeowner's insurance. They compiled the following information for you to review.

Life Insurance

Type	Cory	Tisha
Group life insurance	2 times gross income	1.50 times gross income
Whole life insurance	none	$50,000
Cash value		$1,800
Annual life insurance premiums	$0; employer paid	$0 for employer provided $720 for whole life (due next month)
Beneficiary	Tisha	Cory
Contingent beneficiary	Tisha's parents	Tisha's parents

Health Insurance

Tisha's employer provides a comprehensive major medical insurance policy that covers all members of the Dumont family to a lifetime cap of $3,000,000 per insured. The policy provides an 80/20 coinsurance provision with an annual $5,000 stop-loss provision. The Dumonts are subject to a $500 annual family deductible. Tisha's employer deducts a monthly premium of $225 per month; her employer pays the remainder of the premium. Because Tisha's company offered the better coverage, Cory chose to "opt out" of his coverage and receives a monthly "opt out fee" of $85 per month (included in gross income).

Automobile Insurance (Both Cars)

Type	Personal Auto Policy
Coverages	25/50/25 split-limit liability
Uninsured motorist	25/50/25 split-limit liability
Medical expense coverage	$20,000
Collision	$200 deductible
Comprehensive	$200 deductible
Annual premium car 1	$1,050
Annual premium car 2	$750
Annual premium total	$1,800

Umbrella Liability Insurance

None

Disability Insurance

Tisha: $2,000 per month up to 6 months; premium paid by employer

Cory: None

Homeowner's/Renter's Insurance

HO-4 renter's insurance policy with $25,000 of actual cash value coverage on personal property with an annual premium of $200

Questions

1. After reviewing the earnings multiple approach and the needs approach, Cory and Tisha opt for the simpler earnings multiple approach to estimate their life insurance needs. As Cory explains, "There are just too many unknowns in that needs approach formula. Years of income to be replaced I can understand. If I die tomorrow, I want to know that Tisha can buy a home and the kids can finish college. Chad is 4 and Haley is 2. With 20 years of my income, they should be able to do that." Tisha agrees, although she cautions that before purchasing insurance she would like to confirm their estimates by completing the needs formula. They agree that they could earn a 5 percent after-tax, after-inflation return on the insurance benefit. Do Tisha and Cory have adequate life insurance? If not, how much should each consider purchasing? (*Hint:* Remember that expenses drop by 22 percent for a surviving family of three. Be sure to consult Table 9.2, "Earnings Multiples for Life Insurance.")

2. All of Cory's life insurance and half of Tisha's are provided through their employers. Is this a good idea?

3. Cory's been on the Internet again, this time to read about universal life and variable life insurance. He has asked your opinion about purchasing one of these policies to provide additional insurance coverage for his family. What would you advise him to do? Defend your answer.

4. The Dumonts have asked you to review their life insurance policies and explain them "in plain English." What standard life insurance policy clauses or optional riders would you consider to be most important to Cory and Tisha?

5. An insurance agent recently suggested purchasing whole life policies for Chad and Haley. Costs would be cheap and Cory and Tisha could rest assured that the kids would always be insured. Is this a good idea? Defend your answer.

6. Do Tisha and Cory have adequate health insurance? If not, what changes would you suggest and why?

7. Assume Tisha is injured in a car accident and incurs $5,000 of medical bills. What are the options for paying this bill? How would your answer change if the $5,000 bill resulted from an emergency appendectomy? Assuming that no one else in her family has made a claim this year, how much of the bill would her insurance company pay?

8. Next month is the "annual open enrollment period" for health insurance benefits through Tisha's employer. It is the only time of the year when she can make changes to her policy. Tisha is considering switching to a different HMO or PPO plan. What are the advantages and disadvantages of each form of managed care?

9. Tisha is concerned about a possible layoff due to mergers among several accounting firms. What are some health insurance options available to the Dumonts if Tisha is "downsized"? What are the advantages and disadvantages of Cory "opting out" in this situation? Tisha has considered self-employment from a home office. How will this affect their options for family health care coverage?

10. Both Tisha and Cory are considering the purchase of disability insurance because Cory has none and Tisha's employer-provided policy is very short term. What policy features would you recommend they include?

11. Do Tisha and Cory have adequate renter's insurance? What recommendation would you make? Why?

12. Evaluate the Dumonts' auto insurance. What recommendations for changes, if any, would you make? Why?

13. How much would the Dumonts' policy pay if Cory or Tisha were at fault for an accident that resulted in $65,000 of bodily injury losses? How would the claim be paid?

14. What policy options could the Dumonts select to reduce the cost of their property and liability insurance?

15. What type of homeowner's policy should the Dumonts select when they purchase their first home, assuming they are very cautious about protecting their financial situation? Also, recall that Cory does not like financial surprises, so they will not be considering an older home or a condominium! Should they consider adding an umbrella policy at this time? Explain your answer.

PART 4

Managing Your Investments

You now have an understanding of the financial planning process, including managing your money, and assessing your insurance needs. What's next? It's time to turn your attention to how you make your money grow—that is, how you turn money into wealth—and to do that you need a basic understanding of investments. This all goes back to Principle 1: The Best Protection Is Knowledge; with an understanding of investments not only do you have the ability to manage your own investments, but you are also able to protect yourself against bad, or unscrupulous, investment advice. In effect, investment knowledge serves as an insurance policy against this problem.

In Part 4, we will specifically focus on Principles 8 and 9:

Principle 8: Risk and Return Go Hand in Hand—While this principle focuses on the relationship between risk and return, it also introduces the concept of diversification, which allows you to eliminate risk, without impacting return. In addition, you will see why you can afford to take on more risk when you have a longer period of time until you need your money.

Principle 9: Mind Games, Your Financial Personality, and Your Money—Unfortunately, we all seem to be programmed for failure. Apparently many of the financial mistakes we make are built right into our brains. However, by understanding the behavioral biases we all have, we can avoid these mistakes.

In addition, in Part 4 we will also touch on these principles:

Principle 1: The Best Protection Is knowledge

Principle 2: Nothing Happens Without a Plan

Principle 3: The Time Value of Money

Principle 4: Taxes Affect Personal Finance Decisions

Principle 10: Just Do It!

11 Investment Basics

Learning Objectives

 Set your goals and be ready to invest.

 Calculate interest rates and real rates of return.

 Manage risk in your investments.

 Allocate your assets in the manner that is best for you.

 Understand how difficult it is to beat the market.

In 1995, Ki-Jana Carter didn't know anything about investing. How could he? When he was growing up, money had been tight: Ki-Jana's mother worked 12- to 15-hour days just to make ends meet. Ki-Jana Carter didn't know about investing, but he knew about football.

But that year, Carter, a running back at Penn State, became the first pick in the NFL draft. A pro football career was a dream come true for the 22-year-old. During the preseason, Carter's mind wasn't on money or investments. It was on learning the playbook for the Cincinnati Bengals, his new team. However, a season-ending knee injury in his first preseason game served to teach him a more important lesson, one that many NFL players don't learn until too late: An NFL career—and the pay that comes with it—can vanish in an instant.

When Carter signed with the Bengals, he received a $19.2-million, 7-year contract, which included a $7.125 million signing bonus. Needless to say, he thought that the days of money being tight were over. "I came out of college and felt invincible," says Carter. "After the injury it was like, "Wow, I may not be making more money.'"

Worried that his career might indeed be over and that his income might evaporate, Carter decided to protect the money he already had. Knowing that he didn't know enough, Carter interviewed 14 financial planners and chose Mark Griege, a fee-only planner who was paid a percentage of Carter's investments. Griege and Carter agreed it was time for Carter to learn about investing, so part of Griege's job was teaching Carter this skill. Carter's investing goal was not only to protect his wealth and make money, but to understand investing from a common sense perspective. "I see a lot of guys come into the league and want to go out and spend to show they have a lot of money," says Carter. "That's good now, but I'm trying to live like this when I'm 50, 60, 70."

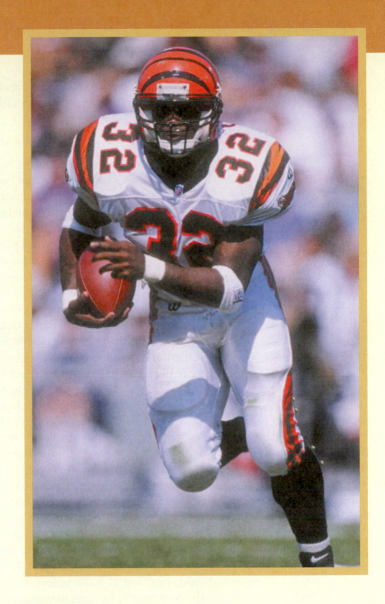

Take a tip from Ki-Jana Carter and remember **Principle 1: The Best Protection Is Knowledge**. A solid grounding in investing will help you reach your financial goals and avoid pitfalls that could upend your financial future. It's worked for Carter and it can work for you. In 1999, after two major knee injuries and a broken wrist over five seasons with the Bengals, the oft-wounded Carter was cut in a salary cap move. After sitting out the 2000 season, he came back with the Redskins and had his best year in the pros averaging 4.9 yards per carry and finally breaking over the 1,000 yards gained mark for his career, and in 2005 his football career ended. Fortunately, his financial future is set.

Principle

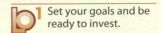
Set your goals and be ready to invest.

Before You Invest

In personal financial planning, everything begins and ends with your goals, and investments are no exception. Before developing an investment plan, you must first decide what your goals are and how much you can set aside to meet those goals.

Before we look at goal setting and making a plan, however, let's look at the difference between investing and speculating.

Investing Versus Speculating

This chapter is about investing, not about speculating. What's the difference? Well, although they both involve risk, when you buy an **investment**, you put your money in an asset that generates value or a return. For example, part of its return or value may come in the form of an **income return** such as dividends or interest payments. Part may also come from the fact that the investment is creating value or wealth—that is, it is earning money and plowing that money back into the investment so that the investment itself appreciates in value. Real estate pays rent, stocks appreciate in value and often times pay dividends, and bonds pay interest. Even if the stock isn't paying dividends now—such as with Google's common stock—it is creating wealth or value and appreciating in price. It is the *return* that the asset generates now and will generate in the future that determines its value.

Speculation on the other hand involves assets that don't generate wealth or a return and involve a much higher level of risk and in general you are hoping for a very high return. Gold coins and baseball cards, for example, are worth more in the future only if someone is willing to buy them at a higher price than you paid when you bought them. Their value depends *entirely* on supply and demand, and demand for these assets can change quickly. As a result, an asset of this type is considered speculation. Other examples of speculation include comic books, autographs, Beanie Babies®, and gems—it's the same as betting on the Super Bowl in hopes that you make a lot of money quickly.

You can make a pretty penny speculating. The first issue of the *X-Men* comic book appeared in September 1963 and cost 12¢. Forty-eight years later it was worth over $13,500 in near mint condition—that's an appreciation rate of over 27 percent per year. But be warned: You can also lose a lot through speculating. Just look at Mark McGwire's 1985 Topps Tiffany card—it sold at a peak price of $10,000, but in 2011 it was down to $15; the same thing happened to Jason Giambi's 1991 Topps rookie card, peaking at $400, before falling to $7 in 2011. Why did the value of these cards drop so much? No one wanted to buy them. It all boils down to supply and demand.

People have speculated for centuries. In the 16th century, for example, Dutch farmers speculated in tulip bulbs. One recorded trade had a single bulb being exchanged for the following: 17 bushels of wheat, 34 bushels of rye, 4 fat oxen, 8 fat swine, 12 fat sheep, 2 goat's-heads of wine, 4 kegs of beer, 2 tons of butter, 1,000 pounds of cheese, a complete bed, a suit of clothes, and a silver drinking cup!

Today's new variation of speculative securities is derivatives. **Derivative securities** are those whose value is derived from the value of other assets—these include options.

An **option** gives its owner *the right* to buy or sell an asset—generally common stock. In other words, if the asset is not of value, you don't have to exercise the option. The price at which the option holder can buy or sell the asset is specified. In addition, options have an expiration date, and there are two basic types of options: a call option, which gives you the option to buy the underlying asset at a set price on or before the option's maturity date,

---

Investment

An asset that generates value or a return. For example, stocks pay dividends and bonds pay interest, so these are considered investments.

Income Return

Investment return received directly from the company or organization in which you've invested, usually in the form of dividends or interest payments.

Speculation

An asset whose value depends solely on supply and demand, as opposed to being based on the return that it generates. For example, gold coins and baseball cards are worth more in the future only if someone is willing to pay more for them.

Derivative Securities

Securities whose value is derived from the value of other assets.

Option

A security that gives its owner the right to buy or sell an asset—generally common stock—at a specified price over a specified period.

STOP & THINK

If an asset doesn't generate a return, its value is determined by supply and demand. Putting money into such an asset is speculating. Gold is a good example. Although recently a number of financial gurus (along with gold sellers trying to push the price of gold up) have been claiming that gold is a good investment, it's simply a form of speculation. While salesmen may make gold sound like a sure bet, it's far from that. In early 1980, the price of gold was a bit over $850. Since 1980, however, the price has bounced a bit, hitting $1,900 in September 2011. While gold did very well in 2010 and early 2011, its average annual return since 1980 was less than 2 percent per year. A typical New York Stock Exchange stock, conversely, increased at an average annual rate of 10.6 percent from 1980 to the beginning of 2011. The bottom line is *invest*, don't speculate.

and a put option, which gives you the option to sell the underlying asset at a set price on or before the option's maturity date.

With options, you find the buyer and seller are, in a sense, betting against each other. For this reason, the options markets are often referred to as a "zero sum game." If someone makes money, then someone must lose money; if profits and losses were added up, the total for all options, ignoring trading costs, would equal zero. To say the least, the options markets are quite complicated and risky. In fact, some experts refer to them as legalized institutions for transferring wealth from the unsophisticated to the sophisticated. These derivatives can be extremely dangerous. For the beginning investor options should be considered speculative in nature. In short, they're not something to rely on to achieve your financial goals.

With *investing*, as opposed to speculating, the value of an asset is determined by what return it earns. Investments have intrinsic value because they produce wealth and income, and although in the short term their price may wander a bit from their intrinsic value, in the long run the price approaches the intrinsic value. Investment is less risky than speculation, and value is based on how much income the investment is producing now along with what it is expected to produce in the future. Certainly, investment is not as exciting as speculation, but "exciting" is not that great if it means losing your nest egg.

Setting Investment Goals

Most of us have goals or at least dreams—we'd like to buy a house, or maybe retire early—but to reach those goals, they must be formalized. That's the point of **Principle 2: Nothing Happens Without a Plan**. When making your plan you must (1) write your goals down and prioritize them, (2) attach costs to them, (3) figure out when the money for those goals will be needed, and (4) periodically reevaluate your goals.

As we said in Chapter 1, when formalizing your goals it's easiest to think about them in terms of short-term, intermediate-term, and long-term time horizons. Short-term goals are any financial goals that can be accomplished within a 1-year period, such as buying a television or taking a vacation. An intermediate-term goal is one that would take between 1 and 10 years to accomplish—perhaps paying for college for an older child or accumulating enough money for a down payment on a new house. A long-term goal is one for which it takes more than 10 years to accumulate the money—retirement, for example.

In setting these goals, the key is to be realistic, which means your goals should reflect your financial and life situations. The following questions might help you focus on what goals are important to you:

- If I don't accomplish this goal, what are the consequences?
- Am I willing to make the financial sacrifices necessary to meet this goal?
- How much money do I need to accomplish this goal?
- When do I need this money?

Once you've set your goals, you then have to use your time value of money skills to translate them into action. For example, if you'd like to retire in 40 years with $500,000, you have to first consider what you can earn on your savings and then determine how much you need to set aside each year.

P2 **Principle**

STOP & THINK

Is it possible to reach your financial goals? Yes, and it may be easier to reach them than you think because time is on your side. A small change in your spending and investment habits could produce big returns later on. For example, if you're 20 now and you save $15 per month—that works out to about 50 cents per day—at 12 percent, 50 years later your savings will have grown to over $585,000. The key is to start early. What could you cut out in order to save $15 per month?

Financial Reality Check

Before you put your investment program into place, it's important that you have a grip on your financial affairs. Make sure you're living within your means, have adequate insurance, and keep emergency funds—in effect, put your financial house in order before you consider investing.

Starting Your Investment Program

The sooner you invest, the more you earn. Keep in mind **Principle 3: The Time Value of Money**. As you know by now, there's no substitute for time when it comes to investments—the earlier you begin planning for the future, the easier it is to achieve your goals. That's why **Principle 10: Just Do It!** is so important. Regardless of your level of income, you can make room for investing.

How do you go about starting an investment program? The first step is to revisit the first two questions you asked when setting up your goals: If I don't accomplish this goal, what are the consequences? And, am I willing to make the financial sacrifices necessary to meet this goal? Once you have the commitment, the next step is to come up with the money. Here are some tips to getting started.

Pay Yourself First   First, set aside your savings, and what's left becomes the amount you can spend. When you pay yourself first, you're acknowledging the fact that your long-term goals are paramount.

Make Investing Automatic   Make your savings automatic. If your employer allows automatic withholding, take advantage of it. Have an amount automatically deducted from your checking account and sent to a brokerage firm or mutual fund.

Take Advantage of Uncle Sam and Your Employer   If your employer offers matching investments, don't pass them by. Matching investments are about as close to something for nothing as you'll ever get. Also, keep an eye out for investments that are tax favored, such as traditional IRAs and Roth IRAs.

Windfalls   If you're ever lucky enough to receive a bit of a windfall—perhaps an inheritance, a salary bonus, a gift, a tax refund, or maybe even something from the lottery—don't fritter it away. Investing some (or all) of it is a speedy way to build your investments.

Make 2 Months a Year Investment Months   Some financial advisors suggest that if you're having trouble starting your investment program, pick 2 months per year to cut back on your spending and make those your investment months. If you know that your "life of poverty" is over at the end of the month, it may be easier to stick to your savings.

Fitting Taxes into Investing

When we compare investment returns we want to make our comparison on an after-tax basis—that is, what we pay to Uncle Sam doesn't count. As we examine the different investment alternatives we'll look more closely at taxes, but several points hold true regardless of what we invest in.

- ◆ The marginal tax rate is the rate you pay on the next dollar of earnings.
- ◆ Tax-free investment alternatives should be compared only on an after-tax basis. Of course, the higher your marginal tax bracket, the more attractive tax-free investments become.

◆ You can make investments on a *tax-deferred* basis, which means that not only does your investment grow free of taxes, but the money you invest isn't taxed until you liquidate your investment.

◆ When it comes to taxes, capital gains and dividend income are better than ordinary income. Recall from Chapter 4 that both the long-term capital gains tax rate and the tax rate on qualified dividends are reduced to 15 percent for taxpayers whose top tax bracket exceeds 15 percent, and for taxpayers in the 10 and 15 percent tax brackets, the tax rate is reduced to 0 percent.

If you were in the 35 percent marginal tax bracket and had $50,000 of additional ordinary income, your tax bill would come to ($50,000 × 35 percent) = $17,500. If this $50,000 of additional income came in the form of long-term capital gains, your taxes would be only ($50,000 × 15 percent) = $7,500. Just as valuable as the tax break on capital gains income is the fact that you don't have to claim it—and, therefore, pay taxes on it—until you sell the asset. That is, you can time when you want to claim your capital gains.

Taxes make some investments better than they would otherwise be and others worse—it all gets back to **Principle 4: Taxes Affect Personal Finance Decisions**.

Investment Choices

Today there are really only two basic categories of investments:

◆ **Lending investments.** Savings accounts and bonds, which are debt instruments issued by corporations and by the government, are examples of lending investments.

◆ **Ownership investments.** Preferred stocks and common stocks, which represent an ownership position in a corporation, along with income-producing real estate, are examples of ownership investments. Let's take a closer look at each of these.

Lending Investments   Whenever you put money in a savings account or buy a bond, you're actually lending someone your money. The amount you've lent them is your investment. A savings account pays you interest on the balance you hold in your account. With a bond, your return is generally fixed and known ahead of time. It has a set **maturity date**, at which time the bond is terminated and the investor is returned the money that has been lent. The face value of the bond, which is the amount you receive when the bond matures, is referred to as the **par value or principal**.

Most bonds issued by corporations trade in units of $1,000, although bonds issued by federal, state, or local governments may trade in units of $5,000 or $10,000. Over the life of the bond, you receive semiannual interest payments, which are set when the bond is issued. The **coupon interest rate** refers to the actual rate of interest the bond pays. Most bonds have fixed interest rates, but some have variable or floating rates, meaning that the interest rate changes periodically to reflect current interest rates.[1]

Let's assume, for example, that you've bought a 20-year bond issued by the government, with a par value of $1,000 and an interest rate of 8 percent. You'll receive $80 per year in interest payments (0.08 × $1,000). Then, at maturity, which in this case is in 20 years, you'll be returned the par value, which is $1,000.

With lending investments, you usually know ahead of time exactly what your return will be, which isn't always a good thing. For example, because you've locked in an 8 percent return on your bond, if inflation suddenly climbs to 16 percent, your return won't even keep up with inflation. However, if inflation drops, your 8 percent may look even better than it did when you purchased the bond.

Maturity Date
The date at which the borrower must repay the loan or borrowed funds.

Par Value or Principal
The stated amount on the face of a bond, which the firm is to repay at the maturity date.

Coupon Interest Rate
The interest to be paid annually on a bond as a percentage of par value, which is specified in the contractual agreement.

---

[1]There are also zero-coupon bonds that make no interest payments to the bondholder. We talk about these in Chapter 14.

The biggest potential problem with lending investments arises when the lender experiences financial difficulties and can't pay the interest on the bond, or can't pay off the bond at maturity. If the firm that issued the bond goes bankrupt, the bondholders most likely lose their entire investment. Unfortunately, even though lending investments let you share a lender's financial pain, they don't let you share any of the pleasure. If the lender suddenly makes a ton of money, you don't.

With lending investments, the best-case scenario is that the issuer pays you all the interest that's owed and at maturity gives you back your principal. Actually, this best-case scenario is much better than it at first seems. If you carefully choose whom you lend money to, whose bonds you buy, or where you open a savings account, there can be much less risk with lending investments than with ownership investments. In addition, the returns can be quite respectable.

Ownership Investments   The two major forms of ownership investment are real estate and stocks. Real estate investments include such things as rental apartments and investments in income-producing property, such as shopping malls and office buildings. In each case, you're investing in something that generates a return: rent. Your home could also be considered a real estate investment. In a sense it generates income because it eliminates rent payments that you would otherwise have to make.

The major disadvantage of real estate investments is that they tend to be quite illiquid. That is, when it comes time to sell off your investment, you may have a hard time getting a fair price for it or even finding someone interested in buying it.

Stock
A fractional ownership in a corporation.

The most popular ownership investment is stocks, but the actual "ownership" isn't of an asset you can hold in your hand or live in. When you purchase 50 shares of General Electric **stock**, you've purchased a small portion of the General Electric Corporation. Although you own only a tiny fraction of GE, buying stock does make you an owner or equity holder, with "equity" being another term for ownership.

What do you get as an owner of GE? Don't count on any free lightbulbs. In the case of common stock ownership, you get a chance to vote for the board of directors, which oversees GE's operations. If GE earns a profit, you'll most likely receive a portion of those profits in the form of **dividends**, which are generally paid out quarterly.

Dividend
A payment by a corporation to its shareholders.

As profits and dividends continue to increase, investors see the stock as more valuable and are willing to pay more to purchase it. Thus, the price goes up. There's no limit as to how high a stock's price can rise. In fact, from 1995 through 1999 the average return on U.S. stocks was 28.6 percent per year! But, from 2000 through 2002 stocks went in the other direction, averaging a loss of 14.6 percent per year, and from 2003 through 2007, they went up again, averaging a 12.8 percent return per year. Then in 2008 stocks dropped by 37 percent, and in 2009 and 2010 they rose by an average of 20.6 percent per year. Remember, those are averages, and individual stocks jumped around more than that. In fact, in October 2008, the stock market dropped by over 18 percent in 1 week—as it appeared to be in free-fall. The bottom line here is that while stocks have done well over longer periods of time, they can fluctuate dramatically over the short term.

In the case of preferred stock, the dividend is generally fixed, with the preferred stockholder receiving an annual dividend as long as the firm has the cash to pay. You can't vote for the board of directors if you own GE preferred stock, unless GE has suffered some financial problems and omitted some preferred stock dividends.

Of course, companies must pay the interest to debt holders before they can distribute dividends to stockholders. Thus, if debt such as bonds eats up a company's

---

STOP & THINK

The average American spends 29 hours a week watching TV. How many hours a week do you think they spend on financial planning and investing?

profits, stockholders get no dividends. Moreover, preferred stockholders take a "preferred" position to common stockholders—that is, they receive their dividends first. Common stockholders receive their dividends from whatever's left over.

The Returns from Investing

When you invest your money, you can receive your return in one of two ways. First, an investment can go up or down in value—in the language of investments, this is referred to as a **capital gain** or **loss**. Although most people associate capital gains and losses with real estate and common stock, these gains and losses also come with bonds. In fact, most of the time when you buy a bond, you buy it for something other than its par value, that is, what the issuer gives you back when the bond matures. That means if you hold it to maturity, you'll experience some capital gains or losses.

Capital Gain or Loss
The gain (or loss) on the sale of a capital asset. For example, any return (or loss) from the appreciation (or drop) in value of a share of stock would be considered a capital gain (or loss).

The second component of the return on your investment is the income return. Income return consists of any payments you receive directly from the company or organization in which you've invested. In the case of bonds, your income return is the interest you receive. In the case of common and preferred stocks, your income return comes in the form of dividends. The rate of return can be calculated as follows:

$$\text{rate of return} = \frac{(\text{ending value} - \text{beginning value}) + \text{income return}}{\text{beginning value}}$$

MONEY MATTERS

Tips from Marcy Furney, ChFC, Certified Financial Planner™

KNOW THYSELF

The typical question at every social gathering is "So, what's good to invest in these days?" My answer is, "It all depends!" The best advice I can give anyone is to invest based on your own personal profile, not on a hot tip from the media, a party, or coffee break conversation. To establish your profile, ask yourself the following questions:

What am I investing for? Is it retirement, a new home, college for the children, and so forth? For some lucky people the goal may just be to make some extra money grow.

When will I need the money? In other words, what is your time horizon? Will you need all the funds at some definite date, or will it be used to provide an income? For example: Many people think they must have all their money accessible on the day they retire. In reality, they need to continue to have their "nest egg" invested so that it will provide for them over many years. Short time limits (a year or two) normally do not allow you to work around the inherent volatility of the market.

How much will I be investing? If you have a large sum, the options are quite different from those open to you with a small monthly amount. In the latter case, you may need to choose among mutual funds that allow as little as $50 monthly purchases rather than attempting to buy one or two shares of stock each time. The dollar amount will also control the level of

diversification you can achieve in individual stocks and bonds versus mutual funds.

What is my volatility or risk tolerance? If you anticipate a panic attack the first time your account statement shows a current balance much lower than what you contributed, you have some decisions to make. Can you learn to cope with it, will you settle for small returns from "safe" investments, or do you need an advisor to help you over the humps?

How knowledgeable am I about the different investment vehicles available? Are you willing to do a lot of "homework," or would you rather pay an advisor for his or her expertise? Your answer to these questions will determine how you go about actually investing using a full-service broker, financial planner, investment advisor, discount broker, or investing directly with mutual fund companies.

So now that you know yourself, "just do it." If fear, lack of time, or inadequate information is holding you up, "Get thee to an advisor!"

Thus, if a stock climbs from $45 to $55 per share over 1 year while paying $3 in dividends, its rate of return over that year would be

$$\text{rate of return} = \frac{(\$55 - \$45) + \$3}{\$45} = \frac{\$10 + \$3}{\$45} = \frac{\$13}{\$45} = 28.89\%$$

If you're calculating the rate of return over a number of years, you may want to break this down into the average annual rate of return. You need only multiply the rate of return by $1/N$, where N is the number of years for which the investment is held. Thus, the average annual rate of return can be calculated as follows:

$$\frac{\text{annual average}}{\text{rate of return}} = \frac{(\text{ending value} - \text{beginning value}) + \text{income return}}{\text{beginning value}} \times \frac{1}{N}$$

If over a 3-year period a stock climbs from $45 to $68 per share and pays a total of $7 over 3 years in dividends, its average annual rate of return would be

$$\text{average annual rate of return} = \frac{(\$68 - \$45) + \$7}{\$45} \times \frac{1}{3} = \frac{\$23 + \$7}{\$45} \times \frac{1}{3}$$

$$= \frac{\$30}{\$45} \times \frac{1}{3} = 0.667 \times 0.333 = 0.222, \text{ or } 22.2\%$$

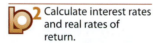 Calculate interest rates and real rates of return.

Market Interest Rates

Interest rates play an extremely important role in determining the value of a share of stock, a bond, or a real estate investment. Interest rates also determine what we earn on savings and are closely tied to the rate of inflation. Therefore, you need to understand interest rates—how they're determined and what affects them—before making any investments. Let's start off by taking a look at what a real interest rate is.

Nominal and Real Rates of Return

Nominal (or Quoted) Rate of Return
The rate of return earned on an investment, unadjusted for lost purchasing power.

Real Rate of Return
The current or nominal rate of return minus the inflation rate.

The **nominal (or quoted) rate of return** is the rate of return earned on an investment without any adjustment for inflation. It's the rate that's quoted in the *Wall Street Journal* for specific bonds or the rate your bank advertises for its savings accounts, and it determines how much interest you earn when you lend money to someone. How much have you *really* earned? The **real rate of return**, which is simply the nominal rate of return minus the inflation rate, tells you how much you've really earned after adjusting for inflation. If you earn 8 percent on an investment while the inflation rate is 3 percent, the nominal rate of return is 8 percent, and the real rate of return is 5 percent (8% − 3%).

Historical Interest Rates

The nominal interest rates for high-quality bonds issued by corporations (corporate AAA bonds), bonds with 10-year maturities issued by the federal government (10-year Treasury bonds), and bonds with 3-month maturities issued by the federal government (3-month Treasury bonds) over the recent past are shown in Figure 11.1. Notice that nominal interest rates have dropped somewhat over the past 20 years. In effect, as inflation slowed down, investors demanded a lower return on money they lent, which resulted in a drop in nominal interest rates. This link between inflation and nominal interest rates has its roots in **Principle 8: Risk and Return Go Hand in Hand.**

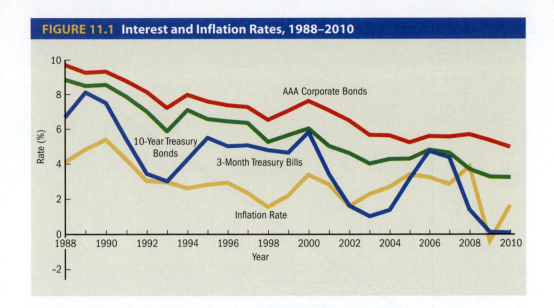

FIGURE 11.1 Interest and Inflation Rates, 1988–2010

Although it's not shown in Figure 11.1, the real rate of interest can be calculated by subtracting the inflation rate from the nominal interest rate. The real rate of return can even be negative. In early 2011, as a result of the downturn in the economy, the Federal Reserve took steps to cut short-term interest rates, the real rate of return on Treasury bills was a negative 1.33 percent (the nominal, or quoted, rate on a Treasury bill with a 1-year maturity was 0.30 percent, minus the inflation rate at that time of 1.63 percent, which equals negative 1.33 percent). That means that if you invested your savings in a Treasury bill in early 2011, your investment wouldn't even have kept up with inflation.

How Interest Rates Affect Returns on Other Investments

The relationship between returns on all the different investment alternatives is extremely tangled. For example, common stocks tend to be riskier than bonds, so you won't invest in common stocks unless they have a higher expected return. That means that if bonds are returning 6 percent, you may be satisfied with a 9 percent return on stocks. However, if bonds were returning 12 percent, you wouldn't invest in stocks if the expected return were only 9 percent. You might demand a 15 percent return on your common stock investment.

In effect, the expected returns on all the investments are related—what you can earn on one investment determines what you demand on another. Interest rates can be thought of as a kind of "base" return. When interest rates go up, investors demand a higher return on all other investments. When interest rates go down, the return investors demand on other investments goes down.

A Look at Risk–Return Trade-Offs

 Manage risk in your investments.

From **Principle 8** you know that risk goes hand in hand with potential return. The more risk you are willing to take on, the greater the potential return—but also, the greater the possibility that you will lose money. What does all this mean? It means you must take steps to eliminate risk without affecting potential return.

There's no question that you must accept some risk to meet your long-term financial goals, so you must balance the amount of risk you're willing to take on with the amount of return you need. Before we examine the sources of risk in investments, let's take a look at the historical levels of risk and return in the investment markets.

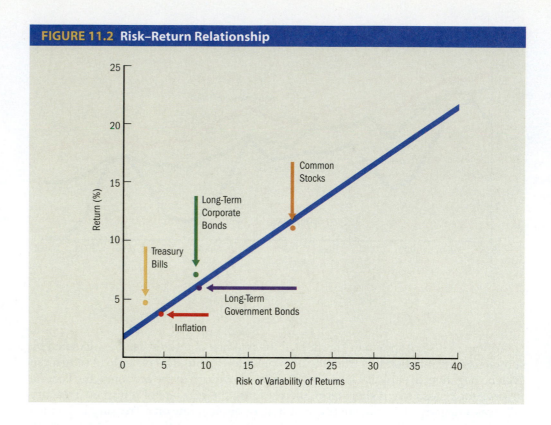

FIGURE 11.2 Risk–Return Relationship

Historical Levels of Risk and Return

Let's look at the historical levels of risk and return for the past 60 years. If you look at these returns graphically, plotting average annual return against risk or variability of returns as your measure of risk, you get the graph in Figure 11.2. As you can see, it bears a strong resemblance to the risk–return trade-off graph presented in Chapter 1.

Remember, when we presented the risk–return relationship described in **Principle 8**, we talked about expected return. Here, you see that what was predicted by **Principle 8** in fact holds. Investments that produce higher returns have higher levels of risk associated with them.

Sources of Risk in the Risk–Return Trade-Off

The compensation that investors demand for taking on added risk differs for every investment because every investment has a different level of risk. The purpose behind presenting these "sources of risk" is to give you an intuitive understanding of what causes fluctuations in the prices and values of different investments.

Keep in mind that these sources are not mutually exclusive—that is, there's a good deal of overlap between some of them. It's very difficult to look at price fluctuation in an investment and try to attribute it solely to one or another "source" of risk. However, some investments are more vulnerable to one source of risk, while some are more vulnerable to another, so understanding these sources can tell you a lot about many investments.

STOP & THINK

Saving and investing are two things that many people view as unpleasant tasks, but they are also good for you. People often procrastinate when it comes to unpleasant tasks that are good for them—stopping smoking, eliminating credit card debt, dieting, exercising. Procrastination is a behavioral trait we all have—remember **Principle 9: Mind Games, Your Financial Personality, and Your Money**—but when it comes to investing it can have a huge impact on your financial future. Do you have a tendency to procrastinate? What about the last term paper you wrote or the last time you crammed for an exam?

Interest Rate Risk One source of risk to investors finds its roots in changes in interest rates. Regardless of their source, interest rate changes can be bad news for investors. For example, when market interest rates rise, the price of outstanding bonds declines, because new bonds with higher interest rates are now available. No one will want to buy your $1,000, 6.5 percent, 10-year bond when $1,000, 8 percent, 10-year bonds are available. The higher the interest rate climbs, the less your bond will be worth.

The same basic relationship holds for common stock. When market interest rates rise, the price of common stock drops. That's because alternative investments such as bonds are paying more when interest rates rise, and that makes stocks look less attractive to them in a relative sense. This fluctuation in security prices due to changes in the market interest rate is a result of **interest rate risk**. Unfortunately, because increases in interest rates affect all securities in the same way, it's impossible to eliminate interest rate risk.

Inflation Risk **Inflation risk** reflects the likelihood that rising prices will eat away the purchasing power of your money, and that changes in the anticipated level of inflation will result in interest rate changes, which will in turn cause security price fluctuations. Inflation risk is closely linked to interest rate risk, but it is important enough in the valuation and investment processes that it's generally treated as a totally separate source of risk.

Business Risk Most stocks and bonds are influenced by how well or poorly the company that issued them is performing. **Business risk** deals with fluctuations in investment value that are caused by good or bad management decisions, or how well or poorly the firm's products are doing in the marketplace. Businesses can go bankrupt, and management does make poor decisions. Look at Omeros, the biopharmaceutical firm. On April 1, 2011, its stock tumbled by 38 percent after one of its experimental drugs failed in late-stage clinical testing.

Business risk is different for different companies. Some companies seem to post even profits year in and year out, regardless of what's happening in the economy, while the profits levels of other firms tend to swing wildly.

Financial Risk **Financial risk** is risk associated with the use of debt by the firm. As a firm takes on more debt, it also takes on interest and principal payments that must be made regardless of how well the firm does. If the firm can't make the payments, it could go bankrupt. Thus, how the firm raises money affects its level of risk.

Liquidity Risk **Liquidity risk** deals with the inability to liquidate a security quickly and at a fair market price. For investments that are infrequently traded, it can be hard to find a buyer. Sometimes it's impossible to find a buyer at a fair market price, and you wind up having to sell for less than an asset's worth—sometimes even for a loss.

Buying a piece of your favorite sports team has long been a popular investment for the super-rich, but there's a good deal of liquidity risk in such a venture. Harvey Lighton, owner of 3.1237 percent of the New York Yankees, learned this lesson when he took out a newspaper ad offering a 1 percent stake in the Yankees for $2.95 million. There were no takers. He then considered a plan to take a 2 percent stake in the Yankees and divide it into 20,000 pieces, each representing one-millionth of the team, and sell them for $500 each. That didn't work either. For investors who need money fast, liquidity risk is an important consideration.

Market Risk **Market risk** is risk associated with overall market movements. There are periods of bull markets—that is, times when all stocks seem to move upward—and times of bear markets, when all stocks tend to decline in price. The same tends to

Interest Rate Risk
The risk of fluctuations in security prices due to changes in the market interest rate.

Inflation Risk
The risk that rising prices will eat away the purchasing power of your money, and that changes in the anticipated level of inflation will result in interest rate changes, which will in turn cause security price fluctuations.

Business Risk
The risk of fluctuations in security prices resulting from good or bad management decisions, or how well or poorly the firm's products are doing in the marketplace.

Financial Risk
The risk associated with a company's use of debt. If a company takes on too much debt and can't meet its obligations, investors risk the company defaulting or dropping in stock value.

Liquidity Risk
Risk associated with the inability to liquidate a security quickly and at a fair market price.

Market Risk
Risk associated with overall market movements.

be true in the bond markets. This is what happened over the 2007–2008 period when stocks dropped 40 percent from their all time highs just 1 year earlier, with virtually all stocks dropping in unison.

Political and Regulatory Risk
Risk resulting from unanticipated changes in the tax or legal environment.

Political and Regulatory Risk **Political and regulatory risk** result from unanticipated changes in the tax or legal environments that have been imposed by the government. Changes in the capital gains tax rate, or in the tax deductibility of interest on municipal bonds, or the passage of any new regulatory reform laws affect investment values and are examples of political and regulatory risk.

> ## STOP & THINK
>
> "Most people get interested in stocks when everyone else is. The time to get interested is when no one else is. You can't buy what is popular and do well."—Warren Buffett. What do you think he meant?

Exchange Rate Risk
The risk of fluctuations in security prices from the variability in earnings resulting from changes in exchange rates.

Call Risk
The risk to bondholders that a bond may be called away from them before maturity.

Calling a Bond
The redeeming of a bond before its scheduled maturity. Many bonds are callable.

Diversification
The elimination of risk by investing in different assets. It works by allowing the extreme good and bad returns to cancel each other out. The result is that total variability or risk is reduced without affecting expected return.

P8 Principle

Exchange Rate Risk **Exchange rate risk** refers to the variability in earnings resulting from changes in exchange rates. For example, if you invest in a German bond, you first convert your dollars into euros. When you liquidate that investment, you sell your bond for euros and convert those euros into dollars. What you earn on your investment depends on how well the investment performed and what happened to the exchange rate. For the international investor, exchange rate risk is simply another layer of risk.

Call Risk **Call risk** is the risk to callable bondholders that a bond may be called away from them before maturity. **Calling a bond** refers to redeeming the bond early, and many bonds are callable. When a bond is called, the bondholder generally receives the face value of the bond plus 1 year of interest payments.

Diversification

Diversification is a simple concept: Don't put all your eggs in one basket. **Diversification** works by allowing the extreme good and bad returns to cancel each other out, resulting in a reduction of the total variability or risk without affecting expected return.

It's important to understand the process of diversification. It not only eliminates a lot of risk, but also helps us understand what risk is relevant to us as investors. It's also important to understand that diversification reduces risk without affecting the expected return. That's what we saw when we introduced **Principle 8** in Chapter 1. It works by allowing the good and bad observations to cancel each other out. As a result, variability, or risk, is reduced.

Portfolio
A group of investments held by an individual.

Diversifying Away Risk As you diversify your investments, much of the risk in the combined holdings of all your investments, which is called your **portfolio**, disappears. This elimination of risk occurs because the stock returns in your portfolio don't always move in the same direction, and as a result, the ups and downs eliminate each other.

To understand how diversification can reduce risk, let's look at a simple example. Suppose you own a sunglasses shop that caters to the tourists on a beautiful Caribbean island, and the only product you sell is sunglasses. During the sunny season, you earn 20 percent on sunglasses, but during the rainy season it's tough to sell sunglasses and you earn 0 percent.

Sunglasses	
Rainy Season	0%
Sunny Season	20%

On average, the sunny and rainy seasons each last half the year. As a result, the expected return on your sunglasses shop is 10 percent (half the year you earn 0 percent, and half the year you earn 20 percent). But, how long the rainy or sunny season actually lasts in a particular year determines your actual return, and that return has varied from year to year, going from 15 percent when three-fourths of the year was sunny to only 5 percent when three-fourths of the year was rainy. To smooth out sales, you add umbrellas to your product line. Umbrellas produce a 20 percent return in the rainy season, and a 0 percent return during the sunny season, giving you an expected return of 10 percent (just as with the sunglasses, half the year you earn 0 percent, and half the year you earn 20 percent).

	Sunglasses	**Umbrellas**
Rainy Season	0%	20%
Sunny Season	20%	0%

What's the end result of this diversification? The expected return hasn't changed. It is still 10 percent (half your investment earned 10 percent in sunglasses, and half your investment earned 10 percent in umbrellas), but the annual ups and downs—the variability of the returns—are totally eliminated. The shop will earn a 10 percent rate of return regardless of how long the sunny or rainy seasons last.

So what can we take away from our foray into diversification? Diversification can reduce risk. However, you should keep in mind that we were able to eliminate *all* the risk because we found two investments that move opposite of each other—and finding two investments that do that is tough. However, most stocks don't move exactly opposite other stocks, and they don't move exactly with other stocks either, so as we add more and more stocks to our investment portfolio, the risk in the portfolio declines little by little. As a result, as you increase the number of stocks, the amount of variability in your portfolio declines, as shown in Figure 11.3.

In the language of investors, we refer to the risk that *can't be eliminated* through diversification as **systematic risk** and the risk that *can be eliminated* through diversification as **unsystematic risk**. It results from factors that affect all stocks. In fact, the term "systematic" comes from the fact that this type of risk systematically affects all stocks and as a result can't be eliminated through diversification. In effect, all risk can be divided up into two types: systematic and unsystematic. Keep in mind that these are *types* of risk, which is different from the *sources* of risk or variability we examined earlier.

Systematic or Market-Related or Nondiversifiable Risk
That portion of a security's risk or variability that can't be eliminated through investor diversification. This type of variability or risk results from factors that affect all securities.

Unsystematic or Firm-Specific or Company-Unique Risk or Diversifiable Risk
Risk or variability that can be eliminated through investor diversification. Unsystematic risk results from factors that are unique to a particular firm.

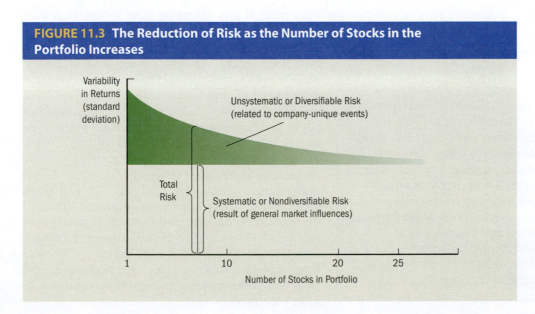

FIGURE 11.3 The Reduction of Risk as the Number of Stocks in the Portfolio Increases

For example, the financial meltdown in the fall of 2008 had a negative effect on the returns of almost all stocks; as a result, that risk could not be diversified away and would be considered a source of systematic risk. On the other hand, unsystematic risk is simply the variability in the returns of an investment that is due to events that are unrelated to the overall market. These returns might be due to the death of the firm's CEO, a product recall, a major fire at a manufacturing plant, or even bad managerial choices. The returns caused by these types of events are not related to the returns of other investments and can be eliminated through diversification. Relating this back to **Principle 8: Risk and Return Go Hand in Hand**, we find that unsystematic risk can be eliminated through diversification. In effect, unsystematic risk doesn't exist for diversified investors. So, when diversified investors talk about risk, they are talking about systematic risk.

Understanding Your Tolerance for Risk

Not everyone has the same tolerance for risk. Some individuals are continuously checking their investments' results. Others can take on risk without looking at a financial page in the newspaper for months at a time. Which is better? That's a judgment call.

It doesn't matter whether you freak out at the slightest sign of risk or you act like a complete daredevil. What's important is recognizing your tolerance for risk, and acting—and investing—accordingly.

One way of developing an understanding of your tolerance for risk is to take one of the many risk-tolerance tests offered in magazines and personal finance self-help books, similar to the one provided in Figure 11.4. The answers are weighted, and according to the number of points you accumulate, you're labeled "more conservative," or "less conservative." A question commonly found on risk-tolerance tests is this: You have a lottery ticket that has a one-in-five chance of winning a $100,000 prize. The minimum you would sell that lottery ticket for before the drawing is:

1. $10,000
2. $15,000
3. $20,000
4. $30,000
5. $40,000

Another way of determining your level of risk tolerance is to review your past actions. Are you willing to switch to a less secure job if it has opportunities your present job doesn't have? Do you worry about losing your job even if it's secure? Are you conservative or aggressive with your investments? Do you keep a very large emergency fund in liquid assets?

If you're willing to take on risks elsewhere but not in your investments, your aversion to this type of risk might be caused by a lack of knowledge. That is, your present investment strategy may be decidedly conservative simply because you do not understand investments and risk. As you learn more about risk–return trade-offs, the effect of diversification on risk, and the time dimension of risk, you'll better realize the investment challenges you actually face. You'll also better understand how important it is not to let your aversion to risk stop you from making lucrative investments to meet your goals.

STOP & THINK

In a study out of Washington University a researcher found that exposure to the opposite sex induces greater risk-taking of about 8 percent in both males and females. Both males and females viewing opposite sex photos displayed a significant increase in risk tolerance, whereas the control subjects—those not looking at photos of the opposite sex—exhibited no significant change; that's a little more of **Principle 9: Mind Games, Your Financial Personality, and Your Money** at work. What this means is that your tolerance for risk is extremely suggestible. Where else have you seen sales people use attractive people to their benefit?

FIGURE 11.4 Risk Tolerance Quiz

Risk Tolerance Quiz

If you're going to be investing, you need to know your risk tolerance. It will help you focus in on the kinds of investment alternatives that make sense for you. Below is a very simple risk tolerance quiz designed to give you an idea of what your risk tolerance is. If you would like to take a more advanced risk tolerance quiz, check out the following Web site:

A Risk Tolerance Quiz[a] developed by Dr. Ruth Lytton at Virginia Tech and Dr. John Grable at Kansas State University: http://njaes.rutgers.edu/money/riskquiz/default.asp

1. You've just invested your savings of $25,000. What range of returns on your investment would you feel most comfortable with after 1 year?
   a. $24,000–$26,500 (1 point)
   b. $23,000–$28,000 (2 points)
   c. $21,000–$31,000 (3 points)
   d. $19,000–$34,000 (4 points)

2. You've already saved and paid for the vacation of your lifetime, but just before you are to leave, your job is "downsized" and you are left without a job. You would:
   a. Cancel the vacation and start looking for a new job. (1 point)
   b. Scale down your vacation to save money. (2 points)
   c. Go ahead with your vacation, and begin putting together a strategy for finding a new job while you're on vacation. (3 points)
   d. Extend your vacation; after all, this may be your last chance to have a vacation like this. (4 points)

3. After you make an investment you feel:
   a. Nauseous (1 point)
   b. Confused (2 points)
   c. Satisfied (3 points)
   d. Excited (4 points)

4. You have just been given $4,000 and you must choose between:
   a. A sure loss of $1,000 (1 point)
   b. A 50 percent chance of losing $2,000 and a 50 percent chance of losing nothing (3 points)

5. The stock market dropped by 10 percent today. You:
   a. Sell all your stock and put it in a money market or savings account; after all, sleeping is important. (1 point)
   b. Just hold tight and wait for things to return to where they were. (3 points)
   c. Invest more because stocks are at bargain prices. (5 points)

Total Score: _____

Scoring:

5–13 points: Low risk tolerance. The lower you score, the more risk averse you are. You should attempt to learn more about risk–return trade-offs. You should make sure you are adequately diversified focusing on safer investments, and attempt to add riskier investments as you gain a better understanding of investing.

14–20 points: High risk tolerance. The higher you score, the less risk averse you are. You are more comfortable with risky investments, being drawn to investments such as common stock rather than money market accounts and CDs. You should make sure your portfolio is adequately diversified._____

[a]J.E. Grable and R.H. Lytton: "Financial risk tolerance revisited: The development of a risk assessment instrument," *Financial Services Review* 8(1999): 163–81.

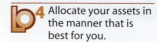 Allocate your assets in the manner that is best for you.

 Principle 8

The Time Dimension of Investing and Asset Allocation

In Chapter 1, when we introduced **Principle 8: Risk and Return Go Hand in Hand**, we asked the question, how much risk can you afford to take? The answer was that as the length of the investment horizon increases, you can afford to invest in riskier assets. Thus, whenever someone asks what they should invest in, the proper response is a question: What is your investment horizon? This is because the returns on those risky assets—stocks—tend to dominate those of less risky assets—CDs and bonds—as the investment horizon lengthens. So even in the worst-case scenario, you'll probably do quite a bit better with stocks than you would do with the more conservative alternative. It doesn't mean that there isn't any risk to investing in common stock. Clearly, there's still a lot of uncertainty as to how much you'll finally end up with. But if your investment horizon is long, you'll probably end up with a lot more if you invest in some risky assets.

Take stocks versus bonds. Without question, common stocks have provided the greatest return over the past 82 years, with large-company stocks earning on average 10.7 percent per year over this period. However, it hasn't been a smooth rise. Common stocks have also had the greatest risk or variability over that same period. In fact, on October 19, 1987, the stock market dropped by 23 percent, on October 27, 1997, it dropped by 7.2 percent, and during the 10-day period from October 1 through October 10 of 2008 the stock market dropped by about 22 percent. The problem with stocks is that "on average" may not be what you actually get. You may, for whatever reason, put your money in the stock market on the wrong day.

Meeting Your Investment Goals and the Time Dimension of Risk

With any long-term investment, you can be sure that there'll be some bad years and some good years. Over time, these offsetting years result in the dispersion of returns converging toward the average. Consequently, when you invest for a longer period, the exceptionally good and exceptionally bad years usually cancel each other out and you end up with less variability, as shown in Figure 11.5. This figure shows the range of compound annual returns for stocks, bonds, and cash over 1-, 5-, and 20-year holding periods since 1950. Let's look at the range of returns on common stock. As you can see, the returns of common stock calculated over 1-year periods range from a high of 52.6 percent to a low of −37 percent. However, as we increase the length of the holding period to 5-year segments or 20-year segments, the picture changes. Over 5-year periods, the average returns range from 29 percent to −2.3 percent, while over 20-year periods they range between 18 percent and 6.5 percent. In effect, during the worst 20-year holding period for stocks since 1950, common stocks still posted a positive 20-year compound annual return of 6.5 percent. Still, there is a lot of risk in stocks, and you are never guaranteed anything—things may change in the future because, let's face it, stocks are risky investments.

So, how much risk should you be prepared to assume or, said differently, what kinds of assets should you invest in—stocks or bonds? If you ask a financial planner that question he or she will most likely answer with a couple of more questions. The first question will deal with your risk tolerance—the less risk tolerant you are, the less risk you should take. The second will deal with your financial situation: how secure your job is, how much you have saved, and whether you have an emergency fund. The final question will probably deal with when you need the money. The longer it is until you need the money, the more risk you can afford to take.

What can we say about the uncertainty regarding how much your investment will eventually grow? There's no question that as your holding period gets longer, the uncertainty surrounding how much your investment will eventually be worth

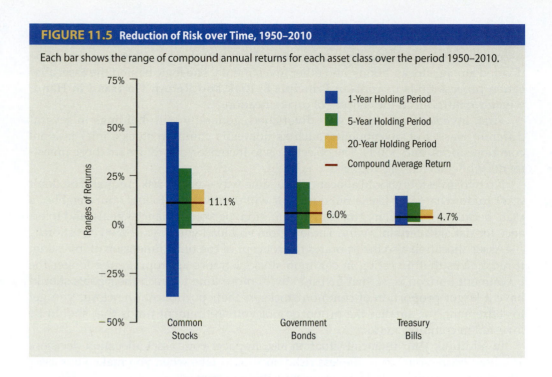

FIGURE 11.5 Reduction of Risk over Time, 1950–2010

Each bar shows the range of compound annual returns for each asset class over the period 1950–2010.

Legend:
- 1-Year Holding Period
- 5-Year Holding Period
- 20-Year Holding Period
- Compound Average Return

Y-axis: Ranges of Returns (75%, 50%, 25%, 0%, −25%, −50%)

X-axis: Common Stocks (11.1%), Government Bonds (6.0%), Treasury Bills (4.7%)

increases. But that shouldn't stop you from taking risk when you have a longer holding period—for example, when saving for your retirement 45 years off in the future. While there may be less uncertainty surrounding the ultimate dollar value of a 45-year investment in bonds versus common stock, you're probably better off investing in "risky" stocks than "safe" bonds. Why? Because even if stocks perform poorly relative to what they've done historically, and bonds perform extremely well relative to what they've done historically, the stock investment will end up larger. That is to say, the investment in bonds will give you less uncertainty about the ultimate value of your investment, but they will also give you a smaller ultimate value. In effect, sometimes it's riskier not to take risks than it is to take them.

What do we know about risk and time? First, if your investment time horizon is long and you invest in something risky such as common stocks, there's still a lot of uncertainty about what the ultimate dollar value of your investment will be. But, at the same time, you'll probably be better off than if you took a more conservative approach. In effect, if your investment time horizon is long, you can afford to take on additional risk. This is an extremely important concept, because it means that your investment horizon plays an extremely important role in determining how you should invest your savings.

There are still other reasons why investors can afford to take more risk as their investment time horizon lengthens. One reason is that they have more opportunities to adjust consumption and work habits over longer time periods. If they are investing with a short time horizon, there isn't much they can do—either save more or spend less—to change their final level of wealth. However, if an investment performs poorly at the beginning of a long investment time horizon, the investor can make an adjustment by saving more, working harder, or spending less.

Another reason often given for investing in stocks when you have a long investment horizon comes from the notion that whatever might cause stocks to crash might also cause bonds to crash. In effect, if stocks crash, there may be no place to hide. That is, if our economic system collapses or the world gets hit by a giant meteor, both stocks and bonds will take a big hit. As a result, investing in less risky assets (bonds) may not really help you if a crash ever comes.

Asset Allocation
An attempt to ensure that the investor's strategy reflects his or her investment time horizon and is well diversified, generally with assets in several different classes of investments, such as domestic common stocks, international common stocks, and bonds.

Asset Allocation

Asset allocation is an investment term that deals with how your money should be divided among stocks, bonds, and other investments. The logic behind the asset allocation process finds its roots in **Principle 8: Risk and Return Go Hand in Hand**, where we introduced the concept of diversification.

First, investors should be well diversified, generally with holdings in several different classes of investments, such as domestic common stocks, international common stocks, and bonds. The objective is to increase your return on those investments while decreasing your risk.

No two investors should allocate in the same way—not all risk is equal. You don't want to do what your Uncle Bill does, nor will you want to follow your neighbor's plan, because your age, income, family situation, personal financial goals, and tolerance for risk will certainly vary. These factors will lead you in your own direction.

Asset allocation also incorporates the concept of the time dimension of investing. It recognizes that investing in common stocks is more appropriate the longer the investment horizon is, so that investors with more time to reach their goals should have a larger proportion of common stocks in their portfolios. The closer you get to retirement, the smaller the proportion of your retirement funds that should be invested in common stocks.

In addition, your financial situation also impacts your asset allocation decision. The less secure your job is, the less risk you should take when you make your asset allocation decision. Table 11.1 summarizes these factors.

Asset allocation is the most important task you'll undertake in your investing career. How you go about your asset allocation will have a far greater impact on your return than will choosing each individual stock or bond you hold.

Asset allocation is not a one-time decision. Adjustments will need to be made as your life circumstances change. As you keep an eye on your portfolio, you may occasionally need to rebalance your mix to keep the percentage of each investment category in line with your current personal financial goals.

TABLE 11.1 Factors Impacting Your Asset Allocation Decision
There isn't a single asset allocation that works for everyone. However, regardless of what asset allocation you use, you should be well diversified with both stocks and bonds. In addition, you should build up an emergency fund before you begin investing for long-term goals. Three factors that you should consider in making your asset allocation decision are:
• **Time horizon.** The more time until you need the money, the more risk you can afford to take. The longer time horizon will give you more time to make adjustments in your portfolio, consumption, and working habits if your investments perform poorly during the early years. If your time horizon is more than 10 years, you should emphasize more risky investments such as stocks that carry higher expected returns to achieve your long-term financial goals.
• **Financial situation or capacity for risk.** How much risk can you afford to take? In answering this question consider: How secure is your job? Do you have a pension plan at work that will provide a steady income at retirement? How much money do you owe or have you saved? Do you have a big enough emergency fund to allow you to avoid tapping into your long-term investments at an inopportune time such as in the midst of a market downturn? If you have a limited capacity for risk you should make sure that you have sufficient short-term bonds and cash investments in your portfolio to cover emergencies in case of the unexpected.
• **Risk tolerance.** Different people have different tolerances for risk. Still, to achieve long-term goals it is probably necessary to take some risks and invest in common stock. If you have a low tolerance for risk, try to learn more about investing—that may make you more comfortable taking the risks you need to take. Still, you will want to balance your investments in such a way that you can still sleep at night even during times of market volatility. You should also try to develop an investment plan you are comfortable with and that you can stick with through market ups and downs.

Asset Allocation and the Early Years—A Time of Wealth Accumulation (Through Age 54)

Because the investment horizon is quite long, investors in this stage should place the majority of their savings into common stocks. These have the highest return associated with them; they also have the highest risk. However, because of the time dimension of investing and the long investment horizon, investing heavily in common stocks makes much more sense.

For investors who are just beginning this investment stage, a strategy of investing only in common stocks can be justified. However, most financial planners recommend that a portion of the investment funds be maintained in bonds. A mix of 80 percent common stocks and 20 percent bonds is relatively common. Although this can be used as a benchmark asset allocation breakdown, remember that your personal situation ultimately determines the appropriate breakdown for you.

Looking at the performance of such an asset allocation breakdown since 1950, we find that the average annual return would have been 11.36 percent (Figure 11.6). The risk associated with such an asset allocation can be seen by examining the fact that in 13 out of 61 years since 1950, it would have recorded losses. The worst annual loss over this period would have occurred in 2008, when such an allocation would have resulted in a 25.14 percent loss. In addition, in 1974 there would have been a 20.67 percent loss.

Asset Allocation and Approaching Retirement—The Golden Years (Ages 55 to 64)

For an individual approaching retirement, the goal becomes preserving the level of wealth already accumulated and allowing this wealth to continue to grow. As the investment horizon shortens, the investor should move some of his or her retirement portfolio into bonds.

FIGURE 11.6 Risk and Return to Benchmark Asset Allocation Breakdown During the Early Years

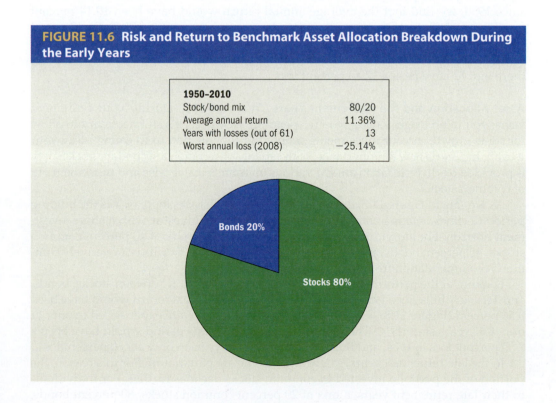

1950–2010	
Stock/bond mix	80/20
Average annual return	11.36%
Years with losses (out of 61)	13
Worst annual loss (2008)	−25.14%

Bonds 20%

Stocks 80%

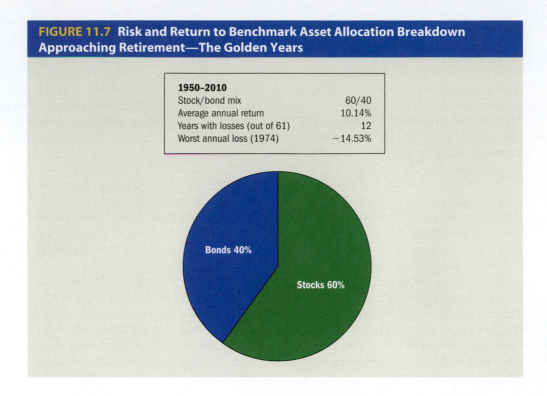

FIGURE 11.7 Risk and Return to Benchmark Asset Allocation Breakdown Approaching Retirement—The Golden Years

1950–2010	
Stock/bond mix	60/40
Average annual return	10.14%
Years with losses (out of 61)	12
Worst annual loss (1974)	−14.53%

In addition, the investor should maintain a diversified portfolio. For individuals approaching retirement, a mix of 60 percent common stocks and 40 percent bonds is a relatively common recommendation from financial planners. Again, depending on the investor's degree of risk tolerance, the proportion invested in common stocks may either increase or decrease.

Looking at the performance of a 60/40 asset allocation between stocks and bonds since 1950, we find that the average annual return would have been 10.14 percent (see Figure 11.7). For this asset allocation, losses were experienced in only 12 out of 61 years since 1950. The worst annual loss would have occurred in 1974, when such an asset allocation would have resulted in a 14.53 percent loss. In addition, in 2008, there would have been a 12.46 percent loss.

Asset Allocation and the Retirement Years (Over Age 65) During your retirement years, you're no longer saving, you're spending. However, it's still necessary to allow for some growth in your investments simply to keep inflation from eating away your wealth. Income is now of importance, with capital appreciation a secondary goal. Safety is provided by diversification among various investment categories and movement out of common stocks.

As we saw in Figure 11.5, the volatility of common stocks increases as the holding period declines, making common stocks riskier for the investor with a short investment horizon. For individuals in their retirement years, a mix of 40 percent common stocks, 40 percent bonds, and 20 percent short-term Treasury bills is a relatively common recommendation from financial planners.

Looking at the performance of a 40/40/20 asset allocation between stocks, bonds, and Treasury bills since 1950, we find that the average annual return would have been 8.56 percent (Figure 11.8). For this asset allocation, losses were experienced in only 11 out of 61 years since 1950. The worst annual loss over this period would have been a 7.55 percent loss in 1974, and in 2008 there would have been only a 4.60 percent loss.

In the late retirement years, safety and income are paramount. For this reason, the portion of the portfolio invested in common stocks declines further. For individuals in their late retirement years, a mix of 20 percent common stocks, 60 percent bonds,

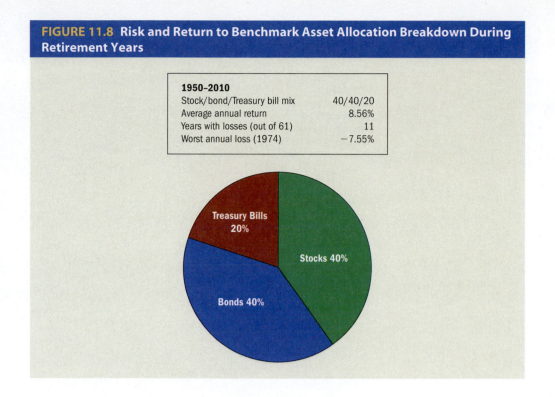

FIGURE 11.8 Risk and Return to Benchmark Asset Allocation Breakdown During Retirement Years

1950–2010	
Stock/bond/Treasury bill mix	40/40/20
Average annual return	8.56%
Years with losses (out of 61)	11
Worst annual loss (1974)	−7.55%

Treasury Bills 20%

Stocks 40%

Bonds 40%

and 20 percent short-term Treasury bills is a relatively common recommendation from financial planners.

Looking at the performance of a 20/60/20 asset allocation between stocks, bonds, and Treasury bills since 1950, we find that the average annual return would have been 7.34 percent (Figure 11.9). Here, only 7 out of 61 years since 1950 experienced losses, with the worst annual loss being 4.56 percent in 1969, while in 2008 there would have actually been a positive annual return of 8.09 percent.

What You Should Know About Efficient Markets

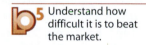

5 Understand how difficult it is to beat the market.

Efficient Market
A market in which all relevant information about the stock is reflected in the stock price.

The concept of **efficient markets** concerns the speed at which new information is reflected in prices. The more efficient the market, the faster prices react to new information. If the stock market were a perfectly efficient market, security prices would equal their true value at all times—in other words, you can't systematically "beat the market." With efficient markets you're just as likely to pick winners as losers. So, is the stock market an efficient market? Well, if it is truly efficient, then there's no benefit to much of what's done by stock analysts.

There is no real definitive answer to this question. Why not? First of all, there's a question of the degree of efficiency. That is, although security analysis may not help small investors earn abnormal profits, it may have value to large investors. Improving your performance by 0.01 percent may be irrelevant for you, but for a manager with a $4 billion portfolio, it means an increase in profits of $400,000 (0.0001 × $4 billion = $400,000). In addition, if someone uncovers a new technique for predicting prices, he or she would be much better off using it rather than publishing it. As a result, we may only see results that indicate that the market is efficient.

However, reports of beating the market don't indicate that the market is inefficient. On average we would expect, just by chance, that half the investors will outperform the market and half will underperform the market. In general, you usually hear about those who beat the market. Not surprisingly,

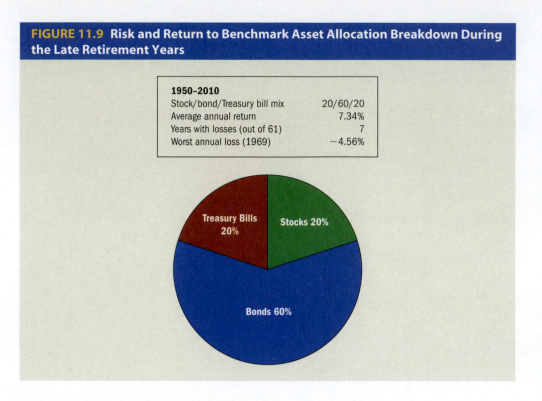

FIGURE 11.9 Risk and Return to Benchmark Asset Allocation Breakdown During the Late Retirement Years

1950–2010	
Stock/bond/Treasury bill mix	20/60/20
Average annual return	7.34%
Years with losses (out of 61)	7
Worst annual loss (1969)	−4.56%

Treasury Bills 20%

Stocks 20%

Bonds 60%

STOP & THINK

Just because a "system" has worked in the past doesn't mean it will in the future. A good example of how misleading good historical results are can be seen by looking at the so-called Super Bowl effect. The market tends to go up when a team from the premerger NFL wins the Super Bowl and tends to go down when a premerger AFL team wins. Through 1997 there were 30 Super Bowls, and in 27 of those years this system correctly predicted the stock market. Statistically, the predictive power of this system appears to shoot right off the scale. Is this a technique that you should let guide your investment strategy? Heavens no! Although there's a strong statistical relationship, there's no cause and effect and no reason to believe that this relationship should hold in the future. While this system did well in the early years, it fell flat, going 0 for 4, between 1998 and 2001 before it rebounded a bit in the 2000s. How did it do in predicting the 2008 market crash? It came close to working, but it fell short. In that game the Giants beat the Patriots when Eli Manning lofted a pass to Plaxico Burress in the end zone to give the Giants a 17–14 lead with 35 seconds left—the NFL won, meaning the market should have gone up. Unfortunately for many investors, the market didn't buy into the Super Bowl effect.

those who underperform the market tend not to publicize their results. The bottom line is that while we can't present a definite answer as to whether you can beat the market, we can give you enough understanding of the difficulties to help you define an investment strategy that makes sense.

Beating the Market

How tough is it to consistently beat the market? Very tough! As we just noted, on average, half the time you should outperform the market, and half the time you should underperform the market. Let's look at the performance of the "superstars" of investing. Every year *Barron's* offers a round-table of Wall Street superstars' predictions for the upcoming year.

Looking at their predictions from 1967 through 1991, an investor who bought each one of the "picks" the day after the publication and held it for 1 year would have earned 0.021 percent above what was expected. If these picks were held for 2 or 3 years, they actually would have performed worse than average.

Actually, the "superstar" picks were not as bleak as they appear. If the stocks were purchased on the day that the picks were made, not on the day they were published in *Barron's*, investors could have earned a return of just over 2 percent above the norm. What does this mean for the average investor? It means it's very difficult to pick underpriced stocks.

If it's so difficult to pick underpriced stocks, should we focus on timing the market—that is, buying stocks before the market rises? To get some perspective on how difficult it is to time the market, let's look at Jim Cramer from the CNBC show *Mad Money*. In the spring of 2007 he predicted that the Dow Jones Industrial Average was headed up to 15,000. While Jim knows his stuff, predicting the market is tough; after all, things are always changing, and in 2007 it was the subprime market that changed. Then in August 2007 he predicted the market would bounce back as a result of the Fed's interest rate cuts and climb up to 14,500. None of that happened, the economy kept on changing, and just over a year later the market was hovering in the mid 8,000s. If Jim Cramer and the other experts have a tough time predicting where the market is going, you can imagine how tough it is for the rest of us.

The bottom line is that you should keep to your plan and invest for the long term. If you try to time the market, you're just as likely to miss an upswing as you are to avoid a downswing.

Checklist 11.1 provides you with the implications of our understanding of efficient markets.

> **STOP & THINK**
>
> If a stranger figured out an incredible investment opportunity or a way to beat the market, do you really think he or she would share that secret with you?

CHECKLIST 11.1

What to Remember About Investing

What does our understanding of efficient markets tell us about investing? It tells us several things.

◆ Systems don't beat the market. It's long-term investing that works. There simply is no foolproof method for beating the market. Beware of "hot tips" and cold calls from stockbrokers. Remember the lessons of **Principle 1: The Best Protection Is Knowledge**. There's an old saying on Wall Street: "Those that know don't tell, and those that tell don't know." If it sounds too good to be true, it probably is. The good news in all this is that if you can do as well as the market, you have done quite well indeed.

◆ Keep to the plan. Don't try to time the market. Keep in mind that stock prices and interest rates go up and go down, but it's almost impossible to buy only when stock prices are low and sell only when they are high. You should invest regularly and view stocks in accordance with your investment horizon.

◆ Focus on the asset allocation process. You should spend your energy on the appropriate asset allocation given your goals, your plan, and where you are in your financial life cycle. Recognize the time dimension of investing. Your asset allocation strategy should reflect your investment horizon.

◆ Keep the commissions down. Because it's difficult to beat the market, make sure you don't give away too much of your return in the way of commissions. Be aware of what the commissions are and shop around.

◆ Diversify, diversify, diversify. The benefits of diversification are still unchallenged.

◆ If you don't feel comfortable, seek help! Don't let the fear of investing keep you out of the game. If you feel uncomfortable, seek the help of a qualified financial advisor.

Thinking Back to Principle 9: Mind Games, Your Financial Personality, and Your Money

If you are going to be a successful investor, it helps to have a basic understanding of some of the behavioral quirks that you may be subject to. After all, if you know the tricks your mind may be playing on you, you may be able to avoid them. So let's take a look at some of the common behavioral biases that affect investors.

Overconfidence   Investors tend to be overconfident. Simply put, "people think they know more than they do."[2] This overconfidence applies to their abilities, their knowledge, and the future. In effect, most investors think they can beat the market. After all, why try to pick stocks otherwise? In reality, even the most professional of all investors, mutual fund managers, consistently underperform the market.

Overconfidence also leads to trading too often. Of course, there is the chance that those who trade more frequently earn higher returns. To test this, one study examined the trading behavior of 78,000 households, dividing the accounts into five groups based upon the level of turnover.[3] They found a net difference of 7 percent between households with the highest and lowest turnover levels, with those that trade more earning less. Moreover, those who trade more often do worse not only because they experience higher trading costs, but because they tend to pick stocks that underperform the market.

> ### STOP & THINK
>
> Do you think overconfidence is a gender thing? Well, it is. Overconfidence afflicts men more than women, and it also leads them to trade too often. Why do you think overconfidence leads to more trades?

Disposition Effect   The disposition effect involves the emotions of fearing regret and seeking pride resulting in selling winners too soon, and keeping losers too long.[4] When confronted with the need to sell, investors are more likely to sell one of their winners and hold on to their losers. Why is this so? According to the disposition effect if they sell a loser they are admitting that purchasing it was a mistake in the first place. On the other hand, if they sell a winner, they now have results they can feel proud about. The problem is that while they can now claim a winner, they also have to claim taxes. The real problem with the disposition effect is the aversion to recognizing bad deals and cutting losses. This is compounded by investors' overconfidence.

House Money Effect   The house money effect really reflects the way that gamblers act and the way they view their winnings. If a gambler enters a casino with $5,000 and immediately doubles it, winning $5,000, that gambler will act differently with the new $5,000, taking on risks that he or she wouldn't normally undertake. The house money effect asserts that this is how investors acted during the dot-com bubble of the late 1990s. Once they made profits on their initial investment, they took risks they normally wouldn't take with these new earnings, which resulted in strengthening the bubble.

---

[2]See Robert J. Shiller, *Irrational Exuberance* (New York: Broadway Books, 2000), 142.

[3]Brad Barber and Terrance Odean, "Trading Is Hazardous to Your Health: The Common Stock Performance of Individual Investors," *Journal of Finance* 55 (2000), 773–806.

[4]Hersh Shefrin and Meir Statman, "The Disposition to Sell Winners Too Early and Ride Losers Too Long: Theory and Evidence," *Journal of Finance* 4 (1984): 777–90.

Loss Then Risk Aversion Effect   Related to the house money effect is the risk aversion effect where investors who lose money are more reluctant to take risks. This relates to the aftermath of the market downturn of the late 2000s. Once investors lost money in stocks, many of them decided stocks weren't for them and got out of the game completely.

Herd Behavior   When investors see stocks moving one way or the other, they have a tendency to join in and follow the crowd.[5] Investors are afraid that others know something about an individual stock or about the market that they don't know or haven't figure out yet. The result is herd behavior. In effect, investors look at behavior and assume that it is based upon knowledge. The end result of this is that they join the crowd and help to push the price in the direction the herd is taking it—a kind of self-fulfilling behavior. Winners are always observed very closely, particularly when a good performance repeats itself a couple of times. New investors are attracted. Finally, no one wants to fight against the massive power of an increasing majority when all investors are running in the same direction.

---

[5]Robert J. Shiller, *Irrational Exuberance* (New York: Broadway Books, 2000), 149–68.

Summary

 Set your goals and be ready to invest.
In personal financial planning, everything begins and ends with your goals. You must first decide what your goals are and how much you can set aside to meet those goals. Once you've done this, you can develop an investment plan.

It's important to know the difference between investments and speculation. Investing involves buying an asset that generates a return. Speculation occurs when an asset's value depends solely on supply and demand. Buying gold coins and baseball cards is considered speculation because they're worth more in the future only if someone is willing to pay more for them.

 Calculate interest rates and real rates of return.
Interest rates play an extremely important role in determining the value of an investment. They are also closely tied to the rate of inflation. The nominal rate of return is the rate of return earned on an investment without any adjustment for lost purchasing power. The real rate of return is simply the current or nominal rate of return minus the inflation rate. It tells you how much you have earned after you've adjusted for inflation.

 Manage risk in your investments.
There are a number of different sources of risk associated with investments, including interest rate risk, inflation risk, business risk, financial risk, liquidity risk, market risk, political and regulatory risk, exchange rate risk, and call risk.

4   Allocate your assets in the manner that is best for you.

As your investment horizon lengthens, you can afford to invest more in riskier assets. This is because the returns of risky assets tend to dominate those of less risky assets as the investment horizon lengthens.

Asset allocation attempts to ensure that the investor is well diversified, generally with investments in several different classes of investments such as domestic common stocks, international common stocks, and bonds. It also incorporates the concept of the time dimension of investing into the allocation process.

 5   Understand how difficult it is to beat the market.

Efficient markets are concerned with the speed at which information is reflected in security prices. The more efficient the market is, the faster prices react to new information. It is very difficult to beat the market and, as a result, you should keep to your plan and invest for the long term.

Review Questions

1. Explain the difference between investing and speculating. Give an example of each.

2. Why is it important to maintain an adequate emergency fund before creating and implementing an investment program?

3. What are five ways to find money to invest?

4. Why should you look for tax-favored investment strategies? How can these strategies help you attain your goals?

5. Name and briefly describe the two basic categories of investments. Provide two examples of each.

6. What are the three primary points of information needed to evaluate the potential total and annual return of a lending investment?

7. Remembering the information from the tax chapter, when it comes to income taxes, why is capital gain income better than dividends or interest income?

8. What is the basic difference between the nominal rate of return and the real rate of return? Which of them might be a better measure of how well an investment has performed? Why?

9. In general how have interest rates changed since the late 1980s according to Figure 11.1?

10. Investors need to be aware of nine sources of risk when calculating the risk–return trade-off. List and briefly describe these nine sources of risk.

11. Differentiate between systematic and nonsystematic risk. Which of these is more important to the average investor? Why?

12. Why might investors not be willing to take risks with their investment portfolios even though they take risks elsewhere? What investment concepts might help them be more willing to take an appropriate amount of risk?

13. What is the long-term relationship between risk and time? Why is this relationship such an important concept to remember when developing and implementing an investment program?

14. What is meant by the term "asset allocation"? What makes asset allocation such a simple and powerful concept? When should an investor change an asset allocation mix?

15. What is the purpose for adjusting your asset allocation as you age? Why wouldn't "the best" or highest returning portfolio always be prudent?

16. What is the relationship between market efficiency and the success of market timing? Does market timing work consistently? What six efficient market concepts should be considered when investing?

Develop Your Skills—Problems and Activities

These problems are available in MyFinanceLab.

1. Everyone needs an emergency fund. Assume your best friend asks you to evaluate a list of investments for an emergency savings fund. Comment on the appropriateness of each of the following:

   a. Certificate of deposit

   b. Three-month Treasury bills

   c. Gold and silver coins

   d. Portfolio of energy stocks

   e. Money market mutual fund

2. Jana just found out that she is going to receive an end-of-year bonus of $40,000. She is in the 35 percent marginal tax bracket. Calculate her income tax on this bonus. Now assume that instead of receiving a bonus, Jana receives the $40,000 as a long-term capital gain. What will be her tax? Which form of compensation offers Jana the best after-tax return? Would your calculation be different if the gain was short term rather than long term?

3. As a savvy student of personal finance, you've just learned that a company in your hometown made so much money last year that they are going to distribute a huge cash distribution this quarter. In order to get in on the deal you've got to make a quick decision. Ignoring the wisdom of such a purchase, which security would you buy to receive the cash payment—stock in the company or a bond offered by the company? Explain your answer.

4. After reading this chapter, it isn't surprising that you're becoming an investment wizard. With your newfound expertise you purchase 100 shares of KSU Corporation for $37 per share. Over the next 12 months assume the price goes up to $45 per share, and you receive a dividend of $0.50 per share. What would be your total return on your KSU Corporation investment? Assuming you continue to hold the stock, calculate your after-tax return. How is your realized after-tax return different if you sell the stock? In both cases assume you are in the 25 percent federal marginal tax bracket and there is no state income tax on investment income.

5. Calculate the nominal rate of interest for a new bond that will mature in 10 years assuming the following bond characteristics and market risks:

   a. Three-month T-bill rate of 4 percent

   b. Anticipated yearly inflation of 3 percent

c. Low or no chance of default

d. A premium of 0.25 percent for every year until maturity

e. No liquidity premium

6. Categorize each of the nine different risk premiums by according to which investment class it applies. If the risk applies to both stocks and bonds then categorize it as "both."

7. You just learned that a blue chip company will issue a bond with a maturity of 100 years. The bond appears to be a good deal because it yields 8.5 percent. Assuming that the inflation rate stays at 4 percent, what is the bond's real rate of return today? If you were looking for a bond to purchase and hold for several years, would you buy this bond? Explain your answer in terms of future inflation projections and the length of the bond's maturity.

8. Tim just retired and put his entire retirement savings of $100,000 in a typical stock on January 1, 2008, when the stock market was near its peak, and sold it on November 20, 2008, when the market was at a low point. As a result, his savings would have dropped to $51,994 for a 48 percent loss. What percent gain does he need for his $51,994 to climb back to $100,000? Would he have been better off if he had employed the principle of asset allocation?

9. Match each of the following behaviors by the appropriate bias as discussed in the chapter.

a. Wanda owns shares in Happy Clam Oil Exploration, but due to recent events the share price is down 30 percent from when she bought. She doesn't want to sell now because it had previously been up as much as 25 percent.

b. Yi was recently reading a *Wall Street Journal* article about the housing crisis and watching one of the *Flip This House* shows on TV. He is certain that the housing market will quickly rebound: after all, "everyone needs to live somewhere." Knowing this he purchases four brand-new, vacant condos overlooking South Miami Beach for a quick flip.

c. Yusuf has been watching the gold market go up and up, so he decides that since everyone is buying gold he needs to do so as well.

10. Outline the typical investment goals associated with each of the following life-cycle stages. Provide a recommended asset allocation for each stage.

a. The early years

b. The golden years

c. The retirement years

d. The late retirement years

Learn by Doing—Suggested Projects

1. Before you can develop an investment plan, you must identify your investment goals. List five short-term and five long-term investment goals for yourself. Ask your spouse or other friends or family if they have identified investment goals. If so, how are your goals similar? Do the goals reflect different stages of the financial life cycle?

2. To learn more about making automatic investments, research the options offered by different brokerage firms or mutual fund companies. Specifically, determine the required minimum monthly contribution amount, time commitment, and any other relevant information for each mutual fund company or brokerage firm. Do the account services, or the costs associated with them, vary with the size of the account? Summarize the information in a group report.

3. Write a list of situations that you can remember as being risky and think about your reaction to each. Do you consider yourself to be a risk-taker or a risk-avoider? Now take one of the online risk tolerance quizzes. Do the results of the quiz support or contradict your belief? Why might the outcomes have been different from what you expected?

4. It is commonly assumed that the older a person gets, the less risk tolerant he or she becomes. Why might this be a standard assumption, and do you believe this assumption? Interview several retired persons about their risk tolerance, and how it has affected their asset allocation. Did their allocation changes, if any, follow the recommendations found in this chapter? What do your results tell you? Were they taking more or less risk with their portfolios than recommended? Why might this be the case? Explain your answers in a one- to two-page report.

5. Most mutual fund and brokerage house Internet sites offer free asset allocation and risk-tolerance assessment services. Visit three or four Internet sites and respond to the questions for the asset allocation programs. Print out the results and write a brief summary of your findings, paying close attention to how accurately the programs assessed your risk tolerance. Were the asset allocation recommendations consistent across the programs?

6. Explain why "your asset allocation mix will have a far greater impact on your return than will the choosing of each individual stock or bond that you hold." Think again about systematic and unsystematic risk as you answer.

7. Finance professors often assert that the stock market is efficient. Explain market efficiency and provide an example of a contradiction to the theory. Explain why the average investor is often unable to take advantage of market "inefficiencies."

8. Search the Internet for investment sites that discuss common behavioral biases and heuristics that people use when selecting what investments to buy and when to buy them. How might each of the topics you find relate to a perceived reduction in risk by the investor? For example, answer the question "do people feel safer or more confident as part of a group?" Write a brief report on your findings.

9. Complete an online search for articles on company earnings or on earnings forecasts for three to five companies. Determine how the announcement affected the share prices by graphing the daily or weekly closing prices for a 4-month time period beginning 3 months prior to the announcement and ending 1 month after. Print your price-time graph and give a brief description of your findings.

Be a Financial Planner—Discussion Case 1

This case is available in MyFinanceLab.

John, age 28, and Emily, age 27, have just had their first child, Lindsey. They have a combined income of $55,000 and rent a two-bedroom apartment. For the past several years John and Emily have taken financial responsibilities one day at a time, but it has finally dawned on them that they now must start thinking about their financial future. Recently John has noticed the stock market begin to move higher, and he is convinced that they should be investing in stocks. Emily is more interested in investing in collectibles such as sports memorabilia, because she's been reading reports of baseball trading card speculators making huge profits. When asked what their goals are John replies that he'd like to save for retirement, and Emily mentions her top priority as saving for Lindsey's college expenses. They both agreed that they'd like to buy a house and pay off $4,000 in credit card bills. When asked to list their investments, all they could come up with was a savings account worth $650.

Questions

1. What should be John and Emily's first priority before investing or making any investment plans?
2. If John and Emily asked you to prioritize their goals, how would you rank their investment objectives? Now match some investment alternatives to their objectives.

3. John and Emily are in the 15 percent tax bracket. Using a financial calculator and the investment category compound average returns given in Figure 11.5, determine the total nominal value (assume inflation is zero) of their portfolio if they invested $2,000 per year for 40 years in common stock. What is the portfolio value if they invested in government bonds? How about Treasury bills?
4. Should John and Emily invest all their money in one investment strategy (stocks or collectibles)? Explain your answer in terms of diversification and the asset allocation process.
5. Given the information in Figures 11.5–11.9, explain why anyone would invest in government or corporate bonds.

Be a Financial Planner—Discussion Case 2

This case is available in MyFinanceLab.

Last year Marcelino graduated from high school and received several thousand dollars from an uncle as a graduation gift. Marcelino, now in his first year of college, just heard of a guy in his dorm that invested in an oil exploration company and made a huge profit in a few months. Marcelino likes the idea of making some money fast and is considering investing his graduation gift money in a similar stock. Marcelino's roommate, Luc, just finished a personal finance course and is concerned that Marcelino may be getting himself into trouble. Luc knows that Marcelino likes to shop online, has run up a fairly large credit card bill, and has trouble balancing his budget on a monthly basis. In addition, Marcelino really doesn't know much about investing or how people actually "make money investing." Luc has asked you to help him work through the following questions so that he can talk to Marcelino about his investment plans.

Questions

1. Before investing any money, what five things should Marcelino do first?
2. Is Marcelino's strategy of investing in an oil exploration stock to make quick profits investing or speculating? Support your answer.
3. Luc started talking to Marcelino about market efficiency and market timing. Based on what you now know, how likely is it that Marcelino can pick a stock that will "beat the market"?
4. Calculate the average annual rate of return Marcelino would receive if he purchases shares in an Internet stock at $25 per share, holds the shares for 3 years, and sells them for $65. What is his after-tax rate of return if he is in the 25 percent marginal tax bracket?
5. What potentially significant disadvantage does Marcelino face if he sells his stock after only 10 months, for $65 per share, and incurs a short-term capital gain?
6. Should Marcelino be concerned about interest rates if he is going to invest in a speculative security? Why or why not?

7. What other financial risks does Marcelino face if he invests in an exploration stock?

8. By investing in two unrelated domestic stocks rather than in just one stock, would Marcelino increase or decrease his systematic risk exposure? What about his unsystematic risk exposure?

9. Luc has urged Marcelino to invest for the long term using a diversified approach. Marcelino is skeptical. Explain why Luc is probably correct.

10. How should Marcelino allocate his assets, given his stage in the life cycle?

12 Securities Markets

Learning Objectives

Identify and describe the primary and secondary securities markets.

Trade securities using a broker.

Locate and use several different sources of investment information to trade securities.

Most parents don't buy stocks on the recommendation of their children, but that's what Mary and Tom Sanchez did. In March 1986, their 13-year-old daughter, Jennifer, a self-proclaimed "computer geek," convinced them to invest $10,000, which was about 15 percent of their total savings, into a stock that was going public at the time—Microsoft. In fact, Jennifer also invested her entire savings—paper route and babysitting money, along with some money from her grandparents—of $750.

Back then, Microsoft was a small firm in Seattle with an unknown future, run by a young, untested computer genius, Bill Gates. In fact, Microsoft was so small and unknown that it was difficult finding a stockbroker who had access to Microsoft shares at its initial price of $21 per share. The Sanchezes did, though, and they're glad of it. They even convinced Mary's brother Jim to invest $5,000 in Microsoft. He wasn't fortunate enough to be able to buy in at $21, but he was able to buy the stock later that month at $26. By mid-2011, the Sanchezes $10,000 investment had grown to over $4.17 million, and Mary's brother Jim's investment of $5,000 had grown to over $1.7 million. It may well be worth considerably more today. As for Jennifer, her $750 would have been worth about $313,000, but instead it took the form of a new Porsche 911 convertible and some other investments.

About 17 years after her first stock recommendation, in March and April 2003, Jennifer made two more recommendations. She had just purchased her first iPod—it was the third generation iPod and the first one to feature an all-touch interface and a dock connector. As Jennifer said, "I truly thought the iPod would change the world—and I was right." On Jennifer's recommendation, both she and her parents invested $50,000 each. By April 2011, that $50,000 investment had grown to over $2.6 million! Her second recommendation was Priceline.com. Jennifer had just booked her first room using Priceline and saved about 50 percent—"I just felt once people discovered it, they wouldn't be able to live without it." Both she and her parents both invested $50,000 each in Priceline. How did this investment

turn out? By April 2011, her $50,000 investment had grown to over $19 million! Needless to say, Jennifer is now known as an "investment wizard" rather than a "computer geek."

Not everyone does as well with investments as the Sanchezes. However, one way to greatly improve your chances for success is to understand the rules of the investment game—in this case, how the securities markets work. Very few people feel comfortable, or should feel comfortable, playing a game without knowing the rules. That's the purpose of this chapter—to introduce you to the rules of the securities markets. We will look at how the investments markets operate and prepare you to go out and make your own investments.

It would be nice if we could all have the same success as the Sanchezes. Unfortunately, that kind of success can't be guaranteed. However, one thing is certain: The first step to becoming rich through a great investment is learning how to make that investment.

Identify and describe the primary and secondary securities markets.

Security Markets

Securities—stocks and bonds—are first bought when they are issued by corporations as a means of raising money. After the initial issue, stocks and bonds are traded—bought and sold—among investors. These trades occur in the securities markets. Just as retail goods are bought and sold in markets such as Wal-Mart or Sears, securities are bought and sold in their appropriate markets.

A **securities market** is a place where you can buy or sell securities. These markets can take the form of anything from an actual building on Wall Street in New York City to an electronic hookup between security dealers all over the world. Securities markets are divided into primary and secondary markets. Let's take a look at what these terms mean.

The Primary Markets

A **primary market** is a market in which new, as opposed to previously issued, securities (i.e., stocks and bonds) are traded. For example, if Nike issues a new batch of stock, this issue would be considered a primary market transaction. Actually, there are two different types of offerings in the primary markets: initial public offerings and seasoned new issues.

An **initial public offering (IPO)** is the first time the company's stock is traded publicly. The initial offering of Microsoft stock was an IPO. Initial public offerings draw a good deal of attention in the press because they show how much a company is worth in the public's eye, and they are opportunities for substantial financial gains—or losses.

It's hard to determine how much people will be willing to pay for a share of a newly traded company's stock. As a result, some IPO prices are set way too low, resulting in huge profits for anyone lucky enough to buy shares at the IPO price. A good example of a company whose low IPO price resulted in huge profits is Jubilant FoodWorks, which operates Domino's Pizza in India and first went public in January 2010. By the end of the year the company's stock had more than tripled.

Of course, some IPO prices are set too high, resulting in tremendous losses for those unlucky enough to buy. Promethean World, an interactive learning technology firm, "went public" (the term used when companies make their initial public offering) in March 2010. By the end of the year, the company's stock had lost over 67 percent of its value.

IPOs are enticing, because they give the investor the chance to get in on the ground floor of a company. It's terrific when you then wind up riding the investment elevator all the way to the penthouse, but you do run the risk that the elevator cable will snap, and your investment will wind up in the basement with a crash. Figure 12.1 provides a listing of the big winners and losers in the IPO market in 2010.

For the small investor, it is often difficult to get shares of IPOs. The most promising companies' initial shares tend to be "bought up" by large investors before the smaller investor has a chance to buy in. In effect, there may not be enough stock to go around.

Seasoned new issues are stock offerings by companies that already have common stock traded in the marketplace. For example, a sale of new shares of stock by Nike would be considered a seasoned new issue.

Stocks and bonds are generally sold in the primary markets with the help of an **investment banker** serving as the **underwriter**. An underwriter is simply a middleman who buys the entire stock or bond issue from the issuing company and then resells it to the general public in individual shares. Morgan Stanley, Goldman Sachs, JP Morgan, Citigroup, and Bank of America/Merrill Lynch all specialize in investment banking. We use the term "investment banker" to refer to both the overall firm and the individuals who work for it.

Securities Markets
A term used to describe where financial securities or instruments—for example, common stocks and bonds—are traded.

Primary Market
A market in which newly issued, as opposed to previously issued, securities are traded.

Initial Public Offering (IPO)
The first time a company's stock is traded publicly.

Seasoned New Issue
A stock offering by a company that already has common stock traded in the marketplace.

Investment Banker
The middleman between the firm issuing securities and the buying public. This term describes both the firms that specialize in selling securities to the public and the individuals who work for investment banking firms.

Underwriter
An investment banker who purchases and subsequently resells a new security issue. The issuing company sells its securities directly to the underwriter, who then sells the issue to the public and assumes the risk of selling the new issue at a satisfactory price.

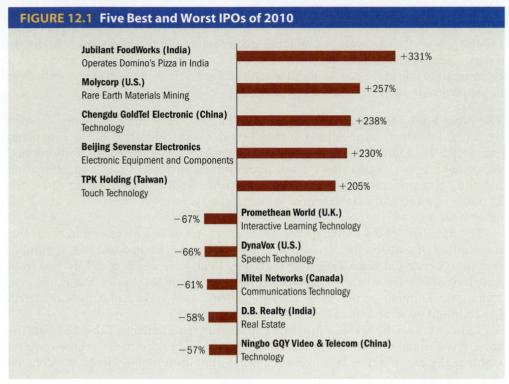

FIGURE 12.1 Five Best and Worst IPOs of 2010

Jubilant FoodWorks (India)
Operates Domino's Pizza in India — +331%

Molycorp (U.S.)
Rare Earth Materials Mining — +257%

Chengdu GoldTel Electronic (China)
Technology — +238%

Beijing Sevenstar Electronics
Electronic Equipment and Components — +230%

TPK Holding (Taiwan)
Touch Technology — +205%

−67% **Promethean World (U.K.)**
Interactive Learning Technology

−66% **DynaVox (U.S.)**
Speech Technology

−61% **Mitel Networks (Canada)**
Communications Technology

−58% **D.B. Realty (India)**
Real Estate

−57% **Ningbo GQY Video & Telecom (China)**
Technology

Source: Standard & Poor's, 2010.

Single investment banking companies rarely underwrite securities issues by themselves. Usually, there is one managing investment banking company handling the issue—advising and working with the issuing company on pricing and timing concerns—that then forms a syndicate of other investment banking companies. This syndicate will underwrite the IPO or seasoned new issue. If investors are interested in the offering, they can contact a member of the underwriting syndicate to request a **prospectus**, which describes the issue and the issuing company's financial prospects.

Secondary Markets—Stocks

Securities that have previously been issued and bought are traded in the **secondary markets**. In other words, if you bought 100 shares of stock in an IPO and then wanted to resell them, you'd have to sell the shares in the secondary market. Only issuing companies (and their underwriters) can sell securities in the primary markets. The proceeds from the sale of a share of IBM stock on the secondary market go to the previous owner of the stock, not to IBM. In fact, the only time IBM ever receives money from the sale of one of its securities is on the primary market.

The secondary markets can take the form of either an organized exchange or an over-the-counter market. An **organized exchange** occupies a physical location where trading occurs such as the New York Stock Exchange. In other words, an organized exchange is actually a building in which stocks are traded. In an **over-the-counter market**, transactions are conducted over the telephone or via a computer hookup. How is it determined where a security will trade? Larger, more frequently traded securities, such as GM, IBM, General Electric, and Disney, are traded on organized exchanges. Those that are less frequently traded, along with many new and high-tech stocks, are relegated to the over-the-counter markets. In either case, the secondary markets make it much easier for sellers to find buyers and vice versa.

Prospectus
A legal document that describes a securities issue and is made available to potential investors.

Secondary Markets
The markets in which previously issued securities are traded.

Organized Exchange
An exchange that occupies a physical location where trading occurs, such as the New York Stock Exchange.

Over-the-Counter Market
A market in which transactions are conducted over the telephone or via a computer hookup rather than in an organized exchange.

Organized Exchanges   There are two major organized exchanges in the United States, the New York Stock Exchange (NYSE) and the American Stock Exchange (AMEX), as well as a number of regional stock exchanges. If a firm's stock trades on a particular exchange, it is said to be *listed* on that exchange. Securities can be listed on more than one exchange. Without question, the NYSE is the big player, with over 80 percent of the typical trading volume.

The New York Stock Exchange (NYSE)   The New York Stock Exchange (owned by NYSE Euronext), also called the "Big Board," is the oldest of all the organized exchanges. It began in the spring of 1792 when 24 traders signed the Buttonwood Agreement, a pact named after the tree under which the traders gathered, obligating them to "give preference" to each other in security trading. When winter came, the 24 traders moved to the backroom of Wall Street's Tontine Coffee House, leaving the other traders out in the cold.

The members of the exchange occupy "seats." A seat is a membership card, and the number of seats on the New York Stock Exchange is limited to 1,366, a number that hasn't changed since 1953. The only way to acquire a seat is to buy one from a current owner for whatever the market price is. The highest price a seat has ever sold for is $4 million in 2005. Large brokerage firms such as Bank of America/Merrill Lynch might own more than 20 seats.

To be listed on the NYSE, a firm must meet strict requirements. Table 12.1 lists the current requirements for the NYSE and demonstrates how restrictive those requirements really are. If a firm fails to maintain the minimum requirements, it's delisted and no longer traded on the NYSE.

In 2011 there were about 2,800 NYSE-listed companies from all over the world, with market value of approximately $15.9 trillion at the beginning of 2011 as shown in Table 12.2. As you can see, the NYSE is the largest organized securities exchange in the world. In 2011, the NYSE became a takeover target of the German stock exchange, Deutsche Boerse. Included among the NYSE-listed stocks are companies such as PepsiCo, AT&T, Walmart, Coca-Cola, and IBM.

When you buy or sell a stock, who do you think you are buying it from or selling it to? The answer most of the time is not a person, it's a computer. Roughly 75 percent of all trades are computer generated. That is, most stock trades come directly from a computer rather than a person.

The American Stock Exchange (AMEX)   The American Stock Exchange is the second most important of the organized exchanges and generally lists stocks of firms that are somewhat smaller than those listed on the NYSE. Although the AMEX operates in a manner similar to the NYSE and is owned by NYSE Euronext, it has only 660 seats and lists over 500 firms. Its trading volume is only 3 percent of that on the NYSE. It may rank

TABLE 12.1 Initial Listing Requirements for the NYSE, 2011
Profitability
Aggregate earnings before taxes (EBT) over the last 3 years must be at least $10 million.
Minimum EBT in each of 2 most recent years of at least $2 million.
Market Value
The market value of publicly held stock must be at least $100 million.
Public Ownership
There must be at least 1.1 million publicly held common shares.
There must be at least 400 holders of 100 shares or more.

TABLE 12.2	Major Stock Exchanges: Year Ended 31 December 2010		
Rank	Location	Stock Exchange	Total Value of All the Listed Stock (billions)
1	United States and Europe	NYSE Euronext	$15,970
2	United States and Europe	NASDAQ OMX	$ 4,931
3	Japan	Tokyo Stock Exchange	$ 3,827
4	United Kingdom	London Stock Exchange	$ 3,613
5	China	Shanghai Stock Exchange	$ 2,717

as number two in terms of the number of companies it lists, but when it comes to the dollar volume of daily trades, it's actually smaller than some regional exchanges.

Over-the-Counter (OTC) Market   The OTC market is a linkup of dealers, with no listing or membership requirements. For the most part, the OTC market is highly automated. A nationwide computer network allows brokers to see up-to-the-second price quotes on roughly 35,000 securities.

Over-the-counter listings are often made up of companies that are too new or too small to be listed on a major exchange. These companies also often have fewer shares available. As a result, in some cases small amounts of buying or selling may have a significant impact on the price of these companies' stocks.

The largest electronic stock exchange is NASDAQ, which allows dealers to post bid and ask prices of OTC stocks on approximately 2,800 stocks. A **bid price** is the highest price a prospective buyer is willing to pay for a security, and an **ask on offer price** is the lowest price at which a prospective seller is willing to sell the security. The asking or offer price should always be above the bid price. Today, NASDAQ provides a marketplace for about 2,800 different stocks and about 15 percent of all the shares traded.

Bid Price
The highest price someone is willing to pay for a security.

Ask on Offer Price
The lowest price at which someone is willing to sell a security.

Secondary Markets—Bonds

Although some bonds are actually traded at the NYSE, most of the buying and selling of bonds doesn't occur on the organized exchanges. Instead, bond dealers transact business and sell bonds out of their holdings. Generally, bond dealers transact business directly only with large financial institutions; the smaller investor can gain access to a bond dealer only through a broker acting as an intermediary. Your broker will buy or sell the bond from the bond dealer and then pass it on to you, charging you a commission for the service.

Secondary markets tend to be for smaller, individual investors, and there just aren't all that many small, individual investors interested in corporate bonds. However, the volume of trading in the secondary market for government bonds is enormous. In fact, the trading volume in government bonds runs in the billions of dollars each month. Government bond trading is dominated by the Federal Reserve, commercial banks, and other financial institutions.

International Markets

International security markets have been around for centuries. In fact, around 2000 B.C. the Babylonians introduced debt financing, and by 400 B.C. the Greeks had developed a security market of sorts. In 2008 the world stock market was valued at over $50 trillion, with over half of that outside the United States. Figure 12.2 provides a breakdown of what the world stock market looks like. As you can see, if you ignore

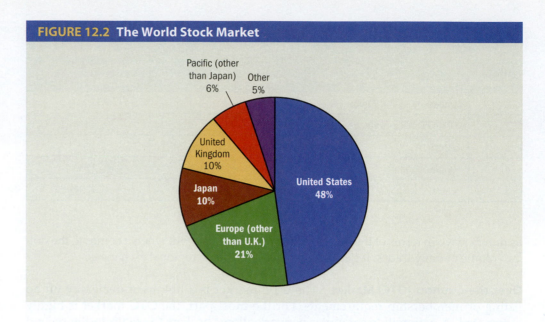

FIGURE 12.2 The World Stock Market

international investments, you're ignoring over half of the stock in the world. The world bond market is also truly international, with a total value of over $25 trillion. In terms of this market, the United States dominates. However, Japan, Germany, the United Kingdom, and France are all major players.

How do you buy a Japanese stock? There are two ways. First, some foreign shares are traded on exchanges in the United States. For example, just over 460 foreign companies are traded on the NYSE and over 60 are traded on the AMEX. In addition, over 400 are traded on the NASDAQ. However, many of these companies are Canadian.

Another way international stocks can be traded is through **American Depository Receipts (ADRs)**. With ADRs, shares of stock aren't traded directly. Instead, the foreign firm's stock is held on deposit in a bank in the foreign firm's country. The foreign bank issues an ADR, which represents direct ownership of those shares. The ADR then trades internationally just like a normal share of stock. Examples of foreign firms with ADRs include Sony and Toyota.

Today, many investment advisors recommend that their clients increase their international investments. They cite relatively low-priced stocks coupled with strong economies. Certainly, there are real opportunities abroad. In fact, since 1980, U.S. foreign holdings have increased more than 100-fold. Foreign equity investments now account for 10 percent of U.S. investors' holdings. However, there are also risks.

For example, the Japanese stock market started plummeting in January 1990 and didn't stop until it lost 63 percent of its value by August 1992. From then until 2011, it continued to slowly slide before rising somewhat —missing the great stock market surges that took place in the United States in the late 1990s. By mid-2011, it still stood at about 75 percent below its high 21 years previously.

Regulation of the Securities Markets

Securities market regulation is aimed at protecting the investor and providing a level playing field so that all investors have a fair chance of making money. There are actually two levels of regulation: general regulation by the Securities and Exchange Commission (SEC, a federal agency) and self-regulation directly by the exchanges (or, in the case of the OTC market, by the Financial Industry Regulatory Authority [FINRA]).

SEC Regulation   The great stock market crash of 1929 inspired much of the legislation that governs the securities markets today. In the period following the crash, the

American Depository Receipt (ADR)
A marketable document (a receipt) that certifies a bank holds shares of a foreign firm's stock that backs the receipt. As a result the ADR trades just like a normal share of stock.

Securities Act of 1933 and the Securities Exchange Act of 1934 were enacted. The Securities Exchange Act of 1934 spoke directly to the secondary market and created the Securities and Exchange Commission or SEC to enforce the trading laws.

The cornerstone of both pieces of legislation is the disclosure of relevant information relating to the offering of a security. Many other acts and laws have been passed to regulate the securities markets. For example, the Investment Advisers Act of 1940 provides investor protection against unethical investment advisors and requires advisors to register with the SEC and provide the SEC with semiannual reports. Under the Investor Protection Act of 1970, the Securities Investor Protection Corporation (SIPC) was established to provide up to $500,000 of insurance to cover investors' account balances in the event that their brokerage firm goes bankrupt.

> **STOP & THINK**
>
> What is the purpose of market regulation? It's to give everyone an equal chance of making money in the stock market. The disclosure principle allows all investors to view the same information at the same time and thereby have an equal chance of making trading profits. That's what guides the majority of the laws governing the securities markets—giving everyone a fair chance at making money. It doesn't always work. Can you name a Wall Street scandal?

Self-Regulation Much of the day-to-day regulation of the markets is left to the securities industry and is performed by the exchanges and the FINRA. The willingness and zeal with which the exchanges approach self-regulation is inspired by the knowledge that if self-regulation doesn't work, government regulation will be imposed.

After the October 1987 market crash, the NYSE self-regulated like mad and imposed a number of "circuit breakers" to head off or slow potential future market crashes. The idea behind these "circuit breakers" is that by closing the market in the event of sharp declines, investors will be given a chance to step back and assess the price decline rather than reacting on instinct.

Insider Trading and Market Abuses Much of the logic behind regulation of the market stems from the desire to level the playing field with respect to the securities markets. The Insider Trading Sanctions Act of 1984 and the Insider Trading and Securities Fraud Enforcement Act of 1988 made it illegal to trade while in the possession of inside information, or "material" nonpublic information held by officers, directors, major stockholders, or anyone with special insider knowledge.

> **STOP & THINK**
>
> Warren Buffett once said "the stock market is designed to transfer money from the active to the patient." What do you think he meant by that?

Has insider trading disappeared? Certainly not. In fact, *Business Week*, after analyzing the largest 100 mergers and takeovers of 1994, came to the conclusion that one out of three of those deals was preceded by stock price run-ups or abnormal volume that could not be explained by the publicly available information at the time.

Another potential abuse involves **churning**, or excessive trading on a client's account, which means the client pays more commissions. Although churning is illegal, it's also practically impossible to prove. Churning can easily take place if the client has relinquished trading control to the broker, but it also takes place on traditional accounts. That's why it's so important to select a broker you can trust.

Churning
Excessive trading in a security account that is inappropriate for the customer and serves only to generate commissions.

How Securities Are Traded

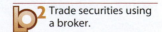
2 Trade securities using a broker.

Let's look now at how to trade securities, and examine the different types of trades and trading mechanisms. You'll notice that when we discuss the different trading mechanisms, we refer to all securities as stocks. We're not favoring stocks or saying that these trading mechanisms apply only to stocks. We're just being lazy, and stocks are the most frequently traded of the different securities.

The Role of the Specialist

Continuous Markets
Markets in which trading can occur at any time, with prices free to fluctuate as trading occurs.

The NYSE and the AMEX both are considered **continuous markets**, which means that trading can occur on them whenever the exchanges are open with prices free to fluctuate as trading occurs. One potential problem in a continuous market is that buyers and sellers don't necessarily come to the market at the same time, which can cause stocks prices to bounce up and down. For that reason, customers can route their orders to the floor for trade where human judgment can make the trading process more efficient, and it is the role of the **specialist** to take care of this potential problem and to "maintain a fair and orderly market." At times specialists buy stock to absorb excess supply and at other times they sell stock out of their inventory to provide for excess demand. In that way they keep the market from fluctuating more than it would otherwise. Today, with most trading done electronically, the role of the specialist is greatly diminished. In 2001, the specialist participated in about 15 percent of all trades on the NYSE, but by 2011, that participation level had dropped to around 3 percent. Still, the specialist maintains an important role in the operation of these markets.

Specialist
An exchange member who oversees the trading in one or more stocks and is responsible for maintaining a "fair and orderly" market in those stocks by buying or selling for his or her own account.

Order Characteristics

When you place an order to buy or sell stock, you need to be clear about the size of the order and the length of time the order is to be outstanding.

FACTS OF LIFE

According to a recent survey by Allianz Life Insurance, 57 percent of women said they wish they had learned more in school about money and finance.

Order Size Common stock is sold in lots or groups of 100 shares on the New York Stock Exchange. These lots are referred to as **round lots**. Orders involving between 1 and 99 shares of stock are referred to as **odd lots** and are processed by "odd lot dealers" who buy and sell out of their inventory.

Round Lot
A group or lot of 100 shares of common stock. Stocks are traded in round lots on the New York Stock Exchange.

Odd Lot
An order involving between 1 and 99 shares of stock.

Day Order
A trading order that expires at the end of the trading day during which it was made.

Open or Good-Till-Canceled (GTC) Order
A trading order that remains effective until filled or canceled.

Discretionary Account
An account that gives your broker the power to make trades for you.

Time Period for Which the Order Will Remain Outstanding When you order a hamburger at Burger King, you want your order filled right away, not in a week. Well, when you order stock, you better specify when you want your order filled, or you just might have to wait a week and pay more than you bargained for. Ordering alternatives include **day orders**, which expire at the end of the trading day during which they were made; **open orders**, also called **good-till-canceled (GTC) orders**, which remain effective until filled or canceled; and fill-or-kill orders, which, if not filled immediately, expire.

You can give your broker the power to make trades for you if you open a **discretionary account**. Because a discretionary account gives your broker power over your money, you should consider it only if you've worked with your broker for years, and only under unusual circumstances. There's no question that problems do occur with discretionary accounts, and the easiest way to avoid the problems is to avoid discretionary accounts.

Types of Orders

Whenever you place an order, you want to make sure that it is carried out in exactly the way you intended. A number of different types of orders act as instructions for how you would like your order to be executed.

Market Orders   A **market order** is an order to buy or sell a set number of securities immediately at the best price available. These orders can generally be executed within minutes of being placed. Once your order is placed with your broker, it's teletyped to the floor of the NYSE, where it's either executed electronically or received by a floor broker. The floor broker takes the order to the location on the exchange floor where that stock trades and executes the trade. As a result, when you place a market order, you can be relatively certain that the order will be executed quickly. However, you can't be certain of the price at which it will be executed.

Market Order
An order to buy or sell a set number of securities immediately at the best price available.

Limit Orders   A **limit order** specifies that the trade is to be made only at a certain price or better. In other words, if a limit order to sell stock is made, the stock will be sold only at a certain price or above. If a limit order to buy is made, the stock is bought only at a certain price or below. Limit orders allow you to limit your bid or ask price to what you feel is an acceptable level. If the specified price isn't available, your trade isn't made. Your order is given to the specialist, who'll execute the limit order if the price moves to your acceptable level.

Limit Order
An order that specifies a securities trade is to be made only at a certain price or better.

Stop Orders   A **stop or stop-loss order** is an order to sell if the price drops *below* a specified level or to buy if the price climbs *above* a specified level. Stop-loss orders are used to protect your profits. They allow you to bail out of the stock if the market starts to tumble, or to buy (a stop order) in if the price starts to rise (these are used to protect profit on short selling, which we'll discuss in a moment).

Stop or Stop-Loss Order
An order to sell a security if the price drops below a specified level or to buy if the price climbs above a specified level.

For example, say you'd purchased stock in Tesoro, the Houston-based refining company, in August 2010 at $10.91 per share, and by early April 2011 it was selling at $28.23 per share. Because you never know when Tesoro might have some problems or when the market might fall, you could lock in some of the gains you'd already made by using a stop-loss order to sell Tesoro at $25.

You wouldn't use a stop-loss order for the full $28.23 current price, because your stock would then be sold immediately while the price remained at $28.23. You also wouldn't use a stop-loss order for an amount very close to $28.23, say $28.00 or so, because market prices commonly fluctuate a bit and you wouldn't want your stop-loss order to be executed on a routine fluctuation just before an uncommon rise up to, say, $50 per share.

You want to set the stop-loss order price just right so that you safeguard against only a major fluctuation. Thus, if the price of Tesoro tumbled to $25, your stop-loss order would activate and sell your Tesoro stock at the best price possible, which may end up being less than $25, because there might not be a buyer for the stock at $25. In this way you can "lock in" some of the paper profits.

> ### STOP & THINK
>
> Limit orders and stop-loss orders are aimed at taking some risk out of investing. The limit order allows you to buy into a stock at what you feel is a good price. Its downside is that if the stock's price continues to rise, your order may never be executed. A stop-loss order allows you to sell the stock quickly if the price falls. Remember, however, that a stop-loss order doesn't guarantee you will sell the stock at the price you set; a stop-loss order becomes a market order when the set price is reached. Do you think it's possible that your stock might continue to fall before someone is willing to buy your shares?

Short Selling

Although it's obvious that you can make money in the stock market when stocks rise in price, you can also make money when prices decline. With **short selling** you're wishing for bad news: The more the stock drops in price, the more money you make. Short selling involves borrowing stock from your broker and selling it. Then, if the stock price goes down, you buy it back and return it to your broker. You make a profit by buying it back for less than you sold it.

Short Selling
Borrowing stock from your broker and selling it with an obligation to replace the stock later.

Beware, however, that if the price of the stock goes up, you have to buy it back at a higher price. You lose! In effect, selling short lets you reverse the order of buying and selling. That is, when you invest in stock, the goal is to buy low and later to sell high. With short selling, the goal is to sell high and later to buy low.

Short selling isn't necessarily free, or even cheap. Because you've borrowed someone's stock and sold it, you not only have to replace it later, you also have to repay any dividends that were paid during the period for which the broker was without the stock. Also, to protect itself from short sellers who might lose the money, the broker keeps the proceeds from the short sale until it gets its stock back. To provide the brokerage firm with a further guarantee that the short seller will be able to repurchase the stock in the future, the short seller must put up some collateral—referred to as a **margin requirement**—during the period of the short sale.

Margin Requirement
The percentage that an investor must have on deposit with a broker when selling short.

Let's suppose you feel strongly that McDonald's stock price is about to fall from its present level of $70 per share, and you want to make money off McDonald's misfortune. First, you call your broker and sell 1,000 shares of McDonald's short. The proceeds of $70,000 are credited to your account, although you can't withdraw those funds. Your broker also has a 50 percent margin requirement, which means you must have an additional $35,000 in cash or securities in your account to serve as collateral. Most short sellers keep Treasury bills or notes in their account for this purpose.

> ### STOP & THINK
>
> Warren Buffett once said "risk comes from not knowing what you're doing." What do you think he meant by that?

Now let's assume that McDonald's drops to $50 per share, and you decide it's time to buy. You call your broker to purchase 1,000 shares of McDonald's for a total cost of $50,000. Thus, you make $20,000 on your short sale by selling high ($70 per share) and later buying low ($50 per share). Remember, though, that when you sell short, you also have to cover any dividends that occurred during the period the broker was without the stock. Thus, your profits are actually equal to the initial price less the total of the ending price and the dividends, as shown in Figure 12.3.

Of course, if McDonald's price goes up, you will lose money, because you will have to buy back the stock. Thus, if McDonald's stock goes up to $90 per share, you'd lose $20,000 on your short sale, in addition to having to cover any dividends that occurred during the period the stock was sold short. You'd also have to listen to your broker laugh when you gave back the more expensive stock. In this case, you'd have sold low ($70 per share) and later bought high ($90 per share). Given the fact that the long-term trend of the stock market is upward, selling short is extremely risky and isn't something most people should consider.

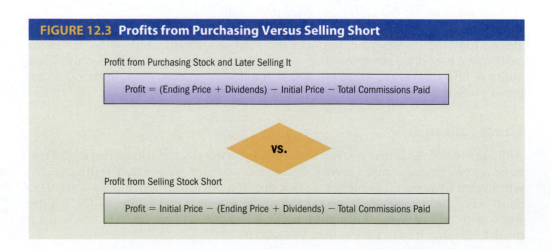

FIGURE 12.3 Profits from Purchasing Versus Selling Short

Profit from Purchasing Stock and Later Selling It

Profit = (Ending Price + Dividends) − Initial Price − Total Commissions Paid

vs.

Profit from Selling Stock Short

Profit = Initial Price − (Ending Price + Dividends) − Total Commissions Paid

Dealing with Brokers

Although you can purchase securities through most financial planners, the most common way to purchase stock is through a stockbroker. A stockbroker is licensed to buy or sell stocks for others. In fact, most financial planners are, among other things, stockbrokers.

There are two general categories of brokers: full-service brokers, and discount and online brokers. You can deal directly with your broker, that is, over the phone or in person, or you can do your trading online without ever interacting directly with a broker. The differences between these two ways of buying stock center on advice and cost. As we'll see later when we examine the cost of trading, the difference in cost can be substantial.

Brokerage Accounts

Just as a bank account represents money you have on deposit at a bank, a brokerage account represents money or investments you have at a brokerage firm. For most investors, this account includes securities and possibly some cash. It can also include other investments. If there are enough different investments, combining these different accounts into an all-in-one account, called an asset management account, might be best.

When we first introduced **asset management accounts** in Chapter 5, we defined such an account as a comprehensive financial services package offered by a brokerage firm that can include a checking account; a credit card; a money market mutual fund; loans; automatic payment on any fixed debt (such as mortgages); brokerage services (buying and selling stocks or bonds); and a system for the direct payment of interest, dividends, and proceeds from security sales into the money market mutual fund.

The major advantage of such an account is that it automatically coordinates the flow of funds into and out of your money market mutual fund. For example, interest and dividends received from securities owned are automatically "swept" into the money market mutual fund. If you write a check for an amount greater than what is held in your money market mutual fund, securities from the investment portion of your asset management account are automatically sold, and the proceeds "swept" into the money market fund to cover the check.

Asset Management Account
Comprehensive financial services packages offered by a brokerage firm that can include a checking account; credit and debit cards; a money market mutual fund; loans; automatic payment of fixed payments, such as mortgages or other debt; brokerage services (buying and selling stocks or bonds); and a system for the direct payment of interest, dividends, and proceeds from security sales into the money market mutual fund.

Types of Brokers

Full-Service Brokers A **full-service broker** or **account executive** is paid on commission, based on the sales volume generated. The companies you think of when you think of stockbrokers, for example, Merrill Lynch, Edward Jones, UBS, and Morgan Stanley Smith Barney are all full-service brokers. The commissions are pretty high with a full-service broker; in fact they run around $150 per trade on average. However, in return for the steep fees, each investor is assigned a broker who oversees his or her account. That broker gives advice and direction to the client, and then executes the trades. The more frequently trades are made, the more the broker earns.

Full-Service Broker or Account Executive
A broker who gives advice and is paid on commission, where that commission is based on the sales volume generated.

Discount and Online Brokers A **discount and online broker** executes trades both with broker assistance and allows for online trading. For example, Fidelity executes trades for anywhere from $7.95 to about $55 depending upon whether the trade is made with the help of a broker, whether it is done directly online, how many trades are made annually, and how large the household's assets are. In spite of the fact that Fidelity is considered a discount and online broker, it provides customers with a wealth of information, including analysts' recommendations and reports along with

Discount and Online Broker
A "no-frills" broker who executes trades without giving any advice and thus charges much lower commission than a full-service broker.

◆ Are you willing to pay a higher commission for investment advice? If so, a full-service broker may be right for you.

◆ Does the brokerage firm provide record-keeping services to help you calculate your taxes?

◆ Are the accounts insured up to $500,000 by the Securities Investor Protection Corporation (SIPC) against the event that the brokerage firm faces financial difficulties?

◆ Does the brokerage firm provide an 800 number and online site for transactions and quotes?

◆ Do you receive interest on idle cash in your account?

earnings estimates. This kind of information was formerly available only through a full-service broker. Now, you can gain access to all the resources your broker has online. The advantages of trading through a discount and online broker are that the costs can be extremely low. In addition, with online trading, you can execute a market order trade immediately, with the confirmation coming back within seconds or a minute at most.

In deciding which type of broker to use, regardless of whether you're considering a full-service or discount and online broker, you need to answer several questions provided in Checklist 12.1. Remember, not all brokerage firms provide the same services at the same cost, so it's a good idea to investigate the alternatives before choosing one to work with.

Cash Versus Margin Accounts

Cash Accounts

Securities trading accounts in which the investors pay in full for their security purchases, with the payment due within 3 business days of the transaction.

Margin Accounts

Securities trading accounts in which the investors borrow a portion of the purchase price from their broker.

Margin or Initial Margin

A maximum limit set on the percentage of the purchase price of a security that must initially be paid for by the investor, which is set by the Federal Reserve.

Investors with **cash accounts** pay in full for their security purchases, with the payment due within 3 business days of the transaction. Investors with **margin accounts** borrow a portion of the purchase price from the broker. In other words, with a margin account, both you and your broker put in $500 to purchase $1,000 worth of stock. The broker comes up with this money by borrowing the funds from a bank and paying what's referred to as the "broker's call money rate," which is generally the prime rate. The broker then charges you this rate plus a 1 to 2 percent service fee.

There's a limit on the percentage of the purchase price that you must initially pay, called the **margin or initial margin**, which is set by the Federal Reserve. For the past 30 years it's been 50 percent. Keep in mind that 50 percent is the minimum margin required by the Federal Reserve and that the broker you work with may require more.

The only time purchasing on margin is to the advantage of the investor is when the return on the stocks is greater than the cost of the borrowing. To demonstrate, let's assume that the margin is 50 percent and that you purchase 200 shares of General Electric stock at $50 per share. In this case, the stock would cost a total of $10,000 (200 × $50), and you'd pay $5,000 and borrow the remaining $5,000 from your broker.

Total cost: 200 shares at $50 per share	$10,000
Amount borrowed: total cost (1 − margin%)	−5,000
Margin: investor's contribution	$5,000

When you purchase securities on margin, they remain in the brokerage firm's name because the shares are used as collateral for the margin loan. What drives investors to make margin purchases is the desire to leverage their profits as those securities go up in price. Let's look at what would happen to your investment if the price of General Electric's stock rose 40 percent to $70 per share.

Total value of 200 shares at $70 per share	$14,000
Margin loan	−5,000
Margin (the net value of your investment)	$9,000

Your initial contribution of $5,000 is now worth $9,000, meaning you made $4,000 on an investment of $5,000—an 80 percent gain on your investment despite a stock price increase of only 40 percent. Actually, your return would be a bit less because you'd also have been paying interest on the portion of the purchase that was financed with borrowed funds, not to mention the commissions you pay when you buy and sell the stock.

Don't get too excited about margin purchases. Although the leverage that margin purchases provide can amplify stock price gains in a positive way, it can also amplify stock price losses in a negative way. Let's assume that the value of the General Electric stock drops to $30 per share.

Total value of 200 shares at $30 per share	$6,000
Margin loan	−5,000
Margin (the net value of your investment)	$ 1,000

Your initial investment of $5,000 is now worth $1,000, meaning you lost $4,000—an 80 percent loss despite only a 40 percent drop in General Electric's stock price. Thus, the leverage that margin purchases produce is often referred to as a "double-edged sword," because it helps you in the good times and hurts you in the bad times.

Margin accounts are set up in such a way that when stock prices fall, only the amount you've put in suffers the loss in value. To protect your broker, a maintenance margin is in place. The **maintenance margin** specifies a minimum percentage margin of collateral that you must maintain—which is often the same as the initial margin. If the margin falls below this percentage, the broker issues a margin call. A **margin call** requires you to replenish the margin account by adding additional cash or securities to bring the margin back up to a minimum level. Alternatively, the broker can sell securities from your margin account to bring the margin percentage up to an acceptable level. Again, you take the loss.

Maintenance Margin
The minimum percentage margin of collateral that you must maintain.

Margin Call
A requirement that you replenish your margin account by adding cash or securities to bring it back to a minimum level.

Registration: Street Name or Your Name

Another choice you have when buying securities is whether you'd like the securities registered in the "street name" or in your name. Securities registered in the "street name" remain in the broker's custody and appear in the broker's computers as a computer entry in your name. You still own the securities and you'll receive any dividends or interest payments just as if the securities were registered in your name, but there are no physical stock certificates. The advantage to registering your securities in street name is that they are more convenient to sell because the stock certificates or bonds don't have to be delivered to your broker.

The only possible disadvantage to leaving your securities in the broker's "street name" is that some brokerage firms impose a maintenance fee on accounts that don't trade within a certain time frame. For example, if you were to make a single purchase of stock,

STOP & THINK

Keep money in perspective. "I'm just not the acquisitive type. I have three cars, and that's as extravagant as it gets for me. My watch cost me $39 and it keeps good time, so why would I need a more expensive one?"— Denzel Washington, two-time Oscar winner. What do you think of Denzel Washington's attitude?

register that stock in the broker's street name, and then not make another trade for some time, the broker may charge you a maintenance fee. This fee could be avoided if you register the stock in your name and have the certificates delivered to you. Before opening an account with a broker, ask whether maintenance charges are imposed against dormant accounts. If they are, try another broker.

Joint Accounts

If you and your spouse are buying securities together, there are several alternative forms of joint accounts, each with different estate planning implications. It's important to either thoroughly understand how these joint accounts work, or confer with a lawyer before setting up your account.

Two of the most common joint accounts are joint tenancy with the right of survivorship and tenancy-in-common. Under an account with **joint tenancy with the right of survivorship**, when one of the individual owners dies, the other receives full ownership of the assets in the account. The assets bypass the lengthy court process called probate where they are transferred according to the instructions left in the deceased's will. However, even with joint tenancy, the assets may be subject to estate taxes. With a **tenancy-in-common account**, the deceased's portion of the account goes to the heirs of the deceased rather than to the surviving account holder.

Choosing a Broker

Using a Full-Service Broker   Much of your decision of whether to go with a discount versus a full-service broker boils down to a choice between service and price—not an uncommon trade-off in many of life's decisions. With a full-service broker you get the personal service, advice, and hand holding that you wouldn't get with a discount broker. If that's the only way you feel comfortable, then a full-service broker is your only choice. However, you should keep in mind that your broker is not a securities analyst and most likely does not evaluate the recommendations he or she receives from analysts, but instead simply passes them on. In effect, when your broker advises you to buy or sell a security, he or she is acting on an analyst's recommendation, not on firsthand research. This doesn't mean you shouldn't take your broker's advice. Rather, you should take that advice and investigate it.

This relates back to **Principle 1: The Best Protection Is Knowledge**. As we have said so often throughout this text, you bear all the consequences of bad decisions, so you *must* take responsibility for your own financial affairs. This is also why it's so important to do your homework when selecting a broker.

Using a Discount/Online Broker   There's one thing you *can* do to increase the performance of your investments and that is to keep the transaction costs—that is, commissions and fees—down to a minimum. Keeping costs down is important, especially if you don't get much for the extra money the commissions and fees represent; remember **Principle 6: Waste Not, Want Not—Smart Spending Matters**. Unfortunately, that's difficult with a full-service broker with commissions 10 to 20 times higher than those charged by a discount broker. Although you might not have an account executive to hold your hand, some discount/online brokers, such as Fidelity for example, provide an abundance of research reports free of charge and an analysis of your portfolio along with downloadable tax information, and on top of that, you'll have a greater return on your investments. In fact, some of the discount/online brokers provide services that are very similar to those offered by full-service brokers. However, remember that not all discount/online brokers are the same—services, planning tools, research materials, and costs can vary dramatically from one to another.

When purchasing bonds, there's no advantage to using a discount/online broker. In general, the commissions charged for bonds by a full-service versus a discount/

Joint Tenancy with the Right of Survivorship
A type of joint ownership in which the surviving owner receives full ownership of the assets in the account when the joint owner dies.

Tenancy-in-Common Account
A type of joint ownership in which the deceased's portion of the account goes to the heirs of the deceased rather than to the surviving account holder.

◆ Look for a broker with a reputation for integrity, intelligence, and efficiency in servicing clients.

◆ Ask business colleagues, your banker, and your friends who are successful investors for recommendations.

◆ Look for a broker with experience and with a record of proven advice. If you work with someone who's been in the business since 1987, that broker will have experienced at least three market downturns.

◆ Look for a broker who understands your investment philosophy and is willing to work within your investment boundaries to achieve your goals.

◆ Interview prospective brokers to find out about background, training, and experience.

◆ Be up-front about your financial circumstances and how much you will invest. Ask for a general recommendation for a person in your situation, and listen.

◆ Ask for a sample portfolio. Be sure to interview several candidates and compare notes to find a good fit.

◆ Look for a broker who has a reputation for allowing customers to say no without undue pressure. Ask for names of clients with financial situations similar to yours whose accounts the broker has handled for at least 3 years, and call them.

◆ Look for a broker who is candid with you regarding costs—both maintenance costs on your account and commissions—and what his or her research recommendations are based on.

online broker will pretty much be the same, especially for larger purchases. If you're going to buy bonds through a broker, you might as well use a full-service broker, because it doesn't cost more. If you're buying Treasury bonds, there's no reason to go through a broker at all. Treasury bonds can be purchased directly from the Treasury Department or from any of the Federal Reserve Banks, and no commission will be charged.

Making the Decision   As with choosing a financial advisor, choosing a broker is a serious decision, one that can have a major impact on your financial future. If you decide on a discount/online broker, look for one with a reputation for honesty and efficiency in servicing clients. If you decide on a full-service broker, take a look at Checklist 12.2.

Remember, your first job is to become knowledgeable (that **Principle 1** at work again). You may feel you have to start off with a full-service broker, but as your understanding of the investment process improves, so will your confidence that you can trade through a discount broker. The advantage that full-service brokers have in terms of research tools, retirement planning tools, and portfolio specialists has been narrowing dramatically in recent years. So, the question remains, "is the added service that full-service brokers provide worth the price?"

The Cost of Trading

We've already touched briefly on the cost of trading in our discussion of full-service and discount/online brokers. We'll now look more closely at what the costs are. Interestingly, the savings can be dramatic. Commissions associated with the purchase of 500 shares of stock at $20 per share—a total purchase of $10,000 of common stock—can range from a high of $230 with an expensive full-service broker down to $5 or less with a discount/online broker. In percentage terms, that's 2.30 percent versus 0.05 percent. Keep in mind that this sales commission is to buy the stock. The broker charges a similar commission to sell the stock. Thus, your stock would have to rise by 4.60 percent before you'd break even and cover your commissions if the stock were purchased from the more expensive full-service broker.

Many brokers also charge a transaction fee, which in general is quite small. What's not quite small is the inactive account annual fee, which is imposed by most full-service brokers at a rate of $25 to $200 per year. If you don't make a certain number of security transactions during the year, your account is debited $25 to $200, which can be a sizable cost for smaller accounts. Moreover, this fee has the effect of encouraging trading when the trade may not be in your best interest. Avoid firms that charge annual fees on inactive accounts.

With smaller transactions, the savings from using a discount/online broker are less noticeable. For a $3,000 purchase (100 shares of stock at $30 per share) the costs might be $75 with a full-service broker but $5 or less with a discount/online broker. In percentage form, that's a cost of 2.5 percent versus 0.17 percent or less. Again, you should keep in mind that these costs are doubled with a "round trip"—that is, buying the stock and later selling it.

So what's the bottom line on the cost of trading? In a nutshell, discount/online brokers are less expensive than full-service brokers, and for larger purchases, this cost difference is even more dramatic. If you make large purchases, you should definitely consider a discount/online broker. If you're a smaller investor, you should and can avoid the potentially costly inactive account fee regardless of whether you choose a full-service or discount/online broker.

If you're purchasing Treasury securities through a broker, you should do so with a full-service broker that doesn't charge an inactive account fee. However, if you're buying Treasury securities, you can totally avoid any fee by purchasing them directly from the Treasury or a Federal Reserve Bank.

Online Trading

Online Trading
Making trades on the Internet.

The two basic ways you can execute your trades are dealing directly with a broker or **online trading**. Although many investors are more comfortable going through a broker, it tends to be less expensive to make the trades yourself online.

Because of the fast pace of online trading—that is, the instant access to your account and nearly instantaneous execution of your trades—it is important to protect yourself. As with everything else in investing or personal finance, this all goes back to **Principle 1: The Best Protection Is Knowledge**. Checklist 12.3 provides a number of tips for online investing—that is, things you need to know if you're considering trading online.

Day Traders
Individuals who trade, generally over the Internet, with a very short time horizon, generally less than 1 day.

While many of these trades are executed by investors with a buy and hold philosophy, many are also executed by **day traders**. A day trader is an individual who trades with a very short-term investment horizon. Typically they station themselves at the computer and look for stocks that are moving up or down in value. Their goal is to ride the momentum of the stock and get out before it changes direction. Day trading is not investing; it is speculating and to say the least, it is risky. In general, day trading should be avoided. However, if you're lured into trying it, keep a few facts in mind:

◆ **Be prepared to suffer severe financial losses.** It is typical for day traders to suffer severe financial losses in their first months, and many never make a penny. That means you should never consider day trading with money you can't afford to lose.

◆ **Don't confuse day trading with investing—they aren't the same.** Day traders aren't interested in value, just in what the stock might do in the next few hours or day.

◆ Online trading is quick and easy, but online *investing* takes time. With a click of a mouse, you can buy and sell stocks from more than 100 discount/online brokers offering executions at $5 or less per transaction. Although online trading saves investors time and money, it does not take the homework out of making investment decisions; making wise investment decisions takes time. Before you trade, know why you are buying or selling and the risk of your investment.

◆ Set your price limits on fast-moving stocks: Place limit orders rather than market orders. For example, if you want to buy some shares of a "hot" stock but don't want to pay more than $20 a share, you can place a limit order to buy the stock at any price up to $20. By entering a limit order rather than a market order, you will not be caught buying the stock at $30 and then suffering immediate losses as the stock drops later in the day or the weeks ahead.

◆ If you cancel an order, make sure the cancellation worked before placing another trade. Although you may receive an electronic receipt for the cancellation, don't assume that means the trade was canceled. Orders can only be canceled if they have not been executed. Ask your firm about how you should check to see if a cancellation order actually worked.

◆ No regulations require a trade to be executed within a certain time. When you enter an order, be sure to indicate that it is "Good for the Day" or "Good Until Canceled."

Source: "Tips for Investing Online," Securities and Exchange Commission, 2011.

◆ **Don't believe claims of easy profits.** People have a tendency to talk more about when they make money, but not about when they lose it. In fact, day trading has been called "a trading method for transferring wealth from unsophisticated investors to sophisticated investors."

◆ **Watch out for "hot tips" and "expert advice" from newsletters and Web sites catering to day traders.** There's no question that someone makes money from these; unfortunately, it isn't the investor. The same is true for those "educational" seminars, classes, and books about day trading—they may not be objective. Many times the seminar speaker, the instructor teaching a class, or the author of a publication about day trading stands to profit if you start day trading.

The bottom line is, avoid day trading. It's speculating, not investing.

Sources of Investment Information

To say the least, there's a wealth of investment information available. A lot of planning and many decisions have to be made before you're at the point of selecting specific securities in which to invest. And once you're ready to invest, you'll want to gather as much information as you can, read it, and interpret it. Fortunately, you

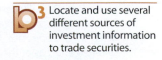
Locate and use several different sources of investment information to trade securities.

don't have to do your own research. That's already done for you, and it's available from the companies themselves, from brokerage firms, from the press—magazines, newspapers, and investment advisory services, and, of course, on the Web.

Corporate Sources

Annual reports are a great source of information. Most annual reports are available for free directly from the company itself. In reading an annual report, the first thing to keep in mind is that although the report is factual, those facts are interpreted in as favorable a light as possible. For example, annual reports generally begin with a letter from the president that highlights the year and gives prospects for the upcoming year. It does so with real attention to public relations. If the president says, "It was a challenging and troublesome year," he or she may really be trying to say, "We lost a lot of money last year."

In looking at an annual report, examine the trends in sales, profits, and dividends, looking for upward movement in all three. Pay attention to the explanation

MONEY MATTERS

Tips from Marcy Furney, ChFC, Certified Financial Planner™

TERMS OF ENRICHMENT

A recent study by a well-known brokerage firm showed that almost 95 percent of individual investors lose money or just break even on stock trades. This is primarily true because they didn't enter into the process armed to make logical, informed decisions. Keep in mind **Principle 9: Mind Games, Your Financial Personality, and Your Money** and be prepared to avoid some of the pitfalls such as these:

"Falling in love" with a stock. Just because you inherited a stock from your favorite grandmother doesn't mean it must always be a viable part of your portfolio. One that has made money for you for several years may become a loser over time. Emotion does not belong in the decision-making process, and there is no "rate of return" for loyalty to a particular investment. Know when to let go.

Investing too heavily in your employer. Many people purchase large amounts of their employer's stock because they feel that they work for a good company. If the company fails, not only have they lost their job, they may have lost a fair amount of their assets. The value of stock in the secondary market may have little to do with how good an employer the company is. (This is not to say that you shouldn't take advantage of some of the excellent company-sponsored stock purchase plans.)

Selling low and buying high. Stock is the one thing in America that people don't seem to want when its "on sale" (when prices are down). Professional money managers normally do not sell just because the price falls or buy because everyone else is. In fact, they more often do the opposite. Their decisions are based on detailed analysis of the stock and how it fits with their portfolio objectives. The key is to be able to evaluate

what may be driving the movement of the price, and avoid making decisions based on panic, fear, rumors, or "hot tips."

The hog factor. Don't be a "hog" and hold on to stocks when they are way up in hopes of them going up further. The saying is "Bears make money. Bulls make money, and hogs get slaughtered" or something like that. Not "selling high" in hopes of "selling higher" can have disappointing results. You may want to sell part of the holdings and keep the rest for a potential continued rise. Alternatively, you could buy the same stock again later and "ride another wave."

Failing to realize the commitment involved. If you are not willing or able to invest the time necessary to do good research and actively tend to your portfolio, perhaps you should seek professional assistance via a mutual fund or other managed account.

Excessive trading costs and taxes. The phrase "playing the market" is sadly appropriate for the actions of some people. They perceive that success in investing lies in moving things around a lot. Consequently, even if they are lucky enough to make some good choices, trading costs and taxes on short-term gains eat up most of what they make.

of how well the firm performed during the year and what management projects for the future. Finally, give close attention to the positives and negatives outlined in the annual report. Are profits up or down? Are new products being introduced? How are the sales on those new products? Are sales climbing or falling? Are new plants being opened or closed?

You look at these items because most of the changes a firm experiences are gradual—things tend to get worse or better over time. By looking at an annual report, you may be able to judge the direction of the changes that are taking place today and that will affect the company's stock price tomorrow.

Brokerage Firm Reports

Most full-service and some discount brokers provide customers access to research reports prepared by the brokerage firm's securities analysts. These reports cover the direction of the economy as a whole. They also look directly at individual companies, analyzing the companies' prospects and concluding with recommendations of buy, hold, or sell. "Buy" indicates a positive recommendation, "sell" a negative recommendation, and "hold" a neutral recommendation.

These reports provide you with the logic behind the recommendation. Even if you don't buy the recommended stocks, the reports are of value to read because they show you the logic that leads an analyst to recommend that a stock be bought or sold. If you're interested in a research report on a specific company, simply call up your broker and request it—it's as simple as that.

The Press

To begin with, every investor should read the *Wall Street Journal* or look at it online. It contains insights, data, and financial news that are essential. A number of other excellent financial magazines are worth a look, including *Forbes*, *Fortune*, and *Barron's*, along with a number of personal finance magazines, such as *Money*, *Smart Money*, and *Kiplinger's Personal Finance*. Remember, the more you read, the more you'll understand what investing is all about. And the more you understand, the more comfortable you'll feel making investments.

Investment Advisory Services

Once you're comfortable reading financial trade magazines and the *Wall Street Journal*, there are more in-depth resources of investment news you may want to take a look at. The primary sources of information on the market and on individual stocks are Moody's Investors Service, Standard & Poor's, and Value Line. They are all available at many libraries. The best way to get started with these resources is to simply head over to your library and ask the librarian what they have in the way of investment advisory services like Value Line or Standard & Poor's.

Among the investment advisory services, the *Value Line Investment Survey* is perhaps the most useful for investors. This publication follows approximately 1,700 companies and provides a one-page summary of each firm's outlook, updating the forecast four times a year. What makes Value Line unique is that it rates every stock on a scale of 1 to 5, with 1 being the most favorable rating on Timeliness™ and Safety™.

In addition to evaluating individual stocks, Value Line examines and ranks different industries, picking out those it feels have the highest investment potential. Value Line also gives weekly evaluations of the economy, as well as the stock and bond markets, advising investors where they should put their money, which direction interest rates are headed, and whether the stock and bond markets are headed up or down.

Internet Sources

There is an incredible amount of corporate information on the Web, including news groups, free software, and discussion groups. For example, the Securities and Exchange Commission filings for corporations and mutual funds that file electronically can be accessed via the Edgar project (**www.edgar-online.com/**) at no charge. Table 12.3 provides a list of several excellent sources of information on the Web. Corporate information is also available from investment companies and commercial online services.

This provides you, regardless of how small an investor you are, with the same opportunities as any other investor. Still, you've got to be careful of where you get your information. Remember that there are no controls on who can post information on the Internet. As a result, that market analysis that seems so astute may have been written by a 12-year-old. Also keep in mind that the agency problem abounds on the Internet. Much of what appears is self-serving in nature. It is either placed there by stockbrokers trying to push stocks on their own Web homepages or by companies trying to improve their stock prices. Look out for those get-rich-quick schemes on the Internet. Someone may get rich, but it's not you.

Investment Clubs

Another excellent source of information is "investment clubs." In recent years, investment clubs have become increasingly popular for their social, educational, and investment value. Every club works a bit differently, but most clubs have required dues (of, say, $10 per month), with the dues then being pooled and invested in the club's name.

TABLE 12.3 Great Sources of Investment Information on the Web

Web Site: **Yahoo! Finance**

Address: **finance.yahoo.com**

- This Web site provides investments and personal finance news, market updates, and a wealth of information on individual stocks including quotes, historical prices, interactive charts, key statistics, analyst opinions, and financial statements. Without question, it is one of the best Web sites out there, and it's free! Go to it and enter a company's name in the "get quotes" box and see what you get. Also, click on "Investing," "News," and "Personal Finance."

Web Site: **CNNMoney.com**

Address: **money.cnn.com**

- Included on this Web site is up-to-date information on the stock market, including articles and prices, along with business news and personal finance.

Web Site: **Money 101—CNNMoney.com**

Address: **money.cnn.com/magazines/moneymag/money101/index.html**

- This is a small section of the CNNMoney.com Web site, but it has a wealth of information on personal finance. It will introduce you to the basics of investing, making a budget, asset allocation, and many other investment and personal finance topics.

Web Site: **The Motley Fool**

Address: **www.fool.com**

- The Motley Fool provides headline investment news and commentary, along with basic advice on investing and retirement.

Web Site: **EDGAR**

Address: **www.sec.gov/edgar.shtml**

- The Securities and Exchange Commission (the government group that oversees stock trading) provides free electronic access to statements, periodic reports, and other forms that firms are required to file.

The real value of these clubs is not what you might earn on your investment, but the knowledge and experience you gain from going through the investment process. With a club, you're often able to gain access to financial planners and investment advisors that you wouldn't be able to access as an individual. Once again, the more you know, the better off you are.

Summary

Identify and describe the primary and secondary securities markets.

The primary securities market is where new securities are sold. A new issue of IBM stock would be considered a primary market transaction. Actually, the primary markets can be divided into two other markets: those for initial public offerings (IPOs) and those for seasoned new issues. An initial public offering is the first time the company's stock is traded publicly. Seasoned new issues are stock offerings by companies that already have common stock traded in the market.

Securities that have previously been issued are traded in the secondary markets. Many securities in secondary markets are traded on organized exchanges, which actually occupy a physical location. The New York Stock Exchange is the oldest of all the organized exchanges, dating back over 200 years. The American Stock Exchange is the second most important of the organized exchanges. The OTC market, in which transactions are conducted over telephone or via a computer hookup, is a highly automated nationwide computer network that allows brokers to see up-to-the-minute price quotes on roughly 35,000 securities and execute trades on those securities.

Trade securities using a broker.

Common stocks are sold in lots or groups of 100 shares on the New York Stock Exchange—this is referred to as a round lot. Orders involving between 1 and 99 shares of stock are referred to as odd lots, and are processed by "odd lot dealers" who buy and sell out of their inventory.

An investor must specify a time period for which the order will remain outstanding. Alternatives include day orders, which expire at the end of the trading day during which they were made; open orders, also called good-till-canceled (GTC) orders, which remain effective until filled; and fill-or-kill orders, which, if not filled immediately, expire.

Investors can specify the price they want to trade on. A market order is simply an order to buy or sell a set number of securities immediately at the best price available. A limit order specifies that the trade is to be made only at a certain price or better. A stop-loss order is an order to sell if the price drops below a specified level or to buy if the price climbs above a specified level.

Investors have a choice of whether to pay cash or borrow from their broker. Investors with cash accounts pay in full for their security purchases, with the payment due within 3 business days of the transaction. Investors with margin accounts borrow a portion of the purchase price from their broker. Short selling involves borrowing stocks from your broker and selling them with an obligation to replace the stocks later. Then, if the price goes down, you buy them back, make a profit, and return the stocks to your broker.

Locate and use several different sources of investment information to trade securities.

If you're going to make informed investment decisions, you have to seek investment information, read it, and interpret it. Fortunately, you don't have to do your own research. That's already done for you, and it's available from the companies themselves, from brokerage firms, and from the press—magazines, newspapers, investment advisory services, and the Web. The Web is the first place you'll want to look, with new investment sites being added almost daily. This provides all investors with the same opportunities. Still, because there are no controls on who can post on the Web, you've got to be careful on where you get your information. You've also got to keep in mind that the agency problem abounds on the Internet. Much of what appears is self-serving in nature or may not be accurate. In addition, joining an investment club can also be a real learning experience and can provide you with access to investment research that you might not otherwise find.

Review Questions

1. What is a securities market? Does a market have to take the form of an actual building? Give an example to support your response.
2. What are the differences between the primary and secondary markets? Which market sells IPOs and seasoned new issues?
3. What two documents alert and inform the public about a pending security issue? What information is contained in each?
4. How does the performance of DynaVox, from Figure 12.1, support the idea that "investing" in IPOs may be a form of speculation?
5. Describe the difference between an over-the-counter market and an organized exchange. What types of stock are generally traded over the counter?
6. Differentiate between the "bid price" and the "ask price."
7. Financial advisors recommend international investments because they help diversify one's portfolio. Name another advantage and risk associated with international investments.
8. What is the difference between foreign shares and American Depository Receipts (ADRs)?
9. Name the two securities regulation organizations. What is their primary purpose for securities market regulation?
10. Much has been written about "insider-trading abuses." What is meant by this term? What two pieces of legislation have been enacted to curb insider-trading abuses?
11. What is "churning"? Why is this of concern to individual investors? What is a discretionary account? Who can make buy and sell decisions in such an account? Why might churning be of greater concern in a discretionary account?
12. What is a continuous market? What is the primary reason stock prices move up and down in a continuous market? Who stabilizes the price in this type of market and how do they accomplish it?
13. The timing of a securities transaction is very important. Differentiate among day orders, open orders, GTC orders, and fill-or-kill orders. In addition to the timing of orders, pricing instructions are also important. Differentiate among the following:
   a. Market order
   b. Limit order
   c. Stop-loss order

   Why would someone consider using a limit or stop-loss order?

14. What is short selling? Should the average investor consider using short selling techniques? Why or why not?

15. What is the primary benefit of an asset management account?

16. How do the services and costs vary with the different types of full-service, discount service, deep discount, and online brokerage accounts?

17. What happens if an investor receives a margin call? How would this relate to the margin requirement or the maintenance margin?

18. Why is **Principle 1: The Best Protection Is Knowledge** so important when choosing a broker?

19. What are the two primary methods of executing trades? What are the service and cost differences?

20. List five publications and three Web sites that can be used to gather financial news or research.

21. What are the major benefits of joining an investment club?

Develop Your Skills—Problems and Activities

These problems are available in MyFinanceLab.

1. After studying the fundamental trends from CDX Company's annual report, you have decided to purchase one round lot of the firm's stock on the open market. On Monday morning you call a stockbroker and ask for the price of CDX stock. The broker indicates that the bid price is $45.20, the ask price is $45.50, and the commission is $38.00. Assuming you wanted to place a market order to purchase shares, what is your cost per share, including the commission, and how much would you pay in total? What percentage of the total cost would you pay in commission?

2. Which securities market regulations deal with each of the following:
   a. Disclosure of relevant information on initial public offerings and registration with the FTC
   b. Created the Securities and Exchange Commission (SEC)
   c. Protected investors against unethical investment advisors by requiring advisors to register with the SEC
   d. Established disclosure and regulation of the mutual fund industry
   e. Established up to $500,000 of insurance to cover investors' account balances in the event that their brokerage firm goes bankrupt
   f. Made it illegal to trade securities while in the possession of inside information

3. Jale Batur, an active investor, recorded the following transactions in her brokerage account:

November 1	Bought 274 shares of OPP
November 7	Bought 50 shares of RSVP
November 11	Sold 150 shares of OPP
November 22	Bought 100 shares of TXBI
November 27	Sold 100 shares of OPP

   Which of the transactions would be considered a round lot? Which were odd-lot transactions?

4. Arianna just made another fantastic investment: She purchased 400 shares in Great Gains Corporation for $21.50 per share. Yesterday the stock closed at $56.50 per share. In order to lock in her gains she has decided to employ a stop-loss order. Assuming she set the order at $56, what is likely to happen? Why

might this not be a wise decision? At what price would you recommend setting the stop-loss order? Why?

5. Uncle John and Aunt Martha own 1,000 shares of AI Inc. in a brokerage account that is titled "John and Martha, Tenancy-in-Common." Explain how the assets would be handled if John passed away. What if both passed away simultaneously? Would these scenarios be different if the account was titled "John or Martha, Joint Tenancy with the Right of Survivorship"?

6. Assume you just purchased 250 shares of Home Depot at $40 per share, and 50 percent of this was purchased "on the margin." Fill in the blanks to determine your contribution to this transaction:

Total cost $_____
Amount borrowed   −_____
Contribution   =====

What would happen to your investment if the price of Home Depot stock rose to $50 per share (ignoring any possible dividends)?

Total value $_____
Loan   −_____
Margin   =====

What was your profit?

What would happen to your investment if the price of Home Depot stock fell to $30 per share (ignoring any possible dividends)?

Total value $_____
Loan   −_____
Margin   =====

What was your loss?

7. Consider the following transaction timeline for XYZ Corp.

November 12—open order placed for 500 shares
November 13—order filled at $25.25 per share
January 4—current market price $61.50 per share
January 5—stop-loss order placed at $55.00 per share
March 29—current market price $58.00 per share
April 2—all 500 shares XYZ Corp. sold at $55.00 per share
April 7—an additional 300 shares short sold at $49.00 per share
April 28—current market price $37.00 per share
May 30—short sell covered at $27.25 per share

Calculate the total amount earned or lost on all trades excluding any possible trading costs.

8. Determine which of the following two companies would be eligible for listing on the NYSE:

	Firm 1	Firm 2
Earnings before taxes for the last 3 years	$5 million	$11 million
Value of publicly held stock	$105 million	$80 million
Number of common shares	3 million	2.5 million
Number of holders of 100 shares	3,000	2,000

9. Last year you sold short 400 shares of stock selling at $90 per share. Six months later the stock had fallen to $45 per share. Over the 6-month period the company paid out two dividends of $1.50 per share. Your total commission cost for selling and buying the shares came to $125. Determine your profit or loss from this transaction.

10. Novice investors sometimes forget to account for trading costs when buying and selling stock. How much would a stock price need to increase (stated as a percentage) in order for Camerin to break even if he purchased stock for $500 and the commission was a flat $19.95 per trade?

Learn by Doing—Suggested Projects

1. Make a list of ten products and services that you use on a daily basis. Examples might include soft drinks, detergents, utilities, and textbooks. Next to each item on the list of products and services make a note of which company produced the good or service. Check online or Standard & Poor's or Value Line to determine the stock exchange on which the companies are traded and a recent closing stock price for them. Further review at least a 2-year price history. Did you notice any relevant trends that might lead to the recommended purchase or sale of stock? Explain your recommendations in a brief written or oral report.

2. Collect the ten most recent tombstone ads you can find using the *Wall Street Journal*. What investment banks consistently show up as underwriters and syndicate participants? Based on your sample of tombstone advertisements, what types of security issues are being offered? As an investor, do you find tombstone advertisements very useful?

3. Using the information from project 2 and information found on the Internet, write a one-page paper on why these types of advertisements are used. Support your answer with information provided in the Securities Act of 1933.

4. Using your local phone book or online listings obtain a list of stockbrokers, financial planners, and investment advisors in your area (check the Yellow Pages using the foregoing titles). Either call or look at their Web sites to determine how each is compensated. Does their compensation method impact your level of trust? Why?

5. Obtain the phone number of a deep discount broker from a personal finance magazine or through an Internet search. Using the five questions presented in Checklist 12.1, "Choosing a Brokerage Firm," as a basis for questioning, interview the discount brokerage firm's representative. Based on the information provided in the interview, does the firm appeal to you? Why or why not?

6. This chapter has pointed out that within the scheme of things at most brokerage firms, small investors fit very "low on the totem pole." Why do you think this is? In terms of receiving timely and unique investment advice, what do you think being "low man on the totem pole" means for you? How might you be able to compensate and "level the playing field"?

7. Some investors continue to hold stock certificates as proof of ownership, but most investors hold their securities in a broker's street name. Ask a relative or friend who owns stocks if they hold the certificates directly or if the certificates are held in a broker's street name, and determine why your friend or relative made this choice. This chapter describes one possible disadvantage of leaving securities in the street name. Do you think this was a consideration in the person's choice?

8. Did you know that every publicly owned and traded company in the United States is required by law to provide both a quarterly and an annual report to anyone who asks for one? Contact a publicly owned company for its annual report or find the annual report on Edgar-online. In looking at the report, do you see any noticeable trends in sales, profits, and dividends? What other useful information is contained in the report? Given your newfound knowledge, would you purchase shares in the company? Why?

9. In this chapter you learned about "churning." However, this is not the only market abuse. Go online to the FINRA compliance homepage (**http://finra.complinet.com/ finra/**) to research other abuses that the FINRA regulates. Write a short report on your findings.

10. To learn more about online brokerage services and fees, visit **www.fool.com**. Click on the "How to Invest" tab and select the "Find a Broker" link and then visit the Discount Broker Center. Use the information you find to make an informed decision about online brokerages. Which brokerage most closely fits your needs? Which one offers the widest range of services? Which one has the lowest cost structure? Do any of the services not offer mutual funds? Is this a deterrent from using that service? Why? Report on your findings in a small group discussion.

Be a Financial Planner—Discussion Case 1

These problems are available in MyFinanceLab.

Miles heard about a fantastic restaurant chain that is issuing an initial public offering (IPO), so he took Dollie to try one of the nearby restaurants. To say the least, they loved it. The restaurant specializes in Thai food and Turkish coffee. According to the tombstone advertisement, the underwriting syndicate appears very reputable. Miles thinks that this opportunity may be the next JetBlue and thinks that buying stock in the IPO is almost a sure thing. Dollie isn't quite so convinced because she reasons that if the investment was such a sure thing, why would she and Miles get a shot at the deal? Miles and Dollie have a brokerage account worth $20,000. They are thinking of investing at least $5,000 in the IPO. What advice would you give Miles and Dollie?

Questions

1. Is Miles correct in thinking that an IPO will dramatically increase in value?
2. What risks might Miles be overlooking when he envisions huge profits?
3. How easy is it for small investors to invest in an IPO? Why might this be the case?
4. Given the lack of information available to small investors about most IPOs, as well as the information you learned in Chapter 11, would you consider IPOs to be investments or speculation? How would you explain this to Dollie and Miles?
5. Based on your perception of risk and return in relation to IPOs, what would you recommend to Miles and Dollie?

Be a Financial Planner—Discussion Case 2

These problems are available in MyFinanceLab.

Hasit and Chandni Kumar are in their early 40s and until now they have always kept their savings in the bank. They liked the idea that a deposit in a bank was insured and guaranteed and that, regardless of what happened in the economy or to the bank, they could always get their money. Hasit and Chandni recently talked with a stockbroker about funding their retirement. The stockbroker pointed out that in terms of reaching their retirement goals, a bank account does not pay enough interest. The broker recommended that they invest in a combination of stocks, bonds, mutual funds, and money market accounts. Both are skeptical about the ultimate safety of their investments. Specifically, Hasit is worried about what would happen to their securities and cash if the brokerage firm went bankrupt, and Chandni is concerned that the markets are rigged and that only those with inside information ever make any money. Both are equally concerned that the markets are unregulated gambles and that there is no way to regulate the ethics of brokers. They've come to you for some advice on what to do.

Questions

1. Should Hasit be concerned about the lack of insurance in his brokerage account? Is there a specific securities act you could cite to back up your answer?

2. Chandni is concerned about insider trading. Do you agree with Chandni's concerns? Why or why not?

3. Name two securities acts that protect investors in terms of regulation. Also name two organizations that oversee the securities markets and the actions of investors.

4. In working with a broker, what should Hasit and Chandni watch for that might lead them to conclude that the broker is not working for their best interest?

5. Provide Hasit and Chandni a list of questions to ask potential brokers to assure the Kumars they will receive the best service at the lowest costs.

6. Hasit and Chandni are considering bypassing the broker and going directly online to trade. What cautions would you share with them? What is the difference between online investing and day trading?

7. If an account titling option is available, would you recommend that Hasit and Chandni own their account as tenants-in-common or as joint tenants with rights of survivorship? Why? What is the primary difference in the two account titling options?

CHAPTER 13

Investing in Stocks

Learning Objectives

Invest in stocks.

Read stock quotes online or in the newspaper.

Classify common stock according to basic market terminology.

Determine the value of stocks.

Employ different investment strategies.

Understand the risks associated with investing in common stock.

Anne Scheiber was a quiet woman who lived alone in a studio apartment in Manhattan. She never traveled; she never bought furniture; she never ate out; she didn't spend money on new clothes. In fact, neighbors claim that when they saw her outside her apartment, which was rare, she always wore the same black coat and hat.

All her life, Anne Scheiber did not attract much attention. But that changed dramatically upon her death in 1995 at 101. In her will, Scheiber revealed that she had a $22 million fortune, almost all of which she bequeathed to Yeshiva University, a small New York school. And by 2002, when the Yeshiva administration finally began to distribute her gift, it had grown to over $36 million. This gift came as a huge surprise, not only because Scheiber had appeared humble, but also because she hadn't attended Yeshiva and, in fact, was totally unknown at the university.

Although the idea of a seemingly poor person leaving a huge fortune to an institution she'd never even visited is fascinating, how Anne Scheiber amassed her fortune is even more interesting. She began her career working as an auditor for the IRS, earning $3,150 per year. In her position she had the opportunity to scrutinize the investment habits of many of the wealthy people she audited.

Over time, Scheiber noticed that most of the fortunes of the wealthy were based on common stock investments. She decided that if it worked for the wealthy, it could work for her, too. When she retired in 1943, Scheiber invested her $5,000 nest egg entirely in common stocks.

At first she stuck to companies she knew, beginning with the popular movie studios Universal and Paramount. Next she bought shares in the then small soft drink companies Coca-Cola and PepsiCo, as well as in a number of drug companies, including Bristol-Myers Squibb and Schering-Plough, which were also small companies at the time.

She continued to dabble in stocks throughout her life. In her later years Scheiber only rarely ventured out of her apartment, usually to see her stockbroker or to read the *Wall Street Journal* at the local library. (In keeping with her frugal ways, she never actually bought the paper.) From 1943 until her death, Anne Scheiber's stock holdings increased in value over 4,000-fold, making her a multimillionaire. One of her best investments was the purchase of 1,000 shares of Schering-Plough for which she paid $10,000 in 1950 and sold in 1994 for over $4 million.

Anne Scheiber may not have lived like a millionaire, but she certainly invested like one. However, even without Scheiber's investing skill, it was not difficult to make money in the stock market if you'd begun investing 60 years ago. For example, if you invested $100 in the common stock a of a typical firm listed on the New York Stock Exchange on the last day of 1950, over the next 60 years it would have grown to $49,151!

Clearly, you can earn serious gains in the stock market, and it doesn't take 60 years. For example, from the end of 1994 through 1999, an investment of $10,000 would have grown to about $28,500! Five years isn't that long to wait to almost triple your money, is it? However, as we've said again and again, investing in the stock market is not without risk: During 2008 stocks dropped by about 38 percent, and at one point were down by around 50 percent! Investing in the stock market is all about risk and return, how to eliminate some of that risk, and sometimes about making a fortune.

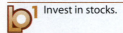 Invest in stocks.

Why Consider Stocks?

Just how does investing in stocks generate returns? When you buy common stock, you purchase a small part of the company. When the company does well, you do well and receive a small part of the profits. If the company does poorly, either you receive no return or you lose money.

Returns from shares of stocks come in the form of dividends and capital appreciation. Remember from Chapter 11 that a *dividend* is a company's distribution of profits to its stockholders. It can be in the form of cash or more company stock, but it's always a liquid asset you can use right away. Capital appreciation refers to an increase in the selling price of your shares of stock, perhaps as the company's earning prospects improve. You can't benefit from capital appreciation until you actually sell your stock.

Neither dividends nor capital appreciation is guaranteed with common stocks. Dividends are paid only when the company earns a profit, and even then they are paid only at the company's discretion. For example, Microsoft, which is consistently profitable, didn't pay dividends for its first 18 years. Capital appreciation takes place only when the company does well, and success is hard to predict. Look, for example, at what happened during the last week of March and first week of April 2011 to the common stock of Horizon Lines, the shipping firm. On March 29th it fell by over 47 percent—then, just about a week later, on April 7th, it jumped up in price by about 29 percent. Stock prices can jump up and down for many reasons or for what appears to be no reason at all.

So why consider investing in stocks? For these reasons:

◆ **Over time, common stocks outperform all other investments.** Although stocks aren't guaranteed to give you any return, they *usually* give you a great return. Figure 13.1 compares the returns on various investments over the period 1951–2010. Common stock clearly blows away the alternatives and exceeds the inflation rate by a wide margin.

◆ **Stocks reduce risk through diversification.** When you include different types of investments that don't move (experience changes in returns) perfectly together over time in your portfolio, you're able to reduce the risk in your portfolio. Stocks move differently than other investments such as bonds and different stocks move in different ways. Holding several types of stock can greatly reduce your risk.

◆ **Stocks are liquid.** You can't be assured of what you'll get when you want to sell your stock, but you won't have difficulty selling it. The secondary markets for common stock are extremely well developed and, as such, you will be able to sell your stock whenever you want with minimum transaction costs.

◆ **The growth in your investment is determined by more than just interest rates.** With some investments, the potential for price appreciation is largely a function of interest rates going down. With common stock, you're not a slave to interest

FIGURE 13.1 Growth of $100 Invested in Different Asset Classes, 1951–2010

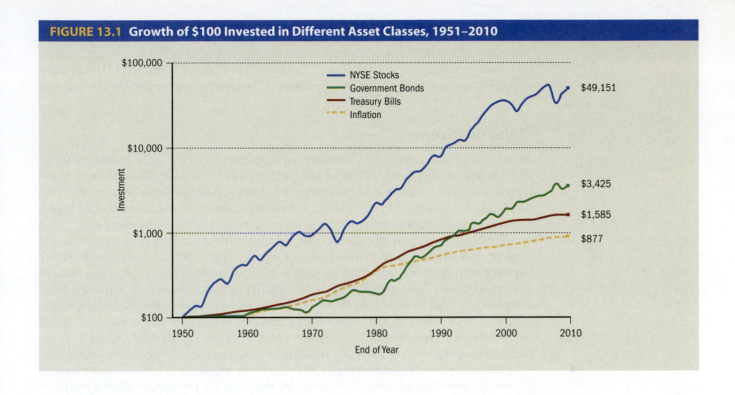

rates. Sure, a change in interest rates can and often will affect your stock prices. However, the earning prospects and performance of the firm will also affect stock prices. If you hitch your star to a company that performs well, you can make money even when interest rates jump.

Once you've made the plunge, you'll want to watch over your investment. Checklist 13.1 provides a number of questions you'll want to consider as your investment progresses.

Now that you know why stocks make good investments, let's take a look at some stock basics.

The Language of Common Stocks

If you're going to invest in common stocks, you certainly ought to know a bit about them and your rights as a common stockholder. Let's look at some specifics.

CHECKLIST 13.1

Investment Progress Checklist

◆ Is the return on my investment meeting my expectations and goals? Is this investment performing as I was led to believe it would?
◆ Is the company making money? How is it doing compared to its competitors?

◆ How much money will I get back if I sell my investment today?
◆ How much am I paying in commission or fees?
◆ Have my goals changed? If so, are my investments still suitable?
◆ What criteria will I use to decide when to sell?

Limited Liability

Although as a common stockholder you're considered one of the many actual owners of the corporation, your liability in the case of bankruptcy is limited to the amount of your investment. The most you can lose, if the company goes broke, is what you invest.

Claim on Income

As owners of the corporation, common stockholders have the right to any earnings that are left after all debt and other obligations have been paid. The dividend is the typical way to distribute these earnings, but the corporation isn't obligated to pay dividends to its stockholders. Instead, the board of directors decides whether to pay dividends or whether to reinvest the leftover earnings back into the company.

Obviously, common stockholders benefit from the distribution of income in the form of dividends. But they also benefit from the reinvestment of earnings. How? Plowing earnings back into the firm results in an increase in the value of the firm, in its earning power, and in its future dividends. These increases in turn cause the price of the common stock to rise. In effect, leftover earnings are distributed directly to the common stockholder in the form of dividends, or indirectly in the form of capital appreciation on the common stock. However, if after paying off debt and other monetary obligations the company has no leftover earnings, the stockholders get zilch.

Although most corporations pay dividends on a quarterly basis, common stock dividends aren't automatic. They must be declared by the corporation's board of directors. On the **declaration date**, the board of directors announces the size of the dividend, which is expressed as the dividend per share, the ex-dividend date, and the payment date.

Because companies need to know who actually owns their stock before they can pay a dividend, they set a cutoff date known as the **ex-dividend date**. On the ex-dividend date, the stock begins trading "without dividend"—that is, if you buy it after the ex-dividend date, you don't get the dividend for that year. On the payment date, the corporation sends out dividend checks to stockholders.

Claims on Assets

When a company does well and has a lot of earnings to distribute, common stockholders receive their share only after the company's creditors are paid. What happens when a company does so poorly that it goes bankrupt? Well, common stockholders are stuck waiting in line again. The creditors have the right to sell off the remaining company assets to regain their money. Only after the claims of the creditors have been paid off do stockholders get to sort through the rubble and try to extract the money they invested. Unfortunately, when companies do go bankrupt, the stockholders are usually plain out of luck.

Voting Rights

Common stockholders are entitled to elect the company's board of directors. Usually, one share of stock equals one vote, although some, but not many, companies issue different "classes" of stock with greater or less voting power. Common stockholders not only have the right to elect the board but also must approve any changes in the charter, or the rules that govern the corporation.

Voting for directors and charter changes occurs at the corporation's annual meeting. Stockholders may attend the meeting and vote in person, but most vote by proxy. A **proxy** is a legal agreement to allow a designated party to vote for a stockholder at the corporation's annual meeting. A proxy vote doesn't mean filling out a voting

Declaration Date
The date on which the board of directors announces the size of the dividend, the ex-dividend date, and the payment date.

Ex-Dividend Date
The date on which the stock "goes ex," meaning it begins trading in the secondary market "without dividend." In other words, if you buy the stock after its ex-dividend date, you don't get the dividend.

Proxy
A legal agreement a stockholder signs to allow someone else to vote for him or her at the corporation's annual meeting.

form and asking your buddy to hand it in for you. Rather, a proxy vote gives your buddy the right to make decisions for you. Usually the firm's management goes after and gets most of the proxy votes. However, in times of financial distress or when management takeovers are threatened, *proxy fights* occur. Proxy fights are battles for proxy votes between rival groups of shareholders who want to take control of the company or aim it in a new direction.

Stock Splits

Occasionally a firm may decide that its stock price is getting too high for the smaller investor to consider purchasing. To keep the price down and thereby encourage more investors to buy, the company "splits the stock." A **stock split** involves substituting more shares for the existing shares of stock. In effect, the number of shares of stock outstanding increases without there being any increase in the market value of the firm. As a result, each share of stock is worth less.

For example, let's assume you own 100 shares of Coca-Cola common stock and that it's just reached $120 per share. Your investment is worth $12,000. The management of Coca-Cola believes that $120 per share is more than the average small investor can afford and wants the price lowered. Coca-Cola's managers decide to split the stock three for one. Thus, investors receive three shares of new Coca-Cola stock for every share of "old" Coca-Cola common stock that they own. There's no gain in wealth to the stockholder, so each new share of stock would be worth $40 ($120/3). You now own 300 shares of Coca-Cola stock, which is selling at $40 per share, but your total investment is still worth $12,000.

Stock Split
Increasing the number of stock shares outstanding by replacing the existing shares of stock with a given number of shares. For example, in a two-for-one split, for every share of existing stock you hold, you would receive two shares of new stock.

> **FACTS of LIFE**
> Berkshire Hathaway's "A" stock has never split. As a result, in mid-2011 one share of its stock was selling at a price of over $120,000 per share.

Stock Repurchases

Sometimes companies buy back their own issued shares of common stock in what's called a **stock repurchase**. This results in fewer shares outstanding, so each remaining stockholder owns a larger proportion of the firm. Stock repurchases are extremely common, with well over 1,000 of these plans announced during most years. For example, for the fiscal year ending January 2011 Walmart spent almost $15 billion repurchasing, or buying back, 257 million shares of its own stock.

Stock Repurchase
A company's repurchasing, or buying back, of its own common stock.

Book Value

The book value of a company is calculated by subtracting the value of all the firm's liabilities from the value of its assets, as given on its balance sheet. To relate book value more easily to the price of the stock, divide the company's book value by the number of shares it has outstanding to get the book value per share.

Book value is a historical number. That is, it reflects the value of the firm's assets when they were purchased, which may be vastly different from their value today. For a firm whose assets were purchased a number of years ago, book value has little or no meaning. Still, this measure of value is often talked about and used in valuing stock.

Earnings Per Share

Earnings per share reflects the level of earnings achieved for every share of stock. Because it focuses on the return earned by the common stockholder, it looks at earnings after preferred stock dividends have been paid.

Preferred stock dividends are subtracted from net income because, as we will see in the next chapter, they're paid before common stock dividends are paid. Net income less preferred stock dividends is available to the common stockholders.

This figure tells investors how much they've earned on each share of stock they own—but not necessarily how much the company will pass along in dividends. This figure is available in the daily stock price listings in most newspapers and can be used to compare the financial performance of different companies. Earnings per share are calculated as follows:

$$\text{earnings per share} = \frac{\text{net income} - \text{preferred stock dividends}}{\text{number of shares of common stock outstanding}}$$

Dividend Yield

Dividend Yield
The ratio of the annual dividends to the market price of the stock.

The **dividend yield** on a share of common stock is the amount of annual dividends divided by the market price of the stock. The dividend yield tells investors how much in the way of a return they would receive if the stock price and dividend level remain constant. For example, if the price of the stock is $50 and it pays $4 per share in dividends, the dividend yield would be 8 percent ($4/$50 = 8%).

Many companies that have tremendous growth possibilities choose to reinvest their earnings rather than pay them out in dividends. As a result, many growth companies simply don't pay dividends. For example, for many years, Microsoft didn't pay dividends, but instead reinvested its earnings, which have now given it the ability to either pay large dividends or buy back its own stock at hefty prices.

> **FACTS of LIFE**
>
> Warren Buffett on excessive trading: "We believe that according the name 'investors' to institutions that trade actively is like calling someone who repeatedly engages in one-night stands a 'romantic.'"

Market-to-Book or Price-to-Book Ratio

The market-to-book or price-to-book ratio is a measure of how highly valued the firm is. When interpreting this ratio, remember that book value reflects historical costs and, as such, may not be overly meaningful. This ratio is calculated as follows:

$$\text{market-to-book ratio} = \frac{\text{stock price}}{\text{book value per share}}$$

Most stocks have market-to-book ratios above 1.0, and they commonly range up to about 2.5.

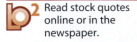 **2** Read stock quotes online or in the newspaper.

Stock Market Index
A measure of the performance of a group of stocks that represent the market or a sector of the market.

Stock Indexes: Measuring the Movements in the Market

Every day you hear financial reports on television or the radio in which someone says: "The market was up today as the Dow rose 27 points." Did you ever wonder just what that person was talking about? "The Dow" is a **stock market index** that measures the performance of various stock prices. There are several stock market indexes, and while they won't tell you exactly how each one of your investments performed, they will provide you with a simple way of measuring stock market performance in general. To understand stock listings and stock performance, you need to be familiar with the Dow and other market indexes.

The Dow

The oldest and most widely quoted of the stock indexes or averages is the **Dow Jones Industrial Average (DJIA),** or **Dow**, started by Charles Dow in 1896. The DJIA's original purpose was to gauge the sense or well-being of the market based on the performance of 12 major companies. The Dow is currently comprised of the prices of 30 large industrial firms, only one of which—General Electric—was in the original group of 12.

Because the DJIA is based on the movement of only 30 large, well-established stocks, many investors believe it reflects price movements for large firms rather than for the general market. Actually, these 30 stocks represent over 25 percent of the market value of the NYSE, making this average more representative than one might think at first glance.

However, the DJIA weights stocks based on their relative prices. As a result, when a high-priced stock moves a small amount, it has an inordinately large impact on the index. Even so, the DJIA does a relatively good job of reflecting market movements. As you can see in Figure 13.2, the DJIA has had its share of ups and down since 1990.

Dow Jones Industrial Average (DJIA) or Dow

A commonly used stock index or indicator of how well stocks have done. This index is comprised of the stock prices of 30 large industrial firms.

FIGURE 13.2 The Dow Jones Industrial Average (DJIA) Since 1990

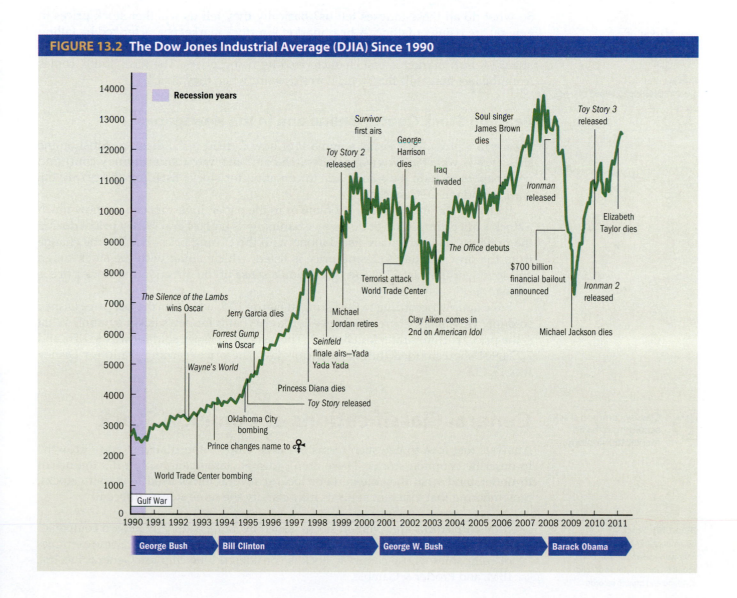

The S&P 500 and Other Indexes

Standard & Poor's 500 Stock Index or S&P 500
Another commonly used stock index or indicator of how well stocks have done based on the movements of 500 stocks, primarily from the NYSE.

Another well known stock market index is the **Standard & Poor's 500 Stock Index or S&P 500**. The S&P 500 is a much broader index than the DJIA, because it's based on the movements of 500 stocks, primarily from the NYSE, but also including some stocks from the AMEX and the over-the-counter (OTC) market. Because the S&P 500 is a broader index, it probably better represents movements in the overall market than does the Dow.

There is also the Russell 1000, which is made up of companies that rank in size from the 1st through 1,000th largest companies; the Russell 2000, which is made up of companies that rank in size from the 1,001st through the 3,000th largest companies; and the Wilshire 5000, which is a very broad-based index made up of stocks from the NYSE, the American Stock Exchange, and the NASDAQ. Also, the NYSE, the AMEX, and the NASDAQ all have indexes that chronicle the movements of their listed stocks, and Standard & Poor's calculates six other general indexes. Still, when investors talk about movements in the market, they generally refer to the Dow.

Market Movements

Bear Market
A stock market characterized by falling prices.

Bull Market
A stock market characterized by rising prices.

So what do all these indexes tell us? Basically they tell us whether stock prices in general are rising or falling. A **bear market** is a stock market characterized by falling prices. The term "bear" comes from the fact that bears swipe downward when they attack. A **bull market** is one characterized by rising prices. The term "bull" comes from the fact that bulls fling their horns upward when they attack.

Reading Stock Quotes Online and in the Newspaper

Figure 13.3 provides a visual summary of how to read NYSE listings. Most online sites (**www.wsj.com**, **www.marketwatch.com**, and **www.smartmoney.com**) and newspapers include the same basic information for stocks listed on the NYSE, the AMEX, and the OTC market.

By looking at the stock quote online or in the paper, investors can see how much a stock's price jumped up or down by examining its highest and lowest prices during the previous day, which are listed along with the closing price. Finally, the change from the previous day's closing price is listed, which, along with the stock's high and low over the past 52 weeks, gives you a sense of the direction the stock price is taking.

For example, according to the listing in Figure 13.3, what was the last price Disney sold for? How many shares traded yesterday? What is Disney's ticker symbol? What is the price/earnings ratio for Disney? (The last price Disney sold for was $41.76, and 7,274,904 shares traded during the prior day! The price/earnings ratio for Disney was 18.43.)

General Classifications of Common Stock

3 Classify common stock according to basic market terminology.

Analysts just love to use such terms as "blue chip," "speculative," and "growth" to describe common stocks. These aren't formal classifications, but it's important to understand what they mean. Let's look at several terms used to classify stocks, remembering that different analysts may classify the same stocks differently.

Blue-Chip Stocks
Common stocks issued by large, nationally known companies with sound financial histories of solid dividend and growth records.

◆ **Blue-chip stocks** are common stocks issued by large, nationally known companies with sound financial histories of solid dividend and growth records. Some examples of companies whose common stock is considered blue chip are General Electric, IBM, and Procter & Gamble.

FIGURE 13.3 How to Read Online Stock Quotes

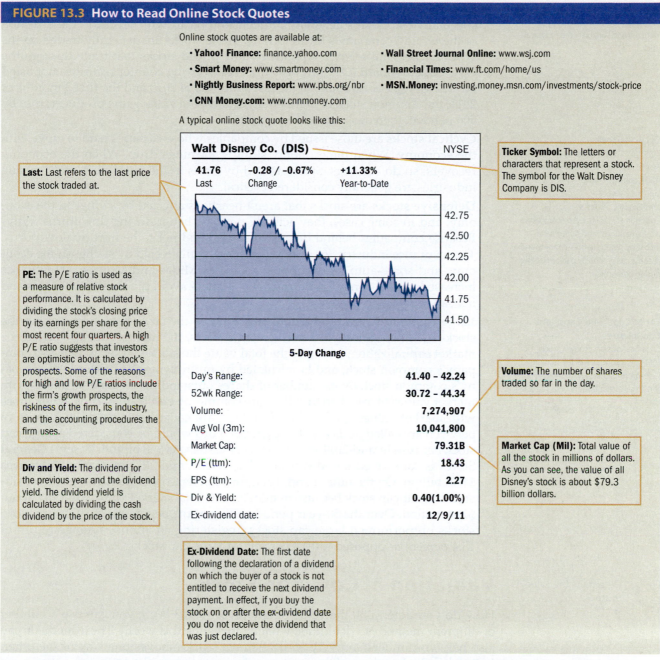

Online stock quotes are available at:

- **Yahoo! Finance:** finance.yahoo.com
- **Smart Money:** www.smartmoney.com
- **Nightly Business Report:** www.pbs.org/nbr
- **CNN Money.com:** www.cnnmoney.com
- **Wall Street Journal Online:** www.wsj.com
- **Financial Times:** www.ft.com/home/us
- **MSN.Money:** investing.money.msn.com/investments/stock-price

A typical online stock quote looks like this:

Walt Disney Co. (DIS)   NYSE

41.76	−0.28 / −0.67%	+11.33%
Last	Change	Year-to-Date

5-Day Change

Day's Range:	41.40 – 42.24
52wk Range:	30.72 – 44.34
Volume:	7,274,907
Avg Vol (3m):	10,041,800
Market Cap:	79.31B
P/E (ttm):	18.43
EPS (ttm):	2.27
Div & Yield:	0.40(1.00%)
Ex-dividend date:	12/9/11

Last: Last refers to the last price the stock traded at.

PE: The P/E ratio is used as a measure of relative stock performance. It is calculated by dividing the stock's closing price by its earnings per share for the most recent four quarters. A high P/E ratio suggests that investors are optimistic about the stock's prospects. Some of the reasons for high and low P/E ratios include the firm's growth prospects, the riskiness of the firm, its industry, and the accounting procedures the firm uses.

Div and Yield: The dividend for the previous year and the dividend yield. The dividend yield is calculated by dividing the cash dividend by the price of the stock.

Ticker Symbol: The letters or characters that represent a stock. The symbol for the Walt Disney Company is DIS.

Volume: The number of shares traded so far in the day.

Market Cap (Mil): Total value of all the stock in millions of dollars. As you can see, the value of all Disney's stock is about $79.3 billion dollars.

Ex-Dividend Date: The first date following the declaration of a dividend on which the buyer of a stock is not entitled to receive the next dividend payment. In effect, if you buy the stock on or after the ex-dividend date you do not receive the dividend that was just declared.

Source: Common information taken from finance.yahoo.com, www.smartmoney.com, www.pbs.org/nbr, www.cnnmoney.com, www.wsj.com, www.ft.com/home/us, and investing.money.msn.com/investments/stock-price.

◆ **Growth stocks** are issued by companies that have exhibited sales and earnings growth well above their industry average. Generally, these are smaller companies, and many times they are newly formed. These companies often pay very low or no dividends; instead, they retain earnings and plow those funds back into the company. An example of a company whose common stock is considered a growth stock is Microsoft, which began as a small company and has only recently begun paying dividends, though it has consistently posted huge increases in earnings.

◆ **Income stocks** are generally associated with more mature firms that pay relatively high dividends, with little increase in earnings. The stocks of most utilities are considered income stocks, because utilities generally pay relatively high dividends and don't experience much growth in earnings.

Growth Stocks
Common stocks issued by companies that have exhibited sales and earnings growth well above their industry average. Generally, these are smaller stocks, and many times they are newly formed.

Income Stocks
Common stocks issued by mature firms that pay relatively high dividends, with little increase in earnings.

Speculative Stocks
Common stocks that carry considerably more risk and variability than a typical stock.

Cyclical Stocks
Common stocks issued by companies whose earnings tend to move with the economy.

Defensive Stocks
Common stocks issued by companies whose earnings tend not to be affected by swings in the economy and in some cases actually perform better during downturns.

Large Caps, Mid Caps, and Small Caps
Classifications of common stock that refer to the size of the issuing firm–more specifically, to the level of the firm's capitalization, or its market value.

◆ **Speculative stocks** carry considerably more risk and variability. Moreover, with speculative stocks it's generally difficult to forecast with precision the direction of the issuing company's future profits. These stocks are generally traded on the OTC market, and many are relatively low priced stocks that trade through the OTC Bulletin Board (OTCBB), which serves over-the-counter securities not listed on NASDAQ. For example, in the last 3 months of 2010 and the first 3 months of 2011, the common stock of Left Behind Games, the video game producer, rose by 500 percent, then dropped by 85 percent.

◆ **Cyclical stocks** are those issued by companies whose earnings tend to move with the economy. When the economy slumps, earnings drop. When the economy recovers, so do earnings. Stocks issued by firms in the auto, steel, and housing industries are generally considered cyclical.

◆ **Defensive stocks** are stocks that aren't nearly as affected by swings in the economy, and in some cases, they actually perform better during downturns. Why? Because companies behind defensive stocks tend not to be hurt by downturns. The insurance industry, for example, is largely unaffected by swings in the economy, and some auto parts suppliers, such as Midas and Monroe, actually see increased sales during downturns as consumers avoid purchasing new cars and instead repair their present cars.

◆ **Large caps, mid caps, and small caps** refer to the size of the firm issuing the stock—more specifically, its market value. Thus, the market cap, also called the market capitalization, is simply the total value the stock market assigns to a company's common stock, and is calculated by multiplying the price of the company's common stock by its number of shares outstanding. In general, stocks with market values of less than $1 billion are commonly called small caps, while those with market values greater than $5 billion are called large caps—and those in between are called mid caps. For example, Ford would be considered a large-cap stock because in mid-2011 its total market value was $58 billion. Casey's General Stores is considered a mid-cap stock because in mid-2011 its market value was $1.48 billion. On the other hand, Bridgford Foods Corporation would be considered a small-cap stock because in mid-2011 its total market value was only about $104 million. Over the 50-year period ending at the beginning of 2011, small-cap stocks outperformed large-cap stocks, registering an annual average return of 13.4 percent as opposed to 10.8 percent for large-cap stocks.

 4 Determine the value of stocks.

Valuation of Common Stock

How do you determine the value of any investment? Well, you can use a number of different methods to determine what an investment is worth. These methods can also help you understand why an investment's price moves one way or the other. Let's take a look at three of the most popular valuation methods.

The Technical Analysis Approach

Technical Analysis
A method of stock analysis that focuses on supply and demand, using charts and computer programs to identify and project price trends for a stock or for the market as a whole.

Technical analysis focuses on supply and demand, using charts and computer programs to identify and project price trends for a stock or for the market as a whole. The logic behind technical analysis is that although economic factors are of great importance in determining stock prices, so are psychological factors, such as *greed* and *fear*.

Technical analysts believe that greed and fear reinforce trends in the market. Greed pushes investors to put their money in the market when the market is rising, and fear has them pull their money out if a downturn appears. In effect, no one wants to be the last aboard a market upturn, and no one wants to be the last out if the market is falling.

Technical analysis takes a number of forms, including the interpretation of charts and graphs and mathematical calculations of trading patterns, all aimed at spotting some trend or direction for stocks. Technical analysts might look into the past for trends or patterns that give some clue as to where investors might be heading. In addition, they might look for price levels where stock prices might get stuck. These price levels are referred to as resistance or support levels.

Unfortunately, although technical analysis may appeal to the novice investor, it's been found to be of little value. Although there appear to be distinct trends in past movements of the market, the problem comes in identifying these trends *before* they surface. Moreover, some of these patterns may have been useful in the past, but without any economic logic behind them, what's to say they'll continue to act as good predictors?

In short, technical analysis should be viewed as something to avoid because it encourages moving in and out of the market, which is dangerous, as opposed to simply buying and holding stocks.

The Price/Earnings Ratio Approach

The **price/earnings (P/E) ratio** is used regularly by security analysts as a measure of a stock's relative value. This price-earnings ratio, or earnings multiplier, is the price per share divided by the earnings per share. It's an indication of how much investors are willing to pay for a dollar of the company's earnings. The more positive investors feel about a stock's future prospects, or the less risk they feel the stock has, the higher the stock's P/E ratio.

Price/Earnings (P/E) Ratio
The price per share divided by the earnings per share. Also called the earnings multiple

For example, a stock that is currently selling for $104 with estimated earnings per share of $6.50 would have a P/E ratio of 16 ($104/$6.50). If the prospects for this stock improved—perhaps the company introduces a new product that in a few years should greatly increase profits—the stock price might rise to $130, which would be a new P/E ratio of 20 ($130/$6.50). A stock with a P/E ratio of 20 would be referred to as "selling at 20 times earnings." How do we use P/E ratios to value stocks? By deciding whether or not the stock's P/E ratio is too high or too low.

How do you determine an appropriate P/E ratio for a specific stock? First, you determine a justified P/E ratio for the market as a whole by looking at past market P/E ratios, taking into consideration the strength of the economy, interest rates, the deficit, and the inflation rate. This overall market P/E ratio is then adjusted depending on the specific prospects for the individual stock. For example, if the growth potential is above average, it is adjusted upward—but how much higher is the

STOP & THINK

Many analysts and investors use the market's P/E ratio as a measure of whether the market is overpriced or underpriced. In recent years they've viewed the average market P/E ratio as being in the 15 to 35 range. If the market's P/E ratio is much above this level, the market is overpriced, and if it's much below this level, the market is underpriced. However, keep in mind that anticipated inflation and the health of the economy and future corporate earnings play a major role in determining the market's P/E ratio. Do you think inflation will increase or decrease in the future?

real question. Although determining an appropriate or justified P/E ratio for a given stock is difficult, we can at least point to some of the factors that drive P/E ratios up and down:

◆ **The higher the firm's earnings growth rate, the higher the firm's P/E ratio.** In effect, the market values a dollar of earnings more if those earnings are expected to grow more in the future.
◆ **The higher the investor's required rate of return, the lower the P/E ratio.** If interest rates rise, or if the firm becomes more risky, the P/E ratio will fall. Likewise, if interest rates drop, or the firm becomes less risky, the P/E ratio should rise.

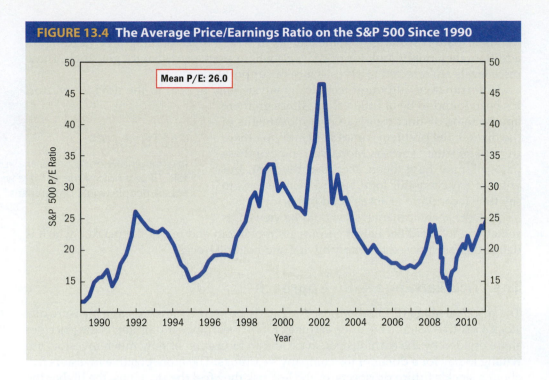

FIGURE 13.4 The Average Price/Earnings Ratio on the S&P 500 Since 1990

Figure 13.4 shows the average P/E ratio since 1990, which should give you an idea of a typical P/E ratio. In recent years, the average has been in the 15 to 35 range. The P/E ratio for growth stocks is much higher—generally beginning at 30 and going on up.

Because this valuation method focuses on such fundamental determinants as future earnings, expected levels of interest rates, and the firm's risk, it's considered to be a type of **fundamental analysis**.

Fundamental Analysis
Determining the value of a share of stock by focusing on such determinants as future earnings and dividends, expected levels of interest rates, and the firm's risk.

The Discounted Dividends Valuation Model

The value of any investment is the present value of the benefits or returns that you receive from that investment. When you purchase a share of common stock, you get dividend payments whenever they're declared, and then at some future point in time you generally sell the stock. Hopefully, you sell it for more than you purchased it for, thus receiving capital gains (the difference between what you purchased the stock for and what you sold it for).

Where does that price you're going to get when you sell your common stock come from? Well, it's based on what the buyer of your shares expects to earn from them: the future dividend payments plus some capital gains. When the buyer eventually sells the shares, the price he will receive for them is based on the next buyer's expectations of future dividend payments plus capital gains. This little exercise can be carried on ad nauseam. This illustrates that the value of a share of stock should be the present value of its future dividends. Moreover, companies can pay out those dividends forever, because common stock has no termination date. Of course, you'll be hoping for capital gains, too, but how much the stock rises in price will be based on what investors feel is going to happen to dividends in the future.

This is an important concept, but it's also one that's difficult for many students to understand, especially when you have stock in a firm such as Apple Computer, which isn't paying dividends right now. However, as Apple earns more and more, the level of its future dividends grows larger and larger, and its price should rise. The point to keep in mind is that earnings eventually turn into dividends, the company pays its shareholders in dividends, and those dividends go on forever.

Thus, the value of a share of common stock is the present value of the infinite stream of dividend payments. It can be written as follows:

$$\text{value of a share of common stock} = \text{present value of the infinite stream of future dividends}$$

When using the discounted dividends valuation model, determining the value of a share of common stock becomes a three-step process. First, we estimate the future dividends, then we estimate our required rate of return, and finally, we discount the dividends back to present values at the required rate of return. Estimating future dividends is a difficult task, however. This means that the answers we get from our valuation formula won't be overly reliable. That is, because the assumption we make might not be accurate, our conclusions might not be accurate. However, this method is still valuable for the insights and implications it yields as to what determines and affects stock prices. Also note that there are alternative valuation techniques available for valuing firms that do not pay dividends.

To simplify the calculations, we must assume that *dividends will grow at a constant rate forever*. Making this assumption, the value of a share of stock can be written as follows:

$$\text{value of common stock} = \frac{\text{dividends next year}}{\text{required rate of return} - \text{growth rate}}$$

Let's look at an example of a share of common stock expected to pay $5 in dividends next year. In addition, let's assume dividends are expected to grow at a rate of 4 percent per year forever, and that given the risk level of this common stock, the investor's required rate of return is 12 percent. Plugging this information into our stock valuation formula, we can calculate the value of the common stock as follows:

$$\text{value of common stock} = \frac{\text{dividends next year}}{\text{required rate of return} - \text{growth rate}}$$

$$= \frac{\$5}{0.12 - 0.04}$$

$$= \frac{\$5}{0.08} = \$62.50$$

Thus, the value of this stock is $62.50. If the stock is selling for less than its value, we should buy it. If it's selling for more than its value, we shouldn't buy it.

Although we now have a value for the share of stock, the formula we used to get it is very limited. In fact, if we try to take this formula and apply it to a company that hasn't paid any dividends in the past, it simply doesn't make sense.

Of course, we used a very simple and basic assumption about dividend values. In the real world, this "discounted dividends valuation model" is used by most major brokerage firms to estimate the value of common stock. However, when analysts use this approach, their calculations are much more complicated than ours. But both calculations are based on the same principles. For our purposes, though, even more important than the exact calculations are this model's implications about stock valuation.

STOP & THINK

Where do you get money to invest in stocks? One way is to use **Principle 9: Mind Games, Your Financial Personality, and Your Money** to help you out. People find it easier to save from a lump sum payment than from regular income. For example, if you earn $50,000 a year, it's tougher to save $10,000 if you are paid that $50,000 in 12 monthly payments than it would be if you were paid $40,000 in 12 monthly payments and another $10,000 as an end-of-year payment. That's because saving from your regular income requires more discipline. One way to overcome this is to have some of your salary automatically deposited in your investment fund. What do you think of this idea?

Why Stocks Fluctuate in Value

Although the assumptions we made with our discounted dividend valuation model limit its use as an accurate tool for valuing stocks, the model does help us understand the underlying factors that affect the price of a share of common stock. Let's examine these factors now.

Interest Rates and Stock Valuation   There's an inverse relationship between interest rates and the value of a share of common stock. As interest rates rise, investors demand a higher return on their common stock. As the required return rises, the present value of the future dividends declines. If you look at the common stock valuation equation, you can see that when required return increases, the value of the stock decreases, and when required return decreases, the value of the stock increases.

Keep in mind that as anticipated inflation declines, investors demand less in the way of a return for delaying consumption (remember **Principle 8: Risk and Return Go Hand in Hand**), and as a result, interest rates also drop. For example, in 1995 declining inflation resulted in a 2 percent drop in interest rates, which in turn saw stocks surge by 37 percent!

Risk and Stock Valuation   As the stock's risk increases, so does the investor's required rate of return. Again, we have to remember **Principle 8: Risk and Return Go Hand in Hand**. In the fall of 2008, the stock market crashed as the financial markets froze up and investors realized that the risk of an extended recession was greater than they thought earlier. As the $700 billion financial rescue plan was put in place, investors perceived there to be more risk in investing in stocks and sent stock prices plummeting. As a result, over the period from October 2007 to March 2009, U.S. stock prices dropped by 50 percent. Investors also felt that the risk of investing in the Russian stock market had increased dramatically; as a result, over that same period the Russian stock market dropped by over 60 percent! On the other hand, Family Dollar and Walmart both did quite well in 2008 as consumers turned to cheaper alternatives for their basic needs.

Earnings (and Dividend) Growth and Stock Valuation   Although the stock valuation equation uses dividend growth to determine value, most analysts think about value in terms of earnings. As earnings grow, so does the company's capacity to pay dividends. As a result, earnings growth is generally viewed as the *cause* of any increase in dividends.

There is a positive relationship between the expected growth rate for earnings and stock prices, which makes sense. As the firm earns more and is able to return more to its shareholders, the stock price should rise. Looking at our valuation equation, you can see that as the growth rate increases, the denominator decreases, and thus, the value of the stock should increase. Let's look back to the crash of 2008: As the economy slowed down, earnings and dividend growth also slowed, which in turn led to a drop in stock prices. In effect, the market crash in 2008 resulted from both an increased level in perceived risk and the expectations of a decrease in earnings and dividend growth in the future. As with changes in risk, different companies can experience changes in earnings and dividend growth that might impact different stocks in different ways.

> ### STOP & THINK
>
> It's a bit intimidating to think about all the analysis that you can do in selecting a stock. Fortunately, much of it's already done for you and it's available online. Take a look at MarketWatch's Investor Tools. Go to **http://www.marketwatch.com/** and click on the Tools & Research tab and you'll find a stock screener.

Stock Investment Strategies

There are several investment strategies you can follow when purchasing stock. As we take a look at a few of them, keep in mind that you can use more than one of these approaches at once. Still, you've got to be alert, especially when your money is on the line. Checklist 13.2 provides a number of things you should look out for.

Dollar Cost Averaging

Dollar cost averaging is the practice of purchasing a fixed dollar amount of stock at specified intervals. The logic behind dollar cost averaging is that by investing the same dollar amount each period instead of buying in one lump sum, you'll be averaging out price fluctuations by buying more shares of common stock when the price is lowest, and fewer shares when the price is highest.

Table 13.1 presents an example of dollar cost averaging, where the investor buys $500 worth of stock each quarter for 2 years instead of investing everything all at once. The reason the investor in this example did better with dollar cost averaging is that the market price bounced from $40 to $55, allowing the investor to buy more shares for the same amount of money when prices dipped.

Lucky people buy stocks when the price is low, and unlucky people buy when the price is high.

5 Employ different investment strategies

Dollar Cost Averaging
A strategy for purchasing common stock in which the investor purchases a fixed dollar amount of stock at specified intervals, for example, quarterly.

STOP & THINK

In a "Getting Going" column in the *Wall Street Journal* Jonathan Clements listed 41 signs that you've become a savvy investor and a smart saver. Sign number two was: "You get excited when stock prices fall." Keep in mind that you're trying to reach long-term goals and you should expect the market to rise and fall between now and then. When stock prices are low, you're buying more shares of stock with your investment dollars—after all, the lower stock prices are today, the easier it is to "buy low, and sell high." Remember, your goal is not to be rich today, but rich when you're ready to retire or meet whatever goal you're saving for. Why does this make sense?

CHECKLIST 13.2
Be Alert

Look out for:
- Recommendations from a sales representative based on "inside" or "confidential information," an "upcoming favorable research report," a "prospective merger or acquisition," or the announcement of a "dynamic new product."
- Telephone sales pitches; NEVER send money to purchase a stock (or other investment) based simply on a telephone sales pitch.
- Representations of spectacular profit, such as, "Your money will double in 6 months." Remember, if it sounds too good to be true, it is!
- "Guarantees" that you will not lose money on a particular securities transaction, or agreements by a sales representative to share in any losses in your account.
- An excessive number of transactions in your account. Such activity generates additional commissions for your sales representative, but may provide no better investment opportunities for you.
- A recommendation from your sales representative that you make a dramatic change in your investment strategy, such as moving from low-risk investments to speculative securities, or concentrating your investments exclusively in a single product.
- Pressure to trade the account in a manner that is inconsistent with your investment goals and the risk you want or can afford to take.

TABLE 13.1 Dollar Cost Averaging

Date	Dollar Cost Averaging, Investing $500 per Quarter					Lump-Sum Investment Buying 80 Shares at $50/Share
	Money Invested	Price	Shares Purchased	Total Shares Owned	Market Value	Market Value
Year 1, quarter 1	$500	$50	10.0	10.0	$500	$4,000
Year 1, quarter 2	500	46	10.9	20.9	961	
Year 1, quarter 3	500	40	12.5	33.4	1,336	
Year 1, quarter 4	500	50	10.0	43.4	2,170	
Year 2, quarter 1	500	55	9.1	52.5	2,888	
Year 2, quarter 2	500	45	11.1	63.6	2,862	
Year 2, quarter 3	500	50	10.0	73.6	3,680	
Year 2, quarter 4	500	52	9.6	83.2	4,327	
Total	$4,000	$48.50	83.2	83.2	$4,327	$4,160

The problem is that no one knows if a given price is going to be a high or a low, because you never know what stocks will do in the future. Dollar cost averaging's intent is to even out your luck by letting the highs and lows cancel each other out.

During the bull market of the 1990s, dollar cost averaging came under some criticism as an inefficient way to invest a lump sum in the market. This criticism centered on the fact that over time, stocks generally tend to rise in price. So if you have a lump sum of money to invest, it's better to get it into the market as soon as possible to get in on those rising prices. For example, look at the stock market from 1995 through the first half of 1999: It went no place but up. That means that the sooner investors got their money in the stock market, the more they made. In fact, history shows that over all the 12-month periods from 1926 through 1991, you would be better off investing in a lump sum 64.5 percent of the time. But with the bouncing around of stock prices in in the 2000s, the dollar cost averaging approach has regained much of its lost popularity.

In spite of all this, dollar cost averaging has merit. First, if you buy stock over an extended period, it's less likely that all your money will be invested right before a market crash. Second, dollar cost averaging keeps you from trying to time the market.

"Timing the market" is attempting to wait for the lowest possible price before buying. It's virtually impossible to do, although admittedly, it's awfully tempting to try. Moreover, in timing the market, an investor can wait and wait for the market to come down and miss a major upturn. That's pretty much the case from 1995 through the first half of 1999—if you were looking for a low point in the market to invest, you never would have entered the market. And very few investors entered the market in March 2009 after it had dropped by 50 percent in less than a year and a half. At that point most people simply couldn't afford to lose any more money in the stock market, and it was also a time when doomsayers were predicting another 50 percent drop in the market. In effect, market timing is similar to an antigravity machine—a great idea, but making it work is the problem. Third, and most important, dollar cost averaging forces investing discipline. You are investing in stocks regularly, and investing becomes part of your budgeting and planning process.

Buy-and-Hold Strategy

As you might guess, a **buy-and-hold** investment strategy involves buying stock and holding it for a period of years. There are four reasons why such a strategy is worth considering. First, it aims at avoiding timing the market. By buying and holding the stock, the ups and downs that occur over shorter periods become irrelevant. Second, the buy-and-hold strategy minimizes brokerage fees and other transaction costs. Constant buying and selling really racks up the charges, but buying and holding has only the charge of buying. By keeping these costs down, the investor retains more of the stock's returns. Third, holding and not selling the stock postpones any capital gains taxes. The longer you can go without paying taxes, the longer you hold your money, and the longer you have to reinvest and earn returns on your returns. Finally, a buy-and-hold strategy means your gains will be taxed as long-term capital gains.

Buy-and-Hold

An investment strategy that involves simply buying stock and holding it for a period of years.

> ### STOP & THINK
>
> If you employ a buy-and-hold strategy while buying stock using the dollar cost averaging method, a downturn in the market isn't necessarily bad. It simply means that when you're buying, you're getting more shares of stocks. Dollar cost averaging is best served by a market that doesn't climb steadily but bounces up and down. Does dollar cost averaging work as well if stocks only move up?

Dividend Reinvestment Plans (DRIPs)

If you want to use common stock to accumulate wealth, you must reinvest rather than spend your dividends. Without reinvesting, your accumulation of wealth will be limited to the stock's capital gains. Unfortunately, many dividends may be small enough that you figure you might as well spend them on a pack of Juicy Fruit rather than reinvest them. Hey, you don't need to pay a brokerage fee to buy Juicy Fruit.

One way to avoid buying too much gum and not enough stock is through a **dividend reinvestment plan, or DRIP**. Under a dividend reinvestment plan, you're allowed to reinvest the dividend in the company's stock automatically without paying any brokerage fees. Most large companies offer such plans, and many stockholders take advantage of them. For example, nearly 40 percent of all PepsiCo stockholders participate in dividend reinvestment plans.

Dividend Reinvestment Plan (DRIP)

An investment plan that allows the investor to automatically reinvest stock dividends in the same company's stock without paying any brokerage fees.

A dividend reinvestment plan is a great way to let your savings grow, but it's not without drawbacks. The major drawback is that when you sell your stock, you'll have to figure out your income taxes—and that can be overwhelming. Each time you reinvest dividends, you're effectively buying additional shares of stock at a different price. Moreover, even though you don't receive any cash when your dividends are reinvested, you still have to pay income tax as if you actually received those dividends.

A final drawback is the fact that you can't choose what to do with your own dividend. What if the company you've invested in is performing moderately well, and you just heard about another company whose stock price is rising faster than the blood pressure of a fat man with a love of salt? You're stuck reinvesting instead of trying something new.

> ### STOP & THINK
>
> Trying to time the market to move in and out of it can be dangerous. The danger lies in missing upturns. For example, a $1,000 investment in stocks at the beginning of 1990 grew to $4,840 by year-end 2009. However, that same $1,000 investment would have only grown to $2,040 if it missed the 10 best months of stock returns. Are you surprised?
>
>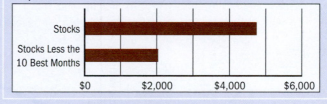

Despite these drawbacks, dividend reinvestment plans appeal to many investors. Two sources of companies offering DRIPs are Standard & Poor's *Directory of Dividend Reinvestment Plans* and Evergreen Enterprises' *Directory of Companies Offering Dividend Reinvestment Plans*, both of which may be available at your library.

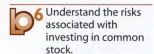

6 Understand the risks associated with investing in common stock.

P8 Principle

Risks Associated with Common Stocks

In Chapter 11 we examined several different sources of risk associated with investing in all securities. Stocks have more risk than other investments, but they also have more potential return. You should already know something about risk and return from **Principle 8: Risk and Return Go Hand in Hand**. Let's take another look at this principle and explore the relationship between stocks and risk to see if we can lower our risk without impacting our return.

Another Look at Principle 8: Risk and Return Go Hand in Hand

We can view stocks as being at the upper end of the risk–return line as shown in Figure 13.5. Watching the DJIA drop by 20 percent during the first 10 days of October 2008, and 40 percent over the previous year, reminds us of the risk associated with common stock. Without those risks, you wouldn't expect the high returns that common stocks provide. Thus, there's a great deal of potential risk if the firm does poorly, and a great deal of potential return if the firm does well.

Fortunately, as we learned in **Principle 8**, you can eliminate much of the risk associated with common stock simply by diversifying your investments. In this way, when one of your stocks goes bust, another investment soars, making up for the loss. Basically, diversification lets you iron out the ups and downs of investing. You don't experience the great returns, but you don't experience the great losses either.

However, when all stocks move in the same direction, as we saw with the October 2008 market crash, diversification simply among stocks doesn't work as well. However, if you had a balanced portfolio of 60 percent stocks, 40 percent bonds, your 12-month loss would have been cut by almost one-half.

Most stocks move up and down when the market as a whole moves up and down. There's an old saying on Wall Street, "a rising tide lifts all boats," meaning when the stock market goes up, it's good for all stocks, and they all seem to rise in value. But when all stocks move up, some tend to move up more than others, and when the stock market moves down, some stocks fall down farther. To measure the movements of an individual stock relative to the movements of the S&P 500 we use **beta**, which can be found in Value Line and other investment publications. The beta for the market is 1.0—that's the benchmark against which specific stock betas are measured. A stock that moves up and down more than the S&P 500 would have a beta greater than 1.0, and a stock that moves up and down less than the S&P 500 would have a beta less than 1.0.

Beta
The measure of of how responsive a stock or portfolio is to changes in the market portfolio, such as the S&P 500 Index.

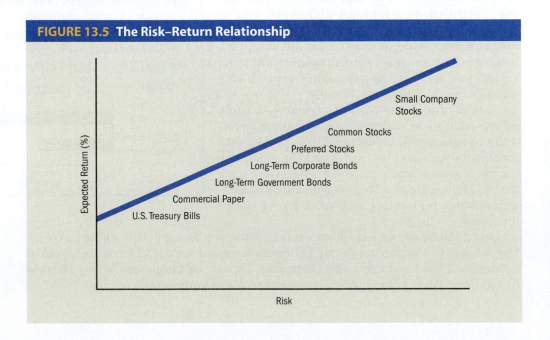

FIGURE 13.5 The Risk–Return Relationship

MONEY MATTERS

Tips from Marcy Furney, ChFC, Certified Financial Planner™

A FOOL AND HIS MONEY

If you are a beginning investor and subject to the adrenaline rush of success, you may fall victim to some of the more complicated and even questionable investment vehicles and strategies. More and more companies are buying prime television time to tell you how you can quickly multiply your money. Remember the caution, "If it looks too good to be true, it probably is," especially when considering the following:

Options (also known as puts and calls). Brokers may tell you that options can multiply the returns on a stock you own (a long position) with only moderate risk. Maybe, maybe not. Options are simply opportunities to buy/ sell stocks at a future date for a particular price. You are essentially betting on a move in the price of the stock. Amateurs should stay away. On some options, the most you can lose is the price you paid for them.

Commodities. Fuel oil, cocoa, wheat, the infamous pork bellies, and many other items are staples in the commodity market. Brokers must have special securities licenses to sell them, and the risks are huge. This is not the place for your kids' college money. Again, you gamble on moves in prices and the potential loss is almost limitless.

Limited partnerships. Though there may be a few good ones, many people still hold the remnants of limited partnerships at values far below what they paid. Such "investments" were sold at one time as tax breaks with big losses in the early years. Now some investors are paying extra taxes and penalties for disallowed deductions. The general partner and the underlying property or objective drive the success of the partnership. There is a very limited secondary market for these holdings.

Gold and precious metals. Besides being offered as an inflation hedge, gold is being sold as the only viable means of exchange in the case of full economic collapse. If you believe that is true, buy it for that purpose, but don't buy simply out of fear. Investigate the assaying and storage costs before taking possession of gold bullion, and remember that the pricing of gold coinage is based on more than just the value of the metal.

Investment systems. According to the infomercials, you can become wealthy in no time with real estate, commodities, currency hedges, day trading, and other stock speculation strategies. All you have to do is buy the right system. These are usually costly, time consuming, and have very low success rates. The traditional methods of investing may not be very exotic or offer such splendid outcomes, but they have served millions of people well for many years. Though history is no guarantee of future performance, you can put heavy odds on the old tried and true when it comes to the future of your money.

The easiest way to interpret beta is to think of it as a measure of the relative responsiveness of a stock to movements in the market. For example, if the market goes up by 20 percent and a stock has a beta of 1.5, then that stock would go up by 30 percent ($20\% \times 1.5 = 30\%$). If the market goes down by 20 percent, that same stock would go down by 30 percent ($-20\% \times 1.5 = -30\%$). In other words, a stock with a beta greater than 1.0 tends to amplify both the up and the down movements in the market. By the same token, a stock with a beta of less than 1.0 tends to mute the movements in the market.

What does all this mean to you as an investor? First, once your stock portfolio is diversified, it tends to move closely with all the other stocks in the marketplace. That is to say, the returns to a diversified portfolio are more a function of major changes in anticipated inflation, interest rates, or the general economy rather than of events unique to any specific company in the portfolio. Second, it means that the only way to fully diversify is to make sure that you invest in more than one type of investment— include domestic and international stocks along with bonds in your portfolio. Finally, if your portfolio is well diversified, you should keep an eye on its beta.

We know that risk and return go hand in hand, so wouldn't it be nice if we could also tolerate a little more risk? Well, we can—as long as we're patient. In the short run, market fluctuations are a killer. Nothing is more painful than experiencing a big fat market downturn and then needing your money. However, the longer your investment time horizon, the more you can afford to invest in riskier assets—that is, stocks.

When you invest in stocks, you're almost certain to experience a bad year or two. Holding on to stock for only a year is very risky, because the year you choose to hold

FIGURE 13.6 A Histogram of Annual Percentage Returns, 1991–2010 (20 years)

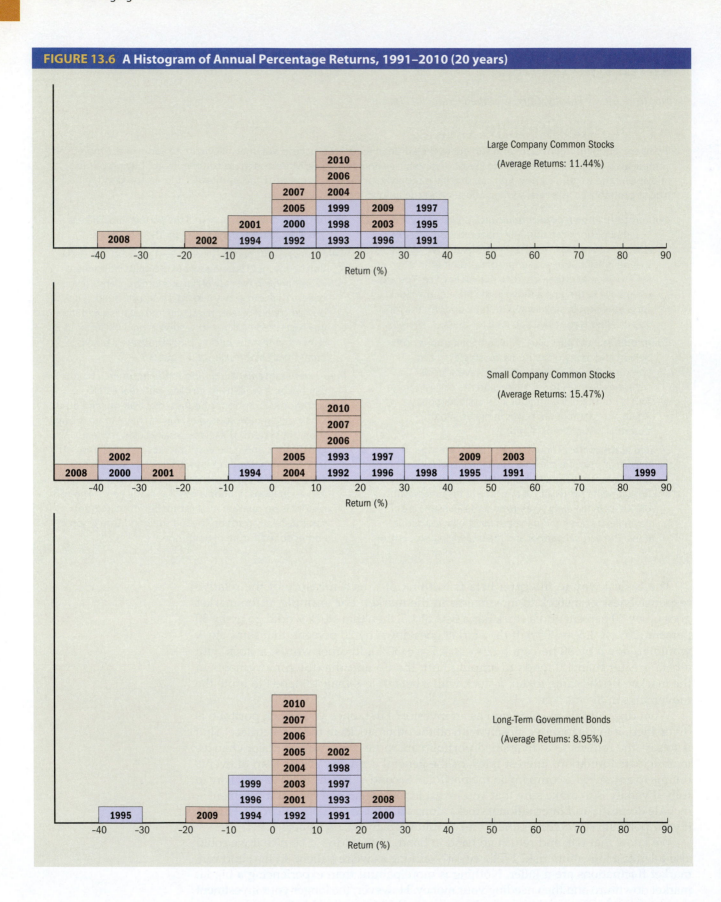

it just might be one of those bad years. Figure 13.6 lists the average yearly return for large- and small-cap stocks and shows how bad a bad year can really be. For example, if you'd chosen to make a 1-year investment in small company stocks in 2008, you'd have been one unhappy camper by year's end. Of course, if you'd made that same investment just 1 year later, you'd have made a hefty return—more than enough to go out and buy you and all your friends the latest iPhone.

As you can see, 1-year returns are amazingly variable, making short-term investments in stocks very risky. However, as the length of the investment horizon increases, you can afford to invest in riskier assets. The longer you hold on to stocks, the more likely you are to hit very good years, such as 1995 through 1999 or 2009. Of course, you're also more likely to hit bad years such as 2000 through 2002, but the very good will cancel out the very bad. Figure 13.7 shows how holding stocks for longer periods reduces the variability of the average annual return on your investment. The truth is, it's hard to beat the long-term return from common stock investments, which is why so many investors favor the buy-and-hold strategy for investing in stocks.

In addition, investors can afford to take on more risk as their investment time horizon increases because they have more opportunities to adjust saving, consumption, and work habits over longer time periods if a risky investment doesn't pan out. If they are investing with a short time horizon, there isn't much they can do to meet their goals.

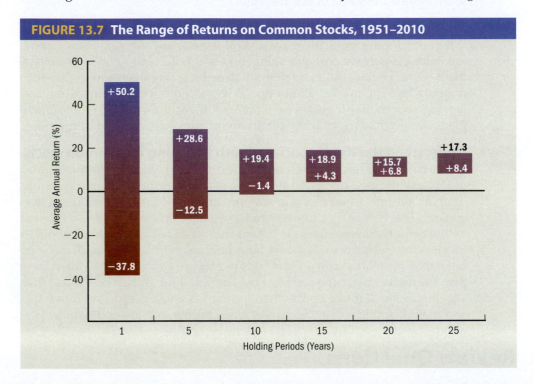

FIGURE 13.7   The Range of Returns on Common Stocks, 1951–2010

Summary

Invest in stocks.
Stocks are a solid investment because over time common stocks outperform all other investments; diversification reduces the risk of stocks; stocks are liquid; and the growth in your investment is determined by more than just interest rates.

Read stock quotes online or in the newspaper.
The health of the stock market is measured by stock indexes. The oldest and most widely quoted of the stock indexes is the Dow Jones Industrial Average

(DJIA) or the Dow. Other useful indexes include the Standard & Poor's 500, the Russell 1000 and 2000, and the Wilshire 5000.

Classify common stock according to basic market terminology.

Stocks can be classified according to the traits of the company issuing the stock. Common classifications include blue-chip, growth, income, speculative, cyclical, defensive, and large-, mid-, and small-cap stocks.

Determine the value of stocks.

A number of methods can be used to determine what a share of stock is worth. One approach is technical analysis. An alternative approach is the price/earnings ratio approach. Under this approach, a justified price/earnings (P/E) ratio is estimated for each stock. This price/earnings ratio, or earnings multiplier, is simply the price per share divided by the earnings per share.

A final approach is the discounted dividend model. We know that the value of any investment is simply the present value of all the returns we receive from that investment. Thus, the value of a share of common stock is simply the present value of the infinite stream of dividend payments. Three factors—interest rates, risk, and expected future growth—combine to determine the value of common stock.

Employ different investment strategies.

When purchasing stock there are several investment strategies you can follow, including dollar cost averaging, buy-and-hold, and dividend reinvestment plans. Dollar cost averaging involves investing over time rather than jumping into the market all at once. Buy-and-hold involves investing and leaving your money invested for a number of years. Dividend reinvestment plans involve having your dividends automatically reinvested in the stock.

Understand the risks associated with investing in common stock.

Stocks have more risk than other securities; however, you can eliminate much of this risk through diversification. Still, sometimes the stock market drops dramatically and when that happens, no amount of diversification can help you out. That type of risk, from overall movements in the market, is measured by the beta. The average beta is 1.0, meaning it moves up or down about as much as the market does. If a stock has a beta greater than 1.0, it will move up more than the market when the market moves up, and will move down more than the market when the market moves down. If the stock's beta is less than 1.0, the stock will move up less than the market when the market moves up, and move down less than the market when the market moves down.

Review Questions

1. Explain how stocks generate returns. Is one form of return preferable over the other? Be sure to consider both liquidity and taxation in your answer.

2. List and describe four reasons why someone should consider investing in stocks.

3. List the six questions an investor should ask periodically to check the progress of stock investments.

4. What is meant by the term "limited liability," and why is this concept important to common stock investors?

5. In terms of a common shareholder's claim on assets, when should a stockholder receive payment if a company declares bankruptcy?

6. Besides having a claim on income what is the most important right of common stockholders? Why is this right important?

7. What is a stock split? Why might a stock split occur?

8. What is the book value of a stock? How is it calculated? What is its relationship to the concept of personal net worth?

9. Two of the most commonly cited stock market indexes are the Dow and the S&P 500. Which of these two indexes better represents movements in the overall market? Why?

10. What is the difference between a bear market and a bull market? How can you easily remember the relevant stock price trends when you hear these terms?

11. Describe the following stock classifications: (a) blue-chip stock, (b) growth stock, (c) income stock, (d) speculative stock, (e) cyclical stock, and (f) defensive stock. Identify one publicly traded company as an example of each.

12. How are large-cap, mid-cap, and small-cap companies defined? Which of these types tend to produce the highest average return?

13. Describe the basic differences between technical analysis and fundamental analysis. List examples of different tools a technical analyst and a fundamental analyst might use when valuing an investment.

14. What three factors influence the value of common stock? Briefly describe each.

15. In terms of the risk–return tradeoff (**Principle 8**), why is there an inverse relationship between interest rates and the value of a share of common stock?

16. What are seven investment strategies to be wary of?

17. What four advantages does dollar cost averaging offer over a buy-and-hold strategy? When is a buy-and-hold approach a better investment strategy?

18. Summarize the advantages and disadvantages of DRIPs.

19. Explain two ways an investor can reduce risk when purchasing stocks.

20. What does beta measure? How can this measurement help you assemble an appropriate portfolio?

Develop Your Skills—Problems and Activities

These problems are available in MyFinanceLab.

1. Assume that you own 200 shares of General Dynamics Corp. (GD) selling at $90 per share. In order to make the stock more affordable for the average investor, GD's management has decided to split the stock.

   a. How much was your investment worth prior to the split?

   b. Assuming GD's management decides to split the stock three-for-one, how many shares would you own after the split?

   c. What is the new price per share immediately after the split?

   d. How much would your investment be worth after the three-for-one split?

2. The Haley Corporation has just announced year-end results as follows:

Value of company assets	$12,500,000
Value of company liabilities	$6,500,000
Net income	$1,600,000
Common stock dividends	$250,000
Preferred stock dividends	$400,000
Number of shares of common stock outstanding	1,000,000
Closing price of Haley Corporation's stock	$45.00 per share

   a. Calculate the book value per share.

   b. Calculate earnings per share.

   c. Calculate Haley Corporation's dividend yield.

   d. Calculate the market-to-book ratio.

3. The Smell Fresh Kitty Litter Company has assets of $10 million, liabilities of $4 million and 2 million shares outstanding. Assuming creditors are paid in full prior to stockholders receiving any money, what is the maximum amount the stockholders would receive in a bankruptcy settlement? What is the amount per share they would receive?

4. You've just learned that Graham Records has purchased the lifetime distribution rights to the music of a new band called the French Fries. Based on this good news you've estimated that Graham Records should pay $4 in dividends next year. You also think that the dividends paid out should increase by 5 percent a year indefinitely. As a knowledgeable investor, you've determined your required rate of return is 9 percent.

a. What is your estimate of the value of Graham Records common stock?

b. What would the value of the stock be if you did not anticipate any increase in the dividend over time?

c. If the required rate of return increased to 12 percent, what would happen to the stock price?

5. Wildcat Corporation recently disclosed the following financial information:

Earnings/Revenue	$1,500,000
Assets	$7,000,000
Liabilities	$1,500,000
Shares outstanding	500,000
Market price	$33.00 per share

Calculate the price/book ratio, the price/earnings ratio, and the book value per share for each of the following separate scenarios:

a. Based on current information

b. Earnings fall to $1,000,000

c. Liabilities increase to $2,500,000

d. The company does a 3:1 stock split with no change in market capitalization

e. The company repurchases 20 percent of the outstanding stock, incurring additional liability to finance the purchase.

6. An investor is considering purchasing one of the following three stocks. Stock X has a market capitalization of $7 billion, pays a relatively high dividend with little increase in earnings, and has a P/E ratio of 11. Stock Y has a market capitalization of $62 billion but does not currently pay a dividend. Stock Y has a P/E ratio of 39. Stock Z, a housing industry company, has a market capitalization of $800 million and a P/E of 18.

a. Classify these stocks according to their market capitalizations.

b. Which of the three would you classify as a growth stock? Why?

c. Which stock would be most appropriate for an aggressive investor?

d. Which stock would be most appropriate for someone seeking a combination of safety and earnings?

7. Use the following data to answer the questions that follow.

Company	Beta
Savoy Corp.	0.70
Hokie Industries	1.35
Graham Records	2.05
Expo Enterprises	0.45
S&P 500	1.00

a. If the S&P 500 goes up by 15 percent, how much should the stocks of Savoy, Hokie, Graham, and Expo change in value?

b. If the stock market drops by 10 percent, which one of these stocks should outperform the others? Why?

8. Use the information in the table below to answer the following questions.

52 Weeks						Vol.	Day			Net
Hi	Lo	Stock	Sym	Div	PE	100s	Hi	Lo	Close	Chg
80.65	58.48	Boeing	BA	1.68	16.82	7976	76.71	75.84	76.28	−0.11

a. What is the current dividend yield for Boeing Company (BA) based on the stock's recent closing price?

b. What is your estimate of Boeing's earnings for the year based on its recent closing price?

c. Based on the net change, at what price did Boeing close yesterday?

9. Assume an investor made the purchases listed in the table below on the first day of every quarter for a year. Use the information provided to fill in the blanks.

Quarter	Price	Money Invested	Shares Purchased	Total Shares Owned	Market Value
1	$30	$200	_____	_____	_____
2	$50	$200	_____	_____	_____
3	$60	$200	_____	_____	_____
4	$35	$200	_____	_____	_____
Total		$800			

10. Using the calculations from problem 9, assume that instead of investing $200 every quarter, the investor decided to make a lump-sum purchase on the first day of the year with $800. If at year-end the price of the stock closed at $35 per share, which investment strategy, dollar cost averaging or lump-sum investing, produced the greater return?

Learn by Doing—Suggested Projects

1. Visit **http://finance.yahoo.com**, **www.morningstar.com**, or a similar Web site. Use these sources to obtain the book value, earnings per share, dividend yield, price-to-book ratio, and P/E ratio on six to eight companies of your choice (please do not restrict yourself to one industry or sector of the market). Based on your knowledge of these companies and the information you obtain categorize each stock using the six general common stock classifications.

2. Rank the suggested questions in Checklist 13.1 in order of importance to you and explain why you gave each question its respective ranking. Then interview a friend or relative who regularly makes his or her own investment decisions. Do you and your interviewee share the same opinions? Write a brief report of your findings. Be sure to include (1) why the similarities and differences occur in the rankings and answers, (2) how your friend or relative feels about brokerage or sales commissions, and (3) whether or not he or she has a strategy for deciding when to sell a stock.

3. Using the Web site **www.dogsofthedow.com/thedow.htm**, look at the list of companies that have been added to and subtracted from the DJIA since 1929 using the "Dow Deletion Table." Use this and the list of the firms that currently make up the DJIA to answer the following questions:

a. Identify the companies by name that have been added or subtracted more than once. Why might this have happened?

b. Identify the types of companies (by sector or industry) that have been added since 1991. What sectors seems to have been the most popular to add and to delete?

c. Identify the highest three and lowest three dividend yielding companies. If these are all supposed to be blue-chip stocks, what might be the explanation for why the dividend yields are so different?

4. Using the Internet, visit the NASDAQ homepage (**www.nasdaq.com**) each day for 1 week. Track the performance of the NASDAQ composite index for the week. Did you notice any significant trend during that time? Do you think that investors were bullish or bearish for the week?

5. Review the general classifications of common stock. Based on your personal comfort level (risk tolerance), which type of stock would most interest you? Why? Be sure to consider current economic conditions, current media coverage, and the current financial market outlook in your response.

6. Every evening the major news networks report that "the market" is up, down, or unchanged. Ask at least ten people what they think is meant by "the market." Report your findings in a one-page summary, and then answer the following questions:

a. How did most individuals define the market?

b. After reading this chapter, do you agree with the definitions given by those you asked? How would you define the market? Why?

c. Is it possible to have multiple markets within a single market? Why or why not?

7. As a group project, use the following stocks to develop a portfolio that has an average beta equal to 1.0. You must include all stocks, but the weighting is yours to develop.

Stock Name	Sector	Beta
SAS Corp.	Financial	0.90
Dipper Group	Industrial	0.65
Startech, Inc.	Technology	2.05
Robust Corp.	Consumer Goods	0.45
Sunlight, Inc.	Energy	−0.20
Medi-serve Group	Health Care	1.10

Given what you have learned about beta as a measure of volatility, have each member of the group individually adjust the allocation of the portfolio in response to an anticipated market decline. Was each member's adjustment appropriate? What was the rationale behind the adjustments? Give a brief presentation on how your group allocated their original portfolio and then defend each member's adjustments in their revised portfolios.

Be a Financial Planner—Discussion Case 1

This case is available in MyFinanceLab.

Although saddened by the death of her favorite aunt, Shannel was extremely surprised to learn that she was named her aunt's only heir. A personal note in the will said, "For your own shop." Shannel and her aunt often visited antique shops and Shannel's dream was to own such a shop. She is expecting to receive approximately $50,000 and hopes to invest this money for her future shop, but she knows very little about stocks or investment strategies. After discussing financial planning topics with Shannel, the following issues became clear. First, the $50,000 is all the money she has saved for her goal. Second, Shannel is very cautious financially and is fearful of investing all her money at once because she has heard conflicting reports concerning stock valuation. Use your knowledge of common stock classifications and investment strategies to answer the following questions.

Questions

1. Which type of stock or combination of stocks would be appropriate for Shannel? Develop your answer in terms of Shannel's risk tolerance, time frame, and goals.

2. What role should cyclical and defensive stocks play in Shannel's portfolio?

3. Would you recommend small capitalization stocks to Shannel? Why or why not?

4. Given Shannel's fear about current stock valuations, what investment strategy would you recommend for her? Why?

5. Why might Shannel consider enrolling in an automatic investment plan?

6. Provide Shannel with four reasons she should consider using a buy-and-hold strategy.

7. Explain a dividend reinvestment plan to Shannel. Would you recommend that she participate in DRIPs with a portion of her portfolio? If so, how much and why?

Be a Financial Planner—Discussion Case 2

This case is available in MyFinanceLab.

Pete and Jessica, on the advice of their next-door neighbor, recently purchased 500 shares of a small capitalization Internet stock, trading at $80 per share. Their neighbor told them that the stock was a "real money maker" because it recently had a two-for-one stock split and would probably split again soon. Even better, according to the neighbor, the company was expected to earn $1 per share and pay a $0.25 dividend next year. Pete and Jessica have so far been less than impressed with the stock's performance–the stock has underperformed the S&P 500 Index this year. Pete and Jessica have come to you for some independent advice.

Questions

1. Assuming that the stock actually splits two for one, how many shares will Pete and Jessica own? What will be the market value of their stock after the split? How will the split affect the value of their holdings? Was their next-door neighbor correct in thinking that the stock split made the stock a "real money maker"?

2. Pete and Jessica aren't sure if they overpaid for their stock. Calculate the value of the stock using the discounted dividends valuation model, assuming a 10 percent required rate of return and a 2 percent growth in dividends. Based on your calculation, did they overpay? How accurate is this valuation model for this type of stock?

3. Using the information provided, calculate the stock's P/E ratio. Would you classify this investment as a growth or value stock?

4. Since Pete, in particular, is worried about the price of the stock, explain to him how and why corporate earnings are so important in the valuation of common stocks.

5. Should Pete and Jessica be using the S&P 500 Index as a benchmark for this stock? Why or why not? What benchmark recommendation would you make?

6. Yesterday they received a cold call from a stockbroker wanting to sell them an initial public offering in a cable television company. Jessica was worried because the broker promised a "no-lose guarantee." Should they invest with this type of broker?

7. Name at least five things Pete and Jessica need to look out for when making stock investments.

8. Pete, the worrier in the family, is concerned about the risk of owning one stock. Should he be? How many stocks should an investor hold in a portfolio in order to reduce systematic risk by at least 60 percent?

14 Investing in Bonds and Other Alternatives

Learning Objectives

 Invest in the bond market.

 Understand basic bond terminology and compare the various types of bonds.

 Calculate the value of a bond and understand the factors that cause bond value to change.

 Compare preferred stock to bonds as an investment option.

 Understand the risks associated with investing in real estate.

Know why you shouldn't *invest* in gold, silver, gems, or collectibles.

For Alec Baldwin, the road of life has been exciting to say the least. He's made headlines, both good and bad, and along the way has made and lost a lot of money. As one of six children born to a schoolteacher and a football coach, he grew up in a family where "we always worried about money," and family fights centered on financial issues.

His life changed part way through college, when, on a dare from a friend, he auditioned for New York University's drama program, was accepted, and transferred to New York University. He soon landed a role in *The Doctors,* a daytime TV soap opera, and from there the prime-time soap *Knots Landing.* Then in 1990, after a decade dominated by television work, he was offered the lead role of Jack Ryan in Tom Clancy's *The Hunt for Red October.* When he was given the chance to reprise the Jack Ryan role in the Clancy sequel, *Patriot Games,* it looked like there was no stopping him, but instead of starring in *Patriot Games,* he turned it down and it was given to Harrison Ford—not a good career move.

Since 2006 he's been on *30 Rock*, playing the role of Jack Donaghy, a slick, humor-challenged, meddling, slightly scary network executive. As far as the critics were concerned, he was perfect, and has won two Emmy Awards, three Golden Globes, and five Screen Actors Guild Awards. In addition, in 2011 he got a star on the Hollywood Walk of Fame.

Throughout his acting career, Alec has taken a lot of chances—for example, turning down that lead role in *The Patriot Games* for the lead in the Broadway revival of *A Streetcar Named Desire*. But when it comes to his financial life, Alec has played it safe by investing a large stash of his money in bonds. He's done well in bonds, but his stock investments haven't always panned out; in fact, he invested quite a bit in telecommunications stocks and lost a ton of money. Alec, in the role of Jack Donaghy, has actually poked fun at his investment losses in

telecom stocks. In one episode of *30 Rock* Tracy Jordan (played by Tracy Morgan), the wild and unpredictable movie star, talks to Jack about money:

Tracy: I need a hundred thousand dollars, or I'm gonna lose both my houses.

Jack: Tracy, I don't understand. You've starred in 14 films. You don't have any money saved?

Tracy: No, I lost all of it.

Jack: Really? Who's your money manager?

Tracy: Grizz.

Grizz (one of Tracy's posse): WorldCom, man. WorldCom.

Tracy: (to Grizz) I forgot about that WorldCom mess; why you gotta be so obsessed with telecommunications?

Similar to a lot of investors, Alec chose bonds because they carry less risk than stocks. Other investors are drawn to bonds because of the steady income they provide. But make no mistake, though bonds are more secure than stocks and though they offer steady income, it doesn't mean that returns are necessarily low. In 1995, for example, long-term Treasury bonds went up in value by over 32 percent! In 2008, when the average price of a stock listed on the New York Stock Exchange dropped by 37.8 percent, the price of a long-term Treasury bond climbed by 25.6 percent—2008 was definitely a year to be invested in bonds as opposed to stocks. Similarly, while stocks dropped by 8.5 percent and 18.2 percent in 2001 and 2002 respectively, bonds grew by 4.1 percent and 17.2 percent. But, bonds can also fall in value. While 2008 was a great year for bonds, 2009 wasn't, with bond prices dropping by 14 percent. The bottom line here is that bonds are a sound source of income and a good way to diversify your investment portfolio.

 Invest in the bond market.

Why Consider Bonds?

A bond is a loan; when you buy a bond, you become a lender. The bond issuer—generally a corporation, the federal government and its agencies, a city, or a state—gets the use of your money and in return pays you interest, generally every 6 months, for the life of the bond. At maturity, the issuer pays you the face value of the bond, which may be more or less than what you originally paid for it.

How exactly do bonds fit into your investment portfolio?

◆ **Bonds reduce risk through diversification.** As you learned earlier, when you put together investments whose returns don't move together over time, you're able to reduce the risk in your portfolio. In the week of April 10–14, 2000, the S&P 500 went down by 10.54 percent and NASDAQ went down 25.30 percent. That same week bond prices rose. The same thing happened in 2001 in the days following the terrorist attack on the World Trade Center and the Pentagon—stock prices fell while bond prices climbed. And again the same thing happened during the stock crash in the fall of 2008. During the 3 months from September through November 2008, the S&P 500 fell by almost 33 percent while long-term government bonds rose by almost 12 percent.

◆ **Bonds produce steady income.** For those needing some income to achieve their financial goals, bonds are a good choice. For example, you may be retired and desire additional income from your investment portfolio to supplement your pension income. With bonds, provided they don't default on their interest payments, you'll receive interest income annually.

◆ **Bonds can be a safe investment if held to maturity.** Interest on bonds must be paid, or the firm can be forced into bankruptcy. So bond interest payments will be made at all costs—unlike dividend payments on common stocks. As a result, bonds are a relatively safe investment. In addition, bond rating services provide reliable information on the riskiness of bonds. If the bond doesn't default and you hold it to maturity, you know exactly what your return will be. In the world of personal finance, it's unusual to find an investment that actually returns exactly what it promises.

Now let's take a look at bond basics.

Basic Bond Terminology and Features

Bonds are similar to just about everything else we've seen so far in this book: If you can't talk the talk, you're going to fall flat on your face when you try to walk the walk. This section should get you fairly conversant in the language of bonds.

LO2 Understand bond terminology and compare the various types of bonds.

Par Value

The **par value** of a bond is its face value, or the amount returned to the bondholder at **maturity**, the date when the bond comes due. For bonds issued by corporations, the par value is generally $1,000. A bond's market price, which is its selling price, is generally expressed as a percentage of the bond's par value. For example, a bond that matures or comes due in the year 2020 that has a $1,000 par value may be quoted as selling for 95.125. This means that the bond is selling for 95.125 percent of its par value, which is $951.25 ($1,000 × 95.125%). At maturity in the year 2020, the bondholder will receive the par value of $1,000 and the bond will be terminated (but not by Arnold Schwarzenegger).

Par Value
The face value of a bond, or the amount that's returned to the bondholder at maturity. It's also referred to as the bond's denomination.

Maturity
The length of time until the bond issuer returns the par value to the bondholder and terminates the bond.

Coupon Interest Rate

The **coupon interest rate** on a bond indicates what percentage of the par value of the bond will be paid out annually in the form of interest. An 8 percent coupon interest rate and a $1,000 par value will pay out $80 (8% × $1,000) annually in interest until maturity, generally in semiannual installments, which would be $40 every 6 months.

Keep in mind that when you purchase a bond and hold it to maturity, your entire return is based on the return of the par value or principal and the payment of interest at the coupon interest rate. The only real risk involved is that the bond issuer won't have the funds to make these payments and will default.

Coupon Interest Rate
The annual rate of interest to be paid out on a bond, calculated as a percentage of the par value.

Indenture

An **indenture** is the legal document that provides the specific terms of the loan agreement, including a description of the bond, the rights of the bondholders, the rights of the issuing firm, and the responsibilities of the bond trustees. A bond trustee, usually a banking institution or trust company, is assigned the task of overseeing the relationship between the bondholder and the issuing firm. A bond indenture may run 100 pages or more in length, with the majority of it devoted to defining protective provisions for the bondholder.

Indenture
A legal agreement between the firm issuing a bond and the bond trustee who represents the bondholders.

Call Provision

A **call provision** entitles the bond issuer to repurchase, or "call," the bonds from their holders at stated prices over specified periods. If interest rates go down, the issuer will call the bonds and replace them with lower-cost debt. The terms of the call provision are provided in the indenture and generally set the call provision at approximately the par value plus 1 year's worth of interest.

While a call provision works to the disadvantage of the investor, bonds with call provisions generally pay higher returns as compensation. Still, if you own high-paying long-term bonds and you're counting on receiving those semiannual interest payments for the next 10 years or so, having them called away from you could rain on your parade. To make callable bonds more attractive, the issuer many times includes in the indenture some protection against calls. Generally, that call protection comes in the form of a **deferred call**. With a deferred call, the bond can't be called until a set number of years have passed since the bond was issued. Although not as safe as a noncallable bond, a bond with a deferred call at least provides protection against an immediate call.

Call Provision
A bond provision that gives the issuer the right to repurchase, or "call," the bonds from their holders at stated prices over specified periods.

Deferred Call
A bond provision stating that the bond can't be called until a set number of years have passed since it was issued.

Sinking Fund

Sinking Fund
A fund to which the bond issuer deposits money to pay off a bond issue.

No one likes to have to pay off debts all at once, and that goes for bond issuers, too. Most set up a **sinking fund** to set aside money on a regular basis to pay off the bonds at maturity. With a sinking fund, the firm either calls, using the bond's call provision, or repurchases a fraction of the outstanding bonds in the open market annually. In this way, the issuer spreads out the large payment that would have otherwise occurred at maturity.

The advantage of a sinking fund for the investor is that the probability that the debt will be successfully paid off at maturity increases, thereby reducing risk. Without a sinking fund, the issuer faces a major payment at maturity. If the issuer is experiencing financial problems when the debt matures, repayment may be jeopardized. The big disadvantage of a sinking fund for investors is the fact that it may result in the bond being called away from them.

Types of Bonds

There's an old science joke that says there are four different types of bonds: ionic, covalent, metallic, and James. Well, in the world of finance there are more types of bonds than that (but James is the only one with a license to kill). There are thousands of outstanding bonds floating around the securities markets, and more are probably on the way as you read this. It's a vast understatement to say that these bonds aren't all alike. The easiest way to explain the differences is to break them down into bonds issued by corporations, by the U.S. government and its agencies, and by states and localities, and examine each group separately. As you'll see, each type of bond has unique advantages and disadvantages to the investor.

FACTS of LIFE

The U.S. bond market is almost twice the size of the combined market value of all U.S. stock markets.

Corporate Bonds

Corporate Bonds
Bonds issued by corporations.

Borrowing money by issuing bonds is a major source of funding for corporations. In fact, **corporate bonds** account for about half of the bonds outstanding. Generally these bonds are issued in denominations of $1,000 in order to appeal to smaller investors. There are several different types of corporate bonds from which you can choose, with one major difference being whether or not the bond is secured.

Secured Bond
Any bond that is backed by the pledge of collateral.

Mortgage Bond
A bond secured by a lien or real property.

Secured Corporate Debt   A **secured bond** is one that's backed by collateral, which, as you remember, is a real asset that can be seized and sold if a debtor doesn't pay off his or her debt. A **mortgage bond** is secured by a lien on real property. Typically, the value of the real property is greater than that of the mortgage bonds issued, providing the investor with a margin of safety in case the market value of the secured property declines.

In the event of bankruptcy, the bond trustees have the power to sell the secured property and use the proceeds to pay the bondholders. If the proceeds from this sale don't cover the bonds, the bondholders fall in line with the other creditors who are owed money.

Debenture
Any unsecured long-term bond.

Unsecured Corporate Debt   The term **debenture** applies to any unsecured long-term bond. When bonds are unsecured, the earning ability of the issuing corporation is of great concern to the investor. Debentures are also viewed as being more risky than secured bonds and, as a result, have a higher yield associated with them.

Firms with more than one issue of debentures outstanding often specify a hierarchy by which some debentures are paid back before others if the firm goes bankrupt.

The claims of the subordinated debentures—bonds lower down in the hierarchy—are honored only after the claims of secured bonds and unsubordinated debentures have been satisfied. As you might imagine, subordinated debentures are riskier than "normal" or unsubordinated debentures and have a higher return associated with them to compensate for the added risk.

Treasury and Agency Bonds

Without question, the biggest single player—and payer—in the bond market is the U.S. government. Given all the news about our national debt, it should come as no surprise that our government spends more than it takes in. The alternatives to financing an unbalanced budget are to sell some assets (anybody want to buy Nebraska?), raise taxes, or borrow more money. The last choice has been found to be the most acceptable approach and has led to the issuance of huge sums of debt by our government. Given the enormous amount of debt financing that goes on, it's not surprising that there are a number of different types of government debt to choose from.

These securities are generally viewed as being risk free, given the government's ability to tax and print more money. When corporations run out of money, they can't just print more, but the government can. Hey, it owns the mints! In addition to there being no default risk on Treasury bonds, there's no risk that government bonds will be called, because the government no longer issues callable bonds.

Because there's no default or call risk associated with government bonds, they generally pay a lower rate of interest than other bonds. In addition, most interest payments received on federal debt are exempt from state and local taxation.[1]

Treasury-issued debt has maturities that range from 3 months to 30 years. When investors speak of Treasury debt with different maturities, they speak of *bills*, *notes*, and *bonds*. The only difference between these is the maturity and the denomination.

If the Treasury debt has a maturity of 3, 6, or 12 months, it's referred to as Treasury *bills*. If, when issued, it has a maturity of 2, 3, 5, or 10 years, it's referred to as Treasury *notes*. Treasury *bonds* are issued with maturities of 30 years. One advantage of purchasing Treasury securities is that you can do it yourself through a program called Treasury Direct, thereby avoiding brokerage fees, which range upward from $25 per transaction. You need only set up an account with the Federal Reserve and Treasury Direct. Then you can make trades and keep track of all your transactions electronically. You can also sell your security before maturity through the Fed for a $34 fee. For instructions, contact the Bureau of Public Debt at **www.publicdebt.treas.gov**.

In addition to the Treasury, a number of other government agencies, such as the Federal National Mortgage Association (FNMA) and the Federal Home Loan Banks (FHLB), issue debt called **agency bonds**. Although these aren't directly issued through the Treasury, they're issued by federal agencies and authorized by Congress. They're still viewed as being virtually risk free and carry an interest rate slightly higher than that carried on Treasury securities. In general, their minimum denomination is $25,000, with maturities that vary from 1 to 40 years, although the average maturity is approximately 15 years.

> **FACTS of LIFE**
>
> In October 2011, the total U.S. federal debt was $14.8 trillion, which works out to about $47,500 per U.S. resident. If you'd like to see how much federal debt there is, go to the U.S. National Debt Clock at **http://www.usdebtclock.org**.

Agency Bonds
Bonds issued by government agencies other than the Treasury.

---

[1]Federal debt issued by FNMA, the Federal National Mortgage Association, is not exempt from state and local taxation.

Pass-Through Certificate
A certificate that represents a portion of ownership in a pool of federally insured mortgages.

(Treasury) Inflation Protected Indexed Securities (TIPS)
U.S. Treasury bonds for which the par value changes with the consumer price index to guarantee the investor a real return (i.e., a return that stays above inflation). These bonds have a maturity of 5, 10, or 20 years and a minimum par value of $1,000.

Pass-Through Certificates Of the agency securities, the most interesting to investors are those issued by the Government National Mortgage Association (GNMA), or "Ginnie Mae," called **pass-through certificates**. A GNMA pass-through certificate represents an interest in a pool of federally insured mortgages. What GNMA does is package a group of mortgages worth $1 million or more, guarantee those mortgages, and sell "certificates" with minimum denominations of $25,000, called pass-through certificates, to finance the mortgages. In effect, pass-through certificates can put an average homeowner with $25,000 to invest on the other side—the lending side—of a mortgage.

Because all the payments from the mortgages financed by the pass-through certificates (less a processing fee and a GNMA insurance fee) go to the certificate holders, the size of the monthly check the investor receives depends on how fast the mortgages are paid off. In addition, the monthly check represents both principal and interest. At maturity there's no return of principal as there is with a bond. With the last payment, the pass-through security is completely paid off, just as your home mortgage would be.

Treasury Inflation Protected Securities (TIPS) The newest and most exciting Treasury bond for investors is the **inflation protected indexed security or TIPS**. These bonds have a maturity of 5, 10, or 20 years and a minimum par value of $1,000. When there are changes in the consumer price index (the government's measure of the effect of inflation on prices), there's a corresponding change in the par value of the bond.

For example, if there's a 3 percent increase in the consumer price index, the par value of these bonds will go up by 3 percent, from $1,000 to $1,030. That means you get a little more interest each year, and at maturity you also get a little more. That's because interest payments are then determined using this new par value. So if the par value of the bond rises to $1,030 and the interest rate on the bond is set at 3.8 percent, the bondholder now gets 3.8 percent of $1,030, or $39.14 (3.8% × $1,030) per year, and at maturity this bond now pays $1,030.

The big headache with respect to these bonds comes in determining taxes. The IRS considers the upward adjustment in the par value of the bonds as interest income, and you have to pay taxes on it during the year the adjustment was made, even though you don't receive this money until the bond matures.

The advantage of these bonds is that investors will be guaranteed a real return—that is, a return above inflation. In addition, the effects of inflation on interest rates will be equalized as the interest payments and the bond's par value rise to reflect inflation. In effect, you win if there's inflation.

U.S. Series EE Bonds The government also issues savings bonds directly aimed at the small investor. United States Series EE bonds are issued by the Treasury with fixed interest rates and denominations so low they can be purchased for as little as $25 each. When a paper Series EE bond is purchased, its price is one-half its face value, with face values going from $50 to $10,000. In other words, you buy a bond, wait a specified amount of time, and get double your money back. If you buy a EE bond electronically, it is sold at face value, that is, you pay $50 for a $50 bond. Series EE bonds are liquid in the sense that they can be cashed at any time, although cashing them before they mature may result in a reduced yield.

I Bonds In addition to Series EE savings bonds, the U.S. Treasury also issues I bonds. An I bond is an accrual-type bond, meaning the interest is added to the value of the bond and paid when the bond is cashed in. These bonds are sold at face value and grow with inflation-indexed earnings for up to 30 years. The return on an I bond is a combination of two separate rates: a fixed rate of return and a semiannual inflation rate. That means you get a fixed rate plus an additional return based on changes in the rate of inflation [as measured by the Consumer Price Index for all Urban consumers (CPI-U)].

With an I bond, you can invest as little as $50 or as much as $10,000 per year. In addition, I bonds also have tax advantages. They allow you to defer federal taxes on earnings for up to 30 years and are exempt from state and local income taxes. In addition, these bonds are very liquid and can be turned into cash any time after 12 months.

Municipal Bonds

Municipal bonds, or "munis," are bonds issued by states, counties, and cities, in addition to other public agencies, such as school districts and highway authorities, to fund public projects. There are thousands of different issues of municipal bonds, with over $1 trillion in outstanding value. Their popularity stems from the fact that they're tax exempt—interest payments aren't taxed by the federal government or, in general, by the state as long as you live in the state in which the bonds were issued.

In fact, if you live in a city and buy a municipal bond issued by that city, your income from that bond would be exempt from city, state, and federal taxes. For example, if you live in New York, which has an income tax, and purchase a municipal bond issued by that city, you'll be exempt from paying taxes on the interest you receive at the federal, state, and city levels. Capital gains from selling municipal bonds before maturity, though, are taxed.

Municipal Bonds, or "Munis"
Bonds issued by states, counties, and cities, as well as other public agencies, such as school districts and highway authorities, to fund public projects.

FACTS of LIFE
Investors held around $3 trillion in taxable and municipal bonds as of April 2011.

There are two basic types of municipal bonds: general obligation bonds and revenue bonds. A **general obligation bond** is backed by the full faith and credit—that is, the taxing power—of the issuer and are exempt from all taxes. **Revenue bonds** derive the funds to pay interest and repay the bonds from a designated project or specific tax and can pay only if a sufficient amount of revenue is generated, and are exempt from state and local taxes but not federal taxes. If a revenue bond derives its funding from a toll road and traffic isn't very heavy, the bond might go unpaid.

Municipal bonds also come with many different maturities. In fact, most municipal bond offerings have **serial maturities**. That is, a portion of the debt comes due, or matures, each year until the issue is exhausted. In effect, it works like a sinking fund. It's important that you choose the maturity date you want so you get the principal back when you need and expect it.

Although municipal bonds are issued by a government, they're not risk free. In fact, there have been several cases in which local governments failed to pay on municipal bonds. Cleveland defaulted on some debt in the late 1970s, and then in the mid-1990s, Orange County, California, defaulted on $800 million of its short-term debt. The primary revenue source for most general obligation municipal bonds is real estate taxes. If local governments overestimate future tax intakes—say, the government thinks more people will move in when instead a bunch of people move out—they get stuck holding a lot of debt they can't handle.

Remember, unlike the federal government, state and local governments can't print more money when they run short. As you might expect, it's very difficult for an investor to judge the quality of a municipal bond offering. Fortunately, the rating agencies that we will discuss shortly, in conjunction with corporate bonds, also rate municipal bonds.

One of the disadvantages of municipal bonds is that if you have to sell them before they mature, it can be difficult to find a buyer. This is especially true for many smaller issues for which there is not a secondary market.

General Obligation Bond
A state or municipal bond backed by the full faith and credit—that is, the taxing power—of the issuer.

Revenue Bonds
State or municipal bonds that have interest and par value paid for with funds from a designated project or specific tax.

Serial Maturities
Bonds, generally municipals, with various maturity dates, usually at set intervals.

Special Situation Bonds

We've already seen the main classification of bonds, but before moving on there are two special types of bonds that deserve mention. They are zero coupon bonds and junk bonds.

Zero Coupon Bonds
Bonds that don't pay interest and are sold at a deep discount from their par value.

Zero Coupon Bonds   Bonds that don't pay interest are called **zero coupon bonds**. Instead, these bonds are sold at a deep discount from their face or par value, and at maturity they return the entire par value. As a result, the entire return is made up by the bond's appreciation in value from its discount purchase price to its price at maturity.

A zero coupon bond can be thought of as something similar to a savings bond and it appeals to those investors who need a lump sum of money at some future date but don't want to be concerned about reinvesting interest payments. Zero coupon bonds are issued by corporations and municipalities, and there are even mortgage-backed zeros, but without question the dominant player in this market is the U.S. government. The government's zero coupon bonds are called STRIPS.

The major disadvantage of these bonds is that while you don't receive any income annually, you're taxed as though you do. The IRS considers any annual appreciation in value (or as the IRS calls it, the undistributed interest) as subject to tax. Another disadvantage of zero coupon bonds is that they tend to fluctuate in value with changes in the interest rate more than traditional bonds do. For example, in 1994, 30-year zero coupon Treasury bonds dropped 18.7 percent, then in 1995 they rose in price by 63.1 percent. Zero coupon bonds aren't a good investment if you may have to sell the bond before it matures. Zero coupon bonds are best suited for tax-deferred retirement accounts such as IRAs or Keogh plans, where the tax disadvantage disappears.

Junk Bonds
Very risky, low-rated bonds, also called high-yield bonds. These bonds are rated BB or below.

Junk Bonds   The second type of special bonds is **junk bonds**, or low-rated bonds, also called high-yield bonds, which are bonds rated BB or below. (We explain bond ratings in the next section.) Originally, the term applied to bonds issued by firms with previously sound financial histories that were currently facing severe financial problems and suffering from poor credit ratings. Today, junk bonds refer to any bond with a low rating. The major issuers of junk bonds are new firms that haven't yet established a performance record.

Because junk bonds carry a much greater risk of default, they also carry an interest rate 3 to 6 percent above AAA grade long-term bonds. The problem with junk bonds is that they haven't been around long enough for us to really know what will happen in a major recession.

Junk bonds are high-risk investments. Moreover, most junk bonds are callable. That means that if the firm does do well and recovers from its difficulties, then the bond will be called. If the firm doesn't do well, the bond could default. Neither alternative is a good one. Prudent investors generally avoid junk bonds. Hey, they're not called junk for nothing!

 3   Calculate the value of a bond and understand the factors that cause bond value to change.

Evaluating Bonds

Not only do you need to know bond terms and what kinds of bonds there are, you also need to know how to evaluate them. That means understanding what a bond yield and a rating are, and knowing how to read a bond quote on the Internet or in the newspaper.

Bond Ratings—A Measure of Riskiness

John Moody first began to rate bonds in 1909. Since that time, two major rating agencies—Moody's and Standard & Poor's—have provided ratings on thousands of corporate, city, and state bonds. These ratings involve a judgment about the future

TABLE 14.1	Interpreting Bond Ratings		
Bond Ratings Category	**Standard & Poor's**	**Moody's**	**Description**
Prime	AAA	Aaa	Highest quality, extremely strong
Very strong	AA	Aa	Very strong capacity to pay
Strong	A	A	Strong capacity to pay
Medium	BBB	Baa	Changing circumstances could impact the firm's ability to pay
Speculative	BB, B	Ba, B	Has speculative elements
Very speculative	CCC, CC	Caa, C	Extremely speculative
Default	C	C	An income bond that doesn't pay interest
Default	D	D	Has not been paying interest or repaying principal

risk potential of a bond—specifically its default risk or the chance that it may not be able to meet its obligations of interest or repayment of principal sometime in the future.

The poorer the bond rating, the higher the rate of return demanded by investors. That's exactly what you'd expect, given **Principle 8: Risk and Return Go Hand in Hand**. Generally, these bond ratings run from AAA for the safest bonds to D for extremely risky bonds. Interestingly, a bond with an A rating is considered only a medium-grade bond rather than a high-grade bond. Table 14.1 provides a description of the different bond ratings.

As an investor, be aware of a bond's rating and its risk. Unfortunately, because bonds are so expensive—selling for around $1,000 each—diversification can be difficult unless you have a great deal of money invested in bonds. So if you buy bonds, avoid the risky ones. Check their ratings, which are available at most local libraries, or ask your broker.

FACTS of LIFE

While AAA is the highest corporate bond rating, you might not want to demand a AAA rating on your bond investments. That's because AAA ratings are relatively rare. Even IBM doesn't have a AAA rating. In fact, only about eight or so of the *Fortune 500* firms are rated AAA. On the other hand, there are plenty of B-rated bonds around; however, although a B may be a good grade in a class, it's only a speculative grade when it comes to bond ratings.

Bond Yield

The bond's yield is simply the return on investment. Note that yield isn't the same as coupon interest rate. The coupon interest rate tells you what your interest payments are as a percentage of the bond's par value. The bond's yield tells you what your return is as a percentage of the price of the bond.

There are two ways of measuring yield. The first, called the current yield, looks at the return from interest payments on the bond at the moment. The second, called the yield to maturity, takes into account total return, including interest and allowing for the fact that you may have purchased the bond for either more or less than it returns at maturity.

Current Yield   The **current yield** on a bond refers to the ratio of the annual interest payment to the bond's market price. If, for example, you're considering a bond with an 8 percent coupon interest rate, a par value of $1,000, and a market price of $700, it would have a current yield of:

Current Yield
The ratio of the annual interest payment to the bond's market price.

$$\text{current yield} = \frac{\text{annual interest payments}}{\text{market price of the bond}}$$

$$= \frac{0.08 \times \$1,000}{\$700} = \frac{\$80}{\$700} = 11.4 \text{ percent}$$

Yield to Maturity
The true yield or return that the bond-holder receives if a bond is held to maturity. It's the measure of expected return for a bond.

Yield to Maturity   The **yield to maturity** is the true yield or return you receive if you hold a bond to maturity. Basically, it's the measure of expected return. In effect, calculating the yield to maturity is the same as solving for the annual interest rate, i, in Chapter 3, where we discussed the time value of money. This measure of return considers the annual interest payments the bondholder receives as well as the difference between the bond's current market price and its value at maturity.

Remember, regardless of whether you bought your bond at a price above or below its par value, at maturity you get exactly its par value. If you paid less than $1,000 for your bond, the bond will appreciate over its lifetime, climbing up to $1,000 at maturity. Conversely, if you paid more than $1,000 for your bond, it will slowly drop in value over its lifetime, falling to $1,000 at maturity when it's redeemed.

If you have a financial calculator, solving for the yield to maturity, or i, is quite easy. If you don't have a financial calculator, you can use a formula to calculate the approximate yield to maturity (you need a calculator to calculate the actual yield to maturity). This formula first determines the average annual return by adding the annual interest payments to the average amount that the bond increases or decreases

MONEY MATTERS

Tips from Marcy Furney, ChFC, Certified Financial Planner™

A BONDING EXPERIENCE

Because you don't have to pay tax on the earnings of Series EE Savings Bonds until you cash them, they can serve as a tax-deferred account for any funds that you need to keep liquid. Consider them an alternative to bank savings accounts for money you don't want to expose to any risk of loss of principal.

Be aware of the potential downside of pass-through certificates. Because they are a pool of mortgages, homeowners' reactions to interest rates determine their outcome. If interest rates fall, a number of mortgages will be refinanced, and you will start getting your principal back in large chunks. Normally the older the mortgage pool, the greater the principal return. This means you must deal with some reinvestment risk throughout the life of the pool rather than just at a future maturity date. In other words, where will you put the return of principal in a falling interest rate environment?

The tax-free nature of municipal bonds may not be truly beneficial to everyone. Compute the equivalent taxable return for your tax bracket before you choose them. If you are in a low bracket, you may find that you can make enough with taxable alternatives to pay the

taxes and still come out ahead. If you are attempting to avoid state income tax, buy municipals for your state of residence. Keep in mind that although dividends are income tax free, capital gains are not.

If you are relying on a steady income flow from bonds, make sure they are not callable and that you hold them to maturity. Laddering the maturity of bonds will help stabilize income and reduce the amount of funds exposed to reinvestment risk at any one time. Liquid funds are available at each maturity, so selling a bond to get money for other needs is seldom necessary.

Even if you are an aggressive investor, don't discount the value of holding some bonds for diversification. They may be boring when the market is riding high, but you'll appreciate them when they slow the downward spiral of your portfolio.

Owning a bond mutual fund is not the same as holding individual bonds. In a fund, the average maturity and manager's trading activity determine the impact of price volatility when interest rates change. If you hold individual bonds to maturity, price volatility is not a factor you must deal with.

in price each year. The annual change in bond price is based on the notion that at maturity the bond will be worth its par value—because it will be redeemed at this price—and calculates the amount the bond must increase or decrease to get to its par value, and divides this by the number of years left to maturity.

This average annual return is then divided by the average value of the bond—the average of its par value and current market price. Thus, the *approximate yield to maturity* is calculated as follows:

$$\text{approximate yield to maturity} = \frac{\text{annual interest payments} + \dfrac{\text{par value} - \text{current price}}{\text{number of years to maturity}}}{\dfrac{\text{par value} + \text{current price}}{2}}$$

Let's look at an example of a bond that has 10 years left to maturity, has a par value of $1,000, a current price of $880, and a coupon interest rate of 10 percent that it pays annually. Thus, it pays $100 annually in interest to the bondholder (coupon interest rate × par value = annual interest payment, or 0.10 × $1,000 = $100). Plugging these numbers into the approximate yield to maturity formula, you get:

$$\text{approximate yield to maturity} = \frac{\$100 + \dfrac{\$1,000 - \$880}{10}}{\dfrac{\$1,000 + \$880}{2}}$$

$$\text{approximate yield to maturity} = \frac{\$100 + \dfrac{\$120}{10}}{\$1,880/2}$$

$$= \$112/\$940 = 11.91 \text{ percent}$$

Calculator Clues

A Bond's Yield to Maturity

Using a financial calculator, let's calculate the yield to maturity on the bond in the previous example. If you don't have a financial calculator, one is available on the MyFinanceLab Web site (**www.myfinancelab.com**). In this example $N = 10$ because there are 10 years to maturity, $PV = -880$ because you would pay $880 if you purchased this bond (the money "leaves your hands"), $PMT = 100$ because that is the amount you receive annually in the form of interest [it is equal to the bond's coupon interest rate (10%) times the bond's par value ($1,000)], and $FV = 1,000$, which is the bond's par value (the amount you receive at maturity). You'll notice the PV took on a negative sign because that is what you would pay for the bond (money "leaves your hands"), while PMT and FV take on positive signs because that money flows to you (the money is "returning to your hands").

Enter:	10			−880.00	100	$1,000
	N	I/Y	PV		PMT	FV
Solve for:		12.14%				

As we noted earlier, you'd need a financial calculator to get the true yield to maturity. If you did calculate the true yield to maturity, you would find it to be 12.14 percent, a difference of only 0.23 percent.

The approximate yield to maturity formula also works for bonds that are selling above their par or maturity value. Let's change the current market price to $1,100 and recalculate the approximate yield to maturity as follows:

$$\text{approximate yield to maturity} = \frac{\$100 + \dfrac{\$1,000 - \$1,100}{10}}{\dfrac{\$1,000 + \$1,100}{2}}$$

$$\text{approximate yield to maturity} = \frac{\$100 - \dfrac{\$100}{10}}{\$2,100/2}$$

$$= \$90/\$1,050 = 8.57 \text{ percent}$$

FACTS of LIFE

Perhaps the most famous bond is James, also known as 007. On an inflation adjusted basis, *Thunderball* had the highest box office receipts of any James Bond, 007, movie.

Calculator Clues

A Bond's Yield to Maturity

Let's calculate the yield to maturity on the previous example using a financial calculator. Again, if you don't have a financial calculator, one is available on the MyFinanceLab Web site. In this example $N = 10$ because there are 10 years to maturity, $PV = 1,100$ because you would pay $1,100 if you purchased this bond (remember, when you're solving for I/Y, there must be both positive and negative cash flows), $PMT = 100$ because that is the amount you receive annually in the form of interest [it is equal to the bond's coupon interest rate (10%) times the bond's par value ($1,000)], and $FV = 1,000$, which is the bond's par value (the amount you receive at maturity).

Enter:	10		−1,100.00	100	$1,000
	N	I/Y	PV	PMT	FV
Solve for:		8.48%			

Thus, the bond's yield to maturity is 8.48 percent. You'll notice that this is different from what you got using the approximation formula. As you might expect, this is the true answer and the other is an approximation.

Equivalent Taxable Yield on Municipal Bonds   The appeal of municipal bonds (munis) is their tax-exempt status. Thus, in comparing municipal bonds to other taxable bonds, the comparison must be between equivalent taxable yield—that is, the yield a taxable bond must offer to match the equivalent taxable yield on the municipal bond. The equivalent taxable yield on a municipal bond is calculated as follows:

$$\text{equivalent taxable yield} = \frac{\text{tax-free yield on the municipal bond}}{(1 - \text{investor's marginal tax bracket})}$$

Keep in mind that the tax bracket referred to includes all taxes avoided by the muni. This bracket could include federal, state, and local taxes. Thus, if the municipal bond yields 7 percent and the investor is in the 38 percent marginal tax bracket, the equivalent taxable yield on a municipal bond would be:

$$\frac{\text{equivalent}}{\text{taxable yield}} = \frac{0.07}{(1 - 0.38)} = \frac{0.07}{(0.62)} = 0.1129, \text{ or } 11.29\%$$

The higher the individual's tax bracket, the more attractive municipal bonds are.

Valuation Principles

The valuation of bonds has its roots in Principles 3 and 8. **Principle 3: The Time Value of Money** allows us to bring the investment returns back to present, while **Principle 8: Risk and Return Go Hand in Hand** tells us what discount rate to use in bringing those returns back to present.

From Chapter 13, you already know that the value of any investment is the present value of all the returns that you receive from that investment. This is how you value stocks, and it's also how you value bonds. In effect, we'll bring the future returns or benefits back to the present and add them up. With bonds, the process is quite simple—you find out the value in today's dollars of the interest and principal payments, and add them together.

Bond Valuation

When you purchase a bond, you get interest payments for a number of years, and then at maturity the bond is redeemed and you receive the par value of the bond back. Thus, *the value of a bond is the present value of the interest payments plus the present value of the repayment of the bond's par value at maturity.* In general, the value of a bond should be approximately the same as its price, because that's what you and other investors would be willing to pay for the bond. Therefore, by understanding how bonds are valued, we can also understand what causes bond prices to rise and fall.

Now, let's bring the interest payments and the repayment of the bond's par value at maturity back to the present. The interest payments come in the form of an annuity—that is, the investor receives the same dollar amount each year. The repayment of par comes in the form of a single cash flow.[2] Thus, the value of the bond can be written as:

$$\frac{\text{value of}}{\text{the bond}} = \frac{\text{present value of the}}{\text{interest payments}} + \frac{\text{present value of repayment}}{\text{of par at maturity}}$$

Rewriting this using the style from Chapter 3, we get

$$\frac{\text{value of}}{\text{the bond}} = \frac{\text{annual}}{\substack{\text{interest} \\ \text{payments}}} \times \frac{\substack{\text{present-} \\ \text{value} \\ \text{interest} \\ \text{factor} \\ \text{of an annuity}}}{} + \frac{\text{par}}{\text{value}} \times \frac{\substack{\text{present-value} \\ \text{interest factor}}}{}$$

Let's look at an example. We're considering buying a bond that matures in 20 years with a coupon interest rate of 10 percent and a par value of $1,000. How much should we pay for it? Well, first we need to decide what return we require on that bond. Let's assume that given the current interest rates and risk level of this bond, our required rate of return is also 10 percent per year. To determine the value of the bond, we need only bring the

---

[2]Actually, the calculation of the value of a bond is slightly more complicated because most bonds pay interest semiannually rather than annually. Although accommodating this complication is relatively simple, the principles behind bond valuation don't change. Moreover, the effect on the value of the bond is only slight. Because our presentation is meant to illustrate how the value of a bond is determined in the marketplace and how changes in interest rates are reflected in bond prices, we won't deal with semiannual interest payments.

interest payments and repayment of par back to the present using our required rate of return as the discount rate. The annual interest payments we'll receive if we buy this bond are equal to the bond's coupon interest rate of 10 percent times the par value of the bond, which is $1,000. Thus, the annual interest payments are $100. Recall that the *present-value interest factor of an annuity* can be determined using a financial calculator or looked up directly in Appendix D, and the *present-value interest factor* can also be determined using a financial calculator or looked up in Appendix B. The value of the bond can now be calculated as follows (using 10 percent for *i*, and 20 years):

$$\frac{\text{value of}}{\text{the bond}} = \frac{\text{present value of the}}{\text{interest payments}} + \frac{\text{present value of repayment}}{\text{of par at maturity}}$$

$$= \$100(\text{present-value interest factor of an annuity})$$

$$+ \$1,000(\text{present-value interest factor})$$

$$= \$100(8.514) + \$1,000(0.1486)$$

$$= \$851.40 + \$148.60$$

$$= \$1,000$$

Thus, the value of this bond would be $1,000. If we purchased it for $1,000, we'd be paying exactly its par value. The reason we'd buy at par is that we'd be earning our entire required rate of return from the interest payments—we required a 10 percent return and we receive a 10 percent return in the form of interest.

Calculator Clues

Value of a Bond

Using a financial calculator, let's calculate the value of a bond that matures in 20 years with a coupon interest rate of 10 percent, which is our required rate of return, and a par value of $1,000. In this example $N = 20$ because there are 20 years to maturity, $I/Y = 10$ because our required rate of return is 10 percent, $PMT = 100$ because that is the amount we receive annually in the form of interest [it is equal to the bond's coupon interest rate (10 percent) times the bond's par value ($1,000)], and $FV = 1,000$ which is the bond's par value (the amount we receive at maturity).

Enter: 20   10   100 $1,000
           [N]   [I/Y]   [PV]   [PMT]   [FV]
Solve for: −1,000.00

Thus, the value of the bond is $1,000. You'll notice that, as expected, we get a negative sign on the *PV*.

STOP & THINK

"The difference between a successful person and others is not a lack of strength, not a lack of knowledge, but rather a lack of will."—Vince Lombardi. What do you think he meant by this?

Now let's look at the same bond and assume that the current level of interest rates has gone up and, as a result, so has our required rate of return—to 12 percent. How much should we pay for this bond now? In this case, the only change is in the value of the discount rate or required rate of return. Recalculating the value of the bond, we find it to be (using 12 percent for *i*, and 20 years):

$$\text{value of the bond} = \text{present value of the interest payments} + \text{present value of repayment of par at maturity}$$

$$= \$100(\text{present-value interest factor of an annuity})$$
$$+ \$1,000(\text{present-value interest factor})$$
$$= \$100(7.469) + \$1,000(0.104)$$
$$= \$746.90 + \$104.00$$
$$= \$850.90$$

Calculator Clues

Value of a Bond When the Required Rate of Return Is 12 Percent

Now let's recalculate the value of this bond when the required rate of return is 12 percent. The only change is that I/Y now equals 12 percent.

Enter: 20   12   100 $1,000
          N   I/Y   PV   PMT   FV

Solve for: −850.61

This is the same number we got using the tables (other than some rounding error).

When we raise our required rate of return to 12 percent, the value of the bond falls to $850.90. As a result, we would want to buy this bond *at a discount*, that is, below its par value. We're requiring a 12 percent return on this bond, but its interest rate is only 10 percent. We'd need to receive the remaining return from the appreciation of the bond in value. So, we would look to buy it for $850.90 and at maturity receive $1,000 for it.

Let's see what happens to the value of this bond when our required rate of return goes down. Assume that the current level of interest rates has gone down and, as a result, so has our required rate of return, this time to 8 percent. Again, the only change is in the value of the discount rate or required rate of return. Recalculating the value of the bond, we find it to be (using 8 percent as i, and 20 years):

$$\text{value of the bond} = \text{present value of the interest payments} + \text{present value of repayment of par at maturity}$$

$$= \$100(\text{present-value interest factor of an annuity})$$
$$+ \$1,000(\text{present-value interest factor})$$
$$= \$100(9.818) + \$1,000(0.215)$$
$$= \$981.80 + \$215.00$$
$$= \$1,196.80$$

Calculator Clues

Value of a Bond When the Required Rate of Return Is 8 Percent

Now let's recalculate the value of this bond when the required rate of return is 8 percent. The only change is that I/Y now equals 8 percent.

Enter: 20   8   100 $1,000
          N   I/Y   PV   PMT   FV

Solve for: −1,196.36

This is the same number we got using the tables (other than some rounding error).

Thus, when the required rate of return drops to 8 percent, the value of the bond climbs to $1,196.80. As a result, we would be willing to buy this bond *at a premium*, that is, above its par value. Again, this makes sense, because if the bond pays 10 percent in interest and we require an 8 percent return, we'd be willing to pay more than $1,000 for it.

In reflecting on this example, notice that as the required rate of return goes up, the value of the bond drops, and when the required rate of return goes down, the value of the bond increases. What can cause the required rate of return to change?

First, if the firm that issued the bond becomes riskier, the required rate of return should rise. The result of this would be a drop in the value of the bond—that certainly makes intuitive sense. A second factor that can cause you to alter your required rate of return on a bond is a change in general interest rates in the market. When interest rates go up, new bonds are issued with higher interest rates. If you own a bond that pays 8 percent interest, and new bonds are available that pay 9 percent interest, no one would want your 8 percent bond unless you lowered its price to make it competitive with the 9 percent bond.

Thus, when interest rates in general rise, the value of outstanding bonds falls. Because the value of these bonds falls, so does their price. Alternatively, when interest rates fall, the value and price of outstanding bonds rise. As we'll see, this inverse relationship between bond values or prices and interest rates is extremely important.

Why Bonds Fluctuate in Value

If you invest in bonds, it's important to know what makes them move up and down in value, and therefore in price. Let's begin by summarizing the key relationship that underlies bond valuation. *There's an inverse relationship between interest rates and bond values in the secondary market: When interest rates rise, bond values drop, and when interest rates drop, bond values rise.*

As interest rates rise, investors demand a higher return on bonds. If a bond has a fixed coupon interest rate, the only way the bond can increase its return to investors is to drop in value and sell for less. Thus, we have an inverse relationship between interest rates and bond values (and prices).

The importance of this relationship can't be overstated. Bond prices fluctuate dramatically, and this relationship explains much of the fluctuation. For example, in 1999 interest rates went up, and as a result long-term Treasury bonds posted average losses of 9.0 percent. Then, in 2000 and in 2002 interest rates fell and those same bonds returned 21.5 and 17.8 percent respectively! The same inverse relationship between interest rates and bond prices showed up dramatically in 2008 and 2009. In 2008, interest rates dropped as the economy slid into a recession, and as a result long-term Treasury bonds climbed by almost 26 percent. Then in 2009, interest rates reversed as investors became concerned about long-term inflation, and as interest rates climbed, long-term Treasury bonds fell by almost 15 percent. Figure 14.1 shows the relationship between bond prices and interest rates since the end of 1970 and illustrates the inverse relationship that exists between them.

Not only do bond values change when interest rates change, but *longer-term bonds fluctuate in price more than shorter-term bonds*. Remember from Chapter 3 that the further in the future a cash flow is, the more its present value will fluctuate as a result of a change in the interest or discount rate. Thus, when interest rates change, longer-term bonds fluctuate in price

STOP & THINK

Can you use this inverse relationship between interest rates and bond prices to make money? Before you forecast interest rates and invest in bonds, you should realize that beating the market is extremely difficult. To use this inverse relationship between interest rates and bond prices, you would not only have to forecast interest rates, but you would have to outforecast the experts. Knowing which way interest rates are going would not be enough if other investors know the same thing: You would need to know which way interest rates are going when no one else knows. What's been happening to interest rates lately?

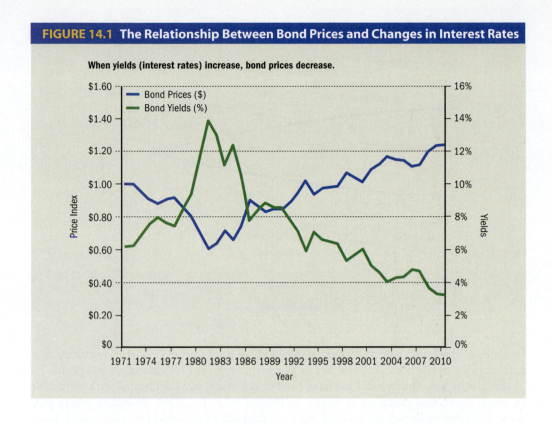

FIGURE 14.1   The Relationship Between Bond Prices and Changes in Interest Rates

more than shorter-term bonds. Figure 14.2 looks at bonds with a 5 percent coupon interest rate and various maturities as market interest rates go up and down. It shows that long-term bonds bounce up and down much more dramatically in response to interest rate changes than short-term bonds.

In addition, *as a bond approaches its maturity date, its market value approaches its par or maturity value.* Without question, a bond will sell for its par or maturity value at maturity. We know this because at maturity the bondholder receives the par value from the

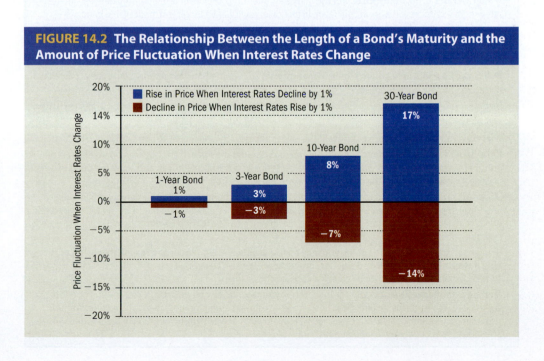

FIGURE 14.2   The Relationship Between the Length of a Bond's Maturity and the Amount of Price Fluctuation When Interest Rates Change

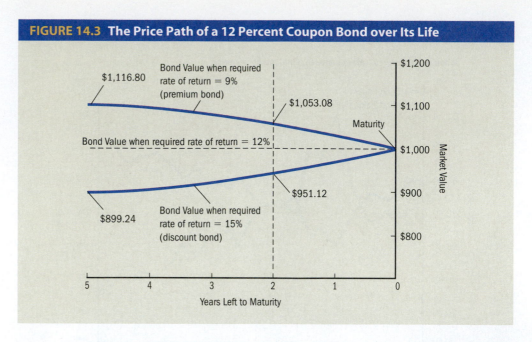

FIGURE 14.3 The Price Path of a 12 Percent Coupon Bond over Its Life

issuer, and the bond is terminated. As a result, as the bond approaches maturity, the market price of the bond approaches its par value. Figure 14.3 illustrates this point.

Finally, *when interest rates go down, bond prices go up, but the upward price movement on bonds with a call provision is limited by the call price.* In effect, investors won't pay more than the call price for a bond, because they know it could be called away from them for that price at any time. Before moving on, let's make sure you understand the pros and cons of bonds. Table 14.2 lists the benefits and dangers of bonds, while Checklist 14.1 looks at picking a good bond.

TABLE 14.2 The Pros and Cons of Investing in Bonds

Benefits of Bonds

- **If interest rates drop, bond prices will rise.** If interest rates drop, that inverse relationship between interest rates and bond prices will work in your favor. In that case, you'll want a long-term, noncallable bond.
- **Bonds reduce risk through diversification.** Any time you add a new investment to your portfolio that doesn't move in tandem with the other investments in your portfolio, you reduce your portfolio risk.
- **Bonds produce steady current income.** What more need we say?
- **Bonds can be a safe investment if held to maturity.** If you hold the bond to maturity and it doesn't default, it'll return exactly what it promises.

Dangers of Bonds

- **If interest rates rise, bond prices will fall.** The longer the maturity, the more the bond will fluctuate.
- **If the issuer experiences financial problems, the bondholder may pay.** If an issuer can't make interest or principal payments, the bond will plummet in value. Minor financial problems can also cause the bond to drop in value. Of course, any time the bond rating drops, bond values drop like a stone.
- **If interest rates drop, the bond may be called.** Most corporate bonds are callable. In theory, when interest rates drop, the value of a bond should rise. However, the issuer may decide to refinance the bond offering with bonds that have a lower interest rate. The bonds may be called away, leaving investors to reinvest the proceeds from the called bonds at lower interest rates.
- **If you need to sell your bonds early, you may have a problem selling them at a reasonable price, particularly if they're bonds issued by a smaller corporation.** There isn't a strong secondary market for the bonds of smaller corporations. In short, bonds aren't a very liquid investment.
- **Finding a good investment outlet for the interest you receive may be difficult.** If you're using bonds to accumulate wealth, it may be difficult to find a good investment outlet for the interest you receive. Without reinvesting the interest payments, there'll be no accumulation of wealth from investing in bonds unless you're investing in zero or very low coupon bonds.

◆ **Think about the effect of taxes.** Consider municipals, particularly if you're in a high tax bracket.

◆ **Keep the inverse relationship between interest rates and bond prices in mind.** If interest rates are very low, the only way they can go is up (which would cause bond prices to drop), so you might want to invest in shorter-term bonds.

◆ **If you're buying a corporate bond, avoid losers.** Look for and avoid firms that might experience major financial problems. All other firms are pretty much the same.

◆ **Limit yourself to bonds rated AA or above.** In this way you minimize any worry regarding a possible default by the issuer.

◆ **Buy your bond when it's first issued, rather than in the secondary market.** The price is generally fair, and the sales commission on a newly issued bond is paid by the issuer.

◆ **Avoid bonds that might get called.** Before you buy a bond, ask your broker or financial planner if the bond is likely to be called. If so, pick another one.

◆ **Match your bond's maturity to your investment time horizon.** In this way you can hold the bond to maturity and avoid having to sell in the secondary market, where you don't always get a fair price.

◆ **Stick to large issues.** If you think you might have to sell before maturity and are buying a corporate bond, make sure you buy a bond issued by a large corporation—the secondary market is generally more active for them.

◆ **When in doubt, go Treasury!** If you're still unsure, it's better to be safe than sorry—buy a Treasury bond.

What Bond Valuation Relationships Mean to the Investor

You can glean several important points from the discussion of bond valuation relationships. You know that bond prices can fluctuate dramatically and that interest rates drive these changes. In addition, you know that there's an inverse relationship between interest rates and bond prices: When interest rates go up, bond prices go down. Conversely, when interest rates go down, bond prices go up. Given this inverse relationship between interest rates and bond prices:

◆ If you expect interest rates to go up (and, therefore, bond prices to fall), you want to mute the inverse relationship by purchasing very short-term bonds. Although there still may be some price fluctuation, it will be minor.

◆ If you expect interest rates to go down, and therefore bond prices to rise, you want to amplify this relationship as much as possible by purchasing bonds with very long maturities that aren't callable. In this case, the bonds will fluctuate as much as possible, and if interest rates go down, the price of the bonds will rise.

Reading Online Corporate Bond Quotes

Figure 14.4 provides a visual summary of how to read online corporate bond listings. Recall that although corporate bonds generally have a par or

FACTS of LIFE

If you're looking for a safe bond, it's hard to beat a Treasury. Sure, they fluctuate when interest rates go up and down just like any other bond, but there is no question about the interest and principal payments being made on time. Treasury bonds issued today are noncallable, won't be downgraded or default, and are liquid. On top of that, you can buy them directly from the Federal Reserve and avoid brokerage commissions.

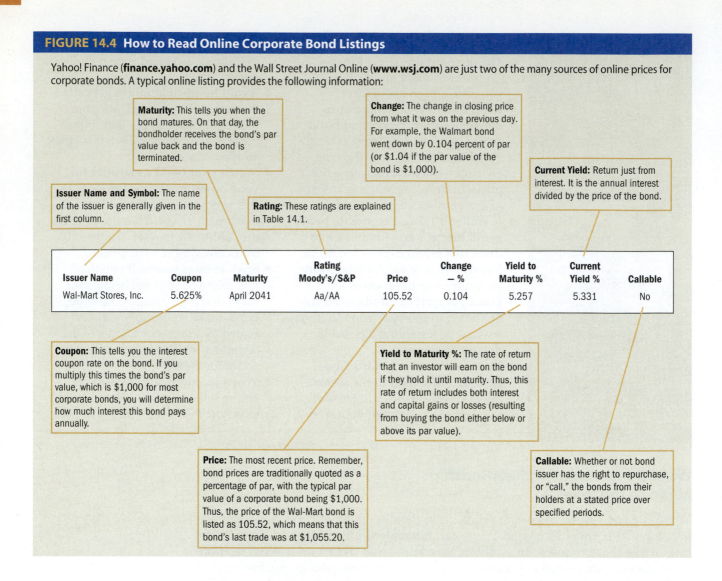

FIGURE 14.4 How to Read Online Corporate Bond Listings

Yahoo! Finance (**finance.yahoo.com**) and the Wall Street Journal Online (**www.wsj.com**) are just two of the many sources of online prices for corporate bonds. A typical online listing provides the following information:

Maturity: This tells you when the bond matures. On that day, the bondholder receives the bond's par value back and the bond is terminated.

Change: The change in closing price from what it was on the previous day. For example, the Walmart bond went down by 0.104 percent of par (or $1.04 if the par value of the bond is $1,000).

Current Yield: Return just from interest. It is the annual interest divided by the price of the bond.

Issuer Name and Symbol: The name of the issuer is generally given in the first column.

Rating: These ratings are explained in Table 14.1.

Issuer Name	Coupon	Maturity	Rating Moody's/S&P	Price	Change — %	Yield to Maturity %	Current Yield %	Callable
Wal-Mart Stores, Inc.	5.625%	April 2041	Aa/AA	105.52	0.104	5.257	5.331	No

Coupon: This tells you the interest coupon rate on the bond. If you multiply this times the bond's par value, which is $1,000 for most corporate bonds, you will determine how much interest this bond pays annually.

Yield to Maturity %: The rate of return that an investor will earn on the bond if they hold it until maturity. Thus, this rate of return includes both interest and capital gains or losses (resulting from buying the bond either below or above its par value).

Price: The most recent price. Remember, bond prices are traditionally quoted as a percentage of par, with the typical par value of a corporate bond being $1,000. Thus, the price of the Wal-Mart bond is listed as 105.52, which means that this bond's last trade was at $1,055.20.

Callable: Whether or not bond issuer has the right to repurchase, or "call," the bonds from their holders at a stated price over specified periods.

face value of $1,000, their selling price is quoted as a percentage of par. Even though a bond may appear to be selling at 101, it's actually selling at 101 percent of its par value, which is $1,000. Thus, a bond listed as selling at 101 is actually selling for $1,010.

What is listed in the paper isn't exactly what you'd pay if you purchased the bond. You're also expected to pay for any **accrued interest** on the bond. Remember, interest is generally paid only every 6 months. Thus, if it's been 5 months since interest was last paid, the bond has accrued 5 months' worth of interest. This accrued interest isn't reflected in the listed price of the bond, but you still need to pay the seller for the accrued interest that's already been earned.

If this bond pays $48 in interest every 6 months, then 5 months' worth of accrued interest would be $\frac{5}{6} \times \$48 = \$40$. That means that although the bond is listed as selling for $1,010, if you purchased it you'd pay $1,010 + $40 = $1,050. This sum of both the quoted or stated price and the accrued interest is often referred to as the **invoice price**.

Accrued Interest

Interest that has been earned on the bond but has not yet been paid out to the bondholder.

Invoice Price

The sum of both the quoted or stated price of a bond and the bond's accrued interest. It's the price you pay if you buy the bond in the secondary market.

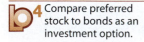
4 Compare preferred stock to bonds as an investment option.

Preferred Stock—An Alternative to Bonds

Preferred stock is often referred to as a hybrid security because it has many of the characteristics of both common stock and bonds. From the investor's point of view, preferred stock is probably closer to bonds. On the one hand, preferred stock is similar to common stock in that it has no fixed maturity date and not paying its dividends won't bring on bankruptcy. On the other hand, preferred stock is similar to bonds in that its dividends are of a fixed size and are paid before common stock dividends are paid. A share of preferred stock is also similar to a bond in that it doesn't carry voting rights.

The size of the preferred stock dividend is generally fixed as a dollar amount or as a percentage of the stock's par value. Because these dividends are fixed, preferred stockholders don't share in profits but are limited to their stated annual dividend. Just as with a bond, if the firm has a great year and earns lots of money, the preferred stock dividend doesn't change.

Features and Characteristics of Preferred Stock

To gain a better understanding of preferred stock, let's take a moment to look at some of its features and characteristics.

Multiple Issues   A firm can issue more than one issue of preferred stock, each with a different set dividend. In fact, some firms have well over ten different issues of preferred stock outstanding.

Cumulative Feature   Most preferred stock carries a **cumulative feature**, which requires that all past unpaid preferred stock dividends be paid before any common stock dividends are declared. This feature provides the preferred stock investor with some degree of protection, because otherwise there would be no reason why preferred stock dividends wouldn't be omitted or passed when common stock dividends are passed.

Adjustable Rate   In the early 1980s, **adjustable-rate preferred stock** was introduced to provide investors with some protection against wide swings in the value of preferred stock that resulted from interest rate swings. With adjustable-rate preferred stock, the amount of quarterly dividends fluctuates with interest rates under a formula that ties the dividend payment to a market interest rate. As a result, when interest rates rise, rather than the value of the preferred stock dropping, the preferred stock's dividend rises and the value of the preferred stock stays relatively constant.

Convertibility   Some preferred stock is also **convertible preferred stock**, which means that its holder can, at any time, exchange it for a predetermined number of shares of common stock. The trade-off associated with convertible preferred stock is that the convertibility feature may allow the preferred stockholder to participate in the company's capital gains, but the preferred stock has a lower dividend associated with it than regular preferred stock.

Callability   Much of the preferred stock outstanding is callable. Just as with bonds, if interest rates drop, there is a good chance that the preferred stock will be called away by the issuing firm.

Valuation of Preferred Stock

When you buy a share of preferred stock, you get a steady stream of dividends that go on forever, because preferred stock never matures. Thus, *the value of a share of preferred stock is the present value of the perpetual stream of constant dividends that the preferred*

Preferred Stock
Stock that offers no ownership or voting rights and generally pays fixed dividends. The dividends on preferred stock are paid out before dividends on common stock can be issued.

Cumulative Feature
A feature of preferred stock that requires all past unpaid preferred stock dividends to have been paid before any common stock dividends can be declared.

Adjustable-Rate Preferred Stock
Preferred stock on which the quarterly dividends fluctuate with the market interest rate.

Convertible Preferred Stock
Preferred stock that the holder can exchange for a predetermined number of shares of common stock.

stockholder receives. As such, the value of a share of preferred stock can be written as follows:

$$\frac{\text{value of}}{\text{preferred stock}} = \frac{\text{present value of the perpetual}}{\text{stream of constant dividends}}$$

Because preferred stock dividends go on forever, they constitute a perpetuity. (Remember this term from Chapter 3?) The calculation of their present value can be reduced to:

$$\frac{\text{value of}}{\text{preferred stock}} = \frac{\text{annual preferred stock divided}}{\text{required rate of return}}$$

When interest rates rise (causing your required rate of return to rise), the value of a share of preferred stock declines. Conversely, when interest rates decline (causing your required rate of return to drop), the value of a share of preferred stock rises. This is the primary valuation relationship in valuing preferred stock and, as we just saw, in valuing bonds.

Let's look at an example. If the Gap has an issue of preferred stock outstanding with an annual dividend of $4, and given the level of risk on this issue, investors demand a required rate of return of 10 percent, its value would be:

$$\frac{\text{value of}}{\text{preferred stock}} = \frac{\$4}{0.10} = \$40$$

As you can see, if the required rate of return on this preferred stock dropped to 8 percent, its value would climb to $4/0.08, or $50. Thus, as market interest rates rise and fall (causing investors' required rates of return to rise and fall), the value of preferred stock moves in an opposite manner.

Risks Associated with Preferred Stock

We've said that preferred stock is a hybrid between bonds and common stock. Unfortunately, when it comes to advantages and disadvantages for the investor, it's also a hybrid, taking disadvantages from both common stock and bonds but advantages from neither. The problems with preferred stock for the individual investor include the following:

◆ If interest rates rise, the value of the preferred stock drops.
◆ If interest rates drop, the value of the preferred stock rises and the preferred stock is called away from the investor (remember, most preferred stock is callable).
◆ The investor doesn't participate in the capital gains that common stockholders receive.
◆ The investor doesn't have the safety of bond interest payments, because preferred stock dividends can be passed without the risk of bankruptcy.

Given all these drawbacks and very few advantages, you may be wondering who buys preferred stock. The answer is, other corporations, because corporations receive a tax break on the dividend income from preferred stock.

If you do decide to invest in preferred stock, you'll want to pay attention to the preferred stock's rating. Similar to bonds, preferred stocks are rated by Moody's and Standard & Poor's. The majority of preferred stock falls into the medium-grade levels. Just as you'd expect from **Principle 8: Risk and Return Go Hand in Hand**, the lower the preferred stock's rating and, therefore, the riskier the preferred stock, the higher the expected return.

Investing in Real Estate

5 Understand the risks associated with investing in real estate.

Since the end of World War II, real estate investments have created more fortunes than almost any other investment. Unfortunately, in the late 1980s, those same real estate investments destroyed quite a few fortunes. Then, from the late 1990s through the mid-2000s, real estate climbed in value and become a popular investment. All that changed around 2006 when real estate prices began to drop.

Most American households—in fact, about two-thirds—own their own homes, and for them, it's the biggest investment they're likely to make. In fact, as we saw in Chapter 8, housing costs take up over 25 percent of after-tax income. The question now becomes: Do you want to go beyond this personal investment and make an additional investment in real estate? For most people, the answer to this question is no. Real estate investment requires time, energy, and sophistication that the majority of us just don't have. There are also a lot of risks with real estate investments. For example, the average price of a house in Miami was $371,000 in 2006, but by mid-2011, that same house was selling for about $166,000—down about 65 percent! However, for some people, investing in real estate is an option. So let's discuss what types of investments in real estate you might consider.

> **FACTS of LIFE**
> Returns on REITs can vary quite a bit from year to year. According to the Morgan Stanley REIT Index, REITs fell by about 75 percent between March 2007 and March 2009. Then between March 2009 and March 2011 much of that loss was recovered, but they were still down 30 percent from their 2007 high.

Real estate investment can be categorized as direct or indirect. With a direct investment, you directly own the property. This type of investment might include a vacation home or commercial property—an apartment building or undeveloped land. With an indirect investment, you're an investor in a group that owns the property and has hired a professional to manage it. Indirect investments include partnerships that buy and manage property, called real estate syndicates, and investment companies that pool the money of many investors and invest in real estate, called real estate investment trusts, or REITs.

Direct Investments in Real Estate

Vacation homes are the most popular of all the direct real estate investments. However, only if your vacation home is viewed as a second home can you deduct your mortgage interest and taxes when you compute your income taxes. However, since 1987 the investment appeal of vacation homes has suffered because of a change in the tax laws. Now, if you rent your vacation home for more than 14 days per year, which many investors do, it's considered rental property, and your deductions are determined by how the property is managed and by your income. In the best case, your income will cover your expenses, providing you with a home rent-free during vacations, but this generally isn't the case. Because of the complexity surrounding the tax benefits of a vacation home, you really need the help of a tax accountant or financial planner to analyze a vacation home before you invest. Even then, it's important to realize that much of your return is likely to depend on future price appreciation. The bottom line is that if you buy a vacation home, buy it for pleasure, not as an investment.

> **FACTS of LIFE**
> When real estate values peaked in 2006, a home in Los Angeles cost the equivalent of 4.5 years' pay. By mid-2011, the average price had since fallen to just over 2 years' income.

Commercial property, such as apartment buildings, duplexes, and office buildings, are best left to professionals who specialize in the management of such investments. First, it's too active an investment for most individuals, requiring a lot of time and energy. It also takes a good deal of sophistication, since evaluating a price for commercial property is complicated.

Investing in undeveloped land, although popular among very rich and sophisticated investors, is risky, and because the land is undeveloped, it doesn't produce any cash flow. In fact, because you have to pay taxes on the undeveloped land, it produces a cash outflow while you're holding it. The purpose of buying undeveloped land is to have it rise in value and then sell it. However, developing the land to the point where it climbs in price can cost a lot of money. Moreover, as we saw in the late 2000s, there's no guarantee that the land will rise in price. As a result, this investment, too, is better left to the experts.

Indirect Investments in Real Estate

Indirect investments in real estate, where you are part of an investment group that works directly with a professional real estate manager, are better suited for the individual investor. Unfortunately, the appeal of real estate syndicates was severely dampened as a result of tax reform in the late 1980s. Moreover, evaluating how attractive an investment a real estate syndicate is can be quite difficult. Therefore, this is another investment alternative that should be left to the experts.

The most attractive real estate alternative is the real estate investment trust, or REIT. Because this type of investment is akin to a mutual fund that specializes in real estate investments, we'll hold off discussion until mutual funds are presented in Chapter 15.

Investing in Real Estate: The Bottom Line

The major advantage for investing in real estate is the income the property can generate coupled with the opportunity for capital gains. Unfortunately, the tax advantages that helped produce real estate fortunes in the past are largely gone or are on the way out. In addition, direct investments in real estate are very active forms of investing, in which time, energy, and knowledge are all important ingredients.

> ## STOP & THINK
>
> "[Gold] gets dug out of the ground in Africa, or someplace. Then we melt it down, dig another hole, bury it again and pay people to stand around guarding it. It has no utility. Anyone watching from Mars would be scratching their head."—Warren Buffet, Harvard, 1998. What do you think he meant by this?

Another drawback to investing in real estate is illiquidity. That is, if you do have to sell your property holdings, it may take months to find a buyer, and there's no guarantee that you'll get what you feel is a fair price. In addition, overbuilding and the real estate bubble of the late 2000s in some areas has in the past, and can in the future, result in a decline of property prices. The bottom line is that real estate investment is not well suited to the novice investor.

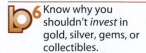

6 Know why you shouldn't *invest* in gold, silver, gems, or collectibles.

Investing—Speculating—in Gold, Silver, Gems, and Collectibles

Don't do it! Putting your money in gold, silver, platinum, precious stones, and the like is not investing—it is speculation. When we differentiated between investing and speculating in Chapter 11, we said that with investing, the value of your asset is determined by what return it earns, not merely by whether that asset is a fashionable one to own or not. If an asset doesn't generate a return, its value is determined by supply and demand, and putting money in it is speculating. Should you speculate? Not if your goal is to create a sound personal financial plan.

Gold, silver, platinum, diamonds, rubies, and collectibles are perfect examples of speculation. Look at gold. In 1980, when the DJIA was below 1,000, gold peaked at around $850 an ounce. Since then gold has bounced a bit and recently has done very well, rising to around $1,900 an ounce in September 2011. While gold did very well in 2010 and early 2011, its average annual return since 1980 was just under 3 percent per year. Over that same period a typical New York Stock Exchange stock increased at an average annual rate of 10.6 percent. Still, on late-night infomercials across the nation you continue to see hucksters proclaiming gold as "the place for your savings." Don't buy into their sales pitch—it's another form of speculation.

Collectibles deserve a bit more discussion because they have entertainment value; a collector often gets joy out of collecting. However, collectibles are not investments as their resale value is speculative. Stamps, coins, comic books, and baseball cards, for example, are worth more in the future only if someone's willing to pay more for them. Their value depends entirely on supply and demand.

Does this mean you should avoid collectibles? Yes, if you're looking to them as an investment. Remember, investment is quite a bit duller and more certain than speculation, but when you're dealing with your future financial security, dull and certain aren't bad things. Collectibles can be fun, but don't expect them to provide for your financial future. I (the author), for example, collect old *Mad* magazines. There's no question that their price may go down, but to me, that's not a concern ("What, me worry?"), because they aren't an investment and aren't intended to be sold.

> ### STOP & THINK
>
> Some people make fortunes dealing in collectibles. Look at Mike Gidwitz, baseball card collector and investment advisor from Chicago. In 1997 he paid a record $640,500 for the hobby's most famous and valuable card, the only T206 Honus Wagner in mint condition. Mike is an extremely nice and very interesting person who also owns the original paintings for the covers of 44 *Mad* magazines. But as Mike says: "I look at baseball cards like gambling—if you can't afford to lose the money then you shouldn't buy them. I don't buy baseball cards for investment, I buy them for the pleasure I get out of them." That's a good philosophy. By the way, Mike sold the card in July 2000 for $1.265 million. What do you collect? Is it of value?

Summary

Invest in the bond market.

Why might you consider investing in bonds? There are several reasons. Bonds reduce risk through diversification, produce steady current income, and if held to maturity, can be a safe investment.

Understand basic bond terminology and compare the various types of bonds.

When you invest in a bond and hold it until it matures, your return is based on two things: (1) semiannual or annual interest payments and (2) the return of the par value or principal. The danger is that the bond issuer will not have the funds to make these payments. There are two measures of return on a bond: current yield and yield to maturity. The current yield on a bond refers to the ratio of the annual interest payment to the bond's market price. The yield to maturity is the true yield or return the bondholder receives if the bond is held to maturity.

Thousands of outstanding bonds have been issued by corporations, the U.S. government and its agencies, states, and localities. There are also a number of special situation bonds, including zero coupon bonds and junk bonds.

3 Calculate the value of a bond and understand the factors that cause bond value to change.

The value of a bond is the present value of the stream of interest payments plus the present value of the repayment of the bond's par value at maturity. There is an inverse relationship between the value of a bond and the investor's required rate of return. Thus, when the required rate of return goes up, the value of the bond drops, and when the investor's required rate of return goes down, the value of the bond increases.

 4 Compare preferred stock to bonds as an investment option.

Preferred stock is a security with no fixed maturity date and with dividends that are generally set in amount and don't fluctuate. Just as with bonds, a firm can issue more than one series or class of preferred stock, each with unique characteristics. In addition, most preferred stock carries a cumulative feature, which requires that all past unpaid preferred stock dividends be paid before any common stock dividends are declared.

 5 Understand the risks associated with investing in real estate.

Real estate investments can be categorized as either direct or indirect. With a direct investment, you directly own the property. With an indirect investment, you're an investor in a group that owns the property and has hired a professional to manage it. These are probably investments best left to the professional.

 6 Know why you shouldn't *invest* in gold, silver, gems, or collectibles.

Gold, silver, platinum, diamonds, rubies, and collectibles are perfect examples of speculation, and should be avoided. As such, you should only consider purchasing them if you aren't concerned about what might happen to their price in the future, because they aren't an investment.

Review Questions

1. What are three reasons why investors should consider adding bonds to their portfolios?
2. Why are bonds generally considered to be relatively safe investments compared to stocks?
3. What is an indenture and why is it an important document for bond investors?
4. Why do firms issue bonds with call provisions? During what type of interest rate environment would you expect an issuer to exercise a call? How do firms make callable bonds more attractive to investors?
5. What is a sinking fund and why is it an advantage to investors?
6. What is meant by the term "subordination" when dealing with corporate debt?
7. Why is U.S. Treasury debt considered risk free? Describe the possibility of default risk associated with Treasury debt.
8. Compare Treasury bills, notes, and bonds in terms of maturity and yield.
9. What is a pass-through certificate, and how is a pass-through both similar to and different from a Treasury security? Give an example of an agency that issues pass-throughs.
10. Describe a Treasury inflation-indexed bond. Who should consider these bonds for an investment portfolio?

11. What advantages do I bonds offer investors? At purchase, how do I bonds differ from EE bonds?

12. What types of entities issue municipal bonds? What significant feature of municipal bonds attracts investors? Given this feature, who should consider investing in municipal bonds?

13. What are the two types of municipal bonds, and which type has the greater default risk? Why?

14. What is a zero coupon bond? Give an example of when the use of zero coupon bonds might be appropriate in an investment portfolio. Do you think these types of bonds should be owned in taxable or tax-deferred accounts?

15. What potential risks do investors face when they purchase junk bonds? How are investors compensated for these risks? What rating would you expect to see a junk bond carry?

16. Explain the difference between current yield and yield to maturity. Which is a more accurate measure of the return an investor will receive?

17. What is the difference between the quoted price and the invoice price? When would you expect the two prices to be equal?

18. What is meant by the terms "premium" and "discount" when referring to the price of a bond?

19. Using sound bond valuation principles, explain in terms of present value why zero coupon bonds sell at such a deep discount to the par value.

20. An investor's required rate of return is important when valuing a bond. What two factors can cause an investor's required rate of return to change?

21. Describe the relationship between interest rates and bond values. If investors' required rate of return decreases, what should happen to the value of bonds? Would this bond be purchased at a premium or discount? How did you make this determination?

22. What features do preferred stock shares offer investors? What feature, similar to a bond, should cause investors to demand a higher dividend yield?

23. Describe the differences between direct and indirect real estate investments.

24. Provide five examples of speculation. What distinguishes these "investments" from stocks, bonds, and real estate?

Develop Your Skills—Problems and Activities

These problems are available in MyFinanceLab.

1. Suppose that you are interested in purchasing a bond issued by the VPI Corporation. The bond is quoted in the *Wall Street Journal* as selling for 88.375. How much will you pay for the bond if you purchase it at the quoted price? Assuming you hold the bond until maturity, how much will you receive at that time?

2. Inflation-indexed bonds pay investors based on a fixed interest rate; however, the semiannual interest payments are calculated on the inflation-adjusted par value. Assuming that the $1,000 inflation-indexed bond in question currently sells for $940 and carries a coupon interest rate of 4 percent, answer the following questions:

   a. If you buy this bond, how much will you receive for your first interest payment, assuming no interest adjustment to principal during this time period?

   b. If there's a 1 percent increase in inflation, what will be the new par value of the bond?

c. What is your new semiannual interest payment?

d. What would the par value be at maturity, assuming a 2.5 percent annual inflation rate and 10-year maturity period?

3. How much will a $500 EE savings bond cost when you initially purchase it? Assuming the bond earns 3.6 percent annually, approximately how long will it take for the bond to reach its stated face value?

4. An investor is considering purchasing a bond with a 5.5 percent coupon interest rate, a par value of $1,000, and a market price of $927.50. The bond will mature in 9 years. Based on this information, answer the following questions:

a. What is the bond's current yield?

b. Calculate the bond's approximate yield to maturity using the formula shown on page 467.

c. What is the bond's yield to maturity using a financial calculator?

5. Three friends, Jodie, Natalie, and Neil, have asked you to determine the equivalent taxable yield on a municipal bond. The bond's current yield is 3.75 percent with 5 years left until maturity. Jodie is in the 15 percent marginal tax bracket, Natalie is in the 25 percent bracket, and Neil is in the 35 percent bracket. Calculate the equivalent taxable yield for your three friends. Assuming a similar AAA corporate bond yields 4 percent, which of your friends should purchase the municipal bond?

6. A highly rated corporate bond with 5 years left until maturity was recently quoted as selling for 103.50. The bond's par value is $1,000, and its initial interest rate was 6.5 percent. If this bond pays interest every 6 months, and it has been 4 months since interest was last paid, how much would you be required to pay for the bond?

7. An XYZ April 2041 bond with a 5.5 percent coupon interest rate and a par value of $1,000 recently had a price of 95.625. Calculate the following:

a. When will the bond mature?

b. How much would you have to pay to purchase this bond?

c. If you owned the bond, how much would someone have to pay to buy it from you?

d. What is the current yield, assuming a closing price of 95.50?

8. According to Figure 14.3, as a bond approaches maturity the premium (or discount) reduces to zero. Prove this by calculating the sales price with 7, 5, and 2 years remaining to maturity for the following two bonds. Assume a constant yield to maturity of 8 percent.

a. A 10-year, 10 percent annual coupon bond

b. A 10-year, 6 percent annual coupon bond

9. Using Appendices C and E, calculate the value of the following bonds:

Par Value	Interest Rate	Required Rate of Return	Years to Maturity
$1,000	5%	5%	10
$1,000	5%	9%	10
$1,000	5%	4%	10

10. What is the value (today's price) of a preferred stock that pays an annual dividend of $3.50 when the required rate of return is 8.5 percent? What is the value when the required rate of return changes to 6 percent and 11.5 percent, respectively?

Learn by Doing—Suggested Projects

1. Connect to the Federal Reserve's Web site (**www.federalreserve.gov**) and locate information about the government's Treasury Direct program. Pay particular attention to the procedures for buying and selling inflation-indexed bonds. Write a brief report explaining how often inflation-indexed bonds are sold and what the minimum investment is for individuals. In your report, discuss the advantages and disadvantages of using Treasury Direct rather than a brokerage firm.

2. Think about the advantages offered by municipal bonds. In terms of marginal tax rates, what type of investor should consider investing in municipal bonds? Is there an advantage to purchasing municipal bonds issued by the state in which you live? If yes, what is that advantage?

3. Classify the four primary features of preferred stock into two groups (1) those that benefit the investor and (2) those that benefit the issuer, and explain how you categorized each. Also, formulate an opinion as to how each of those four features might affect the coupon rate of a new bond issue.

4. Your wealthy uncle has asked you to help him value the bonds in his portfolio. Through the years, he has observed that some bonds sell well below or well above stated par values. He has asked for your assistance in clarifying how to value a bond. What information does your uncle need to provide you before you can begin to value a bond using the formulas provided in the text? If your uncle is worried about losing money in bonds, what rules can he use to reduce his risks? (*Hint:* Think about bond maturities and the relationship between interest rates and bond prices.)

5. Over the years you may have received U.S. savings bonds as gifts. If you don't know whether you have bonds in your own name ask your relatives if they have given you any EE savings bonds. Once you've determined that you have bonds, visit the Treasury Direct Web site at **www.treasurydirect.gov/indiv/tools/tools_savingsbondcalc.htm**. Use the information provided to find out what your bonds are worth, how much interest you are earning, and when your bonds will mature.

6. After reading this chapter, a classmate has come to you confidentially after class to discuss making some money trading bonds based on an interest rate projection formula she learned in economics class. She tells you that it is easy to make money whenever interest rates fall because bond prices always move in the opposite direction of interest rates. Do you think that your classmate is correct in her thinking?

7. Until recently, investors purchased bonds almost entirely for income. Over the past 20 years investors have witnessed increased bond price volatility and the advent of junk bonds. Assume that you were going to advise a favorite relative about picking a good bond. Use as many of this chapter's concepts to put together a discussion list to share with your relative. List at least five points.

8. Take a poll of friends, family, and work colleagues by asking them the following three questions:

a. Do you think that real estate is a safer investment than bonds?

b. Do you think of your house as an investment?

c. Do you think of your jewelry as an investment?

Write a brief summary of your findings, paying close attention to gender and age differences in the way people responded.

9. Provide three or four examples of collectibles. For each, tell whether you agree with the rule that "collectibles are a form of speculation and should be avoided." Explain your answer. Under what circumstances should someone consider purchasing speculative investments?

10. Applying what you have learned about future value, write a short essay explaining why the current market value (CMV) of a long-term bond is more volatile than the CMV of a shorter duration bond. To illustrate your point, present a hypothetical example of each valuation showing a 2 percent increase and decrease in current interest rates.

Be a Financial Planner—Discussion Case 1

This case is available in MyFinanceLab.

While waiting for a plane, you met Miguel, a recent college graduate who once he heard that you knew something about investing, immediately began asking you questions about bonds. Miguel indicated that according to his friends, the stock market was too volatile and that bonds were a safer place to invest. Miguel admitted that he really didn't know much about either stocks or bonds but that he hoped to start saving so that he could purchase a house in the next 5 years. Miguel also mentioned that he had heard about preferred stock and real estate as alternatives to bonds. His roommate recommended that he buy a preferred stock that paid a $4.50 annual dividend or purchase farmland outside of his hometown. Answer the following questions in a way that will help Miguel learn investment concepts.

Questions

1. List four advantages and four disadvantages of investing in bonds.
2. If Miguel thought that interest rates were going to increase, what type and maturity of bond should he purchase? What type and maturity should he avoid? Why?
3. Develop a checklist of rules that Miguel should use when purchasing a bond.
4. To be as safe as possible, what bond maturity should Miguel choose to meet his home purchase goal? What type(s) of risk does this strategy reduce or avoid?
5. Explain to Miguel why he might want to consider investing in preferred stock rather than bonds.
6. What is the fair market value of the preferred stock that Miguel is considering purchasing if his required rate of return is 8 percent?
7. If Miguel really wanted to purchase real estate to meet his objective, would a direct or indirect real estate investment be more appropriate for him? Explain your answer in terms of liquidity, volatility, and safety.

Be a Financial Planner—Discussion Case 2

This case is available in MyFinanceLab.

About 6 months ago, Jinnie inherited a portfolio that included a number of bonds. Jinnie knows very little about investing in general and practically nothing about bonds specifically. She put together the following chart for your review. All Jinnie know for sure is that she now owns seven bonds, ranging in maturity from 3 to 20 years. The following chart includes each bond, its Standard & Poor's rating, its maturity, and its current yield.

Bond Rating Chart

Bond	Standard & Poor's Rating	Years to Maturity	Current Yield
ABC Corp.	AAA	10	4.75%
XYX Industries	AA	3	3.17%
INTL Limited	A	7	6.11%
MED Corp.	BBB	5	4.40%
SPEC, Inc.	B	2	6.67%
LAM Corp.	CCC	3	25.97%
BAD, Inc.	CC	4	10.19%

Questions

1. After a cursory review of the yields, does anything stand out that should cause Jinnie to worry?

2. In terms of bond maturity dates, what should an investor expect? What is happening in this example?

3. In terms of Standard & Poor's ratings, do you think that the differences in yields are reasonable? (Be sure to also consider time remaining to maturity.)

4. Using your responses from questions 2 and 3, is Jinnie being adequately compensated for the risk she is taking?

5. What is the minimum interest rate differential that Jinnie should expect between an AAA-rated bond and a BBB-rated bond? Is this the case in the example?

6. If interest rates were to increase by 1 percent or 2 percent, which of the bonds would be the least affected? Which one would be the most affected? Why?

7. If Jinnie asked for a recommendation on which bonds to sell and which to buy more of, what would you recommend? If she purchases more of one particular issue, even if it offers the best risk and duration-adjusted return, to what other types of risks could Jinnie be exposed? (*Hint:* Review the types of risks found in Chapter 11.)

8. Since Jinnie does not plan to use these funds for many years, would Series EE savings bonds or Series I bonds offer any advantage as an investment alternative?

9. If another investor were to purchase one XYX Industries bond (par value of $1,000), at a price of $945, how much in annual interest would be earned?

10. Use the information from question 9 to determine the new investor's approximate yield to maturity if the XYX Industries bond is purchased.

15 Mutual Funds: An Easy Way to Diversify

Learning Objectives

 Weigh the advantages and disadvantages of investing in mutual funds.

 Differentiate between types of mutual funds, ETFs, and investment trusts.

 Calculate mutual fund returns.

 Classify mutual funds according to objectives.

 Select a mutual fund that's right for you.

For Scott Adams, creator of the *Dilbert* comic strip, it's been a winding climb to the financial top. From 1979 to 1995, Adams worked first at Crocker Bank in San Francisco, and then at Pacific Bell. It was there, in 1989, that he began drawing Dilbert, a mouthless engineer with a perpetually bent necktie. Adams was earning about $70,000 and working in cubicle 4S700R when he was fired from Pacific Bell in 1995—"budget constraints" was the reason given.

Today, *Dilbert* appears in more than 1,200 newspapers in 29 countries. Adams' *Dilbert* books ride the top of the best-sellers lists, and his speaking fee is $10,000 per engagement (he speaks about 35 times per year). In short, he's doing a lot better than he was at Pacific Bell. Adams says he won't reveal his actual earnings though, because, as he says, "my family might expect better gifts from me."

What does Adams do with all his money? He invests it in mutual funds. That might not be what you'd expect from a guy who has often used his cartoon to make fun of mutual funds. In one comic strip, Dilbert was consulting with a financial advisor who was pushing his firm's "churn 'n' burn" family of mutual funds.

"We'll turn your worthless equity into valuable brokerage fees in just three days!" the advisor raved.

In another strip, Dogbert, Dilbert's potato-shaped dog and companion, set himself up as a financial consultant and announced, "I'll tell all my clients to invest in the 'Dogbert Deferred Earnings Fund.'"

"Isn't that a conflict of interest?" Dilbert asks.

"Only if I show interest in the client," replies Dogbert.

Adams tried picking his own stocks for a while, but decided to hand his money over to the professionals. "My years of dabbling versus the experts just showed me that they were better than me." Today he primarily invests in index funds.

Scott Adams, similar to so many novice investors, has found mutual funds to be an ideal way of entering and maintaining a presence in the market. There's an awful lot of comfort in letting a professional manager do all the work for you. As more and more investors have taken advantage of this comfort, mutual funds have seen a dramatic surge in popularity.

In fact, there are over 7,500 mutual funds to choose from today—up from a mere 161 in 1960. Not only has the number of mutual funds skyrocketed, but their total assets have also—to over $12.1 trillion by mid-2011. As Figure 15.1 shows, assets in mutual funds have reflected what has been happening in the stock market.

Mutual funds are not a different category of investments. Instead, they're a way of holding investments such as stocks and bonds. They pool your money with that of other investors and invest it in stocks, bonds, and various short-term securities. Professional managers then tend this investment, making sure it grows nicely. Mutual funds let you diversify even with small investment amounts. In fact, your investment may be only $1,000 or even less, and with that investment you may own a fraction (a very small fraction) of up to 1,000 different stocks.

Mutual Fund
An investment fund that raises funds from investors, pools the money, and invests it in stocks, bonds, and other investments. Each investor owns a share of the fund proportionate to the amount of his or her investment.

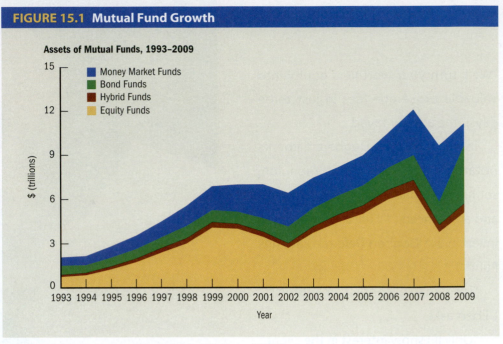

FIGURE 15.1 Mutual Fund Growth

Assets of Mutual Funds, 1993–2009

- Money Market Funds
- Bond Funds
- Hybrid Funds
- Equity Funds

Source: Investment Company Institute *2010 Fact Book,* 48th ed. (Washington, DC, 2010).

It's this instant diversification that makes mutual funds so popular with many investors. Remember, as **Principle 8: Risk and Return Go Hand in Hand** tells us, diversification lets you reduce or "diversify away" some of your risk without affecting your expected return, and mutual funds give smaller investors the same ability to diversify and reduce risk as big investors with lots of money have. Still, not all mutual funds are created equally—at least from the investor's perspective. This chapter will help you to make good choices when selecting mutual funds and avoid the "churn 'n' burn" family of funds.

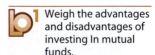
Weigh the advantages and disadvantages of investing In mutual funds.

Why Invest in Mutual Funds?

Investing in mutual funds provides you with a bevy of benefits, especially if you're a small investor. Mutual funds level the investment playing field between large and small investors. Unfortunately, there are also drawbacks to investing in mutual funds. These disadvantages don't outweigh the advantages of mutual funds, particularly for small investors, but it's good to know what they are. After all, forewarned is forearmed. Let's take a look first at the advantages and then examine the disadvantages of investing in mutual funds.

Advantages of Mutual Fund Investing

◆ **Diversification.** Mutual funds are an inexpensive way to diversify. For the small investor, this is an extremely important benefit. If you have only $10,000 to invest, it would be difficult to diversify your holdings without paying commissions. But, when you invest in a mutual fund, you're purchasing a small fraction of the mutual fund's already diversified holdings. Table 15.1 provides a description of

TABLE 15.1 A Listing of Sector Diversification and the 10 Largest Holdings of Vanguard's Windsor II Fund Investments, March 31, 2011

	Equity Sector Diversification		
	Windsor II Fund as of 3/31/2011	Russell 1000 Value Index as of 12/31/2010	10 largest holdings as of 3/31/2011 (26.5% of total net assets)
Consumer Discretionary	7.30%	7.70%	1. ConocoPhillips
Consumer Staples	11.00%	9.90%	2. International Business Machines Corp.
Energy	13.00%	12.50%	3. Pfizer Inc.
Financials	20.00%	27.70%	4. JPMorgan Chase & Co.
Health Care	11.60%	12.50%	5. Wells Fargo & Co.
Industrials	13.00%	9.10%	6. Microsoft Corp.
Information Technology	15.00%	5.50%	7. Philip Morris International Inc.
Materials	2.70%	3.10%	8. Occidental Petroleum Corp.
Telecommunication Services	2.40%	5.20%	9. Raytheon Co.
Utilities	4.00%	6.80%	10. Spectra Energy Corp.

Source: The Vanguard Group, accessed April 16, 2011, **https://personal.vanguard.com/us/funds/snapshot?FundId=0073&FundIntExt=INT#hist=tab%3A2.**

the sector diversification along with a listing of the ten largest holdings out of the 255 securities held by Vanguard's Windsor II Fund. As you can see, that degree of diversification couldn't be obtained by an individual investor with limited funds.

◆ **Professional management.** A mutual fund is an inexpensive way to gain access to professional management. Because fund managers control millions and sometimes even billions of dollars in assets and make huge securities transactions, they have access to all the best research from several brokerage houses. As a result, professional managers are in a much better position to evaluate investments, especially alternative investments. For the small or novice investor, having a professional to lead the way may be essential in taking that first step into the market.

◆ **Minimal transaction costs.** Because mutual funds trade in such large quantities, they pay far less in terms of commissions. For example, if you were trading stocks valued at less than $1,000, the brokerage fees might run up to 50 cents per share. For a mutual fund, those fees might be only 2 cents per share, because volume traders (investors who make a ton of trades) often have the power to negotiate lower fees. Over the long run, these lower transaction costs should translate into higher returns.

◆ **Liquidity.** Mutual funds are easy to buy and sell—just pick up the phone or go online. Although many securities can be hard to trade, mutual funds never keep your money tied up while you're waiting for a transaction to take place. In effect, mutual funds are liquid enough to provide easy access to your money.

◆ **Flexibility.** Given that there are over 8,000 different mutual funds to choose from, it should come as no surprise that they cover many objectives and risk levels. As an individual investor, you should be able to spell out your desired objectives and risk level, and from that find a fund that fits your needs.

◆ **Service.** Mutual funds provide you with a number of services that just wouldn't be available if you invested individually. For example, they provide bookkeeping services, checking accounts, automatic systems to add to or withdraw from your account, and the ability to buy or sell with a single phone call. With a mutual fund, you can also automatically reinvest your dividends, interest, and capital gains distributions.

◆ **Avoidance of bad brokers.** With a mutual fund you avoid the potentially bad advice, high sales commissions, and churning that can come with a bad broker. Remember, a broker's job is trading—brokers don't make money unless you trade. A mutual fund manager's job is to make you money.

Disadvantages of Mutual Fund Investing

◆ **Lower-than-market performance.** On average, approximately 80 percent of actively managed stock mutual funds (non-index mutual funds) underperform the market (the S&P 500 Index). Of course, since that's only an average, it does tend to vary quite a bit from year to year—but it doesn't say much for the ability of mutual fund managers to beat the market. Why is that so? Simply because they have some expenses to pay—administrative and brokerage costs—whereas "the market" has no transaction costs at all—it's just a measure of how much stocks go up or down. Still, if your goal in investing is to make money, mutual funds do quite well.

◆ **Costs.** The costs associated with investing in mutual funds can vary dramatically from fund to fund; investigate their costs before investing. Some funds charge a sales fee or load that can run as high as 8.5 percent, in addition to an annual expense ratio that can run up to 3 percent.

◆ **Risks.** Not all mutual funds are truly safe. In an attempt to beat the competition, many funds have become specialized or segmented. When mutual funds focus on small sectors of the market, such as "health/biotechnology stocks" or "Latin America," they may be diversified within that sector of the market, but they are not diversified across all the different market sectors. As a result, overall they tend not to be very well diversified because the stocks in different sectors tend to move together. As a result, their returns are subject to unsystematic risk.

For example, over the 12-month period ending in April 2010, the Cambiar Aggressive Value Fund climbed by 56.6 percent. Over the same period, the Prasad Growth Fund lost 37.5 percent. A more diversified fund would have been able to smooth out these losses with gains in other areas. Remember, diversification is a huge advantage of mutual funds, but choosing a nondiversified, segmented fund turns that advantage into a disadvantage.

◆ **You Can't Diversify Away a Market Crash.** Many investors view the diversification of mutual funds as eliminating all risk. You should know better. Remember, as **Principle 8: Risk and Return Go Hand in Hand** notes, you can't diversify away a market crash. If there is a market crash, investing in stock mutual funds isn't going to protect you because all stocks will drop together.

◆ **Taxes.** When you invest using a buy-and-hold strategy, you can assure yourself of long-term capital gains, and you don't pay taxes on your capital gains until you sell your stock. Mutual funds, though, tend to trade relatively frequently, and when they sell a security for a profit, you have to pay taxes on your capital gains. Mutual funds don't let you defer your taxes—they make you pay as you go.

 **2** Differentiate between types of mutual funds, ETFs, and investment trusts.

Mutual Fund-Amentals

A mutual fund pools money from investors with similar financial goals. When you invest in a mutual fund, you receive shares in that fund. You're really investing in a diversified portfolio that's professionally managed according to set goals or financial

---

STOP & THINK

"There is some evidence that last year's winners tend to repeat next year. But it is very slight. Mostly the effect comes from the fact that really bad funds stay bad. Their expenses are high, and their choices stay haphazard."—Paul Samuelson. What does this statement tell you about how to choose a mutual fund?

objectives—for example, investing only in international stocks or only in high-yield bonds. These investment objectives are clearly stated by the mutual fund and then used by the fund investment advisor in deciding where to invest.

Your shares in the mutual fund give you an ownership claim to a proportion of the mutual fund's portfolio. In effect, individual investors buy mutual fund shares, the mutual fund managers take this money and buy securities, and the mutual fund shareholders then own a portion of this portfolio. This concept is illustrated in Figure 15.2. It's important to note that mutual fund shareholders don't directly own the fund's securities. Rather, they own a proportion of the overall value of the fund itself.

When you own shares in a mutual fund, you make money in three ways. First, as the value of all the securities held by the mutual fund increases, the value of each mutual fund share also goes up. Second, if a fund receives interest or dividends from its holdings, this income is passed on to shareholders in the form of dividends. Third, if the fund sells a security for more than it originally paid for it, the shareholders receive this gain in the form of a capital gains distribution, generally paid annually.

The shareholder, of course, can elect to have these dividends, interest, and capital gains reinvested back into the fund or receive these earnings in the form of a check from the fund. The tax consequence is the same: All distributions, whether paid out or reinvested, are taxable in the year in which they occur.

Before looking at the different types of mutual funds, let's look at how a mutual fund is organized. The fund itself is generally set up as a corporation or trust and is owned by the fund shareholders, who elect a board of directors. The fund is then run by a management company, generally the group that initially organized the fund. Often a management company will run many different mutual funds. In fact, Fidelity and Vanguard, two of the largest management companies, each have a mutual fund for almost every goal.

Each individual fund then hires an investment advisor, generally from the management company, to oversee that particular fund. The advisor supervises the buying and selling of securities. For this service, the advisor is generally paid a percentage of the total value of the fund on an annual basis. This management fee usually runs about one-half of 1 percent, although it can vary considerably from fund to fund. In addition to the management fee, other operating expenses bring the average total cost of operations to about 1 percent of the fund's total assets per year.

FIGURE 15.2 Pooled Investments

Investors pool their funds and give them to a professional investment manager, who invests those funds in a diversified portfolio.

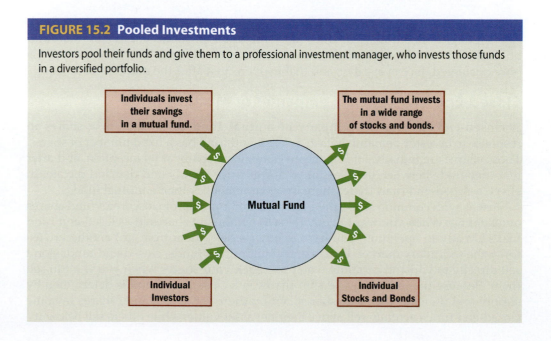

Investment Companies

Investment Company
A firm that invests the pooled money of a number of investors in return for a fee.

Actually, a mutual fund is a special type of **investment company**—that is, a firm that invests the pooled money of a number of investors in return for a fee. In addition to mutual funds, there are a number of other types of investment companies, all of which closely resemble mutual funds.

Open-End Investment Companies or Mutual Funds

Open-End Investment Company or Mutual Fund
A mutual fund that has the ability to issue as many shares as investors want. The value of all the investments that the fund holds determines how much each share in the mutual fund is worth.

By far the most popular form of investment companies is the **open-end investment company** or **mutual funds**. These account for over 95 percent of all the money put into the various investment companies. The term "open-end" means that this type of investment company can issue an unlimited number of ownership shares. That is, as many people who want to invest in the fund can, simply by buying ownership shares.

A share in an open-end mutual fund is different from a share of stock. It doesn't trade in the secondary market; you can buy ownership shares in the mutual fund only directly from the mutual fund itself. When you want out, the mutual fund will buy back your shares, no questions asked.

Net Asset Value (NAV)
The dollar value of a share in a mutual fund. It's the value of the fund's holdings (minus any debt) divided by the number of shares outstanding.

The price that you pay when you buy your ownership shares and the price you receive when you sell your shares are based on the **net asset value (NAV)** of the mutual fund. The net asset value is determined by taking the total market value of all securities held by the mutual fund, subtracting out any liabilities, and dividing this result by the number of shares outstanding.

$$\text{net asset value (NAV)} = \frac{\text{total market value of all securities} - \text{liabilities}}{\text{total shares outstanding}}$$

For example, if the value of all the fund's holdings is determined to be $850 million, the liabilities are $50 million, and there are 40 million shares outstanding, the net asset value would be:

$$\text{net asset value (NAV)} = \frac{\$850 \text{ million} - \$50 \text{ million}}{40 \text{ million shares}} = \$20 \text{ per share}$$

In effect, one share, which represents a one-forty-millionth ownership of the fund, can be bought or sold for $20. Thus, the value of the portfolio that the mutual fund holds determines the value of each share in the mutual fund. Note that the NAV is only calculated once every day, and that happens just after the market close.

Closed-End Investment Companies or Mutual Funds

Closed-End Investment Company or Mutual Fund
A mutual fund that can't issue new shares. These funds raise money only once by issuing a fixed number of shares, and thereafter the shares can be traded between investors. The value of each share is determined both by the value of the investments the fund holds and investor demand for shares in the fund.

A **closed-end investment company or mutual fund** can't issue new shares in response to investor demand. In fact, a closed-end fund has a fixed number of shares. Those shares are initially sold by the investment company at its inception, and after that they trade between investors at whatever price supply and demand dictate. In effect, a closed-end fund trades more like common stock than a mutual fund.

Just as with common stock, there are a limited number of closed-end fund shares outstanding. When you want to buy (or sell) ownership shares in a closed-end fund that's already in operation, you have to buy (or sell) them from (to) another investor in the secondary market. Unlike open-end mutual funds, closed-end funds don't sell directly to you and certainly won't buy back your shares when you want to sell them. Because the price of ownership shares in a closed-end fund is determined by supply and demand for those shares, not by their net asset value, shares in some closed-end funds actually sell above their net asset value, while others sell below it.

In recent years closed-end funds have enjoyed a good deal of popularity because they provide investors with a simple way to invest in some markets. For example, the South Korean government holds a relatively tight reign on the common stock of Korean companies. But one easy way to participate in this market is through a closed-end fund such as the Korea Fund (another efficient way is through ETFs, which we will discuss later in this chapter). In 2010, the Korea Fund rose by almost 30 percent, while the S&P 500 only gained around 13 percent.

Unit Investment Trusts

A **unit investment trust** is a fixed pool of securities, generally municipal bonds, with each unit representing a proportionate ownership in that pool. Although very similar to a mutual fund, a unit investment trust is actually an entirely different beast. For example, unit investment trusts aren't managed. Also, instead of actively trading securities (as mutual funds), unit investment trusts have passive investments. That is, the trust purchases a fixed amount of bonds and then holds those bonds until maturity, at which time the trust is dissolved.

A unit investment trust generally works something like this: First, the investment company announces the formation of the trust, and then advertises and sells the ownership shares through brokers. Generally, there's a minimum required investment of around $1,000, from which a sales commission of 3.5 to 4.9 percent is subtracted. The remaining funds are then invested in municipal bonds. The investment company's role is to collect and pass on the interest and principal payments accruing from the bond portfolio to the investors.

The advantage of unit investment trusts comes from the diversification that they offer. Many municipal bonds are relatively risky, and as a result, diversification holds real value. Unfortunately, because most municipal bonds sell with a minimum price of $1,000, many smaller investors simply don't have the funds to allow for sufficient diversification. A unit investment trust solves this problem handily.

Although most investors hold unit investment trusts until maturity, there's a secondary market for some of the larger units. In addition, most brokers stand ready to repurchase and then resell units, although when units are sold to brokers, they generally are sold at a discount. Unit investment trusts are really aimed at the long-term investor. If your time horizon is less than 10 years, avoid unit investment trusts and stick with mutual funds.

Real Estate Investment Trusts (REITs)

A **real estate investment trust, or REIT**, is similar to a mutual fund in that a professional manager uses the pooled funds of a number of investors to buy and sell a diversified portfolio. In this case, though, all the holdings in the portfolio deal with real estate. Shares in REITs are traded on the major exchanges, and most REITs have no predetermined life span.

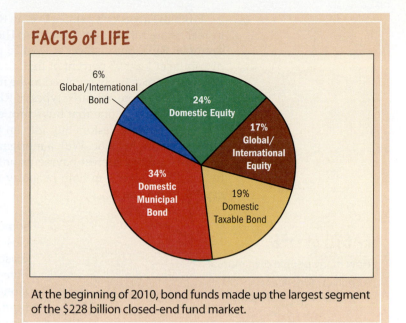

FACTS of LIFE

6% Global/International Bond

24% Domestic Equity

17% Global/International Equity

34% Domestic Municipal Bond

19% Domestic Taxable Bond

At the beginning of 2010, bond funds made up the largest segment of the $228 billion closed-end fund market.

Unit Investment Trust
A fixed pool of securities, generally municipal bonds, in which each share represents a proportionate ownership interest in that pool. The bonds are purchased and then held until maturity, at which time the trust is dissolved.

Real Estate Investment Trust or REIT
An investment vehicle similar to a mutual fund that specializes in real estate investments, such as shopping centers or rental property, or that makes real estate loans.

From the investor's perspective, an REIT looks just like a mutual fund that specializes in real estate rather than securities. There are some technical differences, though. For example, REIT must collect at least 75 percent of its income from real estate and must distribute at least 95 percent of that income in the form of dividends. In addition, most REITs also are actively involved in the management of the real estate that they own.

Note that there are three types of REITs: equity, mortgage, and a hybrid of the two. An equity REIT is one that buys property directly and, in general, also manages that property. When investors buy into an equity REIT, they're hoping that the real estate will appreciate in value. With a mortgage REIT, the investment is limited to mortgages. Investors receive interest payments only, with little chance for capital appreciation. A hybrid REIT invests in both property and mortgages, resulting in some interest and capital appreciation.

Do REITs make sense? They certainly have some diversification value in that they don't move closely with the general stock market. They're also reasonable alternatives for investors who want to invest in real estate, but don't know enough to do it alone. Moreover, although some REITs aren't that liquid, they do tend to be much more liquid than direct investments in real estate.

If you're serious about investing in an REIT, make sure that it's actively traded. (The more heavily traded a security is, the more liquid it is.) However, keep in mind that there are real risks in real estate. As we learned earlier, the real estate market is highly volatile, as the crash in housing prices that began in 2006–2007 demonstrates. As you might have expected, as the housing market plunged in the late 2000s, so did REITS. In fact, the Morgan Stanley REIT Index fell by about 75 percent between March 2007 and March 2009. While it bounced back in the next two years, it still didn't fully recover, and in March 2011 it was still down 30 percent from its 2007 high.

Hedge Funds—Something to Avoid

Hedge Fund
An investment fund that is private, largely unregulated, and very risky and which charges very high fees and only allows wealthy investors to invest.

Hedge funds are investment pools with very few controls—meaning the managers can invest in whatever they want to—that's because they are not regulated by the Securities and Exchange Commission (SEC). They charge very high fees, generally taking "2 and 20"—that is, 2 percent of the assets under management (even when the fund loses money) along with 20 percent of the profits—and some actually take more. For example, the Renaissance Technologies hedge fund takes "5 and 44." On top of that, they won't necessarily give you your money back when you want it, and they generally won't tell you what they're doing with your money. Bernie Madoff ran a hedge fund, and you probably know what happened to it. Because it wasn't truly regulated, Bernie ran it as a Ponzi scheme, where he took money from new investors and used that money to pay the older investors, all the while pocketing most of the money for himself. In the end, around $50 billion was lost, and Bernie ended up behind bars.

Because they pose so much risk, you can't invest in one unless you are an "accredited investor," which means you have to have a net worth of at least $1 million (not including your house) or your income has to have been at least $200,000 ($300,000 if married) for the past 2 years. Why should you avoid them? Because of their fees, their extreme risk, the fact that you have no idea what they're doing with your money, the inability to get your money back when you want it, and their poor performance. How poor is their performance? The average hedge fund earned 20 percent in 2009 and 10.3 percent in 2010, well below the 26.5 percent and 15.1 percent earned on the S&P 500 over the same period. The bottom line is that hedge funds are definitely something you should avoid.

The Costs of Mutual Funds

Although some mutual funds have no sales commission, others impose a commission when you buy into the fund or when you liquidate your holdings, some require a hefty annual management fee, and still others pass on marketing expenses to shareholders. To say the least, the costs associated with mutual funds are complicated.

Load Versus No-Load Funds

Mutual funds are classified as either load or no-load funds. A **load** is mutual-fund speak for a sales commission. **Load funds** are actually mutual funds that are sold through brokers, financial advisors, and financial planners, who tack on the sales commissions/loads for themselves. These commissions can be quite large, typically in the 4 percent to 6 percent range, but they could run all the way up to 8.5 percent. If you decide to buy mutual funds through an advisor or broker, you'll choose from among three different "classes" of funds called Class A, Class B, and Class C shares. These are really the same "pool," or portfolio, of securities, but with different fee arrangements.

Load
A sales commission charged on a mutual fund.

Load Fund
A mutual fund on which a load or sales commission is charged.

- ◆ **Class A shares** have a front-end sales load or fee paid when the funds are purchased.
- ◆ **Class B shares** have a **back-end load** called a contingent deferred sales load (CDSL), which declines to zero after 5 to 10 years, as well as higher expenses. Thus, with Class B shares, the up-front sales commission is eliminated and replaced with an annual charge of around 1 percent, in addition to a back-end load or CDSL, that generally runs at about 5 percent of your initial investment or the market value of your investments, whichever is smaller. The back-end load then declines annually and you might pay 5 percent if you sell the fund in the first year, 4 percent if you sell the fund in the second year, 3 percent if you sell the fund in the third year, and so forth until the fee just disappears.
- ◆ **Class C shares** have you pay both coming and going. Class C shares generally have the highest annual fees; may, although generally don't, have a front-end load; and have a contingent deferred sales load that may disappear after 2 years, or may not disappear at all.

Back-End Load
A commission that's charged only when the investor liquidates his or her holdings.

Bear in mind: Classes A, B, and C are all of the same fund; only the fees and expenses change. Many fund families also have other classes of shares, but those are usually for institutional investors or for investments from tax-deferred savings plans such as 401(k) plans.

A mutual fund that doesn't charge a commission on your ownership shares is referred to as a **no-load fund**. When you purchase a no-load mutual fund, you generally don't deal with a broker or advisor. Instead, you deal directly with the mutual fund investment company via direct mail or through an 800 telephone number. There's no salesperson to pay, and as a result, no load. If you need advice, simply call one of the no-load families of funds such as Vanguard, and an investment advisor will help you out—and they'll do this at no cost.

No-Load Fund
A mutual fund that doesn't charge a commission.

Keeping costs down is always an excellent idea, which makes no-load funds seem the obvious choice. It's a fact that no-load funds perform just as well as load funds—they just don't have salespeople on commission. Without question, you're better off with a no-load fund.

FACTS of LIFE

Empirical studies suggest that fees and expenses should be your primary consideration in picking funds. However, according to the Investment Company Institute, only 43 percent of investors make it a consideration when buying a fund.

Management Fees and Expenses

Managing a mutual fund costs money—a lot of it. Funds run up big expenses paying the investment advisor the management fee, the custodian, the transfer agent, and the underwriter, in addition to the sales commissions on securities trades, operating expenses, legal fees, and so on. You'd be wise to keep an eye on these expenses. Be sure to check out a fund's **expense ratio**, which compares the fund's expenses to its total assets (expense ratio = expenses/assets). Typically, this ratio ranges from 0.25 to 2 percent, although some funds have expense ratios that run in excess of 4 percent.

You want to be sure to invest in a fund with a nice, low expense ratio. Why? Because the funds themselves don't pay the cost of their expenses—you do. Mutual funds are quick to pass their expenses on to you, with these expenses paid for by selling some of the fund's securities and thereby lowering the net asset value. The trading costs make up a good-sized portion of a typical fund's expenses and are closely related to the fund's **turnover rate**, which provides a measure of the level of the fund's trading activity. In general, the higher the turnover rate, the higher the fund's expenses. In addition, the larger the turnover, the greater will be the short- and/or long-term capital gains taxes. Remember, you pay capital gains taxes only when you sell a stock.

12b-1 Fees

Because mutual funds must become known in the marketplace, they tend to have some marketing expenses. Marketing expenses, including advertising and promotional fees, are passed on to the fund shareholders through **12b-1 fees**. These fees can run up to 1 percent annually, and they don't benefit the shareholders in the least. They serve only to allow the fund manager to pass on some of the fund's expenses. Where do these fees really go? According to a 2005 survey by the Investment Company Institute, most of these fees go to brokers and bank trust departments, not for marketing and promotion as initially intended—they do make someone wealthy, but not the investor. In fact, studies have found that funds that charge these fees have higher expense ratios but don't exhibit better performance. In effect, a 12b-1 fee is a hidden (you have to read through the fund's literature or ask to find it) and continuous load, as every year you pay out a portion of your investment to cover the fund's marketing costs.

> ### FACTS of LIFE
>
> Watch out for high fees. Don Philips, president of Morningstar, once said, "If you pay the executives at Sarah Lee more, it doesn't make the cheesecake less good. But with mutual funds, it comes directly out of the batter."

Is there any value to you from the 12b-1 fee? No, no, and no. If your fund earns 10 percent before a 1 percent 12b-1 fee, after the fee it earns only 9 percent. If you invested $10,000 in this fund and left it in for 20 years earning 10 percent, you'd end up with $67,275, but earning 9 percent you'd end up with only $56,044. The 12b-1 fee just cost you $11,231. There is no advantage to that!

A summary of the different mutual fund costs is provided in Table 15.2.

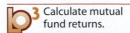
3 Calculate mutual fund returns.

Calculating Mutual Fund Returns

Let's now take a look at returns and how you can figure out the return a mutual fund will make for you. The return from investing in a mutual fund can be in the form of distributions of dividends, capital gains, or a change in NAV (net asset value) of the shares held. To qualify as an investment company and avoid being taxed on the fund's earnings, a fund must distribute a minimum of 97 percent of the interest

TABLE 15.2 Different Mutual Fund Costs

No-Load Funds:	No sales charge
Load Funds:	Sales charge up to 8.5%
Class A Shares:	Front-end load
Class B Shares:	Back-end load, also called a contingent deferred sales load, that generally declines to zero after 5 to 10 years, in addition to an annual charge of around 1%
Class C Shares:	Highest annual fees, and in some cases a contingent deferred load that doesn't disappear
Management Fees:	Fees paid to the fund advisor
Expense Ratio:	The ratio of the fund's expenses to the fund's assets
12b-1 Fees:	Marketing fees passed on to the shareholder, ranging up to 1%

and dividends earned and at least 90 percent of capital gains income. (Capital gains result from selling securities for more than what they were originally bought for.)

Thus, we can calculate the total return from a mutual fund as follows:

$$\text{total return} = \frac{\text{dividends distributed} + \text{capital gains distributed} + \text{ending NAV} - \text{beginning NAV}}{\text{beginning NAV}}$$

For example, let's assume we have a fund with:

$$
\begin{aligned}
\text{beginning NAV} &= \$19.45 \\
\text{ending NAV} &= \$23.59 \\
\text{dividends distributed} &= \$0.60 \\
\text{capital gains distributed} &= \$0.47
\end{aligned}
$$

We can calculate our return as follows:

$$
\begin{aligned}
\text{total return} &= \frac{\$0.60 + \$0.47 + (\$23.59 - \$19.45)}{\$19.45} \\[2mm]
&= \frac{\$0.60 + \$0.47 + \$4.14}{\$19.45} \\[2mm]
&= \frac{\$5.21}{\$19.45} = 26.79\%
\end{aligned}
$$

Thus, the return is 26.79 percent.

If you automatically reinvest any distributions, your return results from both the increase in the NAV of the shares and the increased number of shares you hold. As you automatically reinvest any distributions, the number of shares that you hold increases. As a result, you can calculate your return by taking the value of your ending holdings minus your initial investment and dividing this by the value of your initial investment.

$$\text{total return} = \frac{(\text{number of ending shares} \times \text{ending price}) - (\text{number of beginning shares} \times \text{beginning price})}{(\text{number of beginning shares} \times \text{beginning price})}$$

Thus, if you initially purchase 500 shares at an NAV of $19.45 and, as a result of automatically reinvesting any distributions, you end up with 585 shares with an NAV of $23.59, your return would be:

$$\text{total return} = \frac{(585 \times \$23.59) - (500 \times \$19.45)}{(500 \times \$19.45)}$$

$$= \frac{\$13,800.15 - \$9,725.00}{\$9,725.00}$$

$$= \frac{\$4,075.15}{\$9,725.00} = 41.90\%$$

Thus, the return would be 41.9 percent. Keep in mind, though, that these formulas don't take taxes into account.

Calculating a fund's return should help you spot funds that have been consistent winners over time and avoid those that have performed poorly. Once you've found a fund that fits your objectives, keep a close eye on expenses and fees and try to keep them to a minimum. After that, you might as well go for past winners and avoid losers. There is strong evidence that minimizing fees and expenses can put you on a path toward better returns. There is also evidence that strong performers over the past 3 years remain strong performers for the following 3 years.

STOP & THINK

Look closely at the expenses and fees charged for managing a mutual fund before investing—their impact can be significant. Look, for example, at a mutual fund with an expense ratio of 1.3 percent (the average expense ratio for an actively managed equity fund—that is, a non-index mutual fund—is around 1.5 percent) versus one with an expense ratio of 0.2 percent. If you put $25,000 in both of these funds, each returning 10 percent compounded over the next 25 years, you'd end up with a not so insignificant $58,000 more in the lower expense fund. In choosing a mutual fund, what would you look for?

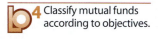 **4** Classify mutual funds according to objectives.

Types and Objectives of Mutual Funds

To make choosing mutual funds a little easier, funds are categorized according to objective. However, these classifications aren't always completely reliable, because fund managers classify their own funds. A fund manager might classify a fund as a stock fund, when in reality its major holdings are bonds. Hey, you don't have to believe everything you read.

When choosing a mutual fund, first figure out what your objectives are. What do you want a mutual fund to do for you? Once you've figured that out, you have but to look, and chances are one of the many mutual funds will suit your needs perfectly—or at least claim to. Before investing, be sure that a given mutual fund actually lives up to its classification.

Money Market Mutual Funds

Money Market Mutual Funds
Mutual funds that invest in Treasury bills, certificates of deposit, commercial paper, and other short-term notes, generally with a maturity of less than 30 days.

Money market mutual funds invest in Treasury bills, CDs, and other very short-term investments, usually those with maturities of less than 30 days. Because these investments are of such short maturity, they're generally regarded as practically risk-free. Money market securities require significant investments—ranging from $10,000 upward, making them out of the reach of the common investor. Money market mutual funds use the pooling principle to make these short-term investments available to the smaller investor.

You may have even seen money market funds offered at your local bank and, in fact, many of these funds work much like interest-bearing checking accounts. For a minimum investment of usually $1,000, you tend to get interest rates that are tied to short-term interest rates and are, thus, higher than you can earn on a basic savings account, as well as limited check-writing privileges. One of the limits on this privilege is that you can't write checks for less than $250 to $500. Money market mutual funds have proved immensely popular because they carry no loads, trade at a constant NAV of $1, and have very minimal expense ratios.

The extreme popularity of money market mutual funds has spawned several specialized variations. One is the **tax-exempt money market mutual fund**, which invests only in very short-term municipal debt. The returns on the funds are exempt from federal taxes, making them popular investments among people in higher tax brackets.

There are also money market mutual funds that invest solely in U.S. government securities in order to avoid any risk whatsoever. These funds are commonly called **government securities money market mutual funds**. They pay a rate slightly lower than traditional money market mutual funds, but in theory are safer. However, because of the very short maturities of their holdings and the extreme diversification associated with money market mutual funds, there's virtually no risk in them anyway.

Stock Mutual Funds

Of the different types of mutual funds, **stock funds** are by far the most popular. In fact, as Figure 15.3 shows, S&P 500 Index stock funds now account for almost 40 percent of all mutual funds. Another 31 percent are domestic equity funds, and 11 percent more are global/international equity funds. Don't think that these funds hold *nothing* but stocks, though. They do have some limited holdings in cash, bonds, and short-term investments. But their main emphasis is indeed firmly on stock.

Because the stock market is so varied and wide-ranging, there are many different types of stock funds to choose from. When reading the following discussion of some of the more popular types of stock funds, think about which ones might be best suited for your investment objectives.

Tax-Exempt Money Market Mutual Fund
A money market mutual fund that invests only in very short-term municipal debt.

Government Securities Money Market Mutual Fund
A money market mutual fund that invests solely in U.S. government securities in order to avoid any risk whatsoever.

Stock Funds
Mutual funds that invest primarily in common stock.

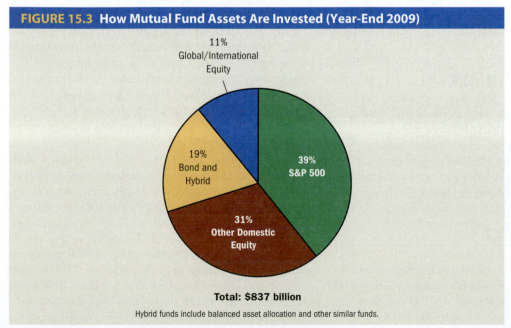

FIGURE 15.3 How Mutual Fund Assets Are Invested (Year-End 2009)

11%
Global/International Equity

19%
Bond and Hybrid

39%
S&P 500

31%
Other Domestic Equity

Total: $837 billion

Hybrid funds include balanced asset allocation and other similar funds.

Source: Investment Company Institute, *2010 Fact Book*, 48th ed. (Washington, DC, 2010).

Aggressive Growth Funds An aggressive growth fund is one that tries to maximize capital appreciation while ignoring income. In other words, these funds tend to go for stocks whose prices could rise dramatically, even though these stocks tend to pay very small dividends. Thus, the dividend yield on stocks in funds of this type tends to be quite low. Stocks with high P/E ratios and those of young companies are perfect for aggressive growth funds. Unfortunately, these stocks can not only gain big, but can lose big, too. As a result, the ownership shares of aggressive growth funds tend to experience wider price swings, both up and down, than do the share prices on other funds.

Small Company Growth Funds Small company growth funds are similar to aggressive growth funds except they limit their investments to small companies. The purpose of small company growth funds is to uncover and invest in undiscovered companies with unlimited future growth. Again, these are very risky funds with a good deal of price volatility.

Growth Funds The differences between aggressive growth funds and growth funds are pretty small, but growth funds generally pay more attention to strong firms that pay dividends. Still, these funds are looking for the potential big gainers. Growth funds are less risky than their aggressive growth cousins, though. Because of the stable dividends, their shares tend to bounce around less in price.

Growth-and-Income Funds This general category of funds tries to invest in a portfolio that will provide the investor with a steady stream of income in addition to having the potential for increasing value. These funds focus on everything from well-established blue-chip companies with strong stable dividends and growth opportunities to stocks with low P/E ratios and above-average dividends. Because of the steady income these funds provide, the shares tend to fluctuate in price less than the market as a whole.

Sector Funds A sector fund is a specialized mutual fund that generally invests at least 65 percent of its assets in securities from a specific industry. For example, there are sector funds dealing with the chemicals, computer, financial services, health/biotechnology, automobile, environmental, utilities, and natural resources industries, to name just a few. Although investing in these funds is much less risky than investing in a single stock, sector funds are riskier than traditional mutual funds because they're less diversified. In fact, the idea behind a sector fund is to *limit* the degree of diversification by limiting investment to a specific industry.

If that industry or part of the world does well, the sector fund does well. If that industry or part of the world has a rough time, so does the sector fund. For example, for the first quarter of 2011, the iShares MSCI All Peru Capped Index fell by over 10 percent and Latin American sector funds were the worst performing sector. On the other hand, precious metals was the hottest of all sectors in the first quarter of 2011, and one of the hottest funds was iShares Silver Trust, which went up by 115 percent. What does this mean for you? Well, if you're going to invest in a sector fund, make sure that you diversify your holdings, perhaps among a number of different mutual funds. Investing in a single sector fund isn't going to provide you with the diversity that makes mutual funds so advantageous.

STOP & THINK

When you see a listing of the best-performing mutual funds, invariably a sector or country fund will appear at the top of the list. However, a sector fund will also appear at the bottom of the list. Their lack of diversity makes sector funds highly volatile and not for the faint of heart. Would you risk putting all your marbles—and dollars—in a single industry? If not, sector funds aren't for you.

Index Funds   An index fund is one that tries to track a market index, such as the S&P 500. It does so by buying the stocks that make up the S&P 500. Much of the value of an index fund comes from its low expense ratio, which can be anywhere from 0.15 to 1.35 percent lower than those of other funds. These funds are great for those who don't want to try to "beat the market" and want the diversification of a mutual fund with costs as low as possible.

International Funds   An international fund concentrates its investments in securities from other countries. In fact, two-thirds of the fund's assets must be invested outside the United States. Some international funds focus on general world regions—the Pacific Basin, Latin America, or other emerging markets. Some focus on specific countries—Japan, Canada, even places like Peru—in an attempt to capture abnormal growth in their specific area of the world. Other international funds look for companies outside the United States that have the potential for abnormal growth, and invest directly in them regardless of location. One advantage of these funds is that they tend not to move perfectly with the U.S. stock market and thus can serve to reduce the variability of returns for all your holdings combined.

Since these funds open you to political and currency risks not present with domestic stocks, it's important to understand the political and economic climate of all the countries represented in an international fund.

Balanced Mutual Funds

A **balanced mutual fund** is one that holds both common stock and bonds, and in many cases, also preferred stock. The objective of these funds is to earn steady income plus some capital gains. In general, these funds are aimed at those who need steady income to live on, moderate growth in capital, and moderate stability in their investments.

Balanced Mutual Fund
A mutual fund that tries to "balance" the objectives of long-term growth, income, and stability. To do this, these funds invest in a mix of common stock and bonds, as well as preferred stock in some cases.

As you might expect, the ratio of bonds to stocks can vary dramatically between balanced funds. Not all balanced funds are equally balanced. In fact, some balanced mutual funds specialize in international securities, hoping to cash in on high returns elsewhere around the world. Still, on the whole, balanced funds tend to be less volatile than stock mutual funds.

Asset Allocation Funds

An **asset allocation fund** is quite similar to a balanced fund in that it invests in a mix of stocks, bonds, and money market securities. In fact, these funds have been described as balanced funds with an attitude. Asset allocation funds differ from balanced funds in that they move money between stocks and bonds in an attempt to outperform the market. That is, when the fund manager feels stocks are on the rise, a higher proportion of the fund's assets are allocated to stocks.

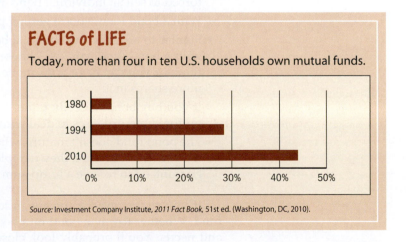

FACTS of LIFE

Today, more than four in ten U.S. households own mutual funds.

Source: Investment Company Institute, *2011 Fact Book*, 51st ed. (Washington, DC, 2010).

Asset allocation funds can be viewed as balanced funds that practice market timing. Unfortunately, the track record for market timers is less than impressive. In fact, market-timing attempts are more likely to produce additional transaction costs rather than additional returns. Think carefully before investing in such a fund.

Asset Allocation Fund
A mutual fund that invests in a mix of stocks, bonds, and money market securities.

Life Cycle and Target Retirement Funds

Life cycle funds are the newest type of mutual fund to hit the market. They're basically asset allocation funds that try to tailor their holdings to the investor's individual characteristics, such as age and risk tolerance. Life cycle funds go beyond the traditional strategies of growth and income and instead focus on where you are in your financial life cycle. For example, in 2011, Vanguard had four LifeStrategy funds, each one aimed at satisfying the objectives of the four different stages of the financial life cycle we discussed in Chapter 1.

With **Target Retirement Funds**, the decision as to how much to invest in stocks, bonds, and money market instruments is made for you, and the only decision you have to make is when you plan to retire. Once you've invested in a Target Retirement Fund, that fund is professionally managed for your stage of retirement planning, with the investments in that fund automatically growing more conservative as your retirement date nears. For example, if you're in your 40s and have 20 years until retirement, you might invest in Vanguard's Target Retirement 2035 Fund. This fund begins with a 60/40 stocks/bonds mix when you have 20 years left to retirement, and gradually declines to a 30/70 stock/bond mix by the time you retire.

Bond Funds

Bond funds appeal to investors who want to invest in bonds but don't have enough money to diversify adequately. In general, bond funds emphasize income over growth. Although they tend to be less volatile than stock funds, bond funds fluctuate in value as market interest rates move up and down.

Bond funds have a number of differences from individual bond purchases.

◆ With an investment of as little as $1,000 you can buy into a diversified bond portfolio. Then you can add to your investment with smaller amounts whenever you wish.
◆ Bond funds offer more liquidity than individual bonds. As we noted in Chapter 14, one of the disadvantages of investing in bonds is that they can be difficult to sell before maturity. With a bond fund, you can both buy and sell at whatever the fund's NAV is, and you don't have to worry about getting a bad price when forced to sell an individual bond at the "wrong time."
◆ With a bond fund, you're getting professional management.
◆ Similar to an individual bond, a bond fund produces regular income. However, with a bond fund, you can choose to receive a monthly check to help your cash flow, or you can have your money automatically reinvested in the fund to buy more shares in it.
◆ If you buy bonds directly rather than through a bond fund, you won't have any mutual fund expenses to deal with.
◆ The bond fund doesn't mature, whereas individual bonds do. When bonds within the bond fund mature, they're replaced with new bonds. As a result, you're never guaranteed to receive a lump-sum payment.

If you're looking for income, a logical place to look is to bonds or to a bond fund. Whether to buy a bond or a bond fund will depend on your individual goals and needs. You'll probably look closer at a bond fund if you want to invest small amounts of money, or you need to keep your investments liquid, and you'll sleep better at night knowing a professional's choosing the securities and keeping them well diversified. Conversely, if you need to know with certainty that in a specific number of years you'll get the principal back, you have a large amount to invest, and you're disciplined enough to reinvest your interest payments, then you might want to stick with individual bonds.

Bond funds can be differentiated both by the type of bonds that they invest in—U.S. government, municipal, or corporate—and by maturity—short term, intermediate term, or long term.

U.S. Government Bond Funds or GNMA Bond Funds

United States government bond funds invest in securities issued by the federal government or its agencies. For example, U.S. Treasury bond funds specialize in Treasury securities. There's no default risk associated with these funds. However, they do fluctuate in value as interest rates move up and down. A number of funds specialize in mortgage-backed securities issued primarily by the Government National Mortgage Association, or GNMA.

These funds hold pools of individual residential mortgages that have been packaged by GNMA and resold to the bond fund. This type of fund also carries interest rate risk in addition to prepayment risk—that is, the risk that as interest rates drop, the mortgages will be refinanced and prepaid. As with other bond funds, a government bond fund is aimed at those who need steady current income.

Municipal Bond Funds

The advantage of municipal bond funds is that the interest is generally exempt from federal taxes. Moreover, if you invest in a municipal bond fund that invests only in bonds from your state, the income may also be exempt from state taxes. In fact, if you live in New York City and invest in a fund that limits its investments to municipal bonds issued by New York City, you avoid federal, state, and local income taxes on the interest payments. For investors in higher tax brackets, avoiding taxes is a big deal.

Corporate Bond Funds

Unless you haven't been paying any attention at all, you've probably guessed that corporate bond funds invest in various corporate bonds. Some corporate bond funds focus mainly on high-quality, highly rated bonds, but others, usually called high-yield corporate bond funds, focus on the much lower rated and much riskier junk bonds. As you know from **Principle 8: Risk and Return Go Hand in Hand**, when you take on more risk, as you do when you invest in junk bonds, your expected return is higher.

Because corporate bonds have the potential for defaulting, it's essential that you diversify if you're going to invest in them. That's where a corporate bond mutual fund comes in—it does the diversifying for you. Of course, you'll want to carry this diversification a bit further by investing in more than just bonds.

When selecting a corporate bond fund, be sure to remember that approximately two-thirds of them carry loads in the 4 to 5 percent range. Although the loads are pretty constant, the returns aren't. As interest rates go up, corporate bond funds and their NAV go down in value. As interest rates drop, corporate bond fund values rise, along with their NAV.

Bond Funds and Their Maturities

Different bond funds also specialize in different length maturities, with short-term (1 to 5 years in maturity), intermediate-term (5 to 10 years in maturity), and long-term (10 to 30 years in maturity) funds. We know from the bond valuation relationships presented in Chapter 14 that there's an inverse relationship between interest rates and bond prices. That is, when interest rates rise, bond prices drop, and when interest rates drop, bond prices rise. We also know that when interest rates change, longer-term bonds fluctuate in price more than shorter-term

---

STOP & THINK

The expense ratios on bond mutual funds can vary dramatically. The average expense ratio in 2010 for bond funds was 1.08 percent. However, this ratio ranged between approximately 0.18 to over 2 percent. Given the fact that long-term government bonds averaged a return of only about 6 percent from 1950 to 2011, it's extremely important to keep expenses low if you're investing in bond funds. If your expenses are 2 percent and your return is only 6 percent, over one-third of your return is already gone. What does this tell you about choosing a mutual fund?

bonds. As a result, the longer the bond fund's maturity, the higher its expected return, but also the greater the fluctuation in its NAV if interest rates change.

ETFs or Exchange Traded Funds

ETFs or Exchange Traded Funds
A hybrid between a mutual fund and an individually traded stock or bond that trade on an exchange just as individual securities do and can be bought and sold throughout the trading day.

ETFs or exchange traded funds, first issued in 1993, are a hybrid between a mutual fund and an individually traded stock or bond. As the name implies, they are mutual funds that trade on an exchange just as individual securities do and can be bought and sold throughout the trading day. In effect, whatever you can do with a stock, you can also do with an ETF. You can, for example, sell short or buy them on margin as discussed in Chapter 12. This trading flexibility is the primary advantage that ETFs have over traditional mutual funds. They trade throughout the day, so you can buy and sell them when you want. Table 15.3 lists a number of differences between mutual funds and ETFs.

Today, about $1.1 trillion is invested in ETFs. Traditionally, ETFs are based on indexes, which means that when you buy an ETF you're really investing in a bundle of stocks or bonds that make up an index, such as the NASDAQ-100, or a sector such as oil services, utilities, or stocks from Japan or Europe. However, in 2008 the Securities and Exchange Commission allowed for the creation of actively managed ETFs. If you're looking to cash in on South Korean, Swedish, or South African companies beyond those that trade on the U.S. exchanges, or on small growth companies, where would you go? You'd look for an ETF. And what is nice about them is that they are diversified within a specific sector or country. That doesn't mean they are totally diversified, just that an ETF made up of energy companies will go the way that energy companies as a whole go and not be dominated by one company.

Because shares in ETFs trade throughout the day just as stocks do, their prices can differ from their NAVs, although in most cases the price differences are quite small. Then, at the end of the trading day, ETFs calculate the value of their holdings to come up with new NAVs for their portfolios, as regular mutual funds do. You can track ETF prices online by name or symbol as you would a share of common stock.

TABLE 15.3 ETFs Versus Mutual Funds

	Mutual Funds	ETFs
How They Trade	Prices are only determined once a day—after the market closes, with the price based upon the closing price of the fund's holdings. Thus, regardless of when you place your buy or sell order, it will not be processed until after the market closes, based upon prices at the market's close.	They trade continuously throughout the day, with the price based upon supply and demand (investors willing to buy or sell).
Assets (mid-2011)	$12.1 trillion	$1.1 trillion
Net Inflows (2010)	$228 billion	$117 billion
Trading Costs and Fees	If purchased directly from the fund company, no commission. If it is a load fund and purchased through a broker, the commissions can go up to 8.5%, and the average annual expense for a mutual fund is 0.98%.	A brokerage commission is generally paid where an ETF is bought or sold, and the average annual expense for index ETFs is 0.56%. However, for the small investor, commissions can add up.
Holdings Transparency	They generally report their holdings only on a monthly or quarterly basis.	They generally report the holdings of the ETF daily on the ETF's Web site.

TABLE 15.4 Advantages and Disadvantages of ETFs

Advantages of Exchange Traded Funds

- ETFs trade on an exchange just as individual securities do and can be bought and sold throughout the trading day.
- ETFs can be sold short or bought on margin.
- ETFs allow you to take an instant position in a sector or country that you may not otherwise have access to, for example, biotechnology or Taiwan.
- ETFs have very low annual expenses.
- ETFs are more tax efficient than most mutual funds.

Disadvantages of ETFs

- Because ETFs trade as common stocks do, you pay commissions.
- ETFs don't necessarily trade at their net asset value.
- You buy the ETF from another investor, so you also have the bid-ask spread to deal with. For example, you might be able to buy the ETF at $25.00, but only be able to sell it later for $24.85.
- For investors who trade frequently, ETFs can be more expensive than typical mutual funds. That's because you incur brokerage costs each time you buy or sell ETF shares.

One advantage to ETFs is that they charge lower annual expenses than most mutual funds, ranging all the way down to about 0.05 percent a year. But, as with stocks, you pay a commission when you buy or sell. Because you buy them from another investor, you also have the bid-ask spread to deal with. That is, you might be able to buy the ETF at $25.00, but be able to sell it for only $24.85. In short, ETFs may be less expensive than regular mutual funds for those who trade infrequently, but they are more expensive than typical mutual funds for those who trade frequently.

Another advantage to ETFs concerns taxes. With a regular mutual fund, the mutual fund manager must occasionally sell holdings to meet the redemption demands of investors. These sales result in taxable capital gains distributions being paid to shareholders. However, with ETFs, most trading is between shareholders, so the funds don't have to sell stocks to meet redemptions. This fact makes ETFs more tax-efficient than most mutual funds.

ETFs have been a huge success because they allow investors who think they know the future direction of a sector, industry, or country to stake out an investment position in that sector, industry, or country. They also allow investors to make their move during the market's trading hours. Table 15.4 lists the advantages and disadvantages of ETFs.

Mutual Funds Services

Aside from the fact that you can probably find a mutual fund with objectives that almost perfectly match your investment goals, what's so special about mutual funds? A lot, actually. Diversification is probably the biggest advantage, but convenience may well be a close second. Mutual funds offer the convenience of being able to buy and sell securities at will, with reduced commissions and professional advice.

That's really just the tip of the convenience iceberg, though. Mutual funds offer myriad services for investors—services that make investing easy and even fun. Let's take a look at a few of the more popular services. As we do, think about which services would be most helpful and appealing to you.

Automatic Investment and Withdrawal Plans An automatic investment plan allows you to make regular deposits directly from your bank account. For example, if you want to invest $100 on the fifteenth of each month, an automatic investment plan lets you do so without lifting a finger. Basically, all you need do is check a box on the mutual fund's account registration form and *voilà*—your $100 will find its way from your savings account to your fund account each and every month. An automatic investment plan is a way of dollar cost averaging when investing in a mutual fund. Recall from Chapter 13 that the logic behind dollar cost averaging is that by investing the same dollar amount on a regular basis, you'll be buying more common stock when the price is lowest and less when the price is highest.

The automatic investment plan is also a good way of moving excess funds from a money market account into the stock market. For example, if you have more money than you feel you need invested in a money market account but are worried about transferring it all at once into the stock market, an automatic investment plan will let you move the funds into the market smoothly over a longer period of time.

Conversely, an automatic or systematic withdrawal plan allows you to withdraw a dollar amount or a percentage of your mutual fund account on a monthly basis. For example, if you were retired and wanted to supplement your income, you might elect to have $250 paid out to you automatically on a monthly basis. Many funds require a minimum fund balance of between $5,000 and $10,000 to participate in an automatic withdrawal plan, with a minimum withdrawal of $50 per month.

Automatic Reinvestment of Interest, Dividends, and Capital Gains   With a mutual fund, you have your choice of receiving interest, dividends, and capital gains payments or having them reinvested by purchasing more shares in the fund. If you're using the mutual fund as a long-term investment, have the distributions automatically reinvested. Reinvestment in the securities markets produces the same growth effects as compound interest—that is, you'll start earning money on your past earnings.

If you're investing in a bond and income fund, you'll get little or no capital appreciation on your holdings. Instead, most of your return will be from dividends, which are distributed back to you each year. If you don't reinvest these distributions, you won't accumulate much wealth. You'll be spending your earnings instead. Over 70 percent of all mutual fund shareholders choose to reinvest their dividends and capital gains.

Wiring and Funds Express Options   If you anticipate needing your funds or your returns fast, you can choose a wiring and funds express option. This option allows you to have your returns/money wired directly to your bank account. It also works the other way and allows you to invest money in the fund immediately by wiring money directly to the fund. In this way you can have your money sent and invested in the fund in the same day. This option is a bit like the automatic investment and withdrawal plan, except the transactions don't happen automatically/monthly.

Phone and Internet Switching   This option allows you to move money from one fund to another simply by making a phone request or making a request on the fund's Web site. If you want to move some of your money from your domestic stock fund to an international stock fund, you can do it easily and generally cost-free with just one phone call or online.

Easy Establishment of Retirement Plans   Most mutual funds provide for the easy establishment of IRS-approved tax-deferred retirement accounts, including traditional and Roth IRAs, 401(k), and Keogh plans. The fund will provide you with everything you need to establish such a plan and then handle the administrative duties. In addition, most funds have representatives available to answer questions you might have when setting the plan up. Retirement plans are a key part of any sound personal financial plan, and getting someone else to set one up and manage it for you is a huge advantage.

Check Writing   Check-writing privileges associated with money market mutual funds can prove very handy when you need to use money from your investments directly for making purchases or in an emergency. As we mentioned before, there are minimum levels, generally in the $250 to $500 range, for which the checks can be written.

Bookkeeping and Help with Taxes   Some of the larger investment companies provide a "tax cost" service that actually calculates your taxable gains or losses when you sell shares. Because the calculation of taxes associated with buying and selling shares in a mutual fund can be enough to drive you crazy, this is a service well worth having. Unfortunately, it's also a service not offered by all mutual funds.

> **FACTS of LIFE**
>
> Why do people invest in mutual funds?
>
> 91 percent are saving for retirement.
>
> 45 percent are saving for emergencies.

Buying a Mutual Fund

5 Select a mutual fund that's right for you.

Now that you know something about mutual funds, you may well be wondering how you go out and buy one. The process of buying a mutual fund involves determining your investment goals, identifying funds that meet your objectives, and evaluating those funds. Your local library and the Internet hold a wealth of information to help your evaluation. Brush up on your math, though, because much of the evaluation process is going to focus on cost. As you learned earlier, mutual fund expenses can vary dramatically from one fund to another.

Step 1: Determining Your Goals

The first step in buying a mutual fund involves determining exactly what your investment goals and time horizon are. In Chapters 1 and 2 we discussed identifying your goals and putting together an investment plan. We described the budgeting and planning procedure as a five-step process. Investing in mutual funds conforms to Step 4: Implement Your Plan. However, before you make it to Step 4, you must have a clear understanding of why you're investing. Is it to provide additional income to supplement your retirement income, or is it to save for your children's education or for your own retirement 30 years from now? Do you want your investments to be tax deferred? How much risk are you comfortable with? Once you've answered these questions, you're ready to go out and find a fund.

Step 2: Meeting Your Objectives

As we saw earlier, there are quite a few different classifications of mutual funds—money market, stock, balanced, asset allocation, life cycle, and bond funds—and within each of these classifications, there can be quite a few different subtypes; for example, subclassifications under stock mutual funds include growth, sector, and index funds among others. Your investment objectives are going to lead you to one of those classifications; for example, if you are saving for an emergency fund, you might want to invest in a money market mutual fund because it is safe and the money is easily accessible, but if you are saving for retirement 40 years from now you might want to invest in a stock index fund. To identify a fund's objectives, the first place to look is in one of the mutual fund evaluation Web sites listed in Table 15.5. For example, the Wall Street Journal Mutual Fund Screener lets you begin by picking a broad category and then from there, move to an expanded list of criteria and categories, while Morningstar Mutual Funds provides fund analysis and classifies funds by objective and management style. One of the advantages of the Yahoo! Finance Mutual Fund Screener Web site is that it's free and lets you begin with a broad category and then immediately filter through that category by relative rank and ratings, making the selection process much simpler. If you find it's easier for you to make decisions based upon visual presentation, take a look at SmartMoney's Mutual Fund Map, which graphically displays information on 1,000 different mutual funds. The addresses for all these Web sites are provided in Table 15.5.

TABLE 15.5 Mutual Fund Information on the Web

Web Site: **Securities and Exchange Commission—Invest Wisely, Mutual Funds**

Address: **http://www.sec.gov/investor/pubs/inwsmf.htm**

Features:

- Explains the basics of mutual fund investing. Covers key points to remember, how mutual funds work, factors to consider, avoiding common pitfalls, what to do if you have problems, and a glossary of key mutual fund terms.
- Includes link to a mutual fund cost calculator: **www.sec.gov/investor/tools.shtml**

Web Site: **SmartMoney Fund Compare**

Address: **http://www.smartmoney.com/fundCompare/**

Features:

- Free.
- Provides Lipper rankings. Rankings are for (1) total returns, (2) consistent returns, (3) preservation, (4) tax efficiency, and (5) expenses. In addition, it provides historical returns, expense ratios, information on any fees or loads, its beta, and the minimum initial purchase.

Web Site: **SmartMoney Mutual Fund Map**

Address: **http://www.smartmoney.com/fundmap/?cid=subnav_mutual_fund_map**

Features:

- Free.
- The map provides a visual presentation of information about 1,000 mutual funds. The format is intuitive and accessible. Each rectangle on the map represents a different fund, and as you glide your cursor over the screen, pop-up data boxes appear, offering statistics about each fund. Each data box includes the fund's name, ticker, net assets, year-to-date return, Morningstar category, and fund family. When you click on a fund, you get a menu that connects you to all kinds of information about the fund, and if you right-click, you zoom in on the fund's category, where you can compare it with its peers.

Web Site: **Wall Street Journal Mutual Fund Screener**

Address: **http://online.wsj.com/public/quotes/mutualfund_screener.html?mod=mdc_h_mfhl**

Features:

- Free.
- Provides the ability to identify funds based upon broad categories (Equity, Fixed Income — Taxable, or Fixed Income — Tax Exempt) to see an expanded list of criteria (International Mid-Cap Growth, Pacific Region Funds, etc.).
- Provides a simple screening tool. You can select a Lipper score for total return that reflects the funds' historical total return performance relative to peers. You can also screen funds by historical returns, fees and expenses, portfolio characteristics, and P/E ratios for equity funds, and average quality rating for bond funds.

Web Site: **Yahoo! Finance Mutual Fund Screener**

Address: **http://screen.yahoo.com/funds.html**

Features:

- Free.
- Provides a criteria-based screening tool. Criteria include Morningstar ratings, performance returns, fees and loads, minimum initial investment, and turnover.

Web Site: **Yahoo! Finance Mutual Fund Top Performers**

Address: **http://biz.yahoo.com/p/top.html**

Features:

- Free.
- Provides a list of top performers. Includes both overall top performers and top performers for U.S. stock funds, international stock funds, bond funds, and hybrid funds. Once you select a fund by clicking on its symbol, you are provided with a fund profile, performance information, historical prices, holdings, risk levels, technical analysis, and purchase information.

Web Site: **Morningstar Mutual Funds**

Address: **www.morningstar.com**

Features:

- Free subscription needed, but not all features are free; it is available at some libraries.
- Provides analysis and classifies funds by objective and management style. Features an investment style box showing whether the fund stresses value- or growth-oriented investments and company size.

<table>
<tr><td>

CHECKLIST 15.1

Buying a Mutual Fund

</td><td>

Before you buy a mutual fund, can you answer these questions?
- How has this fund performed over the long run?
- Have I obtained an independent evaluation of this fund?
- What specific risks are associated with this fund?
- What type of securities does the fund hold? How often does the portfolio change?
- How does the fund perform compared to other funds of the same type or to an index of the same type of investment?
- What is the fund's expense ratio?
- How much will the fund charge me when I buy shares? What other ongoing fees are charged?
- How tax efficient is this fund?

</td></tr>
</table>

In assessing a fund's objective, pay close attention to past performance. If it's intended as a long-term investment, how has it done over the past year, 3 years, and 10 years? If it's intended to produce current income, what is it paying out in terms of its current yield?

Step 3: Selecting a Fund

Once you've found some funds with objectives that match your own, it's time to evaluate them. Evaluation means looking closely at past performance and scrutinizing the costs associated with the funds. Although past performance doesn't necessarily predict future results, it can give you further insights into the investment philosophy and style of the fund. In addition, when making any investment, you want to pick the one that's going to cost the least and return the most (see Checklist 15.1).

Where to Look—Sources of Information   You may be thinking, "I have a hard time finding my socks. How am I supposed to find all this stuff about mutual funds?" There is plenty of help to be had. Some places you'll want to look at include the mutual fund's prospectus, the *Wall Street Journal*, and, most importantly, on the Web. You can get the **mutual fund prospectus** simply by calling the mutual fund and asking. Investment companies are required by law to offer a prospectus, and Table 15.6 provides a brief overview of what is provided in a prospectus.

Mutual Fund Prospectus
A description of the mutual fund, including the fund's objectives and risks, its historical performance, its expenses, the manager's history, and other information.

TABLE 15.6   What's in a Mutual Fund Prospectus?

- **The fund's goal and investment strategy.**
- **The fund manager's past experience.** You'll want to look closely at this. Many times when the mutual fund manager changes so does the style and performance of the fund.
- **Any investment's limitation that the fund may have.** For example, can the mutual fund invest in foreign securities?
- **Any tax considerations of importance to investors.**
- **The redemption and investment process for buying and selling shares in the fund.**
- **Services provided to investors.** For example, does the mutual fund provide 24-hour telephone service?
- **Performance over the past 10 years or since the fund has been in existence.** Most funds generally show this by demonstrating what would have happened if you had put $10,000 in the fund 10 years earlier or when the fund was formed.
- **Fund fees and expenses.** Look closely at the fund's sales and redemption charges. In addition, information on the management fee and fees for marketing expenses, called 12b-1 fees, are included.
- **The fund's annual turnover ratio.** There's also an additional part to the prospectus, which can be obtained separately and contains a listing of the fund's holdings, as well as additional information on the fund management.

For the most recent returns, you'll want to look online. Figure 15.4 shows how a typical fund listing generally appears on one of the many online finance Web sites (**finance.yahoo.com**, **www.smartmoney.com**, or **www.wsj.com**), along with an explanation of the terminology.

There's plenty of mutual fund material available on the Web, with some of the best sources listed in Table 15.7. Perhaps the best thing about Internet sources of information is that they're interactive—that is, you can use them to screen through different criteria easily and find the fund that fits your needs.

Internet Screening to Find the Right Mutual Fund   Internet screening involves using an Internet program that searches out funds that meet the criteria that you've selected. That is, you may want a growth stock fund with low expenses that has been one of the top performers for the past 3 years—with a mutual fund Internet screening program, all you have to do is select that criteria and the program will instantly deliver to you the names of the mutual funds that fit that criteria.

Two of the best Web sites are Morningstar (**www.morningstar.com**), and Yahoo! Finance (**finance.yahoo.com**). Most brokerage Web sites also provide screening tools. Table 15.7 provides a description and summary of the screening capabilities of those Web sites.

What kind of things should you be screening for? Table 15.8 provides a listing of possible screening criteria.

Step 4: Making the Purchase

After all of your figuring, matching, picking, evaluating, and calculating, you should now know exactly what fund you want. Now it's time to do some buying. Load funds are generally sold through salespeople—perhaps a broker or a financial advisor. No-load funds, though, tend to be sold directly by the investment company. If you decide to keep costs down and go for a no-load fund, you have two choices. You can deal directly with the investment company that runs the fund, or you can purchase the no-load fund through a "mutual fund supermarket."

Buying Direct   The easiest way to buy a mutual fund is to pick up the phone or go on the Internet. Vanguard and Fidelity, the two largest mutual fund families, both have 800 numbers and Web sites that you can use to set up an account, to move money into

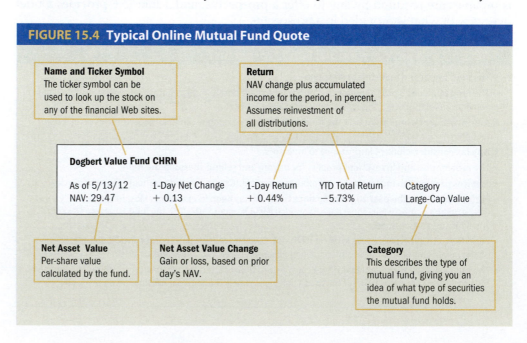

FIGURE 15.4 Typical Online Mutual Fund Quote

Name and Ticker Symbol
The ticker symbol can be used to look up the stock on any of the financial Web sites.

Return
NAV change plus accumulated income for the period, in percent. Assumes reinvestment of all distributions.

Dogbert Value Fund CHRN

| As of 5/13/12 | 1-Day Net Change | 1-Day Return | YTD Total Return | Category |
| NAV: 29.47 | + 0.13 | + 0.44% | −5.73% | Large-Cap Value |

Net Asset Value
Per-share value calculated by the fund.

Net Asset Value Change
Gain or loss, based on prior day's NAV.

Category
This describes the type of mutual fund, giving you an idea of what type of securities the mutual fund holds.

TABLE 15.7 Web Sources for Screening Mutual Funds

Web Site: **Morningstar**

Address: **http://screen.morningstar.com/FundSelector.html**

Features:

- Free, but you need to register.
- Extremely easy to use.
- Provides explanations if you aren't familiar with the terms (simply click on the light bulb next to the term).
- Allows for screening by fund type, manager's tenure, initial investment, cost, expenses, Morningstar rating, returns over different periods, turnover, and size.
- You can enter any fund ticker symbol in the "Quotes" box and Morningstar will provide stats, Morningstar ratings, and Morningstar style boxes, along with quite a bit of other data free of charge.

Web Site: **Yahoo! Finance**

Address: **http://screen.yahoo.com/funds.html**

Features:

- Free
- Allows for screening by fund type, fund family, rank in category, manager's tenure, Morningstar rating, returns over different periods, initial investment, front loads, expense ratio, and size.

Web Site: **Mutual Fund Education Alliance, Mutual Fund Investor's Center**

Address: **http://www.mfea.com/FundSelector/default.asp**

Features:

- Free.
- Allows for screening by load, minimum required investment, Morningstar rating, expense ratio, management fee, 12b-1 fee, and redemption fee.
- "Fund Quicklist"—if you're overwhelmed by the screening process—lists low-fee funds, top 5 funds by category, and funds with low initial investment.

Web Site: **Various Brokerage Web sites**

Address: **www.fidelity.com** (other brokerage Web sites also provide screening features)

Features:

- If you have an account with an online brokerage, chances are there is an excellent screening feature provided.
- You can enter any fund ticker symbol and will be provided with information on risk, performance, ratings, composition, fees, and features.

and out of your funds, to switch funds, and to request educational material. You can transfer money electronically, or send a check to Vanguard or Fidelity through the mail. When you sell your holdings, you can receive a check in the mail or have the proceeds automatically deposited into an account you hold with these companies or into your checking account.

Buying Through a "Mutual Fund Supermarket"   The downside of buying directly from different mutual funds is that if you have money in eight different mutual fund

TABLE 15.8 Screening Criteria for Mutual Funds

- **Load Funds**—Avoid both front load funds and those with deferred sales charges.
- **12b-1 Fees**—Avoid them; there are plenty of good funds that don't charge them.
- **Expenses Ratio**—Keep it under 1.25%.
- **Turnover Ratio**—Focus on funds with low turnover; they are liable for less taxes and they produce higher returns.
- **Morningstar Rating**—Morningstar's star rating compares historical returns to risk; you want to start out screening for five-star funds.
- **Historical Returns**—Look for strong returns over the past 1-year and 3-year periods.
- **Morningstar Risk**—Lower is better; that way, you know the fund hasn't just done well because it made risky bets.
- **Initial Investment**—Make sure you pick a fund that you can invest in. Some funds require a high initial investment.
- **Manager's Tenure**—Avoid a fund if the manager has just left because historical returns mean nothing once the manager leaves.

MONEY MATTERS

Tips from Marcy Furney, ChFC, Certified Financial Planner™

THE FEELING IS MUTUAL

When deciding how and where to invest, many people fail to take into account their particular tax situation. Consequently, income taxes eat up a large part of their return. Understanding some of the tax implications of mutual funds may allow more of the earnings to end up in your pocket.

Mutual funds pass along to shareholders the taxable income from their investments in the form of dividends and capital gains. Even if all distributions are automatically reinvested, the tax liability is your responsibility. The percent of total return that these taxable elements comprise could be of great concern to anyone attempting to lower his or her income taxes.

When funds pay out capital gains (normally at the end of the year), the price per share decreases by the amount paid out. If you buy just before a capital gain distribution is made, you pay the higher share price and part of your original investment is immediately returned to you in the form of a taxable capital gain. In other words, don't buy a tax liability by investing right before a distribution date.

Consider tax implications when moving money from one fund to another. Even if you "transfer" within the same fund family, the IRS deems the transaction a sale and a purchase and you are taxed on any gain from the sale.

Unlike individual stocks for which you control when gains will be taken, mutual funds have capital gains when the manager decides to sell appreciated assets. Morningstar and other analyses give an estimate of the percent of the fund's assets with such exposure. This information may sway your choice when selecting from a group of similar funds. Some have extremely large unrealized capital gains, which could become the shareholders' tax liability at any time.

Fund companies that provide cost-basis information for shareholders may not do so if you make several partial redemptions. It is important to keep records of all purchases, distributions, and withdrawals so that you can determine the gain or loss from any sale. When selling part of your shares, you may be able to choose an average cost per share figure or designate specific shares to sell. It all depends on whether you are trying to reduce or increase your taxable gain at that time. Beware: Once you choose a method of determining cost basis, you normally cannot change it for the life of that particular fund.

You may wish to consult your financial planner or tax advisor before any purchases or redemptions are made. Ownership of the fund (e.g., parent versus child), taxability of the income, and use of gains and losses are important aspects of your overall financial picture.

families, you'll have eight different statements to deal with. If you decide you want to move money from one family to another, you're in for a real headache.

Luckily, there are "mutual fund supermarkets" such as Charles Schwab & Co. and Fidelity, where you can pick mutual funds from different mutual fund families. However, you should also be aware that you may be charged a small transaction fee when you buy a no-load fund through a mutual fund supermarket. You can avoid transaction fees altogether by purchasing these funds directly from their mutual fund families. In addition, many banks also sell mutual funds. Unfortunately, investors often don't realize that mutual funds sold by banks aren't insured by the federal government, as are most bank accounts. Moreover, most mutual funds sold by banks are load funds.

Summary

Weigh the advantages and disadvantages of investing in mutual funds.

When you invest in a mutual fund, you're buying a fraction of a very large portfolio. This portfolio may include stocks, bonds, short-term securities, and even cash. Your money is pooled with that of other investors to purchase the fund's holdings. The shareholders then own a proportionate share of the overall portfolio. The value of mutual fund shares goes up and down as the value of the mutual fund's investments goes up and down.

 Differentiate between types of mutual funds, ETFs, and investment trusts.

Investment companies invest the pooled money in return for a fee. An open-end investment company is actually an open-end mutual fund. It has the ability to issue and redeem shares on a daily basis, and the value of the portfolio that it holds determines the value of each ownership share in the mutual fund. The price paid for an open-end mutual fund share, or received when the share is sold, is the net asset value (NAV).

A closed-end fund has a fixed number of shares. Those shares are initially sold by the fund at its inception, and after that they trade between investors at whatever price supply and demand dictate. A unit investment trust is a pool of securities, generally municipal bonds, with each share representing a proportionate ownership in that pool. A real estate investment trust, or REIT, is similar to a mutual fund, with the funds going either directly into real estate, real estate loans (mortgages), or a combination of the two.

 Calculate mutual fund returns.

Although some mutual funds have no sales commission, others impose a sales commission, and still others require a hefty annual management fee. A load is a sales commission; thus, a load fund is one that charges a sales commission. A mutual fund that doesn't charge a commission is referred to as a no-load fund.

Be very aware of any and all mutual fund expenses and try to avoid them. The return from investing in a mutual fund can be in the form of dividends or capital gains distributions, or a change in the NAV of the shares held. Capital gains result from selling securities for more than what they were originally bought for.

 Classify mutual funds according to objectives.

To allow you to more easily choose from over 8,000 mutual funds available, funds are categorized according to objective.

 Select a mutual fund that's right for you.

The process of selecting a mutual fund involves determining your investment goals, identifying funds that meet your objectives, and evaluating those funds. There's a wealth of information and screening tools available to aid you online for evaluating mutual funds.

Review Questions

1. What is a mutual fund? What makes a mutual fund different from owning a stock or bond directly?

2. List and explain the seven advantages associated with owning a mutual fund. Which of these advantages relates to **Principle 8**? How?

3. List and explain the five disadvantages of mutual funds.

4. If diversification is a primary advantage of mutual funds, why can't a mutual fund diversify away systematic risk?

5. Mutual fund investors make money in three ways. Name and briefly describe each. How are these reflected in the formula for calculating total return?

6. Describe the organization of a mutual fund. What is the role of the investment manager or advisor? How is he or she typically compensated?

7. Describe the four most common types of investment companies.

8. Define net asset value. When is the net asset value of a mutual fund calculated?

9. How do closed-end funds differ from open-end funds? What asset class dominates the closed-end mutual fund market?

10. What is an REIT and how is one similar to and different from a mutual fund?

11. What is a hedge fund? Why are they not a recommended investment for most investors?

12. What is the primary difference between a load fund and a no-load fund? What is a back-end load? A 12b-1 fee?

13. What is the "typical" range of an expense ratio? What costs are paid out of the expense ratio? What expense is not included in the expense ratio? How can these costs and expenses affect long-term earnings?

14. List the six major categories of mutual funds. What is the fundamental difference among these categories? What two categories are most alike? Why?

15. Why are money market mutual funds considered practically risk free?

16. What is an index fund and why should most investors consider purchasing shares in an index fund versus another type of stock fund?

17. What are the three main categories of bond funds? What is the primary advantage of each category?

18. What is an ETF and how is it similar and dissimilar to a mutual fund?

19. What is the primary disadvantage of an ETF for an investor who might like to trade in and out of the market?

20. List the seven special services offered to investors by most mutual fund companies. For each, explain its benefit to a specific type of investor.

21. How does an automatic investment plan facilitate **Principle 10?**

22. Summarize the three steps involved in the mutual fund selection process.

23. What is a "mutual fund supermarket"? What are the advantages and disadvantages of buying funds this way versus buying them directly?

Develop Your Skills—Problems and Activities

These problems are available in MyFinanceLab.

1. Calculate the net asset value (NAV) for a mutual fund with the following values:

Market value of securities held in the portfolio	= $1.2 billion
Liabilities of the fund	= $37 million
Shares outstanding	= 60 million

2. The following information pertains to the Big Returns Fund:

Cost	Class "A"	Class "B"	Class "C"
Front-end load	5.50	0.00	0.00
Back-end load	0.00	5.00	1.00
		Declining 1% per year	First year only
Management fee	0.90	0.90	0.90
12b-1 fee	0.25	0.50	1.00

For each share class, calculate (1) how much you would pay in initial commissions, (2) how much you would pay in back-end commissions if you sold after 2 years, (3) how much in annual expenses you would pay over a 2-year holding period. Assume you purchased $2,500 worth of shares in this fund, and that prior to reductions for management and 12b-1 fees the gross fund return was 10 percent each year.

3. Match the following types of stock funds shown below to the appropriate stocks that would typically be found in each portfolio.

Growth funds	(a) Foreign stocks
U.S. Government Bond Funds	(b) Moves money from stocks to bonds to maximize return
Growth and income funds	(c) Market basket that represents the S&P 500
Life cycle funds	(d) Mix of stocks, bonds, and money market securities
Sector funds	(e) 65 percent of stocks from the technology industry
Index funds	(f) Dividend-paying blue-chip stocks
Balanced funds	(g) Tailored to investor characteristics
International funds	(h) High growth and high P/E companies
Small company funds	(i) Companies with strong earnings and some dividends
Asset allocation funds	(j) Federal agency securities
Aggressive growth funds	(k) Companies that probably trade on the OTC market

4. Zap Fund is the mainstay of your portfolio. The investment company just announced its year-end distributions. The long-term capital gain per share is $4.60 and the dividend per share is $2.10. Assuming the NAV increased from $39.10 to $46.21, calculate your total annual return.

5. At the beginning of last year Thomas purchased 200 shares of the Web.com Fund at an NAV of $26.00 and automatically reinvested all distributions. As a result of reinvesting Thomas ended the year with 265 shares of the fund with an NAV of $32.20. What was his total return for the year on this investment?

6. Calculate the after-withdrawal future value of $10,000 invested for 5 years in each share class in the table below. In terms of costs, which would be the best investment for someone who knows the fund will be sold at the end of the 5-year period? Assume that each fund's gross (before fees) total return is 12 percent per year.

Cost	Class "A"	Class "B"	Class "C"
Front-end load	5.75	0.00	0.00
Back-end load	0.00	5.00	1.00
		Declining 1% per year	First year only
Management fee	0.55	0.90	1.00
12b-1 fee	0.25	0.50	1.00

7. Melanie is considering purchasing shares in an international bond fund. She has limited her search to one open-end and one closed-end fund. Information on the funds follows:

	Open-End	Closed-End
NAV	$12.00	$24.05
Sales price	no-load	$21.95
Annual expenses	1.45%	1.15%
YTD return	12.00%	12.50%

a. How much would Melanie pay for the open-end fund? How much would she pay for the closed-end fund?

b. Is the closed-end fund selling at a discount or a premium to its NAV?

c. Given both funds' similar returns and expense ratios, would you recommend that Melanie purchase the closed-end fund? Why or why not?

8. The reinvestment of capital gains and dividends can make a significant difference in your total return. Consider the following situation to determine the difference reinvestment can make over a 5-year period.

Initial purchase amount	$10,000
Initial purchase date	January 1
Initial purchase price	$19.30 per share
Annual capital gains distribution rate	1.5%
Annual dividend distribution rate	0.6%
Annual price appreciation rate	7.4%

Assume all distributions are made on the last day of the year at the closing net asset value (NAV). Ignore tax consequences for the scenarios in a and b, below.

a. Calculate the ending investment value plus the total of distributions received assuming no reinvestment.

b. Calculate the ending investment value assuming all distributions are reinvested.

c. Calculate and explain the difference.

9. Calculate the total cost for purchasing 100 shares of each of the following funds. Remember to include both sales commission and any transaction costs.

a. A load mutual fund that sells for an NAV of $19 per share and charges a sales commission of 4 percent of the purchase amount

b. A closed-end fund that has an ask price of $19.50 and bid price of $19 per share

c. An ETF that has an ask price of $19.25, a bid price of $19, and a transaction fee of $15

10. You must choose between a no-load, open-end mutual fund with an annual expense ratio of 0.85 percent but no transaction cost or an ETF with an annual expense ratio of 0.25 percent and a transaction cost of $20.00.

a. Calculate which is the lower cost alternative to purchase.

b. Calculate which is the lower cost to own over 6 months, if you sell after 7 percent gain.

c. Calculate which is the lower cost to own over 2 years, if you achieve a 10 percent per year gain.

d. Calculate which is the lower cost to own over 2 years, if you experience a 10 percent per year loss.

Learn by Doing—Suggested Projects

1. Actively managed mutual funds tend to underperform in comparison to the S&P 500 Index. Why is this? Using the Web or another source (e.g., mutual fund newsletter, magazine, or financial professional), identify three to five funds that have beat the market for the past year. Using the Web sites **www.morningstar .com**, **www.smartmoney.com**, or **finance.yahoo.com**, research the individual stocks or sectors of the economy that comprise the fund. Can you explain why these funds are beating the market? Is the S&P 500 Index always the appropriate method to measure performance? Why or why not?

2. Use your favorite search engine to do a search on life cycle funds. Read several of the articles that you find and prepare a short report on why life cycle funds have become so popular. Also do some research on the average expense ratios

for these fund types and include an editorial from a financial publication on whether or not the benefits justify any additional costs.

3. Use **finance.yahoo.com** to sort mutual funds according to their expense ratios. Is there a correlation between low expense ratios and better performance? If all other areas of comparison are equal, why are mutual funds with low expense ratios always a good recommendation?

4. Visit a personal finance Web site and read about mutual funds. What are the current trends with mutual funds?

5. According to Checklist 15.1, tax efficiency is a key area to research when choosing a mutual fund. Look up five different large-cap, growth mutual funds at **finance.yahoo.com/funds** (*note:* there is no www in front of this Web address) and **www.morningstar.com**, or the fund's Web site and make note of the portfolio turnover rate, the performance, and the tax efficiency of each fund. According to your research, does there seem to be any correlation between either the turnover rate or the performance of the fund and its tax efficiency?

6. Call one of the two largest brokerage firms that offer a "mutual fund supermarket" (Charles Schwab at 1-800-435-4000 or Fidelity at 1-800-544-9697) or visit its Internet site. Obtain a list of funds available through the supermarket. According to the information provided, what are some of the advantages of purchasing funds through a supermarket? Does the information describe how the brokerage firms selling the funds are paid? How do you think they are compensated for offering this service?

7. Use the three-step process described in the text to select a mutual fund based on your current circumstances. What classification of fund(s) would be appropriate given (a) the amount of money you have available to open an account, (b) your time horizon for using the money, (c) your goal or investment objective for the money, and (d) your risk tolerance?

Be a Financial Planner—Discussion Case 1

This case is available in MyFinanceLab.

Rick Phillips has usually been just a market watcher and not a market participant; however, he recently received $15,000 for the movie rights to his new book. Rick has never before had the resources to invest and therefore owns no other security investments, but he has followed several telecom stocks over the past year. The share prices have fluctuated dramatically, but Rick is definitely interested in this type of stock. He feels that wireless telecommunication companies offer great possibilities. When you asked Rick if he was comfortable with the risk associated with such an investment, he indicated that he would be if superior returns could be obtained.

Questions

1. Given the fact that Rick only has $15,000 to invest, explain why he should consider investing in mutual funds rather than individual stocks.

2. In what type(s) of stock mutual fund(s) would you recommend Rick invest? Why?

3. In helping Rick make an investment choice, what factors would you explain to him are most important when choosing a mutual fund?

4. Although most mutual funds will provide Rick with some level of diversification, what type of risk will Rick still be exposed to if he purchases a single mutual fund?

5. To assure Rick of the liquidity and marketability of his investment, would you recommend that he invest in an open-end or closed-end mutual fund? Why?

6. In terms of costs, would you recommend load or no-load funds to Rick? Why?

7. Develop a model portfolio of three mutual fund types (e.g., index, growth, bond, etc.) to help Rick understand the benefits of diversification. Explain your choices. Be sure to consider issues of risk and volatility.

Be a Financial Planner—Discussion Case 2

This case is available in MyFinanceLab.

Mahalia has decided that she needs to invest her savings somewhere other than a bank account where she is only earning 1.25 percent annually. She has heard that money market mutual funds and short-term bond funds may provide higher yields than bank accounts and offer stability of principal similar to the bank. Mahalia's primary investment goal is to keep her savings (about $15,000 when she last checked) secure and accessible so that she can make a down payment on a house within the next 3 years. She has several questions regarding investing in mutual funds and has come to you for help.

Questions

1. What are the types of mutual funds that would be appropriate in meeting Mahalia's objective?
2. What sources could Mahalia use to obtain specific information and ratings on different funds?
3. When reviewing a fund's prospectus or an analysis provided by Morningstar, for what specific type of information should Mahalia look?
4. When evaluating a fund, how much importance should Mahalia place on a fund's past performance?
5. Given Mahalia's goal and your response to question 1, how important are loads, fees, and expenses in her search for a good mutual fund?
6. Provide Mahalia with six reasons why she should consider purchasing shares in a bond fund.
7. What type of bond fund would you recommend? Why?
8. In terms of the risk–return trade-off, what length of maturity for a bond fund would be appropriate for Mahalia?
9. Name and describe at least four services provided by mutual funds that should appeal to Mahalia.

Be a Financial Planner—Continuing Case: Cory and Tisha Dumont

As Cory and Tisha Dumont have reviewed your answers to their previous questions, they have recognized that their need for financial planning assistance was far greater than they realized. They have taken your advice and consistently reduced expenses. To their great surprise, they have already accumulated $1,500 for an emergency fund. They feel that they are getting a handle on their basic money management skills and are more confident in their insurance knowledge and product selection. Now they want to develop an investment plan.

Recall that Cory and Tisha have $13,000 invested in a market index mutual fund for a house down payment. They also have $2,500 in a savings account earning 3 percent interest and an average of $1,800 in their checking account earning 0.75 percent interest. (Their $1,500 in emergency funds is in addition to these savings amounts and has been temporarily deposited in their savings account.) The shares of Great Basin Balanced Mutual Fund, given to Tisha by her father, are worth $2,300. After completing a risk tolerance questionnaire on an investment Web site, Tisha and Cory confirmed that their attitudes toward risk were very different. Tisha is much more comfortable with "gambling" higher risks for higher returns, whereas Cory wants a "safe bet." Help the Dumonts answer the following questions regarding the management of their investments.

Questions

1. Fundamentally, what must Cory and Tisha understand about themselves *and* the risk–return trade-off of investments to achieve their long-term investment goals?

2. As Pogo, the cartoon character said, "We have met the enemy and he is us." To protect their investment plan, what mind games and behavioral quirks should Cory and Tisha avoid?

3. Based on the Dumonts' stage in the life cycle, what type of investment asset allocation would be appropriate, assuming they want to establish a retirement savings fund? What types of stocks, mutual funds, or exchange traded funds (ETFs) should they consider for the equity portion of their asset allocation plan? Should they consider international common stocks, mutual funds, or ETFs? Why or why not? What types of bonds, bond funds, or bond ETFs would be appropriate for the fixed-income portion of their asset allocation plan? (*Hint:* Be sure to consider the bond maturity, rating, and type of issuer.)

4. Briefly explain the concept of efficient markets for Cory and Tisha. Based on that understanding, what six strategies should they use to guide their investment management?

5. Give Cory and Tisha a simple explanation of brokerage accounts, asset management accounts, and margin accounts. Help the Dumonts consider each of these alternatives, noting advantages and disadvantages.

6. Explain to Cory and Tisha the advantages and disadvantages associated with managing an investment portfolio through a full-service brokerage firm versus a discount or online brokerage firm. How will the trade-off between service and price affect their choice of a broker?

7. Online investing, not day trading, seems to be the simplest and cheapest approach for the Dumonts. If they choose to use an online brokerage, what strategies would you recommend regarding orders, trades, margins, and other account activity?

8. Explain to the Dumonts how owning a combination of securities can reduce risks as addressed by **Principle 8: Risk and Return Go Hand in Hand.** Why is it important to know, and be able to interpret, the beta of a diversified portfolio?

9. The Dumonts, in the 15 percent marginal tax bracket, are concerned about the federal taxes paid on investment earnings. Show the calculations to answer the following questions. (*Hint:* See Chapter 4 or Chapter 14.)

   a. A tax-free money market mutual fund is currently yielding 2.40 percent. Should the Dumonts move their savings or keep their money in the bank earning 3 percent?

   b. If a U.S. Treasury note is currently yielding 8 percent, what is the minimum interest rate that the Dumonts must receive in order to purchase an equivalent municipal bond?

10. Calculate the amount of money the Dumonts will have in their savings account if they add no other funds and keep it invested at 3 percent over the next 25 years. Calculate how much they can accumulate over 25 years if they move the money into a money market mutual fund earning 5 percent. Based on your calculations, should the Dumonts reallocate their savings into a money market mutual fund? What advantages and disadvantages should be considered? (*Hint:* Use your financial calculator or see Chapter 3.)

11. Cory's parents recently gave the Dumonts $40,000 to start education funds for Chad and Haley. A stockbroker has recommended that Cory and Tisha include a

10-year corporate bond in the portfolio. The bond currently yields 8 percent and sells for $1,000. If interest rates increase 2 percentage points and the bond is sold, how much will the bond sell for at that time? Calculate the bond price if rates fall 1 percent. What investing rule does this prove?

12. The same stockbroker who recommended a bond for Chad's college savings also recommended that Haley's college savings portfolio include a preferred stock currently selling for $53 and paying a $5 dividend. If the Dumonts' required rate of return is 10 percent, for how much should the preferred stock sell?

13. Should the Dumonts take the stockbroker's advice on education savings and buy the bond for Chad and the preferred stock for Haley? Defend your answer and provide other investment alternatives that the Dumonts should consider.

14. Explain to Cory and Tisha why mutual funds may be a good alternative for meeting their investment objectives. What specific types of mutual funds would be appropriate for meeting the following investment objectives, given their time horizon and risk tolerance? (*Hint:* Try to develop an asset allocation strategy by suggesting percentages for each fund type(s) included.)

   a. Emergency fund

   b. House down payment savings

   c. College fund for Chad

   d. College fund for Haley

   e. Retirement fund for Cory

   f. Retirement fund for Tisha

15. Recall that when Tisha turned 21 her father gave her shares in the Great Basin Balanced Mutual Fund. Today the fund is worth $2,300. Assuming that Tisha will use this fund as a long-term investment (maybe for retirement), and given her risk tolerance and age, does this type of fund match her objective? What investment risk is most important when thinking about investments for a college fund or retirement? Would this be a good fund if she decided to use it to save for college expenses for Chad and Haley? Defend your answers.

16. Cory and Tisha invested in a stock market index mutual fund to save for their "dream house," which they expect to purchase in 3 to 5 years. Would you recommend that they maintain, increase, or decrease their holdings in this type of fund given their objective? Explain your answer. What type of fund or other investment would you recommend?

17. What mutual fund services would you recommend that the Dumonts use to save for their goals systematically? Why? How might these services be integrated with a portfolio accumulation strategy?

18. Would you recommend no-load or load funds to the Dumonts? Why? What other factors are important to consider when comparing different mutual funds with the same objective?

19. Should the Dumonts consider using a mutual fund supermarket? What are the advantages and disadvantages of using this investment strategy? Might a bank offer a better option?

20. Given the time horizon of their goals and their knowledge of investment strategies, what are the advantages and disadvantages of considering ETFs for the house, college, or retirement?

21. When Cory and Tisha do purchase a house, should they consider this an investment? Explain your answer in terms of (a) liquidity and (b) how market values for real estate are determined.

22. What sources of investment information can Cory and Tisha use to learn more about potential stock, bond, and mutual fund investments? Recall that Cory likes to use the Internet for research.

PART 5
Life Cycle Issues

Part 5: Life Cycle Issues focuses on financial planning for the future—your retirement years, and beyond, with a look at estate planning. The key word here is planning. Without a plan, nothing will happen, and to put a plan into place requires an understanding of the issues you face and the alternatives available that will take you where you want to go. Moreover, without an understanding of the issues confronting you and the importance of putting a plan into place, it's easy to become complacent and procrastinate.

Part 5 closes by tying the different personal finance topics together to provide you with a step-by-step action plan by looking at ten "Financial Life Events." In addition, it examines a dozen financial and lifestyle decisions that will have a major impact on your financial future, and offers a close look at the keys to successful debt management.

In Part 5, we will specifically focus on Principle 10:

Principle 10: Just Do It!—After all, making the commitment to financial planning may be the most difficult step in the financial planning process. In addition, in Part 5 we will also touch on the following principles:

Principle 1: The Best Protection Is Knowledge

Principle 2: Nothing Happens Without a Plan

Principle 3: The Time Value of Money

Principle 4: Taxes Affect Personal Finance Decisions

Principle 5: Stuff Happens, or the Importance of Liquidity

Principle 6: Waste Not, Want Not—Smart Spending Matters

Principle 7: Protect Yourself Against Major Catastrophes

Principle 8: Risk and Return Go Hand in Hand

Principle 9: Mind Games, Your Financial Personality, and Your Money

16 Retirement Planning

Learning Objectives

 Understand the changing nature of retirement planning.

 Set up a retirement plan.

 Contribute to a tax-favored retirement plan to help fund your retirement.

 Choose how your retirement benefits are paid out to you.

 Put together a retirement plan and effectively monitor it.

Most people assume that if you make it big early in life, you'll surely retire to a life of luxury. Not so. Retiring comfortably takes planning. Just look at musical icon Tina Turner.

Turner was born in 1939 to cotton plantation workers in Brownsville, Tennessee, and moved to St. Louis to live with relatives when she was in her teens. It was there she met Ike Turner, her future husband and singing partner. Together they hit the big time, becoming huge stars in the 1970s with hits such as "River Deep, Mountain Wide," and an R&B-style version of Creedence Clearwater Revival's "Proud Mary." Unfortunately, the big time isn't all that Ike hit. After being beaten bloody in July 1976, Tina Turner finally walked out of her 20-year abusive marriage to Ike. When she left, she had no recording contract, no savings, no fancy cars or homes—just 36 cents and a Mobil gas card.

For a while, Turner and her four children lived on food stamps. Although facing poverty, she refused any financial help from Ike when the couple finally divorced in 1978. Instead, she managed to support herself and her family by playing

Holiday Inns and other minor clubs. By 1979, she was $500,000 in debt, with no prospects and no one to lend a helping hand. It looked as if Tina Turner had retired to a life of poverty and obscurity.

Fortunately, along came Roger Davies, a young Australian promoter, who signed on as her manager. With his help, Turner paid off her bills, put together a new backup band, and got a fresh start. Despite record company skepticism, she managed to get a new recording contract, and by 1984 she had a number-one hit with "What's Love Got to Do with It." Today Turner continues to be a major star, and in 2010, at age 70, she rose to the top of the UK charts one more time just after finishing her Tina!: 50th Anniversary Tour, one of the highest grossing tours of all time. While this time around Turner has surely planned for her retirement, let's hope she never stops performing!

You may think you're too young or not wealthy enough to worry about retirement. Think again. Regardless of your age, you need to start planning for retirement. By doing so, you're focusing on a specific financial goal. As you learned in Chapters 1 and 2, you're going to have a lot of financial goals in your life. Retirement, though, is a biggie. After all, how well you do in achieving your retirement goal is probably going to determine how much you enjoy the last 20 or more years of your life.

It's hard to think about retiring when you're young. For most people, today looms larger than tomorrow. That car loan or mortgage you're trying to pay off this year will no doubt seem far more important than your financial situation 30 to 40 years from now. But just think how worried you'll be when you're 65 and you don't have a dime to retire on. Big money in a second career may have worked for Tina Turner, but it's a long shot for most of us. Fortunately, with a sound plan and a little discipline, you can retire to a life of relative ease without ever having to fret or fear.

There used to be a time when retirement planning wasn't necessary—retirement meant taking a pension from your employer and letting Social Security pick up any slack. Not anymore. Thanks to the recent drive to cut spending, employers tend not to pay pensions, and those that still do have reduced them to as little as possible. That leaves a lot of slack for Social Security, but given some of the Social Security reform proposals that have been tossed around, coupled with the government's drive to cut its own spending, there might not be such a thing as Social Security by the time you retire.

Nowadays, you've got to come up with the funds for your retirement all by yourself. Sound scary? Well, it's actually not. We'll explain exactly how to make a good retirement plan. But first we should explain how Social Security and employer-funded pensions work. No, we're not trying to rub it in and show you what you're missing. You simply need to know about past retirement plans before you can dive into the present ones.

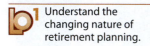 Understand the changing nature of retirement planning.

Social Security

For many senior citizens, Social Security is their primary source of retirement income. For younger workers who won't face retirement for 40 years, the Social Security system may no longer be available then, or may have changed dramatically. Still, for many of the millions of individuals receiving benefits today, Social Security is the difference between living in poverty and modest comfort. Let's take a look at how the Social Security system currently functions.

Financing Social Security

To begin with, Social Security isn't an investment. When you pay money into Social Security, you're purchasing mandatory insurance that provides for you and your family in the event of death, disability, health problems, or retirement. Moreover, the benefits paid by Social Security aren't intended to allow you to live in comfort after you retire. They're intended to provide a base level of protection.

Whether you want to or not, you fund Social Security during your working years by paying taxes directly to the Social Security system. If you're not self-employed, both you and your employer pay into the system—each pays 7.65 percent of your gross salary up to $106,800 in 2010.[1] This deduction appears on your pay slip as "FICA," which stands for the Federal Insurance Contributions Act.

These funds actually go to both Social Security and to Medicare (the government's health insurance program for the elderly, which we discussed in Chapter 9). Medicare also keeps on taxing after the Social Security cap has been reached, taking an additional 1.45 percent from both you and your employer.

If your salary were $106,800 in 2010, your FICA contribution would be $8,170.20. If you're self-employed, you have to pay both the employer and employee portions of FICA, at a rate of 15.3 percent up to the $106,800 limit, paying a total of $16,340.40. In addition, you pay Medicare 2.9 percent on all net earnings above $106,800.

---

[1]For 2011, Congress reduced the employee portion of the Social Security FICA tax by 2 percent. This reduction is scheduled to last for only 1 year, returning to the previous level in 2012.

These funds cover the payments currently being made to today's retirees by Social Security, while allowing for a "built-in surplus" for payouts in the future. The Social Security Trust Fund is up to $2.6 trillion so far, and is invested in special-issue Treasury bonds. These bonds are housed in a Bureau of the Public Debt safe in Parkersburg, WV; on the bond, a congressional instruction declares, "the United States is pledged to . . . the obligation with respect to both principal and interest." In other words, the FICA taxes being paid by today's workers are providing the money for benefit payments for today's retirees, and any excess collected by the government is lent to itself (by buying Treasury bonds from the government). The money you pay to FICA isn't saved up and invested in an account just for you. Instead it gets pooled with the money all other current workers are paying to FICA and goes into a senior citizen's Social Security benefits check.

> **FACTS of LIFE**
>
> "Isn't this exciting! I earned this. I wiped tables for it, I steamed milk for it, and it's—(opening her paycheck)—not worth it! Who's FICA? Why is he getting my money?" These are the words of Rachel Green on the TV show *Friends*, seeing her first Central Perk paycheck in the episode "The One with George Stephanopoulos."

The plan is that when you retire, the FICA taxes paid by people working then and money accumulated in the Social Security Trust Fund will go into your benefits check. Unfortunately, the proportion of current workers to current Social Security recipients is shrinking rapidly. Whereas 40 years ago there were 16 workers for every Social Security recipient, today the ratio is down to 3 workers to every recipient. And the problem won't go away. In fact, it will only get worse—in 40 years the ratio of working contributors to recipients will be down to 2-to-1. The bottom line here is that there will be some changes in Social Security by the time it's your turn to collect, and some of these changes—perhaps increasing the retirement age or limiting benefits for the wealthy—may happen in the next few years.

Eligibility

Roughly 95 percent of all Americans are covered by Social Security. The major groups outside the system include police officers and workers continuously employed by the government since 1984, both of whom are covered by alternative retirement systems.

To become eligible for Social Security, all you have to do is pay money into the system. As you do, you receive Social Security credits. In 2011, you earned one credit for each $1,120 in earnings, up to a maximum of four credits per year. To qualify for benefits, you need 40 credits.

Once you've met this requirement, you become eligible for retirement, disability, and survivor benefits. Earning beyond 40 credits won't increase your benefits. If you die, some of your family members may also be eligible for Social Security benefits, even if they never paid into the system.

Retirement Benefits

The size of your Social Security benefits is determined by (1) your number of years of earnings, (2) your average level of earning, and (3) an adjustment for inflation. The formula attempts to provide benefits that would replace 42 percent of your average earnings over your working years, adjusted upward somewhat for those in lower income brackets and downward for those in higher income brackets. Thus, the benefits are slightly weighted toward individuals in lower income brackets because they, in general, have less savings to rely on at retirement.

The retirement age to receive full benefits gradually rises until it hits 67 for those born in 1960 or later. Those who retire as early as age 62 can receive reduced benefits. However, those benefits are *permanently* reduced by five-ninths of 1 percent for the first 36 months and five-twelfths of 1 percent for subsequent months before the

TABLE 16.1 Estimated Monthly Social Security Benefit for Retiree Born in 1990 (2012 Dollars)

Year	Retirement Age	Average Earnings Base			
		$20,000	$40,000	$60,000	$100,000
2052	62	$681	$1,056	$1,374	$1,726
2057	67	$967	$1,500	$1,952	$2,452
2060	70	$1,199	$1,861	$2,420	$3,040

Source: Social Security Administration, http://www.ssa.gov/retire2/AnypiaApplet.html.

"full" retirement age. That means people scheduled to receive full benefits at age 67 and who retire at age 62 will receive only 70 percent of their full benefits, and this reduced level of benefits is permanent.

If you delay retirement, you can increase your Social Security benefits. The longer you work, the higher the average earnings base on which your benefits are calculated. In addition, those who delay retirement also have a percentage added to their benefits. For example, if you were born in 1943 or later, Social Security adds 8 percent per year to your benefit for each year that you delay signing up for Social Security beyond your full retirement age. Table 16.1 provides an estimate of the size of the Social Security benefits at retirement for someone who was 22 in 2012. Keep in mind that, depending on the level of your income and how you file your tax return, your Social Security benefits may be taxed.

FACTS OF LIFE

According to the 2010 Social Security Trustees Report, the Social Security Trust Fund will be exhausted in 2037, at which point it will be able to pay only about 75 percent of promised benefits.

You must notify your Social Security office and file an application 3 months before you want your first check to arrive; the government won't automatically start sending you your Social Security check just because you're officially retired.

How important is Social Security today? Take a look at Figure 16.1. As you can see, many low-income retirees depend on Social Security benefits to get by. The poverty rate for retirees, if they did not receive Social Security, would be almost half (46 percent), with Social Security reducing the poverty rate to 1 in 10. For women, Social Security is particularly important. In fact, half of women 65 years and older would be living in poverty but for Social Security. As we saw in Chapter 1, the financial difficulties that women face are particularly difficult, and as a result, elderly women are particularly dependent upon Social Security. Why is Social Security so important to women?

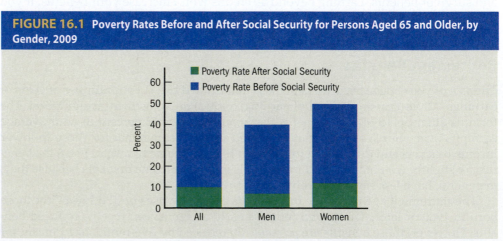

FIGURE 16.1 Poverty Rates Before and After Social Security for Persons Aged 65 and Older, by Gender, 2009

Source: U.S. Congress, *Unnecessary Risk: The Perils of Privatizing Social Security*, Report by the U.S. Congress Joint Economic Committee, October 2010.

◆ Women live longer than men; 60 percent of Social Security beneficiaries are women.

◆ As Figure 16.1 shows, half of all women 65 and older would be poor without Social Security.

◆ Social Security is the only source of income for 1 of every 4 unmarried women over 75 years of age.

Disability and Survivor Benefits

Although retirement benefits are the focus of our attention in this chapter, Social Security is actually a mandatory insurance program. Insurance against poverty at retirement is only one portion of its coverage. Social Security also provides disability and survivor benefits.

Disability benefits provide protection for those who experience a physical or mental impairment that is expected to result in death or keep them from doing any substantial work for at least a year. "Substantial work" is generally defined as anything that generates monthly earnings of $500 or more.

Social Security also provides survivor benefits to families when the breadwinner dies. These payments include a small, automatic one-time payment at the time of death to help defray funeral costs, as well as continued monthly payments to the spouse if he or she is over 60, over 50 if disabled, or any age and caring for a child either under 16 or disabled and receiving Social Security benefits. Continued monthly payments are also available to your children if they're under 18 or under 19 but still in elementary or secondary school, or if they're disabled. Your parents can also qualify for survivor benefits if you die and they're dependent on you for at least half of their support.

Employer-Funded Pensions

Twenty years ago, a "guaranteed" pension provided by your employer was the norm. You'd work for one company for most or all of your working life, and that company would reward your loyalty and hard work by taking care of you during retirement. In today's job scene, where companies aren't quite so generous and where employees change jobs often, pension plans are rare. However, some companies do still offer pensions, usually referring to them as "defined-benefit plans."

Defined-Benefit Plans

Under a **defined-benefit plan**, you receive a promised or "defined" payout at retirement. These plans are generally **noncontributory retirement plans**, which means you don't have to pay anything into them. (With a **contributory retirement plan**, you, and usually your employer, do pay into the plan.) The payout, which you receive as taxable income, is generally based on a formula that takes into account your age at retirement, salary level, and years of service.

The formulas can vary dramatically from company to company. Some focus only on salary during the final few years of service, which is better for you, while others use an average of all your years' salary as a base to calculate pension benefits. One commonly used formula is to pay out 1.5 percent of the average of your final 3 to 5 years' worth of salary times your number of years of service.

annual benefit = average salary over "final years" × years of service × 0.015

Thus, if you retired after 25 years of service with an average salary of $70,000 over the final years, you'd receive $26,250 ($70,000 × 25 × 0.015 = $26,250), which would

Defined-Benefit Plan
A traditional pension plan in which you receive a promised or "defined" pension payout at retirement. The payout is based on a formula that takes into account your age at retirement, salary level, and years of service.

Noncontributory Retirement Plan
A retirement plan in which the employer provides all the funds and the employee need not contribute.

Contributory Retirement Plan
A retirement plan in which the employee, possibly with the help of the employer, provides the funds for the plan.

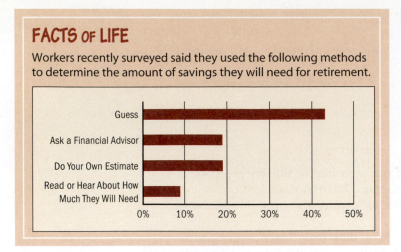

FACTS OF LIFE

Workers recently surveyed said they used the following methods to determine the amount of savings they will need for retirement.

be 37.5 percent of your final average salary. In general, the most that employees, even those who've spent their entire careers with the same company, ever receive from a defined-benefit pension is 40 to 45 percent of their before-retirement income.

One nice thing about a defined-benefit plan is that the employer bears the investment risk associated with the plan. That is, regardless of what the stock and bond markets do, you're still promised the same amount. You also have the option of extending pension coverage to your spouse. When you die, your spouse will continue to receive payments.

Companies are able to change their pension policies with little notice, and since corporate retirement plans are under pressure to drop traditional pensions, they often do. What has caused this pressure? First, since we live much longer in retirement, that means more pension costs. On top of that, health care costs have soared in recent years. In addition, low interest rates and a weak stock market have caused pension funding problems for most corporations. However, the biggest factor pushing corporations to ditch pension funds is competition. While older companies are dumping their pension plans, younger companies just don't offer them to begin with. Look at Microsoft, Walmart Stores, and Southwest Airlines—none of these younger companies offer pension plans.

One additional problem with defined-benefits programs is that they lack **portability**—that is, if you leave the company, your pension doesn't go with you. If you're **vested**, meaning you've worked long enough for the company to have the right to receive pension benefits, you'll eventually get a pension. However, it'll likely be small because pensions are generally based on years of service and salary levels. If you're not yet vested and you leave, you can kiss your pension good-bye.

Another problem with defined-benefit plans is that few of them—in fact only 1 in 10—adjust for inflation once the benefits begin. The benefit level stays constant over your retirement while inflation reduces the spending power of each dollar.

A final problem with defined-benefit plans is that they're not all **funded pension plans**, in which the employer makes regular pension contributions to a trustee who collects and invests the retirement funds. In other words, the employer sets up a separate account to guarantee the payment of pension benefits.

In an **unfunded pension plan**, pension expenses are paid out of current company earnings. These are pay-as-you-go pension plans. Needless to say, a funded plan is much safer than an unfunded plan, which would disappear if the company went under. Fortunately, the law requires employers to notify employees if their pension fund is less than 90 percent funded.

Cash-Balance Plans: The Latest Twist in Defined-Benefit Plans

In recent years, many large companies, including Eastman Kodak, CBS, Citigroup, and IBM, have switched from traditional defined-benefit plans to **cash-balance plans**. Cash-balance plans use a different formula for accumulation of benefits, one in which workers are credited with a percentage of their pay each year, plus a predetermined rate of investment earning or interest. Typically, this account earns interest at close to the long-term Treasury bond rate.

This sounds an awful lot like a defined-contribution plan, but it's not. That's because the accounts grow at this set rate, regardless of how much is actually earned. In addition, workers don't get to make investment decisions and they generally get lower returns on their cash balances than they would have been able to earn.

Portability
A pension fund provision that allows employees to retain and transfer any pension benefits already earned to another pension plan if they leave the company.

Vested
To gain the right to the retirement contributions made by your employer in your name. In the case of a pension plan, employees become vested when they've worked for a specified period of time and, thus, gained the right to pension benefits.

Funded Pension Plan
A pension plan in which the employer makes pension contributions directly to a trustee who holds and invests the employees' retirement funds.

Unfunded Pension Plan
A pension fund in which the benefits are paid out of current earnings on a pay-as-you-go basis.

Cash-Balance Plan
A retirement plan in which workers are credited with a percentage of their pay, plus a predetermined rate of interest.

Let's look a bit closer at how they work. Under a cash-balance plan, employers contribute a percentage of your salary each year into your account. This generally ranges between 4 and 7 percent. The contribution then grows, generally at the 30-year Treasury bond rate, although some companies will allow its growth to be tied to the S&P 500 index. Then, if you leave the company, you can generally roll the balance into an IRA (i.e., an individual retirement account, explained later in this chapter).

What's the good news? First, your retirement benefits are much easier to track. It is also better for young employees, because they start to build up benefits much earlier. In addition, if you leave the company, you can take your cash balance with you. Why have a third of all large companies in the United States converted to cash-balance plans? It's not because these companies are trying to shower their employees with money; it's because they save money with them as a result of reduced future benefits for older workers.

Plan Now, Retire Later

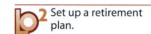 Set up a retirement plan.

It's incredibly easy to avoid thinking about retirement. This brings us back to **Principle 2: Nothing Happens Without a Plan**. Saving isn't a natural event—it must be planned. Unfortunately, planning isn't natural either. Although an elaborate, complicated plan might be ideal, you might be better off with a modest, uncomplicated retirement plan. Once the plan becomes part of your financial routine, you can modify and expand it. But a retirement plan can't be postponed; the longer you put it off, the more difficult accomplishing your goals becomes. Figure 16.2 shows the seven steps of the retirement planning process. Let's take a look at each step in depth.

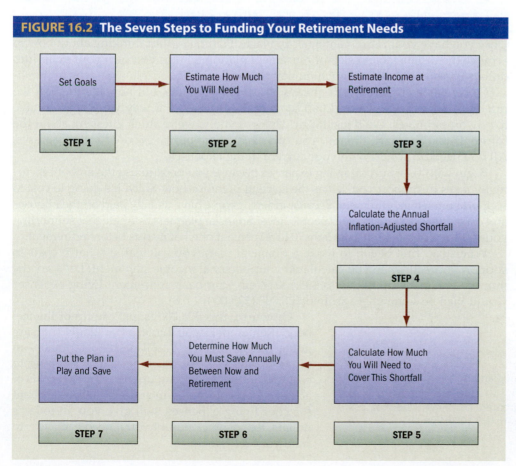

FIGURE 16.2 The Seven Steps to Funding Your Retirement Needs

- Set Goals — **STEP 1**
- Estimate How Much You Will Need — **STEP 2**
- Estimate Income at Retirement — **STEP 3**
- Calculate the Annual Inflation-Adjusted Shortfall — **STEP 4**
- Calculate How Much You Will Need to Cover This Shortfall — **STEP 5**
- Determine How Much You Must Save Annually Between Now and Retirement — **STEP 6**
- Put the Plan in Play and Save — **STEP 7**

Step 1: Set Goals

The first step in planning for your retirement is figuring out just what you want to do when you retire. Naturally, you'll want to be able to support yourself and pay any medical bills, but that could cost a little or it could cost a whole lot. Therefore, you need to start by asking yourself some basic questions: How costly a lifestyle do you want to lead? Do you want to live like a king or more economically, perhaps like a minor duke or nobleman? Do you currently have any medical conditions that you know are going to be costly later in life?

Once you've answered these questions, you can pretty much set your basic goal of being able to support yourself and pay your medical expenses. Then it's time to think about other goals. Do you want to stay in your current house, or will you want to move to Florida and eat early-bird specials? Do you want to live in a retirement community or your own residence? Do you want to travel? Do you want to be able to buy that Dodge Viper and hit the open road? Do you want to have money set aside for your family? It may be hard to sit down and consider everything you might want to do when you retire, but you'll need to be as exhaustive as possible when setting your goals.

As you learned in Chapter 1, goals aren't entirely useful unless you include the element of time and decide when you hope to achieve them. In the case of retirement, you need to figure out exactly when you'd like to retire. The typical retirement age is 65, but more and more people are putting off retirement until 70 or even later.

The time frame for achieving your goals is more important than you might think. For example, if you want to retire at age 60, you'll need to save up a lot of money to be able to pay for a lengthy retirement. If you really love your job and don't want to retire until you're 70, you won't need to save as much because your period of retirement will likely be shorter, and you'll be giving yourself an extra 10 years to prepare for it.

Step 2: Estimate How Much You Will Need

Once you have your retirement goals in place, it's time to start thinking about how to achieve them. The second step of retirement planning helps you turn your goals into dollars by estimating how much money you will need.

Of course, estimates aren't always accurate or reliable, but hey, it's the best we can do. It'd be nice if we could all see into the future—that way we wouldn't have to rely on estimates. We'd just know. Unfortunately, we're stuck guessing about the future. If you're smart, though, you can make some pretty good educated guesses. All you need do is start with your current living expenses.

Begin with your current living expenses because you need to use the amount it currently takes to support yourself as the starting point for how much it's going to cost to support yourself in retirement. Because elderly people have usually paid off their houses and consume less than younger people, most financial planners estimate that supporting yourself in retirement will cost only 70 to 80 percent of what it costs before retirement.

When you first began to make a financial plan, you calculated what it costs to support yourself when you calculated your personal income statement. Let's say the number you came up with was $35,000. Well, your basic retirement living expenses would then be somewhere around $28,000 ($35,000 × 0.8).

Of course, this $28,000 is just the tip of the iceberg. Remember, you have other goals that are going to cost money. You'll need to estimate—in today's dollars—how much each goal is going to cost you annually. Adding up the estimated costs of achieving all your goals, including the base amount for your living expenses, will give you, in today's dollars, the income amount you'll need each year to fund your retirement.

FACTS OF LIFE

Average time annually spent planning for vacations: 4 hours
Average length of vacation: 1 to 2 weeks
Average time spent on retirement planning: 1 hour or less
Average time spent in retirement: 19 years

TABLE 16.2 The Average Tax Rate

Retirement Income	Average Tax Rate	
	Couples Filing Jointly	Individuals
$20,000	7%	10%
30,000	10	14
40,000	12	17
50,000	14	20
60,000	17	22
70,000	19	23
80,000	21	24
90,000	22	25
100,000	23	26
150,000	28	30

Note: To estimate your anticipated average tax rate at retirement, you can use the table above based on current tax rates. If you anticipate a change in future tax rates—for example, a flat tax—use that number.

However, you're not done yet. Don't forget the government. Yes, you need to factor in the effect of taxes. Table 16.2 gives you a rough idea of the average tax rate you'll pay on your required retirement income. To convert an amount of after-tax retirement income into before-tax income, simply divide the amount of after-tax retirement income you'll need by (1 − your average tax rate), using Table 16.2 to find your average tax rate. For example, if you need $60,000 of after-tax income and you are filing jointly, your tax rate is 17 percent, then you'd need $60,000/(1 − 0.17) = $72,289.

Figure 16.3 provides a summary and overview of the calculations involved in funding your retirement needs, while a detailed illustration of these calculations is provided in the appendix to this chapter.

FIGURE 16.3 Funding Your Retirement Needs

A detailed example of the calculations for funding your retirement needs appears in the appendix to this chapter.

Step 1: Set Goals

Step 2: Estimate How Much You Will Need
- Begin with 80% of your present living expenses
- Add in the cost of other goals
- Add in the taxes you'll incur

Step 3: Estimate Income at Retirement
- Income from Social Security
- Any pension benefits
- Any other income

Step 4: Calculate the Annual Inflation-Adjusted Shortfall
- Look at the difference between the totals in Steps 2 and 3
- Adjust for inflation

Step 5: Calculate How Much You Need to Cover This Shortfall
- Consider what you'll be earning on your savings after inflation

Step 6: Determine How Much You Must Save Annually Between Now and Retirement
- Determine how much you'll need to save annually to cover the shortfall calculated in Step 5

Step 7: Put the Plan in Play and Save

Step 3: Estimate Income at Retirement

As you've probably guessed, once you know how much income you're going to need when you retire, the logical next step is figuring out just how much income you're going to have. First, estimate your Social Security benefits. The Social Security Administration mails out annual earnings and benefit statements to all workers age 25 and older (about 125 million) who are not already receiving monthly Social Security benefits. The statement provides estimates of the Social Security retirement, disability, and survivors' benefits they and their family could be eligible to receive now and in the future. (If you didn't save your Social Security statement, call or visit a local Social Security office [1-800-772-1213] or visit the Web site, **www.ssa .gov**.) You can also get an estimate of Social Security benefits from the Social Security benefits calculator located at **www.ssa.gov/OACT/quickcalc/**. To the Social Security benefits, you add any projected pension benefits in today's dollars plus any other retirement income available.

To determine how much your pension will pay, stop at your company's employee benefits office. Get a copy of your individual benefit statement, which describes your pension plan and estimates how much your plan is worth today and the level of benefits you'll receive when you retire. There are a number of basic questions included in Checklist 16.1 that you should be able to answer about your company's pension fund.

Step 4: Calculate the (Annual) Inflation-Adjusted Shortfall

Now it's time to compare the amounts from Steps 2 and 3. For most people, there's a big difference between the retirement income they need and the retirement income they'll have. As pensions are phased out and Social Security becomes less certain, that difference is going to get bigger and bigger.

Step 5: Calculate How Much You Need to Cover This Shortfall

By now you know how much of an annual shortfall you'll have in your retirement funding. That is, you'll know how much additional money you'll need to come up with each year to support yourself in retirement. The question then becomes: How

---

CHECKLIST 16.1

Questions You Should Be Able to Answer About Your Company's Pension Plan

- Is this a noncontributory or contributory plan?
- What are the pension requirements in terms of age and years of service?
- Is there an early retirement age, and if so, what are the benefits?
- What is the full benefits retirement age?
- How does the vesting process work?
- If I retire at age 65, how much will I receive in the way of pension payments?
- If I die, what benefits will my spouse and family receive?
- What is the present size of my pension credit today?
- If I am disabled, will I receive pension benefits?

- Can I withdraw money from my retirement fund before retirement?
- Can I borrow on my retirement fund, and if so, what are the terms?
- If my company is taken over or goes bankrupt, what happens to the pension fund?
- Is the plan funded? If not, what portion of the benefits could the company pay today?
- Is my pension plan a defined-contribution plan or a defined-benefit plan?
- What are the choices available to me regarding ways that the pension might be paid out?

much must you have saved by retirement to fund this annual shortfall?

In determining how much you need to cover this shortfall you'll want to take into consideration what you can earn on your investments and the fact that each year you'll want a bit more in the way of retirement funds to counteract the effects of inflation.

Step 6: Determine How Much You Must Save Annually Between Now and Retirement

Now you know the total amount you'll need to have saved by the time you retire, but you're not about to put it all away at once. Instead, you'll need to put money away little by little, year by year. Now you need to know how much to put away each year.

Once you know how much you need to have saved by the time retirement comes around, determining how much you need to save annually is pretty easy. You can use the financial calculator on the Web site that accompanies this book to solve for PMT, the annual annuity, just as you did in Chapter 3 when you looked at amortized loans. If you'd like a bit of help in determining just what you need to save for retirement, there are several excellent online retirement planning Web sites highlighted in Table 16.3.

Step 7: Put the Plan in Play and Save

OK, you've finally figured out exactly how much you need to save each year to achieve your retirement goals. Now all you need to do is save. This last step should be the easiest, right? Wrong. It's actually one of the hardest. There are countless ways to save for retirement, and choosing the one that's best for you requires knowing something about what's available out there.

In the next few sections, we'll walk you through the various types of retirement savings plans, and we'll give you plenty of good advice to get you on your way. Whatever you decide to do, be sure you don't take saving too lightly in the retirement planning process. Watch out for that last step—it's a doozie!

What Plan Is Best for You?

What's the best way to save for retirement? Well, that really depends on your circumstances. There are so many options available, some of them very job or occupation specific, that it's hard to make general statements about what plans are right for everyone. However, it's safe to say that you should certainly try to use a tax-favored retirement plan.

Most plans are tax deferred and work by allowing investment earnings to go untaxed until you remove these earnings at retirement. In essence, they allow you to put off paying taxes so that you can invest the money that would otherwise have gone to the IRS. In addition, some plans allow for the contributions to be made on either a fully or partially tax-deductible basis. In retirement planning, **Principle 4: Taxes Affect Personal Finance Decisions** can't be overstressed.

There are several advantages to tax-deferred plans. First, because the contributions may not be taxed, you can contribute more. You can contribute funds that would otherwise go to the IRS. Second, because the investment earnings aren't taxed until they're withdrawn at retirement, you can earn money on earnings that also would have otherwise gone to the IRS. In other words, you can earn compound interest on money that would normally have gone to the IRS.

> ### STOP & THINK
>
> In a survey by Lincoln Financial Group and *Money* magazine, working and retired Americans were asked when their children should start saving for retirement. Their average answer was at age 22. This may sound soon for most of you, but it's an answer based on experience. The bottom line is that the time to start your retirement savings is now: It will never be easier to reach your goal. Why do you think it's so important to start early?

TABLE 16.3 Online Retirement Planning

Web Site: WealthRuler™ by TDAmeritrade

Address: http://www.tdameritrade.com/planningretirement/wealthruler.html

Features:

- Free.
- Extremely easy to use.
- Considers the impact of expenses during your retirement years. If you're unsure of what those expenses might be, it will provide the estimates for you.
- Allows you to analyze your plan based on different scenarios.
- Tools and calculators are also provided on the TDAmerica Web site.

Web Site: Financial Engines

Online Availability: Web site is available through many employers and investment product providers like Vanguard and T. Rowe Price. For example, for Vanguard customers with $50,000 or more in assets at Vanguard: **https://personal.vanguard.com/us/insights/retirement/financial-engines**

Features:

- Often free availability with many employers and investment product providers.
- Extremely easy to use.
- One of the most sophisticated of all the retirement planning tools.
- Simulates thousands of scenarios for future years' interest rates, inflation, and returns.

Web Site: CNN Money Retirement Planner

Online Availability: http://cgi.money.cnn.com/tools/retirementplanner/retirementplanner.jsp

Features:

- Free.
- Basic and extremely easy to use.
- Helps determine how much you'll need at retirement.
- Calculates your chances of getting there.
- Provides suggestions if it looks like you'll fall short.

Web Site: myPlan by Fidelity

Address: https://www.fidelity.com/retirement/calculators then click on **myPlan^SM Snapshot**.

Features:

- Free.
- Extremely easy to use.
- With five easy questions, it helps you gain a general understanding of how much you need to retire.
- The Retirement Resource Center provides plenty of easy-to-understand guidance and answers to common questions.

Web Site: Retirement QuickPlan by eTrade

Address: https://us.etrade.com/e/t/retirementplanning/planyourretirement

Features:

- Free.
- Extremely easy to use—takes as little as 10 minutes.
- Provides scenarios based on savings, investments, expenses, and goals.
- In the Retirement Tools & Education section, tools and calculators are provided as well as stock and fund screeners.

Figure 16.4 shows just how dramatic this compounding can be. Let's assume you wish to invest $2,000 of before-tax income on an annual basis in a retirement account. Let's also assume you can earn 9 percent compounded annually on this investment and your marginal state and federal tax rate is 31 percent.

If you invest in a tax-deferred retirement account to which the contributions are fully tax deductible, you'll start off and end up with more money. You'll start with

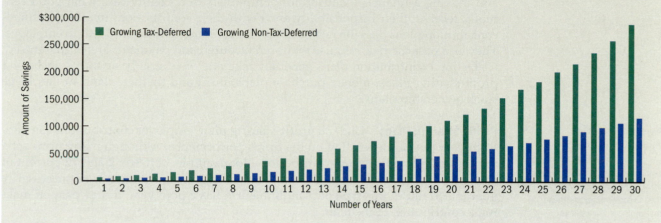

FIGURE 16.4 Saving in a Tax-Deferred Retirement Account Versus Saving on a Non-Tax-Deferred Basis

Assuming an investment of $2,000 of before-tax income on an annual basis in a retirement account where those contributions are fully tax deductible versus investing $2,000 of before-tax income on a non-tax-deferred basis. A 9 percent annual return is assumed on these investments, with investment earnings in the tax-deferred account being tax deferred, and earnings in the other account being taxed annually. A marginal state and federal tax rate of 31 percent is also assumed.

more money because, after taxes, you'll still have your full $2,000 to invest. You'll end up with more money because you'll be able to compound more of your earnings instead of paying them to the IRS.

Investing in a fully taxable retirement account is a different story. To begin with, you won't be able to invest the entire $2,000 because 31 percent of this amount will go toward your state and federal taxes, leaving you with only $1,380 to invest. In addition, the investment earnings will also be taxed annually, at a rate of 31 percent.

Figure 16.4 compares these retirement plans with annual investments of $2,000 of before-tax income for 30 years. After 10 years you'd have accumulated $33,121 in the tax-deferred account, but only $19,511 in the taxable account. After 20 years the tax-deferred account would have grown to $111,529, whereas the taxable account would be at $55,150. Finally, after 30 years the tax-deferred account would have grown to $297,150, whereas the taxable account would have accumulated only $120,250.

Of course, Uncle Sam does catch up eventually. When you withdraw your retirement funds, the interest earned on them over the years is taxed, but at least you had the chance to earn plenty of extra interest.

There are major advantages to saving on a tax-deferred basis. It's pure and simple smart investing. Before you look into any other types of retirement investments, check out the ones that are tax favored. There are plenty of these plans currently available. Some are employer-sponsored, and others are aimed at the self-employed. Let's take a look.

FACTS OF LIFE

Median income of older women and men by age, 2008:

Age	Women	Men
70–74	$16,800	$27,043
80–plus	$15,600	$19,412

Employer-Sponsored Retirement Plans

Defined-Contributions Plans

Under a **defined-contribution plan**, your employer alone or you and your employer together contribute directly to an individual account set aside specifically for you. In effect, a defined-contribution plan can be thought of as a personal savings account

Defined-Contribution Plan
A pension plan in which you and your employer or your employer alone contributes directly to a retirement account set aside specifically for you. In effect, a defined-contribution plan can be thought of as a savings account for retirement.

for retirement. Your eventual payments aren't guaranteed. Instead, what you eventually receive depends on how well your retirement account performs. Many defined-contribution plans allow you to choose how your account is invested.

In recent years the popularity of such programs has skyrocketed because they involve no risk for the employer. The employer's job involves a bit of bookkeeping and making a financial contribution. Employers don't really care what you eventually receive; their responsibility ends with their contribution. In effect, defined-contribution plans pass the responsibility for retirement from employer to employee. They also pass the risk, because they aren't insured and payments aren't guaranteed.

Defined-contribution plans generally take one of several basic forms, including profit-sharing plans, money purchase plans, thrift and savings plans, or employee stock ownership plans.

Profit-Sharing Plans

Profit-Sharing Plan
A pension plan in which the company's contributions vary from year to year depending on the firm's performance. The amount of money contributed to each employee depends on the employee's salary level.

Profit-Sharing Plans   Under a **profit-sharing plan**, employer contributions can vary from year to year depending on the firm's performance. Although many firms set a minimum and a maximum contribution—for example, between 2 and 12 percent of each employee's salary annually—not all firms do. A contribution is not necessarily guaranteed under this type of plan. If the firm has a poor year, it may pass on making a contribution to the plan.

Money Purchase Plan
A pension plan in which the employer contributes a set percentage of employees' salaries to their retirement plans annually.

Money Purchase Plans   Under a **money purchase plan**, the employer contributes a set percentage of employees' salaries to their retirement plans annually. For the employer, such a plan offers less flexibility, because contributions are required regardless of how well the firm does. For the employee, these plans are preferable to profit-sharing because of the guaranteed contribution.

Thrift and Savings Plan
A pension plan in which the employer matches a percentage of the employees' contributions to their retirement accounts.

Thrift and Savings Plans   Under a **thrift and savings plan**, the employer matches a percentage of employees' contributions to their retirement accounts.

Employee Stock Ownership Plan or ESOP
A retirement plan in which the retirement funds are invested directly in the company's stock.

Employee Stock Ownership Plan   Under an **employee stock ownership plan (ESOP)**, the company's contribution is made in the form of company stock. Of all the retirement plans, this is the riskiest, because your return at retirement depends on how well the company does. If the company goes bankrupt, you might lose not only your job, but also all your retirement benefits. Of course, if the company's stock price soars, you could do extremely well. However, an ESOP doesn't allow for the degree of diversification that you need with your retirement savings. In short, an ESOP isn't something you can safely rely on.

401(k) Plan
A tax-deferred retirement savings plan in which employees of private corporations may contribute a portion of their wages up to a maximum amount set by law ($15,500 in 2008 and thereafter these limits will rise with inflation in $500 increments). Employers may contribute a full or partially matching amount, and may limit the proportion of the annual salary contributed (typically to 15 percent).

401(k) Plans   A **401(k) plan** is really a do-it-yourself variation of a profit-sharing/thrift plan. These can be set up as part of an employer-sponsored defined-contribution plan, with both the employer and the employee contributing to the plan, or with only the employee making a contribution. Over the past 20 years these plans have exploded in terms of popularity. In fact, about nine out of ten large employers—that is, companies employing over 500 workers—provide 401(k) plans for their workers. Corporations love them because they allow the retirement program to be handed over entirely to the employee.

A 401(k) plan is a tax-deferred retirement plan in which both the employee's contributions to the plan and the earnings on those contributions are tax deductible, with all taxes being deferred until retirement withdrawals are made.[2] In essence, a 401(k) is equivalent to the tax-deferred retirement plan presented earlier in Figure 16.4.

---

[2] A **403(b)** plan is essentially the same as a 401(k) plan except that it's aimed at employees of schools and charitable organizations. Although our discussion will focus on 401(k) plans, it also holds true for 403(b) plans.

The advantages to such an account are twofold. First, you don't pay taxes on money contributed to 401(k) plans, which means you can add money into your retirement account that would have otherwise been paid out as taxes. Second, your earnings on your retirement account are tax deferred. Thus, you can earn a return on money that would otherwise have been paid out in taxes.

The end result, as shown in Figure 16.4, is that you can accumulate a much larger retirement nest egg using a 401(k) account than you otherwise could. So you should invest the maximum allowable amount in your 401(k) account. You should do this before you consider any other taxed investment alternatives. Moreover, this should be automatic—that is, *your 401(k) should be paid* before you receive anything. Only after you have maxed out on your 401(k) contributions should you consider other investments.

Many 401(k) plans are set up as thrift and savings plans, in which the employer matches a percentage of the employee's contribution, although in the recent economic downturn, about 15 percent of companies with match programs suspended their contributions. For example, Coca-Cola Bottling and Black & Decker both dropped their matching contributions, with Black & Decker later reinstating it, while Burton Snowboards kept its 401(k) match but reduced it from 4 percent to 1 percent. As you might expect, not all 401(k) match programs are the same. For example, Home Depot matches $1.50 for every participant dollar up to 1 percent of pay, and then 50 cents per dollar on the next 2 percent to 5 percent. McDonald's, on the other hand, has a supersized 401(k) match program, with employees who save just 1 percent of pay getting $3 from the company for every $1 stashed in their 401(k). The next 4 percent of pay contributed is matched by the company dollar for dollar.

Needless to say, a matching 401(k) program increases participation. In addition, a matching plan is an offer too good to refuse. It's free money, and you should take advantage of any matching the company is willing to do.

Also, 401(k) plans offer a wide variety of investment options. In fact, over half of all 401(k) plans offer five or more investment choices. These options range from conservative guaranteed investment contracts (GICs) to aggressive stock funds.

How Much Can You Contribute?

The limits on contributions to these plans are on the rise. For 2008 the limits on employee contributions to 401(k) and 403(b) plans (also SEP-IRA plans, which will be covered shortly) were set at $16,500 and thereafter these limits rise with inflation in $500 increments. Also, taxpayers over 50 are allowed to make additional annual "catch up" contributions of $5,500, with that limit also indexed for inflation.

FACTS OF LIFE

How do you stack up if you're **35 to 44?**

◆ Average 401(k) contribution of a person between 35 and 44: 6.4 percent of salary.
◆ Average retirement savings of a person between 35 and 44: 0.8 times annual income.

FACTS OF LIFE

Less than 1 in 10 workers contributes the maximum to their 401(k) plan.

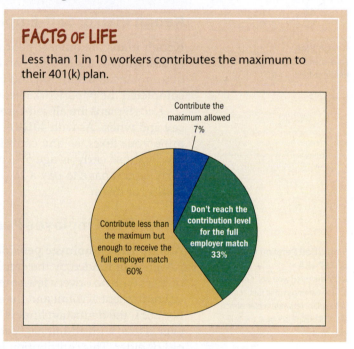

Contribute the maximum allowed
7%

Don't reach the contribution level for the full employer match
33%

Contribute less than the maximum but enough to receive the full employer match
60%

FACTS OF LIFE

Behavioral finance, and **Principle 9: Mind Games, Your Financial Personality, and Your Money**, play a major role in how you save for retirement. In fact, Congress acknowledged this when it enacted the Pension Protection Act of 2006, which allows employers to enroll workers automatically in defined-contribution plans.

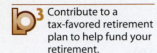 Contribute to a tax-favored retirement plan to help fund your retirement.

Retirement Plans for the Self-Employed and Small Business Employees

Fully tax-deductible retirement plans for the self-employed or small business employee—which includes anyone who has his or her own business, works for a small business, or does freelance work on a part-time basis—hold the same basic advantages as employer-sponsored plans available in large corporations. You qualify for such a plan if you do any work for yourself (even if you work full-time for an employer and are covered by another retirement plan there).

It's surprising how many individuals qualify for these plans and either don't realize it or do nothing to take advantage of another tax-deferred retirement tool. Examples of those who are eligible are lawyers, doctors, dentists, carpenters, plumbers, artists, freelance writers, and consultants. Basically, if you're self-employed, either full-time or part-time, or work for a small business, you can contribute to a Keogh or self-employed retirement plan, a simplified employee pension plan (SEP-IRA), or the newer savings incentive match plan for employees (SIMPLE) plan.

Keogh Plan or Self-Employed Retirement Plan

Keogh Plan
A tax-sheltered retirement plan for the self-employed.

Keogh plans are quite similar to corporate pension or profit-sharing plans and the establishment of a Keogh plan is relatively easy. You select a bank, mutual fund, or other financial institution and contact it. In general, the institution will have already completed the paperwork needed to establish the plan.

Keogh plans are all self-directed, meaning you decide what securities to buy and sell and when. As with 401(k)s, the payment to the plan comes out before you determine your taxes, so any contributions reduce your bill to Uncle Sam. Withdrawals can begin as early as age 59½ and must begin by age 70½ If you need your money early, you'll have to pay a 10 percent penalty, except in cases of serious illness, disability, or death.

Simplified Employee Pension Plan

Simplified Pension Plan or SEP-IRA
A tax-sheltered (you don't pay taxes on any earnings while they remain in the plan) retirement plan aimed at small businesses or at the self-employed.

A **simplified employee pension plan (SEP-IRA)** is similar to a defined-contribution Keogh plan funded by the employer. SEP-IRAs are used primarily by small business owners with no or very few employees. Each employee sets up his or her own individual retirement account and the employer makes annual contributions to that account. For 2011, the deduction limit is 25 percent of the employee's salary or $49,000, whichever is less, with additional "catch-up" contributions for individuals who are 50 years old or older. This contribution limit is indexed annually for inflation.

In addition, there's flexibility in making contributions. For example, they can be made one year and not the next, and when they are made, they're immediately vested. The advantage of a SEP-IRA program is that it works about the same as a Keogh plan but is easier to set up. In addition, a SEP-IRA doesn't have the reporting requirements of a Keogh.

FACTS OF LIFE

While most workers—70 percent of them—feel confident they will have enough money to live comfortably at retirement, only 43 percent have actually tried to calculate how much they will need.

Savings Incentive Match Plan for Employees

Savings Incentive Match Plan for Employees or SIMPLE Plan
A tax-sheltered retirement plan aimed at small businesses or the self-employed that provides for some matching funds by the employer to be deposited in to the employee's retirement account.

Small employers can establish a **savings incentive match plan for employees** or **SIMPLE plan**—SIMPLE IRAs and SIMPLE 401(k)s. These new SIMPLE plans may be set up by employers with fewer than 100 employees earning $5,000 or more, covering all their employees, including themselves. Employee contributions are excluded from income, and the earnings in the retirement plan are tax deferred. In addition to employee contributions, there are some matching funds provided by the employer—although the employer does have some flexibility in determining how much to contribute.

Why did Congress decide to establish one more type of retirement plan? Because many smaller businesses were put off by complex and expensive alternative plans and, thus, didn't provide retirement plans for their employees. That's where the SIMPLE plans fit in, because the rules governing them are, as the name implies, simple.

Individual Retirement Arrangements (IRAs)

There are three types of IRAs to choose from: the traditional IRA, the Roth IRA, and the Coverdell Education Savings Accounts, previously called Education IRA. Let's look at each of them.

Traditional IRAs

Individual retirement arrangements (IRAs), often called individual retirement accounts, are personal savings plans that give you tax advantages for saving for retirement. Contributions to a traditional IRA may be tax deductible—either in whole or in part, depending on the level of your earnings and whether you or your spouse has a company retirement plan. Also, you don't pay any taxes on the earnings on the amounts in your IRA until they are distributed. In addition, the portion of the contributions that was tax deductible also is not taxed until distributed.

The maximum amount you can contribute to an IRA in 2011 is $5,000, and thereafter it is adjusted for inflation in $500 increments. In addition, individuals age 50 and over are permitted to make additional annual contributions of $1,000.

If both you and your spouse are employed and aren't covered by a company retirement plan, you can contribute annually up to the maximum, which was $5,000 in 2011, on a tax-deferred basis to your IRA. A married couple with only one spouse working outside the home may both contribute to an IRA, provided the "working spouse" has at least earned income up to the amount contributed. If neither of you is an "active participant" in a retirement plan at work, or if your joint adjusted gross income is below the IRS cutoff, your IRA contributions are entirely tax deductible.

What's an "active participant"? If you have a defined-benefit retirement plan, you're considered an "active participant." In addition, if you have a defined-contribution plan and either you or your employer contributed to it during the year, you're considered an "active participant" and there is an income limit after which your IRA contributions are no longer tax deductible. However, if neither you nor your employer contributed to your defined-contribution plan during the year or your income is below the cutoff level, you can make a fully deductible contribution to your IRA.

There's also a provision that allows a nonworking spouse to make a deductible contribution to an IRA even if the working spouse is covered by a qualified retirement plan or his or her income is high. Under this provision, a nonworking spouse can make a fully deductible contribution to an IRA as long as his or her "modified" adjusted gross income (AGI) is below $169,000, even if the other spouse is covered by a qualified retirement plan, where "modified" AGI is adjusted gross income before subtracting IRA deductions. In addition, a partial deduction is allowed until income hits $179,000. Partial tax deductions are also available for IRA contributions, again depending on income level.

For the tax year 2011 the trigger point for full deductibility of IRA contributions is $56,000 of "modified" AGI for those filing single returns and $90,000 for those filing jointly. Once "modified" AGI reaches $66,000 for single returns and $110,000 for those filing a joint return, deductibility is totally phased out.

Individual Retirement Account or IRA
A tax advantaged retirement account. The contribution may or may not be tax deductible, depending on the individual's income level and whether he or she, or his or her spouse, is covered by a company retirement plan.

> **FACTS OF LIFE**
> The average monthly Social Security benefit for retired workers as of March 2011 was $1,178.80.

If all contributions to your IRA are tax deductible, then all withdrawals from your IRA will be taxed, unless you're just moving your money into another IRA. There are also restrictions on the timing and amount of IRA withdrawals, as follows:

◆ Distributions before age 59½ are subject to a 10 percent tax penalty with few exceptions.

◆ After you turn 70½ you must start receiving annual distributions under a life expectancy calculation.

◆ You can make penalty-free withdrawals provided you (a) are making them to buy your first home, (b) are using them for college expenses, (c) you become disabled, (d) you need the money to pay medical expenses in excess of 7.5 percent of your AGI, or (e) you need the money to pay medical insurance payments if you've been unemployed for at least 12 consecutive weeks. There is, however, a limit of $10,000 on penalty-free withdrawals to buy a first home.

In addition to annual contributions to an IRA, you can roll over a distribution from a qualified employer plan or from another IRA into a new IRA. Why would you ever do this? If you get a new job or if you retire early, you may be faced with that 10 percent early distribution penalty. To get around this penalty, you can instead have your distributions rolled over into a new IRA. If you're going to roll over your distributions into a new IRA, make sure you see a financial advisor or tax accountant ahead of time because there are a number of rollover rules you need to follow to avoid taxes.

What are your investment choices with an IRA? You can go with stocks, bonds, mutual funds, real estate, CDs—almost anything. It's your call because IRAs are self-directed, and you can change your IRA funds from one investment to another at any time without paying taxes. The only things you can't invest in are life insurance or collectibles, other than gold or silver U.S. coins. You also can't borrow from your IRA, and you can't use it as collateral for a loan.

Saver's Tax Credit   Low- and moderate-income workers are also provided with help in saving for retirement in the form of the Saver's Tax Credit. The saver's credit helps offset part of the first $2,000 workers voluntarily contribute to IRAs and to 401(k) plans and similar workplace retirement programs and is available in addition to any other tax savings that apply. The maximum saver's credit is $1,000 for individuals, and $2,000 for married couples, with the taxpayer's credit amount based on his or her filing status, adjusted gross income, tax liability, and amount contributed to qualifying retirement programs.

The idea behind it is to encourage low- and moderate-income workers to save for retirement. There are income limits on this tax credit; for example, a married couple filing a joint return who earned more than $56,500 in 2011 would not be eligible. Similar to other tax credits, the saver's credit can increase a taxpayer's refund or reduce the tax owed. Needless to say, this is a credit that you'll want to take advantage of if you qualify.

The Roth IRA

Roth IRA
An IRA in which contributions are not tax deductible. That is, you'd make your contribution to this IRA out of after-tax income. But once the money is in there, it grows tax free and when it is withdrawn, the withdrawals are tax free.

A **Roth IRA** is also a personal savings plan similar to a traditional IRA, except it operates somewhat in reverse manner. For instance, while contributions to a traditional IRA may be deductible, contributions to a Roth IRA are *not* tax deductible.

However, while distributions (including earnings) from a traditional IRA are taxed, the distributions (including earnings) from a Roth IRA are distributed on an after-tax basis. One similarity between the traditional IRA and the Roth IRA is that with both, you don't pay any taxes while your money is in the IRA.

The big advantage of the Roth IRA is that you can avoid taxes when you finally withdraw your money. Of course, as with everything else in the tax code, there are some exceptions. First, to avoid taxes, you must keep your money in your Roth IRA for at least 5 years.

Who's eligible to put money into a Roth IRA? A lot of people! The income limits are inflation adjusted and in 2011 didn't begin until $107,000 for single taxpayers and $169,000 for couples (but there is a backdoor around those limits which we will mention in a moment). Keep in mind that even if you have a 401(k) account, you can also contribute to an IRA. You can have both a traditional IRA and a Roth IRA; however, your total contributions to both are limited to the maximum IRA contribution levels of $5,000 in 2011 and thereafter it is adjusted for inflation in $500 increments.

Another great feature of the Roth IRA is that, at any time, you can pull out an amount up to your original contribution without getting hit with a tax penalty. Also new with the Roth IRA, there is no requirement that distributions begin by age 70½.

In addition to your annual contribution, you can also roll money from your existing IRA into your Roth IRA without incurring a 10 percent penalty. For the tax year 2011 and thereafter (unless Congress closes this loophole), you can use this conversion loophole to fund a Roth IRA regardless of your income level. This is the backdoor method of funding a Roth IRA mentioned earlier that sidesteps the income limits on Roth IRAs. Since anyone can make after-tax contributions to a traditional IRA regardless of their income level, you can put after-tax money in a traditional IRA, then convert it to a Roth IRA, thereby sidestepping the income eligibility requirements attached to the Roth IRA. Remember, when you convert a traditional IRA to a Roth IRA you have to pay taxes on any pre-tax contributions as well as any growth in the investment value, but since your contributions were done on an after-tax basis, you would only pay taxes on any growth in investment value.

FACTS OF LIFE

If you are 27 right now and you contribute $5,000 (remember that's the maximum contribution in 2011, and it will be small in comparison to allowable future contributions) to a Roth IRA and if you earn 9.67 percent on your investments (that's the average return on large company stocks since 1960), when you turn 67 you'll have $2,023,481 and no taxes! Not too shabby, eh? If you started when you were 22 you'd end up with over $3.24 million.

Traditional Versus Roth IRA: Which Is Best for You?

Mathematically, you end up with the same amount to spend at retirement if you use a traditional IRA or a Roth IRA, provided both are taxed at the same rate. So which one should you choose? If you can afford it, the answer is the Roth IRA. That's because you can take care of taxes ahead of time and end up with more money to spend at retirement. In effect, you're putting more money into the Roth IRA because the Roth IRA includes a $5,000 contribution *plus* the taxes you'd pay on that $5,000 contribution.

In terms of after-tax contributions, if you are in the 28 percent tax bracket a $5,000 contribution to a Roth IRA would cost you $6,944 of before-tax income—$5,000 for the contribution and $1,944 for taxes ($6,944 × 0.28 = $1,944). If you put $5,000 in a traditional IRA and let it grow at 10 percent for 40 years, you end up with $226,296 before you paid any taxes—after taxes, at 28 percent, you'd have $162,933. If you'd put $5,000 in a Roth IRA, you'd need a bit more money on the front end (as we just showed, $6,944), because you'd have to pay taxes, but you'd end up with $226,296 after 40 years and no taxes!

MONEY MATTERS

Tips from Marcy Furney, ChFC, Certified Financial Planner™

RETIRE RIGHT

Don't consider your retirement funds as a source of dollars for emergencies. Withdrawal from qualified retirement accounts can result in taxes, penalties, and even investment company charges. Money in employer-sponsored plans is normally not even accessible as long as you're employed by the company, unless the plan allows for loans or special IRS-defined hardship withdrawals.

Include medical insurance costs in your calculation of retirement needs, especially if you are planning to retire before you are eligible for Medicare. Many employers are paring down or eliminating post-retirement medical coverage. Even with Medicare, you may need a supplement plan, which could cost several hundred dollars a month for you and your spouse.

Get information on the shortfalls of Medicare coverage for nursing home and custodial care and on the eligibility requirements for Medicaid. You may find that you need long-term care insurance before retirement and must include its cost in your calculation of annual financial needs. If you anticipate having to care for elderly family members, it could be advantageous to assist them in purchasing such coverage.

If you plan to "roll over" money from a company retirement plan to an IRA, get assistance from your financial advisor or IRA investment company in executing a "trustee-to-trustee transfer." Through this process, the money flows directly to the IRA account or comes to you via a check made payable to the IRA. If you take possession of the funds at any time or even receive a check made out to you, 20 percent withholding applies to the distribution.

If you are in a low income-tax bracket and meet the requirements to fund a Roth IRA or a regular deductible IRA, give the potential outcome great consideration when deciding which to use. Foregoing a small tax deduction now (doing the Roth IRA) could result in a sizable source of tax-free money at retirement.

Investigate joint and survivor annuity payment options from qualified retirement plans carefully. Once you make a decision, it is usually irrevocable. You will receive a lower monthly payment while you are living so that income can go to your spouse when you die. If your spouse dies before you, your monthly amount probably won't go up. You may find that you can take the larger single life payment, use some of the money to pay for life insurance to provide your spouse an income when you die, and still net more income than the joint and survivor arrangement would provide. This "pension maximization" process also provides potential funds to beneficiaries if the annuitant and spouse die before all equivalent retirement assets are spent.

Saving for College: The Coverdell Education Savings Accounts or ESA

Coverdell Education Savings Account or Education IRA
An IRA that works just like the Roth IRA, except with respect to contributions. Contributions are limited to $2,000 annually per child for each child younger than 18, with income limits beginning at $95,000 for single taxpayers and $190,000 for couples. The earnings are tax free and there is no tax on withdrawals to pay for education.

Sure, college isn't retirement, but if you don't save properly for your children's college education, you may end up having to postpone retirement after dipping into your retirement savings. Fortunately, there are some tools out there meant to both help and inspire you to save for college. Let's first look at the **Coverdell Education Savings Account**, which was previously called the **Education IRA**. It works just like the Roth IRA, except with respect to contributions. Contributions are limited to $2,000 annually per child for each child younger than 18 (and beyond for special needs beneficiaries), with income limits beginning at $95,000 for single taxpayers and $190,000 for couples. Again, the earnings are tax free and there is no tax on withdrawals to pay for education with the definition of what qualified education expenses are now, including certain elementary and secondary school expenses.

In addition, individuals have until April 15 of the following year to make contributions for the taxable year. Taxpayers can also claim an American Opportunity credit or a Lifetime Learning credit in the same year as taking a distribution from a Coverdell Education Savings Account, provided that the same expenses aren't used for both purposes.

Savings must be withdrawn by the time the child reaches age 30, although any leftover amounts can be rolled over into accounts for younger siblings. If the money in the Coverdell Education Savings Account isn't used for college, you may have to pay taxes plus a 10 percent penalty on its withdrawal.

How much can you save using a Coverdell Education Savings Account? If you contribute $2,000 every year and assume an 8 percent return on investment, you'd have just under $75,000 in 18 years—not bad, eh? Now let's add some reality to that number. Consider the fact that in 2011 the cost of 1 year at a 4-year, in-state public university was $19,388 and $39,028 for a 4-year private college, according to the College Board. If those prices should increase by 4 percent each year, they would climb to $39,277 and $79,064 respectively in 18 years for the first year of college—and the 4-year total would be $166,786 and $335,741 for each. Now that $75,000 would be helpful, but you'd still be short, and that's if you contributed $2,000 per year for 18 years. If you got a late start, say you began investing with 12 years to go, you'd end up with just under $38,000, which wouldn't even cover 1 year at a private college.

Although the Coverdell Education Savings Account is a great way to save for your child's education, tax-advantaged 529 plans hold several advantages over it. However, if you're so inclined, you can open both types of accounts. Let's now take a look at 529 plans.

Saving for College: 529 Plans

The **529 plans** are tax-advantaged savings plans used only for college and gradu-ate school, allowing you to contribute up to $250,000 to $330,000 (depending on the state-sponsored plan), which can then grow tax free. These plans began in the 1990s because of the rule that doesn't allow the federal government to tax money that's given to a state. The result was that these accounts were tax deferred, a situation that was later made permanent by Congress.

529 Plans
Tax-advantaged savings plans used only for college and graduate school.

Although these plans are all sponsored by individual states, they are open to all applicants regardless of where you live. Thus, a resident of North Carolina can put money in a 529 plan in Michigan or in any state for that matter. You can also invest directly or you can invest through a financial advisor (and, of course, pay a commis-sion). In addition in some states, part or all of your contribution may be tax deductible.

As with any other investment, you've got some decisions to make. The first decision is what type of plan to choose. There are two basic types of 529 plans: "prepaid college tuition plans" and "college savings plans." The college savings plans offer you much more flexibility—both in terms of how you can use them and the investment alternative. One problem with prepaid college tuition plans is that they generally guarantee that you will be covered only if your child chooses to go to a public in-state college or university. That loss of flexibility may

FACTS of LIFE

The most expensive college in the United States, based upon the 2010–2011 tuition, fees, room, and board, was Sarah Lawrence College in Bronxville, New York, at $57,556, and this doesn't include books, personal expenses, or the $1,780 the school charges for accident and sickness insurance, which students must buy unless they have a waiver. It also does not include any late night pizzas, spring break excursions, or any tattoos you might get. If you included them you'd easily be above $60,000 per year.

not seem important when college is 10 years away, but when the day comes to pick a college, that loss of flexibility may become extremely important.

Next, you've got to decide whether to go it alone or pay a commission for it and ask an advisor. There are some quality no-commission programs offered by fund families such as Fidelity and T. Rowe Price that would make selecting a plan relatively easy. However, given the fact that this is an area of constant change, there may be some advantages to having an advisor. In any case, that decision shouldn't keep you away from 529 plans. You'll also want to take a look at the investment alternatives within the plan, since they are generally limited. Also, check out how flexible the plan is. For example, find out if there are time limits on when the account must be used and what expenses can be covered by the plan. Finally, check the enrollment fee as well as any annual fees. Those things can mount up if you aren't careful.

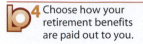 **4** Choose how your retirement benefits are paid out to you.

Facing Retirement—The Payout

You might think that once you've saved enough for retirement, coming up with a plan for distributing those savings would be simple. Think again. Your distribution or payout decision affects how much you receive, how it's taxed, whether you're protected against inflation, whether you might outlive your retirement funds, and a host of other important concerns. Checklist 16.2 provides a listing of key ages associated with retirement planning.

Some plans have more flexibility than others—for example, traditional (non-Roth) IRAs allow for withdrawals to begin at age 59½ and at age 70½ withdrawals become compulsory. Still, there are also several basic distribution choices that include receiving your payout as a lump sum, receiving it in the form of an annuity for a set number of years or for your lifetime, or some combination. Unfortunately, there isn't one best way to receive your retirement distribution. However, there are a number of important points to keep in mind when making this decision.

◆ Make sure you plan ahead before you decide how to receive a payout. Make sure you understand the tax consequences of any decision.

◆ In deciding how to receive a payout, make sure you look at all your retirement plan payouts together. You may want to take some plan distributions in a lump sum and others as an annuity.

◆ Once you receive your retirement plan payout, make sure you use your understanding of investing, including diversification and the time dimension of risk, when deciding what to do with those funds.

Let's now take a look at some of the specifics behind these distribution options.

An Annuity, or Lifetime Payments

An annuity provides you with an annual payout. This payout can go for a set number of years, it can be in the form of lifetime payments for either you or you and your spouse, or it can be in the form of lifetime payments with a minimum number of payments guaranteed. In short, just deciding on an annuity isn't enough—you must also decide among several variations of an annuity.

Single Life Annuity
An annuity in which you receive a set monthly payment for your entire life.

Annuity for Life or a "Certain Period"
A single life annuity that allows you to receive your payments for a fixed period of time. Payments will be made to you for the remainder of your life, but if you die before the end of the time period (generally either 10 or 20 years), payments will continue to be made to your beneficiary until the end of the period.

Single Life Annuity   Under a **single life annuity**, you receive a set monthly payment for your entire life. Think of this type of annuity as the Energizer® bunny—it just keeps going and going, at least as long as you do. If you die after 1 year, the payments cease. Alternatively, if you live to be 100, so do your payments.

An Annuity for Life or a "Certain Period"   Under an **annuity for life** or a **"certain period,"** you receive annuity payments for life. However, if you die before the end of the "certain period," which is generally either 10 or 20 years, payments will continue to your beneficiary until the end of that period. Because a minimum number of payments must be made (payments must continue until the end of the certain period), an

CHECKLIST 16.2
A Retirement Checklist for the Ages

◆ **Age 50:** At 50 you are eligible to make extra or "catch-up" contributions beyond what younger individuals can contribute to your 401(k) or similar retirement plan, and to your IRA. For 401(k), 403(b), 457, SIMPLE IRA, or salary reduction SEP plans the catch-up amount was $5,000 in 2008 and indexed to inflation in the future. For an IRA, the catch-up amount is $1,000.

◆ **Age 55:** If you leave your job or retire and you're 55 or older, you can begin withdrawals from your 401(k) without paying a 10 percent early withdrawal penalty. However, unless you roll the money over into an IRA or another 401(k), you will have to pay income taxes on your withdrawal.

◆ **Age 59½:** Once you reach 59½, regardless of whether you've retired or left your job, the 10 percent penalty on early withdrawals from your 401(k) or your IRA no longer applies. Unless you roll the money over into an IRA or another 401(k), you'll have to pay income tax on it (**www.irs.gov/pub/irs-pdf/p590.pdf**).

◆ **Age 62:** At 62 you've finally reached the Social Security early retirement age. At that age you become eligible to start receiving Social Security. However, the longer you wait (up until age 70), the higher your benefit will be (**www.ssa.gov/planners/calculators.htm**). Also, the more money you make at your job, the less you will receive in Social Security benefits (**www.ssa.gov/OACT/COLA/rtea.html**).

◆ **Age 62 to 70:** The longer you wait to begin receiving Social Security, the larger your benefit will be. The exact size of your benefit depends on your "full retirement age," which is determined by the year you were born (**www.ssa.gov/retire2**).

◆ **Age 65:** At 65 you qualify for Medicare coverage. You'll want to take it, even if you want to postpone Social Security a bit longer (**www.medicare.gov/Publications/Pubs/pdf/10050.pdf**). One thing you'll want to make sure of is that you have health insurance if you retire before you turn 65. You don't want to be retired without health care coverage—that's a recipe for financial disaster.

◆ **Age 70½:** Once you've reached 70½ you can no longer contribute to your 401(k) or traditional IRAs (but you can continue to contribute to a Roth IRA as long as you have earned income) and you must begin withdrawing money in the form of a "required minimum distribution" (RMD), which is based on a formula that looks at your life expectancy. In addition, you'll have to pay income taxes on these withdrawals unless they're from a Roth IRA.

annuity for life or a "certain period" pays a smaller amount than a single life annuity. In addition, the longer the "certain period," the smaller the monthly amount.

Joint and Survivor Annuity A **joint and survivor annuity** provides payments over the life of both you and your spouse. Under this choice, the two most common options are: (1) a 50 percent survivor benefit, which pays your spouse 50 percent of the original annuity after you die; or (2) a 100 percent survivor benefit, which continues benefits to your spouse at the same level after you die. Of course, the higher the survivor benefit, the lower the size of the annuity. Many firms provide medical benefits to pensioners and their spouses over their entire life when this type of annuity is chosen as the payout method.

Joint and Survivor Annuity
An annuity that provides payments over the life of both you and your spouse.

Most individuals who are married choose this option. In fact, if you're married and you choose another option, your spouse must sign a waiver giving you permission to accept that alternative payout.

The advantages of an annuity include the fact that it can be set up in such a way that you or you and your spouse will continue to receive benefits regardless of how long you live. In addition, some firms continue to pay for medical benefits while an annuity pension payout is being received.

The disadvantages include the fact that there's no inflation protection. Although you know for certain how much you'll receive each month, the spending power of this amount will be continuously eroded by inflation. In addition, such an annuity payout method doesn't allow for flexibility in payout patterns. For example, if there's a financial emergency, the pattern can't be altered to deal with it. In addition, under the annuity there is little flexibility to leave money to heirs.

Annuities are usually available with employer-sponsored retirement plans, but insurance companies also sell them. Depending on how attractive your employer's annuity options are, you may be better off taking a lump-sum distribution and purchasing an insurance company annuity on your own. The point here is that you aren't restricted to the annuity options offered by your employer. You should compare them with the other options available from the highest-rated insurance companies before making a decision.

A Lump-Sum Payment

Lump-Sum Option
A payout arrangement in which you receive all your benefits in one single payment.

Under a **lump-sum option**, you receive your benefits in one single payment. If you're concerned about inflation protection, or if you're concerned about having access to emergency funds, a lump-sum distribution, or taking part of your money in a lump sum and putting the rest toward an annuity, may be best. If you do take your benefits in a lump sum, you'll be faced with the job of making your money last for your lifetime and for your loved ones after you're gone. That's not all bad—you get to invest the money wherever you choose, and you may end up earning a high return.

The big advantage to a lump-sum payout is the flexibility it provides. Unfortunately, you'll run the risk of making a bad investment and losing the money you so carefully saved. Table 16.4 provides a listing of some of the advantages and disadvantages of an annuity versus a lump-sum payout.

TABLE 16.4 An Annuity or Lifetime Payments Versus a Lump-Sum Payout	
Annuity or Lifetime Payments	**Lump-Sum Payout**
Advantages	**Advantages**
Payments continue as long as you live. Employer health benefits may continue with the annuity.	Flexibility to allow for emergency withdrawals. Allows for big-ticket purchases—for example, a retirement home if desired. Potential for inflation protection. Allows for money to be passed on to heirs. Control over how the money is invested.
Disadvantages	**Disadvantages**
In general, no inflation protection. No flexibility to make withdrawals in the event of a financial emergency. Doesn't allow for money to be passed on to heirs— payments stop when you die.	You could run out of money. You might not have the discipline to keep from spending the money. Complicates the financial planning process because you're responsible for your own retirement funding.

Tax Treatment of Distributions

If you receive your payout in the form of an annuity, those payments will generally be taxed as normal income.

With a lump-sum payout, you pay taxes all at once. An alternative to paying taxes on a lump-sum payout is to have the distribution rolled over into an IRA or qualified plan. This rollover makes a lot of sense if you've taken a new job or retired early and don't need the money now. You avoid paying taxes on the distribution while the funds continue to grow on a tax-deferred basis.

Putting a Plan Together and Monitoring It

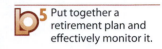

5 Put together a retirement plan and effectively monitor it.

For most individuals, there won't be a single source of retirement income: Most people rely on retirement savings from a combination of different plans. What works best for you depends on where you work and what your retirement benefits are. However, the place to start is with the seven steps outlined at the beginning of this chapter. In addition, you should make sure you invest the maximum allowable amount in tax-sheltered retirement plans because they both reduce your taxes and allow your retirement funds to grow on a tax-deferred basis.

Your investment strategy should also reflect your investment time horizon. Early on you should be willing to take on more risk—going with a strong dose of stocks in your retirement portfolio. As retirement draws near, you should gradually switch over to less risky investments. If you're uncertain about putting together your plan, or if you'd like another opinion, don't hesitate to see a professional financial planner. Figure 16.5 illustrates the typical sources of retirement income for a senior family unit (that is, a couple over 65 or an individual over 65 living alone). As you can see, income comes from four primary sources, with Social Security accounting for 36.5 percent, earnings for 29.7 percent, pensions for 18.5 percent, and asset income (investments) for 12.7 percent. Only 2.7 percent comes from other sources (including public assistance). Social Security is much more important for senior family units with lower incomes. In fact, if you rank senior family units by total income

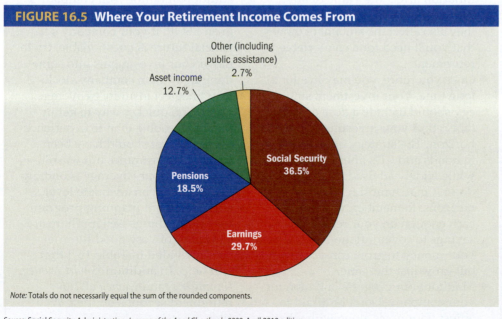

FIGURE 16.5 Where Your Retirement Income Comes From

Other (including public assistance) 2.7%

Asset income 12.7%

Social Security 36.5%

Pensions 18.5%

Earnings 29.7%

Note: Totals do not necessarily equal the sum of the rounded components.

Source: Social Security Administration, *Income of the Aged Chartbook, 2008,* April 2010 edition.

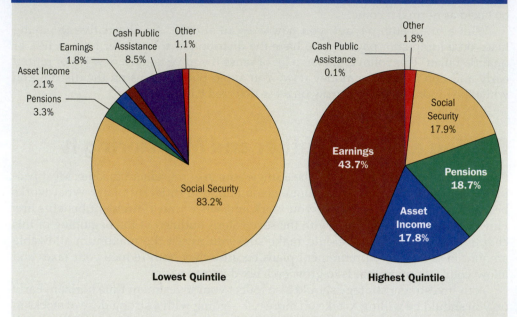

FIGURE 16.6 Where Retirement Income Comes from for the Highest and Lowest Income Quintiles

Lowest Quintile:
- Earnings 1.8%
- Cash Public Assistance 8.5%
- Other 1.1%
- Asset Income 2.1%
- Pensions 3.3%
- Social Security 83.2%

Highest Quintile:
- Other 1.8%
- Cash Public Assistance 0.1%
- Social Security 17.9%
- Earnings 43.7%
- Pensions 18.7%
- Asset Income 17.8%

Notes: The quintile limits for aged units for 2008 are $12,082, $19,877, $31,303, and $55,889. Totals do not necessarily equal the sum of the rounded components.

Source: Social Security Administration, *Income of the Aged Chartbook, 2008,* April 2010 edition.

CHECKLIST 16.3

Possible Complications

◆ Changes in inflation can have a drastic effect on your retirement. Not only do changes in anticipated inflation affect the value of any stocks and bonds that you own, they also affect the amount of money that you'll need for a comfortable retirement.

◆ Once you retire, you may live for a long time. Your investment strategy should include a dose of stocks that reflect your investment time horizon. The strategy of investing in bonds and CDs after retirement, while widely advised, probably doesn't match most retirees' time horizons. Remember, you want to earn enough on your retirement savings to cover inflation and allow your money to grow conservatively, but grow just the same.

◆ Monitor your progress and monitor your company. Don't be afraid to adjust your goals along with what's necessary to meet those goals. Make sure you track the performance of your retirement investments. In addition, monitor your company's health, especially if you participate in an ESOP. If your company's financial future is questionable, try to move your investments into something other than company stock.

◆ Don't neglect insurance coverage. There's no quicker way to get in financial trouble than to experience a disaster that should have been covered by insurance but wasn't. Make sure your coverage is both up to date and at an adequate level.

◆ An investment planning program may make things easier. There are a number of very good Internet sites provided in Table 16.3 that will help. In addition, *Smart Money*, *Kiplinger's*, and *Money* all have retirement sections on their Web sites.

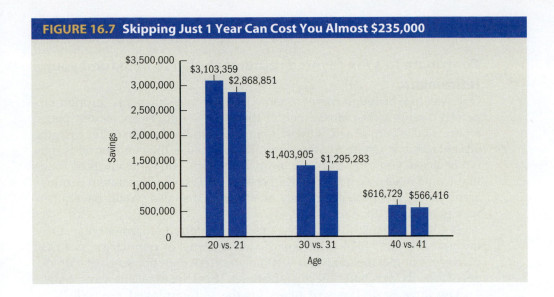

FIGURE 16.7 Skipping Just 1 Year Can Cost You Almost $235,000

and divide them into five equal groups or quintiles, Social Security only provides 17.9 percent of the income to the highest income quintile, but provides a whopping 83.2 percent of the income to the lowest income quintile as shown in Figure 16.6.

Monitoring your retirement planning, both before and after you retire, is an ongoing process in which adjustments are constantly made for new and unexpected changes in your financial and personal life. Although it's impossible to point out all the complications that might occur, a number of things that should be kept in mind are provided in Checklist 16.3.

Saving for Retirement—Let's Postpone Starting for 1 Year

Why is it so important that you not delay beginning to save for retirement? Because that 1 year can cost you a lot—in fact, that 1 year can cost almost $235.000. Just look at the results in Figure 16.7. This example assumes that on your birthday at the specified age you contribute $5,000 to an IRA that earns 8 percent per year and you continue making contributions until age 70. You can see that not only do you end up with more when you begin earlier, but you also lose quite a bit just by postponing your savings by 1 year.

Summary

Understand the changing nature of retirement planning.

For many individuals, Social Security is the primary source of retirement income. About 95 percent of all Americans are covered by Social Security. The size of your Social Security benefits is determined by (1) the number of years of earnings, (2) the average level of earning, and (3) an adjustment for inflation.

Set up a retirement plan.

Funding your retirement needs can be thought of as a seven-step process: Set goals, estimate how much you'll need to meet your goals, estimate your income at retirement, calculate the inflation-adjusted shortfall, calculate the funds needed to cover this shortfall, determine how much you must save annually between now and retirement, and put the plan in place and save.

Contribute to a tax-favored retirement plan to help fund your retirement.

One way in which you can earn more on your investments is through tax-deferred retirement plans. Some of these are employer-sponsored plans, whereas others are aimed at the self-employed individual. In either case, the advantages are essentially the same. First, because the contributions may not be taxed, you can contribute more. In essence, you can contribute funds that would otherwise go to the IRS. Second, because the investment earnings aren't taxed, you can earn money on earnings that also would have otherwise gone to the IRS.

A 401(k) plan is really a do-it-yourself tax-deferred retirement plan. Over the past 20 years, 401(k)s have exploded in terms of popularity. A 403(b) plan is essentially the same as a 401(k) plan except that it is aimed at employees of schools and charitable organizations. These are excellent ways to save.

The three basic types of plans for the self-employed are SEP-IRAs, SIMPLE plans, and Keogh plans. Another method to fund retirement is via an individual retirement account, or IRA. There are three types of IRAs: traditional IRAs, Roth IRAs, and Coverdell Education Savings Accounts.

Choose how your retirement benefits are paid out to you.

Another important retirement decision is the distribution or payout decision, which affects how much you receive, how it is taxed, whether you are protected against inflation, whether you might outlive your retirement funds, and a host of other important concerns. Your basic distribution choices are to receive your payout as a lump sum, to receive it in the form of an annuity or lifetime payments, or some combination of the two.

Put together a retirement plan and effectively monitor it.

You must monitor your progress toward your retirement goal, both before and after you retire, constantly allowing for new and unexpected changes that occur in your financial and personal life.

Review Questions

1. What are you purchasing with your payroll tax paid to Social Security? How will your benefits be paid for in 40 years?

2. How many credits do you need to qualify for Social Security benefits? How is a credit earned? How many can you earn each year?

3. How is the amount of someone's Social Security benefit determined? What percentage of income does Social Security typically replace? What percentage of full benefits do those retiring at age 62 receive?

4. Why is the amount available from personal savings and Social Security retirement benefits even more important for women than for men?

5. What is meant by the term "disability and survivor benefits"? How does the Social Security Administration define "substantial work"?

6. Describe a pension plan, the most common example of a defined-benefit retirement plan. What are the advantages and disadvantages of this type of plan? Why are defined-benefit plans declining?

7. What is vesting? What does it mean for an employee? An employer? Why is it important when initially considering a job offer? When thinking about changing jobs?

8. Describe a cash-balance retirement plan. What are the advantages and disadvantages for the employee? What advantages, if any, does this defined-benefit plan offer an employer?

9. List and briefly explain each of the seven steps and the calculations involved in retirement planning.

10. What are the two fundamental principles and advantages of a tax-deferred retirement plan?

11. Compare and contrast a defined-contribution plan and a defined-benefit plan. Who is responsible for the investment of funds for each plan? How are benefits determined? How are these plans advantageous to an employer?

12. List the five most common examples of a defined-contribution plan. For each, cite a unique advantage or disadvantage for the employee.

13. What is a 401(k) plan and how does it differ from a 403(b) plan? Describe two advantages associated with contributing to such plans.

14. What is a "catch-up" provision? Who can use it? Why?

15. Who is eligible to participate in a self-employed or small business retirement plan? Would a public school teacher who moonlights as a photographer qualify for a SEP-IRA?

16. Briefly describe a Keogh, SEP-IRA, and SIMPLE plan, noting how each is funded. Generally, what advantages do these plans share with other tax-deferred plans?

17. Who manages the investments in a Keogh, SEP-IRA, or SIMPLE plan? If withdrawals are made prior to age 59½, will the IRS typically impose a penalty? If so, when might the penalty be waived?

18. How does the traditional IRA differ from the Roth IRA? What characteristics are common to both?

19. Can a nonworking spouse have a traditional IRA? If so, what restrictions apply?

20. What penalty-free withdrawals are allowed from a traditional IRA?

21. What is meant by the term "rollover?" Why is this important?

22. Explain the benefit of the Saver's Tax Credit. What restrictions apply?

23. Once the taxes are paid, what advantages are available from rolling money from a traditional to a Roth IRA?

24. Describe the Coverdell Education Savings Account. How does it differ from the 529 plan?

25. What is a 529 plan? What restrictions on funding, contributions, and withdrawals apply?

26. What advantages does a 529 plan offer over a Coverdell Education Savings Account? May a household fund both plans?

27. What is an annuity? Describe the different annuity variations for retirement distributions.

28. Explain two examples of how the advantages and disadvantages of an annuity and a lump-sum distribution counter, or offset, each other. Why is this important to understand when choosing a of distribution method?

29. Explain why Social Security benefits are more important for lower income households than for higher income households.

30. Timing is essential to retirement planning. Why?

Develop Your Skills—Problems and Activities

These problems are available in MyFinanceLab.

1. Jazmin earned $51,250 this year. Calculate her total FICA contribution for the year. How much did her employer pay toward FICA? (*Hint:* Do not use the special 2011 FICA limits.)

2. Grady Zebrowski, age 25, just graduated from college, accepted his first job with a $50,000 salary, and is already looking forward to retirement in 40 years. He assumes a 3.5 percent inflation rate and plans to live in retirement for 20 years. He does not want to plan on any Social Security benefits. Assume Grady can earn an 8 percent rate of return on his investments prior to retirement and a 5 percent rate of return on his investments post-retirement to answer the following questions using your financial calculator.

   a. Grady wants to replace 90 percent of his current income. What is his annual need in today's dollars?

   b. Using Table 16.2, Grady thinks he might have an average tax rate of 13 percent at retirement if he is married. Adjusting for taxes, how much does Grady really need per year, in today's dollars?

   c. Adjusting for inflation, how much does Grady need per year in future dollars when he begins retirement in 40 years?

   d. If he needs this amount for 20 years, how much does he need in total for retirement? (*Hint:* Use the inflation-adjusted rate of return.)

   e. How much does Grady need to save per month to reach his retirement goal assuming he does not receive any employer match on his retirement savings?

3. Sedki earned $119,750 in 2010. How much did he pay in Social Security taxes? In Medicare taxes? In total FICA taxes? (*Hint:* Don't forget the annual Social Security earnings cap.)

4. Anne-Marie and Yancy calculate their current living expenditures to be $67,000 a year. During retirement they plan to take one cruise a year that will cost $5,000 in today's dollars. Anne-Marie estimated that their average tax rate in retirement would be 12 percent. Yancy estimated their Social Security income to be about $22,000 and their retirement benefits are approximately $35,000. Use this information to answer the following questions:

   a. How much income, in today's dollars, will Anne-Marie and Yancy need in retirement assuming 70 percent replacement and an additional $5,000 for the cruise?

   b. Calculate their projected annual income shortfall in today's dollars.

   c. Determine, in dollars, the future value of the shortfall 30 years from now, assuming an inflation rate of 5 percent.

   d. Assuming an 8 percent nominal rate of return and 25 years in retirement, calculate their necessary annual investment to reach their retirement goals.

5. Russell and Charmin have current living expenses of $97,000 a year. Estimate the present value amount of income they will need to maintain their level of living in retirement. Assume an average tax rate of 20 percent and an 80 percent income replacement ratio.

6. Anita currently has 25 years of service and an average annual salary of $37,000 over her last 5 years of employment. She was looking forward to retirement but has been offered a promotion. If she continues to work for 5 more years and increases her average annual salary to $47,000, how will her monthly pension benefit change according to the typical pension benefit formula as described in this chapter? If Anita's plan is similar to most pension plans, how will it adjust for inflation?

7. Reece is comparing retirement plans with prospective employers. ABC, Inc., offering a salary of $38,000, will match 75 percent of his contributions up to 10 percent of his salary, his maximum contribution. XYZ Company will match 100 percent of his contribution up to 6 percent of salary, but he can contribute up to 15 percent of his income. XYZ Company is offering a $35,000 salary. If Reece assumes that he will contribute the maximum amount allowed and keep these first-year retirement funds invested for 30 years with a 9 percent return, how much would each account be worth? How can he use this information when choosing an employer?

8. Peter and Blair recently reviewed their future retirement income and expense projections. They hope to retire in 30 years and anticipate they will need funding for an additional 20 years. They determined that they would have a retirement income of $61,000 in today's dollars, but they would actually need $86,000 in retirement income to meet all of their objectives. Calculate the total amount that Peter and Blair must save if they wish to completely fund their income shortfall, assuming a 3 percent inflation rate and a return of 8 percent.

9. Min-Jun and Min-Suh want to contribute $120,000 to a 529 plan for the benefit of their new grandchild. If done shortly after the birth of the child, with a 7 percent annual return and no other contributions, what will the account be worth when the child is 18 and ready to enter college? (*Hint:* Use your financial calculator.)

10. Assuming a 7 percent annual return with a Coverdell Education Savings Account, how much would $2,000 annual contributions be worth when the child from the previous question is 18 and ready to enter college? (*Hint:* Use your financial calculator.)

Learn by Doing—Suggested Projects

1. Take a survey of friends, relatives, and classmates to determine if they think Social Security is a funded or unfunded plan. Did they understand the difference? Were you surprised at the responses? Did your respondents consider Social Security as a part of their retirement plan? Report your results.

2. Visit the Web sites of several mutual fund families to determine the minimum initial investment needed to open an individual, nonretirement account and an IRA account. Are the amounts different? What might be the reason? Review the account application (available on the Web or by calling the toll-free number) to determine if there are questions applicable only to the nonretirement or IRA account. Report your findings.

3. Make a list of factors that you would want to consider before establishing your own retirement goals. How would these factors change if you were assisting a close, older relative to set retirement goals?

4. Contact your current employer, or an employer you would like to work for, and request a retirement benefits package summary. Specifically, what types of plans does the organization offer? A defined-benefit plan? A defined-contribution plan? A cash-balance plan? Rank the plans offered, noting the advantages and disadvantages of each. Which plan would you choose?

5. "Pay yourself first" and start early are fundamental strategies when planning for retirement. Interview a group of young professionals to determine if they are implementing these strategies. Are they eligible to participate in their companies' retirement plan(s)? If not, when will they be eligible? How did they decide the amount to save for retirement? Are they taking advantage of the companies' match, if applicable? Prepare a report of your findings.

6. Some people argue against investing in a traditional IRA if the contribution is not deductible. Ask a benefits administrator, a human resource specialist, or a

financial planner if they agree with this assertion. Why or why not? Discuss the short- and long-term tax advantages of a Roth and a traditional IRA. What criteria do these professionals consider when educating clients to make IRA choices?

7. Ideally, retirement preparation spans most of your lifetime. Ask a relative or friend who appears to be enjoying retirement about his or her retirement planning. Consider both financial and personal implications. Review the principles listed in Chapter 1 and ask how those strategies, in retrospect, impacted his or her retirement planning.

8. Talk with someone who is currently retired about his or her sources of retirement income. Is current income sufficient to meet needs? What unexpected expenses (e.g., appliance replacements, home maintenance, recreation, or medical care) have had a major impact on his or her retirement level of living? Do you think he or she is putting enough effort into monitoring the plan? Together, develop a list of recommendations to keep in mind for monitoring a retirement plan.

9. Talk with an employee assistance professional or benefits administrator about common mistakes employees make when planning for retirement. Organize your questions around the time frames of (a) the early to middle years of employment, (b) the latter years of employment, (c) the retirement decision and distribution options, and (d) the early and later years of retirement. Report your findings.

Be a Financial Planner—Discussion Case 1

This case is available in MyFinanceLab.

Bill (age 42) and Molly Hickok (age 39), residents of Anchorage, Alaska, recently told you that they have become increasingly worried about their retirement. Bill, a public school teacher, dreams of retiring at 62 so they can travel and visit family. Molly, a self-employed travel consultant, is unsure that their current retirement plan will achieve that goal. She is concerned that the cost of living in Alaska along with their lifestyle have them spending at a level they could not maintain. Although they have a nice income of more than $100,000 per year, they got a late start planning for retirement, which is now just 20 years away. Bill has tried to plan for the future by contributing to his 403(b) plan, but he is only investing 6 percent of his income where he could be investing 10 percent. Use what they told you along with the information below to help them prepare for a prosperous retirement.

Molly's income	$78,000
Bill's income	$42,000
Social Security income at retirement	$2,600/mo
Current annual expenditures	$70,000
Bill's Roth IRA	$20,000
Bill's 403(b) plan	$47,800
Marginal tax bracket	25%

Questions

1. Do Bill and Molly qualify for any other tax-advantaged saving vehicles? If so, which ones? To what extent?

2. Since Bill does not receive a company match, should he invest the maximum amount in his Roth IRA annually or just invest more in his 403(b)? Defend your answer.

3. Assuming Bill and Molly can reduce expenses and invest more, how do their retirement savings limits differ before and after age 50?

4. Calculate the future value income need for their first year in retirement, assuming a 3 percent inflation rate and an 80 percent income replacement.

5. Calculate the projected annual income at retirement that will be generated by their portfolio assuming an 8 percent nominal rate of return, a 20-year retirement period, and no further contributions.

6. Given their projected Social Security and investment income, how much will Bill and Molly need to invest annually to make up their income shortfall? Into what account(s) would you suggest they make the investments?

7. What Social Security survivor benefits are currently available to Bill and Molly?

8. Given Molly's concerns about their retirement preparation, what changes might they implement based on **Principle 10: Just Do It!** to secure their travel plans?

Be a Financial Planner—Discussion Case 2

This case is available in MyFinanceLab.

Timur and Marguerite recently met with the benefits administrator at Timur's employer to establish his retirement date and to discuss payout options for his pension. Timur just turned 67, while Marguerite, a self-employed artist, will be 62 in 6 months. The benefits administrator was helpful in outlining potential sources of income that they can expect in retirement. Annual estimates are as follows:

Social Security	$9,000
Defined-benefit plan	$12,000 (single life annuity)
Marguerite's work	$5,000
Defined-contribution plan	$10,000 (single life annuity)
Other	$4,000

The defined-contribution payout was calculated based on a 401(k) balance of $250,000 earning approximately 8 percent. The benefits administrator indicated that a 100 percent joint and survivor annuity would decrease yearly benefits by about $2,000 in the defined-benefit plan and $1,500 in the defined-contribution plan.

Questions

1. What are the advantages associated with taking the pension payouts in the form of an annuity? What are the disadvantages?

2. Based on the information provided, which type of annuity would you recommend that Timur and Marguerite choose given the difference in their ages and earnings?

3. Would you advise them to take the annuity offered in the defined-contribution plan, which guarantees a 4 percent rate of return, or would you recommend the lump-sum payment? Why? What are the disadvantages associated with your recommendation?

4. What recommendations would you make to Timur and Marguerite to help them monitor expenses and safeguard their retirement lifestyle?

5. Timur is anxious to replace work with babysitting his new grandson. He and Marguerite want to establish a 529 account this year, but are unsure of the differences, if any, in the prepaid college tuition plan and the college savings plan. Compare the two plans for them.

6. If all of the relatives together can contribute an average of $6,500 per year for the next 18 years and the 529 account earns 7.5 percent, how much will be available for Timur's grandson's college expenses in 18 years? (*Hint:* Use your financial calculator.)

Appendix

Crunchin' the Numbers— Funding Your Retirement Needs

Step 1: Set Goals

Step 2: Estimate How Much You Will Need

Take a look at Larry and Louise Tate, introduced in Chapter 2. They calculated their annual living expenditures to be $52,234. To obtain an estimate of their annual living expenses at retirement in today's dollars, they'd multiply this amount by 0.8, which would come to $41,787. They would then need to adjust this amount for any additional expenditures to meet their other goals. For example, the Tates may wish to move to a more expensive area of the country, or they may wish to travel more after retirement.

Let's assume that the Tates wish to take two additional vacation trips annually at $2,000 per trip, measured in today's dollars, for an increase in expenses of $4,000 per year. They would thus need a total of $45,787 for their annual living expenditures at retirement in today's dollars, as calculated on line D of Figure 16A.1. The Tates now must adjust this number for taxes. Using Table 16.2, we see that the average tax rate for retirement income between $40,000 and $50,000 is approximately 12 percent. However, since the Tates intend to retire in a state with a relatively high state income tax, they have decided to use 14 percent rather than 12 percent as their estimated tax rate. The Tates must divide their annual living expenditures by $(1 - 0.14)$, or 0.86, resulting in $53,241. In effect, 14 percent of this $53,241, or $7,454, will go to pay taxes, leaving $45,787 to cover living expenditures.

Step 3: Estimate Income at Retirement

The Tates estimate their Social Security income to be $18,000 and their pension benefits to be $25,000, giving them a total level of retirement income of $43,000 in today's dollars.

Step 4: Calculate the (Annual) Inflation-Adjusted Shortfall

For the Tates, the before-tax income level they need is $53,241 (line F of Figure 16A.1), whereas their available income is only $43,000 (line J), leaving a shortfall of $10,241 (line K).

Of course, this shortfall is in today's dollars, as are all our calculations so far. To determine what the shortfall will be in retirement dollars 30 years from now, the Tates must project $10,241 into the future. This is a problem involving the future value of a single cash flow.

As you should recall, we need an inflation rate to work a future value problem. Let's assume that the inflation rate over the next 30 years will be 4 percent annually. To move money forward in time 30 years, assuming a 4 percent rate of inflation, multiply it ($10,241) by the *Future-Value Interest Factor*, which is 3.243 (as found in Appendix A in the 4% column and 30 year row), yielding an inflation-adjusted shortfall of $33,212.

FIGURE 16A.1 Worksheet for Funding Retirement Needs

		The Tates Example	Your Numbers

Step 1: Set Goals

Step 2: Estimate How Much You Will Need

A. Present level of living expenditures on an after-tax basis — $52,234 _____

B. Times 0.80 equals: Base retirement expenditure in today's dollars — × 0.80 = $41,787 _____

C. Plus or minus: Anticipated increases or decreases in living expenditures after retirement — + $4,000 _____

D. Equals: Annual living expenditures at retirement in today's dollars on an after-tax basis — = $45,787 _____

E. Before-tax adjustment factor, based on average tax rate of 14% (If the average tax rate is not known, it can be estimated using Table 16.2, "The Average Tax Rate.") This is used to calculate the before-tax income necessary to cover the annual living expenses in line D. In this case, assume an average tax rate of 14%. Thus, line F, the before-tax income = line D/line E, where line E = (1 − Average Tax Rate) — ÷ 0.86 _____

F. Equals: The before-tax income necessary to cover the annual living expenses in line D — line D divided by line E = $53,241 _____

Step 3: Estimate Income at Retirement

G. Income from Social Security in today's dollars — $18,000 _____

H. Plus: Projected pension benefits in today's dollars — + $25,000 _____

I. Other income in today's dollars — + $0 _____

J. Equals (lines G + H + I): Anticipated retirement income, in today's dollars — = $43,000 _____

Step 4: Calculate the (Annual) Inflation-Adjusted Shortfall

K. Anticipated shortfall in today's dollars (line F minus line J) — = $10,241 _____

L. Inflation adjustment factor, based on anticipated inflation rate of 4% between now and retirement with 30 years to retirement (FVIFs are found in Appendix A): $FVIF_{\text{inflation rate \%, no. years to retirement}}$ — × 3.243 _____

M. Equals: Inflation-adjusted shortfall (line K × line L) — = $33,212 _____

Step 5: Calculate How Much You Need to Cover This Shortfall over the Number of Years You Expect to Be Retired (assuming an inflation-adjusted return of of 5% [return (9%) minus the inflation rate (4%)] during your retirement period, with retirement anticipated to last 30 years)

N. Calculate the funds needed at retirement to cover the inflation-adjusted shortfall over the entire retirement period, assuming that these funds can be invested at 9% and that the inflation rate over this period is 4%. Thus, determining the present value of a 30-year annuity assuming a 5% inflation-adjusted return (PVIFAs are found in Appendix D): $PVIFA_{\text{inflation-adjusted return, no. years in retirement}}$ — = 15.373 _____

O. Equals: Funds needed at retirement to finance the shortfall (line M × line N) — × line M = $510,568 _____

Step 6: Determine How Much You Must Save Annually Between Now and Retirement (30 years until retirement and earning a 9% return) to Cover the Shortfall

P. Future-value interest factor for an annuity for 30 years, given a 9% expected annual return: $FVIFA_{\text{expected rate of return, no. years to retirement}}$ (FVIFAs are found in Appendix C) — = 136.305 _____

Q. Equals: PMT, or the amount that must be saved annually for 30 years and invested at 9% in order to accumulate the line O amount at the end of 30 years — line O divided by line P $3,746 _____

Calculator Clues

Calculating Step 4: Inflation-Adjusted Shortfall

Calculating the inflation adjusted shortfall is easy with a financial calculator. Remember, if you don't have a calculator handy, there's one waiting for you on MyFinanceLab. In the example above we want to determine how much the shortfall of $10,241 will be in 30 years assuming it grows at the 4 percent rate of inflation.

Enter:	30	4	10,241	0	
	N	I/Y	PV	PMT	FV
Solve for:					−33,216

Due to rounding error, this answer is slightly different from the one calculated using the tables. In addition, as expected, the *FV* takes on a negative sign.

Step 5: Calculate How Much You Need to Cover This Shortfall

We know the Tates have an annual shortfall of $33,212 in retirement (future) dollars. They don't want inflation to erode the value of their savings. That means they'll want their retirement savings to grow by 4 percent each year just to cover inflation. In addition, assume they can earn a 9 percent return on their retirement funds. That is to say, whereas the shortfall payout will increase by 4 percent per year to compensate for inflation, they earn 9 percent per year on their investment. In effect, they earn an inflation-adjusted rate of 5 percent (that is, 9% − 4%) per year.[3]

Thus, in determining how much the Tates need to have saved if they wish to withdraw $33,212 per year while earning a 5 percent inflation-adjusted return, you're really determining the present value of an annuity. In this case, it's a 30-year annuity, because the Tates want this retirement supplement to continue for 30 years, and it's discounted back to the present at 5 percent. To do this, we multiply the inflation-adjusted shortfall of $33,212 by the *Present-Value Interest Factor for an Annuity* of 15.373 (found in Appendix D in the 5% column and the 30 year row), and find that $510,568 is the amount that the Tates need to accumulate by retirement.

Calculator Clues

Calculating Step 5: Funds Needed to Cover the Shortfall

Let's try the above problem using a financial calculator. We are solving for the *PV* of a 30-year annuity of $33,212 at 5 percent.

Enter:	30	5		32,212	0
	N	I/Y	PV	PMT	FV
Solve for:			−510.550		

Again, due to rounding error in the tables, this answer is slightly different from the one we just calculated. In addition, as expected, the *PV* takes on a negative sign.

---

[3]Actually, the inflation-adjusted or real rate of return would be a bit less because of the cross product or Fisher Effect, but for pedagogical purposes we will ignore it. This relationship was first analyzed by Irving Fisher and shows that $R_{nominal} = r_{real} + I_{inflation} + (r_{real} \times I_{inflation})$. A detailed examination of the Fisher Effect is presented in Peter N. Ireland, "Long-Term Interest Rates and Inflation: A Fisherian Approach," *Federal Reserve Bank of Richmond, Economic Quarterly*, 82 (Winter 1996): 22–26.

Step 6: Determine How Much You Must Save Annually Between Now and Retirement

The Tates know they need to accumulate $510,568 by the time they retire in 30 years. To determine how much they need to put away each year to achieve this amount, they need to know how much they can earn on their investments between now and when they retire. Let's assume they can earn 9 percent. This then becomes a simple future value of an annuity problem, solving for *PMT* in the formula where *Future-Value Interest Factor for an Annuity* is found in Appendix C in the 9% column and 30 year row.

$$FV = PMT \text{ (Future-Value Interest Factor for an Annuity)}$$

$$\$510,568 = PMT \text{ (136.305)}$$

$$PMT = \$3,746$$

Therefore, the Tates must save $3,746 each year for the next 30 years at 9 percent to meet their retirement goals.

Calculator Clues

Calculating Step 6: Calculating How Much the Tates Need to Save Annually

Calculating the inflation adjusted shortfall is easy with a financial calculator. Remember, if you don't have a calculator handy, there's one waiting for you on MyFinanceLab. In the example above, we want to determine how much the shortfall of $10,241 will be in 30 years assuming it grows at the 4 percent rate of inflation.

Enter:

30	9	0		510,568
N	I/Y	PV	PMT	FV

Solve for: −3,746

You'll notice that *PMT* takes on a negative sign.

Step 7: Put the Plan in Play and Save

17 Estate Planning: Saving Your Heirs Money and Headaches

Learning Objectives

 Understand the importance and the process of estate planning.

 Draft a will and understand its purpose in estate planning.

 Avoid probate.

In life, George Steinbrenner beat the Red Sox—and in death, he beat the IRS. For 37 years, from 1973 until his death in July 2010, George was the owner of the New York Yankees. During that time the Yankees were the American League champs 11 times and won the World Series 7 times. The son of a wealthy shipping magnate, he had a brief career as a college football coach, then moved into the shipping business and from there tried his hand at producing Broadway plays. But his best investment by far was when he bought a 55 percent interest in the Yankees for $8.8 million in 1973. At his death, according to *Forbes*, those same Yankees were valued at $1.6 billion, and his personal fortune was estimated at $1.1 billion.

Given the way estate taxes work, Steinbrenner should have paid at least a half a billion dollars in estate taxes, but once again Steinbrenner came out on the winning end. He paid nothing in estate taxes because Congress let the estate tax disappear in 2010 as they argued whether it should be reformed or repeated forever.[1] His heirs will eventually pay some capital gains taxes if they ever sell their 55 percent interest in the Yankees, but they still saved millions because in death George won the World Series of Taxes.

Steinbrenner wasn't the only wealthy American to die in 2010 and avoid federal estate taxes. Dan Duncan (gas and oil pipelines) saved $4.5 billion and John Kluge (TV and radio) saved around $3.4 billion, merely because they also died in 2010—and all because Congress didn't act in time.

Most people cringe at the thought of **estate planning**, mostly because it involves death. As a result, many individuals avoid it, ignoring the inevitable or assuming that only the rich need to deal with it. However, there's value in estate planning for practically everyone. Once you're dead, there might not be anyone to provide for your spouse or kids.

With estate planning you're ensuring that you preserve as much as possible of your wealth—no matter how little that may be—for your heirs. It also ensures that the guardianship of your children will fall to whomever you wish. Basically, estate planning finds much of its logic in **Principle 7: Protect Yourself Against Major Catastrophes**—in this case, the catastrophe is your death. You'll also

Estate Planning
The process of planning for what happens to your accumulated wealth and your dependents after you die.

7
Principle

---

[1]However, not paying estate taxes doesn't mean that Steinbrenner escaped taxes altogether. In addition to the estate taxes disappearing in 2010, the step-up in basis rule also came close to disappearing, being limited to $1.3 million, with an extra $3 million for the surviving spouse. Under the old step-up in basis rule, heirs who inherited property got to step-up, or raise, the property's income tax basis to the property's fair market value at the owner's death. Then, when the heirs sell the property, they would only pay capital gains tax on the difference between the future sales price for the property and the property's value at the time they inherited it. But when Steinbrenner's heirs sell the estate's property, they will pay capital gains tax on the difference between the future sales price for the estate and the original cost (with some minor adjustments) of the property. Still, this is a pretty big break for the Steinbrenner family, and it's all because Congress didn't act.

find that much of what happens in estate planning is done to keep taxes to a minimum, which brings us back to **Principle 4: Taxes Affect Personal Finance Decisions**. As you'll see, the basic choices available to you with respect to minimizing taxes and passing on your estate are the use of a will, gifts, and trusts.

You'll also see that estate planning can be an extremely complicated process. Our purpose here isn't to make you an expert in estate planning but to alert you to its benefits and challenges. After studying this chapter you'll have a better understanding of the concepts, terminology, process, techniques, and tools of estate planning. And you'll be better able to plan for the disposition of whatever you have accumulated.

Estate planning is planning for what happens to your wealth and your dependents after you die. And regardless of how large your estate is, the basic objectives remain the same. First, you want to make sure your property is distributed according to your wishes and your dependents are provided for. Providing for your dependents will involve, among other things, selecting a guardian for your children if they're under 18. Second, you want to pass on as much of your estate as possible, which means you'll want to minimize estate and inheritance taxes. Finally, you'll want to keep settlement costs, including legal and accounting fees, to a minimum. In essence, you'll be developing a strategy to give away and distribute your assets while paying the minimum in taxes and fees. Estate planning may seem a bit gloomy because it forces you to think about your own demise. Fortunately, there's one aspect of estate planning that doesn't deal with your own death. Unfortunately, it deals with your incapacitation. Yes, the final objective of estate planning is determining who is to have decision-making authority in the event that you become unable to care for yourself as a result of physical or mental impairment.

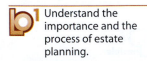

Understand the importance and the process of estate planning.

The Estate Planning Process

Once you recognize these basic objectives of the estate planning process, you'll want to fine-tune them to meet your specific needs and goals. For example, you might want to protect your current spouse from claims on your assets by your ex-spouse. You might also want to induce your kids to go to college by leaving all of your money to them in a fund that they can access only after they graduate. No matter how you choose to fine-tune the basic objectives of estate planning, the financial planning process remains the same for everyone. Let's take a look at that process.

The estate planning process has four steps.

Step 1: Determine the Value of Your Estate

Estate planning starts with determining the value of your assets. After all, you can't determine how to distribute what you own if you don't know what you own. The easiest way to figure out what you've got and what it's worth is by looking at your personal balance sheet (see Chapter 2). It should list all of your assets and their respective values, as well as your net worth.

Your net worth was calculated by determining what you own and subtracting from that what you owe.

$$\text{your estate's net worth} = \text{value of your estate} - \text{level of estate's liabilities}$$

In estate planning, your net worth must be recalculated slightly differently. First, you must keep in mind that when you die, your life insurance will pay off. In calculating the value of your life insurance, you should use the death benefit as its value rather than its cash or surrender value. In addition, you should include any death benefits associated with an employer-sponsored retirement plan.

It's important to get a sense of your wealth, not only because you'll need to know what you have to distribute, but also because its level will determine how much tax planning you'll need. For example, in 2012 the first $5 million of your estate can be passed on tax free. Then in 2013, things change, and the estate tax exemption is scheduled to drop down to $1 million and the maximum tax rate is scheduled to jump to 55 percent, but that is only what's scheduled to happen, and it is more likely that Congress will act to change that before it actually happens. You'd approach estate planning differently if your estate were worth $100,000 than you would if it were worth $10 million.

> ### FACTS of LIFE
>
> Most people are surprised to see how much their estate is worth. Once you start adding a home plus furnishings to a couple of automobiles, savings, and investments, things add up. The only way to determine what your estate is worth is to go through the numbers.

Step 2: Choose Your Heirs and Decide What They Receive

Once you know just what you have, you can figure out who's going to get it when you go. Most married people will just leave everything to their spouse. However, you may want to consider the relationships you have with various people and the needs of your dependents and potential heirs.

If, for example, you have a child with special needs who requires special schooling, you may want to make sure that need is taken care of first. Or perhaps some of your children have already completed college. In this case you may want to earmark college funds to those children who haven't yet finished or even started college.

Step 3: Determine the Cash Needs of the Estate

Once you know what you've got and who's going to get it, your estate planning is done, right? Nope. Before your property can be distributed to your heirs, uncovered medical costs, funeral expenses, all legal fees, outstanding debt, and estate and inheritance taxes must be paid. It's a good idea to have enough funds in the form of liquid assets—Treasury bills, stocks, and bonds—to cover your estate tax needs, or to provide tax-free income to your heirs from a life insurance policy that will cover your estate taxes. While every estate is different, a general rule of thumb is that funeral and settlement costs generally run at around $15,000 or 4 percent of the estate.

Step 4: Select and Implement Your Estate Planning Techniques

The final step is determining which estate planning tools are most appropriate to achieve your goals. In general, you'll need a combination of several planning techniques. Some of the most commonly used include a will, a durable power of attorney, joint ownership, trusts, life insurance, and gifts.

These tools can be a little tricky to use, and once you've figured out how to use them, implementing your estate plan can be complex. As a result, you should consult a legal specialist in estate planning to help you with the tools and to handle the details of implementing your plan.

Principle **1**

But just because you'll need a professional to help you use them doesn't mean you don't need to understand the tools of estate planning. After all, you'll need to be able to speak the same language as the professional so you can fully understand his or her advice. Remember **Principle 1: The Best Protection Is Knowledge**. We examine and explain all the major tools of estate planning that you need to understand. First, however, we need to discuss taxes, because the use of most estate planning tools is based on tax consequences.

Understanding and Avoiding Estate Taxes

Estate taxes are a central element to consider in estate planning because of the high tax rate imposed on estates. Earlier we mentioned that in 2012 the first $5 million of an estate can be passed on tax free.

This $5 million tax-free transfer will be reduced to $1 million by 2013 unless Congress acts. Of course, the IRS likes to make everything as complicated as possible, so we'd better explain how this tax-free transfer works.

To understand how estate taxes work, you need to understand the estate tax exemption or unified tax credit. To do this let's look at the 2012 tax year. If you die in 2012, instead of charging no taxes at all on the first $5 million of your estate, the IRS actually will charge a hefty 18 percent tax rate on the first $10,000 of your estate and keep raising this rate all the way up to 35 percent when the amount hits $5 million. To offset the taxes on the first $5 million of your estate, the IRS will then issue an estate tax credit, called a **unified tax credit**, which effectively nullifies the taxes on the first $5 million of your estate. Above this tax-free threshold of $5 million, the estate pays at a tax rate of 35 percent. What does all this really mean? Over one-third of any amount that you pass on beyond $5 million will be lost to taxes! But in 2013, things could get more taxing, because the estate tax exemption is set to drop from $5 million to $1 million with the maximum tax rate soaring to 55 percent! That probably won't happen—Congress will most likely step in and change things— but relying on what Congress might do in the future is a risky path to take.

Unified Tax Credit
An estate and gift tax credit that, in 2012, allows the first $5 million of an estate and lifetime gifts (beyond the annual gift exclusion) to be passed on tax free.

One thing you should keep in mind is that the estate tax exemption is portable, which means that when one spouse dies, the unused amount goes to the surviving spouse and can be used at his or her death. So if the husband dies and used $2 million of his credit, at his wife's death, she can use her $5 million credit in addition to the remaining $3 million of her husband's credit.

An awful lot of wills have to be rewritten to make sure that full advantage of the exemption is taken. It also means there's a moving target as to how big an estate can be passed on tax free. As a result, sometimes we'll refer to this amount as the "estate-tax-free transfer threshold" and not even mention the dollar amount because it changes each year.

Given the high estate tax rates imposed, your personal tax strategy should shift toward estate tax planning once your net worth climbs above the tax-free transfer threshold. Individuals with a net worth below the tax-free transfer threshold should focus on income tax strategies and on nontax estate planning concerns.

To deal with your estate taxes properly, you'll need to calculate what those taxes will be. However, before you can calculate these taxes, there are a couple other taxes— gift and generation-skipping taxes—as well as a deduction that we need to consider.

STOP & THINK

For years there has been a debate on whether to repeal estate taxes, often referred to as "death taxes," entirely. While this would benefit the wealthy, not all wealthy individuals are in favor of its repeal.

"Without the estate tax, you in effect will have an aristocracy of wealth, which means you pass down the ability to command the resources of the nation based on heredity rather than merit. [Repeal would be like] choosing the 2020 Olympic team by picking the eldest sons of the gold-medal winners in the 2000 Olympics."
—Warren Buffett. What do you think?

Gift Taxes

Gifts are an excellent way of transferring wealth before you die. They reduce the taxable value of your estate and allow you to help out your heirs while you're still alive—*and the recipient of the gift isn't taxed.* Under the present law, you're permitted to give $13,000 per year tax free in 2011 to as many different people as you like.

Let's look at a couple with four children and eight grandchildren and an estate valued at $12 million. Over a 5-year period, the couple could transfer to each of their children and grandchildren a total of $26,000 per year tax free—$13,000 from the husband and $13,000 from the wife for a total of $130,000 to each child and grandchild. These gifts would reduce the couple's taxable estate from $12 million to $10.44 million and result in significantly lower estate taxes. Remember that the exclusion for annual gifts applies to each spouse. That is, a husband and wife can give up to $26,000 jointly to each of their children or to whomever they wish without paying any taxes.

If you'd like to give more than that, you can. However, the gift tax and the estate tax *work together with a total lifetime tax-exempt limit (which is $5 million in both 2011 and 2012) on gifts over and above the yearly tax-free limit of $13,000 per recipient.* Therefore, in 2012 the first $5 million of your estate *minus* total lifetime non-tax-exempt gifts (that portion of gifts in excess of $13,000 per year per person) can be transferred tax free. If your lifetime non-tax-exempt gifts total $100,000, in 2012 the first $4.9 million rather than the first $5 million of your estate would not be taxed. Since 2011 the lifetime gift tax exemption has been linked to the estate tax exemption, which is $5 million. That means if you gift away any amount of your lifetime gift tax exemption (remember, gifts of up to $13,000 per year don't count against this—just the amount over $13,000), then this amount will be subtracted from your estate tax exemption after you die.

The $13,000-per-year tax-free gift is indexed to inflation in $1,000 increments. In fact, it started out as a $10,000 per-year level in 1997 and, as a result of inflation, increased to $11,000 in 2002, to $12,000 in 2006, and in 2009 rose to $13,000. Then, in the future, it will rise to match inflation in $1,000 increments.

Unlimited Marital Deduction

The U.S. tax code allows for an unlimited marital deduction for gift and estate tax purposes, which means that there's no limit to the size of transfers between spouses that can be made on a tax-free basis. In other words, when a husband or wife dies, the estate, regardless of size, can be transferred to the survivor totally tax free. Whereas an estate valued at up to the tax-free transfer threshold (which is $5 million in 2012) can be transferred tax free to any beneficiary, there's no limit on the value of an estate that can be transferred to a spouse. All federal estate taxes can be avoided through the use of the unlimited marital deduction.

The unlimited marital deduction doesn't apply to spouses who aren't U.S. citizens. The logic behind this law is to prevent non-U.S. spouses from returning to their home countries with an untaxed estate. Once they left the United States, Uncle Sam would never get any more tax dollars from the estate, and the IRS isn't about to let that happen.

The Generation-Skipping Transfer Tax

There's an additional tax imposed on gifts and bequests that skip a generation— for example, gifts or bequests that pass assets from a grandparent to a grandchild. The purpose of the **generation-skipping tax** is to wring potentially lost tax dollars from the intervening generation. In effect, the assets are taxed as if they moved from the grandparents to their own children, and then from their children to the grandchildren.

Generation-Skipping Tax
A tax on wealth and property transfers to a person two or more generations younger than the donor.

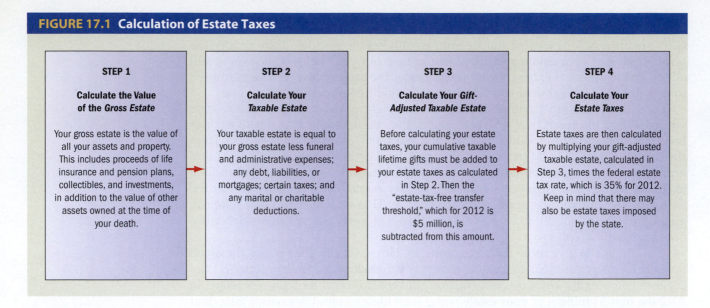

FIGURE 17.1 Calculation of Estate Taxes

STEP 1	STEP 2	STEP 3	STEP 4
Calculate the Value of the *Gross Estate*	**Calculate Your *Taxable Estate***	**Calculate Your *Gift-Adjusted Taxable Estate***	**Calculate Your *Estate Taxes***
Your gross estate is the value of all your assets and property. This includes proceeds of life insurance and pension plans, collectibles, and investments, in addition to the value of other assets owned at the time of your death.	Your taxable estate is equal to your gross estate less funeral and administrative expenses; any debt, liabilities, or mortgages; certain taxes; and any marital or charitable deductions.	Before calculating your estate taxes, your cumulative taxable lifetime gifts must be added to your estate taxes as calculated in Step 2. Then the "estate-tax-free transfer threshold," which for 2012 is $5 million, is subtracted from this amount.	Estate taxes are then calculated by multiplying your gift-adjusted taxable estate, calculated in Step 3, times the federal estate tax rate, which is 35% for 2012. Keep in mind that there may also be estate taxes imposed by the state.

Calculating Estate Taxes

You can view the calculation of estate taxes as a four-step process, as outlined in Figure 17.1. To walk you through this process, we use the example with the 2012 tax-free transfer threshold of $5 million presented in Figure 17.2.

The process of calculating your estate taxes starts by calculating the value of your gross estate, which is the value of all your assets and property at the time

FIGURE 17.2 Calculation of Estate Taxes for the 2012 Tax Year

	Amount	Total Amount
STEP 1: Calculate the Value of the *Gross Estate*		$5,900,000
A. Value of gross estate		
STEP 2: Calculate Your *Taxable Estate*		
Less:		
Funeral expenses	$10,000	
Estate administrative expenses	40,000	
Debt	0	
Taxes	0	
Marital deduction	0	
Charitable deduction	50,000	
Total		− $100,000
Equals:		
B. Taxable estate		= $5,800,000
STEP 3: Calculate Your *Gift-Adjusted Taxable Estate*		
Plus:		
Cumulative taxable lifetime gifts (in excess of annual tax-free gift allowance per person)		+ $200,000
Less:		
Estate-tax-free transfer threshold		− $5,000,000
Equals:		
Gift-adjusted taxable estate		= $1,000,000
STEP 4: Calculate Your *Estate Taxes*		
Gift-adjusted taxable estate X 0.35		$350,000

of your death. Remember to include the death benefits of any insurance policy or retirement plan you have. The example in Figure 17.2 assumes you have a gross estate of $5.9 million.

In Step 2, you calculate your taxable estate by subtracting the funeral and estate administrative expenses, along with any debts and taxes you owe, from the gross estate calculated in Step 1. Keep in mind that in Step 2 you need to subtract any and all liabilities or mortgages existing at the time of death. In addition, you subtract any allowable deductions, such as the unlimited marriage deduction and any charitable deductions you have made. Remember, gifts to charity are tax deductible, and there's no limit on the size of charitable gifts. Our example in Figure 17.2 assumes that your expenses, debt, and income and other taxes owed totaled $100,000.

To calculate the gift-adjusted taxable estate in Step 3, the Step 2 value must be adjusted for any taxable lifetime gifts that you've made. Remember that the annual gift tax exclusion allows for only one $13,000 (in 2012) gift per year per individual. Let's assume over your life you have given heavily to your children, and one of your gifts exceeded the allowable gift tax exclusion by $200,000. Thus, the gift-adjusted taxable estate is $1 million, which results in taxes of $350,000.

How about state death taxes? These depend upon which state you live in. Some states have eliminated estate taxes completely, while others don't impose a state tax on estates that fall below the federal estate-tax-free transfer threshold, which is $5 million in 2012. Still other states have implemented separate estate tax systems, which mean higher tax bills.

Wills

A **will** is a legal document that describes how you want your property to be transferred to others. Within your will you designate **beneficiaries**, or individuals who are willed your property; an **executor**, sometimes called a **personal representative**, who'll be responsible for carrying out the provisions of your will; and a **guardian**, who'll care for any of your children under the age of 18 and manage their property. Wills are the cornerstone of solid estate planning.

Wills and Probate

Probate is the legal process of distributing an estate's assets. The first step in the probate process is the validation of the will. Once the court is satisfied that the will is valid, the process of distributing the assets begins. First, the probate court appoints the executor, generally selecting whoever was designated in the will. The executor usually receives a fee ranging from 2 to 5 percent or more of the value of the estate for overseeing the distribution of the estate's assets and managing those assets during the probate process. Once the assets have been distributed and the taxes have been paid, a report is filed with the court and the estate is closed.

The advantage, and really the only purpose, of going through the probate process is to validate the will—to allow for challenges and make sure that this is in fact the last will and testament of the deceased. In the case of a challenge to the will, probate allows for the challenge or dispute to be settled. Probate also allows for an orderly distribution of the assets of an individual who dies intestate, or without a valid will.

Will
A legal document that describes how you want your property to be transferred to others after your death.

Beneficiary
An individual who is willed your property.

 Draft a will and understand its purpose in estate planning.

Executor or Personal Representative
An individual who is responsible for carrying out the provisions of your will and managing your property until the estate is passed on to your heirs.

Guardian
An individual who'll care for any children under the age of 18 and manage their property.

Probate
The legal procedure that establishes the validity of a will and then distributes the estate's assets.

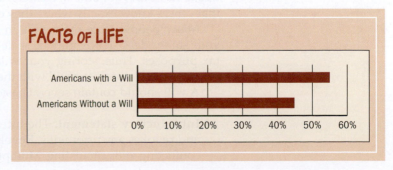

FACTS OF LIFE

	0%	10%	20%	30%	40%	50%	60%
Americans with a Will							
Americans Without a Will							

The disadvantages associated with probate center on its cost and speed. There are numerous expenses—legal fees, executor fees, court costs—that make the probate process expensive. In fact, probate can run from 1 to 8 percent of the value of the estate, depending on the laws of the state in which the deceased lived. In addition, the probate process can also be quite slow, especially if there are challenges to the will or tax problems.

Wills and Estate Planning

Because all wills must go through the potentially slow and costly probate process, wills aren't the preferred way to pass on your property. However, wills still play an extremely important role in the estate planning process. There are a number of reasons why you need to have a will, including the following:

◆ If you don't have a will, the court will likely choose a relative as the guardian to your children under the age of 18 and their property. This relative may or may not be someone you would choose; therefore, it is important to specify in your will a guardian for your children.

◆ In the case of children with special needs, a will may be the most appropriate way of providing for those needs.

◆ Property that isn't co-owned or in trusts is transferred according to your wishes as expressed in your will.

◆ You can make special gifts or bequests through a will. You can even handle the future care of your pets through a will.

◆ If you don't have a will, the court will appoint an administrator to distribute your assets. Not only might this distribution conflict with your desires, but the costs of an administrator for your estate will be more than the cost of drawing up a will, leaving less for your heirs.

Writing a Will

Although it's possible to write your own will, it's not a particularly good idea. Handwritten wills, and even oral wills, are accepted in some states, but they're a lot riskier than a formally prepared legal will. You're taking the chance that the probate court might disallow your will on the grounds of some overlooked technicality.

You should have a lawyer either draw up or review your will. Fortunately, a simple will costs only around $250. Of course, the more complicated the will is, the more expensive its preparation will be.

Once your will has been drawn up, you must sign it, and the signing must be witnessed by two or more people. It must then be stored in a safe place and periodically reviewed and updated. The most common storage place is with your lawyer. If you change lawyers, you need to remember to retrieve and relocate your will. An alternative is to store it at home in a safe, fireproof place. Of course, you should make sure that others know exactly where they can find it.

Many people store their wills in safety-deposit boxes. However, after you die your safety-deposit box may be sealed until it can be examined and inventoried for tax purposes. Thus, storing your will there isn't a particularly good idea. In some states you can store your will with the clerk of the probate court.

A will should contain several basic features or clauses, including the following:

◆ **Introductory statement.** The introductory statement identifies whose will it is and revokes any prior wills. Revoking prior wills is important so that there aren't conflicting wills circulating. Multiple wills can really make a mess out of the probate process and slow things down terribly (to the point that your heirs might drop dead from old age before your estate is settled).

◆ **Payment of debt and taxes clause.** This clause directs the payment of any debts, death and funeral expenses, and taxes.

◆ **Disposition of property clause.** This clause allows for the distribution of money and property. It states who is to receive what, and what happens to the remainder of the estate after all the bequests have been honored.

◆ **Appointment clause.** This clause names the executor of the estate and the guardian if there are children under 18.

◆ **Common disaster clause.** This clause identifies which spouse is assumed to have died first in the event that both die simultaneously.

◆ **Attestation and witness clause.** This clause dates and validates the will with a signing before two or more witnesses.

Approximately 1 in 3 wills is challenged. For that reason, it's important that you understand the requirements for a valid will. First, you must be mentally competent when the will is written. Second, you can't be under undue influence of another person. For example, if you're physically threatened or forced to sign the will, it will be invalidated. Finally, the will must conform to the laws of the state.

Updating or Changing a Will—The Codicil

A **codicil** is an attachment to a will that alters or amends a portion of the will. You should periodically review your will to make sure it conforms to your present situation. If your family expands or if you get married or divorced, you should alter your will appropriately. If the changes are substantial, it's best to write a new will and expressly revoke all prior wills. If the changes are minor, they can be effected through a codicil. A codicil should be drawn up by a lawyer, witnessed, and attached to the will.

Codicil
An attachment to a will that alters or amends a portion of the will.

Letter of Last Instructions

A **letter of last instructions** isn't a legally binding document. It's a letter, generally to the surviving spouse, that provides information and directions with respect to the execution of the will. Much of what's contained in the letter of last instructions is information such as the location of the will, legal documents such as birth certificates, Social Security numbers, and tax returns. It also has information as to the location of financial assets, including insurance policies, bank accounts, safety-deposit boxes, stocks, and bonds. Also, this letter indicates everyone who should be notified of your death.

A letter of last instructions often includes a listing of personal property and valuables as well. Finally, the letter contains funeral and burial instructions, along with your wishes regarding organ donation. The purpose of such a listing is to make dealing with your estate easier on your survivors. Generally, if you have an attorney prepare your will, he or she will also prepare a letter of last instructions. Although it doesn't carry the same legal weight as a will, it's honored in most states.

Letter of Last Instructions
A letter, generally to your surviving spouse, that provides information and directions with respect to the execution of the will.

Selecting an Executor

An executor takes on the dual role of (1) making sure that your wishes are carried out and (2) managing your property until the estate is passed on to your heirs. To say the least, this is both an important and a time-consuming task. You should take care in naming your executor. For smaller estates it may be a family member, but for larger estates, it should be a lawyer or a bank trust officer with experience as an executor.

Generally, executors are paid for their services, but on smaller estates, family members many times accept money only to cover expenses.

Not only does the executor deal with personal matters such as sending copies of the will to all the beneficiaries and publishing death notices, but he or she is also responsible for paying any necessary taxes, paying off the debts of the estate, managing the financial matters of the estate, distributing the assets remaining after bequests have been honored as specified in the will, and reporting a final accounting of the distribution to the court.

Other Estate Planning Documents

A **durable power of attorney** provides for someone to act on your behalf in the event that you become mentally incapacitated. In effect, it empowers someone to act as your legal representative. The durable power of attorney is, of course, separate from your will, and it goes into effect while you're alive but unable to act on your own. You can set up the power of attorney so that any degree of legal power is transferred. It should be very specific as to which aspects of your affairs it covers and does not cover, and should mention specific accounts.

A **living will** allows you to state your wishes regarding medical treatment in the event of a terminal illness or injury. Included with the living will should be a health care proxy, which designates someone to make health care decisions should you become unable to make those decisions for yourself. A **durable health care power of attorney**, or health care proxy would allow you to designate a trusted friend to make life support decisions for you if you lose the capacity to decide.

Avoiding Probate

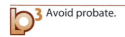
3 Avoid probate.

Unless you really want to tie up the time and money of your heirs, it's a good idea to avoid probate. Think of probate as a necessary evil. It's essential to validate your will and ensure that its provisions are carried out, but it can be a time- and money-consuming hassle. The three simplest ways of avoiding probate are through joint ownership, gifts, and trusts.

Joint Ownership

When assets are owned jointly, they're transferred to the surviving owner(s) without going through probate. In effect, the surviving owner(s) immediately assumes your ownership share of the property. There are three different forms of joint ownership: tenancy by the entirety, joint tenancy, and tenancy in common. **Tenancy by the entirety** ownership exists only between married couples. Property held by a married couple under tenancy by the entirety can be transferred only if both husband and wife agree. In addition, upon the death of one, the property automatically passes directly to the survivor.

Under **joint tenancy with the right of survivorship**, two or more individuals share the ownership of assets, which many times are held in a joint account at a bank or a brokerage firm. When one joint owner dies, the ownership passes directly on to the surviving owner or owners, bypassing the will.

With **tenancy in common**, two or more individuals share ownership of the assets. When one of the owners dies, that owner's share becomes part of the deceased's estate and is distributed according to the deceased's will. The other joint owner or owners don't receive the deceased's ownership shares unless the deceased's will states so expressly.

Although joint ownership—particularly tenancy by the entirety and joint tenancy— is probably the simplest way of avoiding probate, it does have some drawbacks. If the

Durable Power of Attorney
A document that provides for someone to act on your behalf in the event that you become mentally incapacitated.

Living Will
A directive to a physician that allows you to state your wishes regarding medical treatment in the event of an illness or injury that renders you unable to make decisions regarding life support or other measures to extend your life.

Durable Health Care Power of Attorney
A document that designates someone to make life support decisions for you if you lose capacity to decide.

Tenancy by the Entirety
A type of ownership limited to married couples. Property held this way can be transferred only if both the husband and wife agree. In addition, upon the death of one, the property automatically passes directly to the survivor.

Joint Tenancy with the Right of Survivorship
A type of ownership in which two or more individuals share the ownership of assets, usually in a joint account at a bank or a brokerage firm. When one joint owner dies, the ownership passes directly on to the surviving owners, bypassing the will.

Tenancy in Common
A type of ownership in which two or more individuals share ownership of assets. When one of the owners dies, that owner's share isn't passed on to the other owners. It becomes part of the deceased's estate and is distributed according to the deceased's will.

MONEY MATTERS

Tips from Marcy Furney, ChFC, Certified Financial Planner™

ALL IN THE FAMILY

If you have any assets, a spouse, and/or children—GET A WILL! If you die without one, your state will "write one for you" based on intestacy laws. Often those laws are directly opposed to your intent. For example, part of your estate may go to your parents when you would have wanted your spouse to inherit everything, or the guardian appointed for your children may be someone you always detested.

Beware of do-it-yourself will packages or computer software. Although many are good, some leave out very important sections of a viable will or are not valid in your state. Also, such tools may not provide any coaching on how bequests should be worded to avoid confusion at probate. One error could run your beneficiaries more in probate costs than the attorney's fee to do it right the first time.

Although living trusts are excellent tools for certain people, do your homework before deciding if one is right for you. Unfortunately, they are often "sold" by persons quoting highly exaggerated probate costs and using other scare tactics. Be sure your situation warrants the time and expense. Probate costs vary greatly from state to state and you may find the expense of such a trust is much more than your estate would pay for probate. If you do choose a living trust, use a qualified attorney to set it up.

One of the biggest erosions of large estates with business or real estate holdings is forced sale of assets at "fire sale" prices to pay taxes. If your assets are primarily illiquid, you may want life insurance to provide the funds necessary to preserve those valuable holdings.

Consider using an irrevocable life insurance trust as a source of money for estate taxes. If structured properly, the trust may use annual exclusion gifts ($13,000 in 2012) to beneficiaries to pay insurance premiums. Proceeds from the policy are not your assets, and you are able to reduce the size of your estate with the annual gifts. By purchasing the life insurance through the trust initially, rather than using a policy you may already have, you avoid the chance of proceeds reverting to your estate if you die within 3 years.

Business owners who do not wish to burden their beneficiaries with trying to run a company after their death should investigate a "buy-sell agreement." There are several types of such plans that provide for another shareholder, partner, or even key employee to purchase the business from the estate. Funding is often provided through life insurance. In such a win-win situation, forced sale of the company is avoided and the deceased owner's family receives the liquidity they may need.

relationship between those involved deteriorates, one of the joint owners could use up the asset. For example, if a bank account is jointly owned, one of the joint owners could "take the money and run." This nasty kind of rip-off is illegal, but it's also difficult to stop.

In addition, because joint ownership takes mutual agreement or a divorce settlement to dissolve, there can be problems if the relationship between the parties deteriorates. For example, one individual may wish to sell some jointly owned property for a great profit, but another joint owner might block the sale just out of spite.

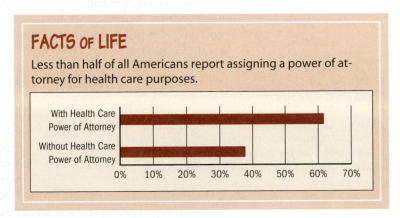

FACTS OF LIFE

Less than half of all Americans report assigning a power of attorney for health care purposes.

Without cooperation between the parties, joint ownership can seem like a prison.

Still, there are situations in which joint ownership is an excellent idea. For example, a jointly owned bank account allows survivors to access funds immediately, which can help pay for funeral expenses. In addition, joint property is also valuable in a divorce because it gives both parties some bargaining power, thereby forcing compromises that might not otherwise occur.

The concept of **community property** represents another form of joint ownership. Community property is any property acquired during a marriage, assuming both husband and wife share equally in the ownership of any assets acquired during the marriage. It doesn't include assets each spouse owned individually before the marriage or gifts and inheritances acquired during marriage that have been kept separate.

Upon the death of either the husband or the wife, the surviving spouse automatically receives one-half of the community property. The remaining portion of the property is disposed of according to the will, or in the absence of a will, according to state law. Currently only a few states, located primarily in the West, recognize community property.

Gifts

Not only can you give away $13,000 per year (in 2012) tax free to as many people as you want, but since anything you have given away is no longer yours, these gifts don't go through probate. Gifts avoid probate, reduce the taxable value of your estate, and allow you to help out your heirs while you're still alive. And the recipient doesn't pay taxes on the gift.

Gifts are also a good way of transferring property that grows in value, such as stocks or real estate. If, for example, you hold on to a stock investment that continues to grow in value, your estate will continue to grow in value, and the more your estate is worth over the estate-tax-free transfer threshold, the more your heirs will lose to estate taxes. If you can afford to part with the stock investment and you know you want to pass it on to someone else anyway, you might consider giving it as a gift.

One major exception to the annual gift exclusion rule deals with life insurance policies. If a life insurance policy is given away within 3 years of the owner's death, it is included in the estate for tax purposes. Here's how it works. Let's assume that you gave your daughter a $500,000 policy that had a cash value of $13,000. First, there'd be no gift tax on the gift because its cash value would fall into the $13,000 or less category. Then let's assume that 3 years and 1 day later you die.

In this case, the $500,000 insurance policy payout wouldn't be included in your estate for tax purposes. If, however, you'd died 1 day before 3 years was up since you gave the policy to your daughter, the entire $500,000 would be included in your estate for tax purposes. The bottom line is that if you're intending to give away a life insurance policy, it's much better to do it sooner rather than later.

In addition to the $13,000 gift tax exclusion, there is an *unlimited gift tax exclusion on payments made for medical or educational expenses*. You can make this type of gift to anyone regardless of whether the person is related to you or not. The only requirement is that you make the payment directly to the school, in the case of education expenses, or to the institution providing the service, in the case of medical expenses. In fact, the unlimited gift tax exclusion for medical expenses can even cover health insurance payments. You can give someone $13,000 and then pay for his or her health insurance, medical, and educational expenses!

The primary disadvantage to gifts is that once you've given your assets away, you might find that you need them. In addition, because you no longer have control over the assets you give, they may be squandered. Wouldn't it just stink to give your son $13,000 to go buy a car and watch him squander it on a full-body tattoo? Still, you should give a lifetime gift-giving program serious consideration.

FACTS OF LIFE

When it comes to estate planning, ignorance is bliss. One in ten American adults who do not have any elements of an estate plan say it's because they don't want to think about dying or becoming incapacitated.

Up to this point we've been talking about avoiding probate by giving gifts to your family and other individuals. You can also avoid probate by giving gifts to charity, in which case you don't have to worry about any limits on what you can give tax free, because there aren't any. You can give an unlimited amount of your estate away to federally recognized charities on a tax-free basis. In fact, your charitable gifts are even tax deductible, so you not only reduce your estate taxes by giving to charity, you also reduce your yearly income tax. See, it pays to be charitable!

Naming Beneficiaries in Contracts—Life Insurance and Retirement Plans

Insurance contracts and employee retirement plans can also be used to transfer wealth while avoiding probate. Insurance policies, either term or cash-value, can be set up so that someone other than the insured owns the policy. For example, a wife could own an insurance policy on the life of her husband, or a child could own an insurance policy on the life of a parent. One of the major advantages of life insurance is that the proceeds don't go through probate.

Many employee retirement plans pay benefits to spouses upon the death of the employee. These benefits don't go through probate and begin immediately upon the death of the worker. In addition, Social Security benefits go directly to the surviving spouse and dependent children.

Trusts

A **trust** is a legal entity that holds and manages an asset for another person. A trust is created when an individual, called a grantor, transfers property to a trustee, which can be an individual, an investment firm, or a bank, for the benefit of one or more people, the beneficiaries. Virtually any asset can be put in a trust—money, securities, life insurance policies, and property.

Trust
A legal entity in which some of your property is held for the benefit of another person.

Why do people use trusts? Here are some of the more common reasons:

◆ **Trusts avoid probate.** Trusts bypass the costly and time-consuming process of probate.

◆ **Trusts are much more difficult to challenge in court than are wills.** If there are concerns that a will may be challenged, placing the property in a trust can minimize the problem. Challenges to the will don't affect a trust unless the challenge is that the deceased was incompetent or was under undue influence when the trust was formed.

◆ **Trusts can reduce estate taxes.** Trusts can be used to shelter assets from estate taxes.

◆ **Trusts allow for professional management.** If a spouse doesn't have the understanding or desire to manage money effectively, a trust can provide the desired professional management.

◆ **Trusts provide for confidentiality.** Whereas a will becomes a matter of public record, a trust does not. Thus, if you want privacy, perhaps to keep from offending a relative who doesn't receive all he or she may expect, a trust may be just the thing for you.

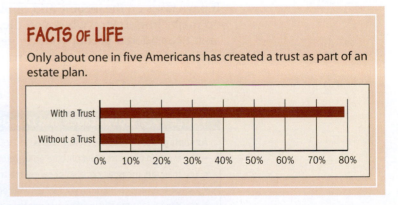

FACTS OF LIFE
Only about one in five Americans has created a trust as part of an estate plan.

◆ **Trusts can be used to provide for a child with special needs.** A trust can be set up to provide the necessary funds for a child with special needs. A special needs trust can provide funds for disabled children of majority age without eliminating government benefit programs such as Medicaid.

◆ **Trusts can be used to hold money until a child reaches maturity.** Because most children don't have the maturity or understanding necessary to handle large sums of money, a trust can be used to hold those funds until the children reach a designated age. The funds don't have to be immediately dispersed. Instead, they can be distributed over any period of time that is desired.

◆ **Trusts can ensure that children from a previous marriage will receive some inheritance.** If you leave your estate to a second spouse, children from your previous marriage may never receive any inheritance. A trust can ensure that they receive what you wish.

Because there are so many different types of trusts, many people find them confusing. However, all trusts can be classified as being either living trusts or testamentary trusts.

Living Trusts

Living Trust
A trust created during your life.

A **living trust** is one in which you place your assets while you're alive. There are two types of living trusts, revocable and irrevocable.

Revocable Living Trust
A trust in which you control the assets in the trust and can receive income from the trust without removing assets from the estate.

Revocable Living Trusts With a **revocable living trust**, you place the assets into the trust while you're alive, and you can withdraw the funds from the trust later if you wish. It's an alternative way to hold your assets. While your assets—for example, your house—are in a revocable living trust, you have access to them, can receive income from them, and can use them. In addition, you pay taxes on whatever income your assets earn.

In other words, there isn't much difference between assets in a revocable living trust and assets owned outright until you die or become incompetent, at which point the trust beneficiary takes control of the assets in the trust. It's important to remember that there are no tax advantages to a revocable living trust—they don't reduce your estate taxes. However, when you die, assets held in a living trust go directly to your beneficiary. Revocable living trusts allow you to avoid the high costs of probate and ensure the privacy that a will does not afford. Table 17.1 summarizes the advantages and disadvantages of revocable living trusts.

Irrevocable Living Trust
A trust in which you relinquish title and control of the assets when they are placed in the trust.

Irrevocable Living Trusts An **irrevocable living trust**, as the name suggests, is permanent. It can't be changed or altered once it's been established, because you no longer hold title to the assets in the trust. The trust becomes a separate legal entity. It pays taxes on the income and capital gains that its assets produce. This fact takes on major importance when you die, because assets in an irrevocable living trust aren't considered part of your estate, and any appreciation of assets would not be subject to estate tax. This type of trust also bypasses probate.

TABLE 17.1 Advantages and Disadvantages of Revocable Living Trusts
Advantages of Revocable Living Trusts
• The assets in the trust avoid probate upon your death.
• You maintain the power to alter or cancel the trust.
• If you become incompetent, your assets will continue to be professionally managed by the trustee.
• You can replace the trustee if you do not have confidence in his or her skills.
Disadvantages of Revocable Living Trusts
• There are no tax advantages—you pay taxes on any income and capital gains on the assets in the trust.
• The assets in the revocable living trust are considered part of your estate for estate tax purposes.
• The assets in the revocable living trust cannot be used as collateral for a loan.

TABLE 17.2 Advantages and Disadvantages of Irrevocable Living Trusts

Advantages of Irrevocable Living Trusts

- The assets in the trust avoid probate upon your death.
- Any price appreciation on assets in the trust is not considered part of your estate, and no estate taxes are imposed on it when you die.
- Income earned on assets in the trust can be directed to the beneficiary, which can result in tax savings if the beneficiary is in a lower tax bracket.

Disadvantages of Irrevocable Living Trusts

- You no longer maintain control over the assets in the trust.
- The assets in the trust cannot be used as collateral for a loan.
- It may be more expensive to set up than the probate costs you are trying to avoid.
- Setting up the trust can involve a lot of paperwork.

The major difference between a revocable and an irrevocable living trust centers on the fact that with a revocable trust, you retain title to and have control of the assets in the trust. Table 17.2 summarizes the advantages and disadvantages of irrevocable living trusts.

Testamentary Trusts

A **testamentary trust** is one created by a will: It doesn't exist until probate has been completed. There are a number of different purposes for testamentary trusts, including reducing estate taxes, providing professional investment management, and making sure your estate ends up in the right hands. Let's look at some of the more common types of testamentary trusts.

Standard Family Trusts (also known as A-B Trusts, Credit-Shelter Trusts, and Unified Credit Trusts)   For years standard **family trusts** were a cornerstone of estate planning for married couples. The primary objective of these trusts for married couples was to ensure that the estate tax exemption of the first spouse to die could be used by the surviving spouse. This was done by setting up a trust for the survivor, thus keeping the value of those assets out of the survivor's taxable estate. In this way, the surviving spouse was able to take advantage not only of their own estate tax exemption at death, but also their spouse's exemption, thus sheltering twice the amount than would otherwise be possible. However, among other provisions in the 2010 Tax Relief Act that went into effect in 2011 was the **portable estate exemption** that allows a deceased spouse's unused estate tax exclusion to be shifted to the surviving spouse. In effect, the initial spouse to die not only leaves his or her assets to the surviving spouse, but also leaves any unused estate tax exemption to be used at the surviving spouse's death. This is in addition to the surviving spouse's own exemption. The only thing you have to do to receive this benefit is to indicate on the estate tax return, Form 706, filed when the first spouse dies, that you would like this feature. Keep in mind that you still have to file this form even if the estate is not otherwise required to file a Form 706. Also, only the last spouse's exemption is portable, so you can't build up a huge exemption by remarrying and outliving a lot of spouses.

For example, since the estate tax exemption is $5 million, if the husband dies first and has $3 million in his estate, the $3 million would be transferred directly to his surviving spouse, leaving no taxable estate. Then when his wife dies, she would be able to use her deceased husband's unused estate tax exclusion amount. As a result, the wife's estate tax exclusion would now be $7 million (her $5 million basic exclusion amount plus $2 million unused exclusion from her late husband).

This portable estate exemption makes one of the primary features of a standard family trust irrelevant. still, family trusts are a good idea for a number of reasons.

Testamentary Trust
A trust created by your will, which becomes active after you die.

Family Trust
A trust established to transfer assets to your children, while allowing the surviving spouse access to funds in the trust if necessary. Upon the death of the surviving spouse, the remaining funds in the trust are distributed to the children tax free.

Portable Estate Exemption
An exemption that allows a deceased spouse's unused estate tax exclusion to be shifted to the surviving spouse.

First, as we have seen many times, tax laws come and go, and to base an estate plan on a law that may not be there when needed is not a good idea. Remember, this portability feature makes it possible for a married couple to transfer up to $10 million free of federal estate tax without having to use a family trust; however, without further Congressional action this feature will expire in 2013 when the estate and gift tax exemption is scheduled to drop to $1 million per person and the top estate tax rate jumps to 55 percent. Most likely Congress will act before then, but exactly what Congress does, and it is not guaranteed that they do anything at all, is far from certain. In addition, family trusts also provide other benefits, two of which include protecting assets from a lawsuit against the surviving spouse and protecting assets in the event the surviving spouse remarries.

Qualified Terminable Interest Property Trust (Q-TIP)   A **qualified terminable interest property trust**, or **Q-TIP**, gives the individual establishing the trust the ability to direct income from the trust to his or her spouse over the spouse's life, and then, at the spouse's death, to choose to whom the assets go. The primary reason for using a Q-TIP trust is to keep your estate from ending up in the hands of your spouse's future husband or wife rather than your children after you die. Q-TIP trusts are generally set up so that your spouse receives the income on your estate while he or she is alive, and after your spouse's death, the assets in the trust are passed on to your children.

Sprinkling Trusts   A **sprinkling trust** is a trust that distributes income according to need rather than to some preset formula. The trustee is given discretion to determine who needs what among a designated group of beneficiaries, and then "sprinkles" the income among them according to need.

Qualified Terminable Interest Property Trust (Q-TIP)

A trust that gives the individual establishing the trust the ability to direct income from the trust to his or her spouse over the spouse's life, and then, at the spouse's death, to choose to whom the assets go.

Sprinkling Trusts

A trust that distributes income according to need rather than to some preset formula. The trustee is given discretion to determine who needs what among the designated beneficiaries and then "sprinkles" the income among them according to need.

CHECKLIST 17.1

Estate Planning

Do you and the members of your family know . . .
- The location of your will, durable power of attorney, and living will (with the name of the attorney who drafted them)?
- The name of your attorney?
- Where to find your letter of last instructions, including burial requests and organ donor information?
- Your Social Security number?
- The location of your safety-deposit box and the key to it?
- Where you stored your birth certificate? Your marriage certificate? Any military discharge papers?
- Where to find your insurance policies (life, health, and property/liability) along with the name of your insurance agent?
- The whereabouts of deeds and titles to property (both real estate and, for example, automobiles)?

- The site of your stocks, bonds, and other securities, and who your broker is?
- How to find any business agreements, including any debts owed you?
- All checking, savings, and brokerage account numbers, along with the location of those accounts?
- The name of your accountant?
- Your last year's income tax return?
- The name of past employers, along with any pension or retirement benefits information?

You should also . . .
- Calculate the size of your estate.
- Estimate how much of your estate would be lost to taxes if you died.
- Know who the executor of your will is and who your beneficiaries are.
- Select a guardian for your children if they are under 18.

A Last Word on Estate Planning

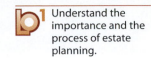

Understand the importance and the process of estate planning.

The complexities associated with estate planning, coupled with the fact that estate planning is essentially about your death, cause many of us to put off the process. Don't. Now that you have a basic understanding of the process, objectives, and tools of estate planning, approach a professional. By no means should you attempt your own estate planning. Finally, make sure your family knows where your estate planning documents are. Checklist 17.1 will help you organize your affairs.

Summary

 Understand the importance and the process of estate planning.

Estate planning involves planning for what happens to your accumulated wealth and your dependents after you die. Estate planning can be viewed as a four-step process: Determine the value of your estate; choose your heirs, determine their needs, and decide what they receive; determine the cash needs of the estate; select and implement your estate planning techniques.

The purpose of going through the probate process is to allow for validation of the will—to allow for challenges and make sure this is in fact the last will and testament of the deceased. A will is a legal document that describes how you want your property to be transferred to others.

 Draft a will and understand its purpose in estate planning.

Within your will, you designate beneficiaries or individuals who are willed your property. You also designate an executor who will be responsible for carrying out the provisions of your will. In addition, you can also designate a guardian who will care for any children under the age of 18 and manage their property. You should periodically review your will to make sure that it conforms to your present situation.

 Avoid probate.

Trusts are legal entities that hold money or assets. Some of the more common reasons for trusts are (1) trusts avoid probate, (2) trusts are much more difficult to challenge in court than are wills, (3) trusts can reduce estate taxes, (4) trusts allow for professional management, (5) trusts provide for confidentiality, (6) trusts can be used to provide for a child with special needs, (7) trusts can be used to hold money until a child reaches maturity, and (8) trusts can ensure that children from a previous marriage will receive some inheritance.

With a revocable living trust, you place the assets into the trust while you are alive, and you can withdraw the funds from the trust later if you wish. An irrevocable living trust, as the name suggests, is permanent. A testamentary trust is one that is created by a will. Because these trusts are established by a will, they aren't created until probate has been completed.

Review Questions

1. Define estate planning. List the objectives to accomplish through estate planning.
2. Describe the four steps in the estate planning process.
3. What is the estate-tax-free transfer threshold for 2012 and 2013, and how does this relate to the unified tax credit?
4. Explain the annual gift tax exclusion. How is it used as an estate planning tool?

5. Explain the importance of having the lifetime gift tax exemption linked to the estate tax exemption.

6. Describe the unlimited marital deduction. What exclusions apply?

7. What is the generation-skipping transfer tax?

8. List and briefly describe the four steps involved in the process of calculating estate taxes.

9. What is probate and why is it often prudent to take steps to avoid probate?

10. List five reasons why having a will is important.

11. Describe the basic clauses in a will. What individuals are typically designated in a will?

12. List three characteristics of a valid will. Are handwritten or oral wills acceptable?

13. Describe the following estate planning documents: (a) codicil, (b) letter of last instructions, (c) durable power of attorney, (d) living will, and (e) health care proxy.

14. What are the roles and duties of an executor?

15. List four strategies for transferring property that will avoid probate.

16. List and briefly describe (a) the three forms of joint ownership and (b) the advantages and disadvantages of these approaches of owning property with others.

17. What is community property? What restrictions apply to this form of ownership?

18. Why is gifting an important estate planning tool? Why are assets that grow in value recommended as gifts?

19. Briefly explain the gifting exceptions that apply to (a) life insurance, (b) medical and educational expense, and (c) charitable gifts.

20. What is a trust? Name five possible advantages of using trusts in estate planning.

21. What are the fundamental differences between a living and a testamentary trust? Categorize the following as living or testamentary and briefly describe each: irrevocable trust, qualified terminable interest property trust (Q-TIP), revocable trust, and sprinkling trust.

22. Explain how the portable estate exemption, resulting from the 2010 Tax Relief Act, altered estate planning using family trusts.

Develop Your Skills—Problems and Activities

These problems are available in MyFinanceLab.

1. As the first gift from their estate, Lily and Tom Phillips plan to give $20,000 to their son, Raoul, for a down payment on a house.

   a. How much gift tax will be owed by Lily and Tom?

   b. How much income tax will be owed by Raoul?

   c. List three advantages of making this gift.

2. Following his death in 2012, Zane Wulster's gross taxable estate was valued at $3,300,000. He has made a total of $200,000 of gifts that exceeded the annual gift tax exclusion.

   a. What is the amount of his gross gift-adjusted taxable estate? (*Hint:* Use Worksheet 17.)

   b. Are estate taxes payable?

3. Morgan, a widow, recently passed away. The value of her assets at the time of death was $5,600,000. The cost of her funeral was $18,000, while estate administrative costs totaled $52,000. As stipulated in her will, she left $100,000 to charities. Based on this information (see Worksheet 17) answer the following questions:

   a. Determine the value of Morgan's gross estate.

   b. Calculate the value of her taxable estate.

c. What is her gift-adjusted taxable estate value?

d. Assuming she died in 2012, how much of her estate would be subject to taxation?

e. Calculate the estate tax liability.

4. May Yee had a $950,000 net worth at the time of her death in 2012. In addition, she owned a $250,000 whole life policy with $40,000 of accumulated cash value; her niece was designated as the beneficiary. She also had a $150,000 pension plan benefit, also payable to her niece.

a. What is the value of May Yee's gross estate?

b. How much of her estate is taxable?

c. How much of her estate must pass through probate?

5. Determine which of the following 2012 annual gifts are subject to gift taxes and to what extent they need to be included in an estate.

a. Grandparents gave a grandchild $24,000 for the purchase of a new car.

b. Father gave $35,000 to a son to start a small business.

c. Parents paid $35,000 to Wellesley College for their daughter's tuition.

d. Sister paid $47,000 of her brother's qualified medical expenses to Duke Medical Center.

e. Widow gave $105,000 to charity.

f. Mother gave a daughter a life insurance policy with a face value of $50,000 and a cash value of $10,000 two years prior to the mother's death.

6. So-hyun Joo, and her husband KJ, Each own assets valued at $3,000,000. If KJ dies in 2012 and leaves all of his assets to So-hyun, without the use of a trust arrangement, how much of his estate will be subject to tax? If So-hyun were also to pass away in 2012, after receiving KJ's assets, what will be her estate tax liability?

7. Elsa and Ludvik Hansen have $5.8 million of assets: $2,400,000 in Ludvik's name, $2,400,000 in Elsa's name, and $1 million of jointly owned property. Their jointly owned property is titled using joint tenancy with right of survivorship. Elsa also co-owns a $500,000 beach house with her sister as tenants in common.

a. What are the advantages or disadvantages of the Hansens' plan to rely on the unlimited marital deduction?

b. What could the Hansens do to reduce their expected estate tax liability prior to either spouse's death?

c. Who would receive Elsa's half share in the beach house if she were to die?

Learn by Doing—Suggested Projects

1. Locate three to five articles about problems experienced by individuals or families who failed to develop estate plans or to identify responsible parties in the event of physical or mental impairment. Summarize your findings. In your opinion, is the cost of "failing to plan" worth the price of avoiding the issue(s)?

2. Conduct an online estate planning article search on current and future estate tax law changes. Write a brief summary of recommendations from the articles showing how future changes in the tax code might alter the way people plan for the distribution of their assets at death.

3. The text of a simple will can be found on the Internet. Locate and print at least two wills. Compare the language and clauses, as described in your text. What are the advantages and disadvantages of using this approach to prepare a will? Who might benefit from this alternative? Write a brief summary and present your findings to the class.

4. Will preparation kits are available on the Internet and in book stores and office supply stores. Research the cost, availability, and descriptions of at least three kits.

What are the advantages and disadvantages of using this approach to prepare a will? Who might benefit from this alternative? Write a brief summary and present your findings to the class.

5. Research the probate court procedures in your state of residence. Interview a representative of the court, observe the court proceedings, or learn how to access a probated will. Summarize your findings.

6. Make a list of criteria that you would use in selecting the executor of your estate and the heirs named to inherit your assets. How would these criteria change if you were selecting a guardian for your children?

7. Contact three law firms to determine the cost of preparing a simple will and the kinds of information needed by the attorney. Prepare a report of your findings.

8. Prepare a letter of last instructions. Discuss it with one or more family members. Have they prepared a letter of last instruction or implemented other estate planning strategies?

9. Locate a list of medical treatments generally included in living wills prepared in your state of residence. Research the meaning of these procedures. Write a report describing your feelings regarding medical treatment in the event of a terminal illness or incapacitation. Whom would you select as a health care proxy?

10. Discuss with a close adult friend or relative his or her estate plans including the use of a will, trusts, lifetime gifting, a living will, and/or a durable power of attorney. Write a one-page report of your findings.

Be a Financial Planner—Discussion Case 1

This case is available in MyFinanceLab.

Lee and Marta Howard are in their early 70s. Recently they have grown concerned about probate and estate taxes. They calculated that this year they will have a combined net worth of $ 6,100,000. In addition, Lee owns a $500,000 whole life insurance policy on his life. Marta is the beneficiary. They are also considering giving their recently divorced son $100,000 to start a financial counseling practice. He is their only child, but he has two children of his own. One, age 25, is disabled, lives in a group home, and receives Medicaid. The other is a freshman in college. Although a bit ashamed to admit as much, the Howards do not have a will and have made no plans for their estate. Their overriding fear is that they will outlive their money.

Questions

1. Should Lee and Marta be concerned about probate? Why or why not?

2. What should Lee and Marta include in a letter of last instructions?

3. Help the Howards understand the differences between revocable and irrevocable living trusts by listing the advantages and disadvantages of both.

4. How might the Howards use trusts to benefit their grandchildren? How might these strategies affect their estate taxes?

5. What options does Lee have for gifting his whole life insurance policy, either to an individual or a charity? What are the consequences for his estate tax planning?

6. Would you recommend that Lee and Marta write their own will or should they hire an attorney? Explain your answer.

7. Once they have a completed and signed will, where should they keep it? Where should they definitely not keep the will?

8. Assume that Lee and Marta (a) own all assets jointly, except for the life insurance policy that Lee owns, and (b) decide not to gift or establish trusts. If Lee were to die in 2012 and leave his assets to Marta through a marital transfer, how much of the estate would be subject to taxes if Marta dies later in 2012 (assuming the estate growth is offset by all expenses incurred in 2012)?

9. If after Lee's death, Marta decided to (a) give her son the $100,000, (b) establish two $1,000,000 irrevocable trusts for the grandchildren, and (c) give another $500,000 to charity, how much

of the estate would be subject to taxes if Marta were to die later in 2012 (assuming the estate growth is offset by all expenses incurred in 2012)?

10. Given the ages of the Howards, should they consider naming their son in a durable power of attorney document? What are the advantages and disadvantages of this?

Be a Financial Planner—Discussion Case 2

This case is available in MyFinanceLab.

Cindy and Ned Lipman were recently married, each for the second time. Both are concerned about leaving assets to the adult children from their previous marriages and are reluctant to combine their individual assets. Together, they have an estate valued at $5.25 million, of which $2,100,000 is in Cindy's name and $2,350,000 is in Ned's name. They live in Cindy's $800,000 home that she received in her divorce settlement. Cindy and Ned have not revised their wills since their marriage. The wills still name their previous spouses as executor and beneficiary of their respective estates.

Planning for incapacitation is another estate planning concern. Cindy's 86-year-old mother and 84-year-old uncle both have Alzheimer's disease and she is concerned that it may be hereditary. Ned recently lost his father to a long-term illness and has vowed never to be kept "alive" by medical technology, confined to a hospital bed. Cindy, on the other hand, believes all steps should be taken to prolong a person's life.

Questions

1. What type of trust is appropriate for remarried couples such as the Lipmans? How might your answer change if the individuals have sufficient assets to provide for himself or herself independently following the death of either spouse?

2. Should either of them die in 2012, how much estate tax would Cindy and Ned owe on their respective estates? How does the portable estate exemption affect their potential tax liability?

3. What can Cindy and Ned do to address their concerns about estate planning in the event of incapacitation?

4. Would Cindy and Ned make good health care proxies for one another? Why or why not?

5. Since Cindy and Ned both have valid wills, are revisions necessary? If so, what changes should be made?

Be a Financial Planner—Continuing Case: Cory and Tisha Dumont

After finding the Web site deathclock.com, Cory talked Tisha into checking out their life expectancies. The "pessimistic" view projected that Cory would die at age 53. Cory jokingly commented, "Forget the life insurance premiums and saving for retirement, I'm living it up *now*!" The "normal" perspective projected that Cory would live to age 73, whereas Tisha was projected to die at the age of 79. Her reply to Cory, "You may live it up now, but I've got 6 years to live it up without you! And, if I inherit all our assets, I could be a wealthy old lady! We need to save and invest even more. I wonder how much fun a wealthy old lady could have?" Although Cory and Tisha could joke about their deathclock.com experience, it did raise some important financial issues for them to consider. They don't plan to retire or to transfer their estate anytime soon, but their concerns are clearly a part of the financial planning process.

With your assistance, they have reviewed their spending, credit usage, insurance needs, and investment plans. In short, by developing a financial plan and changing a few spending habits, they are building an estate for the future. They are concerned about financial independence during their "golden years"—however long they might be—and want to make the most of their retirement options. They are also concerned about preserving their estate for the benefit of Chad and Haley, regardless of the timing of their deaths.

Questions

1. Assuming the "deathclock" projection is accurate, Cory is concerned about getting back as much as possible of his Social Security taxes. At what age can he retire and receive full Social Security benefits? If he delays retirement, what percentage increase in his benefits can he expect? What is the earliest age that Cory can retire and receive Social Security? How will early retirement affect his benefits?

2. If Cory or Tisha were to die tomorrow, what kind of Social Security benefits, if any, would the surviving spouse, Chad, and Haley receive? For how long?

3. Both Cory and Tisha are contributing to a "qualified" or tax-favored 401(k) retirement plan at work.

   a. What are two unique benefits of such a plan?

   b. Why are these benefits and the time value of money particularly important in retirement planning?

   c. What must the Dumonts do to be "active participants"?

   d. What are "catch-up" provisions? Why and how are they used?

4. Cory and Tisha are interested in other retirement saving strategies. What is the maximum amount they could contribute to an IRA? If they decided to contribute to a traditional IRA, would they receive a full or partial tax deduction? Why? What are the advantages and disadvantages of opening a Roth IRA instead of a traditional IRA? What advantages are common to both plans?

5. Cory's company is planning to convert all employees to a cash-balance retirement plan. Explain this plan, noting advantages and disadvantages for Cory.

6. The Dumonts estimate their current living expenses at approximately $64,000, which they joke could be very comfortable *without the kids* that they won't have during retirement. (*Hint:* To answer the following questions, consult Worksheet 16, use a financial calculator as discussed in Chapter 3, or the Money in Motion calculator, which is available in MyFinanceLab.)

   a. How much income, before and after taxes, will they need to retire, assuming an average tax rate of 17 percent during retirement?

   b. Assume that through a combination of savings, Social Security, and retirement plan distributions Cory and Tisha are able to receive $45,000 annually in retirement. Determine their retirement income shortfall. Assuming a 4 percent inflation rate and 35 years until retirement, calculate their inflation-adjusted shortfall.

   c. If Cory and Tisha can earn a 5 percent inflation-adjusted return, determine how much they must accumulate in savings over the 35 years to fund the annual inflation-adjusted shortfall as calculated earlier.

   d. How much do the Dumonts need to start saving each year for the next 35 years at 9 percent to meet their saving accumulation goal as calculated in part c?

7. If, for 30 years, Cory and Tisha invested $2,000 at the end of every year in a tax-free account, what would be the future value of the account if they earned 9 percent annually? If, instead, they first paid taxes (marginal tax rate of 15 percent) and then made the investment, how much would the account be worth at the end of 30 years? Based on these calculations, what advice would you give to Cory and Tisha regarding their retirement savings? What principle of saving in an IRS tax-deferred plan does this example demonstrate? Use a financial calculator as discussed in Chapter 3, or the Money in Motion calculator that is available in MyFinanceLab.

8. Recall that Cory has $2,500 in retirement funds with a former employer. When Cory resigned, the account value was almost $4,000, but only part of it was available to him. Explain how vesting rules explain the difference between the two

dollar amounts. What options and tax implications should Cory compare to claim his retirement benefits?

9. Cory has considered using the $2,500 for a surprise vacation for the family, an IRA account, or another mutual fund account to fund a 25-year anniversary trip with Tisha. Could he roll over the distribution from the qualified plan to a traditional IRA invested in a mutual fund (remember, no income taxes have been paid on the contributions), and in 19 years take money out for the trip? What are the tax implications of this plan instead of funding a taxable mutual fund account?

10. Tisha has considered offering accounting services to small businesses. She has obtained a business license and plans to work out of her home. Would she qualify for a small business/self-employed retirement plan? If so, what plan should she consider?

11. Tisha has indicated that she thinks a single life annuity will be her choice when she begins to receive retirement pension benefits. She thinks this is the best pay-out structure because (a) she has earned the entire benefit, (b) she can control the investment of the funds, and (c) Cory will receive his own pension. Will Tisha automatically be able to choose a single life annuity payout option? Assuming that Cory does not want Tisha to have a single life annuity, what type of joint and survivor annuity will provide the greatest immediate payout and provide Cory a guaranteed income should he outlive Tisha?

12. After retirement, what expected and unexpected changes should the Dumonts monitor to safeguard their future?

13. At this stage of the life cycle, which of the objectives of estate planning are most important to the Dumont household? Preparation of what two estate planning documents would enable them to accomplish these objectives? Where should the documents be kept?

14. Recall that Cory's parents recently gave each of the children a $20,000 gift to be invested for college. How much federal income tax and gift tax are due on this trans-fer? Will there be any generation-skipping transfer tax due? The senior Dumonts planned to give Chad $30,000 instead of $20,000 but were advised not to. Why?

15. Cory and Tisha want to develop other saving strategies to fund education costs. What are the advantages or disadvantages of opening a Coverdell Education Savings Account or a 529 plan for each of the children? Could they establish both types of accounts?

16. The Dumonts are curious as to why someone would want to avoid probate. Having the court oversee the will and the distribution of assets sounds like a good thing. Explain why avoiding probate may be an important issue in estate planning. What four steps could the Dumonts take to avoid probate?

17. Recently, Cory reluctantly agreed to be named as executor for his older sister Emily's estate. Does serving as executor include acting as guardian for her child, who is younger than Chad and Haley? What are the duties that Cory would be expected to perform as executor?

18. The Dumonts recently noticed on their bank statement that their accounts are owned jointly with right of survivorship. Provide a simple explanation of this term.

19. The Dumonts have always considered a trust a financial tool of the wealthy. But they do want to learn more about estate planning. Provide a simple explanation of how both living and testamentary trusts, which by definition are quite different, can accomplish the same purpose of reducing estate taxes.

20. Cory's parents have always joked that they plan to cheat the "tax man" by dying broke. Their estate planning strategy involves utilizing the unlimited marital deduction. Explain how relying on the unlimited marital deduction may not always be an effective planning strategy.

Compound Sum of $1

n	1%	2%	3%	4%	5%	6%	7%	8%	9%	10%
1	1.010	1.020	1.030	1.040	1.050	1.060	1.070	1.080	1.090	1.100
2	1.020	1.040	1.061	1.082	1.102	1.124	1.145	1.166	1.188	1.210
3	1.030	1.061	1.093	1.125	1.158	1.191	1.225	1.260	1.295	1.331
4	1.041	1.082	1.126	1.170	1.216	1.262	1.311	1.360	1.412	1.464
5	1.051	1.104	1.159	1.217	1.276	1.338	1.403	1.469	1.539	1.611
6	1.062	1.126	1.194	1.265	1.340	1.419	1.501	1.587	1.677	1.772
7	1.072	1.149	1.230	1.316	1.407	1.504	1.606	1.714	1.828	1.949
8	1.083	1.172	1.267	1.369	1.477	1.594	1.718	1.851	1.993	2.144
9	1.094	1.195	1.305	1.423	1.551	1.689	1.838	1.999	2.172	2.358
10	1.105	1.219	1.344	1.480	1.629	1.791	1.967	2.159	2.367	2.594
11	1.116	1.243	1.384	1.539	1.710	1.898	2.105	2.332	2.580	2.853
12	1.127	1.268	1.426	1.601	1.796	2.012	2.252	2.518	2.813	3.138
13	1.138	1.294	1.469	1.665	1.886	2.133	2.410	2.720	3.066	3.452
14	1.149	1.319	1.513	1.732	1.980	2.261	2.579	2.937	3.342	3.797
15	1.161	1.346	1.558	1.801	2.079	2.397	2.759	3.172	3.642	4.177
16	1.173	1.373	1.605	1.873	2.183	2.540	2.952	3.426	3.970	4.595
17	1.184	1.400	1.653	1.948	2.292	2.693	3.159	3.700	4.328	5.054
18	1.196	1.428	1.702	2.026	2.407	2.854	3.380	3.996	4.717	5.560
19	1.208	1.457	1.753	2.107	2.527	3.026	3.616	4.316	5.142	6.116
20	1.220	1.486	1.806	2.191	2.653	3.207	3.870	4.661	5.604	6.727
21	1.232	1.516	1.860	2.279	2.786	3.399	4.140	5.034	6.109	7.400
22	1.245	1.546	1.916	2.370	2.925	3.603	4.430	5.436	6.658	8.140
23	1.257	1.577	1.974	2.465	3.071	3.820	4.740	5.871	7.258	8.954
24	1.270	1.608	2.033	2.563	3.225	4.049	5.072	6.341	7.911	9.850
25	1.282	1.641	2.094	2.666	3.386	4.292	5.427	6.848	8.623	10.834
30	1.348	1.811	2.427	3.243	4.322	5.743	7.612	10.062	13.267	17.449
40	1.489	2.208	3.262	4.801	7.040	10.285	14.974	21.724	31.408	45.258
50	1.645	2.691	4.384	7.106	11.467	18.419	29.456	46.900	74.354	117.386

n	11%	12%	13%	14%	15%	16%	17%	18%	19%	20%
1	1.110	1.120	1.130	1.140	1.150	1.160	1.170	1.180	1.190	1.200
2	1.232	1.254	1.277	1.300	1.322	1.346	1.369	1.392	1.416	1.440
3	1.368	1.405	1.443	1.482	1.521	1.561	1.602	1.643	1.685	1.728
4	1.518	1.574	1.630	1.689	1.749	1.811	1.874	1.939	2.005	2.074
5	1.685	1.762	1.842	1.925	2.011	2.100	2.192	2.288	2.386	2.488
6	1.870	1.974	2.082	2.195	2.313	2.436	2.565	2.700	2.840	2.986
7	2.076	2.211	2.353	2.502	2.660	2.826	3.001	3.185	3.379	3.583
8	2.305	2.476	2.658	2.853	3.059	3.278	3.511	3.759	4.021	4.300
9	2.558	2.773	3.004	3.252	3.518	3.803	4.108	4.435	4.785	5.160
10	2.839	3.106	3.395	3.707	4.046	4.411	4.807	5.234	5.695	6.192
11	3.152	3.479	3.836	4.226	4.652	5.117	5.624	6.176	6.777	7.430
12	3.498	3.896	4.334	4.818	5.350	5.936	6.580	7.288	8.064	8.916
13	3.883	4.363	4.898	5.492	6.153	6.886	7.699	8.599	9.596	10.699
14	4.310	4.887	5.535	6.261	7.076	7.987	9.007	10.147	11.420	12.839
15	4.785	5.474	6.254	7.138	8.137	9.265	10.539	11.974	13.589	15.407
16	5.311	6.130	7.067	8.137	9.358	10.748	12.330	14.129	16.171	18.488
17	5.895	6.866	7.986	9.276	10.761	12.468	14.426	16.672	19.244	22.186
18	6.543	7.690	9.024	10.575	12.375	14.462	16.879	19.673	22.900	26.623
19	7.263	8.613	10.197	12.055	14.232	16.776	19.748	23.214	27.251	31.948
20	8.062	9.646	11.523	13.743	16.366	19.461	23.105	27.393	32.429	38.337
21	8.949	10.804	13.021	15.667	18.821	22.574	27.033	32.323	38.591	46.005
22	9.933	12.100	14.713	17.861	21.644	26.186	31.629	38.141	45.923	55.205
23	11.026	13.552	16.626	20.361	24.891	30.376	37.005	45.007	54.648	66.247
24	12.239	15.178	18.788	23.212	28.625	35.236	43.296	53.108	65.031	79.496
25	13.585	17.000	21.230	26.461	32.918	40.874	50.656	62.667	77.387	95.395
30	22.892	29.960	39.115	50.949	66.210	85.849	111.061	143.367	184.672	237.373
40	64.999	93.049	132.776	188.876	267.856	378.715	533.846	750.353	1051.642	1469.740
50	184.559	288.996	450.711	700.197	1083.619	1670.669	2566.080	3927.189	5988.730	9100.191

n	21%	22%	23%	24%	25%	26%	27%	28%	29%	30%
1	1.210	1.220	1.230	1.240	1.250	1.260	1.270	1.280	1.290	1.300
2	1.464	1.488	1.513	1.538	1.562	1.588	1.613	1.638	1.664	1.690
3	1.772	1.816	1.861	1.907	1.953	2.000	2.048	2.097	2.147	2.197
4	2.144	2.215	2.289	2.364	2.441	2.520	2.601	2.684	2.769	2.856
5	2.594	2.703	2.815	2.932	3.052	3.176	3.304	4.436	3.572	3.713
6	3.138	3.297	3.463	3.635	3.815	4.001	3.196	4.398	4.608	4.827
7	3.797	4.023	4.259	4.508	4.768	5.042	5.329	5.629	5.945	6.275
8	4.595	4.908	5.239	5.589	5.960	6.353	6.767	7.206	7.669	8.157
9	5.560	5.987	6.444	6.931	7.451	8.004	8.595	9.223	9.893	10.604
10	6.727	7.305	7.926	8.594	9.313	10.086	10.915	11.806	12.761	13.786
11	8.140	8.912	9.749	10.657	11.642	12.708	13.862	15.112	16.462	17.921
12	9.850	10.872	11.991	13.215	14.552	16.012	17.605	19.343	21.236	23.298
13	11.918	13.264	14.749	16.386	18.190	20.175	22.359	24.759	27.395	30.287
14	14.421	16.182	18.141	20.319	22.737	25.420	28.395	31.691	35.339	39.373
15	17.449	19.742	22.314	25.195	28.422	32.030	36.062	40.565	45.587	51.185
16	21.113	24.085	27.446	31.242	35.527	40.357	45.799	51.923	58.808	66.541
17	25.547	29.384	33.758	38.740	44.409	50.850	58.165	66.461	75.862	86.503
18	30.912	35.848	41.523	48.038	55.511	64.071	73.869	85.070	97.862	112.454
19	37.404	43.735	51.073	59.567	69.389	80.730	93.813	108.890	126.242	146.190
20	45.258	53.357	62.820	73.863	86.736	101.720	119.143	139.379	162.852	190.047
21	54.762	65.095	77.268	91.591	108.420	128.167	151.312	178.405	210.079	247.061
22	66.262	79.416	95.040	113.572	135.525	161.490	192.165	228.358	271.002	321.178
23	80.178	96.887	116.899	140.829	169.407	203.477	244.050	292.298	349.592	417.431
24	97.015	118.203	143.786	174.628	211.758	256.381	309.943	374.141	450.974	542.791
25	117.388	144.207	176.857	216.539	264.698	323.040	393.628	478.901	581.756	705.627
30	304.471	389.748	497.904	634.810	807.793	1025.904	1300.477	1645.488	2078.208	2619.936
40	2048.309	2846.941	3946.340	5455.797	7523.156	10346.879	14195.051	19426.418	26520.723	36117.754
50	13779.844	20795.680	31278.301	46889.207	70064.812	104354.562	154942.687	229345.875	338440.000	497910.125

n	31%	32%	33%	34%	35%	36%	37%	38%	39%	40%
1	1.310	1.320	1.330	1.340	1.350	1.360	1.370	1.380	1.390	1.400
2	1.716	1.742	1.769	1.796	1.822	1.850	1.877	1.904	1.932	1.960
3	2.248	2.300	2.353	2.406	2.460	2.515	2.571	2.628	2.686	2.744
4	2.945	3.036	3.129	3.224	3.321	3.421	3.523	3.627	3.733	3.842
5	3.858	4.007	4.162	4.320	4.484	4.653	4.826	5.005	5.189	5.378
6	5.054	5.290	5.535	5.789	6.053	6.328	6.612	6.907	7.213	7.530
7	6.621	6.983	7.361	7.758	8.172	8.605	9.058	9.531	10.025	10.541
8	8.673	9.217	9.791	10.395	11.032	11.703	12.410	13.153	13.935	14.758
9	11.362	12.166	13.022	13.930	14.894	15.917	17.001	18.151	19.370	20.661
10	14.884	16.060	17.319	18.666	20.106	21.646	23.292	25.049	26.924	28.925
11	19.498	21.199	23.034	25.012	27.144	29.439	31.910	34.567	37.425	40.495
12	25.542	27.982	30.635	33.516	36.644	40.037	43.716	47.703	52.020	56.694
13	33.460	36.937	40.745	44.912	49.469	54.451	59.892	65.830	72.308	79.371
14	43.832	49.756	54.190	60.181	66.784	74.053	82.051	90.845	100.509	111.120
15	57.420	64.358	72.073	80.643	90.158	100.712	112.410	125.366	139.707	155.567
16	75.220	84.953	95.857	108.061	121.713	136.968	154.002	173.005	194.192	217.793
17	98.539	112.138	127.490	144.802	164.312	186.277	210.983	238.747	269.927	304.911
18	129.086	148.022	169.561	194.035	221.822	253.337	289.046	329.471	375.198	426.875
19	169.102	195.389	225.517	260.006	299.459	344.537	395.993	454.669	521.525	597.625
20	221.523	257.913	299.937	348.408	404.270	468.571	542.511	627.443	724.919	836.674
21	290.196	340.446	398.916	466.867	545.764	637.256	743.240	865.871	1007.637	1171.343
22	380.156	449.388	530.558	625.601	736.781	865.668	1018.238	1194.900	1400.615	1639.878
23	498.004	593.192	705.642	838.305	994.653	1178.668	1394.986	1648.961	1946.854	2295.829
24	652.385	783.013	938.504	1123.328	1342.781	1602.988	1911.129	2275.564	2706.125	3214.158
25	854.623	1033.577	1248.210	1505.258	1812.754	2180.063	2618.245	3140.275	3761.511	4499.816
30	3297.081	4142.008	5194.516	6503.285	8128.426	10142.914	12636.086	15716.703	19517.969	24201.043
40	49072.621	66519.313	89962.188	121388.437	163433.875	219558.625	294317.937	393684.687	525508.312	700022.688

APPENDIX
B Present Value of $1

n	1%	2%	3%	4%	5%	6%	7%	8%	9%	10%
1	.990	.980	.971	.962	.952	.943	.935	.926	.917	.909
2	.980	.961	.943	.925	.907	.890	.873	.857	.842	.826
3	.971	.942	.915	.889	.864	.840	.816	.794	.772	.751
4	.961	.924	.888	.855	.823	.792	.763	.735	.708	.683
5	.951	.906	.863	.822	.784	.747	.713	.681	.650	.621
6	.942	.888	.837	.790	.746	.705	.666	.630	.596	.564
7	.933	.871	.813	.760	.711	.665	.623	.583	.547	.513
8	.923	.853	.789	.731	.677	.627	.582	.540	.502	.467
9	.914	.837	.766	.703	.645	.592	.544	.500	.460	.424
10	.905	.820	.744	.676	.614	.558	.508	.463	.422	.386
11	.896	.804	.722	.650	.585	.527	.475	.429	.388	.350
12	.887	.789	.701	.625	.557	.497	.444	.397	.356	.319
13	.879	.773	.681	.601	.530	.469	.415	.368	.326	.290
14	.870	.758	.661	.577	.505	.442	.388	.340	.299	.263
15	.861	.743	.642	.555	.481	.417	.362	.315	.275	.239
16	.853	.728	.623	.534	.458	.394	.339	.292	.252	.218
17	.844	.714	.605	.513	.436	.371	.317	.270	.231	.198
18	.836	.700	.587	.494	.416	.350	.296	.250	.212	.180
19	.828	.686	.570	.475	.396	.331	.277	.232	.194	.164
20	.820	.673	.554	.456	.377	.312	.258	.215	.178	.149
21	.811	.660	.538	.439	.359	.294	.242	.199	.164	.135
22	.803	.647	.522	.422	.342	.278	.226	.184	.150	.123
23	.795	.634	.507	.406	.326	.262	.211	.170	.138	.112
24	.788	.622	.492	.390	.310	.247	.197	.158	.126	.102
25	.780	.610	.478	.375	.295	.233	.184	.146	.116	.092
30	.742	.552	.412	.308	.231	.174	.131	.099	.075	.057
40	.672	.453	.307	.208	.142	.097	.067	.046	.032	.022
50	.608	.372	.228	.141	.087	.054	.034	.021	.013	.009

n	11%	12%	13%	14%	15%	16%	17%	18%	19%	20%
1	.901	.893	.885	.877	.870	.862	.855	.847	.840	.833
2	.812	.797	.783	.769	.756	.743	.731	.718	.706	.694
3	.731	.712	.693	.675	.658	.641	.624	.609	.593	.579
4	.659	.636	.613	.592	.572	.552	.534	.516	.499	.482
5	.593	.567	.543	.519	.497	.476	.456	.437	.419	.402
6	.535	.507	.480	.456	.432	.410	.390	.370	.352	.335
7	.482	.452	.425	.400	.376	.354	.333	.314	.296	.279
8	.434	.404	.376	.351	.327	.305	.285	.266	.249	.233
9	.391	.361	.333	.308	.284	.263	.243	.225	.209	.194
10	.352	.322	.295	.270	.247	.227	.208	.191	.176	.162
11	.317	.287	.261	.237	.215	.195	.178	.162	.148	.135
12	.286	.257	.231	.208	.187	.168	.152	.137	.124	.112
13	.258	.229	.204	.182	.163	.145	.130	.116	.104	.093
14	.232	.205	.181	.160	.141	.125	.111	.099	.088	.078
15	.209	.183	.160	.140	.123	.108	.095	.084	.074	.065
16	.188	.163	.141	.123	.107	.093	.081	.071	.062	.054
17	.170	.146	.125	.108	.093	.080	.069	.060	.052	.045
18	.153	.130	.111	.095	.081	.069	.059	.051	.044	.038
19	.138	.116	.098	.083	.070	.060	.051	.043	.037	.031
20	.124	.104	.087	.073	.061	.051	.043	.037	.031	.026
21	.112	.093	.077	.064	.053	.044	.037	.031	.026	.022
22	.101	.083	.068	.056	.046	.038	.032	.026	.022	.018
23	.091	.074	.060	.049	.040	.033	.027	.022	.018	.015
24	.082	.066	.053	.043	.035	.028	.023	.019	.015	.013
25	.074	.059	.047	.038	.030	.024	.020	.016	.013	.010
30	.044	.033	.026	.020	.015	.012	.009	.007	.005	.004
40	.015	.011	.008	.005	.004	.003	.002	.001	.001	.001
50	.005	.003	.002	.001	.001	.001	.000	.000	.000	.000

n	21%	22%	23%	24%	25%	26%	27%	28%	29%	30%
1	.826	.820	.813	.806	.800	.794	.787	.781	.775	.769
2	.683	.672	.661	.650	.640	.630	.620	.610	.601	.592
3	.564	.551	.537	.524	.512	.500	.488	.477	.466	.455
4	.467	.451	.437	.423	.410	.397	.384	.373	.361	.350
5	.386	.370	.355	.341	.328	.315	.303	.291	.280	.269
6	.319	.303	.289	.275	.262	.250	.238	.227	.217	.207
7	.263	.249	.235	.222	.210	.198	.188	.178	.168	.159
8	.218	.204	.191	.179	.168	.157	.148	.139	.130	.123
9	.180	.167	.155	.144	.134	.125	.116	.108	.101	.094
10	.149	.137	.126	.116	.107	.099	.092	.085	.078	.073
11	.123	.112	.103	.094	.086	.079	.072	.066	.061	.056
12	.102	.092	.083	.076	.069	.062	.057	.052	.047	.043
13	.084	.075	.068	.061	.055	.050	.045	.040	.037	.033
14	.069	.062	.055	.049	.044	.039	.035	.032	.028	.025
15	.057	.051	.045	.040	.035	.031	.028	.025	.022	.020
16	.047	.042	.036	.032	.028	.025	.022	.019	.017	.015
17	.039	.034	.030	.026	.023	.020	.017	.015	.013	.012
18	.032	.028	.024	.021	.018	.016	.014	.012	.010	.009
19	.027	.023	.020	.017	.014	.012	.011	.009	.008	.007
20	.022	.019	.016	.014	.012	.010	.008	.007	.006	.005
21	.018	.015	.013	.011	.009	.008	.007	.006	.005	.004
22	.015	.013	.011	.009	.007	.006	.005	.004	.004	.003
23	.012	.010	.009	.007	.006	.005	.004	.003	.003	.002
24	.010	.008	.007	.006	.005	.004	.003	.003	.002	.002
25	.009	.007	.006	.005	.004	.003	.003	.002	.002	.001
30	.003	.003	.002	.002	.001	.001	.001	.001	.000	.000
40	.000	.000	.000	.000	.000	.000	.000	.000	.000	.000
50	.000	.000	.000	.000	.000	.000	.000	.000	.000	.000

n	31%	32%	33%	34%	35%	36%	37%	38%	39%	40%
1	.763	.758	.752	.746	.741	.735	.730	.725	.719	.714
2	.583	.574	.565	.557	.549	.541	.533	.525	.518	.510
3	.445	.435	.425	.416	.406	.398	.389	.381	.372	.364
4	.340	.329	.320	.310	.301	.292	.284	.276	.268	.260
5	.259	.250	.240	.231	.223	.215	.207	.200	.193	.186
6	.198	.189	.181	.173	.165	.158	.151	.145	.139	.133
7	.151	.143	.136	.129	.122	.116	.110	.105	.100	.095
8	.115	.108	.102	.096	.091	.085	.081	.076	.072	.068
9	.088	.082	.077	.072	.067	.063	.059	.055	.052	.048
10	.067	.062	.058	.054	.050	.046	.043	.040	.037	.035
11	.051	.047	.043	.040	.037	.034	.031	.029	.027	.025
12	.039	.036	.033	.030	.027	.025	.023	.021	.019	.018
13	.030	.027	.025	.022	.020	.018	.017	.015	.014	.013
14	.023	.021	.018	.017	.015	.014	.012	.011	.010	.009
15	.017	.016	.014	.012	.011	.010	.009	.008	.007	.006
16	.013	.012	.010	.009	.008	.007	.006	.006	.005	.005
17	.010	.009	.008	.007	.006	.005	.005	.004	.004	.003
18	.008	.007	.006	.005	.005	.004	.003	.003	.003	.002
19	.006	.005	.004	.004	.003	.003	.003	.002	.002	.002
20	.005	.004	.003	.003	.002	.002	.002	.002	.001	.001
21	.003	.003	.003	.002	.002	.002	.001	.001	.001	.001
22	.003	.002	.002	.002	.001	.001	.001	.001	.001	.001
23	.002	.002	.001	.001	.001	.001	.001	.001	.001	.000
24	.002	.001	.001	.001	.001	.001	.001	.000	.000	.000
25	.001	.001	.001	.001	.001	.000	.000	.000	.000	.000
30	.000	.000	.000	.000	.000	.000	.000	.000	.000	.000
40	.000	.000	.000	.000	.000	.000	.000	.000	.000	.000

C Compound Sum of an Annuity of $1 for *n* Periods

n	1%	2%	3%	4%	5%	6%	7%	8%	9%	10%
1	1.000	1.000	1.000	1.000	1.000	1.000	1.000	1.000	1.000	1.000
2	2.010	2.020	2.030	2.040	2.050	2.060	2.070	2.080	2.090	2.100
3	3.030	3.060	3.091	3.122	3.152	3.184	3.215	3.246	3.278	3.310
4	4.060	4.122	4.184	4.246	4.310	4.375	4.440	4.506	4.573	4.641
5	5.101	5.204	5.309	5.416	5.526	5.637	5.751	5.867	5.985	6.105
6	6.152	6.308	6.468	6.633	6.802	6.975	7.153	7.336	7.523	7.716
7	7.214	7.434	7.662	7.898	8.142	8.394	8.654	8.923	9.200	9.487
8	8.286	8.583	8.892	9.214	9.549	9.897	10.260	10.637	11.028	11.436
9	9.368	9.755	10.159	10.583	11.027	11.491	11.978	12.488	13.021	13.579
10	10.462	10.950	11.464	12.006	12.578	13.181	13.816	14.487	15.193	15.937
11	11.567	12.169	12.808	13.486	14.207	14.972	15.784	16.645	17.560	18.531
12	12.682	13.412	14.192	15.026	15.917	16.870	17.888	18.977	20.141	21.384
13	13.809	14.680	15.618	16.627	17.713	18.882	20.141	21.495	22.953	24.523
14	14.947	15.974	17.086	18.292	19.598	21.015	22.550	24.215	26.019	27.975
15	16.097	17.293	18.599	20.023	21.578	23.276	25.129	27.152	29.361	31.772
16	17.258	18.639	20.157	21.824	23.657	25.672	27.888	30.324	33.003	35.949
17	18.430	20.012	21.761	23.697	25.840	28.213	30.840	33.750	36.973	40.544
18	19.614	21.412	23.414	25.645	28.132	30.905	33.999	37.450	41.301	45.599
19	20.811	22.840	25.117	27.671	30.539	33.760	37.379	41.446	46.018	51.158
20	22.019	24.297	26.870	29.778	33.066	36.785	40.995	45.762	51.159	57.274
21	23.239	25.783	28.676	31.969	35.719	39.992	44.865	50.422	56.764	64.002
22	24.471	27.299	30.536	34.248	38.505	43.392	49.005	55.456	62.872	71.402
23	25.716	28.845	32.452	36.618	41.430	46.995	53.435	60.893	69.531	79.542
24	26.973	30.421	34.426	39.082	44.501	50.815	58.176	66.764	76.789	88.496
25	28.243	32.030	36.459	41.645	47.726	54.864	63.248	73.105	84.699	98.346
30	34.784	40.567	47.575	56.084	66.438	79.957	94.459	113.282	136.305	164.491
40	48.885	60.401	75.400	95.024	120.797	154.758	199.630	295.052	337.872	442.580
50	64.461	84.577	112.794	152.664	209.341	290.325	406.516	573.756	815.051	1163.865

n	11%	12%	13%	14%	15%	16%	17%	18%	19%	20%
1	1.000	1.000	1.000	1.000	1.000	1.000	1.000	1.000	1.000	1.000
2	2.110	2.120	2.130	2.140	2.150	2.160	2.170	2.180	2.190	2.200
3	3.342	3.374	3.407	3.440	3.472	3.506	3.539	3.572	3.606	3.640
4	4.710	4.779	4.850	4.921	4.993	5.066	5.141	5.215	5.291	5.368
5	6.228	6.353	6.480	6.610	6.742	6.877	7.014	7.154	7.297	7.442
6	7.913	8.115	8.323	8.535	8.754	8.977	9.207	9.442	9.683	9.930
7	9.783	10.089	10.405	10.730	11.067	11.414	11.772	12.141	12.523	12.916
8	11.859	12.300	12.757	13.233	13.727	14.240	14.773	15.327	15.902	16.499
9	14.164	14.776	15.416	16.085	16.786	17.518	18.285	19.086	19.923	20.799
10	16.722	17.549	18.420	19.337	20.304	21.321	22.393	23.521	24.709	25.959
11	19.561	20.655	21.814	23.044	24.349	25.733	27.200	28.755	30.403	32.150
12	22.713	24.133	25.650	27.271	29.001	30.850	32.824	34.931	37.180	39.580
13	26.211	28.029	29.984	32.088	34.352	36.786	39.404	42.218	45.244	48.496
14	30.095	32.392	34.882	37.581	40.504	43.672	47.102	50.818	54.841	59.196
15	34.405	37.280	40.417	43.842	47.580	51.659	56.109	60.965	66.260	72.035
16	39.190	42.753	46.671	50.980	55.717	60.925	66.648	72.938	79.850	87.442
17	44.500	48.883	53.738	59.117	65.075	71.673	78.978	87.067	96.021	105.930
18	50.396	55.749	61.724	68.393	75.836	84.140	93.404	103.739	115.265	128.116
19	56.939	63.439	70.748	78.968	88.211	98.603	110.283	123.412	138.165	154.739
20	64.202	72.052	80.946	91.024	102.443	115.379	130.031	146.626	165.417	186.687
21	72.264	81.698	92.468	104.767	118.809	134.840	153.136	174.019	197.846	225.024
22	81.213	92.502	105.489	120.434	137.630	157.414	180.169	206.342	236.436	271.028
23	91.147	104.602	120.203	138.295	159.274	183.600	211.798	244.483	282.359	326.234
24	102.173	118.154	136.829	158.656	184.166	213.976	248.803	289.490	337.007	392.480
25	114.412	133.333	115.616	181.867	212.790	249.212	292.099	342.598	402.038	471.976
30	199.018	241.330	293.192	356.778	434.738	530.306	647.423	790.932	966.698	1181.865
40	581.812	767.080	1013.667	1341.979	1779.048	2360.724	3134.412	4163.094	5529.711	7343.715
50	1668.723	2399.975	3459.344	4994.301	7217.488	10435.449	15088.805	21812.273	31514.492	45496.094

n	21%	22%	23%	24%	25%	26%	27%	28%	29%	30%
1	1.000	1.000	1.000	1.000	1.000	1.000	1.000	1.000	1.000	1.000
2	2.210	2.220	2.230	2.240	2.250	2.260	2.270	2.280	2.290	2.300
3	3.674	3.708	3.743	3.778	3.813	3.848	3.883	3.918	3.954	3.990
4	5.446	5.524	5.604	5.684	5.766	5.848	5.931	6.016	6.101	6.187
5	7.589	7.740	7.893	8.048	8.207	8.368	8.533	8.700	8.870	9.043
6	10.183	10.442	10.708	10.980	11.259	11.544	11.837	12.136	12.442	12.756
7	13.321	13.740	14.171	14.615	15.073	15.546	16.032	16.534	17.051	17.583
8	17.119	17.762	18.430	19.123	19.842	20.588	21.361	22.163	22.995	23.858
9	21.714	22.670	23.669	24.712	25.802	26.940	28.129	29.369	30.664	32.015
10	27.274	28.657	20.113	31.643	33.253	34.945	36.723	38.592	40.556	42.619
11	34.001	35.962	38.039	40.238	42.566	45.030	47.639	50.398	53.318	56.405
12	42.141	44.873	47.787	50.895	54.208	57.730	61.501	65.510	69.780	74.326
13	51.991	45.745	59.778	64.109	68.760	73.750	79.106	84.853	91.016	97.624
14	63.909	69.009	74.528	80.496	86.949	93.925	101.465	109.611	118.411	127.912
15	78.330	65.191	92.669	100.815	109.687	119.346	129.860	141.302	153.750	167.285
16	95.779	104.933	114.983	126.010	138.109	151.375	165.922	181.867	199.337	218.470
17	116.892	129.019	142.428	157.252	173.636	191.733	211.721	233.790	258.145	285.011
18	142.439	158.403	176.187	195.993	218.045	242.583	269.885	300.250	334.006	371.514
19	173.351	194.251	217.710	244.031	273.556	306.654	343.754	385.321	431.868	483.968
20	210.755	237.986	268.783	303.598	342.945	387.384	437.568	494.210	558.110	630.157
21	256.013	291.343	331.603	377.461	429.681	489.104	556.710	633.589	720.962	820.204
22	310.775	356.438	408.871	469.052	538.101	617.270	708.022	811.993	931.040	1067.265
23	377.038	435.854	503.911	582.624	673.626	778.760	900.187	1040.351	1202.042	1388.443
24	457.215	532.741	620.810	723.453	843.032	982.237	1144.237	1332.649	1551.634	1805.975
25	554.230	650.944	764.596	898.082	1054.791	1238.617	1454.180	1706.790	2002.608	2348.765
30	1445.111	1767.044	2160.459	2640.881	3227.172	3941.953	4812.891	5873.172	7162.785	8729.805
40	9749.141	12936.141	17153.691	22728.367	30088.621	39791.957	52570.707	69376.562	91447.375	120389.375

n	31%	32%	33%	34%	35%	36%	37%	38%	39%	40%
1	1.000	1.000	1.000	1.000	1.000	1.000	1.000	1.000	1.000	1.000
2	2.310	2.320	2.330	2.340	2.350	2.360	2.370	2.380	2.390	2.400
3	4.026	4.062	4.099	4.136	4.172	4.210	4.247	4.284	4.322	4.360
4	6.274	6.363	6.452	6.542	6.633	6.725	6.818	6.912	7.008	7.104
5	9.219	9.398	9.581	9.766	9.954	10.146	10.341	10.539	10.741	10.946
6	13.077	13.406	13.742	14.086	14.438	14.799	15.167	15.544	15.930	16.324
7	18.131	18.696	19.277	19.876	20.492	21.126	21.779	22.451	23.142	23.853
8	24.752	25.678	26.638	27.633	28.664	29.732	30.837	31.982	33.167	34.395
9	33.425	34.895	36.429	38.028	39.696	41.435	43.247	45.135	47.103	49.152
10	44.786	47.062	49.451	51.958	54.590	57.351	60.248	63.287	66.473	69.813
11	59.670	63.121	66.769	70.624	74.696	78.998	83.540	88.335	93.397	98.739
12	79.167	84.320	89.803	95.636	101.840	108.437	115.450	122.903	130.822	139.234
13	104.709	112.302	120.438	129.152	138.484	148.474	159.166	170.606	182.842	195.928
14	138.169	149.239	161.183	174.063	187.953	202.925	219.058	236.435	255.151	275.299
15	182.001	197.996	215.373	234.245	254.737	276.978	301.109	327.281	355.659	386.418
16	239.421	262.354	287.446	314.888	344.895	377.690	413.520	542.647	495.366	541.985
17	314.642	347.307	383.303	422.949	466.608	514.658	567.521	625.652	689.558	759.778
18	413.180	459.445	510.792	567.751	630.920	700.935	778.504	864.399	959.485	1064.689
19	542.266	607.467	680.354	761.786	852.741	954.271	1067.551	1193.870	1334.683	1491.563
20	711.368	802.856	905.870	1021.792	1152.200	1298.809	1463.544	1648.539	1856.208	2089.188
21	932.891	1060.769	1205.807	1370.201	1556.470	1767.380	2006.055	2275.982	2581.128	2925.862
22	1223.087	1401.215	1604.724	1837.068	2102.234	2404.636	2749.294	3141.852	3588.765	4097.203
23	1603.243	1850.603	2135.282	2462.669	2839.014	3271.304	3767.532	4336.750	4989.379	5737.078
24	2101.247	2443.795	2840.924	3300.974	3833.667	4449.969	5162.516	5985.711	6936.230	8032.906
25	2753.631	3226.808	3779.428	4424.301	5176.445	6052.957	7073.645	8261.273	9642.352	11247.062
30	10632.543	12940.672	15737.945	19124.434	23221.258	28172.016	34148.906	41357.227	50043.625	60500.207

D Present Value of an Annuity of $1 for n Periods

n	1%	2%	3%	4%	5%	6%	7%	8%	9%	10%
1	.990	.980	.971	.962	.952	.943	.935	.926	.917	.909
2	1.970	1.942	1.913	1.886	1.859	1.833	1.808	1.783	1.759	1.736
3	2.941	2.884	2.829	2.775	2.723	2.673	2.624	2.577	2.531	2.487
4	3.902	3.808	3.717	3.630	3.546	3.465	3.387	3.312	3.240	3.170
5	4.853	4.713	4.580	4.452	4.329	4.212	4.100	3.993	3.890	3.791
6	5.795	5.601	5.417	5.242	5.076	4.917	4.767	4.623	4.486	4.355
7	6.728	6.472	6.230	6.002	5.786	5.582	5.389	5.206	5.033	4.868
8	7.652	7.326	7.020	6.733	6.463	6.210	5.971	5.747	5.535	5.335
9	8.566	8.162	7.786	7.435	7.108	6.802	6.515	6.247	5.995	5.759
10	9.471	8.983	8.530	8.111	7.722	7.360	7.024	6.710	6.418	6.145
11	10.368	9.787	9.253	8.760	8.306	7.887	7.499	7.139	6.805	6.495
12	11.255	10.575	9.954	9.385	8.863	8.384	7.943	7.536	7.161	6.814
13	12.134	11.348	10.635	9.986	9.394	8.853	8.358	7.904	7.487	7.103
14	13.004	12.106	11.296	10.563	9.899	9.295	8.746	8.244	7.786	7.367
15	13.865	12.849	11.938	11.118	10.380	9.712	9.108	8.560	8.061	7.606
16	14.718	13.578	12.561	11.652	10.838	10.106	9.447	8.851	8.313	7.824
17	15.562	14.292	13.166	12.166	11.274	10.477	9.763	9.122	8.544	8.022
18	16.398	14.992	13.754	12.659	11.690	10.828	10.059	9.372	8.756	8.201
19	17.226	15.679	14.324	13.134	12.085	11.158	10.336	9.604	8.950	8.365
20	18.046	16.352	14.878	13.590	12.462	11.470	10.594	9.818	9.129	8.514
21	18.857	17.011	15.415	14.029	12.821	11.764	10.836	10.017	9.292	8.649
22	19.661	17.658	15.937	14.451	13.163	12.042	11.061	10.201	9.442	8.772
23	20.456	18.292	16.444	14.857	13.489	12.303	11.272	10.371	9.580	8.883
24	21.244	18.914	16.936	15.247	13.799	12.550	11.469	10.529	9.707	8.985
25	22.023	19.524	17.413	15.622	14.094	12.783	11.654	10.675	9.823	9.077
30	25.808	22.397	19.601	17.292	15.373	13.765	12.409	11.258	10.274	9.427
40	32.835	27.356	23.115	19.793	17.159	15.046	13.332	11.925	10.757	9.779
50	39.197	31.424	25.730	21.482	18.256	15.762	13.801	12.234	10.962	9.915

n	11%	12%	13%	14%	15%	16%	17%	18%	19%	20%
1	.901	.893	.885	.877	.870	.862	.855	.847	.840	.833
2	1.713	1.690	1.668	1.647	1.626	1.605	1.585	1.566	1.547	1.528
3	2.444	2.402	2.361	2.322	2.283	2.246	2.210	2.174	2.140	2.106
4	3.102	3.037	2.974	2.914	2.855	2.798	2.743	2.690	2.639	2.589
5	3.696	3.605	3.517	3.433	3.352	3.274	3.199	3.127	3.058	2.991
6	4.231	4.111	3.998	3.889	3.784	3.685	3.589	3.498	3.410	3.326
7	4.712	4.564	4.423	4.288	4.160	4.039	3.922	3.812	3.706	3.605
8	5.146	4.968	4.799	4.639	4.487	4.344	4.207	4.078	3.954	3.837
9	5.537	5.328	5.132	4.946	4.772	4.607	4.451	4.303	4.163	4.031
10	5.889	5.650	5.426	5.216	5.019	4.833	4.659	4.494	4.339	4.192
11	6.207	5.938	5.687	5.453	5.234	5.029	4.836	4.656	4.487	4.327
12	6.492	6.194	5.918	5.660	5.421	5.197	4.988	4.793	4.611	4.439
13	6.750	6.424	6.122	5.842	5.583	5.342	5.118	4.910	4.715	4.533
14	6.982	6.628	6.303	6.002	5.724	5.468	5.229	5.008	4.802	4.611
15	7.191	6.811	6.462	6.142	5.847	5.575	5.324	5.092	4.876	4.675
16	7.379	6.974	6.604	6.265	5.954	5.669	5.405	5.162	4.938	4.730
17	7.549	7.120	6.729	6.373	6.047	5.749	5.475	5.222	4.990	4.775
18	7.702	7.250	6.840	6.467	6.128	5.818	5.534	5.273	5.033	4.812
19	7.839	7.366	6.938	6.550	6.198	5.877	5.585	5.316	5.070	4.843
20	7.963	7.469	7.025	6.623	6.259	5.929	5.628	5.353	5.101	4.870
21	8.075	7.562	7.102	6.687	6.312	5.973	5.665	5.384	5.127	4.891
21	8.176	7.645	7.170	6.743	6.359	6.011	5.696	5.410	5.149	4.909
23	8.266	7.718	7.230	6.792	6.399	6.044	5.723	5.432	5.167	4.925
24	8.348	7.784	7.283	6.835	6.434	6.073	5.747	5.451	5.182	4.937
25	8.442	7.843	7.330	6.873	6.464	6.097	5.766	5.467	5.195	4.948
30	8.694	8.055	7.496	7.003	6.566	6.177	5.829	5.517	5.235	4.979
40	8.951	8.244	7.634	7.105	6.642	6.233	5.871	5.548	5.258	4.997
50	9.042	8.305	7.675	7.133	6.661	6.246	5.880	5.554	5.262	4.999

n	21%	22%	23%	24%	25%	26%	27%	28%	29%	30%
1	.826	.820	.813	.806	.800	.794	.787	.781	.775	.769
2	1.509	1.492	1.474	1.457	1.440	1.424	1.407	1.392	1.376	1.361
3	2.074	2.042	2.011	1.981	1.952	1.923	1.896	1.868	1.842	1.816
4	2.540	2.494	2.448	2.404	2.362	2.320	2.280	2.241	2.203	2.166
5	2.926	2.864	2.803	2.745	2.689	2.635	2.583	2.532	2.483	2.436
6	3.245	3.167	3.092	3.020	2.951	2.885	2.821	2.759	2.700	2.643
7	3.508	3.416	3.327	3.242	3.161	3.083	3.009	2.937	2.868	2.802
8	3.726	3.619	3.518	3.421	3.329	3.241	3.156	3.076	2.999	2.925
9	3.905	3.786	3.673	3.566	3.463	3.366	3.273	3.184	3.100	3.019
10	4.054	3.923	3.799	3.682	3.570	3.465	3.364	3.269	3.178	3.092
11	4.177	4.035	3.902	3.776	3.656	3.544	3.437	3.335	3.239	3.147
12	4.278	4.127	3.985	3.851	3.725	3.606	3.493	3.387	3.286	3.190
13	4.362	4.203	4.053	3.912	3.780	3.656	3.538	3.427	3.322	3.223
14	4.432	4.265	4.108	3.962	3.824	3.695	3.573	3.459	3.351	3.249
15	4.489	4.315	4.153	4.001	3.859	3.726	3.601	3.483	3.373	3.268
16	4.536	4.357	4.189	4.033	3.887	3.751	3.623	3.503	3.390	3.283
17	4.576	4.391	4.219	4.059	3.910	3.771	3.640	3.518	3.403	3.295
18	4.608	4.419	4.243	4.080	3.928	3.786	3.654	3.529	3.413	3.304
19	4.635	4.442	4.263	4.097	3.942	3.799	3.664	3.539	3.421	3.311
20	4.657	4.460	4.279	4.110	3.954	3.808	3.673	3.546	3.427	3.316
21	4.675	4.476	4.292	4.121	3.963	3.816	3.679	3.551	3.432	3.320
22	4.690	4.488	4.302	4.130	3.970	3.822	3.684	3.556	3.436	3.323
23	4.703	4.499	4.311	4.137	3.976	3.827	3.689	3.559	3.438	3.325
24	4.713	4.507	4.318	4.143	3.981	3.831	3.692	3.562	3.441	3.327
25	4.721	4.514	4.323	4.147	3.985	3.834	3.694	3.564	3.442	3.329
30	4.746	4.534	4.339	4.160	3.995	3.842	3.701	3.569	3.447	3.332
40	4.760	4.544	4.347	4.166	3.999	3.846	3.703	3.571	3.448	3.333
50	4.762	4.545	4.348	4.167	4.000	3.846	3.704	3.571	3.448	3.333

n	31%	32%	33%	34%	35%	36%	37%	38%	39%	40%
1	.763	.758	.752	.746	.741	.735	.730	.725	.719	.714
2	1.346	1.331	1.317	1.303	1.289	1.276	1.263	1.250	1.237	1.224
3	1.791	1.766	1.742	1.719	1.696	1.673	1.652	1.630	1.609	1.589
4	2.130	2.096	2.062	2.029	1.997	1.966	1.935	1.906	1.877	1.849
5	2.390	2.345	2.302	2.260	2.220	2.181	2.143	2.106	2.070	2.035
6	2.588	2.534	2.483	2.433	2.385	2.339	2.294	2.251	2.209	2.168
7	2.739	2.677	2.619	2.562	2.508	2.455	2.404	2.355	2.308	2.263
8	2.854	2.786	2.721	2.658	2.598	2.540	2.485	2.432	2.380	2.331
9	2.942	2.868	2.798	2.730	2.665	2.603	2.544	2.487	2.432	2.379
10	3.009	2.930	2.855	2.784	2.715	2.649	2.587	2.527	2.469	2.414
11	3.060	2.978	2.899	2.824	2.752	2.683	2.618	2.555	2.496	2.438
12	3.100	3.013	2.931	2.853	2.779	2.708	2.641	2.576	2.515	2.456
13	3.129	3.040	2.956	2.876	2.799	2.727	2.658	2.592	2.529	2.469
14	3.152	3.061	2.974	2.892	2.814	2.740	2.670	2.603	2.539	2.477
15	3.170	3.076	2.988	2.905	2.825	2.750	2.679	2.611	2.546	2.484
16	3.183	3.088	2.999	2.914	2.834	2.757	2.685	2.616	2.551	2.489
17	3.193	3.097	3.007	2.921	2.840	2.763	2.690	2.621	2.555	2.492
18	3.201	3.104	3.012	2.926	2.844	2.767	2.693	2.624	2.557	2.494
19	3.207	3.109	3.017	2.930	2.848	2.770	2.696	2.626	2.559	2.496
20	3.211	3.113	3.020	2.933	2.850	2.772	2.698	2.627	2.561	2.497
21	3.215	3.116	3.023	2.935	2.852	2.773	2.699	2.629	2.562	2.498
22	3.217	3.118	3.025	2.936	2.853	2.775	2.700	2.629	2.562	2.498
23	3.219	3.120	3.026	2.938	2.854	2.775	2.701	2.630	2.563	2.499
24	3.221	3.121	3.027	2.939	2.855	2.776	2.701	2.630	2.563	2.499
25	3.222	3.122	3.028	2.939	2.856	2.776	2.702	2.631	2.563	2.499
30	3.225	2.124	3.030	2.941	2.857	2.777	2.702	2.631	2.564	2.500
40	3.226	3.125	3.030	2.941	2.857	2.778	2.703	2.632	2.564	2.500
50	3.226	3.125	3.030	2.941	2.857	2.778	2.703	2.632	2.564	2.500

E Monthly Installment Loan Tables ($1,000 loan with interest payments compounded monthly)

Loan Maturity (in months)

Interest	6	12	18	24	30	36	48	60	72	84	96
4.00%	168.62	85.15	57.33	43.42	35.08	29.52	22.58	18.42	15.65	13.67	12.19
4.25%	168.74	85.26	57.44	43.54	35.19	29.64	22.69	18.53	15.76	13.78	12.31
4.50%	168.86	85.38	57.56	43.65	35.31	29.75	22.80	18.64	15.87	13.90	12.42
4.75%	168.98	85.49	57.67	43.76	35.42	29.86	22.92	18.76	15.99	14.02	12.54
5.00%	169.11	85.61	57.78	43.87	35.53	29.97	23.03	18.87	16.10	14.13	12.66
5.25%	169.23	85.72	57.89	43.98	35.64	30.08	23.14	18.99	16.22	14.25	12.78
5.50%	169.35	85.84	58.01	44.10	35.75	30.20	23.26	19.10	16.34	14.37	12.90
5.75%	169.47	85.95	58.12	44.21	35.87	30.31	23.37	19.22	16.46	14.49	13.02
6.00%	169.60	86.07	58.23	44.32	35.98	30.42	23.49	19.33	16.57	14.61	13.14
6.25%	169.72	86.18	58.34	44.43	36.09	30.54	23.60	19.45	16.69	14.73	13.26
6.50%	169.84	86.30	58.46	44.55	36.20	30.65	23.71	19.57	16.81	14.85	13.39
6.75%	169.96	86.41	58.57	44.66	36.32	30.76	23.83	19.68	16.93	14.97	13.51
7.00%	170.09	86.53	58.68	44.77	36.43	30.88	23.95	19.80	17.05	15.09	13.63
7.25%	170.21	86.64	58.80	44.89	36.55	30.99	24.06	19.92	17.17	15.22	13.76
7.50%	170.33	86.76	58.91	45.00	36.66	31.11	24.18	20.04	17.29	15.34	13.88
7.75%	170.45	86.87	59.03	45.11	36.77	31.22	24.30	20.16	17.41	15.46	14.01
8.00%	170.58	86.99	59.14	45.23	36.89	31.34	24.41	20.28	17.53	15.59	14.14
8.25%	170.70	87.10	59.25	45.34	37.00	31.45	24.53	20.40	17.66	15.71	14.26
8.50%	170.82	87.22	59.37	45.46	37.12	31.57	24.65	20.52	17.78	15.84	14.39
8.75%	170.95	87.34	59.48	45.57	37.23	31.68	24.77	20.64	17.90	15.96	14.52
9.00%	171.07	87.45	59.60	45.68	37.35	31.80	24.89	20.76	18.03	16.09	14.65
9.25%	171.19	87.57	59.71	45.80	37.46	31.92	25.00	20.88	18.15	16.22	14.78
9.50%	171.32	87.68	59.83	45.91	37.58	32.03	25.12	21.00	18.27	16.34	14.91
9.75%	171.44	87.80	59.94	46.03	37.70	32.15	25.24	21.12	18.40	16.47	15.04
10.00%	171.56	87.92	60.06	46.14	37.81	32.27	25.36	21.25	18.53	16.60	15.17
10.25%	171.68	88.03	60.17	46.26	37.93	32.38	25.48	21.37	18.65	16.73	15.31
10.50%	171.81	88.15	60.29	46.38	38.04	32.50	25.60	21.49	18.78	16.86	15.44
10.75%	171.93	88.27	60.40	46.49	38.16	32.62	25.72	21.62	18.91	16.99	15.57
11.00%	172.05	88.38	60.52	46.61	38.28	32.74	25.85	21.74	19.03	17.12	15.71
11.25%	172.18	88.50	60.63	46.72	38.40	32.86	25.97	21.87	19.16	17.25	15.84
11.50%	172.30	88.62	60.75	46.84	38.51	32.98	26.09	21.99	19.29	17.39	15.98
11.75%	172.42	88.73	60.87	46.96	38.63	33.10	26.21	22.12	19.42	17.52	16.12
12.00%	172.55	88.85	60.98	47.07	38.75	33.21	26.33	22.24	19.55	17.65	16.25
12.25%	172.67	88.97	61.10	47.19	38.87	33.33	26.46	22.37	19.68	17.79	16.39
12.50%	172.80	89.08	61.21	47.31	38.98	33.45	26.58	22.50	19.81	17.92	16.53
12.75%	172.92	89.20	61.33	47.42	39.10	33.57	26.70	22.63	19.94	18.06	16.67
13.00%	173.04	89.32	61.45	47.54	39.22	33.69	26.83	22.75	20.07	18.19	16.81
13.25%	173.17	89.43	61.56	47.66	39.34	33.81	26.95	22.88	20.21	18.33	16.95
13.50%	173.29	89.55	61.68	47.78	39.46	33.94	27.08	23.01	20.34	18.46	17.09
13.75%	173.41	89.67	61.80	47.89	39.58	34.06	27.20	23.14	20.47	18.60	17.23
14.00%	173.54	89.79	61.92	48.01	39.70	34.18	27.33	23.27	20.61	18.74	17.37
14.25%	173.66	89.90	62.03	48.13	39.82	34.30	27.45	23.40	20.74	18.88	17.51
14.50%	173.79	90.02	62.15	48.25	39.94	34.42	27.58	23.53	20.87	19.02	17.66

Loan Maturity (in months)

Interest	6	12	18	24	30	36	48	60	72	84	96
14.75%	173.91	90.14	62.27	48.37	40.06	34.54	27.70	23.66	21.01	19.16	17.80
15.00%	174.03	90.26	62.38	48.49	40.18	34.67	27.83	23.79	21.15	19.30	17.95
15.25%	174.16	90.38	62.50	48.61	40.30	34.79	27.96	23.92	21.28	19.44	18.09
15.50%	174.28	90.49	62.62	48.72	40.42	34.91	28.08	24.05	21.42	19.58	18.24
15.75%	174.41	90.61	62.74	48.84	40.54	35.03	28.21	24.19	21.55	19.72	18.38
16.00%	174.53	90.73	62.86	48.96	40.66	35.16	28.34	24.32	21.69	19.86	18.53
16.25%	174.65	90.85	62.97	49.08	40.78	35.28	28.47	24.45	21.83	20.00	18.68
16.50%	174.78	90.97	63.09	49.20	40.91	35.40	28.60	24.58	21.97	20.15	18.82
16.75%	174.90	91.09	63.21	49.32	41.03	35.53	28.73	24.72	22.11	20.29	18.97
17.00%	175.03	91.20	63.33	49.44	41.15	35.65	28.86	24.85	22.25	20.24	19.12
17.25%	175.15	91.32	63.45	49.56	41.27	35.78	28.98	24.99	22.39	20.58	19.27
17.50%	175.28	91.44	63.57	49.68	41.39	35.90	29.11	25.12	22.53	20.73	19.42
17.75%	175.40	91.56	63.69	49.80	41.52	36.03	29.24	25.26	22.67	20.87	19.57
18.00%	175.53	91.68	63.81	49.92	41.64	36.15	29.37	25.39	22.81	21.02	19.72
18.25%	175.65	91.80	63.93	50.04	41.76	36.28	29.51	25.53	22.95	21.16	19.88
18.50%	175.77	91.92	64.04	50.17	41.89	36.40	29.64	25.67	23.09	21.31	20.03
18.75%	175.90	92.04	64.16	50.29	42.01	36.53	29.77	25.80	23.23	21.46	20.18
19.00%	176.02	92.16	64.28	50.41	42.13	36.66	29.90	25.94	23.38	21.61	20.33
19.25%	176.15	92.28	64.40	50.53	42.26	36.78	30.03	26.08	23.52	21.76	20.49
19.50%	176.27	92.40	64.52	50.65	42.38	36.91	30.16	26.22	23.66	21.91	20.64
19.75%	176.40	92.51	64.64	50.77	42.51	37.04	30.30	26.35	23.81	22.06	20.80
20.00%	176.52	92.63	64.76	50.90	42.63	37.16	30.43	26.49	23.95	22.21	20.95
20.25%	176.65	92.75	64.88	51.02	42.75	37.29	30.56	26.63	24.10	22.36	21.11
20.50%	176.77	92.87	65.00	51.14	42.88	37.42	30.70	26.77	24.24	22.51	21.27
20.75%	176.90	92.99	65.12	51.26	43.00	37.55	30.83	26.91	24.39	22.66	21.42
21.00%	177.02	93.11	65.24	51.39	43.13	37.68	30.97	27.05	24.54	22.81	21.58
21.25%	177.15	93.23	65.37	51.51	43.26	37.80	31.10	27.19	24.68	22.96	21.74
21.50%	177.27	93.35	65.49	51.63	43.38	37.93	31.24	27.34	24.83	23.12	21.90
21.75%	177.40	93.47	65.61	51.75	43.51	38.06	31.37	27.48	24.98	23.27	22.06
22.00%	177.52	93.59	65.73	51.88	43.63	38.19	31.51	27.62	25.13	23.43	22.22
22.25%	177.65	93.71	65.85	52.00	43.76	38.32	31.64	27.76	25.27	23.58	22.38
22.50%	177.77	93.84	65.97	52.13	43.89	38.45	31.78	27.90	25.42	23.74	22.54
22.75%	177.90	93.96	66.09	52.25	44.01	38.58	31.91	28.05	25.57	23.89	22.70
23.00%	178.02	94.08	66.21	52.37	44.14	38.71	32.05	28.19	25.72	24.05	22.86
23.25%	178.15	94.20	66.34	52.50	44.27	38.84	32.19	28.33	25.87	24.20	23.02
23.50%	178.27	94.32	66.46	52.62	44.39	38.97	32.33	28.48	26.02	24.36	23.19
23.75%	178.40	94.44	66.58	52.75	44.52	39.10	32.46	28.62	26.18	24.52	23.35
24.00%	178.53	94.56	66.70	52.87	44.65	39.23	32.60	28.77	26.33	24.68	23.51
24.25%	178.65	94.68	66.82	53.00	44.78	39.36	32.74	28.91	26.48	24.83	23.68
24.50%	178.78	94.80	66.95	53.12	44.91	39.50	32.88	29.06	26.63	24.99	23.84
24.75%	178.90	94.92	67.07	53.25	45.03	39.63	33.02	29.20	26.78	25.15	24.01
25.00%	179.03	95.04	67.19	53.37	45.16	39.76	33.16	29.35	26.94	25.31	24.17

Index

*Note: **Boldface** page numbers indicate definitions of key terms.*